FILM THEORY
AND PHILOSOPHY

Film Theory and Philosophy

EDITED BY
RICHARD ALLEN
AND
MURRAY SMITH

CLARENDON PRESS · OXFORD
1997

Oxford University Press, Great Clarendon Street, Oxford OX2 6DP
Oxford New York
Athens Auckland Bangkok Bogota Bombay Buenos Aires
Calcutta Cape Town Dar es Salaam Delhi Florence Hong Kong
Istanbul Karachi Kuala Lumpur Madras Madrid Melbourne
Mexico City Nairobi Paris Singapore Taipei Tokyo Toronto Warsaw
and associated companies in
Berlin Ibadan

Oxford is a trade mark of Oxford University Press

Published in the United States
by Oxford University Press Inc., New York

British Library Cataloguing in Publication Data
Data available

Library of Congress Cataloging in Publication Data
Film theory and philosophy / edited by Richard Allen and Murray Smith.
Includes bibliographical references and index.
1. Motion pictures—Philosophy. I. Allen, Richard, 1921– .
II. Smith, Murray (Murray Stuart), 1962– .
PN1995. F4673 1997 791.43′01—dc21 97–12930
ISBN 0–19–815921–8

1 3 5 7 9 10 8 6 4 2

Typeset by Best-set Typesetter Ltd., Hong Kong
Printed in Great Britain
on acid-free paper by
Bookcraft Ltd.,
Midsomer Norton, Somerset

Acknowledgements

We have benefited from the advice, encouragement, and criticisms of many people over the course of developing this anthology. We would like to thank Deborah Knight, Alex Neill, David Rodowick, and Malcolm Turvey for their valuable comments on the introduction, and Renata Jackson for her thorough proofing and meticulous index. Thanks also to the team at OUP: Andrew Lockett for being receptive to the project, Mick Belson for cracking the whip, and Edwin Pritchard for his careful copy-editing. Bridget Sisk and Miri Song have provided moral support throughout. We are especially grateful to Paisley Livingston, whose enthusiasm for this project sustained us through moments of doubt and whose candid, yet generous criticisms have made the volume better than it otherwise would have been. Any problems that remain are, needless to say, entirely our own responsibility.

Contents

Notes on Contributors

RICHARD ALLEN is Associate Professor and Chair of Cinema Studies at New York University. He is author of *Projecting Illusion: Film Spectatorship and the Impression of Reality* (New York: Cambridge University Press, 1995) and is currently writing a book arguing against theory.

EDWARD BRANIGAN is a Professor in the Department of Film Studies at the University of California, Santa Barbara. He is author of *Narrative Comprehension and Film* (New York: Routledge, 1992); and *Point of View in the Cinema* (New York: Mouton, 1984) as well as general editor (with Charles Wolfe) of the American Film Institute Film Readers series (Routledge). He has received two teaching awards including a USCB Distinguished Teaching Award.

NOËL CARROLL is Monroe C. Beardsley Professor of the Philosophy of Art at the University of Wisconsin-Madison. He is the author of *Theorizing the Moving Image* (New York: Cambridge University Press, 1996); *The Philosophy of Horror* (New York: Routledge, 1990); *Mystifying Movies* (New York: Columbia University Press, 1988); *Philosophical Problems of Classical Film Theory* (Princeton: Princeton University Press, 1988); and co-editor of the volume *Post-Theory: Reconstructing Film Studies* (Madison: University of Wisconsin Press, 1996). His forthcoming book is on the philosophy of mass art.

GREGORY CURRIE is Professor of Philosophy and Head of the School of Arts at Flinders University, Adelaide, Australia. He is a fellow of the Australian Academy of the Humanities. He is the author of *An Ontology of Art* (London: Macmillan, 1989), *The Nature of Fiction* (Cambridge: Cambridge University Press, 1990), *Image and Mind: Film, Philosophy, and Cognitive Science* (New York: Cambridge University Press, 1995) and of articles in *Mind*, *American Philosophical Quarterly*, and other philosophical journals. He is currently working on a theory of the imagination.

DIRK EITZEN is Assistant Professor of Film and Media Studies at Franklin and Marshall College. His previous publications include essays on the subjects of film historiography, textuality and discourse, and cognition and illusion. He has also written on the documentary film and is an award-winning documentary film-maker.

BERYS GAUT teaches in the Department of Moral Philosophy, University of St Andrews, Scotland. He has published articles on film theory, aesthetics, ethics, and political philosophy. He is co-editor of the volume *Ethics and Practical Reason* (Oxford University Press, forthcoming).

JENNIFER HAMMETT teaches in the Cinema Department at San Franscisco State University. She is currently working on a book-length pragmatist critique of film theory.

PETER KIVY is Professor of Philosophy at Rutgers University. His many books on the philosophy and aesthetics of music include *The Fine Art of Repetition and Other Essays in the Philosophy of Music* (New York: Cambridge University Press, 1993); *Sound and Semblance: Reflections on Musical Representation*, 2nd edn. (Princeton: Princeton University Press, 1991); *Music Alone: Philosophical Reflections on the Purely Musical Experience* (Ithaca, NY: Cornell University Press, 1990); *Osmin's Rage: Philosophical Reflections on Opera, Drama, and Text* (Princeton: Princeton University Press, 1988); and *The Corded Shell: Reflections on Musical Expression* (Princeton: Princeton University Press, 1980).

DEBORAH KNIGHT is Assistant Professor and Queen's National Scholar at Queen's University, Kingston, Canada. She has published in the areas of film theory, feminist film theory, philosophy of language, philosophy of mind, and Canadian cinema in journals such as *New Literary History*, *Philosophy Today*, *Metaphilosophy*, *Philosophy and Literature*, and *Cinemas*. She is currently completing a book on intentional agency and the interpretation of action, and pursuing research into film genres.

FLO LEIBOWITZ is Professor of Philosophy at Oregon State University, where she teaches courses in aesthetics and philosophy of mind. She has published many essays on film genre and the aesthetics of film in such journals as *Philosophy and Literature* and the *Journal of Aesthetics and Art Criticism*.

PAISLEY LIVINGSTON is Professor of English and Philosophy at McGill University, Montreal, Canada. He is the author of *Ingmar Bergman and the Rituals of Art* (Ithaca, NY: Cornell University Press, 1982); *Literary Knowledge: Humanistic Inquiry and the Philosophy of Science* (Ithaca, NY: Cornell University Press, 1988); *Literature and Rationality: Ideas of Agency in Theory and Fiction* (Cambridge: Cambridge University Press, 1991); and *Models of Desire: René Girard and the Psychology of Mimesis* (Baltimore: Johns Hopkins University Press, 1992).

TOMMY LOTT is Professor of Philosophy at the University of Missouri-St Louis. He has published several articles in areas of modern philosophy. He is author of *Like Rum in the Punch: Alain Locke and the Theory of African-American Culture* (University of Massachusetts Press, forthcoming). He is also editor of *Subjugation and Bondage: Critical Essays on Slavery and Social Philosophy* (Roman & Littlefield, forthcoming), and co-editor with John Pittman of *Blackwell's Companion to African-American Philosophy* (forthcoming).

CARL PLANTINGA is Associate Professor of Film at Hollins College in Roanoke, Virginia. His book *Rhetoric and Representation in Nonfiction Film* will be published in 1997 by Cambridge University Press. With Greg Smith, he is currently editing a collection of essays, *Passionate Views: Thinking about Film and Emotion*.

TREVOR PONECH, Assistant Professor of English at McGill University, is currently at work on a book-length study on the nature of non-fiction cinema.

HÉCTOR RODRÍGUEZ lectures in the Humanities at Hong Kong Baptist University. He has published on the sociology of Hong Kong cinema and the aesthetics of Japanese director Shohei Imamura, and he is completing a book on Taiwanese cinema.

MURRAY SMITH is Lecturer in Film Studies at the School of Arts and Image Studies, University of Kent. He is the author of *Engaging Characters: Fiction, Emotion, and the Cinema* (Oxford: Clarendon Press, 1995), and co-editor, with Steve Neale, of *Contemporary Hollywood Cinema* (Routledge, forthcoming).

MALCOLM TURVEY is a Ph.D. candidate in the Department of Cinema Studies at New York University. He is pursuing research on the relevance of Wittgenstein's philosophy for film theory.

KENDALL L. WALTON is James B. and Grace J. Nelson Professor of Philosophy at the University of Michigan. He is the author of *Mimesis as Make-Believe: On the Foundations of the Representational Arts* (Cambridge, Mass.: Harvard University Press, 1990), as well many essays in various journals of philosophy and cultural criticism.

GEORGE WILSON is Professor of Philosophy at Johns Hopkins University. He is author of *Narration in Light* (Baltimore: Johns Hopkins University Press, 1986) and *The Intentionality of Human Action* (Stanford, Calif.: Stanford University Press, 1989); and several essays on the philosophy of language and philosophy of mind.

Instructions for Use

With this collection of essays we hope to address at least two different audiences who have, hitherto, had relatively little to say to each other—those within the discipline of film studies, and those working within philosophy, especially the philosophy of art, of mind, and of language. We have tried to provide a context for both of these audiences through the main introduction and the shorter introductions which frame each part. There is, however, a division of labour between the main introduction and the part introductions. On the one hand, the main introduction aims to provide a map of the influence of various traditions of philosophy on film theory, with a polemical emphasis on the undersung virtues of analytic philosophy, a neglected and misunderstood tradition within film studies. On the other hand, the part introductions frame the individual chapters within the context of ongoing debates and issues of concern within film studies. Thus, while the main introduction seeks to situate film theory in relation to philosophy as a whole, the part introductions seek to contextualize each chapter in the volume within specific debates within film studies. We hope that together these will help the reader find a path through the complex and fascinating material gathered here.

Introduction:
Film Theory and Philosophy

RICHARD ALLEN AND MURRAY SMITH

> What distinguishes analytical philosophy from other contemporary
> philosophy (though not from much philosophy of other times) is a
> certain way of going on, which involves argument, distinctions, and, so
> far as it remembers to try to achieve it and succeeds, moderately plain
> speech. As an alternative to plain speech, it distinguishes sharply be-
> tween obscurity and technicality. It always rejects the first, but the
> second it sometimes finds a necessity. This feature peculiarly enrages
> some of its enemies. Wanting philosophy to be at once profound and
> accessible, they resent technicality but are comforted by obscurity.[1]

It is widely recognized that the field of film studies is in a state of flux, or
even crisis or impasse. While it would be a misrepresentation to suggest that
the field was once wholly unified and is now fragmented, there is little doubt
that the discipline is no longer governed by the cluster of aims, methods, and
assumptions (drawn from structural linguistics and psychoanalysis) which
arose in the late 1960s and held sway, in institutional terms, until sometime
in the 1980s. The picture is further complicated by shifts in the very
definition and delimitation of the field, which, in the opinion of many, will
ultimately be swallowed by the emergent and broader fields of media and
cultural studies. These conditions make for a moment of great potential—
a potential which arises from the fact that it is during such periods of
relative intellectual insecurity that new connections and alliances may be
forged, new perspectives discovered, and old questions recast in fresh and
dynamic ways.[2] This is a propitious context in which to focus the attention
of film studies and the fields adjacent to it on an approach which has
become increasingly visible over the last decade, without assuming the
dimensions of anything like a 'movement' or a 'school' within film studies:
the approach associated with the tradition of analytic philosophy.[3]

The influence of Continental philosophy on film studies and the humanities in general need not be laboured: the names of Nietzsche, Lacan,
Althusser, Adorno, Benjamin, Derrida, Heidegger, Foucault, Deleuze, and
Bourdieu will be familiar in literary, media, and arts departments, even if
their arguments are better known through English-language digests and
primers than from the originals. By contrast, for those in film, media, and
cultural studies, the phrase 'analytic philosophy' conjures up a range of

mostly negative associations. Throughout the 1970s and for much of the 1980s, analytic philosophy was disdained if not abhorred by most members of the academic film community. While Continental philosophy was assumed to be ambitious, speculative, and politically engaged, analytic philosophy was considered narrow, technical, and oblivious to political implication. Such philosophy was identified with positivism, viewed as arid and asocial, regarded as the province of conservatives alone, and, as such, deemed anathema to the socially progressive goals dear to the discipline.

Yet these assumptions about analytic philosophy and its differences from Continental philosophy were and are either gross simplifications or simply wrong. Anyone who has tackled early Derrida should know that Continental philosophy can be extremely technical; anyone who has read Kendall Walton's *Mimesis as Make-Believe* ought to question the idea that analytic philosophy is necessarily lacking in ambition. Equally it is mistaken to think that analytic philosophy has any intrinsic political colouring—conservative or otherwise—just as the same claim would be mistaken if applied to Continental philosophy. There are politically conservative analytic philosophers (like Roger Scruton, Robert Nozick, and John Finnis), liberals (like John Rawls and Ronald Dworkin), and radicals of various sorts (analytic Marxists like Jon Elster, G. A. Cohen, and Andrew Levine; feminists such as Alison Jaggar and Laurie Shrage).[4] It is true that analytic philosophy is characterized by explicitness, precision, and clarity in argument, in contrast to the ambiguity and obscurity that often besets writing inspired by the Continental tradition. In general analytic philosophy strives to avoid the pitfalls of both dogmatism (the subordination of argumentative rigour and consistency to the defence of a particular doctrine) and uncritical pluralism (the acceptance of a range of positions with little interest in argument about their relative and particular merits, or attention to inconsistencies among them).[5] The goal of this volume is to give momentum to work in an analytic vein, while at the same time dispelling the mistaken assumptions about its nature. Our hope is that we can galvanize interest in such work, so that the analytic tradition is viewed as a rich resource for film studies, not a toxic waste dump to be avoided at all costs.[6]

Given prevailing attitudes—pro-Continental, anti-analytic—it is insufficient, however, simply to rescue analytic philosophy from misconceptions. It is also necessary to understand why it is that Continental modes of thought have been so tenacious. Undoubtedly some of the reasons are institutional, having to do with the fact that Continental thought was given credence in departments of literature where it was free from the kind of scrutiny analytic philosophers routinely bring to their own work and to the writing of others. However, there are also philosophical reasons for the influence of certain recent schools of Continental philosophy in the humanities and film theory in particular. These reasons, we shall argue, are, by and large, bad reasons. The questions that Continental philosophy seeks to answer are best answered by embracing the analytic modes of enquiry exemplified in this volume.

In this introduction we describe and clarify the characteristic methods and strategies of analytic philosophy and the film theory it informs, and provide some indication of the breadth of issues, methods, and substantive doctrines examined, criticized, and defended by exponents of analytic philosophy. A sense of the diversity of analytically informed work can be gleaned by considering the development of cognitive science—a field which has had a major impact on film studies over the last decade. Cognitive theory has developed in part through dialogue with analytic philosophy of mind (in the work of, for example, Daniel Dennett, Stephen Stich, and Alvin Goldman).[7] However, that dialogue has been characterized as much by disagreement as agreement between philosophers and experimental cognitive scientists. Indeed, in the opinion of some philosophers influenced by the late Wittgenstein, the philosophy of mind challenges the very intelligibility of a science of the mind.[8] Thus, while this anthology contains some work informed by cognitive theory (Currie, Carroll, Ponech, Branigan, Smith), other authors within this volume have pursued a critique of aspects of cognitivism or the paradigm as a whole (Wilson, Gaut, Hammett, Allen, Turvey). Analytic philosophy is thus a broad enough church to shelter divergent and indeed incompatible perspectives on cognitivism. What then differentiates the approach we advance here—what we might call 'analytic' film theory—from cognitive film theory? What gives 'analytic' film theory its coherence and importance?

OPENING UP THE ANALYTIC TOOLBOX

The origins of the modern analytic tradition lie in a reaction to the idealism dominating British philosophy at the beginning of the twentieth century. Led by Moore and Russell, this reaction drew on the anti-psychologistic logic of Frege, which discriminated truth from the judgement that something is true. The idealists argued that it was necessary to distinguish between reality as it appears to the senses, which is discrete and multiple, and therefore contradictory, and the reality which underlies appearance that consists in the indivisible unity of mind or spirit. The shift from idealism to analysis is neatly captured in a remark made by Cambridge philosopher C. D. Broad, who noted that Russell's *The Principles of Mathematics* had taught him 'not to welcome contradictions as proofs that such and such features in the apparent world are unreal' but rather to suspect that the contradictions in fact lie in the argument of the philosopher.[9] In contrast to idealism, philosophy was conceived by Moore and Russell (in different ways) as the analysis of thoughts or 'propositions', that rendered perspicuous their logical form (their relationship to other propositions) and their epistemic status (their relationship to the world). Since thoughts are conveyed by language, the practice of analysis became identified with the task of clarifying the meaning of linguistic expressions, the relations between them, and with the relationship of meaning to truth. For Russell, 'analysis' consisted of a critical examination of the misleading picture of reality afforded by natural language. The tools of the philosopher, formal and symbolic logic, provided the means to build an accurate picture of the world. In the post-war period the writings of Quine were decisive in consolidating analytic philosophy as a practice of theory-building modelled upon science, or a 'naturalized philosophy' by, amongst other things, assailing the distinction between truths that are grounded independently of facts (analytic truths) and those that are not, and thereby undermining the assumption that the subject-matter of philosophy was essentially different from that of science.[10]

Other figures in the tradition, however, repudiate this conception of philosophy. In the hands of Oxford philosophers such as Austin, Ryle, and Grice (sometimes referred to as 'ordinary language' philosophers, although they were not only interested in ordinary language) and in the writings of the later Wittgenstein, analysis became not a process of correcting the distortions of ordinary language, but a clarification of the range of functions or uses of language beyond simply that of reference (the key function for Russell, the early Wittgenstein, and the logical positivists), a range which cannot be reduced to a formal, systematized logic. Here, analysis is more like topography than geology or seismology: it aims at a careful description of the landscape of language and the life it is integrated with, rather than a penetration to a purportedly more fundamental and accurate level of representation. Philosophical problems are regarded as chimera thrown up by too brusque a dismissal of ordinary language, attention to the subleties of which is seen to 'dissolve', if not solve, in the traditional sense, many traditional questions. As Michael Devitt and Kim Sterelny write, 'When the naturalistic philosopher points his finger at reality, the linguistic philosopher discusses the finger.'[11]

This is only a thumbnail sketch of two of the most widely recognized conceptions of 'analytic' practice; many other definitions have been offered. Indeed, analytic philosophy tends to be described by those who practise it as a style or approach, rather than a doctrine or body of knowledge. In order to respect these varied conceptions of and perspectives on 'analysis'—as well as other manifestations of diversity that we will describe later in this chapter—we have chosen to write of an 'analytic tradition' rather than 'analytic philosophy' *per se.*[12] As we have seen, what defines this tradition is its attention to the analysis of concepts and their interrelations. Even where the goal and methods of analysis have been various, there is a consistent—and salutary—emphasis on the various kinds of logical relationships that hold between concepts. Symbolic logic is the most abstract and formalized method of undertaking such analysis, but not the only one. A good, preliminary example of this kind of precise attention to logical relations is given by David Gorman, commenting on the following exposition of Derridean theory by Christopher Norris: 'Always there is the appeal—however covert, metaphorical, or tucked out of sight—to some analogue of writing whose role in the argument turns out to be crucial to its whole working system of assumptions.'[13] Gorman points out that the 'always' in the sentence is fatally ambiguous, between the contingent claim that this habit is 'routine', and the much stronger claim that it is logically 'necessary'. In addition to this disambiguation of terms, typical strategies for authors in the analytic tradition in pursuit of logical precision would be the discrimination of strict, logical implication from implicature (the implied or indirect assertion of a proposition), and of deductive from inductive and abductive reasoning;[14] the unearthing of hidden premises (see, for example, Berys Gaut's chapter on authorship); the scrutinizing of an argument for the presence of circularity, or question-begging; the attention to paradox, but also to its dissolution (a concern in the chapters of both Deborah Knight and Richard Allen); and the discrimination of logical contradictories from logical contraries. Carroll, for example, points to the confusion that arises from a failure to distinguish between the contradictory of 'fiction' (the heterogeneous body of 'non-fiction' films) and a contrary of 'fiction' (the more specific body of 'documentary' films, which Carroll analyses as 'films of presumptive assertion').

The influence of both strains of the analytic tradition can be felt in the various essays in this volume, and in many we find a kind of amalgam of them. Both Carroll in his chapter on documentary, and Livingston in his chapter on authorship, for example, advance 'truth-tracking' analyses of the conceptual frameworks of their chosen domains, which distinguish between ordinary (linguistic) usage, and the concepts which lie behind such usage. The investigation of use provides a starting-point for analysis, but use is not a reliable guide to the nature of the concept being analysed. This does not so much suggest that the ordinary use of language is misguided as that it is merely rough-and-ready, and therefore capable of clarification for technical and theoretical purposes. A good analysis should not merely, and need not at all, mimic that which it analyses; analysis would be facile if it did no more than reflect or restate the tangle of assumptions and theses that make up a given field. Livingston's description of his goal is particularly telling and useful in this regard: 'What is wanted is a semi-technical notion of authorship that avoids at least some of the confusion and ambiguity of ordinary language without merely stipulating a usage that is theoretically self-serving or historically inaccurate.'[15] On this view, analysis steers a path between an arbitrary stipulation of concepts—a sort of Humpty Dumpty theoretical world in which success is guaranteed because it does not track or aim to clarify anything outside itself—and a straightforward acceptance of what 'ordinary language' seems to imply about the concepts and phenomena of a given domain.[16] Analysis along these lines does not (at least not uniformly or necessarily) amount to the reduction—or 'purging' or 'repression', as it is sometimes called—of the ambiguity or complexity of experience. Rather, it represents an attempt to recognize and clarify the constituents of such complexity.[17] As Carroll emphasizes in the conclusion to his chapter, the point is not to reform ordinary linguistic usage, but to reveal the conceptual structure which such usage depends upon, and thereby to clarify the extension of the phrase 'documentary film'. Similarly, Livingston works through a series of hypothetical authorial case-studies, in order to reveal the assumptions deployed in our thinking about authorship, and to identify the range of cases in which the term is appropriately used.

One response to the claims being made here for the methodological virtues of the analytic tradition is that such techniques are not the unique possession of analytic philosophy, but the mark of sound argument and good scholarship in general. To the extent that the analytic tradition builds upon recognized aspects of logic—syllogistic logic, principles like Ockham's razor—which have accrued over the long history of Western philosophy prior to the split which started to open at the beginning of the twentieth century, there is some truth in this. But there can be little doubting the refinement and elaboration of such techniques within the analytic tradition, as well as the emphasis placed upon their observance. This last point can best be highlighted by considering the characteristic strategies of film and cultural theory which would seek to distance itself from the analytic tradition. It is not, obviously enough, that one finds a total absence of recognized argumentative strategies and adherence to logic in Continentally inspired theory. But the embrace of such standards by 'Continental' thinkers is a fickle one. The striking feature which places such work in contrast to analytic theory is the opportunistic attitude it frequently displays towards argumentative rigour, as well as a willingness to embrace rather more dubious argumentative strategies.

Three such strategies stand out: first, a disabling habit of deference and quotation with respect to authoritative figures; secondly, the misleading use of examples (and a related confusion between analogy and example), a practice which we will term 'the fallacy of exemplification'; and thirdly, a strategic use of obscurity (that is to say, deliberate though unacknowledged obfuscation). No tradition of thought, or particular argument made within a tradition, can be entirely free of dependence on authority, for the simple reason that no argument can question and explore every assumption made within it, and many of these assumptions rely on the authority either of tradition (long and pervasive acceptance) or of a particular figure. Some assumptions must be made so that others can be critically examined; and the making of assumptions usually involves an appeal to authority. Nevertheless, there is an important distinction between a self-conscious bracketing of certain assumptions as ones which will be accepted in a given context for the sake of examining other concepts, and the wholesale acceptance of a particular doctrine, the Truth of which can be alluded to at will. Ironically, of course, the very concept of authority, along with its association with tradition, has been the subject of critique within Continentally inspired theory—most famously, in Roland Barthes's attack on the notion of authorship. As several authors have shown, however, such claims merely occlude the fact that they are supported by a specific and identifiable tradition of Romantic thought, replete with valued authors and their authoritative (within the tradition) arguments.[18]

Deconstructive critics have a habit of adducing evidence in support of their arguments—how could they not do so?—but their attitude to evidence is inconsistent. What we call the fallacy of exemplification is committed when a generalization (about the nature of cinema, for example) is made solely on the basis of the analysis of a single, putatively exemplary case. By definition, an 'exemplary case' is one which ought to be representative of a large number of cases. Jacqueline Rose, for example, makes the claim that a certain type of paranoia and attendant aggressivity is 'latent' in the pervasively used technique of reverse-field editing.[19] This claim is made as part of a theory of cinematic spectatorship, evidence for which is provided by an analysis of Hitchcock's *The Birds*. One problem with this analysis is the way that it makes a claim about a technique on the basis of a very particular, if not simply loaded, example: paranoia, fear, and aggressivity are central thematic concerns of *The Birds*, so we should not be surprised that reverse-field editing at some points in the film evokes 'aggressivity'. In other words, the theme of the film actually makes this a very poor example as the basis of a claim about something supposedly inherent to a technique: much better would be a demonstration that reverse-field editing even in a love scene creates a counter-current of aggressivity. Setting these qualms aside for the sake of argument, let us allow the example as evidence, evidence for the generalization Rose makes about the effects of reverse-field editing in cinema. It then becomes apparent that little or no effort is made even to gesture towards the supposedly large body of other films of which this example is allegedly representative; and absolutely none is made to account for obvious counter-examples—in other words, films which apparently falsify the generalization, or would at least force it to be recast in much narrower terms ('the films of Hitchcock ...', 'the films of classical Hollywood ...').[20]

By 'strategic obscurity' we mean to pick out certain modes of argument—or pseudo-argument—which run counter to the clarificatory impetus of the analytic tradition. Chief among these would be punning (the use of mere phonetic analogy to advance an argument in a particular direction) and association. A good example of association can be found in Jonathan Crary's *Techniques of the Observer*.[21] Discussing the rise of physiological optics in the first half of the nineteenth century, Crary explicates the theory of Johannes Müller, who posited the notion of 'specific nerve energies', and argued that our experience of light is the result of nervous excitation, such stimulation deriving not only from light but from pressure or electricity applied to the nerves (in contrast to the directness of human perception as modelled by the camera obscura). Crary writes: 'Müller showed that a variety of different causes will produce the *same* sensation in a given sensory nerve. In other words, he is describing a fundamentally arbitrary relation between stimulus and sensation.'[22] It does not follow, however, from the fact that Müller argues that various kinds of stimulation can give rise to the experience of light, and that the same kind of stimulation gives rise to different experiences depending on the kind of nerve excited, that the relation between stimulus and sensation is arbitrary. On the contrary, it is constrained by the physiological features that Müller examines. Crary arrives at the 'arbitrariness' of perception by a conceptual slide from the indirectness or mediation of perception that Müller's account of the nervous system introduces. Association is, then, a kind of conceptual punning: leaping from one concept (indirectness or mediation) to a related but different one (arbitrariness). Crary seeks to associate Müller's theory of visual perception with 'arbitrariness' in the Saussurian sense, the *sine qua non* of semiotic theory, so that he can mount the larger argument that such apparently referential and indeed resemblance-based media as photography and film in fact impose 'arbitrary' cultural and ideological constructs upon spectator-subjects. There may be something to this thesis, but it cannot be convincingly established through association.[23]

Association and punning are encouraged by Derrida's arguments concerning the drift of utterances away from their intended meaning, and more generally by the post-structural emphasis on language as a mysterious veil which interposes itself between human agents and the world, whose philosophical implications we shall explore in more detail in the next section. They are also strategies which could hardly constrast more dramatically with the rigorous discrimination between entailment and various weaker forms of relation, typically distinguished by those in the analytic tradition. As the quotation from Bernard Williams at the head of this introduction emphasizes, the obscurity which often arises from the sustained use of association and punning should not be confused with the technicality often found in analytic philosophy—a technicality which attempts to maintain clarity in the face of dense and complex phenomena, the intricacy of which may outstrip conventional idioms. Often the substitution of poetic for argumentative strategies is justified by the argument that there is no clear line between philosophical and literary discourse, and that a resonant word or multifaceted image—of the type conjured by a pun—is as legitimate a strategy as any more traditional use of logic.[24] This confuses a truth about the use and availability of various kinds of strategy to all sorts of writing, with a refusal to recognize the different goals of different types of writing and the contrasting emphasis placed on different techniques as a consequence. Philosophy of all types makes use of 'literary' devices—punning, narrative, metaphor—and literature makes use of arguments, both implicit and explicit. But it does not follow from this that philosophical and literary writing are identical, unless one is making the trivial argument that both are forms of writing. And the consequence of the 'dissolution' view is a great deal of 'Theory' which is bad philosophy (because of its on-again, off-again adherence to the standards of careful argument) and still worse literature (because of the deflection away from the goals of literary discourse by the pretence that it is also philosophy).[25] This is not to deny that there are some extraordinary authors who can pull off such a genre-bending hybrid, but to argue rather that the interest of such authors arises partly from a background in which the two practices are defined by different overarching goals, even while they may share certain linguistic techniques. However, since such a clear distinction between the goals of philosophy and the goals of literature is one that is likely to be resisted by Continentally inspired film theory, it is worth pausing here to consider two related questions: what does such film theory conceive its goals to be? And are these goals really best served by ignoring the aims and strategies of analytic philosophy?

CONTINENTAL PHILOSOPHY AND FILM THEORY

The philosophical inspiration for the dominant paradigm of film theory in the 1970s and 1980s, the psycho-semiotic theory of subject-positioning, lies in the unlikely confluence of two distinct philosophical traditions—one leading from Hegel and Sartre to Lacan, the other leading from Husserl and Derrida's critique of Husserl to Kristeva—that united in an overarching theory of the construction of the subject in language. Drawing on Barthes's and Kristeva's theories of literary narration and Brecht's ideas about the theatre, film theorists like Stephen Heath grafted the theory of subject construction onto the idea that modernist art—art that drew attention to and often questioned its own status as a medium of representation—

provided a model for the emancipation of consciousness. The result was an ambitious, overarching theory that aimed to 'deconstruct' the subject 'constructed' by dominant forms of representation, like classical Hollywood cinema, in a manner that was thought to parallel certain strategies of modernist art. To be sure, psychoanalytic semiotics, along with the political modernism it supported, has lost status in recent years to cultural studies because of its perceived failure to afford a conceptual space for agency. Yet despite the distance of cultural studies from psychoanalytic semiotics, the theory of subject positioning that psychoanalytic semiotics served to articulate remains in currency, even if in an attenuated form and a version that is not specific to the cinema.[26] Furthermore, what is often taken to be the philosophical cutting edge of contemporary visual theory—postmodern theories of the image—carry over many of the philosophical assumptions that underlie the political modernism they have displaced.

The philosophical traditions underlying Continentally influenced film theory of the recent past are united by two assumptions. First, the primary purpose of philosophy is taken to be the critique of epistemology; the task of philosophy is to demonstrate that the apparent justifications of our beliefs have no objective grounding. Secondly, the critique of epistemology is identified with the ethical critique of modernity, conceived as a capitalist, scientific culture that apparently enhances, but in fact devalues and degrades, human existence. The fact that philosophy is conceived of as a discourse that reveals the absence of any objective grounding for what we take to be knowledge lends philosophy itself a decided air of paradox, for the demonstration of the impossibility of knowledge undermines itself in the act of being stated. However, contemporary philosophers in the Continental tradition do not regard this as a devastating circularity. Thinkers like Theodor Adorno, Jacques Derrida, and Michel Foucault have embraced this contradiction as *the* defining feature of philosophy and the only legitimate path that philosophy can take in response to modernity. As we have already suggested, it is a path that leads the philosopher to conceive of the practice of philosophy as one that is akin to modernist art—a practice which, at its worst, leads to the damaging equivocations, pseudo-arguments, and obscurity discussed above. Such 'post-epistemological' philosophy endlessly reflects on its (in-)ability to make knowledge claims, paralleling the focus in much modernist art on the limitations and paradoxes of representation.[27] (One consequence of this stance is that the line between philosophers as such and writers nomimally in other disciplines becomes difficult to mark.) We do not claim that these two assumptions—the emphasis on the critique of epistemology, and the identification of that critique with an ethical critique of modernity—are distributed in equal measure or in the same way in the thought of every Continental thinker who has influenced film theory of the recent past. The tradition of phenomenology, for example, does not share all of these assumptions. Nor are these claims, individually or jointly, the province of Continental philosophers alone (one need only think of Richard Rorty here). Nonetheless, with great consistency, these epistemological and ethical concerns have coalesced in Anglo-American film theory taking its cue from Continental philosophy.

These two assumptions about the nature of philosophy unite with a third in Continentally inspired film theory that pertains to the role that cinema might play for the philosopher-as-modernist-artist. In a great deal of this theory, the ethical critique of modernity is promoted by using the cinema to model the idea of knowledge and/or its critique, as it is conceived by philosophy. Sometimes cinematic representation is thought of simply as a model for the idea of consciousness or knowledge, as in the theory and practice of certain avant-garde film-makers.[28] Frequently, however, philosophers and film theorists are seduced into thinking of cinema as a medium that either causally governs consciousness and knowledge, and/or the critique of knowledge, in a manner that philosophy can only theorize. Now it is certainly true that there are ways of using Continental philosophy to think about film which do not focus in this way on cinematic representation as such—for example, analyses of single films or genres of film from a Lacanian or Deleuzian perspective. Nevertheless, even where the focus is a particular film, the film often serves to illustrate or 'allegorize' the theory in question.[29] In either the general or the particular case, film is used to dramatize or represent metaphorically some philosophical notion.

We will now consider in turn each of the three broad, interlocking assumptions that animate Continentally inspired film theory.

The purpose of philosophy is to critique epistemology

The traditions of Continental philosophy influential on Anglo-American film theory of the recent past share in common a scepticism about the possibility of knowledge. This is no ordinary scepticism. Garden variety scepticism arises from the thought that we can be certain of the existence only of that which we immediately apprehend: the contents of our consciousness or the ideas we survey with our mind's eye. We can at best only *infer* the existence of the outside world, and since, in any given case, our inference may fail, we cannot be *certain* of the truth of our knowledge claims. The ordinary sceptic does not categorically deny that knowledge is possible; he is in this sense an epistemic agnostic. By contrast, the nature of the scepticism that has influenced film theory is an epistemic atheism that draws its inspiration from Nietzsche. For the epistemic atheist it is not just that knowledge claims cannot be justified with certainty, it is that knowledge claims by their very definition are somehow self-defeating. Is such epistemic atheism justified?

Epistemic atheism is closely identified with the thought of Derrida. While Derrida exerted less direct influence in film studies in the 1970s and 1980s than he did on literary theory, his ideas nonetheless entered into film theory through literary and political modernism.[30] Derrida's version of epistemic atheism emerged from a critical reading of Husserl, who had tried at the turn of the century to put epistemology on firm foundations by refuting scepticism once and for all.[31] Husserl acknowledged that from the 'natural standpoint' of sensory experience the mind perceives an infinite series of partial, perspectival views of the object that seem to license sceptical questions about whether or not it is one and the same object that we see in a given place at any given time. However, he argued that sceptical doubt is eradicated once we 'step back' from or 'bracket' the natural standpoint with its limited vision of the object in order to 'see' the whole object within the single mental glance of the mind's eye. But how do we identify and reidentify this object in the mind's eye? Isn't the sceptical dilemma restored at a different level of analysis?

Husserl tried to head off scepticism by pointing out that we use the linguistic sign to reidentify the object in the mind's eye. Derrida countered that the aspect of the linguistic sign that allows us to identify and reidentify the object over time—its sensuous aspect or 'the signifier', to use Saussure's term, as Derrida does—is precisely the aspect of the sign that must be bracketed (according to Husserl) together with the rest of perceptual experience. Now in keeping with the analytic response to idealism we would do well to conclude from this that Husserl's conception of knowledge is mistaken because it is based upon a contradiction—recall Broad's insight into idealist thought cited earlier—but Derrida's conclusion is quite to the contrary: Husserl's argument demonstrates, albeit inadvertently, that knowledge is founded upon contradiction. The presence of an object in the mind's eye is guaranteed only by the presence of something—the material signifier—that is by definition absent. Thus, for Derrida, any knowledge claim, founded by definition upon the presence of the object in the mind's eye, must make reference to its own impossibility in the very act of being made. The impossibility is founded upon the present/absent structure of the sign, a structure that Derrida strategically, if implausibly, equates with the arbitrariness of the Saussurian signifer.

For an epistemic atheist like Derrida, the failure of a knowledge claim is a conceptual feature of the claim itself: knowledge claims are self-defeating by their nature, for they necessarily run up against the opacity of language.[32] However, once the derivation of Derrida's contention is made apparent, it is easy to see that such a radical deconstructive scepticism is entirely parasitic upon the conception of knowledge it purports to undercut.[33] Derrida's epistemic atheism presupposes that knowledge must necessarily take the form specified by Husserl. Epistemic atheism results from the thought that the only possible epistemology is an idealist one in which beliefs are grounded or justified because they are true in some absolute or presuppositionless sense of Truth. But why should we accept this definition of knowledge in the first place? Philosophers writing within the analytic tradition propose a number of ways of understanding knowledge. Many, though by no means all, of these take the idea of scientific knowledge as the paradigm case of knowledge, but as we shall see, whether or not science is the paradigm, no philosopher working within the analytic tradition conceives of knowledge in terms of some absolute transparency of the world to the self.[34]

Derrida exemplifies epistemic atheism in its purest form, but there is an important sense in which epistemic atheism lurks within the thought of those contemporary thinkers of a more metaphysical bent, like Lacan, whose thought has been so influential upon film theory of the recent past. For while Lacan is certainly prepared to tell us what really is the case, what really is the case is also what eludes knowledge. Lacan borrows from Heidegger the idea of Being as No-thing-ness, but, contrary to Heidegger, he places No-thing-ness at the origins of the subject's psychical development.[35] For Lacan, the real identity of the subject lies in a condition of existence prior to identity and difference, a condition of 'no-thing-ness' that he calls the 'Real'. He describes the emergence of the ego, the subject capable of knowledge, out of this condition with his famous mirror metaphor, a reinterpretation of Freud's theory of narcissism.[36] Before the mirror of the other, the subject appears as an entity, an object. Although the subject is really no-thing-ness, when 'it' is reflected in the mirror of the other it conceives of itself as something, a self, which it is not. The mirror-stage marks the emergence of the subject capable of recognizing identity and difference from the pre-lapsarian condition in which identity and difference are not yet established. Once the subject symbolizes itself in language, the illusion of the ego—which Lacan labels 'the subject supposed to know'—is consolidated upon the concealment of the no-thing-ness that the subject really is.

In Lacan's theory, language enables knowledge of self and world, but what is in fact known is a world of appearance (the symbolic order) made possible only by the exclusion of the ineffable, the unknown (no-thing-ness, or the Real). However, if no-thing-ness or the Real lies beyond the form of knowledge available to the ego, then it does not affect the coherence and value of the knowledge afforded by the world of appearance. The existence of the ineffable or unknowable undermines the possibility of knowledge only with the addition of the premiss that knowledge must necessarily be conceived in Absolute terms. Either language affords us transcendental guarantees or it is a veil cast over the abyss of the Real, affording a structure to our experience in place of no-thing-ness. Yet Lacan gives us no reason to accept the idea that knowledge, if it is not transcendentally grounded, is an illusion, at least for the everyday purposes of say, understanding what movies are, as opposed to meditating upon the meaning of life in face of death in a universe where God does not exist. Yet for many, epistemic atheism seems to provide the framework for intellectual enquiry in the humanities in general and in film studies in particular. Why is this so? Clearly it is not on account of a disinterested evaluation of its intellectual merits, but on account of its usefulness: epistemic atheism seems to afford a short cut to the ethical critique of Western culture.

Philosophy's critique of epistemology is identified with the ethical critique of modernity

The link between philosophy as a critique of knowledge and the ethical critique of modernity recurs in twentieth-century Continental thought as a whole but it is a defining theme of those Western Marxist thinkers who theorized the failure of social revolution. It emerges fully fledged in the writings of the Frankfurt School philosopher and social theorist Theodor Adorno and is echoed, in different ways, in the work of Louis Althusser, whose thought inspired a whole generation of film theorists, and Michel Foucault, whose ideas have been especially influential in the emerging field of cultural studies. Reduced to a barest sketch the argument is this. In the modern world, scientific reason embodies a form of knowledge in which thought is assumed to mirror nature. Science proceeds as if the individual were empowered to discover reality through observation. However, in the name of discovering reality, it merely projects its own definitions of the world upon it, to which the world is made to conform; it creates the world as it appears. The critique of epistemology gives the lie to this appearance and exposes the falsity of scientific claims to neutral description. But modernity is not simply defined by scientific knowledge; it is also defined by a coercive application of 'scientific rationality' to the shaping of useful social agents, that is, members of society who maintain the social order. Maintenance of the social order is guaranteed precisely by cultivating human subjects who act as if they have been empowered to understand the world by observing it, and who thereby never penetrate beyond the world as it appears. The critique of epistemology, ethically motivated, exposes the coercive nature of modernity, revealing the modern individual, often equated with the 'humanist subject', to be created in subjection. All power to the theorist!

Adorno discusses what he regards as the illusion of scientific reason, in which a concept is projected upon an object in the belief that it is discovering the object, through the concept of 'identity thinking'; Althusser labels it the 'empiricist conception of knowledge'.[37] For both, ideology is conceived not as 'false consciousness', merely a set of beliefs whose contents are false, but as the 'logic' of a system that produces the falsity that is 'consciousness' or 'the ego'. While Adorno emphasizes the role of market forces in moulding human needs, Althusser theorizes the manner in which social institutions repeatedly appeal to the narcissism of human beings by calling upon them to occupy a place in the social world. By responding to this call, human beings define themselves as individuals who believe that their place is freely chosen, while it is in fact determined in advance by a system that 'interpellates' the subject.[38] Althusser suggested erroneously that the interpellated subject was like the subject before Lacan's mirror, the 'subject supposed to know' who is defined by misrecognition, by a failure of understanding that is constitutive of its identity. His error was to assimilate Lacan's 'no-thing', who isn't in a position to recognize much, with a subject whose narcissism can be appealed to. Picking up on this reference, Althusserian film theorists, compounding error upon error, swiftly assimilated Lacan's mirror to the cinematic image, and discovered in the cinema both a model and vehicle for a 'semiotic' theory of subject construction. For film theorists of the 1970s and 1980s, representation itself is coercive, echoing in semiotic language Adorno's claim that the primal form of ideology is 'rationality' or 'logic' itself.

The critique of epistemology is defined as an ethical imperative in modernity, then, because knowledge in the form of science sustains a coercive social order by at once engendering modern subjectivity—the autonomous individual who assumes the capacity to understand the world—and perpetuating human misery, for the autonomy of the subject and the knowledge that appears afforded to it is an illusion. The subject necessarily fails to understand its own condition of existence in subjection (save for the heroic critic of ideology/epistemology who exposes this condition). When the critique of epistemology is cast as the ethical critique of modernity, the mode of enquiry of analytic philosophy exemplified in this volume—precise delimitation of answerable, domain-specific questions—might appear at best irrelevant, incapable of addressing the important questions, and at worst perniciously scientistic, in a manner that exemplifies the very form of discourse that it is philosophy's task, for someone like Adorno, to contest. The first and more moderate claim assumes that the critique of epistemology is a viable way to foster ethical criticism, the key to which is the capacity of the theorist to imagine an alternative to the condition of modernity. The second and more damning claim assumes that analytic philosophy is based upon scientific explanation and hence is incompatible with an ethically informed understanding of human action and the products of human action. Both claims are mistaken.

It is hard to discern anything other than the abandonment of ethics in the argument that the knowing subject, by making a knowledge claim, is ethically compromised. So inescapable is the veil of illusion cast by representation that merely to expose the nature of the veil, however remorselessly, ends up as an empty gesture, a form of left-wing pessimism.[39] Adorno assumes there was once a pre-enlightenment condition of true rather than false mimesis, a sacred or mythical world where what was the case was inseparable from what was thought to be the case, where representation was not yet distinct from what it represented. Yet, like the Lacanian Real, this is no more than a fiction that serves rhetorically to legitimate its theoretical opposite, the mantle of illusion cast by representation. Even a more serious attempt to 'historicize' modernity such as Michel Foucault's offers no real way to imagine an alternative. Foucault agrees with Adorno that the scientific imperative to map the correspondence between words and things, which emerges in the Enlightenment, displaces a prior conception of knowledge where language and object are undifferentiated, but he also pinpoints modernity as the moment when science turned towards understanding Man.[40] The manner in which it does so is at once insidiously coercive and ultimately illusory, as the discourses that constitute man necessarily fail to understand their own conditions of emergence. However, Foucault offers us no consistent place outside the modern 'episteme' (until another epistemic shift seizes us and places us in the next episteme) and hence no position from which to contest the tyranny of the discourses that 'produce' us.

The contradictions undermining Foucault's project have been brilliantly dissected by Charles Taylor. While Foucault's analyses of the development of modern institutions and practices (prisons, clinics, psychoanalysis) seem to be driven by a negative evaluation of them, and thus provide grounds for the rejection or reform of them, the strong relativism of his position with regard to such notions as 'freedom' and 'truth' neutralizes any such moral stance. Taylor reveals the incoherence of Foucault's (Nietzschean) reduction of 'truth' and 'freedom' to power. 'Power', for example, is defined by 'some notion of contraint imposed on someone by a process in some way related to human agency'.[41] Such an idea depends, logically, on a contrasting idea of liberation or freedom—freedom from the constraint imposed in the exercise of power. Similarly, Taylor demonstrates how Foucault's claims regarding the insinuation of forms of subjugation into the minds of subjects depends on notions of masking and illusion—in other words, on deception and falsehood, which 'make no sense without a corresponding notion of truth'.[42] So long as Foucault insists upon the wholesale relativism implicit in a phrase like 'regimes of truth', the possibility of any ethical criticism is foreclosed.[43]

The intellectually compromised nature of an ethical critique that is cast within the framework of epistemic atheism is apparent in the film theory that emerged under its aegis. Here we will focus on one underlying argument of feminist film theory. According to this argument, the position of the 'subject supposed to know' that representation affords coincides with the position of the heterosexual male. The authority of the male subject is established upon the concealment of his own no-thing-ness or insufficiency that is understood in terms of castration. The male subject's awareness of his own potential lack of a penis stands for a more metaphysical sense of lack that is defended against by ascribing a visible lack or insufficiency to women, who are perceived as fetish-images at once adored and vilified. When the 'position' of the subject supposed to know, afforded by representation, is identified in this way with the 'position' of the male subject, the options for the feminist thinker are invidious: either (*a*) adopt the patriarchal standpoint of the one who is supposed to know; or (*b*) resign herself to the lack she is defined by; or (*c*) imagine that there is some position for women to exist outside any framework of representation (feminist essentialism); or (*d*) be constrained ceaselessly to expose the way that representation structures a relationship of subordination between knower and known across the axis of sexual difference. As Jennifer Hammett shows in her contribution to this volume, when feminist criticisms of the representations of women are cast in terms of a critique of the way in which the category of 'woman' is constituted—that is, in terms of an epistemological critique—the moral force of feminist argument as an alternative set of beliefs to those promoted by a patriarchal culture is blunted, for women appear trapped within a patriarchally structured prison-house of representation from which there is no escape. But this prison is not a real one. It is, rather, imagined by the theorist who erroneously concludes from the 'discovery' that any beliefs about women are mediated by the forms of representation that make possible the articulation of those beliefs, that women are merely an effect of representation.

Even if it is conceded that the radical critique of epistemology is an impediment rather than an aid to ethical criticism, and that ethical criticism is better conceived as the criticism of particular beliefs rather than of the idea of knowledge itself, the question arises as to whether analytic philosophy provides a legitimate framework for the conduct of ethical argument. For example, in the writings of Adorno, 'non-dialectical' philosophy exemplifies a form of thinking that trivializes ethical problems by simplifying them. Ethical problems are defined in such a way that they admit of ready solution, and these solutions are then presented as purely factual discoveries: 'What may or may not be reflected upon, however urgent, is regulated by a method blithely modelled after the current methods of exact science. Approved modes of proceeding, pure means, gain primacy over ends, the goals of cognition. Experiences that balk at being unequivocally tagged get a dressing down: the difficulties they cause are said to be due solely to loose, pre-scientific nomenclature.' Adorno's criticism is arguably a just one if its target is specifically positivism in philosophy and the social sciences: in fact,

it echoes the claim of later analytic philosophers that positivism is a profoundly anti-realist doctrine.[44] Of course, Adorno writes from the dogmatic
perspective of one who believes that Hegelian philosophy conclusively
demonstrates that logical and epistemological questions are inseparable
from substantive ethical ones. He implies that, outside his own very specific
tradition, *all* contemporary philosophical thought is tarnished with a blindness to the conceptual assumptions that underpin its claims. This is clearly
not the case.

Yet beyond Adorno's dogmatism and the caricature of analytic philosophy that results from it lies an issue of importance. Much of Continental
thought is motivated by the underlying idea that science, however it is
conceived, cannot deliver a satisfactory understanding of human action and
the products of human action. This is a topic that we shall explore a little
more in the next section; suffice it to say here that the insight is completely
obscured when scientific knowledge is characterized in terms of a simplistic
positivism, and an ethical critique of the limits of scientific explanation is
cast as the radical critique of epistemology that issues from the definition of
knowledge in Absolute terms. The problem attached to scientific explanation is more coherently conceived not as the problem of science *per se* (that
is undermined, like knowledge, by a constitutive failing) but a problem
about the role and limits of scientific explanation.

It is indeed true that many analytic philosophers are wedded to science as
a model for philosophical enquiry into human action. Science held an
exhalted place in the pursuit of knowledge for Russell, an attitude sustained
in Quine's project of a 'naturalized epistemology'. Many analytic philosophers are interested in posing and answering questions of an ethically
neutral character. However, it would be rash to conclude from these facts
that Continental philosophy's suspicion of the analytic tradition is justified.
First, while contemporary analytic philosophy has demonstrated the fertility
of a scientific approach to philosophical enquiry, there is also a strong
counter-current to the scientific paradigm within analytic philosophy which
emphasizes the limitations of science—centrally, causal explanation—in
exploring questions of human value, a strain of argument sustained in
different ways by the late Wittgenstein and Charles Taylor. As we have
suggested, analytic philosophy is best defined by a method of argument,
rather than a doctrine: the methods of argument used by analytic philosophers do not need to appeal to science for their justification. Rather than
being a symptom of the tyranny of science, analytic philosophy provides
precisely the conceptual tools necessary for discussing the strengths and
limits of scientific explanation. Secondly, the existence of questions of an
ethically neutral character does not pose a threat to the conduct of an ethical
enquiry. On the contrary, ethical enquiry surely benefits from the perspicuous delimitation of questions that are not ethical in nature, central to which

is the general demarcation of the ethical from the epistemological. Continental philosophers may resist this distinction, but this resistance is ill-conceived, for the maintenance of the distinction is indispensable to the ethical enquiry they deem to be the essence of philosophy.

The ethical critique of modernity is promoted through a theorization of cinema as a model of, or process governing, knowledge and/or the critique of knowledge

What is specific to film theory informed by Continental philosophy are the ways in which the cinema is related to the critique of epistemology. This theorization takes place in two related but distinct stages. In the first, a philosophy that aspires to the condition of modernist art finds in cinema a form of expression that can be used to model the idea of knowledge and its critique. This way of conceiving of cinema is encouraged by a fact about philosophy and a fact about film. Cartesian and post-Cartesian epistemology thinks about knowledge in terms of visual metaphors; thus the use of film to model epistemology simply involves the application of existing visual metaphors to the medium. This move is encouraged by what many theorists have seen as the unique realism of film, whether understood in terms of iconic resemblance or indexicality (the causal relationship between object and image).[45] The second way of conceiving the relationship between cinema and the idea of knowledge takes the analogy to an altogether different stage: philosophy discovers in the cinema a social apparatus that causally governs the operation of consciousness. Film no longer simply models the idea of knowledge through the congruence between the medium and the metaphors of knowledge as vision. Rather, the cinema is now conceived as a form of mass culture whose effect is perniciously manipulative, as in the writings of Adorno, or it is celebrated as a new art form with the potential not simply to model, but to engineer a state of liberated consciousness that is historically unprecedented, as in the more hyperbolic formulations of both Soviet and post-'68 film theorists.

Although arguments that conceive of cinematic representation as an analogy for the idea of knowledge may be based upon an incoherent conception of epistemology, the aspiration to use the apparatus of cinema to imagine the relationship between consciousness and the world is not itself incoherent; indeed, it has given rise to some imaginative and evocative films (in the work of Hollis Frampton and Michael Snow, for example). However, the theorist who uses the cinema to model the idea of knowledge in this way easily slips into incoherence when the model for a philosophical proposition takes on the status of empirical evidence for its truth: analogy is confused with example. The confusion of analogy with example is a particularly insidious error, for it compounds the fallacy of exemplification with equivocation. Analogy leads the theorist to the example, which then becomes proof of the theory. When the idea of cinema as a model of consciousness is linked to the idea that modernist art is a weapon to transform consciousness, the claim that the cinema models a certain relationship between consciousness and world tends to be taken quite literally. This move is particularly true of post-'68 film theory, where Brecht's arguments about illusion and distantiation in theatre are cast within the framework of the radical critique of epistemology propagated within contemporary French philosophy.

In an argument that was highly influential upon the development of film theory, Jean-Louis Baudry suggests that the cinema places the spectator in the position of Husserl's transcendental subject, whose integrity is assured by the fact that it appears to grasp the object or reality in its fullness, for the material signifier in the cinema—the image—is transparent (that is, we seem to see the object represented itself, rather than a representation of the object). Since the image is really a material signifier, however, and not the reality it appears to be, this 'position' of the transcendental subject and the reality it appears to grasp are a fabrication. Using the language of Lacan, Baudry suggests that the transcendental subject misrecognizes itself in the cinematic image like the subject in the mirror. The cinema is an apparatus that embodies the subject's fantasy of certitude in itself and the world, but it is equally capable of exposing the fictive nature of both subject and object.[46] For apparatus theorists, following Baudry, the cinema could be used in such a way that denies this liberating insight, through the deployment of realist strategies of narration that perpetuate the illusion of a unified, centred subject (classical cinema); or it can be used in a fashion that realizes its potential to explore and expose the subject's disunity, through the deployment of modernist techniques like montage (the avant-garde).

This argument not only echoes Brecht's views on theatrical illusion, it also rehearses in a different language Adorno's strictures on commercial cinema as a medium that dupes the masses by virtue of its form, and which is emblematic of the manner in which 'identitarian logic' has permeated the social sphere to produce a population unable to distinguish reality from illusion. The very same properties of the medium that engender illusion can also have an emancipatory function. But as Noël Carroll has demonstrated thoroughly, the argument is incoherent.[47] The semiotic theory of illusion is false: representations—cinematic and otherwise—do not in general cause us to believe that what they represent is real. The claim about emancipation is self-contradictory—for in the case of the theorist, the subject constructed in representation is one who is supposed to be able to recognize the real character of representation and hence his or her own constructed nature. If this is possible, the theory cannot be true. Film theory that weds the critique of epistemology to the critique of modernity in a manner that is other than metaphorical is thus mistaken. It is based upon a profound over-valuation of the power of representations that indicates a misunderstanding of the way in which representation affects cognition (whether positive or negative).

Postmodernist reflection on the cinema rehearses the same confusions that characterize modernist thinking about the cinema. For some contemporary thinkers influenced by the critique of epistemology, images have so permeated everyday life that it is no longer possible to make the distinction between what is imagined and what is real, a distinction that grounds ethically informed criticism as well as avant-garde practice. If, for Adorno, 'real life is becoming indistinguishable from the movies', he still retains a conception of what real life is like apart from the movies.[48] However, for Jean Baudrillard, influential theorist of the postmodern, 'the very definition of the real becomes: *that of which it is possible to give an equivalent reproduction. . . .* the real is not only what can be reproduced, but *that which is always already reproduced.* The hyperreal.'[49] The 'always already' here is used as a trope to discount the possibility that representations could have a relationship to something outside themselves.[50] Taken at face value, Baudrillard's assertion constitutes a particularly absurd application of the fallacious argument that since what we understand of a phenomenon is mediated by our representation of it, then the phenomenon itself is simply an effect of that representation. This error is compounded by the fallacy of exemplification (yet again): one or two cases where we do confuse representation and reality are taken as the basis of a theory of the nature of reality as a whole! Ironically, this is a profoundly positivist error—in so far as it is only concerned with inductively confirming a hypothesis—but one as often as not committed, as it is here, by those working in a tradition which sees itself as beyond such epistemic naivety.

Like Baudrillard, the French philosopher Gilles Deleuze conceives of the cinema as a simulacrum, a simulation that defies any distinction between what is real and what is merely a representation of reality. However, unlike Baudrillard, Deleuze's point of departure is not a characterization of the social effects of an apparatus but the idea that cinema models the critique of epistemology. Yet, in contrast to contemporary film theory that draws on transcendental phenomenology and psychoanalysis, Deleuze relies on a materialist interpretation of the philosophy of Bergson. Like Husserl, Bergson confronts the problem of scepticism that Cartesianism gives rise to, but unlike Husserl he posits an alternative conception of reality—the temporal *durée* that encompasses thought and substance alike. Deleuze uses Bergson to challenge any theory of the image as a form of illusion, for, he argues, spatial reality together with our image or thought of it are one and the same thing. Because of its capacity to realize fully any imagined space-time continuum, cinema is identical with reality conceived in Bergsonian terms; the cinema models a Bergsonian universe. For Deleuze, however, the cinema does not merely *model* a Bergsonian world. Like many of his modernist predecessors, Deleuze is concerned with the idea that the cinema emerges at a particular historical moment. The cinema, he claims, produces 'its own evidence' of reality as it is described by Bergson.[51] This claim is indefensible for it again conflates analogy with example. Yet without it Deleuze's theory, relying so heavily as it does on Bergsonism, seems merely a curiosity.

Over and above the conceptual failings of these theories, what is striking about the Continental philosophy that has been taken to the cinema is the way in which extraordinarily sweeping claims that pertain to the end of epistemology, the construction of the subject, or theses concerning the ultimate constituents of reality, are all rooted in one aspect of the cinema— the causal or indexical nature of the photographic image—as if within this feature of cinematic representation somehow lies an answer to every signifi-cant question we might seek to ask about the cinema (and even modernity or knowledge in general). However, this feature of the cinema achieves its salience only because of the philosophical presuppositions that are brought to bear upon it. Once these presuppositions are abandoned, as we have argued that they must be, then the place of indexicality in our overall understanding of cinematic representation becomes a question to be inves-tigated. Three chapters in this volume—by Currie, Walton, and Allen— address this question. Furthermore, it becomes clear that there are many questions about the nature of cinema and our responses to it that do not pertain to the causal or indexical character of the photographic image, nor, to anticipate the future direction of such arguments, to its digital character.

SCIENCE, SIGNIFICANCE, AND RATIONALITY

As we have seen, many within the analytic tradition regard science highly, seeing it principally as a resource and a paragon of practice rather than a reductive, insidious, and/or ethnocentric practice. It is important, though, to recognize how distant the science so prized by many analytic philosophers is from the caricatural description of it to be found in a great deal of film and cultural theory. We allude here, once again, to two of the great bogey-men stalking the pages of many works of Continentally informed theory: empiricism and positivism. It is remarkable that for many theorists, analytic philosophy can be reduced to logical positivism—a doctrine which came under attack almost as soon as it was expounded in the 1920s and 1930s, and whose central principle has long been recognized as self-refuting by other philosophers in the analytic tradition.[52] Since then, philosophers of science have demonstrated in numerous ways how science is a far more complex matter than the inductive accumulation of independently verifiable facts, without, however, suggesting that there are no differences between scientific and other kinds of knowledge or practice.

There is space here only to discuss a few of these developments. Perhaps the most well-known of these is Karl Popper's notion of falsification—the argument that science advances not, or not solely, through inductive confirmation, but through the falsification of hypotheses. The validity of a scientific hypothesis lies in its availability to falsification whilst remaining unfalsified; a hypothesis supported by evidence is said by Popper to be 'corroborated', a more tentative notion than 'confirmation'. Other important arguments concern the 'theory-dependence' of observation statements, of observation itself, and of experiment; and the 'underdetermination' of theory by data. All of these, in their different ways, point to the constructive role of theoretical models and assumptions in experimental practice, and to the fact that facts do not simply pile up independent of the 'equipment' used by scientists (in the broadest sense—theoretical concepts as well as technological devices). As John Hyman puts it, 'Metaphor and analogy are the scaffolding of science.'[53]

Along with this, few would now argue with the idea that science does not float entirely free from social and political—in general, historical—matters. The question is: at what level(s) do these social and political issues affect scientific concepts, practices, and research goals? Many scientific discoveries may have been driven and enabled by military and imperialistic goals, but does that make the scientific theories themselves equally contingent or 'socially constructed'? Can the 'context of discovery' be kept apart from the 'context of justification'? Some philosophers—social constructionists— argue that the context of discovery is not in principle separate from the epistemology of science or the norms of justification. Our view is that this is an unsustainably relativistic perspective. Social constructionism—and more broadly, the sociology of science—draws attention to a host of important phenomena: the social forces which determine the distribution of research funds and thus which problems are prioritized; the way in which the application of epistemic norms may be undermined in particular instances (e.g. where the political expediency of a certain outcome affects the conduct and interpretation of research);[54] and, more generally, the fact that it is not only the truth or plausibility of scientific claims which leads to their acceptance. Nevertheless, if epistemological norms of justification are entirely relative to social acceptability and political expediency, we might well ask, with Paisley Livingston: 'Are we to imagine that airplanes can fly only because they are useful in warfare and business?'[55] Moreover, epistemological questions immediately reassert themselves with respect to the claims of the social constructionists themselves. The sociology of science is, therefore, to be welcomed for all the reasons given above, but it cannot actually replace epistemology. The sociology of science thus remains distinct from the epistemology of science. The important point to be made here, though, is that a range of views on this matter are held by philosophers in the analytic tradition, including social constructionist views.[56]

It may come as a shock to some to discover that there are a number of philosophers in the analytic tradition who abandon a commitment to 'realism' in their account of science, in favour of an instrumental account. 'Realism' refers here to the ontological assumption that the observable items of ordinary experience exist, and that they exist independently of our mental experience or apprehension of them. 'Scientific realism' is the more specific doctrine that the unobservable entities of science exist, and do so in a mind-independent fashion. 'Instrumentalism', by contrast, names the anti-realist belief that the theories and concepts of science are merely tools or 'convenient fictions'[57] which happen to work reasonably well in our efforts to predict and manipulate the physical world. Still more radically, some very distinguished philosophers of language, such as Michael Dummett and Hilary Putnam, argue against realism more generally ('metaphysical', 'common sense', or 'natural' realism). Moreover, it has been argued that logical positivism, far from being an extreme form of empiricism or naive realism, is a profoundly (if covertly) anti-realist doctrine.[58] The attitude of the analytic tradition to science, then, is a sophisticated matter which bears little resemblance to the lumpen positivism so often used as a stick with which to beat it.[59]

The point of this discussion of post-positivist philosophy of science is to highlight its sophistication and variety. Those who model film theory on a 'naturalized' philosophical practice, which sees itself as an element of natural science, are rarely guilty of the epistemic ingenuousness of which they are so often accused. But as we have already suggested, this is not to say that the casting of film theory as a science—especially a natural science—is beyond challenge. Central to such a challenge is the idea that much of film theory, and all of film criticism, is concerned with the human significance and evaluation of film, and that scientific methodology is simply inappropriate for the examination of such questions. The concerns of film theory lie, rather, in the domains of ethics and aesthetics. While science occurs in a context of human interests and raises questions of value, it aspires to a value-neutral description and explanation of the natural world (however this neutrality is qualified by the considerations discussed above). Wherever questions of significance and evaluation become the explicit object or content of a practice, however, science can hardly be the model for it.

Charles Taylor has made this point by arguing that humans are uniquely 'self-interpreting' animals, in the sense that much of their reality is constituted by culturally informed interpretations of themselves and their fellows.[60] According to Taylor, this fact circumscribes the explanatory reach of natural science, for in so far as it aspires to an 'experience-independent' description of the world, it cannot account for 'experience-dependent' phenomena—for example, complex emotions like shame. The language of science is, in this sense, unable to grasp the significance of human beliefs, emotions, values, and practices; the most it could conceivably achieve is the description of physical states (e.g. brain states) which correspond to these experiences, which is not the same as describing the experiences *qua* experiences. Importantly, however, Taylor also shows that this argument against naturalism does not necessarily parlay into an argument for strong conceptual or ethical relativism; he is as critical of the all-encompassing pretensions of naturalism as of 'a debilitating relativism'.[61] This is clear from his sympathetic but critical discussion of Foucault, which we have already discussed. Taylor thus avoids the false dichotomy of, on the one hand, an exclusive commitment to natural science as the model of all knowledge, and, on the other hand, a complete rejection of science along with the embrace of deconstructive scepticism and post-structural belle-lettrism. His work offers a model for a politicized criticism of national and international film culture, balancing the dangers of insidious ethnocentrism (of which film studies is well aware) with an awareness of the absurdities of relativism (of which film studies is virtually oblivious).

Similar anxieties about 'naturalism' or 'scientism' are given voice, directly or indirectly, in several chapters in this volume, including those of Allen, Rodriguez, Wilson, and Hammett. Elsewhere, Karen Hanson has directly challenged the modelling of film theory on science, while at the same time arguing that many of the core features of philosophical argument which are taken to be scientific in character—for example, rigorous argument, attention to countervailing evidence—are ones in fact shared by other domains of thought unconcerned with causal explanation, the generation of laws, and prediction. Quoting William James, Hanson identifies this philosophical impulse with a 'passion for distinguishing . . . [and] Loyalty to clearness and integrity of perception, dislike of blurred outlines, of vague identifications . . .'[62] Hanson, in other words, is among those who would distinguish philosophy from science, while allowing that much of what counts as good scientific practice is good practice in other, directly value-laden endeavours. Arguing that some of the questions of film theory cannot be addressed on a natural scientific basis does not amount to an argument against clear and precise reasoning.

In response to Hanson's argument, one can point to the possibility of a 'naturalized ethics' and 'aesthetics', that is, to contributions that the sciences might make even to these domains: evolutionary arguments about the origins and function of morality, for example, or psychological arguments about our perception of form, movement, colour, sound, and so forth. But it would be a serious mistake, akin to a Rylean 'category mistake', to assume that such theories could ever supplant the making of value-judge-ments within or between value systems: we might learn from perceptual psychologists about the effects of rapid editing or Steadicam-style camera movement, for example, but this will hardly conjure up an evaluation of films using such techniques.[63] Scientific knowledge can inform, but it cannot make, aesthetic judgements, any more than it can make political decisions. 'Film theory'—and philosophy of film—cuts across many different sorts of question, as the essays in this volume amply demonstrate, and may therefore legitimately draw upon the methods of both natural and social scientific practice, as well as those of conceptual investigation and value theory. What defines 'film theory' is an empirical object of study, not any one aspect of its nature or uses.[64] What is ill-conceived is the attempt to unify all of the practices used to investigate this empirical object under the same rubric, whether of 'science' or any other.

For some, this position still grants too much to science—some radical conceptual and cultural relativists regard science as simply a culturally specific practice with no special claim to knowledge.[65] Such relativism faces obvious difficulties in explaining away the differences in success in manipu-lating the physical world between sciences like physics and non-scientific belief systems like astrology. And as we have seen in our discussions of Derrida and Foucault, relativism is also self-defeating to the extent that it disallows knowledge claims and ethical judgements. Rather than dwelling on these problems further, however, one might ask whether the goals underlying such relativism are in fact best served by it (an echo of the question we have already posed about Continentally inspired film theory). Relativism has been sustained by a desire to respect cultural difference and variation, and to undermine the triumphalist and hubristic modernism which sees itself as superior to traditional or 'primitive' culture. As we will see, however, there are powerful arguments for the existence of non-relative, cross-cultural norms of agency, rationality, and personhood, which nevertheless respect the complexity of diverse cultural situations. The con-cerns of relativism, in other words, are in fact better served through a basic, universal framework of agency and rationality. Indeed, we shall argue that it is only through acknowledging such norms that one can avoid writing off cultures radically different from our own as either irrational, inscrutable, or irreducibly 'other'. Many of these arguments have been influential on the emerging body of analytic film theory: arguments from speech act theory and linguistic pragmatism, philosophical psychology, theories of rationality and of personal identity.

Concepts and arguments drawn from the speech act theories of John Searle and Paul Grice are most in evidence in discussions of documentary and non-fiction film-making. Noël Carroll, Carl Plantinga, and Trevor Ponech have all developed accounts of documentary which define it as a specific kind of 'utterance' (an action performed with expressive or communicative intent) intended to be understood as a direct assertion or truth-claim about reality (as contrasted with an utterance which we are to entertain as a fiction).[66] All three authors are motivated by the inability of purely textual accounts (those based on the structural and/or stylistic features of films in isolation from a context of intention or reception) to explain the differences in our attitudes toward documentaries and fiction films, and even our ability to identify a documentary, without an implicit appeal to the intention of an agent. A pragmatic framework has also been applied to the analysis of the fiction film by Gregory Currie, again developing and adapting concepts from Grice.[67]

The concept of 'intentionality'—the 'directedness' or purposiveness of cognition—embedded within speech act theory is also a crucial ingredient in theories of rational action and agency. Although 'rationality' is another concept which has been attacked as no more than an item in a patriarchal and ethnocentric ideology of Western cultural imperialism, Paisley Livingston has persuasively argued for the inescapability of a basic 'heuristic of practical reasoning' in the understanding of human agency in general. The heuristic states that we invariably operate within the assumption that the actions of other human agents are explicable in terms of the beliefs and desires (motivational states) that they hold. This heuristic is fallible in two ways: actions may turn out to be irrational or a-rational (for example, the product of some purely organic process, like an aneurism, rather than an intentional state). But we begin by assuming a rational principle of explanation, rather than an a-rational or an irrational one (and the latter is, of course, only definable against a background notion of rationality). The rationality assumed here is not, however, the perfect rationality assumed in theories of logic or economic calculation, but a 'bounded and minimal' one operating in the context of human cognitive limitations.

Once this last point is understood, far from losing its relevance when it comes to the analysis of non-Western cultures, the necessity of the heuristic of practical rationality becomes all the more apparent. In order to obtain any purchase on what could easily be dismissed as irrational behaviour, we have to discover the society's network of beliefs, values, and associated motivations—that is, the constituents of the heuristic of practical reasoning. And this is also true of the symbolic artefacts of the culture, such as narratives, in so far as understanding the actions of characters in terms of practical reasoning is basic to comprehending narratives.[68] Why does Soma continuously shout at a wooden post wrapped in cloth, carried by two companions, in Solomani Sise's *Yeelen* (1987)? Because he wants to find his son and believes that the 'Magic Pestle' will aid him in this task; and as the opening titles of the film indicate, belief in the power of the Magic Pestle 'to find what has been lost' is standard in the elite caste of Bambaran society to which he belongs. Once again, this does not rule out instances where an action is explained by a brain lesion or by the subversion of the agent's reasoning by some unconscious mental process. But we begin with the heuristic of practical reasoning, and in a great many cases have no need to turn to non-rational forms of explanation.

Two objections to this argument can be quickly laid to rest. The first is that any talk of 'intentionality' in relation to literary or filmic works lapses back into the 'intentional fallacy'.[69] The argument here, however, is that attention to the intentional and rational acts leading to the production of a text is a necessary feature of a full understanding of it, not that it is sufficient for such an understanding. Unintended meanings may still be legitimately recognized in a work, and may indeed be crucial. The second objection is that too much explanatory weight is placed upon an isolated moment of intentional deliberation, as if such discrete intentional states are not situated within the larger networks of desires, beliefs, and attitudes, of both the individual and society. This objection has been one of the justifications for anti-intentionalist frameworks of literary and cultural understanding: meaning simply cannot be controlled by the intentions of an individual, so we must look elsewhere if we are to understand cultural dynamics.[70]

A very different response to the limitations of examining isolated, discrete intentional states is pursued by Livingston and Ponech, drawing on the work of Michael Bratman and Jon Elster.[71] Accepting that 'time-slice' analyses of the isolated actions of human agents are overly abstract and idealized—implausibly positing 'agents who are always starting from scratch in their deliberations'[72]—they argue that individual actions must be seen in the context of various and multiple goals and plans that the agent may have, short and long term, overt and covert, neutral and politicized, which may complement or conflict with one another to varying degrees. Moreover, actions are often 'strategic' (that is, made in the light of judgements concerning what other agents are likely to do) and collective. Finally, they recognize that the activities of readers and viewers of texts must also be analysed in terms of their practical reasoning, taking account of all of the complicating factors just outlined. This is exemplified by the kind of textual 'appropriation' or 'reading through' texts discussed by Tommy Lott in his chapter on black cinema criticism. In short, rather than jettisoning intentionality or rationality, their complexity is recognized. Other facets of the debates on agency and intentionality, especially as they bear upon questions of authorship, are broached by both Livingston and Berys Gaut in their chapters in this volume.

Much of this introductory essay has been concerned with describing the methods, debates, and principles of analytic philosophy, with only occasional reference to the contributions such philosophy has made to film theory. This is partly because, so far, there have been relatively few such contributions: for most members of the film, media, and cultural studies communities, analytic philosophy is an undiscovered country. As often happens with such territories, its occupants have been misrepresented and simplified, and so it is that the task of this essay has been to expose such intellectual xenophobia for what it is. Another consequence of the quarantining of analytic philosophy has been an exaggerated sense of the purism of both the Continental and analytic traditions. The work of Taylor is a case in point. In fact, notwithstanding all that has been said so far, the image of a mutually exclusive and exhaustive constrast between analytic and Continental philosophy is in many respects misleading and inadequate as a picture of Western philosophy, past and present. At the most basic level, many members of one tradition or the other venture onto the terrain of the other for useful or telling insights and intuitions (as well as the better-known put-downs): witness Kivy's references to Adorno and Eisler in his chapter in this volume; Livingston's to Adorno and Merleau-Ponty in a recent essay on characterization in fiction; and the unexpected conjunction of Jacques Derrida and David Bordwell in an essay by another contributor to this volume, Deborah Knight.[73] This cross-over extends to more ambitious attempts to expound the arguments of speculative, Continental philosophers in an analytic fashion: examples include Taylor on Heidegger, Hegel, Gadamer, and Foucault; G. A. Cohen and Jon Elster on Marx; Ivan Soll on Nietzsche; Samuel Wheeler on Derrida; the ambitious synthesis of various analytic and Continental perspectives on language in the work of Charles Altieri; and, closer to home, Alan Casebier's work on Husserlian phenomenology and film, which provides a very different conception of Husserl's thought from the one that has been most influential in film theory. Finally, writers are beginning to trace historical commonalities between the two traditions of philosophy. Michael Dummett, for example, has written that 'the roots of analytical philosophy . . . are the *same* roots as those of the phenomenological school, which appears to many the antithesis of analytical, or of what they think of as "Anglo-American" philosophy.'[74] His analysis focuses on the overlapping philosophical interests, as well as the separate paths of development, of Frege and Husserl.

We have noted that analytic philosophy is often conceived of as a pedantic, conservative discipline by scholars of film, media, and culture, in comparison with the imaginative richness and moral and ideological focus of much Contintental thought. To be sure, the analytic tradition places rigorous thinking at a premium, and we have emphasized just how important this virtue is at a time when critical discourse in the humanities is too often governed by sloppiness, sophistry, and dogma. However, analytic thought does not entail political conservatism, nor do analytic philosophers lack imagination. On the contrary, the analytic tradition is rich and diverse: the analytic toolbox contains not only a variety of useful instruments, but ones which can and have been put to a variety of purposes. A vast array of phenomena has been examined by analytic philosophers, and many different doctrines defended by them. The aim of analytic film theory is not to block the pursuit or defence of any particular intuition or doctrine, but to improve the rigour with which such defences are made. Its purpose is not to put certain positions out of bounds, but to ensure that any position taken is argued for in such a way that it can clearly be argued with.

NOTES

1. Bernard Williams, *Ethics and the Limits of Philosophy*, 3rd edn. (London: Fontana, 1993), p. vi.
2. For other symptoms of this pluralism, see David Bordwell and Noël Carroll (eds.), *Post-Theory: Reconstructing Film Studies* (Madison: University of Wisconsin Press, 1996), in which the editors argue for a range of theoretical models focused on 'small' or 'middle-range' problems, rather than a single, all-encompassing Theory. Warren Buckland (ed.), *The Film Spectator: From Sign to Mind* (Amsterdam: Amsterdam University Press, 1995), represents another line of development within this pluralistic context, in this case exploring the intersection of semiotics with Chomskian cognitivism and linguistic pragmatism.
3. Both 'analytic' and 'analytical' are used in the literature; for the sake of consistency we will only use 'analytic' in this introduction (other than in quotes where the author uses 'analytical').
4. Of particular interest in this regard is Peggy Zeglin Brand and Carolyn Korsmeyer (eds.), *Feminism and Tradition in Aesthetics* (University Park: Pennsylvania State University Press, 1995), in which a number of analytic philosophers address the intersection of gender and aesthetics.
5. Noël Carroll dubs this 'peaceful coexistence pluralism'; Bordwell and Carroll, *Post-Theory*, 62–3.
6. In this respect this collection also differs from another recent collection with a philosophical emphasis: Cynthia A. Freeland and Thomas E. Wartenberg (eds.), *Philosophy and Film* (New York: Routledge, 1995). According to the editors' own description, this volume contains work 'from widely divergent schools of thought: analytical, "Continental," Marxist, feminist, pragmatist, post-modern, anti-post-modern, classical' (4). Our aim, by contrast, is to make a case for the contribution that a specific kind of philosophy—analytic philosophy—might make to film theory, while at the same time demonstrating its breadth and countering certain mis-descriptions of it.
7. Discussion of the nature of this dialogue can be found in Alvin Goldman, *Liaisons: Philosophy Meets the Cognitive and Social Sciences* (Cambridge, Mass.: MIT, 1991).
8. This point of view is represented in John Hyman (ed.), *Investigating Psychology* (New York: Routledge, 1991).
9. C. D. Broad, 'Critical and Speculative Philosophy', in J. H. Muirhead (ed.), *Contemporary British Philosophy*, 1st series (London: Allen and Unwin, 1924), 78, quoted in P. M. S. Hacker, *Wittgenstein's Place in Twentieth Century Philosophy* (Oxford: Blackwell, 1996), 67.
10. The classic statement of this argument is W. V. Quine, 'Two Dogmas of Empiricism', *From a Logical Point of View* (Cambridge, Mass.: Harvard University Press, 1953). Quine provides an overview of his perspective in W. V. Quine, *From Stimulus to Science* (Cambridge, Mass.: Harvard University Press, 1995). Other arguments for

naturalistic philosophy can be found in Michael Devitt and Kim Sterelny, *Language and Reality* (Cambridge, Mass.: MIT Press, 1987); and David Papineau, *Philosophical Naturalism* (Oxford: Oxford University Press, 1993).

11. Devitt and Sterelny, *Language and Reality*, 229.

12. Some commentators characterize the most influential contemporary Anglo-American philosophy as 'post-analytic', a phrase intended to suggest the relative lack of consensus concerning the central problems and methods of philosophy, as well as the self-questioning of basic assumptions within the tradition to the point where it ceases to be recognizable as a tradition. Needless to say, we regard this as an exaggerated claim. See John Rajchman, 'Philosophy in America', in John Rajchman and Cornel West (eds.), *Post-Analytic Philosophy* (New York: Columbia University Press, 1985).

13. David Gorman, 'From Small Beginnings: Literary Theorists Encounter Analytic Philosophy', *Poetics Today*, 11: 3 (Fall 1990), 653.

14. Abductive reasoning is defined as 'inference to the best explanation', or accepting a conclusion on the grounds that it explains the available evidence, as contrasted with acceptance on the basis of inference from the particular to the general (induction), or acceptance on the basis of entailment from the general to the particular (deduction).

15. This volume, 134.

16. Cf. Gregory Currie's remarks on 'revisionism' in *Image and Mind: Film, Philosophy, and Cognitive Science* (New York: Cambridge University Press, 1995), 216.

17. On moves away from reduction as a goal in philosophy, see Stephen Stich's remarks in *From Folk Psychology to Cognitive Science: The Case against Belief* (Cambridge, Mass.: MIT, 1983), 76–8. Cf. also John Searle's remarks on precise theories of 'indeterminate phenomena', quoted in Carl Plantinga, 'Defining Documentary: Fiction, Non-Fiction, and Projected Worlds', in *Persistence of Vision*, 5 (1987), 50.

18. Deborah Knight, 'Women, Subjectivity, and the Rhetoric of Anti-Humanism in Feminist Film Theory', *New Literary History*, 26: 1 (1995), 46; Knight draws on Sandra M. Gilbert and Susan Gubar, 'The Mirror and the Vamp: Reflections on Feminist Criticism', in Ralph Cohen (ed.), *The Future of Literary Theory* (New York: Routledge, 1989).

19. Jacqueline Rose, 'Paranoia and the Film System', *Screen* 17: 4 (Winter 1976/7), 89.

20. For further diagnosis of ills related to the fallacy of exemplification, see Richard Levin, 'The New Interdisciplinarity in Literary Criticism', in Nancy Esterlin and Barbara Riebling, *After Poststructuralism: Interdisciplinarity and Literary Theory* (Evanston, Ill.: Northwestern University Press, 1993), 13–43.

21. Jonathan Crary, *Techniques of the Observer: On Vision and Modernity in the Nineteenth Century* (Cambridge, Mass.: MIT Press, 1990).

22. Ibid. 90.

23. For other critical discussions of the use of punning and association in film theory, see Noël Carroll, 'Address to the Heathen', *October*, 23 (Winter 1982), 114–17, 153–7; David Bordwell, *Making Meaning: Inference and Rhetoric in the Interpretation of Cinema* (Cambridge, Mass.: Harvard University Press, 1989); and David Bordwell, 'Contemporary Film Studies and the Vicissitudes of Grand Theory', in Bordwell and Carroll, *Post-Theory*, 23–4.

24. For a defence of Derrida along these lines, see Richard Rorty, *Contingency, Irony, Solidarity* (Cambridge: Cambridge University Press, 1989), 122–37.

25. For a related discussion, see Paisley Livingston, 'The Poetic Fallacy', in Dwight Eddins (ed.), *The Emperor Redressed: Critiquing Critical Theory* (Tuscaloosa: University of Alabama Press, 1995), 150–65.

26. See David Bordwell, 'Contemporary Film Studies and the Vicissitudes of Grand Theory', in Bordwell and Carroll, *Post-Theory*, 3–36.

27. See J. G. Merquior, *From Prague to Paris: A Critique of Structuralist and Post-structuralist Thought* (London: Verso, 1986), 237–44, for a delightfully tart commentary on this tendency in Continental philosophy.

28. Thus with particular reference to the work of Michael Snow, Annette Michelson has written of 'cinematic works that present themselves as analogues of consciousness . . . as though inquiry into the nature and processes of experience had found in this century's art form, a striking, a uniquely direct presentational mode. The illusionism of the new, temporal art reflects and occasions reflection upon, the conditions of knowledge.' 'Toward Snow', in P. Adams Sitney (ed.), *The Avant-Garde Film: A Reader of Theory and Criticism* (New York: Anthology Film Archives, 1978), 172. Elsewhere, Michelson speaks of cinema in its function as a metaphor for consciousness or knowledge as a 'philosophical toy'. See Annette Michelson, 'On the Eve of the Future: The Reasonable Fascimile and the Philosophical Toy', *October*, 29 (Summer 1984), 3–20.

29. Consider, for example, the way in which Slavoj Žižek uses the films of Hitchcock and other texts of popular culture to illustrate Lacan's theories. *Enjoy Your Symptom!: Jacques Lacan in Hollywood and Out* (New York: Routledge, 1992); and *Looking Awry: An Introduction to Jacques Lacan through Popular Culture* (Cambridge, Mass.: MIT Press, 1992).

30. See D. N. Rodowick, *The Crisis of Political Modernism: Criticism and Ideology in Contemporary Film Theory* (Urbana: University of Illinois Press, 1988).

31. Derrida addresses Husserl in a number of works. Our focus is a central argument of his essay 'Speech and Phenomenon', in *Speech and Phenomena, and Other Essays on Husserl's Theory of Signs* (Evanston, Ill.: Northwestern University Press, 1973).

32. The a prioristic nature of deconstructive scepticism is emphasized by M. H. Abrams in 'What is Humanistic Criticism?', and by Frederick Crews in 'The End of the Poststructuralist Era', both in Eddins (ed.), *Emperor Redressed*, 13–44 and 45–61 respectively.

33. For a more detailed presentation of this argument seem, Thomas Pavel, *The Feud of Language: A History of Structuralist Thought* (Oxford: Blackwell, 1989), 38–73; Raymond Tallis, *Not Saussure: A Critique of Post-Saussurian Literary Theory* (London: Macmillan, 1988), 164–234; Richard Allen, *Projecting Illusion: Film Spectatorship and the Impression of Reality* (New York: Cambridge University Press, 1995), 47–80; and Paisley Livingston, *Literary Knowledge: Humanistic Inquiry and the Philosophy of Science* (Ithaca, NY: Cornell University Press, 1988), 42–55.

34. This point is well argued by Susan Haack in her demolition of Richard Rorty's fashionable debunking of epistemology, in *Evidence and Inquiry: Towards Reconstruction in Epistemology* (Oxford: Blackwell, 1993), 182–202.

35. For a critical discussion of Lacan's relationship to Heidegger and Hegel, see Mikkel Borch-Jacobson's ironically titled *Lacan: The Absolute Master*, trans. Douglas Birck (Stanford, Calif.: Stanford University Press, 1991).

36. Jacques Lacan, 'The Mirror Stage as Formative of the Function of the I', in *Écrits: A Selection*, trans. Alan Sheridan (New York: Tavistock, 1977), 1–7.

37. Theodor W. Adorno, *Negative Dialectics*, trans. E. B. Ashton (New York: Continuum, 1983), 149; Louis Althusser and Étienne Balibar, *Reading Capital*, trans. Ben Brewster (London: Verso, 1979), 35.

38. See Louis Althusser, 'Ideology and Ideological State Apparatuses (Notes towards an Investigation)', *Lenin and Philosophy and other Essays*, trans. Ben Brewster (New York: Monthly Review Press, 1971), 127–86.

39. Adorno writes: 'the fact that cognition or truth is a picture of its object is the substitute and consolation for the irreparable cutting off of like from like. As false illusion the picture character of cognition conceals the fact that the subject and object no longer resemble one another. And that means nothing else than that they are

alienated from one another.' *Against Epistemology: A Metacritique*, trans. Willis Domingo (Cambridge, Mass.: MIT, 1983), 143.

40. See Michel Foucault, *The Order of Things: An Archaeology of the Human Sciences* (New York: Vintage/Random House, 1973).

41. Charles Taylor, 'Foucault on Freedom and Truth', in *Philosophy and the Human Sciences: Philosophical Papers* 2 (Cambridge: Cambridge University Press, 1985), 174.

42. Ibid. 176.

43. On this point, see also Mary Midgeley, 'On Trying out One's New Sword', in *Heart and Mind: The Varieties of Moral Experience* (London: Methuen, 1981).

44. Adorno, *Negative Dialectics*, 211. Adorno's target is not precise and he does not speak of analytic philosophy as such. This almost accidental point of agreement is thrown up in the curious 'debate' between Adorno and Popper, recorded in Theodor W. Adorno, Hans Albert, Ralf Dahrendorf, Jurgen Habermas, Harald Pilot, and Karl R. Popper, *The Positivist Dispute in German Sociology*, trans. Glyn Adey and David Frisby (London: Heinemann Educational Books, 1976).

45. Martin Jay paints in broad strokes the connection between film theory and the visual metaphors of Cartesian and post-Cartesian philosophy in *Downcast Eyes: The Denigration of Vision in Twentieth Century French Thought* (Berkeley and Los Angeles: University of California Press, 1994).

46. Jean-Louis Baudry, 'Ideological Effects of the Basic Cinematographic Apparatus', trans. Alan Williams, in Philip Rosen (ed.), *Narrative, Apparatus, Ideology* (New York: Columbia University Press, 1986), 286–98.

47. Noël Carroll, *Mystifying Movies: Fads and Fallacies in Contemporary Film Theory* (New York: Columbia University Press, 1988).

48. Theodor Adorno and Max Horkheimer, *Dialectic of the Enlightenment*, trans. John Cumming (New York: Continuum, 1972), 126.

49. Jean Baudrillard, *Simulations*, trans. Paul Foss, Paul Patton, and Philip Beitchman (New York: Semiotext(e), 1983), 146.

50. On the 'always already' argument, see Livingston, *Literary Knowledge*, 176–86.

51. Gilles Deleuze, *Cinema 1: The Movement Image*, trans. Hugh Tomlinson and Barbara Habberjam (Minneapolis: University of Minnesota Press, 1986), 56.

52. Adorno et al., *The Positivist Dispute*, provides a good instance of the term 'positivism' being interpreted so loosely that it is used to characterize the work of one of the first critics of logical positivism, Karl Popper.

53. John Hyman, *The Imitation of Nature* (Oxford: Blackwell, 1989), 1. An introductory overview of the concepts in the philosophy of science mentioned here is A. F. Chalmers, *What is this Thing called Science?* 2nd edn. (Buckingham: Open University Press, 1982). On the theory-dependence of observation, see N. R. Hanson, *Patterns of Discovery* (Cambridge: Cambridge University Press, 1958); and on the theory-dependence of observation statements, see Karl Popper, *The Logic of Scientific Discovery* (London: Hutchinson, 1959) (original German version, 1935).

54. See e.g. Willard Rowland's investigation into the way in which the results of audience research into TV violence are framed by both network TV and governmental agendas, in *The Politics of TV Violence: Policy Uses of Communication Research* (Beverly Hills, Calif.: Sage, 1983).

55. Livingston, *Literary Knowledge*, 77.

56. One of the founding works of social constructionism within the philosophy of science was, of course, Thomas Kuhn's *The Structure of Scientific Revolutions* (Chicago: Chicago University Press, 1962). For a later and more radical example, see David Bloor, *Knowledge and Social Imagery* (London: RKP, 1976). For critical commentary, see Livingston, *Literary Knowledge*, 67–79.

57. Chalmers, *What is this Thing called Science?*, 147.

58. See Devitt and Sterelny, *Language and Reality*, 190; and Ian Hacking, *Representing and Intervening* (Cambridge: Cambridge University Press, 1983), ch. 3.

59. Noël Carroll makes numerous pertinent and incisive remarks on the issues of truth, evidence, empiricism, and more generally on the value of debates in post-positivist philosophy of science in relation to film theory, in his introductory essay in Bordwell and Carroll, *Post-Theory*, 37–70.

60. Charles Taylor, 'Self-interpreting Animals', in *Human Agency and Language: Philosophical Papers 1* (Cambridge: Cambridge University Press, 1985), 47. Related arguments have been made by Daniel Dennett, Thomas Nagel, and John Searle.

61. Charles Taylor, 'Understanding and Ethnocentricity', in *Philosophy and the Human Sciences*, 131.

62. James cited in Karen Hanson, 'Provocations and Justifications of Film', in Freeland and Wartenberg, *Philosophy and Film*, 45. See also Susan Haack, *Evidence and Inquiry*, 137.

63. It may be possible for scientific research to discover some innate human predilections and aversions for certain types of perceptual and cognitive experience, but it is most unlikely that these will be sufficient to explain the huge diversity of aesthetic forms and evaluative criteria which human history displays. Providing an evolutionary argument for the basis of aesthetic or moral experience is one thing; providing such an argument for specific aesthetic or moral criteria is quite another.

64. On the contrast between empirical object or 'problem' and 'doctrine' driven theory, see also Bordwell, 'Grand Theory', in Bordwell and Carroll, *Post-Theory*, 28.

65. See, for example, Steve Fuller, *Philosophy, Rhetoric, and the End of Knowledge: The Coming of Science and Technology Studies* (Madison: University of Wisconsin Press, 1993); and Bloor, *Knowledge and Social Imagery*.

66. See Carl Plantinga, 'Defining Documentary', 44–54; Carroll (this volume); and Ponech (this volume).

67. Gregory Currie, *The Nature of Fiction* (New York: Cambridge University Press, 1990), and *Image and Mind*.

68. Paisley Livingston, *Literature and Rationality: Ideas of Agency in Theory and Fiction* (Cambridge: Cambridge University Press, 1991), 8, 54.

69. In their essay on the intentional fallacy, W. K. Wimsatt and Monroe Beardsley argue that 'the design or intention of the author is neither available nor desirable as a standard for judging the success of a literary work.' 'The Intentional Fallacy', in W. K. Wimsatt, with Monroe Beardsley, *The Verbal Icon: Studies in the Meaning of Poetry* (London: Methuen, 1954), 3.

70. As Wimsatt and Beardsley put it, in a phrase that would not be wholly out of place in a post-structural context: 'The poem is not the critic's own and not the author's (it is detached from the author at birth and goes about the world beyond his power to intend about it or control it).' Ibid. 5.

71. Michael Bratman, *Intentions, Plans, and Practical Reasoning* (Cambridge, Mass.: Harvard University Press, 1987); Jon Elster, *Sour Grapes: Studies in the Subversion of Rationality* (Cambridge: Cambridge University Press, 1983).

72. Bratman, *Intentions*, 29, quoted in Livingston, *Literature*, 43.

73. Paisley Livingston, 'Characterization and Fictional Truth in the Cinema', in Bordwell and Carroll, *Post-Theory*; Knight, 'Anti-Humanism', 47. Knight notes the similarities between Derrida's arguments in *Dissemination*, trans. Barbara Johnson (Chicago: University of Chicago Press, 1981), about the value imbalances in binary oppositions, and the notion of 'proportional series' discussed by Bordwell in *Making Meaning*, 118–20.

74. Michael Dummett, *Origins of Analytical Philosophy* (Cambridge, Mass.: Harvard University Press, 1994), p. ix. Dummett also points out the inaccuracy of this latter ascription in terms of the contribution of non-English speaking, especially Scandinavian, philosophers to the analytic tradition, and the fact that many of

the key figures in the emergence of analytic philosophy wrote in German, not English.

In a critical commentary on Dummett's argument, Ray Monk has suggested that by overstressing the 'linguistic turn' Dummett merely replaces one oversimplified account of the intellectual history of analytic philosophy with another. Monk nevertheless agrees with Dummett's assessment that the Germanic roots of the analytic tradition have not been properly recognized. See Ray Monk, 'Bertrand Russell's Brainchild; Analytic Philosophy: Its Conception and Birth', *Radical Philosophy*, 78 (July–Aug. 1996), 2–5.

PART I

What is Cinematic Representation?

'What is cinematic representation?' has been the concern of film theorists since the early days of cinema when intellectual enthusiasts of the medium at once celebrated the capacity of the mechanically reproduced image to capture reality in a way that seemed peculiarly modern, yet also viewed with suspicion the power of the new medium upon the minds of the masses. The question was taken up with renewed insistence by post-'68 film theorists who developed a semiotic theory of 'filmic illusion' to explain the power of movies. The cinematic image was conceived as a sign that produces in the spectator the impression that what it represents is real. The cinema was said to be an 'imaginary signifier', to use Christian Metz's influential formula—a form of representation which 'disavowed' its status as representation. Film theory became locked into two problematic assumptions. The first of these was the implausible idea that we routinely entertain false beliefs about the status of the image, mistaking representation for referent, a phenomenon that psychoanalysis was thought to explain. In addition, an uncritical and idiosyncratic use of semiotics—loosely allied with anti-illusionist, modernist aesthetic practice—was wielded as a weapon to combat the purported illusionism of the image. Isolated within the boundaries of a narrow range of Continental thinking, often ill-digested and articulated at second or third hand, film theory betrayed a striking lack of knowledge of and interest in the wide and diverse corpus of analytic thought on the subject of aesthetic representation—for example, Beardsley, Hospers, Goodman, Wollheim, Gombrich, Walton, and Wittgenstein—to say nothing of the long tradition of philosophical aesthetics, all of which was swept aside in the manner we have detailed in the introduction.

The chapters here address anew the question 'What is cinematic representation?' in more fertile and nuanced terms than those which have hitherto characterized academic film theory. Together, they support our claim that analytic philosophy is a broad church that encompasses a variety of approaches to given problems and thus affords a diversity of competing solutions. In contrast to Noël Carroll, whose practice of analytic film theory is one of 'piecemeal theorizing', Gregory Currie argues that an analytic philosophy of film can and should rival in its ambition and scope the claims of psychoanalytic semiotics. In pursuit of this overarching theory, he sketches the contours of the realist approach to cinematic representation developed in his recent book *Image and Mind*, an approach that marries conceptual enquiry with the empirical discoveries of cognitive science. Specifically, he argues, (1) that films are literally moving images, rather than illusions of movement; and (2) that moving images resemble in certain ways the objects they depict and hence are realistic, although they are not realistic because they in some sense afford perceptual access to the world. Moreover, (3) visual fictions invite us to imagine the events they depict taking place, rather than inviting us to believe or to imagine that we are seeing those events.

In his book *Mimesis as Make-Believe*, Kendall Walton has offered a general theory of representation that is equally ambitious in scope but whose assumptions about representation in general and photography in particular differ sharply from those of Currie. Walton argues that while visual representations are not illusions, they allow us to imagine that we see what they depict, and photography (and by extension film) affords the further possibility of indirectly seeing objects themselves. In his contribution to this volume Walton defends his theory of visual representations from the criticisms of Currie and Carroll, and offers further justification for the discrimination he has drawn between looking at paintings and looking at photographs or movies. Writing from the perspective of the later philosophy of Wittgenstein, however, Richard Allen takes issue with the theories of both Currie and Walton. He argues that contemporary cognitive and analytic theories of the perception of motion pictures, like his own psychoanalytically inspired theory, are vitiated by their reliance, implicit or explicit, upon the causal theory of perception. He claims that what we see when we look at a moving picture is specified not by a causal theory but by the perceptual reports that articulate what it is that we see. His chapter may profitably be read in conjunction with the article by Malcolm Turvey later in the volume, which draws on Wittgenstein's remarks on 'aspect-seeing' in order to argue that mistaken assumptions about what we see when we look at films taint theories of emotional response to films.

Edward Branigan rounds off the section with a chapter on the relative status of sound and image in the cinema. As both an aspect of our experience of films and as an object of study, sound has traditionally been subordinated to the image in film theory. However, more recent theorists, like Michel Chion, have argued for the perceptual and aesthetic equality of sound and image within film. Branigan's essay brings to bear ideas drawn from cognitive science as well as arguments from various philosophers on this disputed issue. Reflecting on what sound is and how it is perceived, he argues that there is truth both to the claim that sound is subordinate to the image in our perception of movies, and to the idea that sound and image may function as equal partners. Certain features of the physical world and our 'bottom-up' perception of it, mirrored in our concepts, produce an asymmetry in the way we ascribe visible properties and aural properties to objects. Objects appear to be made out of their visible (and tactile) properties, whereas sounds appear detachable and transient (they exist in time rather than space). This asymmetry results in, among other things, the privilege given to vision in the understanding of film. However, higher-order, 'top-down' forms of cognitive processing allow us to experience sound in a manner that is contrary to our customary perception. Under certain conditions, Branigan argues, we can perceive sound as a 'spatial' phenomenon in a manner that creates an equality between sound and image.

The Film Theory that Never Was:
A Nervous Manifesto

GREGORY CURRIE

This is a manifesto for a film theory I would like to have, and for the way I would like to see theory done. I shall begin with a glimpse of an ideal theoretical structure, a theory/methodology I should be pleased to have made a contribution to. Manifestos usually try to sum up in a slogan what they represent. I shall resist this. The rest of this chapter will have to do. But I will say something about the philosophical background against which the manifesto should be seen.

1. FILM THEORY AND PHILOSOPHY OF FILM

'Analytical philosophy of film' is not a very satisfactory description, but I do not know a better short title for the approach I adopt. It is unsatisfactory primarily because it suggests a commitment to the 'philosophy is conceptual analysis' equation which few of us now accept and to an Olympian perspective from which the philosopher hopes to see further than other beings. But it does suggest a basis of thought within the Anglo-American tradition, with its emphasis on clarity of expression and argument, on the role of logic, and on respect for science. In this sense, analytical philosophy is a thriving enterprise. But analytical philosophy *of film* is a cottage industry existing on the margins of academic philosophy as practised in English-speaking countries. Unlike the more familiar psychoanalytic approach to film, it does not have an established and overarching theoretical structure, and indeed some of its practitioners actively discourage the search for one.[1] Its only distinctive features might be these: (i) a dissatisfaction with the kind of philosophy appealed to in recent film theory; (ii) a commitment to the broadly analytical approach as defined above, as well as the integration, where appropriate, of philosophical ideas with results about the mind and other relevant phenomena from the most predictive research in psychology, cognitive science, and other empirical disciplines; (iii) a desire to approach particular films, film genres, and film styles with as light a theoretical baggage as possible, so that the films themselves should not disappear or become distorted under the burden of theory.[2] What I aim to do here is to offer an absurdly ambitious conception of what an analytical philosophy of film would look like if it took seriously the aim of constructing a systematic and globally connected theory. Secondly I should like to indicate how some of my own work might be seen as a modest contribution to such an approach. I shall describe a connected set of questions, of roughly increasing specificity, which would jointly constitute a budget of central problems in relation to film, from the most general questions about the nature of the medium to the most specific ones about the interpretation of individual films. Any set of answers to these questions, or to some substantial subset of them, where the answers derive from some roughly coherent set of theories, would then constitute a philosophy of film.

So I say that practitioners of philosophy of film should take seriously the search for grand theory. The grand theory in question need not be arrived at all at once, and the best way to get it might not be for many or any of us to spend our time looking for a synthesis; it might just grow naturally. But still, other things being equal, a theory that is strongly integrated across the domain of film and strongly linked to successful work in other areas will be better—more simple, coherent, and therefore more credible—than a bunch of disparate theories isolated from other branches of knowledge. And since simplicity and coherence are epistemic virtues that admit of degrees, achieving the aim is not crucial; a partially realized grand theory could be preferable to a disparate collection of partially realized small theories.

What is the budget of questions that we should be aiming to answer? The questions will resolve themselves into rough groupings. One group will concern film's *nature*: what distinguishes film from other media? What are film's near relatives and what its distant cousins? What is the minimal set of features a work must have to be a film? (The answer to that last question might be 'none'.) Another group will concern the *modes* of filmic representation: the kinds of contents which film is capable of conveying, or is most apt to convey. A third concerns the appropriate or standard kinds of *engagement* with film: how is the viewer drawn into the diegesis? How does the viewer construct/understand the narrative presented? A fourth concerns the *individuation* of filmic elements and their connections: scene, shot, point of view, montage, etc. A fifth group concerns film *production*: is there a distinctive filmic process, and how do we weigh the important elements within that process? How does the filmic process bear on the understanding and appraisal of the outcome, the finished film? Next will be questions about film *kinds*: what are filmic genres, and how does grouping by genre compare with grouping by authorship? Then there will be questions about film *style*: what elements of film, if any, can be designated as stylistic elements? What stylistic features, if any, are invariant across filmic kinds identified in terms of genre, authorship, or other non-stylistic features?

Finally there will be questions about *individual* films—questions which, ideally, would be informed by the answers given to earlier questions in our list. So when we try to understand and appreciate a particular film we shall want to bear in mind our decisions about the nature of film and filmic representation, together with general principles concerning the viewer's response. But we shall also and more specifically need to understand the particular elements of *this* film and their connection in the light of our theory of individuation, to understand how far the facts about *this* particular filmic process affect the nature and value of the outcome, and to locate *this* film in its appropriate kind or kinds and to identify *its* stylistic features.

On this view, film theory aims at a body of knowledge organized along an axis of increasing specificity, where everything is (potentially) relevant to everything else and everything (actually) comes together in the analysis of particular films. Whatever we call it, it will be at least in part a philosophical activity, for various reasons. First, some of its questions—concerning essence, representation, individuation, kind, style, and the relations between process and result—are themselves ineluctably philosophical; deciding what content these notions have requires philosophical reflection. But it will be philosophical also in the sense that any large-scale theoretical undertaking is, because it will depend for its success on a sensitivity to the logical and conceptual connections between different components.

Of course different and conflicting theories can be constructed along these lines; how are we to choose between them? Internal coherence will be one consideration, but it cannot be the only one. Another will be simply: coherence with the rest of our knowledge. We ought not to say anything about film which we cannot, ultimately, integrate with our beliefs about other things. And we certainly should not insulate our beliefs about film from our other beliefs by convincing ourselves that film is *sui generis*. What we say about film genres ought to cohere with what we say about genres in other artistic and representational forms; similarly for film style, and the other issues announced above. That is not to say that there is nothing distinctively filmic about film genre or film style. Rather, the claim is that applying a notion like genre or style to film in a special way needs justification in terms of the special features of the filmic medium or by reference to some other consideration available within the theory itself. That way we avoid the accusation that we are reshaping general notions in an ad hoc way to fit a special purpose. But the most important constraint on a theory of the kind I have described will be that it lead to interesting and enlightening analyses of particular films. 'Contemporary interpretation-centred criticism . . . has become boring', says David Bordwell, and I am inclined to agree with him.[3] We must never forget that what we are doing as theorists would have no application or even any meaning without there being a body of particular films, many bad and some good, which give point to the questions we ask. Unless we can, in answering these questions, help to make the best of these individual works that can be made of them, we might as well be doing something else.[4]

But this 'bottom up' constraint on theory—that theory be interpretively fecund—offers no universal methodology for film studies, for there is no theory-neutral conception of what is to count as an illuminating interpretation. I suspect that we are never going to get a universally applicable standard for appraising theories of film, or any other art for that matter.[5] But that does not mean that every theory of film will be self-validating, for it will be possible for a theory of film to generate interpretations which are, by its own lights, dull and pedestrian.

The constraint of interpretive fecundity will affect the ways we have of satisfying the constraint of coherence. We can always achieve coherence in a top-down fashion, rejecting hypotheses lower down if they conflict with higher-level hypotheses already accepted. But fecundity requires us to regard our theoretical system as reticulated, with clashes between components resolvable in any direction; a critical judgement of a particular film cannot, if it is to be taken seriously, depend on a theoretical notion for which no defence can be given, but high-level theory may have to give way if it leads to dull or highly counter-intuitive criticism. Indeed there is an argument for saying that items lower down ought to be given more weight than items higher up. This is a consequence of the demand for *respect for common sense*. G. E. Moore said that we ought never to put more faith in a high-level philosophical theory than we put in a common-sense judgement like 'I have two hands'. Consequently, in his view, we ought never to believe any philosophy which has as its conclusion the non-existence of material things. In film theory we are not likely to be met with such a stark contrast between arid theory and rock-bottom intuitive conviction. But we ought to start from the assumption that our judgements about particular films are more likely to be reliable than our theories of medium, style, genre, and the rest. Consequently, a theoretical principle would have to have a lot going for it in other areas if it is to force us to abandon an intuitively illuminating interpretation of a particular work.[6]

It is not just that our judgements about particular films are fashioned in response to the direct experience of the particularity and detail of those works, whereas our general conceptions of medium, style, and the rest are rather remote from direct experience. There is another reason that judgements about particular works should count more heavily than judgements about theoretical concepts. It is that, in the case of judgements about particular works, our judgements themselves are partly *constitutive* of the phenomenon, but our judgements about concepts like genre are not. Genre is a theoretical-explanatory notion, and our views about genre can be quite radically wrong, as can our views about quarks and gluons. But at least some of our views about particular works do not seem to be so fallible. Thus, as has frequently been observed, it makes questionable sense to suppose that everyone could find a film frightening, funny, moving, or dull, and yet the work itself should not actually be frightening, funny, moving, or dull. It is possible for an individual to be wrong about these things, as would be the case where that individual's response was a perverse or otherwise radically atypical one. But this point can be made: to the extent that I take seriously my judgement about this particular work—that it is funny—then to that extent I must see my judgement as constitutive of its being funny, and not see my judgement as a guess, even an informed one, about some quality the work has quite independent of my response to it. But if I take some stand on the notion of genre, thinking of genres in, say, an Aristotelian way, then that really is just a hypothesis on my part, and it is a hypothesis which is only as good and reliable as the methods of theory-formation by which I arrived at it. I cannot cite the simple fact of my holding that view of genre as supportive of the view.

It is this approach to film that the manifesto aims to promote: open to criticism from outside, struggling for inner coherence, giving strong weight to intuitive judgement and searching for comprehensiveness. I do not have a theory which exemplifies the structure I have described, and I do not know of one. But I would like to think of my own work so far as contributing to the construction of such a theory, and in particular to the forging of connections between film and other areas like cognitive psychology. In the rest of this chapter, I shall say something about where I have got to. It will be evident from what follows that I have so far been working in largely top-down mode; thus the nervousness of this manifesto. It is not yet clear whether the theory I am developing will really exemplify the theory structure I favour. Indeed, as I shall make clear later on, there are points at which I have recklessly ignored my own directives.

I shall begin this brief outline of my own views in an appropriately general way with a hypothesis about the film *medium*. I end it with some remarks on the connection between theory of film and experimental psychology.

2. MOVING PICTURES

Film is moving picture. Literally, that is. No talk here of an illusion of movement, for if the movement of film were illusory there would not really be any movement, and film could not be moving pictures. But isn't there in fact only a sequence of static images, each displayed so briefly and all in such quick succession that we think we see movement when in fact there is none? To this objection I offer two responses, a strong one and a weak one.

I vacillate between the two, and for the moment I say only that if the strong one is too strong the weak one will do in its stead. The strong defence claims, defiantly, that the motion we seem to see is real motion. This motion is, I grant, partly a product of the mind, in the sense that the explanation for our seeing movement appeals ineliminably to our perceptual apparatus. Creatures constituted differently from us might not see motion on the screen (though of course many creatures other than humans *do* seem to see motion there). But then you can say the same for colours; the explanation of our seeing US mail boxes as blue appeals ineliminably to our perceptual apparatus; Martians, for all we know, would see them as red and dogs, we know, do not see them in colour. But still they are blue, really blue, though that may mean only that they are blue for us. Just as colours are real, so is the movement on the screen. That is the strong response.

The weaker response does not insist that screen movement is real. Instead, it makes a tripartite distinction between what is real, what is illusory, and what is apparent, with the category of the apparent lying between the other two. Perhaps (I grant this just for the sake of the argument) things which depend on our subjective responses in the way that screen motion does cannot count as real (there probably is at least one legitimate sense of 'real' which would make that true). But if our standards of reality are high, we ought not to let everything else fall into the illusory basket. For the illusory is what causes error. If colours, for instance, are not real by our strong criterion of reality, are we to say that we suffer an illusion when we think we see things as coloured? It is surely more appropriate to say that colours belong to the category of the (non-illusory) apparent. We are not in error when we see colours, nor are we in error when we claim to see motion on the screen. Indeed, it is hard to see how we *could* be in error. For screen motion, like colour, is one of those concepts defined in terms of a certain kind of response. Roughly, for things to be red they merely have to look red to us in normal conditions. Similarly, the filmic apparatus achieves the condition of presenting screen motion when, in (suitably defined) normal circumstances, people will see screen motion there. So it is not possible for us to discover that we have all been in error in thinking that US post boxes are blue, and nor can we all be in error in seeming to perceive screen motion.[7]

So films are moving pictures. But of course they are usually more than that. They contain other elements, notably sound. Granted. My point is merely that a minimal definition of the kind *film* requires reference only to moving images, because anything which displays moving images will count as a film, whatever other features it has. Moving pictures are the essence of film.[8]

My second thesis is that these moving pictures which are the essence of film are *realistic*. By that I mean there is an important relation of similarity between the film image and what the film image represents, and this similarity is what enables film images to represent things in the way they do. So the realism I am arguing for here is a version of representational realism. Since it is a special case of a more general thesis about pictorial representation, I shall begin with pictures in general, of which film images are a special case—or so I shall argue.

Certain pictures do seem to be like their subjects; not so like them as to be indistinguishable from them, except under very peculiar circumstances, but like them nonetheless. In particular, cinematic images often have a quality of extraordinary realism, depicting their subjects in a way which is vastly more lifelike than, say, painting or still photography. This sense of likeness is not simply a matter of being 'true to' the subject. A description of a horse can be accurate, without the description being in any interesting way like the horse. When we read a description, we may recognize what is being described, and when we look at a depiction we may recognize what it depicts, but we do these things in fundamentally different ways. To comprehend the description I deploy my linguistic capacities, my understanding of the semantics and syntax of the language. To see that the picture is a picture of a horse, I deploy my horse-recognition capacities. That is, I use the same capacity to recognize the picture of a horse that I use to recognize a horse.[9]

If that is the only respect in which picture and horse are alike, it is a rather weak respect. It would be like saying that Julius Caesar and tonight's concert are alike in that I thought about both of them today; true, but not the sort of thing we usually think of when we hear that two objects are alike. In particular, it is not immediately clear how an account of the likeness between pictures and their subjects based on our deployment of a common recognitional capacity in both cases could ground the notion that picture and subject are alike in *appearance*. Yet I think it can.[10]

When I see an object and recognize it, that must be because there is something in the appearance of the object which enables me to recognize it. I might not be able to say what it is, as I cannot say what it is about the budget director's walk that enables me to recognize that unwelcome person from a considerable distance. But there must be some aspect of the information conveyed to me by sight from the budget director which enables me to recognize him when I see him, and the information conveyed to me by sight just *is* his appearance. And if it is true that I recognize a picture as a picture of the director by the same means by which I recognize the director, it must be true that I recognize the picture because I am sensitive to those properties of the picture's appearance it has in common with the director himself.

What, then, are those properties? It would be an error to try to answer this question by locating some single property of the director's appearance—a size, shape, or colour property for instance—and insisting that it is a sensitivity to *this* property which enables me, in every case, to recognize a depiction of the director when I see one. There could be an indefinite list of properties in virtue of which I might recognize the director, and different pictures will possess different of those properties. One way to go from here would be to speak of 'family resemblance', in something like Wittgenstein's sense, between pictures of the director. But I have never thought this a very satisfactory or illuminating move in any context. A better move would be to say that the likeness between the director and depictions of him consists in their having the following single property in common: the property of *having a property to which someone able to recognize the director is sensitive, and in virtue of which sensitivity they possess that ability*. Thus the single property shared by the director and his depictions is a higher-order property: the property of having a property within a certain class. It is in virtue of sharing this property that the director and his depictions are alike in appearance.

Note that their sharing this property is consistent with picture and subject being very unalike in all sorts of ways, including ways to do with appearance. Cinematic images, and indeed images of all kinds, are different in various ways from the things they depict and one would not easily mistake an image of Cary Grant for Cary Grant. All that the realism of pictures thesis, as I present it, says is that Grant and the image have in common some property by means of which I am able to recognize Grant when I see him.

Cinematic images are, of course, moving, and therefore rather different from, say photographs and paintings. But that makes the theory of pictures just outlined more applicable to screen images, not less so. For moving pictures are like the things they represent along a further dimension, that of movement. Just as I have a capacity visually to recognize certain objects when I see them, so do I have the capacity to recognize the movement of objects (recognized and unrecognized) when I see it. And in general, if I can detect the movement of objects seen, I can detect the movement visible in a cinematic image which records such an object moving. How so? The obvious answer is this: because the same capacity to recognize movement is deployed in both cases.[11]

Because cinematic images are moving pictures, they depict for us, not just colours and shapes, but movement and change in general. When we detect change, we normally detect it as occurring in time, and as having a duration. Thus when we observe a process we can track it through time, either by means of our (not very reliable) subjective sense of the passage of time, or by our (more reliable) clocks (by a 'clock' here I mean any regular process which can be recruited to the task of measuring time). Just so with processes as depicted cinematically. As long as they occur within a single shot, we can measure the duration of the process by measuring the duration of the representation of the process—assuming that we are not dealing with slow or fast motion. And we have exactly the same means of measuring the duration of the representation of the process on screen as we have of measuring the process itself. So just as we can recognize the objects depicted in a cinematic image by using the same capacities we use to recognize those objects themselves, so we recognize the duration and order of depicted events and processes in just the same way we recognize the duration of those events and processes themselves. So in the same way that film depicts objects realistically, it depicts time realistically also, within the confines of the single shot.

The same holds for the depiction of spatial relations between objects. We see that objects are spatially related thus and so largely because we see this surface as occluding that one, where principles of good continuation indicate that the visible parts of the further object are connected by occluded parts. This and like principles apply also to the sense we get of spatial relations between objects depicted in film—so long, once again, as the objects are visible within the same shot. Thus film is capable of the realistic portrayal of space and time; that is the truth in Bazin's doctrine of the realism of long-take, deep focus style. But we must be careful—more careful than Bazin was—in connection with metaphysical arguments about the nature of representational realism with the justification of realist style. That film is capable of representing objects and their spatio-temporal relations realistically does not entail that films must be shot and edited so as to maximize the use of this capacity, any more than the (true) thesis that film is capable of depicting people entails that films are better the more people they depict.

3. CONVENTION, INTENTION, AND GENRE

It is wholly different with language; my capacity to identify a man when I see one, and my capacity to identify a *name* or *description* of a man are different capacities. Current psychological evidence suggests, in fact, that these are competencies which tap into different functional areas of the brain, and develop along quite different trajectories. Annette Karmiloff-Smith and her colleagues have done some interesting work on the understanding of preliterate children of pictorial and linguistic systems of representation. Toddlers were asked to 'draw' a dog, and to 'write' its name.

When children objected that they did not know how to draw or write, we encouraged them to pretend to be doing so. . . . video tapes show that preliterate toddlers lift the pen much more frequently when pretending to write than when pretending to draw [footnote omitted]. The toddler goes about the process of writing and drawing differently, even though the end product sometimes turns out similarly.[12]

It seems that children have some understanding, at least at a functional level, of the difference between pictures and language before they can manually produce items of either kind! Also, the child's understanding of language develops in a quite different way from her understanding of pictures. Children understand pictures and what they depict very early, while the process of first-language acquisition, while astonishingly fast from one point of view, takes much longer and develops stepwise, with patterns of characteristic errors followed by breakthroughs of understanding. Further, the ability to draw and the ability to write can be selectively impaired; brain damage can affect the one and not the other, suggesting that these are quite distinct mental capacities. None of this bodes well for the suggestion that our understanding of works in visual, depictive media like film can be illuminated by discovering 'languages' of depiction.

That is unsurprising, given the basic difference between pictures and language. For all the languages we are familiar with, the capacity to understand words and sentences in that language depends on a knowledge of conventions which associate words (which are, after all, arbitrary signs) with things.[13] My capacity to process cinematic images is not in this or any comparable sense convention-driven. If there are conventions of film, they play a peripheral role, like the use of the fade-out to indicate the passage of time, the use of a black outfit to identify the bad guy, or the chequered table cloth proclaiming 'poor but honest'. Peripheral in this sense: such conventions are not what make the communication of meaning in cinema possible. Film can, and often does, communicate its meanings without such conventions. But without convention there can be no communication of meaning in language for any of the languages we know anything about. With language, the conventions are basic and systematic; in film they are peripheral and adventitious. Later I shall argue that the absence of a film language has some negative consequences for the development of a psychology of film.

'Convention' has more than one sense. Here I have been using 'convention' in the sense that word has when it appears in the phrase 'linguistic convention', for the issue has been whether there is anything like a language of film. In connection with film we also talk of genres as conventions or as conventional. But generic conventions are not language-like, for they are not arbitrary. It is a convention that 'red' means red partly because other assignments of meaning would do as well; it would be no loss to us if we had called red 'black'. But generic conventions are not arbitrary. Thus it is a convention of revenge tragedy (and incidentally of the closely related filmic genre, the gangster film) that the story will follow the rise and fall of a talented and ruthless man who seeks power. If what you seek to construct is a revenge tragedy, that is one of the constraints you must observe. If instead you trace the humdrum day of a well-meaning family man you will not produce a revenge tragedy or anything like one. The conventions of a genre are constitutive of the genre and to that extent non-arbitrary. But can't we push at the limits of a genre, and bend it out of shape, by flouting its conventions? To some extent yes. But flouting some of the conventions requires that you observe sufficiently many of them so that what you produce gives the sense of being located in relation to that genre, even if it is not comfortably within its limits. The malleability of generic conventions does not make them arbitrary.

But couldn't a filmic or other genre such as the screwball comedy have developed in other ways, and might not those other ways have been as good as the way it did develop? And doesn't that make the way it has developed, and the conventions that constitute it, arbitrary in some sense? We are in the grip of a false picture here, a picture according to which there is one thing, the screwball comedy, for which there are various equally appropriate paths of development and various corresponding results. You might just as well say it is conventional that tigers have legs, because the creatures that developed tiger characteristics in the process of evolution might have developed other characteristics. So they may. Only then they wouldn't be tigers; and instead of tigers evolution would have given us something else. So it is with genres. There is nothing inevitable or supremely right about the genres we have. They are just what history has happened to throw up, though like species they tend to survive and flourish because they find a niche. Genres are not inevitable, but they need not on that account be arbitrary.

So genres are not conventional in the way that linguistic meaning is: that is, genres are not arbitrary, and it is not, therefore, a convention which genres we adopt. But genres might be conventional in a much weaker sense, a sense roughly synonymous with 'depending on mutual knowledge and expectation'.[14] Here we need to distinguish between two questions that often get run together: what is a genre? And what is it for a work to belong to a genre? In answering the first question we need appeal to no facts about mutual knowledge. A genre is a set of features, features which works should possess if they are to belong to that that genre. Thus there are sets of features definitive of the detective novel, the encomium, the screwball comedy, and all the other literary, filmic, and generally artistic genres there can be. Thus genres are defined purely formally, by specification of their constitutive features. But for a work to belong to a genre is not merely for it to have the features definitive of the genre. On some distant planet there may now be playing films with all the defining features of the screwball comedy, but they will not be, merely on that account, screwball comedies. Works in a genre have the features definitive of the genre, but in addition their having them must have a certain kind of salience for the community in which they are produced. To simplify somewhat, a work belongs to a genre only if it possesses the features constitutive of that genre and it is common knowlegdge between the work's maker and its audience that the work possesses those features in virtue of its having been influenced by other works which also possess them. This is a simplification because, for example, there are different kinds of genre membership and a work can be marginally or retrospectively a work within a genre, and these notions are not covered by the definition just given. The definition given covers what we might call central membership in a genre, a notion in terms of which other kinds of genre membership can be defined in somewhat complex terms.[15] These other kinds of genre membership are, I believe, essentially normative ones, and in this sense they contrast with the notion of central membership in a genre. So there is not, in my view, any value-judgement implicit in the claim that, for example, *Stagecoach* is a western, though that information, in conjunction with other facts about the film, might be the basis for a value judgement about it. That this film is a western is an assertion of central genre membership and as such is true or false simply according to whether the film has the requisite features and whether its audience had the requisite common knowledge. But to speak, as Stanley Cavell does, of a genre of the Comedy of Remarriage is to apply the notion of genre retrospectively, and Cavell's claim is well taken if we find it illuminating, interesting, aesthetically pleasing, or whatever to group the films of which he speaks under the concepts he identifies. We are being asked, in effect, to see these films as if they were centrally members of this genre; that, at least, is the best I can make of Cavell's claim. So I do not think that there is, straightforwardly, a fact of the matter as to whether Cavell is right about this genre and its exemplars. It is at least partly a question of value.[16]

Exactly how genre membership, centrally conceived, relates to normative conceptions of genre is a complex issue. But the example of central membership will suffice for my present purpose. It illustrates the point that, while there is a sense in which genres are conventional, that is nothing like the sense in which linguistic meaning is conventional.

To deny that film is a matter of arbitrary code is not to say that film is 'a slice of life', or that it pretends to give us unmediated access to visible reality. In particular, comprehension of film cannot consist entirely in the recognition of visually depicted objects and their movements; that is merely the easily identifiable tip of an iceberg marked 'interpretation'. To interpret a film requires us to go below the visible (and audible) surface, to make coherent sense of the sequence of images the film presents us with, and to extract from them, together with the order of their occurrence, a story. The fact that, for the most part, we do this with little effort and little resulting disagreement between subjects has obscured the difficulty of the task and the puzzling nature of our 'narrative competence'. What, beyond our naturally given capacity to recognize visually depicted objects, is responsible for

that competence? My answer is that it is our capacity to recognize intentions: we figure out what story is told in the film by figuring out what story
someone who put just those images together in just that way would have
intended to tell. Filmic comprehension does not differ in this respect from
comprehension of narrative in other media. Films and novels are alike in
that they require us to make inferences to the intentions of a maker; they are
unalike in that, while literature requires also a linguistic competence on the
reader's part, film requires only a naturally given competence with visual
depiction.

4. THE VIEWER

Realism, or conformity to the natural appearances of things, is the principle
characteristic of the film medium. What are the psychological effects of this
kind of realism? Does it, in particular, give rise to what film theorists have
called a 'reality effect': the causing in the viewer of an illusion of the reality
of what is on the screen? Along with others, I have argued that it does not.[17]
The arguments are well known, and I will not rehearse them here. But I do
want to observe that it is sometimes difficult to know with whom one is
disagreeing in this area. In an interesting attempt to breathe new life into the
illusionistic paradigm, Richard Allen has recently argued that film is an
especially efficient producer of a kind of illusion which he calls a projective
illusion. Allen holds that this phenomenon involves no creation of a false
belief; it is not an 'epistemic illusion'. Instead, you as a viewer

> imagine that you perceive a world inhabited by zombies . . . you do not mistake a
> staged event for actuality in the manner of a reproductive illusion; rather, you lose
> awareness of the fact that you are watching a recorded event that is staged before the
> camera. . . . when you imagine that you look upon the events of the film 'from
> within', the frame of the image circumscribes the limits of your visual field rather
> than signalling to you that what you see is a projection of a recorded image. . . . In
> projective illusion, the spectator occupies the perceptual point of view of the camera
> upon the events of the film.[18]

I have argued that film does not engender an illusion of the reality of its
fictional events and characters. But while Allen describes here what he calls
an illusion, it is not clear that we disagree; we seem to agree, for example,
that the viewer does not make, and is not prone to make, any *mistake*. We
both say that the viewer *imagines* things. Perhaps there is nothing more
between us on this score than a choice about how to use the word 'illusion'.
But we do definitely disagree about something; for Allen says that we
imagine perceiving the world of the zombies. And I take it that when he says
that the spectator occupies the point of view of the camera he means that the
spectator imagines occupying it. I, on the other hand, hold that our imagi-

native engagement with the film does not go so far as this. Let me explain.

Kendall Walton has said that fictions are props in games of make-believe.[19] I think Walton is quite right to assert a continuity between childhood games of make-believe and fictions of even the most sophisticated kind. Perhaps the reader or viewer of a fictional work really is engaging in a game of this kind. But there is a difference in my view between at least the standard children's games of make-believe and the games authorized by fictional works. While standard games of pretence are *self-involving*, fictions usually are not. When we play games of pretence, we are to imagine things of ourselves, including things about relation, between ourselves and other objects and people incorporated into the game. The player of cowboys and Indians imagines that he is hiding from an Indian, or sneaking up on one, or that he is a fearless warrior, or whatever. Games of pretence can be less overtly behavioural, as with daydreaming, but here again we usually imagine things of ourselves; we engage in what I call *personal imagining*.

With fictions, on the other hand, we generally imagine things of the characters and not of ourselves. There are interactive fictions where the reader plays the role of a character, but this is not the usual form of fiction. In fact I have argued that for standard fictions, where there is no obvious indication of there being a place in the fiction for the reader or observer, then the reader/observer engages in what I call *impersonal* imagining; he or she imagines the events of the fiction taking place, but does not imagine being in specific spatio-temporal relations to those events. So on my view the reader imagines Huck floating down the river, but does not imagine being there with him, and the film viewer imagines Marion being attacked in the shower, but does not imagine being there in the shower to share the experience.[20]

This is not to deny that readers or viewers of fictions play roles within the games of pretence authorized by those fictions. They may for instance play the role of being someone who is gaining information about true events. What I deny is that the standard mode of audience role-play in film watching consists in playing the role of someone who is seeing those events as they happen.

There are various reasons why I think my view is highly plausible, but I have argued for it in detail elsewhere and will not repeat those arguments here.[21] Instead I want to note that it is at this point that our theory of film most decisively makes contact with the empirical realm. There are two aspects to this I want to consider. First, it ought to be empirically decidable whether or not I am right in claiming that the mode of imagining character-istic of film watching is impersonal imagining. This matter was somewhat belatedly brought to my attention by a paper by Paul Harris of the Depart-ment of Experimental Psychology at Oxford.[22] Harris has done important work on the psychology of imagination, and in this paper he extends his work by arguing, on the basis of various studies, that we typically engage with fictions by imagining that we are located within the spatio-temporal structure of the fictional world; in my terms, Harris is arguing that we engage in personal imagining. The results Harris appeals to belong to a very small body of work on this topic, and in fact I believe these results are not decisive either way on the issue of personal versus impersonal imagining.[23] But we are at least beginning to treat this matter as the respectably empirical issue it certainly is, and not a subject exclusively for armchair philosophy. I look forward to further progress in this area. But progress may require us to overcome some difficulties in the analysis of film narrative which are not present in the case of literature.

I argued earlier that there is no film language. In particular, shots, scenes, and filmic representations generally are not analysable in the way that linguistic items are. We cannot break a filmic narrative down sentence by sentence, nor can we pick out the grammatical parts from a filmic sentence, since there are no such sentences; film images have no grammatical structure, no 'atoms' or minimal semantic parts out of which they are composed. But without the possibility of this kind of segmentation it is difficult to give any analysis of exactly what the viewer's reaction is a reaction to. Thus the results Harris cites in his study of imaginative involvement with fictions concern, for example, the comparing of the times it takes to read various sentences, with shorter times indicating the reader's greater readiness to integrate the sentence with the rest of the narrative. Similar techniques have been applied to study the reader's processing of verbal metaphors. Moving from language to the study of visually presented narratives is going to require us to devise ways of *isolating narrative elements without recourse to language*; it is not clear how this can be done.

The other point I want to make about imagination and empirical psychology is this. The methodology I outlined at the beginning of this chapter enjoins us not to invent psychological processes and mechanisms simply to suit the convenience of film theory. The psychology of film must sit comfortably with, and eventually be derived from, the best overall psychological theory we have. Do we have a general psychological theory of the imagination? I think we are beginning to understand imagination by a method often used elsewhere in the empirical study of the mind: the examinationn of psychological deficits. One of the most useful approaches to vision and its various components is via cases of damaged vision. If we have subjects with identifiable sites of damage in the brain, and identifiable deficiencies of vision—loss of colour vision or ability visually to discriminate faces, for example—we can learn a great deal about how normal vision works. Is there any such procedure available to us when it comes to imagination? Here the question is not so easily answered because, while it is relatively uncontroversial as to what is a visual capacity and what isn't, it is often controversial as to what is an imaginative capacity and what isn't. Still, there does seem to be a class of subjects who typically show a pattern of deficits rather naturally describable as 'lack of imagination'. People with autism tend to have interests which are confined to the rote learning of lists of items, or concern mechanical, repetitive activities. As children they are often noticeable for their absence of pretend play. Their language skills can be quite sophisticated, yet they often seem to lack insight into the give-and-take of conversational speech. Their behaviour is often inappropriate because they lack intuitive understanding of other people's attitudes and knowledge, having to substitute rote-learned rules of thumb which have limited applicability.[24] While they may be fascinated by video and cinematic displays, they seem to lack an interest in or understanding of the fictional contents of these and other media.

The theoretical study of autism is at too early a stage for us to derive firm conclusions about the nature of imagination, but this seems to me one direction in which to look. I suggest that the study of childhood autism and the related study of the ordinary development of play and imaginative understanding in children is going to be a more fruitful direction for people interested in the psychology of fictional media such as film than, say, Lacanian speculations on a supposed 'mirror stage' in the child's development.[25]

I have laid out, very briefly, some of the theses and arguments I have been working on. I have also described the outline of what I regard as an ideal abstract structure for the theory of film. I hope that some of my arguments will contribute to the exemplification of that structure.

NOTES

1. See David Bordwell and Noël Carroll (eds.), *Post-Theory: Reconstructing Film Studies* (Madison: University of Wisconsin Press, 1996).
2. Exemplary of this approach is George Wilson's *Narration in Light* (Baltimore: Johns Hopkins University Press, 1986).
3. David Bordwell, *Making Meaning: Inference and Rhetoric in the Interpretation of Cinema* (Cambridge, Mass.: Harvard University Press, 1989), 261. Not that I agree with Bordwell's own theoretical recommendations; see Berys Gaut, 'Making Sense of Films: Neoformalism and its Limits', *Forum for Modern Language Studies*, 31 (1995), 8–23, for criticism.
4. For the idea that the aim of criticism is to make the best of the work of art, see Ronald Dworkin, *Law's Empire* (London: Fontana, 1986).
5. See my 'Interpretation and Objectivity', *Mind*, 102 (1993), 413–28.
6. What is to count as an intuitive judgement is ineluctably vague. But vague notions are not thereby incoherent notions. Indeed, since almost all our notions are vague, vagueness could not be a sign of incoherence. Vagueness is not even a drawback; for

many purposes vague notions are more usable than precise ones, the boundaries of which one has constantly to track.

7. Actually it is more complicated than that, because standard conditions cannot be defined in terms of how all or most people actually are constituted. For example, there is nothing incoherent about the idea that we discover that we all have a disease which is affecting our eyesight and which is causing us to see (erroneously) post boxes as blue. But I shall ignore such complexities here, clinging dogmatically to the belief that such things as colour and cinematic motion are somehow defined in terms of subjective responses.

8. A full definition of film might say something about how the moving pictures are produced and displayed, thus allowing us to distinguish between different screen media. I take this to be largely a bookkeeping exercise. See my *Image and Mind* (Cambridge: Cambridge University Press, 1995), Introduction.

9. See Noël Carroll, 'The Power of Movies', *Daedalus*, 114 (1985), 79–103. See also Flint Schier, *Deeper into Pictures: An Essay on Pictorial Representation* (New York: Cambridge University Press, 1986); 'triggering recognitional capacities' is Schier's phrase.

10. Here I disagree with Flint Schier, who argued that an account of the nature of pictures in terms of recognitional capacities does not ground any thesis of resemblance between picture and subject. See his *Deeper into Pictures*.

11. Compare this with the auditory case. I can understand what is said to me on the phone just about as well as I understand the speech of someone talking to me face to face. How so? Obviously, because the same capacity for speech recognition is deployed in both cases. So what is said here about the visual images of film applies also to film sound.

12. Annette Kamiloff-Smith, *Beyond Modularity* (Cambridge, Mass.: MIT Press, 1992), 143–4.

13. Systems of picturing lack other features important for language, like recursiveness. See my *Image and Mind* (New York: Cambridge University Press, 1995), ch. 4.

14. On mutual knowledge see David Lewis, *Convention* (Cambridge, Mass.: Harvard University Press, 1969), and Stephen Schiffer, *Meaning* (Oxford: Clarendon Press, 1972).

15. See my 'Genre', in preparation. It is these days quite standard to think of concept possession, for at least many cases, not in terms of understanding necessary and sufficient conditions for the application of the concept but in terms of the capacity to judge whether a given object has many of a set of 'prototypical' features (see Alvin Goldman, *Philosophical Applications of Cognitive Science* (Boulder, Colo.: Westview Press, 1993), 127–8). My account of genre here is, in this sense, an account (or the beginnings of one) of a genre-prototype.

16. Thanks here to Richard Allen.

17. See Noël Carroll, *Mystifying Movies: Fads and Fallacies in Contemporary Film Theory* (New York: Columbia University Press, 1988); Kendall Walton, 'Fearing Fictions', *Journal of Philosophy*, 75 (1978), 5–27, and my *Image and Mind*, ch. 3.

18. *Projecting Illusion* (New York: Cambridge University Press, 1995), 107.

19. *Mimesis as Make-Believe* (Cambridge, Mass.: Harvard University Press, 1990).

20. In his *Engaging Characters: Fiction, Emotion and the Cinema* (Oxford: Clarendon Press, 1995), Murray Smith draws on Richard Wollheim's distinction between central and acentral imagining in order to underline his claim that accounts of our relations to film characters in terms of a single notion of 'identification' are inadequate. While identification-theorists emphasize something akin to central imagining, Smith's own approach through the idea of sympathy lays greater stress on acentral imagining. How close is my account to Smith's? There are definite similarities, but in rejecting centralist theories of film-response Smith seems to have in mind theories which have the viewer apprehend the film-world through a character (see

e.g. ibid. 80). In so far as I reject personal imagining, I reject a more inclusive set of possibilities, for I reject the idea that the the viewer imagines himself to be located *anywhere* within the space of the action, including places unoccupied by any character. ('In so far as' is an important qualification here. I do admit some atypical cases of personal imagining in film viewing; see *Image and Mind*, ch. 6.) In general though, our views are close, particularly in respect of the role we assign to empathy and its contemporary variant, simulation. See my *Image and Mind*, ch. 5, and my 'Identification, Empathy, Simulation', forthcoming in *Passionate Views* (Baltimore: Johns Hopkins University Press), ed. Carl Plantinga.

21. See my *Image and Mind*, ch. 5.
22. Paul Harris, 'Fictional Absorption: Implications for Culture', forthcoming in S. Bruton (ed.), *Intersubjective Communication and Emotion in Ontogeny* (Cambridge: Cambridge University Press).
23. See my 'Fiction and Imagination: A Reply to Paul Harris', forthcoming.
24. For a readable introduction to the nature of the condition containing many illustrative examples of these kinds of behaviours, see Üta Frith, *Autism: Explaining the Enigma* (Oxford: Basil Blackwell, 1989).
25. See my 'Simulation-Theory, Theory-Theory and the Evidence from Autism', in Peter Carruthers and Peter K. Smith (eds.), *Theories of Theories of Mind* (Cambridge: Cambridge University Press, 1995), and my 'Realism of Character and the Value of Fiction', in Mette Hjort and Sue Lavers (eds.), *Emotion and the Arts* (New York: Oxford University Press, 1996).

2

On Pictures and Photographs: Objections Answered

KENDALL L. WALTON

Nearly all films are representational; more specifically, they are visual or depictive representations, pictures. And the vast majority of films are photographic depictions. The *depictive* and the *photographic* are two of the most fundamental categories that need to be explained if we are to understand the medium of film. I have elsewhere offered an account of depiction: pictures—both still pictures and moving ones—are props in visual games of make-believe. By this I mean, in part, that in looking at a picture the spectator imagines seeing what it portrays.[1] I have also argued that photographs are special among pictures in that they are *transparent*: to look at a photograph is actually to see, indirectly but genuinely, whatever it is a photograph of.[2]

Both of these claims have elicited a wide variety of reactions, some sympathetic and some sceptical. Noël Carroll and Gregory Currie are among the more thoughtful sceptics, and have discussed these matters with special attention to the medium of film. In what follows I consider their objections and examine alternatives that they propose. I should add that Currie endorses the main features of my theory of representation and incorporates them in his own. My focus now is on points of disagreement.

PICTURES

The question of what pictures are, and in particular how they differ from descriptions, is a lot more difficult than it seems. Given how obvious it is that a picture of a mountain and the word 'mountain' are animals of very different kinds, the nature of the difference is disconcertingly elusive. Many attempts to account for it manage to do little more than point to the fact that there is a difference.[3] This much seems clear, however: there is something especially visual about pictorial representation and depiction of other kinds. Currie observes that painting, theatre, and film are *visual* media.[4] But how so? Pictures are to be looked at. But so are written words, and we use our eyes on graphs and diagrams as well.

The answer lies in the particular nature of the visual experiences that pictures provide. What is distinctive about these experiences shows in our ways of talking about them. We speak of 'seeing an ox', when we look at a picture of an ox. We may point to the area of the canvas that our eyes are fixed on and say, 'There is an ox *there*' or '*That* is an ox'. Remarks like these are not appropriate when we look at the word 'ox', or a written description of an ox—the Blue Ox in the Paul Bunyan stories, for instance.

Such remarks, when one is observing a picture, are not to be taken literally. To look at a picture of an ox is not actually to see an ox, and it is (virtually always) obvious to the viewer that he is not seeing one.[5] The person who points to the canvas saying 'That is an ox' knows that there is only a piece of canvas there. Nevertheless, seeing a picture of an ox involves thinking of oneself as looking at an ox. We can put this by saying that one *imagines* seeing an ox, as one looks at the picture.[6] I do not mean that one deliberately undertakes to imagine this. Rather, one finds oneself imagining it, more or less automatically, as a result of perceiving the picture. In watching a film, the images on the screen induce spectators to imagine seeing the characters and events that are portrayed. And we imagine seeing them from a certain perspective or point of view, one determined by the position of the camera, or rather by features of the screen images that result from the position the camera was in when the film was photographed.

This is not the whole story. Words sometimes stimulate readers to imagine seeing. A reader of the Paul Bunyan stories might call up a visual image, and might describe his experience by saying, 'I see an ox'. But this comment (taken in a non-literal way, of course) does not characterize an aspect of the reader's visual experience of the text, as it does one's experience of a picture of an ox; the reader's eyes might be closed when he calls up the image. And it will not be appropriate for the reader to point to the words on the page and say (in the same spirit that one does while pointing to the picture), 'An ox is *there*' or '*That* is an ox.' One's perception of the text is merely a cause of an experience involving the thought of seeing an ox. In the case of picture perception, not only does looking at the picture induce us to imagine seeing an ox, we also imagine our actual visual experience, our perceiving the relevant part of the canvas, to be an experience of seeing an ox.

Carroll and Currie are concerned with the first part of my account, the idea that the perception of pictures—moving pictures in particular—involves imagining seeing.

Currie claims that if viewers were to imagine themselves to be seeing the things and events portrayed by a film, they would have to imagine being in various bizarre situations, undergoing strange and unlikely transformations, and enjoying magical modes of access to the fictional happenings.[7] We do not ordinarily engage in these latter imaginings when we watch movies, he thinks, so we cannot ordinarily be imagining seeing what they portray. In watching a sequence of shots from different points of view we will imagine seeing from different points of view. According to Currie, this means that the spectator will have to imagine jumping around from one place to another. In the scene in Hitchcock's *The Birds* in which Melanie Daniels crosses Bodega Bay in a hired boat, '[t]he transitions between the first three shots would require [the spectator] to imagine her position shifted instantly through ninety degrees twice, around the edge of the bay. . . . The transitions between 5 and 14 would then have her imagine herself shifting back and forth nine times between Melanie's own position . . . and different points on the shore, all within the space of a minute or two.'[8]

This is simply not so. Nothing is easier than, first, to imagine watching a boat from the shore, and then to imagine observing it from on board, without ever imagining moving or being transported somehow from the shore to the boat. One just imagines the one visual experience, and then imagines the other. In deciding where to go to observe a launching of a space shuttle you might imagine watching the moment of blast-off from one vantage-point, and then imagine watching it from another. There is no requirement that you imagine being in both places at once. The principle here is simple: one need not imagine the conjunction of other things that one imagines. Imagining *p* and imagining *q* does not have to involve imagining that both are true. If viewers of *The Birds* imagine watching the boat in Bodega Bay from the shore, and then, in the next shot, imagine being on the boat, it does not follow that they must ever have imagined even having *been* in both places, let alone moving from one place to the other.

Even if the spectator does imagine being on shore at one moment and on board the boat a moment later, this does not require imagining moving or being transported from the shore to the boat, imagining *changing* locations. One need not, in one's imaginative experience, follow out the implications of what one imagines.[9] This is especially obvious if, as Currie thinks, imaginings are necessarily *occurrent* mental events, if there is no such thing as dispositional imagining.[10] Obviously, when thoughts occur to us, many of their consequences do not.

Currie concedes that one needn't imagine the logical consequences of what one imagines,[11] effectively undercutting many of his objections to the idea that in watching a film one imagines seeing what is portrayed. He contends that if in watching *The Birds* the viewer imagines seeing from the perspective of the camera, one of the shots would require her 'to imagine herself suddenly in the water by the boat'. This wrongly assumes that she is required to work out the consequences of what she imagines. The viewer is likely not even to consider the question of where one would have to be in order to see the boat from the point of view she imagines seeing it from.[12] (Also, the fact that a sudden change in the images on the screen induce spectators suddenly to imagine a certain event does not mean that they must imagine the event occurring suddenly.)

'Do I imagine myself on the battlefield, mysteriously immune to the violence around me?', Currie asks rhetorically. The answer is: probably not. One *just* imagines seeing the violence of the battle from a particular perspective, if that is what the film portrays.

In the case of 'subjective' shots, shots portraying the view of a character in the fiction, Currie thinks that on the imagining seeing hypothesis the spectator would have to identify himself with the character, to imagine that he is the character.[13] This is not so. We imagine seeing things from a certain point of view, noticing certain aspects of them, and so forth. And we understand that what we imagine seeing is what fictionally the character sees; we imagine that that is what the character sees. The film thus *shows* us what the character's visual experience is like. This need not involve identifying with the character, imagining ourselves to be him.

Nevertheless, we do, sometimes, identify in one sense or another with characters, empathize with them, and subjective shots often encourage such identification.[14] I leave open the question of whether this involves imagining oneself to *be* the character. It certainly involves *simulating* the experience of characters, including their visual experience. And even when we do not empathize with the 'prominent attitudes and objectives' of a character (when in watching subjective shots from the point of view of a homicidal maniac our sympathies are with the victim, for instance[15]), there is no reason why we shouldn't simulate their visual experiences. Subjective shots induce exactly this kind of simulation.[16]

'If we are to imagine ourselves seeing fictional things and events when we watch a film, we shall have to imagine that our visual powers are strangely restricted, and that what I see depends in no way on our own decisions. The camera is often placed to restrict our view of the action for dramatic purposes, and in these cases one would often like to see more or see differently. But if we are imagining ourselves to be seeing the fiction itself, what are we to imagine concerning the source of this restriction?'[17] There is a confusion here between restrictions on what one imagines seeing, and imagining there to be restrictions on what one sees.[18] If what I imagine seeing depends not on my decisions but on the images projected on the screen, this does not force me to imagine that my decisions have nothing to do with what I see. Nothing prevents me from imagining that I could see something different by looking in a different direction or stepping around an obstruction, even if the screen images guiding my imaginings do not allow me to imagine actually doing so. And if I should imagine that my vision is restricted, I needn't imagine anything at all about why or how this is so, about the source of the restriction. Nor must I imagine that the restriction is a strange one.

Currie argues for one exception to the idea that one need not imagine the logical consequences of what one imagines: 'You cannot imagine, of a certain scene represented to you onscreen, that you are seeing it, but not that you are seeing it from any point of view.' This is so, he says, because 'the concepts of seeing and of point of view are linked more intimately than by entailment alone.' His point is obscure. 'To see *is* to see from a point of view,' he says; 'there is no such thing as nonperspectival seeing.'[19] Let's agree. And let us grant, for the sake of argument, that the connection is so 'intimate' that one cannot imagine seeing without imagining that there is a point of view from which one is seeing, that one's seeing is perspectival. This is innocuous.[20] But Currie seems to mean something much stronger: that to imagine seeing is necessarily to imagine seeing from some *particular* perspective, i.e. that there must be a particular perspective such that one imagines seeing from *that* perspective. This is certainly not so—not at least if, as Currie seems to think, to imagine seeing is just to imagine *that* one sees. I can easily imagine that I see something without there being a particular point of view which I imagine that I see it from. I need not imagine that I see from above, or that I see it from the side, or that I see it from nearby, or from afar.

I argued that imagining seeing does not reduce to imagining that I see.[21] And perhaps imagining seeing, or the kind of imagining seeing depictions provoke, is imagining seeing from one or another particular perspective.[22] Even so, there is no paradox. What Currie finds strange is not the idea that spectators of films imagine seeing from a given perspective, but the idea that they imagine certain consequences of their seeing from the perspective in question: their being in the water, being immune to bullets, changing position, etc. Imagining seeing from the relevant perspective does not require imagining these consequences. The perspective might be defined simply as being a certain approximate distance and direction from the object seen. And it is likely that the imaginer, or a person who actually sees something from a certain perspective, cannot specify in words even the distance and direction from which he sees or imagines seeing.[23]

Currie presents another objection: 'Suppose I am watching a movie in which the murderer enters unseen.' On the imagining seeing hypothesis, he thinks, it would have to be true that 'I imagine that there is an unseen murderer which I see.' But '[i]t is implausible to suppose that in the case described the audience is called on to imagine something contradictory.' I refer the reader to *Mimesis as Make-Believe*, where I considered exactly this objection.[24] What I say here will be brief, and is not meant to replace my discussion there.

In the first place, it is simply a mistake to suppose that if the spectator imagines seeing something and also imagines that that thing is not seen by anyone, he must be imagining a contradiction. Imagining *p* and imagining *not-p* do not entail imagining the conjunction, *p and not-p*. Currie's hypothetical movie might be understood to induce viewers to imagine seeing a murderer creeping silently into a building, and to induce this imagining as a way of indicating what the viewers are to imagine occurring without being seen. If, understanding this, they do imagine that the murderer is unseen, they needn't ever have imagined that the murderer is both seen and unseen.

The main point to be noticed, however, is that appreciators regularly are required to imagine incompatible and otherwise conflicting propositions, in any case, even apart from any imagining seeing, and that they do imagine these propositions, ordinarily, without feeling any particular tension or sense of paradox.[25] The idea that the spectator imagines seeing things which he also imagines to be unseen introduces no special difficulties, and constitutes no reason to reject the imagining seeing hypothesis.

It is a commonplace that dreams often contain paradoxes—what on reflection, on awakening, we recognize as paradoxes—which are not felt as such while we are dreaming. Here is one example:

Last night I had a dream . . . Mrs. Terry . . . told us that Marion and Florence were at the theatre, 'the Walter House,' where they had a good engagement. 'In that case,' I said, 'I'll go on there at once, and see the performance—and may I take Polly with me?' 'Certainly,' said Mrs. Terry. And there was Polly, the child, seated in the room, and looking about nine or ten years old: and I was distinctly conscious of the fact, yet without any feeling of surprise at its incongruity, that I was going to take the *child* Polly with me to the theatre, to see the *grown-up* Polly act! Both pictures— Polly as a child, and Polly as a woman, are, I suppose, equally clear in my ordinary waking memory: and it seems that in sleep I had contrived to give the two pictures separate individualities.[26]

In *Mimesis* I described numerous incongruities in what we imagine in appreciating the most ordinary representational works of art and discussed various ways of treating them, incongruities that involve only imaginings that Currie will surely allow. What is important is that no additional theoretical resources are needed to accommodate (apparent) incongruities arising from viewers' imagining seeing, and we should be neither surprised nor dismayed that there are such.

If imagining seeing is not the key to the notion of depiction, what is? Noël Carroll thinks there is an easy way of understanding pictorial representation, without invoking make-believe or imagining seeing. 'Pictorial or depictive representations are those whose subjects we recognize by looking (rather than by reading or decoding).'[27] This is not a solution. It is by looking that we recognize what (written) names and descriptions refer to. Yes, we *read* them, so this must not be the kind of 'recognition by looking' Carroll has in mind. But what is the difference? This is itself the heart of the problem. What is it to perceive pictures and how does picture perception differ from reading? (It is not a matter of ascertaining what is portrayed immediately or non-inferentially or automatically. Reading is often immediate, non-inferential, and automatic. Nor is it a matter of how much or what kind of training is required; we want to know how picture perception and reading themselves differ, regardless of how they or the capacities for them may have come about.)

Gregory Currie's answer is more elaborate, but no more successful. 'What makes the experience of cinema, painting and the other pictorial media an essentially visual one is that it gives rise to perceptual imaginings. Poetry and the novel, on the other hand, give rise to symbolic imaginings . . .'[28] What are 'perceptual imaginings'? We imagine that things have a certain appearance, when we see a film or picture of them, he says. But of course we will imagine this on reading a novelist's description of their appearance as well. Three further characteristics are supposed to make the imaginings elicited by paintings and films 'perceptual': (*a*) We imagine things' possessing certain clusters or bunches of features, corresponding to those we might perceive something as possessing: both colour and shape, for instance, rather than just one or the other. By contrast, 'If we had been reading a novel we might, at a certain point, have read something that prompted us to imagine that the character's eyes were blue. [But] we would be in no position to imagine anything about their shape, because we are told nothing about shape.' (*b*) We imagine very specific features. '[W]hen we see the screen we imagine that the character's eyes are exactly *that* shape, *that* colour, and *that* size in relation to the character's other features', whereas if we were reading a novel we 'would be in no position . . . to imagine that the [character's] eyes are some specific shade of blue.' And (*c*) our imaginings are sensitive to fine variations in the perceptual qualities of the stimulus (e.g. the film image). 'If what we saw on the screen were shaped or coloured in a slightly different way, what we would then have imagined about the character's features would have been correspondingly different.' Written descriptions are not similarly sensitive, he says. And some features are irrelevant: 'It would be a matter of indifference to our imaginings, moreover, whether the text was composed in this type face (or size, or colour) or that one.'[29]

The imaginings elicited by novels and stories do not differ as sharply as Currie suggests from those elicited by pictures. And differences of the kinds he describes do not begin to account for the distinctively perceptual nature of our experiences of pictures. A monochrome drawing or print will prompt us to imagine the shape of a person's eyes but tells us nothing about their colour. Novels often do describe both the shape and colour of a character's eyes, and we could introduce words specifying both shape and colour (e.g. 'blare' = blue square) without making descriptions containing them the least bit pictorial. There are words and phrases specifying particular shades of colour ('burnt sienna', 'the colour of *x*'), and a description of a character as being 'exactly five feet eleven inches tall' requires the reader to imagine his height more precisely than a picture is likely to. If typefaces, sizes, or colours of linguistic symbols, or fine differences in their shapes, were semantically significant and so affected what appearance the reader of a novel is supposed to imagine a character having, it is hard to believe that the experience of reading would thereby be even slightly more like the experience we describe as 'seeing a man', which perceivers of a picture of a man enjoy.[30]

The inadequacy of Currie's account of depiction is especially apparent when he tries to explain the fact that pictures depict things from certain points of view or perspectives, without endorsing what is surely the most natural way of doing this: understanding a picture to induce an experience one thinks of as seeing them from that point of view. Currie thinks that a picture, a cinematic image of a man, for instance, induces 'perspectival' imaginings, but he means by this no more than that it induces spectators to imagine that the man has a certain appearance from a certain perspective.[31] Beliefs can be perspectival in the same sense, as Currie insists. One may believe that Uncle Albert 'appears thus and so from a certain perspective'. Holding this belief is nothing like the kind of perspectival perceptual experiences we have when we look at pictures and other depictions, and neither does imagining that Uncle Albert has a particular appearance from a certain perspective. Perspectival imagining, in Currie's weak sense, doesn't begin to account for these experiences.

PHOTOGRAPHY

I turn now to photography, and to my claim that photographic pictures are transparent.

The idea that photographs have a 'mechanical' connection with what they are photographs of, that they differ fundamentally in this respect from drawings, sketches, and paintings, which are humanly mediated, and that because of this photographs somehow put us in closer contact with the world than 'handmade' pictures do, has been a constantly recurring theme in discussions of photography. It persists in the face of determined objections, and despite the difficulty of spelling it out coherently. We hardly need to be reminded that most photographs, like pictures of other kinds, are made by people, and that they reflect the photographer's interests, desires, vision, etc. Don't photographs, like other pictures, put us in contact, in the first instance, with a human being's conception of reality, rather than reality itself? Isn't photography just another method people have of making pictures, one that merely uses different tools and materials—cameras, photosensitive paper, darkroom equipment, rather than canvas, paint, and brushes? And don't the results differ only contingently and in degree, not fundamentally, from pictures of other kinds? I answered that the difference is indeed fundamental, that (with some qualifications) photographs are transparent and handmade pictures are not, and that this difference is entirely compatible with the fact that photographs, like paintings, result from human activity and reflect the picture maker's interests, intentions, beliefs, etc.

Noël Carroll and Gregory Currie misconstrue the transparency thesis in one important respect. Both take transparency to be incompatible with representation. According to Carroll, I 'deny that [documentary] photographs are representations, preferring to think of them as prosthetic devices, like binoculars, that enhance our ability to *see* whatever they are photographs of. So for Walton there is no imagining seeing when it comes to this sort of photograph.'[32] My position is that photographs, documentary photographs included, induce imagining seeing and are representations (depictions, pictures), in addition to being transparent.[33] In viewing a photograph of a class reunion, for instance, one actually sees the members of the class, albeit indirectly via the photograph, but at the same time one imagines seeing them (directly without photographic assistance). In the case of non-documentary films, what we actually see (the actors and the movie set) may be different from what we imagine seeing (the characters, a murder, a chariot race). As I emphasized in 'Transparent Pictures', the combination of actual and imagined seeing, and interaction between the role of photographs as aids to vision and their role as representations, is one of photography's most important and intriguing characteristics. To construe transparency as excluding imagining seeing is to miss out on it completely.

The question, then, is not whether photographs are representations, pictures, but whether they are pictures of a special kind. Currie agrees with most of what I said on this score. He agrees that photographs differ from other pictures in the respect which, I hold, prevents the latter from being transparent. Photographs are counterfactually dependent on the scenes they portray: if the scene had been different the photograph would have been different. The same is often true of paintings, in particular when the artist painted from life aiming to portray accurately what he saw. But—this was my main point—a painting from life depends counterfactually on the scene because the beliefs of the painter depend counterfactually on it. The counterfactual dependence of a photograph on the photographed scene, by contrast, is independent of the photographer's beliefs. It is because a difference in the scene would have affected the painter's beliefs about what is there, that it would have made the painting different. But a difference in what is in front of the camera would have made the photograph different even if it didn't affect the photographer's beliefs. The painter paints what he thinks he sees. The photographer captures with his camera whatever is in front of it, regardless of what he thinks is there.[34]

Currie concurs with all of this. As he puts it, photographs have 'natural' counterfactual dependence on the photographed scenes, whereas handmade paintings possess only 'intentional' counterfactual dependence on what they portray. He also agrees that this makes for a significant similarity between seeing a photograph of something and seeing the thing itself in the ordinary manner, and a respect in which both differ from seeing a painting of the thing. One's visual experience is naturally counterfactually dependent on the thing when one either sees it directly or sees a photograph of it, but not when one sees a painting of it.[35]

What Currie disagrees with is my decision to bring out this similarity by regarding viewers as actually *seeing* things when they see photographs of them. In saying this I was not especially concerned to be faithful to the ordinary sense of the word 'see' (if there is such a thing). So I could almost declare victory at this point, as far as Currie is concerned, and dismiss the remaining disagreement as semantic rather than substantive. But my transparency claim reflects more than just the natural counterfactual dependence of photographs on photographed scenes. I did not settle on an account of what it is to see something.[36] But even without such an account, comparisons with other aids to vision show how natural it is to think of seeing a photograph as a way of seeing the thing, as akin to seeing it directly.

In 'Transparent Pictures' I presented a challenge: we see things in (through) mirrors. We also see them with the aid of telescopes and microscopes. Why not regard live television as an aid to vision as well? And if we do, it is hard to see why we should not regard photography similarly. There are differences among these various means of access to things, of course. The challenge is to specify a difference that justifies denying that we see via some of these devices but not others, one that allows mirrors, telescopes, and microscopes, at least, to be transparent, as surely we must, while excluding photography. I gave reasons in 'Transparent Pictures' for taking the difference just outlined between photographs and handmade pictures as a reason to draw the line between them, to deny that the latter are transparent while allowing that the former are. I have not seen a compelling rationale for drawing the line earlier, somewhere between mirrors and photography.

Carroll and Currie take up the challenge. 'With ordinary seeing we get information about the spatial and temporal relations between the object seen and ourselves. . . . Call this kind of information "egocentric information". . . . Photographs, on the other hand, do not convey egocentric information.'[37] I can 'orient my body' spatially to what I see, either with the naked eye or through a telescope or microscope. But when I see a photograph I cannot orient my body to the photographed objects. The space of the objects is 'disconnected phenomenologically from the space I live in'.[38]

There can be no doubt that an important function of vision in human beings is to provide information about how things we see are related temporally and spatially to us. The ability to see evolved in humans and other animals primarily, no doubt, because such information is so important for survival.[39] But why suppose that seeing occurs only when this function is actually served? If the capacity to feel pain evolved in humans and other animals mainly as an indicator of damage to the body and as a device to prevent behaviour that would exacerbate the damage, it certainly does not follow that pain felt when there is no bodily damage (e.g. when neural pain receptors are stimulated artificially) is not really *pain*. And the egocentric information that is important to survival is primarily information about an organism's *immediate* surroundings, yet the capacity that has evolved allows us to see stars and other remote objects. An account of what it is to see should explain how seeing enables organisms to acquire information about their environment. There is no reason to assume that it must limit seeing to cases in which that is done.

Carroll and Currie agree that mirrors are aids to vision, that we literally see an object when we see it in or through a mirror. Consider an array of mirrors relaying the reflection of a carnation to a perceiver. Suppose that it is not evident to the perceiver how many mirrors are involved or how they are positioned, so he has no idea what direction the carnation is from him or how far away it is. Does he see the carnation through the mirrors? Surely he does.

Currie bravely bites the bullet. Although we normally see through mirrors, Currie says; when there is a confusing iteration of mirrors, such that egocentric spatial information is lost, we do not.[40] Carroll will have to agree. 'I do not speak of literally *seeing* the objects in question,' he says, 'unless I can perspicuously relate myself spatially to them—unless I know where they are in the space I inhabit.'[41]

If this result is not bad enough, consider a variation of the example. Suppose I see a carnation in the ordinary way, right in front of my eyes. But suppose that there are lots of mirrors around, or I suspect that there are. None of them actually affects my perception of the carnation, but I cannot tell that they do not; I think I may be seeing the image of a carnation reflected in one or many mirrors. So I have no idea where the carnation is in relation to me. Currie and Carroll are forced to deny that I see the carnation at all!

This does not exhaust the peculiar blindness that the Carroll–Currie conception of seeing would induce in us. Currie's blanket contention that photographs supply no egocentric information at all goes too far. He does acknowledge, in a footnote, that 'photographs can serve, along with information from other sources, in an inference to egocentric information'.[42] But he insists that this doesn't count, that it doesn't render the photographs in question transparent. Now, however, it will be hard for him to make room for the fact—a fact he endorses—that single, simple mirrors are transparent, in normal instances. The person who sees something in a mirror is likely to know where the reflected object is in relation to him, but only by relying on information from other sources. He must take into account facts about the reflective properties of mirrors. The spatial orientation of the mirror through which he sees is crucial, and this may not be apparent from his current visual experience. He may not be able to see even that there is a mirror; he may not see its edges or any other sign of it. And if the mirror's edges are visible, their significance is clear only in light of other background information, information he acquired from previous experience. Moreover, when no mirrors are involved or even suspected, when, in the most ordinary of cases, I see a carnation in front of my eyes, my egocentric knowledge that it is there depends on the realization that I am *not* seeing it through a mirror. It is a commonplace that what we learn from perception, in general, egocentric information included, depends on a wealth of background information not available from the perception itself, information by means of which we interpret perceptual cues.

Yes, the background information may be internalized, rather than consciously appealed to; the perceiver may not need to pay attention to the cues and explicitly draw the inference.[43] But this is true in the case of photographs, as well as those of mirrors and ordinary unassisted seeing. And it doesn't matter whether or not conscious inferences are made, anyway. If I must consciously figure out that an object which I see is in front of me, or behind me, using the information that there is or is not a mediating mirror, I am not *seeing* that it is where it is. But I am still seeing it. The transparency thesis is a thesis about direct object seeing, not about seeing *that* something is the case. When I see a photograph of a carnation I see the carnation, whether or not I see that it bears such and such spatial relations to me. (Seeing an object may require seeing that *something* is true of it; this may follow from a requirement that to see something is in a relevant sense to recognize it.[44] But it does not require seeing that egocentric facts obtain—facts about its spatial relation to oneself.)

The Carroll–Currie proposal amounts to ad hoc linguistic legislation, although it was not intended that way. So understood it is not pointless. 'See', in Carroll's and Currie's unusual sense, does at least mark out an important class of cases (not a sharply delineated one, and not one that separates photographs neatly from other pictures). But the same is true of 'see' as I understand it. Carroll and Currie have provided no reason for preferring their construal of the word to one on which (most) photographs are transparent.

My proposal may or may not be a departure from 'ordinary language', but if it is it is an especially natural one. We *do* speak of 'seeing' Uncle Fred when we see a photograph of him. Sometimes we say things like this in the same spirit in which we speak (non-literally) of seeing Fred while looking at his painted portrait. (Both are pictorial representations.) But sometimes the spirit is very different. In explaining why the *Star* tabloid planted a photographer on a neighbouring rooftop to catch political operative Richard Morris with a call girl, news editor Dick Belsky remarked, 'We wanted to see it with our own eyes.'[45] A sketch of the liaison, even by the most credible artist-reporter, would surely not have satisfied the desire Belsky expressed.

Who is to have proprietary rights to the word 'see' is not the issue, however. My proposal was meant to bring out the important similarities and differences that I sketched above (and explained more fully in 'Transparent Pictures')—especially the kinship which seeing a photograph of something bears to other ways of seeing it, and seeing a painting of it does not. Other terminology might serve this purpose. But the restricted notion of seeing that Carroll and Currie recommend risks losing sight of these similarities and differences. Carroll himself, following a suggestion of Francis Sparshott, mentions an alternative to his special sense of 'see' which does not run this risk. We might describe our experience of film, when we have no clear sense of the spatial relations the photographed objects bear to us, as 'alienated vision'.[46] In calling this *vision* Sparshott allows that what Carroll and Currie count as seeing—'unalienated' vision—is only one variety. Seeing through photographs and through confusing batteries of mirrors, notwithstanding any 'alienation', is another.

In their discussion of transparency, Carroll and Currie focus almost entirely on the role of perception in acquiring information. One of the larger objectives of 'Transparent Pictures' was to show that information gathering is not the only important function of perception. We sometimes have an interest in seeing things, in being in perceptual contact with them, apart from any expectations of learning about them. This interest helps to explain why we sometimes display and cherish a photograph of a loved one (or a movie star or athelete or personal hero), even a fuzzy and badly exposed photograph, long after we have extracted any interesting or important information it might contain, and why we may sometimes prefer such a photograph to a realistic painting or drawing that is loaded with information. We value the experience of seeing the loved one (even indirectly), the experience of being in perceptual contact with him or her, for its own sake, not just as a means of adding to our knowledge.[47]

NOTES

1. *Mimesis as Make-Believe: On the Foundations of the Representational Arts* (Cambridge, Mass.: Harvard University Press, 1990).

2. 'Transparent Pictures', *Critical Inquiry*, 11: 2 (1984), 246–77. See also 'Looking again through Photographs: A Response to Edwin Martin', *Critical Inquiry*, 12 (Summer 1986), 801–8.

3. This is true of many traditional attempts to define depiction in terms of visual resemblance. The point is not that visual resemblance is not part of what makes pictures pictures, but that the main work of devising an informative account consists in specifying what kind of resemblance is involved and how it is involved. I hold that the relevant kind of resemblance is to be explained in terms of imagining or make-believe. And nothing is lost by simply explaining depiction in terms of imagining or make-believe, without mentioning 'resemblance'.

4. Gregory Currie, *Image and Mind: Film, Philosophy and Cognitive Science* (Cambridge: Cambridge University Press, 1995), 169, 181.

5. Unless it is a photograph of an ox (as well as a photographic picture of one). But 'I see an ox' said while observing such a photograph, understood in one natural way, is not literally true.

6. Imagining seeing an ox is not reducible to imagining that one sees an ox. Cf. *Mimesis*, §1.4 'Imagining about Oneself'. Carroll neglects this distinction, and Currie explicitly collapses it: 'I take it to be a distinctive thesis of classical film theory that cinema encourages a certain kind of imagining which I have called imagining seeing: imagining that you are seeing the fictional events of the film, and seeing them from the point of view of the camera.' (*Image and Mind*, 168.)

7. *Image and Mind*, 172.

8. Ibid. 177.

9. Cf. *Mimesis as Make-Believe*, especially ch. 4.

10. Currie, 'Imagination and Simulation', in Martin Davies and Tony Stone (eds.), *Mental Simulation: Evaluations and Applications* (Oxford: Blackwell, 1995), 160.

11. *Image and Mind*, 177.

12. Given the propositions that a work initially induces us to imagine, which of their consequences are we also to imagine and which of them can we ignore? The answer varies from medium to medium and genre to genre. We should not expect a simple systematic formula. Cf. *Mimesis as Make-Believe*, 165–6.

13. *Image and Mind*, 174–6.

14. Cf. *Mimesis*, 32–4, 255.

15. Currie, *Image and Mind*, 176.

16. Currie himself says that in watching *Stagecoach* 'we *see* Dallas the prostitute from Lucy's point of view' (ibid. 175, my italics).

17. Ibid. 172–3.

18. Cf. *Mimesis and Make-Believe*, 359. See also §6.4 'Restrictions on Participation'. The restrictions I discuss obviously do not make it fictional that one is restricted.

19. *Image and Mind*, 178.

20. It is also questionable, especially if Currie is right in assuming that all imagining is occurrent. Must one who imagines seeing be imagining *occurrently* that his seeing is perspectival? (Not imagining that one's seeing is perspectival is not the same as imagining that one's seeing is not perspectival, of course.)

21. See note 6.

22. But I am sceptical. See *Mimesis as Make-Believe*, §8.7.

23. Currie's claim of a more-intimate-than-entailment connection between seeing and points of view is part of an argument against an Imagined Observer Hypothesis weaker than the one he attributes to the 'classical' film theorists, Panofsky and Balázs in particular. The weaker alternative postulates 'a kind of *purely* visual imagining, unconnected with any imaginings about where we are seeing from or how it is that we are able to see', one that does not involve imagining ourselves 'placed anywhere in the scene, or as undergoing any changes of position' (*Image and Mind*, 177). The mistake here is in thinking that an alternative that is weaker in the ways mentioned

would have to postulate an incoherent 'imagined nonperspectival seeing' (169). It is not clear that, on a charitable reading, Belasz and Panofsky have to be understood as holding the strong view he outlines, rather than a more reasonable one of the kind I have been defending.

24. See especially §6.6 'Seeing the Unseen', which relies on principles developed in §4.5 'Silly Questions', and elaborated elsewhere in *Mimesis*. My discussion in *Mimesis* was in response to an early statement of the objection by Nicholas Wolterstorff, directed to an earlier presentation of my account of depiction.

25. It is not hard to nurture a sense of paradox, however, even cases like that of the unseen murderer. One can make them feel like M. C. Escher's prints and some absurdist stories which emphasize the conflicts in what they ask us to imagine.

26. Lewis Carroll, quoted in S. D. Collingwood, *The Life and Letters of Lewis Carroll* (1899). From Stephen Brook, *The Oxford Book of Dreams*, 202–3.

27. 'Critical Study: Kendall L Walton, Mimesis as Make-Believe', *Philosophical Quarterly*, 45: 178 (Jan. 1995), 97.

28. *Image and Mind*, 184.

29. *Image and Mind*, 184. See also pp. 182–3.

30. Currie's account fails for much the same reasons that Nelson Goodman's does, with which it has considerable affinity. But Goodman doesn't claim to be defining a distinctively visual or perceptual notion of representation.

31. *Image and Mind*, 188.

32. 'Critical Study', 97. See Currie, *Image and Mind*, 50–1, 71, 72.

33. See 'Transparent Pictures', 251–4, and *Mimesis as Make-Believe*, 88, 330, 331 n. Patrick Maynard makes a good case for regarding certain things as photographs but not pictures. Cf. *The Engine of Visualization: A Philosophical Primer of Photography* (Ithaca, NY: Cornell University Press, forthcoming). I was concerned only with what he calls photographic pictures.

34. This paragraph is a gloss on my more precise formulation in 'Transparent Pictures', 262–5. Carroll seems to have missed the point about counterfactual dependence. Paintings are not counterfactually dependent on the objects they depict, he says. (Carroll, 'Towards an Ontology of the Moving Image', in Cynthia A. Freeland and Thomas E. Wartenberg (eds.), *Philosophy and Film* (New York: Routledge, 1995), 70).

35. Currie also reiterates my reasons for dismissing as irrelevant several considerations that are often adduced against the transparency thesis and the idea that photographs are special (*Image and Mind*, 56–8).

36. Neither the natural counterfactual dependence of one's visual experiences on objects, nor that plus a correspondence between similiarity relations and the likelihood of discriminatory errors, is sufficient for seeing an object. So I do not subscribe to the account of transparency Currie outlines in *Image and Mind*, 63. I did make some tentative suggestions about what else is required. Cf. 'Looking again through Photographs', 804.

37. Currie, *Image and Mind*, 66.

38. Carroll, 'Towards an Ontology of the Moving Image', 71. See also 'Critical Study', 97–8. Nigel Warburton made a similar point in 'Seeing through "Seeing through Photographs"', *Ratio*, NS 1 (June 1988), 64–74.

39. See Carroll, *Theorizing the Moving Image* (New York: Cambridge University Press, 1996), 62–3.

40. *Image and Mind*, 70.

41. 'Towards an Ontology of the Moving Image', 71.

42. *Image and Mind*, 66.

43. See Walton, 'The Dispensability of Perceptual Inferences', *Mind* (1963), 357–67.

44. Looking again through Pictures', 804.

45. *Newsweek*, 9 Sept. 1996, p. 36.

46. 'Ontology', 71; *Theorizing*, 62.
47. Some readers may be interested in how I would treat several examples that Currie thinks make trouble for the transparency thesis:

(a) Suppose scenes cause visual experiences not directly, but only with the mediation of a Malebranchian God, who in his benevolence acts 'to maintain [the] counterfactual dependence' we observe (*Image and Mind*, 62). Currie thinks we would still see things, in this case, and hence that natural counterfactual dependence is not necessary for perception. I think it is at least as plausible that, in the situation imagined, 'see' would pick out a different natural kind from the one it actually picks out, and that there would then be instances of the former but not the latter. Also, it is not easy to be sure that any inclination to say that seeing occurs, in this exotic example, does not depend on thinking of the Malebranchian God as something more like a force of nature than a human intentional agent, even if we describe it in intentional terms (as we do computers).

(b) Suppose two clocks are linked mechanically, so their hands always move in tandem. Do I see one of the clocks by looking at the other? (*Image and Mind*, 65) No, and for a reason that Currie himself endorses in connection with another example. Suppose a person's eyes lack lenses, and unfocused light stimulates his retinas. He sees mere homogeneous fields of white or black or grey, depending on the intensity of the incident light. Does he see the objects that reflect light to his eyes? No. The reason, I argued, is that his visual experiences are not richly enough counterfactually dependent on the reflecting objects, and Currie concurs ('Looking again through Photographs', 803–4. *Image and Mind*, 57). Only the intensity of light reflected by the scene affects his visual experience. Likewise in the clock example: Only the position and/or movement of the hands of the second clock affects the visual experiences of the person looking at the first one. This is not enough for him to qualify as seeing the second clock (or even its hands). If the example is changed so that the first clock is dependent in many respects on the second one (and other conditions are met), I would recommend speaking of seeing the second by looking at the first. Even so, the perceiver will not *know* he is seeing the second clock, and may not even have the impression of seeing it, unless he realizes that the rich counterfactual dependence obtains.

(c) Do I see heat, by looking at the column of mercury in a thermometer? (*Image and Mind*, 63–4.) Not, I think, if I explicitly infer how hot it is from the length of the column. (In that case there would seem to be *nothing* that I *see* to be true of the heat. I could not be said to recognize or notice it, in a sense that, arguably, is required for perceiving it. Cf. 'Looking again through Photographs', 804.) And not if, as is plausible, heat is by definition something that can only be felt, not perceived in other ways. Currie thinks that seeing heat is not ruled out by definition. He thinks we might see heat if things looked darker the hotter they were. I am sceptical. In any case, we wouldn't see heat if we have to infer, explicitly, how hot things are from how bright or dark they appear. Suppose we don't have to, suppose the lightness or darkness functions simply as a perceptual cue. If this counts as seeing heat, then surely we would be seeing heat if the height of the mercury in a thermometer serves as the cue instead.

3

Looking at Motion Pictures

RICHARD ALLEN

> When I see the picture of a galloping horse—do I merely *know* that this
> is the kind of movement meant? Is it superstition to think that I *see* the
> horse galloping in the picture?
>
> Wittgenstein

What is it we see when we look at a motion picture? This is a central
question addressed by all film theory. It derives from a much older question:
what is it we see when we look at a picture? But the answer to this question
depends in turn upon how we understand the activity of seeing itself. The
philosophical understanding of what seeing is has been dominated by causal
theories of perception. Very broadly speaking, causal theories of perception
define seeing as the presence of a causal relationship between the object and
one's perception of the object. Seeing is understood as a form of experience,
a perceptual one, that is caused by the presence of the object in front of
one's eyes. When seeing is conceived in this way, pictorial perception
generates a paradox. Arrayed before us is the disposition of pigment on a
canvas or colours on photographic paper, but that is not what we report
that we see when we see a painting or colour photograph: we report that we
see what the photograph or painting depicts. But how can we see what a
photograph or painting depicts when it does not lie before us?

Visual theorists have sought to resolve the paradox of pictorial perception
in a way that conforms to the causal theory of perception. As they have been
applied to the problem of perceiving motion pictures, these theories are of
at least four kinds: illusion theories, transparency theories, imagination
theories, and recognition theories. According to illusion theories of pictorial
perception we see what a picture depicts because a picture causes us to have
a visual experience that is like the visual experience that we have when we
see the object. We may be deceived by the illusion, in which case it is a
cognitive or epistemic illusion, or the illusion may be merely sensory or

My special thanks to Macolm Turvey for realizing so clearly the significance of
Wittgenstein for film theory and for his comments on this paper. Thanks also to Berys
Gaut, Paisley Livingston, Murray Smith, and Michael Zryd for their helpful criticisms.
The faults that undoubtedly remain are entirely my own.

perceptual. Theories of illusion were highly influential in the film theories of the 1970s and early 1980s that sought to explain the special power of movies to shape the imagination. Transparency theories are associated with the realist tradition of film theory: Bazin, Kracauer, and Cavell. Transparency theorists claim that the unique properties of the photographic image allow us, in some sense, to actually see the object when we look at a motion picture. The object of sight is not absent from us but indirectly made present to us via its photographic reproduction. Imagination and recognition theories of pictorial perception are of more recent vintage and are associated with the turn toward 'cognitive' approaches to understanding motion picture perception within film theory. Imagination theorists of pictorial perception deny the fact that we see what is depicted in a motion picture: rather than seeing what a picture depicts, we imagine seeing what a picture depicts. Recognition theorists, like imagination theorists, resolve the paradox of pictorial perception by denying that, strictly speaking, we see what is depicted in a picture. However, they may also deny that we imagine that we see something and simply claim that what we see is the disposition of colours on a flat surface that cues our recognition of what the picture is of.

Each of these theories attempts to resolve the paradox of looking at pictures by rejecting one or other horn of the dilemma. Either we see what a picture depicts because what we see *is* the object itself or an illusion of it, or we do not see the object itself and instead we either imagine that we see what the picture is of or it affords us a recognition of what it depicts. I shall argue neither solution is satisfactory: we require an understanding of seeing pictures that, contrary to imagination and recognition theorists, respects that fact that seeing what a picture is of is a genuine case of seeing, without commitment to the idea that what we see is the object itself or an illusion of it. Both the paradox and the proposed solutions to it presuppose that any genuine perceptual report consists of the description of the physical properties of an object, for seeing is taken to be a causal process that links a physical object with our perception of it. Once we abandon the conceptual straight-jacket imposed by the causal theory of perception, as I argue that we should, we can recognize that an object of sight is not always a physical object and the paradox of pictorial perception dissolves.

Following Wittgenstein, I shall argue that the content of our perceptual reports is specified not by a theory but simply by what we report that we see when we make veridical reports using perceptual verbs. Wittgenstein draws attention to the fact there are many cases of seeing that involve the seeing of an aspect, for example, seeing a face in the clouds, seeing a resemblance to another family member in the face of a person, seeing the expression of fear in a face or in a portrait, or seeing the movement of an animal in a sketch of an animal.[1] In aspect seeing, the specification of what is seen cannot be couched in terms of the physical properties of an object, yet I am, nonetheless, seeing something, not simply imagining that I see it. Pictorial perception exemplifies aspect seeing. When we look at a motion picture we see what the motion picture depicts, but what we see is neither the thing itself nor an illusion of it. But how can I *explain* this fact? I do not offer an alternative theory here about what it is we see when we look at motion pictures. Instead, my strategy will be to diagnose what it is that impels the theorist of vision to insist there is something strange about our talk of seeing something that is depicted in a motion picture. Dispel the strangeness, or recognize how widespread this strangeness is, and the pressure is allayed to revise our customary ways of speaking on account of a theory.

Film theory whether in its realist, psychoanalytic, or cognitive forms, has conceived its task as one of explaining the relationship between the image and the spectator's experience of that image or the relationship between properties of the object that is seen and the psychological impact of those properties upon the spectator. That is, visual theory is founded upon the causal theory of perception. For this reason, abandoning the causal theory of perception does not simply involve relinquishing *a* theory of motion picture perception, it involves the abandonment of film theory itself as the route to understanding what it is we see when we look at motion pictures. What it is that we see when we look at motion pictures can be specified only by describing it, and this points to the central role of criticism for under-standing movies.

My concern is to address the paradox of looking at pictures. However, contained within the problem of whether or not we can see what a picture depicts is a problem posed by a certain class of pictures: pictures of fictions. Fictional objects do not exist. How can something that is non-existent be depicted, and if it cannot be depicted how can we see it in a picture? The idea that we can perceive fictional objects is surely nonsensical: a 'meta-physical impossibility'.[2] My approach to the problem of perceiving fictions is simply this. Assuming that fictions can be depicted, then the arguments that I make about looking at pictures in general apply to pictures of fictions as well. That is, just as we might report that we saw Larry Hagman acting the part of J.R. being shot, we might also report, if we were avid *Dallas* watchers, 'J.R. has been shot . . . I just saw it.' Similarly, assuming that what is fictional can be depicted, then we can see what is depicted in a painting, whether the painting is of a horse or a unicorn. However, I shall not argue the case here.

I

The illusion thesis is one that is associated with contemporary film theory though its roots are ancient. The theory that pictures are cognitive or epistemic illusions that cause us to believe mistakenly that what we see is real has been thoroughly debunked and can be laid to rest.[3] Illusions do not necessarily cause us to have mistaken beliefs about the object, but elsewhere I have tried to defend a weaker version of the illusion thesis: cinema and other forms of pictorial representations can function as a form of perceptual or sensory illusion that I call 'projective illusion'. I define projective illusion as a form of illusion that is akin to our experience of an illusion like the Müller-Lyer illusion, where we know that what we see is an illusion yet our senses are still deceived. However, it is also a weaker form of illusion than this kind of sensory deception since in projective illusion, as I define it, I can bring to bear my knowledge of the fact that the representation is a depiction to prevent projective illusion taking hold, or to break the hold of the illusion entirely.[4]

This idea of projective illusion is both empirically false and conceptually confused. What is distinctive about an illusion is that it is a special form of representation that is configured in such a way as to confound our senses: our senses become unreliable guides to what lies before us. For example, in the Müller-Lyer illusion we seem to see two lines of unequal length, even though we know that the two lines are of the same length. However, representations do not, in general, drive such a wedge between perception and belief in this way; we do not customarily take a representation for something other than it is. I try to build into the theory of projective illusion a recognition of the fact that my knowledge: that the representation is a depiction is sufficient to break the hold of the putative illusion. However, the kind of mistaken perception engendered by an illusion is not one that can be corrected by my knowledge: that is what makes it an illusion. I argue that the correction occurs in the manner that I can change my perception when I perceive an ambiguous figure like Jadstrow's 'Is it a duck? Is it a rabbit?' However, the idea that the correction of our perception of projective illusion occurs in this way still presupposes that I see the image as an illusion in the first place. As Noël Carroll points out, if the illusion theory is wrong, then so is the explanation of how the spectator's experience of the illusion is countered.[5]

I attempt to circumvent this kind of objection to the theory by revising the concept of projective illusion to one in which we entertain in thought or imagine that we see the represented object.[6] However, it is not appropriate to label the thesis of imagined seeing projective *illusion* for it is not an illusion theory at all. If I imagine seeing I do not see, just as if I imagine eating I do not actually eat. If imagined seeing is not seeing, then it is not the seeing of an illusion either. Film theorists have tried to reconcile the thesis of imagined seeing with the illusion theory by recourse to psychoanalytic theory. Psychoanalysis offers a putatively empirical theory of how the mind works in such a way as to confuse what is imagined with what is real. This theory is not necessary to sustain the thesis of imagined seeing, but it is necessary to convert the thesis about imagined seeing into a thesis about what we see, that is, into the idea that the camera somehow allows the spectator to be an invisible visual witness to events they see on the screen.[7] However, even if psychoanalytic theory were cogent it would not turn imagined seeing into the seeing of an illusion. For if imagined seeing is confused with seeing, the result is not the perception of an illusion but a hallucination. Hallucinations, unlike illusions, are visual deceptions that are internally rather than externally caused. Thus psychoanalytic theory offers no support to an illusion theory of depiction.

The confusion that characterizes my own theory is, I think, typical of illusion theories. However, before leaving the topic of illusion it is important to recognize the feature of looking at motion pictures that illusion theories, however confusedly, are trying to explain. Illusion theories take seriously the fact that it is meaningful to speak of looking at what a motion pictures depicts, whether actual or fictional, and that we emotionally respond to those depictions with an immediacy that is on a par with the way that we respond to actual objects and people. As Malcolm Turvey argues elsewhere in this volume, this is a feature of our response to motion pictures that critics of the illusion theory overlook, for in abandoning the illusion theory they also abandon any explanation of looking at motion pictures that is based on the fact that we see what they depict.[8] Nonetheless, illusion theories err in the explanation they offer of seeing motion pictures, for they rely upon the assumption that what we specify in our perceptual reports must be the properties of a physical object that have caused us to see it. Since we make our perceptual reports in the presence of a picture and not the object itself, we must be under the spell of an illusion that causes us to have a visual experience of the object without the object being present.

The causal theory of perception is based on the assumption that the content of my visual experience can be detached from the specification of what it is that I see, and that seeing an illusion of x shares the same content—a visual experience—with seeing x. The theory of what it is to see an illusion of x—that it involves the same visual experience as the one involved in seeing x—is an integral part of the causal theory of perception since it demonstrates how it is that our visual experience of seeing can be detached from the specification of what it is I actually see: the visual experience is the same, but what we see is different.[9] However, as John Hyman has pointed out in a carefully argued critique of the causal theory of perception, it is not clear what it could mean to have a visual experience of something without seeing it.[10] We cannot usually experience an activity, say playing the piano, without actually doing it. We can at best imagine doing it. Why is the case of seeing different? The difference seems to be that when we see the illusion of an object we just do have a visual experience of something without seeing it. However, if we accept that to see an illusion of *x* is to have a visual experience of *x*, this does not entail that the visual experience we have is the same as the visual experience of actually seeing *x*. For example, the person who looks at a sensory illusion of *x* will obviously distinguish their experience from the case where they actually see *x* or where someone else actually sees *x*. They will report that they seem to see *x* or that what they see looks like *x*, rather than reporting that they see *x*.

The causal theorist might respond in the following way. Surely the person who believes they are seeing an object (as in the case of epistemic or cognitive illusion) thinks that they are seeing the same thing as a person who is seeing the object. Looking at an illusion of *x*, a person will report that they are seeing *x*, and they might report that what they are seeing in this case is the same as what they saw in a previous case of seeing *x*. But what is the nature of what is shared here, and is it a sufficient basis for the causal theory? It *is* true that there is nothing in the visual experience of a person who believes that she sees *x* that allows her to make the claim that what she sees is not what she thinks she sees. The person who believes she sees *x* believes that she is having the same experience as a person who actually sees *x* or the same experience as when she actually saw *x* before. In this sense we can speak of what someone believes they see as being, from the subject's point of view, indistinguishable from what they actually saw before or from what another actually sees. However, for the person who experiences an illusion to *believe* that she is having the same experience does not mean that she *has* the same experience. For although reports about what we see in general provide a sound basis for ascribing a certain kind of visual experience to us, these reports, like any other first-person avowal may be defeated by (anomalous) circumstances. The defeating circumstances are in this case precisely that the person is seeing not *x* but an illusion of *x*, and thus although she reports that she sees *x*, she actually only seems to see *x*.

Furthermore, as Hyman also points out, the idea of there being something in common between these two forms of visual experience is not only false but unintelligible. For there are only two ways in which one visual experience could be similar to another. They could be similar in visual appearance or they could be similar in the way they feel. But one visual experience cannot be similar to another on the basis of its visible properties, because what can be seen of a visual experience is only the behaviour of the person who is having the visual experience. But neither can the visual experiences be similar in the way they feel for a visual experience is not a physical sensation. Since the idea of there being a visual experience in common between actually seeing *x* and imagining or thinking that we see *x* is either false or nonsensical, then so is the idea that our seeing *x* consists in a report about what we seem, think, or appear to see. The causal theory of perception requires that we can separate out a mental component of perception from the physical component to make room for an explanation of the causal connection between them. But there is no room to be had. Mental and physical are indissolubly linked in our perceptual reports.

I have argued, following Hyman, that the causal theory of perception mistakenly assumes (*a*) that the content of my visual experience can be detached from the specification of what it is that I see, and (*b*) that the seeing of an illusion shares the same content—a visual experience—with actual seeing. It is these mistaken ideas that motivate the analogy between pictures and illusions: in seeing a picture I am said to have the same visual experience as when I see the object. However, as we have seen, what is shared between the seeing of an illusion of *x* and seeing *x* is simply the belief that one is seeing the same thing, and, in the cases where the illusion is merely sensory, not even this belief is shared. Clearly, in the case of seeing what is depicted in a picture I do not erroneously believe that I am seeing the object itself but neither do I seem to see something in a way that confounds my knowledge that what I see is only an illusion. Once we abandon the causal theory of perception together with the conception of illusion it entails, the argument that seeing the object depicted in a picture is like seeing an illusion and hence like seeing the object itself loses its appeal.

II

Kendall Walton has provided a rigorous, defensible version of the central claim of the realist tradition in film theory, that what we see in a photograph or motion picture is not simply a representation of the object but the object itself. Bazin claimed that 'No matter how fuzzy, distorted or discolored, no matter how lacking in documentary value the image may be, it shares, by the process of its becoming, the being of the model of which it is the reproduction; it is the model.'[11] This assertion is based upon a conflation of photographic representation with what the photograph is of. Walton revises Bazin's account in the following way. He argues that when we look at a photograph or a motion picture we may speak with justification of seeing an object photographed just in those cases where the object depicted in the photograph is something that existed in front of the camera when the photograph was taken (something that we can assume in the case of the standard photograph of a non-fictional object). However, we can see the object not because the representation *is* in some sense the object photographed as Bazin claimed, but because the photograph allows us to see the object indirectly. The object photographed is, in this case, seen *through* the photograph in a manner that is akin to the way that we look through eyeglasses or a telescope at an object.[12] We thus really are looking at

William Shatner when we see *Star Trek: The Motion Picture*, but he is not directly present to us, nor do we believe that he is present to us in the manner of an illusion.

Walton's reasoning is that photographs maintain the putative counterfactual dependence that obtains between how an object is and how it appears to me. That is, according to the causal theory of perception, under normal conditions of viewing, an object appears to me in a certain way by virtue of the causal connections between it and my visual experience. If we were to entertain a situation that is counter to the facts at hand—if the object were different or I was looking at it from a different perspective—my visual experience of it would be different in a manner that corresponded to the different situation. Photography preserves this counterfactual dependence in a manner that, unlike painting, is not relative to the intention of the artist. Regardless of what actually stands before the painter when he paints, what he paints and we see is what he intends to paint and for us to see. However, even if the photographer intends to photograph something else, in the standard case he photographs and we see what was before the camera. The counterfactual dependence in photography is natural rather than intentional. Natural counterfactual dependence is not sufficient to establish transparency because we can imagine, for example, a light sensitive machine that printed out descriptions of what it records that would obviously fail to produce representational transparency. Thus Walton argues that visual transparency is only guaranteed by the fact that photographs, unlike verbal descriptions, preserve real similarity relationships between objects: the word 'house' is more likely to be confused with 'hearse' than with 'barn', but a photograph of a house can be confused with a barn just as a house can be mistaken for a barn. The range of discriminatory error is alike in the case of seeing photographs and seeing things.   .

Walton's argument about photography and cinema has the advantage that it can make sense of the fact that we do speak of seeing the object depicted without resorting to an illusion theory. However, it does so upon the basis of a theory that draws a sharp distinction between looking at photographic depictions of existing objects or persons, like William Shatner, and looking at photographs of fictional objects or persons, like Captain Kirk, or looking at a painting of either William Shatner or Captain Kirk. For Walton, when we look at a representational painting or a motion picture fiction we imagine seeing what the painting or the fiction represents. Walton is committed to the idea that there is a sharp or categorical difference between what we report on when we exclaim 'There is William Shatner' when we look at a painted poster of *Star Trek: The Motion Picture* and when we look at the film. In the first case, we imagine that we see what is depicted, in the second case, we are reporting upon what we actually see via its photographic reproduction. Yet, is my exclamation that I can see what is depicted justified only in the case of looking at photographs or motion pictures and not in the case of representational paintings (or looking at fictions)?

Gregory Currie suggests that Walton's account of looking at photographs errs in his supposition that the counterfactual dependence that looking at photographs shares with ordinary seeing is a test of transparency. Currie argues that since natural counterfactual dependence is neither necessary nor sufficient for transparency, the counterfactual dependence that seeing photographs shares with seeing does not serve to make photographs more like seeing an object than seeing a representation of it.[13] Photographs are therefore not transparent in the manner claimed by Walton. I agree with Currie that Walton draws too sharp a distinction between looking at photographs and looking at paintings, but I believe that Currie argues against Walton for the wrong reasons. I shall contend that the problem in Walton's account lies not in the putative link between a natural counterfactual dependence displayed by seeing and photography, and transparency, but in the idea that the counterfactual dependence manifested by photographs reproduces the counterfactual dependence found in seeing. In fact, there is no room for the concept of counterfactual dependence within our concept of seeing. Why not?

What does it mean to say that if the scene before my eyes were different my visual experience of that scene would be different, other than the tautology that if what I saw was different what I saw would be different? For the counterfactual conditional to be meaningful, the subjective aspect of what I see must be specifiable in a manner that is independent of the fact of seeing. As I have already noted, precisely the same specification is required for the causal theory of perception. Thus the idea of counterfactual dependency can be understood in terms of the causal theory in the following way: when I see an object x, I have a visual experience that corresponds to what lies before my eyes, and I have this experience by virtue of the causal connections between the scene and the visual experience. What establishes the case that I see x rather than y is the causal relationship between x and the visual experience I have when seeing x. These causal connections are such that if the scene before my eyes were different my visual experience would be correspondingly different. I have argued against the causal theory of perception on the grounds that we cannot specify the content of our visual experience independently of what it is we see. Now while the idea of counterfactual dependency need not be expressed in causal terms—the nature of the connection between visual experience and the object of sight may remain unspecified—the idea of counterfactual dependency in perception is based, nonetheless, on the same requirement as the causal theory: the possibility of specifying the content of our visual experience independently of what it is that we see. Thus the theory of counterfactual dependency fails as an account of perception, whether or not it is expressed in terms of the causal theory of perception.

The idea of counterfactual dependency explains only the difference in relationship that a representational painting or drawing has to the scene painted and a photograph to what is photographed. It suggests the fact that, as Currie puts it, photographs are natural representations whereas paintings are intentional representations.[14] This difference between paintings and photographs is crucial to understanding the evidential nature of photographs and films. However, this difference justifies the thesis that when we look at a photograph we are brought into perceptual contact with the object only if it is coherent to ascribe to seeing the same counterfactual dependency. But it is not. Once we abandon the causal theory of perception, the difference between seeing photographs and seeing paintings cannot be conceptualized in terms of a difference between a case of genuine seeing and a case in which we do not, properly speaking, see the object depicted at all.

III

I have suggested that illusion and transparency theorists are right to take seriously the idea that we see what is depicted in a picture, but they mistakenly try to fit their explanation of what it is that we see within the framework of the causal theory of perception; it is this attempt that leads to error. Pictures are not like illusions and the transparency thesis draws too sharp a contrast between looking at representational paintings and looking at photographs. However, one may agree with this criticism of illusion and transparency theories without accepting that the reason for their failure is the fact they rely on a particular theory of perception. Instead, the reason for their failure might seem to lie in their mistaken assumption that when we look at what is depicted in a picture we actually see what it depicts.

As we have seen, other than in the case where we look at a standard photograph of a non-fictional object, Walton argues that looking at what is depicted in a picture is a form of imagined seeing rather than seeing, though he emphasizes that the activity in which we imagine seeing the object depicted is bound up with our actual seeing of the surface of the picture. Referring to Hobbema's picture *Wooded Landscape with a Water Mill*, Walton writes: 'Rather than merely imagining seeing a mill, as a result of actually seeing the canvas (as one may imagine seeing Emma upon reading a description of her appearance in *Madame Bovary*), one imagines one's seeing of the canvas to be a seeing of a mill and this imagining is an integral part of one's visual experience of the canvas.'[15] Walton's thesis of imagined seeing is advanced as a general thesis about seeing pictures; he offers the transparency thesis as a further thesis that pertains to looking at photo-graphs alone.[16]

But why is the case of looking at what is depicted in a picture a case of imagined seeing rather than seeing? Walton derives his thesis of imagined seeing, in part, from Richard Wollheim's characterization of looking at paintings in terms of 'seeing-in'. However, unlike Walton, Wollheim claims that 'seeing-in' is not a form of imagined seeing but a case of seeing. But what is it, then, that we see? According to Wollheim, a picture is not an illusion because seeing what is depicted does not preclude our attention to the surface of the painting. The term 'seeing-in' is designed to capture what he terms the 'two-foldedness' of the experience of seeing what a picture depicts. Yet, in spite of his intention, Wollheim's account of 'seeing-in' becomes an illusion theory since his analysis of seeing is cast in terms of the causal theory of perception.[17] He defines 'seeing-in' as the capacity to have 'perceptual experiences of things not present to the senses': the picture of an object causes us to have a mental state that is like the mental state of those who actually see the object.[18] Of course, this experience of seeing something not present to the senses is meant to coincide with the experience of seeing the surface of the picture, but how is this coincidence of illusion and veridical perception to be achieved?[19] While Wollheim may be right to conceive of looking at pictures as a form of seeing, his understanding of pictorial perception is vitiated by his dependence on the causal theory of perception.

Wollheim's discussion of seeing-in is derived from Wittgenstein's contem-plation in the *Philosophical Investigations* on looking at pictures, to which I shall now turn in order to further evaluate the thesis of imagined seeing. What we see when we see something in a picture is a part of a family of cases that Wittgenstein calls the seeing of aspects. Consider the simple drawing in the figure. Wittgenstein points out that this shape can be seen in a number of ways: as a solid object, as the geometrical drawing of a triangle, as standing on its base, as hanging from its apex, as a mountain, as a wedge, as an arrow, as a pointer, as an overturned object which is meant to stand on the shorter side of the right angle, as a half-parallelogram, and as various other things.[20] It is tempting to consider seeing the aspects of the triangle as a case of imagined seeing. At least two considerations lead us to this. First, what we see is not specifiable in terms of the physical properties of what we see, for we cannot discriminate one aspect from another on the basis of the physical properties of the object depicted. Secondly, it undoubtedly requires imagination to see the triangle as one thing and another just as it requires imagination to see the shape of creatures in the clouds as Leonardo asked of the aspiring painter. Aspect seeing in this case is subject to the will in a way that ordinary seeing is not.[21] The first consideration is not conclusive. Despite the fact that we do not discriminate aspects on the basis of different

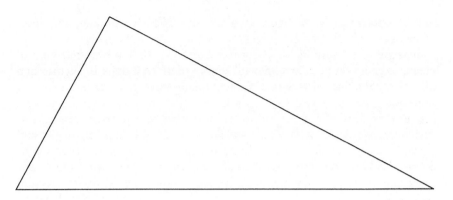

Fig. 3.1

sets of physical features, it is the physical features of the triangle that lead us to see it one way or another; we do not simply project properties onto the triangle at random. Yet it is hard to conceive of our perception of the different aspects as the perception of something different, for the aspect lacks the fixity or permanence that typically characterizes an object of sight. The 'perception' of the aspects of the triangle does seem to be a good candidate for imagined seeing. However, to concede that seeing the aspects of a triangle is a case of imagined seeing is not to concede that the thesis of imagined seeing provides a general explanation of what we see when we look at a picture, for it is only an unusual type of picture that elicits or encourages this kind of imaginative activity. Typically, a picture will endow a given aspect with a sense of permanence, that is, a given aspect becomes a property that the picture compels us to see: this is a picture of a wedge, this is a picture of an arrow. While we must be able to recognize what the picture is of in order to see picture of a wedge or an arrow, in these cases, it takes no distinctive activity of the imagination to do so: our recognition of what the picture is of is immediate and the aspect is a permanent feature of the picture.

The affinity of looking at what is depicted in a picture with seeing (as opposed to an activity of the imagination or imagined seeing) can be illustrated by considering Jastrow's drawing 'Is it a duck? Is it a rabbit' and Wittgenstein's discussion of it. The duck-rabbit figure contrasts with the triangular figure for we are not free to interpret the object in different ways. Instead, we are compelled to see the figure one way or another. Imagination is not required to see the two aspects of the duck-rabbit figure, simply the capacity to recognize ducks and rabbits. Seeing the figure, say, as a duck, is like seeing a duck, for two main reasons. First, the perception is immediate and direct. Someone who has only seen the duck-rabbit figure as a duck, that is, who perceives the figure as an unambiguous picture, will not report when asked what it is that he sees: 'Now I am seeing the figure as a duck', as if seeing the figure as a duck was the product of some special kind of mental activity on her part. She will simply point to a duck or picture of a duck, or make duck noises in order to explain what it is that he sees in the same way that he would explain what it is that he sees when he sees an actual duck. It would make as little sense for me to say, 'Now I am seeing the figure as a duck', as it would for me to say at the sight of a knife and fork, 'Now I am seeing this as a knife and fork'. Wittgenstein writes: 'One doesn't "take" what one knows as the cutlery at a meal for cutlery; any more than one ordinarily tries to move one's mouth as one eats or aims at moving it.'[22] Secondly, like a visual perception, our seeing the duck aspect is a mental state with a measurable duration. For example, we might say, 'I saw the figure as a duck for exactly two minutes, but now I am seeing the figure as a rabbit and I shall do so for a further five minutes.'

So where does this brief discussion of seeing-aspects in the context of pictorial perception leave us? While seeing-aspects may involve an activity of the imagination that in certain cases may license us to speak of imagined seeing, no distinctive activity of the imagination is commonly required to recognize what a picture is a picture of. In the typical case of pictorial representation where what the representation is a representation of is determinate, the affinities between seeing-aspects and seeing are striking. Of course in the standard case of pictorial representation, just as in the case where we perceive the aspects of the triangle, our perception of the aspect is not specifiable in terms of the physical properties of what we see. However, given the affinities that looking at a pictorial representation bears to seeing in general, it is surely only the prejudicial adherence to a mistaken theory of perception that prevents visual theorists from acknowledging that seeing what is depicted in a picture is a form of seeing and not simply a form of imagined seeing.

IV

Some visual theorists agree that the thesis of imagined seeing is not required to explain the activity of looking at pictures, but argue instead that the activity can be explained through the idea of recognition, without resorting to the claim that we see what is depicted in a motion picture. For example, Noël Carroll argues against the thesis of imagined seeing on the grounds that it seems unnecessary to postulate the activity of imagining looking in at least one class of depictions: non-fictional depictions. What is in common between looking at non-fiction and fictional depictions is simply the fact that we recognize what they are by looking, rather than, say, by reading:

'Recognition, without the additional process of imagining seeing, is basic to analyzing depictive representation.'[23]

Gregory Currie has offered a detailed elaboration of the recognition thesis. Currie, like Carroll, proceeds from the assumption that 'cinematic images, like paintings, are representations, that we perceive representations of things when we see photographs'.[24] However, this is obviously only a starting-point for an analysis of what it is we see when we look at a picture, for we can easily imagine circumstances in which we look at a picture but we cannot see what it is the picture is of: our glasses are misty or the room is dark, we see a rectangular shape on the wall but we cannot see that it is a still life. The difference between seeing a picture and seeing what is depicted in it consists, for Currie, in recognizing what the picture is of. The apparent advantage of the concept of recognition is that it allows us to capture what is in common between seeing an object and seeing a picture of the object in a manner that is consistent with the causal theory of perception. When we see a horse, seeing the horse involves recognition that it is a horse we see; when we see a picture of a horse we recognize by looking at the picture that it is a horse depicted. What lies in common between seeing a horse and a picture of a horse is that both activities deploy horse-recognition capacities, but in the one case we see a horse, in the other case we merely look at the picture of a horse. But since our recognition of something depends upon our seeing it, how is it that when we recognize that the picture is a picture of a horse by looking, we do not see a horse?

The specifics of Currie's account of how we draw upon our object-recognition capacities when looking at pictures develops a theory of pictorial cognition proposed by Flint Schier.[25] Following Dennett, Fodor, and others, Currie argues that the brain is organized into a number of relatively autonomous subsystems that operate on a hierarchy of the complex to the primitive. Primitive subsystems of the brain act to categorize the 'visual input' as the object itself, whether or not what we see is a depiction of the object or the object itself. More complex subsystems then operate to correct this diagnosis if it is erroneous and allow us to recognize the depicted object as a depicted object, or alternatively, if what we see is the object, they confirm the diagnosis. He admits that his view of picture recognition constitutes a sort of illusionism about pictures 'but this is an illusionism we can live with. It allows, exactly, that the person seeing can recognize a picture as representing a horse without him supposing he is actually looking at one'.[26]

Is this an illusionist theory and can we live with it? Presumably Currie does not want to maintain that the primitive subsystem of the brain actually sees the visual input, so the 'deception' here is scarcely an illusion. Furthermore, it seems inappropriate in this context to speak of recognition or deception at all, since the failure involved is more like that of a robot that lacks the capacity to discriminate between certain sensory inputs than the response of a human being. Can a robot display the shock of recognition, can he be aware of his mistake without quite knowing how to correct it? So why does Currie personify the parts of the brain as homunculi that see and are confused by what they see? It is, I think, because he perceives a need to explain what it is that we *see* when we recognize what is depicted in a picture, while at the same time holding to the assumption that what we see must be specifiable in terms of the physical properties of an object. Since we do not see an actual object when we look at a picture of it, the only way of explaining how it is we do see what is depicted is the illusion theory. But the illusion theory is untenable as a theory of consciously looking at pictures, so it is buried in the subsystems of the brain, in the cognitive unconscious, so to speak, where it is hoped it can do no harm. But the illusion thesis cannot be buried there without entailing conceptual confusion.[27] If we subtract from Currie's discussion the misleading talk of homunculi in the brain doing the seeing and being confused, we are still bereft of an explanation of how seeing enters into our recognition of the depicted object.

Perhaps it is meaningful to speak of recognizing something by looking in a manner that does not imply that we are looking at the thing we recognize. Carroll's formulation, quoted earlier, certainly implies this. He suggests we can recognize by reading or by looking in such a way that the concept of recognition is detached from the concept of seeing what it is that we recognize. However, as Kendall Walton argues in this volume, the concept of recognition here is detached from the idea of seeing what it is that we recognize only by ignoring the distinction between reading about something and seeing a picture of it.[28] When we read we certainly look, but the recognition is not visual recognition. Yet it is precisely the latter that we are seeking to understand. Currie accounts for the difference between our experience of written and visual fictions in the following terms: visual fictions as opposed to written fictions involve 'perceptual imagining'; for example, 'I see displayed on the screen a man with a knife, and I imagine that there is a murderer,' but I do not, *contra* Walton, 'imagine that I see this unseen murderer.'[29] However, when Currie writes, 'I see displayed on the screen a man with a knife', he means that my man-with-knife recognition capacities are triggered by the image. Since the recognition thesis already leaves us bereft of a distinction between seeing something and reading about it, the thesis of 'perceptual imagining' that presupposes the prior deployment of our recognition capacities—what we recognize cues our imagination—cannot restore the distinction that has been elided.[30] Against Currie, Walton opts for the thesis of imagined seeing to explain the visual basis of looking at pictures, but as I have argued, the thesis of imagined seeing also fails to account for what it is we see when we look at a picture.

Looking at a picture, whether a painting, a photograph, or a film, we recognize what the picture is of because we see what it depicts.

V

I have addressed what are, arguably, the four main kinds of theses that film theorists and philosophers have offered to explain what it is we see when we look at a motion picture: illusion theories, the transparency theory, the thesis of imagined seeing, and the recognition thesis. I have suggested that all these theories are individually flawed, but that their underlying problem is the assumption that they share in common: the causal theory of perception. By requiring that we separate our perceptual reports into a mental component and a physical component, the causal theory of perception imposes a conceptual straight-jacket upon our understanding of what it is to look at a picture: what it is that we see when we look at something must be specifiable in terms of a physical object array that causally affects our senses. This profoundly distorts our understanding of what it is we see when we see depictions, because it entails that we are mistaken in claiming that we do see what is depicted in pictures. Each of the explanations I have examined thus far as to what it is to see a motion picture conforms to the strait-jacket of the causal theory of perception either by producing a theory of what it is we do see or by denying that we really see anything at all. It is for this reason that none of them provides a satisfactory understanding of what it is we see when we look at what a picture or motion picture depicts.

The insight afforded by the illusion theory is to take seriously the idea that we do see the object depicted when we see a motion picture. However, that insight is then distorted when it is construed as the claim that we have a visual experience that is identical to the visual experience we have when we actually see an object that is not a depiction. Walton is correct to recognize that there are differences in the way we look at paintings and motion pictures. However, the transparency thesis misconstrues the distinctive character of cinematic depiction by claiming that in photography and cinema we see the object itself. As a generalized account of seeing pictures, the thesis of imagined seeing acknowledges that there is more to seeing a picture than simply recognizing what it is of, but it mistakenly construes seeing what a picture is of as a mental activity that is added on to the activity of looking; but looking at what a picture is of does not require a further activity other than simply looking. Finally, the recognition thesis either fails to offer an explanation of the visual basis of pictorial recognition at all (Carroll) or it offers this only by recourse to an illusion theory (Currie).

But surely one of these theories, or a theory like them, must be right? Is it not superstition to say that we can see what is depicted in a picture? It *would* be superstitious to claim that when we look at what a picture depicts we see some *thing* that is absent or non-existent. But, of course, this is not what we do see. But then how can I claim that we see what is depicted in a picture at all? One answer is because, as Wittgenstein points out, the verb 'to see' has many uses, only one of which is captured in reports about the deployment of objects in space, and we react to pictures in the same spontaneous way that we react in the presence of actual objects. Another answer is that a picture is an unusual object of vision. It is unusual because, as Hyman has written: 'when looking at a painting, the natural answer to the question "What do you see?" is a description of the depicted scene, and not a description of the disposition of pigments. This is not simply because we have learned to assume that this is what the question is after. We can see what is depicted; but it is generally more difficult, and it may be very difficult indeed, to see how the pigments are disposed.'[31]

Although it may be quite hard to see paintings in terms of the disposition of pigments on the canvas, it is normally possible to do so. However, it is typically impossible to attend to the surface features of a photographic image, as opposed to the paper that it is printed on. To be sure, photographs like paintings have a surface, but we are only made aware of this surface when the photograph is developed in a way that exposes the grain. In the case of the cinema—a projected moving image—it is impossible to attend to the surface features of the image, since the projected image has no surface other than the screen upon which it is projected. These considerations suggest that we can revive Walton's transparency claim once it is shorn of the argument that what we see when we look at a photograph or motion picture is the object itself. The standard photograph is transparent because even though it has a surface, we cannot see its surface. The projected moving image is transparent for it lacks a surface. Paintings, by contrast, tend to lack transparency, though paintings that mimic photographs appear transparent. The divide does not correspond to two categorically different ways of seeing, but it does point to a difference in what we see when we look at paintings and photographs or films. This interpretation of transparency has the distinct advantage that it is indifferent to whether or not a photograph is mechanically or digitally produced. That is, the standard photograph remains transparent whether or not its causal origins lie in the registration of reflected light from an object.

NOTES

1. The main source for Wittgenstein's discussion of seeing aspects is *Philosophical Investigations*, 2nd edn. trans. G. E. M. Anscombe (Oxford: Blackwell, 1958), Pt II, xi. Further extensive discussion of the concept is contained in three volumes of

Wittgenstein's notes on the philosophy of psychology: *Remarks on the Philosophy of Psychology*, vols. i, ii (Chicago: University of Chicago Press, 1980) and *Last Writings on the Philosophy of Psychology*, vol. i (Chicago: University of Chicago Press, 1982).

2. See, for example, Noël Carroll, *Theorizing the Moving Image* (Cambridge: Cambridge University Press, 1996), 368.

3. See Noël Carroll, *Mystifying Movies: Fads and Fallacies in Contemporary Film Theory* (New York: Columbia University Press, 1988), 89–146.

4. See Richard Allen, *Projecting Illusion: Film Spectatorship and the Impression of Reality* (New York: Cambridge University Press, 1995), 106–14.

5. Noël Carroll, *Theorizing the Moving Image*, 368.

6. This revision occurs in the transition between an earlier version of my argument 'Representation, Illusion, and the Cinema', *Cinema Journal*, 32: 2 (Winter 1993), 21–48, and the later version in *Projecting Illusion*, 81–119.

7. The most influential example of this argument is Christian Metz in 'The Imaginary Signifier', trans. Ben Brewster in *The Imaginary Signifier: Psychoanalysis and Cinema* (Bloomington: Indiana University Press, 1982), 3–87.

8. See Malcolm Turvey, 'Seeing Theory: On Perception and Emotional Response in Current Film Theory', in this volume.

9. Contemporary philosophical discussion of the causal theory of perception orginates with H. P. Grice, 'The Causal Theory of Perception', *Proceedings of the Aristotelian Society*, suppl. vol. 35 (1961), 121–52, and subsequent articles by Peter Strawson, 'Causation in Perception' in *Freedom and Resentment and Other Essays* (London: Methuen, 1974), 66–84; and 'Perception and its Objects,' in G. F. Macdonald (ed.), *Perception and Identity* (London: Macmillan, 1979), 41–60. A recent defence of the theory from its critics is to be found in William Child, *Causality, Interpretation and the Mind* (Oxford: Clarendon Press, 1994), 140–77.

10. John Hyman, 'The Causal Theory of Perception', *Philosophical Quarterly*, 42: 168 (1992), 284. My argument against the causal theory of perception is indebted entirely to this article.

11. André Bazin, 'The Ontology of the Photographic Image', *What is Cinema?*, vol. i, trans. Hugh Gray (Berkeley and Los Angeles: University of California Press, 1967), 14.

12. Kendall Walton, 'Transparent Pictures: On the Nature of Photographic Realism', *Critical Inquiry*, 11: 2 (1984), 252.

13. Gregory Currie, *Image and Mind: Film, Philosophy and Cognitive Science* (Cambridge: Cambridge University Press, 1995), 61.

14. Ibid., 77.

15. Kendall Walton, *Mimesis as Make-Believe: On the Foundations of the Representational Arts* (Cambridge, Mass.: Harvard University Press, 1990), 301.

16. See Walton, *Mimesis and Make-Believe*, 330, and 'On Pictures and Photographs: Objections Answered', in this volume.

17. For criticism of Wollheim on this point that links his analysis to the causal theory of perception, see John Hyman, *The Imitation of Nature* (Oxford: Blackwell, 1989), 20–4.

18. See Richard Wollheim, *Art and Its Objects*, 2nd edn. (New York: Cambridge University Press, 1980), 217.

19. Flint Schier challenges Wollheim in a related manner in *Deeper into Pictures: An Essay on Pictorial Representation* (New York: Cambridge University Press, 1986), 202–3.

20. Ludwig Wittgenstein, *Philosophical Investigations*, Pt II, xi, 201.

21. The role of the imagination in aspect seeing is emphasized by T. E. Wilkerson in 'Pictorial Representation: A Defense of the Aspect Theory', *Midwest Studies in Philosophy*, 16 (1991), 152–66. While this emphasis is valuable as an account of aspect seeing it distorts the role of the imagination in looking at pictures.

22. Wittgenstein, *Philosophical Investigations*, Pt II, xi, 195.
23. Noël Carroll, 'Critical Study: Kendall L Walton, Mimesis as Make-Believe', *Philosophical Quarterly*, 45, 178 (1995), 97.
24. Currie, *Image and Mind*, 78.
25. See Schier, *Deeper into Pictures* (New York: Cambridge University Press, 1986), 188–95.
26. Currie, *Image and Mind*, 86.
27. On the 'reckless application of human-being predicates to insufficiently humanlike objects' see Anthony Kenny, 'The Homunculus Fallacy', in John Hyman (ed.), *Investigating Psychology* (New York: Routledge, 1991), 155–65.
28. See Kendall Walton's remarks in 'On Pictures and Photographs: Objections Answered', in this volume.
29. Currie, *Image and Mind*, 179.
30. In 'On Pictures and Photographs: Objections Answered', Walton offers further good reasons for thinking that the Currie thesis of 'perceptual imagining' should be rejected.
31. Hyman, *The Imitation of Nature*, 42–3.

4

Sound, Epistemology, Film

EDWARD BRANIGAN

Film theorists may have moved too quickly in recent years in declaring the sound track of a film an equal partner with the image in some grand democracy. One need not return to the problematical argument that 'film is a visual medium' in order to raise questions about the status of sound in film.[1] It is important, I believe, to begin by examining more closely our intuitive perception of sound.

A phenomenology may provide important clues to what we believe sound to be. Sound and light may have the same physical basis in wave motion, but they are perceived differently. Lightness and colour appear to reside *in* an object—to be a quality of the object—rather than to emanate *from* an object.[2] By contrast, we think of sound as coming from a source, from an object: a radio, a door, a boot. Colour is (seemingly) possessed, but sound is made. Thus we tend to hear sound as transitory and contingent—an on/off phenomenon—while vision is more absolute (a reference-point, if you like). We do not think of objects as fundamentally colourless (which of course they are); instead, we believe the book has a red cover even when the lights are off. We do, however, think of background noise, room tone, our own breathing, and silence as having no sound and hence of objects as being fundamentally quiet unless touched, or otherwise put into motion. Sound comes and goes while light seems permanent. Furthermore, these sorts of beliefs may well be tied to universal features of human language. There is evidence that in many languages the five major sense modalities have been arranged into a hierarchy with verbs of sight given precedence over verbs of hearing.[3]

An early version of these arguments was presented at the Society for Cinema Studies conference in May 1987 and was published as 'Sound and Epistemology in Film' in the *Journal of Aesthetics and Art Criticism*, 47: 4 (Fall 1989), 311–24. I would like to thank David Alan Black, David Bordwell, and Charles Wolfe for contributing valuable comments and ideas to the 1989 article which was translated into Czech as 'Zvuk A Epistemologie Ve Filmu' and will be reprinted with some corrections and minor revisions in *Iluminace*. Zdeněk Böhm, Michal Bregant, Nataša Ďurovičová, and Ivan Záček kindly assisted in this translation. The present essay is an expansion and substantial rewriting of the above arguments. This rethinking of sound would not have occurred without the encouragement and acute commentary of Richard Allen, Arnt Maasø, Murray Smith, and Melinda Szaloky.

It would seem, therefore, that a persistence to vision and a transience to sound is built into our perceptual activity and into our use of language. These facts will need to be addressed at a theoretical level when analysing how a spectator confronts sound and image in film. Is sound less closely tied to the Kantian category of substance than vision? If so, what presuppositions about sound direct our search for knowledge from the visual features of film? May these presuppositions be altered to change our perception of the relationship between sound and light? More generally, how do we expect sound to be of use to us in describing the world and in imagining a real world through the fictional depictions of a film? How does sound relate to the structures of language? I will refer to these problems collectively as the 'epistemological' issue of film sound.

I will address the epistemology of film sound by developing an argument along the following lines. Certain features of the world and how it impinges on us are deeply embedded in our language, cognition, and actions. The result is an asymmetry in the way we ascribe visible and audible properties to objects. It appears that objects are composed of visible (and other) properties while sound seems detachable and transient. This asymmetry accounts for the privileged position of vision in understanding objects depicted in the medium of film. Nevertheless sound may be perceived in a manner that overcomes our customary bias. This, however, involves a different mental orientation ('top-down' rather than 'bottom-up') with a different sense of 'time' that utilizes a different procedure for placing objects under 'description'. When these aspects of perception are carefully sorted out, many contradictory statements about the nature of sound can be reconciled and many simple pronouncements about the basic constituents of film (e.g. motion, editing, sound, and the camera) can be discarded.

I. SOUND AS ADJECTIVE

There is no doubt that we have a bias toward *material* objects: the car will hit me, not its light or sound. The question is why lightness and colour seem more tightly bound to a material object than sound and thus able to provide a more reliable guide for our bodily movements in the world. The answer may lie in the physics of light and sound waves. Consider, for example, the much shorter wavelength (thus higher frequency) of light as compared to sound.[4] Most of the light we see as colour is *reflected* from or passed through surfaces whereas most of the sound we hear comes *directly* from a source. The information we gain about the position and source of a sound which comes from reflected sound (e.g. reverberation) is usually slight compared to the information which comes from direct sound through loudness, pitch, and timbre. This is perhaps another way of saying that as human beings we are unable to utilize a sonar-like ability in navigating our environment (as do bats and whales) and instead rely on vision to guide our body movement (for the reason that the human ear is not sensitive to the much higher frequency of sound necessary for propagation in a narrow beam and accurate reflection off surfaces). The straight-line propagation of light is able to resolve the edges and shape of an object with great accuracy though unable to bend around corners; hence, the colour of an object is sharply defined and does not spread out into a blur. By contrast, the sound processed by the human ear is less precise but more flexible: it is able to bend around corners or come up behind an auditor, reporting its object more globally as a 'motion-event', a disturbance within the surrounding space.[5] Light and sound differ, then, in their ability to resolve the relative position, and material configuration, of an object because their operating frequencies are different. For humans, visual information is much more important in perceiving space than auditory information.[6] This fact may be easily verified by looking around one's environment and noting how few objects and obstructions are making sounds.

A second major difference between light and sound concerns motion. Because sound waves are mechanical and require a medium of transmission, such as air or water or human bone, the presence of sound implies *two* motions: a vibrating aural source and a vibrating medium. By contrast, the electromagnetic radiation of light needs no medium—if it did, we would see no stars at night—and does not imply motion in the same way since it involves the movement of photons associated with, for example, the oscillation of an electric charge or a change in the energy state of an atom. Sound depends upon a motion within the medium which surrounds the human body. This means that the motion of a given object must be converted (within the limits of resolution provided by the medium) into a scale of action commensurate with the scale of the human body. The sounds we hear, though ultimately derived from molecular interactions, are encountered by us through large-scale movements of a medium. In the medium of air, for example, a mechanical disturbance causes successive air molecules to oscillate in a direction *parallel* to the direction of propagation of large changes in pressure which will be perceived by us as sound. Interruptions in a sound (and other changes in sound quality) not only point to a vibrating aural source but characterize *an elastic medium* within which various aural sources are distributed. Sound allows us to hear the *interior* of a (vibrating) object, and one might add, to hear the surface which is turned away from our sight as well as hear a multiplicity of surfaces which may be too numerous to be seen in the particularity of their interactions (e.g. the sudden stirring of leaves in a tree when a breeze hits or the sounds made by a race car engine or the sounds of a church organ). Hence also, even 'silence' acquires *a structure* with a spatial interpretation: the medium has returned to its initial state (room tone).[7] By contrast, visible light is sensed directly because its motion requires no movement of an intervening medium. Electromagnetic fields oscillate in a direction *perpendicular* to the direction of propagation of the radiation which will be perceived by us as light. Thus light and sound are generated by different kinds of forces that are acting in different directions with respect to the direction of propagation. Furthermore, sound, but not light, requires a medium of propagation. Light may have an effect on a medium, such as a sunset turning the atmosphere red, but in such cases the medium has merely become a lighted object. Light reveals its properties through the objects which reflect it whereas sound reveals its properties through a medium which moves and rubs against us.

The way in which human biology is able to exploit the physical difference between light and sound results in sound having a lesser survival value for humans than light. This fact may underlie the claim by Christian Metz that sound is basically *adjectival* while vision is a *noun*. Metz addresses the epistemological issue of sound by arguing that all perception derives from the *naming* function of verbal language. When we see a 'lamp' and can name it, the identification is complete and all that could be added would be merely adjectival—a 'tall, reading' lamp.[8] When we hear and name a sound, however, the identification remains incomplete. A 'whistling' sound still needs to be specified: the whistling *of* what? *from* where? the whistling *of* the wind *in* the trees *from* across the river.[9] According to Metz, sounds function as adjectives which merely describe or characterize substances which are fundamentally *visual* and properly named by a noun. This is true even if our identification of a sound happens to be expressed linguistically as a noun: 'I heard the whistling.' Again, who or what is *making* the sound that whistles? Metz traces this notion of vision and audition to the subject-predicate structure of Indo-European languages and to the distinctions among primary, secondary, and tertiary qualities made by the Western philosophical tradition. Language and philosophy, in turn, are seen as social and cultural phenomena. What we take to be 'intelligible' depends on how we have learned to classify and categorize as well as, presumably, what social actions and goals are encouraged or permitted under specific descriptions of the world.[10] In this way Metz is able to follow Roland Barthes and others in holding that the world is determined by the goals of a particular society and its modes of expression, and is not simply a universal 'nature' seen by an unbiased eye.

In dismantling the notion of a naive perception and raising instead social and historical factors, Metz flirts with a linguistic determinism. He says that a percept and the word which names it form a tight, unbreakable bond.[11] Although we need not, of course, speak the word when we see or hear something, a word or words must be called forth in our mind as a 'thought' in order for the perception to be intelligible. (This fits with Metz's assertion in another context that an image of a revolver in a film translates not into 'revolver', but into the verbal exclamation, 'Here is a revolver!') However, one need not accept this variety of linguistic determinism in order to preserve a fundamental distinction between visual and aural objects in the world and in film.[12] If natural language is taken as merely one sort of mental computation, then linguistics need not be designated as the master epistemological paradigm in describing the operation of our perception.

Light has an intrinsic advantage over sound when the goal is to identify and locate objects, and their attributes, in the space around us or in the space depicted by a film. (However, as we will discuss later, this advantage may be lost when there are other goals, such as to reason, recall, search, revise, plan, learn, intend, desire, or imagine.) When we aim to discover what and where things are (i.e. to conceive existential statements), light appears to us to be simply possessed by distant objects and permanent while sound appears to be created and contingent. Nonetheless, sound as an adjective is not merely a pale imitation of light. The intermittent sensation of sound heightens our impression of movement because it entails the stress and relaxation of the medium that is carrying the sound. The result is that the presence of sound in an environment or in a film opens up our sense of space because it implies continuous motion somewhere in between: a vibrating source causing a large medium to vibrate. In film, of course, the motion is created by loudspeakers which literally create a disturbance within the three-dimensional space of the movie theatre. Sound draws our attention to a particular motion-event and thus achieves a greater 'intimacy' than light because it seems to put the spectator directly in touch with a nearby action through a medium of air which traverses space, touching both spectator and represented event.[13]

The reproduction of aural objects in three dimensions contrasts with the reproduction of visual objects in two dimensions on a film screen. (Light from the projector, though moving through the three-dimensional space of the theatre, represents in that space by essentially illuminating only one surface—the screen—without disturbing the medium of air.) Therefore one possible outcome of juxtaposing sound and image is that the sound may allow the *inference* that the space represented by the image contains motion and volume which is both *nearby* and contemporaneous; or, to state it differently, the space of the theatre sound may come to stand for the space implied by the image.[14] This interrelationship is possible only because of the fundamental differences between sound and light. In the proper circumstances, each vanishes into the higher-level (emergent) perceptual category of 'space'.

In film, the technique of 'synchronizing' sound and image produces a single, continuous representation of space.[15] Considered broadly, synchronized sound includes much more than matching word sounds to the visible movements of a character's lips. There are many other types of visual movements which may be matched with sounds to delineate a unified space: body motion (dance and 'Mickey Mousing'), objects in motion, camera movement, pulsing light, and even more abstract changes related to editing, plot, and story-telling (e.g. a 'stinger chord' to underscore a dramatic revelation).[16] Against this background, asynchronous sound may be interpreted as simply the result of a technical failure. Asynchronous sound may, however, pose more complex problems for the spectator if it signifies a true discontinuity in the depicted space—another 'scene' not yet visible and perhaps not yet narrativized: for example, when sound is used to bridge, or overlap, shots or scenes; or, used to foreshadow an event; or, used as closure for a narrative; or, used as a diegetic or nondiegetic metaphor. In such a case, sound is somehow 'ahead' of light, not following in its wake but somewhere else: sound seems to be anticipating and creating space, addressing questions about the how and why of the objects seen. In order to understand the manner in which sound may come to dominate light in our comprehension of film, we will need to consider more carefully the relationship among sound, motion, and space.

2. SOUND IN THE MIDDLE WORLD

There is an important connection between motion and the perceived extent of an aural or visual space. Motion and space are distinct but not independent. In order for 'motion' to exist, there must be (1) a place and (2) another place to move to. Alternatively, in order for 'space' to exist, there must be (1) a place and (2) some *other* place with at least the possibility of movement, or causal interaction, between the places; otherwise in what sense could the second place be said to exist in sufficient proximity to the first in order to be able to be joined with it into a conceptual unity called 'space'? Our perception of a 'space' is thus founded on appreciating at least some of the possible movements among places for a group of objects which includes, most importantly, the perceiver as one of those objects. Space and motion, then, are interconnected. They are not, however, equal and symmetrical, for there may be two places without actual movement but no actual movement without place. The reason is that motion in the common-sense view is identified with one of its properties, velocity, which, in turn, is equivalent to the distance between two places divided by time. Thus conceived, motion is not as fundamental as space but depends on a relationship between places and time. Or, to put it differently, although an appropriate movement may transform a visible distance into a 'length' of time, space has a distance and time a duration even without movement.

In ordinary perception, space and time appear as distinct and invariant which leaves motion in a subordinate relation to space and time. As we shall see, it is better to avoid characterizing sound in absolute terms in favour of relating it to a particular framework in which it may be known and to a particular set of questions one wishes to answer. The frame of reference I have implicitly chosen in order to characterize sound (and motion) is human perception and the questions involve the relation between perceiving sound in our daily environment and perceiving sound in a movie theatre. My assumption has been that human experience is confined to the 'world of middle dimensions' described by Newtonian mechanics and does not extend to the large-scale structure of the universe described by Einstein nor to the microworld of quantum mechanics.[17] The mechanisms of human perception and thought are adapted to the spatial, temporal, and causal framework of a middle world dominated by solid objects.[18] In such a world sound is at a disadvantage for the two reasons we have examined: first, it operates at a different frequency than light (resolving an object's properties in a more diffuse manner) and, second, it is intimately related to the continuous movement of an elastic medium which, in turn, is perceived as dependent upon place (i.e. motion is interpreted as a movement from place to place of solid objects *within* a space). Light seems to take precedence over sound because it is better able to reveal the solid objects which constitute the events deemed most important in the middle world. Relative to sound, light comes to possess the properties of the solid objects it illuminates (e.g. permanence, distinctness, and conservation of action). When light is thought of as a 'solid' object (i.e. when it becomes transparent), it is more likely to be represented in the form of a noun. Sound, by contrast, appears more ephemeral and governed by motion, making it more likely to be represented in the form of a verb or adjective—as a predicate or attribute of some *other* object whose materiality is taken for granted (even if unseen). Our ability to hear sounds *being made* exists in parallel with our ability *to make* sounds (which we then hear) whereas light can only be sensed, *not* made by us. Again, lightness seems to have a distant quality, 'outside' and apart from the human body whereas sound seems to be part of us and our movements. In these ways, language, human biology, and the physics of the middle world converge to frame an initial condition for the perception of sound: its measurement against distant, lighted objects. That is, we seem to make judgements about the sound we hear by using knowledge obtained through the action of light.

We have not reached a conclusion, however. We must still consider what relationship sound may have to 'time'. Our usual beliefs about time are displayed in the root metaphor, 'river of time'.[19] We believe time to be independent of space: it begins and ends at the shoreline of the river. We also believe time to be flowing continuously in an irreversible direction. As

Heraclitus observed, 'One cannot step twice into the same river, for other waters and yet other waters are ever flowing on.'[20] It is not the 'water' which is time in the metaphor, but the 'motion' of the water 'passing away'. It is motion that continually creates a new river. Thus time is seen as immaterial and ephemeral, always fleeing, escaping our grasp, running out or running down. Time becomes a limited resource which may be conserved, but only temporarily. Hence we speak of time as invested, saved, budgeted, and possessed but only because it may be spent, lost, wasted, taken, stolen, or borrowed (e.g. 'This project took time that I did not have').[21] Like energy, time seems precious, but invisible and changing, and thus difficult to hold onto. It is no surprise, then, that time is likely to be thought of as a verb, or attribute, or inevitable process *directed at* something (forcing objects to decay) or going some*where* (leaving us behind). Therefore describing sound as a temporal process would seem merely to confirm its status as secondary to light. We think of sound as filling a rigid space defined by light much like water fills and responds to a glass. Again, what appears ephemeral (and liquid) is likely to be represented in the form of a verb or adjective.[22]

Having reached a conclusion about sound, at least as to its initial perception when juxtaposed with light, let us now consider the limits of this perception. I will argue that there is a second way in which time is ordinarily conceived in the middle world. When we imagine time to be functioning in a way different from, say, a river, then our perception of sound will be altered.

3. TWO PERCEPTIONS OF TIME AND TWO TYPES OF PERCEPTION

Tom Levin argues that sound has a special and unique relationship to time and space which is fundamentally different from the relationship that a film image has to time and space: 'the closer word and image are coupled the greater the *contrast* between them becomes manifest.'[23] He believes that sound and image may be made commensurable on some scale of value, or one made dominant, but only within an ideological practice. He asserts, for example, that because sound and image are fundamentally different there is no genuine acoustic equivalent to the freeze frame.[24] William Johnson, however, reaches exactly the opposite conclusion. He argues that just as a single image may be repeated many times in a 'freeze frame' to suggest that time has stopped, so a single note may be repeated in order to halt a melody and stop its time.[25] Johnson wishes to demonstrate that sound and image are intrinsically equal and ideologically neutral; that they are subject to the same aesthetic techniques and manipulations; and that any inequality, or dominance of one by the other, reveals some unjustified prejudice—a theoretical deafness or blindness, as it were. In the same spirit Noël Burch declares, 'It seems that the essential nature of the relationship between sound and image is due not to the difference between them, but rather to the similarity between them.'[26]

In fact, I believe that the intuitions which underlie each of the two arguments are valid because they are addressed to two different cognitive skills—two different types of perceptual activity. Levin's argument is based on a 'direct' perception of sound where sound exists by its very nature *in* time; it persists and has a duration. In this view, sound, like the river of time, cannot stop moving even though new sounds are heard which are very similar to the old ones. Levin's view, I believe, is consistent with the notion of sound which I have presented so far; that is, sound as a verb or adjective. If sound were to be frozen, there would be nothing to hear. It must always move *toward* something, or emanate *from* some (more permanent) object or state of being. Johnson's argument, on the other hand, is based on an 'indirect' perception of sound where sound is evaluated within some larger context; for now, let us say, it is evaluated within a 'discourse' or within a 'narrative' structure.[27] For Johnson, then, in the proper circumstances sounds which are very similar may be *taken as identical*, and one may imagine that time has stopped or slowed, or reversed and started again, or is discontinuous. Indeed, in the proper circumstances (against the proper background) time may be imagined to undergo any number of transformations, to trace out even bizarre 'configurations'. My use of a spatial metaphor here to describe time is justified because the notion of time has been expanded and is being seen as part of a larger event or pattern. The spatial metaphor arises, for example, when we talk about such relational aspects of time as order, repetition, and symmetry. Temporal *duration* is now being interpreted as comparable to the *extent* of a solid object (e.g. 'It's been a long day.' 'He's not *long* for this world.') and so may be conceived as something fixed and solid, not moving though still movable, capable of being shrunk, expanded, shifted or relocated; capable even of being perfectly duplicated and repeated.[28] In this new view, time becomes a substance described by a noun or gerund. (Chunks of ice are now floating on the 'river of time'.) Thus if time may come to be seen in different ways as the occasion warrants, or come in different varieties some measured in lengths, then sound, too, may escape its adjectival status when perceived indirectly.[29] In order to examine what may happen to sound, we must briefly sketch these two general ways of perceiving time.

Ordinary language reflects our basic understanding of time in the expression, 'tick-tock'.[30] Why do we not say, 'tick-tick'? I believe that the change in vowel sounds in the preferred version serves to define time as a pure duration, a short interval of *spoken time* marked by a slight difference in sound. A 'tock' is really another 'tick' but slightly displaced. By contrast, 'tick-tick' is ambiguous. It will mark off a short interval of time if the second 'tick' is understood as a *replica* of the first 'tick'; or, alternatively, it will mark only an instant of time (an acoustic freeze frame) if the second 'tick' is understood as *identical* to the first, as a repetition of the previous 'tick', the same 'tick' (somehow) heard again.[31]

A 'tock', then, is normally understood as another sort of 'tick', a second *instance*, a replica. The change of vowel sound is just enough to preserve a distinction between two equivalent entities and so measure an interval, or duration, between them. On the other hand, a second 'tick' may not be a new and distinct 'tick'. It may be construed as merely the reappearance of a prior one (i.e. where there is only one 'tick', only one *instant* of time, no matter how many times we may hear it); in such a case, however, we must imagine a *new* frame of reference for time arising out of a more basic duration in which, after all, two very similar words were pronounced (and heard) at different times. Identity of 'ticks' (on the new, higher level) is purchased at the cost of overlooking difference and separation somewhere else. The 'distance' which has been achieved from duration by spatializing (and freezing) it allows time to be mentioned in a new sense, that is, within some larger analysis of experience on a higher level. It is as if a person were to decide to view two marks on a paper from a distance sufficient to make of them one mark in order to gain a new view of the environment. There is nothing, of course, illegitimate in this play of identity and difference, of measured similarities, for such a play is at the centre of classification, language, and comprehension. The test for the usefulness of some newly created (higher-level) temporal frame—which momentarily freezes other frames—must be sought on other grounds. The only point I wish to make here is that 'tick-tock' better represents our basic understanding of time (in the middle world) as a change through an interval—as a movement, a duration, a river of time—because it is less ambiguous than 'tick-tick' which may suggest either an interval or an instant, and moreover, may suggest that time is reversible, malleable, or lacks direction. ('Tick-tick' is symmetrical.)

Since an appropriate reframing may bend time into whatever shape may be desired, and even make it the equal of a suitably reframed 'space', William Johnson decides that sound must essentially be the equal of image. In effect, Johnson seizes on this potential of sound to declare that sound is a free and independent variable. It would be more accurate, however, to say that sound may acquire its equality within a particular activity of perception in which it may be known, and in relation to a particular set of questions one wishes to answer. Sound (and time) gains its equality when it is indirectly perceived ('tick-tick') by being fixed within a context that is larger than identifying and locating objects in space. The basic issue concerns not what sound is, free of any context, but how sound is made useful to us through one or another type of perception in conjunction with one or another kind of goal.

Corresponding to the approaches of Levin and Johnson, there are, I believe, two broad ways of perceiving sound (and light) in film. Some perceptual processes operate upon data from the loudspeakers (and data appearing on the screen) primarily in a direct, 'bottom-up' manner by examining the data in very brief periods of time (with little or no associated memory) and organizing it automatically into such features as aural pitch, loudness, edge, depth, motion, size, shape, colour, texture, and so on.[32] Bottom-up perception is serial and 'data-driven', and produces only 'short-range' effects. This is the perceptual context within which Levin evaluates sound. Other perceptual processes, however, based on acquired knowledge, memory, and schemas (frames, scripts), are not constrained by stimulus time, and work primarily 'top-down' on the data using a spectator's expectations and goals as principles of organization. These goals of the spectator may be considerably broader than answering such existential questions as what and where things are. For example, one prominent top-down goal for organizing data in a film is the creation of a 'narrative', or story world; other goals may involve states of reasoning, imagination, desire, intention, anticipation, recall, hypothesis, search, and making the future (un)predictable.[33] Top-down processes must be flexible and general in order to be effective across a wide range of situations while allowing for (unpredi\ct!able) variations among specific cases. Top-down procedures are 'indirect' in the sense that they may reframe data in alternative ways independently of the stimulus conditions (e.g. temporal duration) which govern the initial appearance of the data. Top-down processes often treat data as an inductive sample to be projected and tested within a variety of parallel frames of reference while bottom-up processes are serial, highly specialized, and atomistic (e.g. detecting motion). Top-down perception becomes the backdrop against which Johnson evaluates sound.

The problem is that there is no general set of necessary and sufficient conditions which determine how the results of bottom-up processing must be judged and interpreted. Perceptual illusions and constancies demonstrate that we may easily see what is not present, or fail to see what is present according to criteria in effect for a given mode of processing. The fact of 'juxtaposition' on the screen, for example, carries no necessary implication about temporal sequence, causality, or spatial relationship within a story world. Similarly, the perception of continuous or discontinuous screen time may lead equally to judgements of either continuous or discontinuous story time. Even a repetition of the *same shot* need not signify that the *same time* is again being represented in the story. The reason is that more complex events may be represented in film than what only occurs in front of the camera (or microphone) and/or occurs only once. These examples are meant to illustrate that certainty cannot be achieved through a strict empirical (bottom-up) testing of the data on the screen since *any* temporal, causal, and spatial configuration *may denote or refer to any other* configuration, given the proper circumstances. Therefore, in cases where it is *knowledge* that is being measured and evaluated, and used to make predictions, sound is on its way toward equality. Sound achieves its equality when it is taken as a form of knowledge rather than taken as a state of the real world, for, as Nelson Goodman might say, there are many worlds, if any, and so, many sounds, if one.

Because top-down processes are active in watching a film, a spectator is not restricted to a film's screen or projection time, i.e. to the strict duration ('tick-tock') of an image on the screen. Instead the spectator is able to move forward and backward through screen data in order to experiment with a variety of syntactical, semantic, and referential hypotheses, i.e. to cancel differences ('tick-tock') in favour of applying new frames of reference which create new similarities ('tick-tick') throughout, and beyond, the film. By experimenting with various methods for ordering data, the spectator creates temporal experiences which do not derive directly from screen time. This suggests that sound, too, need not be limited to its existence as a bottom-up percept responsive to the beat of the speakers. If true, this also suggests that there is no definitive answer to the problem of where to locate a microphone with respect to a camera in order to best record the auditory and visual properties of an object—to make manifest *the* reality of a situation—for sound does not exist outside perceptual context, goal, and use.[34]

It would seem that a diversity of top-down and bottom-up processes are at work every moment creating a variety of representations with varying degrees of compatibility and certainty. Thus cognition as a whole is perhaps best thought of as a system which struggles to manage incomplete, ambiguous, deceptive, and often conflicting interpretations of data. The perceiver must actively search, compare, test, discriminate, remember, and speculate within many realms and imagined contexts. Conflicts arise between top-down and bottom-up processing, between story and screen, and between the fictional world of the characters (the 'diegesis') and what seems external to it. This amounts to saying that human comprehension does not proceed by progressively refining sensory data from lower to higher stages until a single thought is perfected and grasped by a singular Self. Rather, the human mind seems to be organized into modules that operate in parallel, are often too specialized to 'communicate' with one another (or even to make use of 'words'), and produce criss-crossing outputs which conflict as well as unify.[35] Perception resembles a fluctuating, unstable equilibrium. Watching a film, then, might better be described as watching many films at once; and hearing a sound as hearing many sounds. There is no absolute notion of sound or time which fits all circumstances.

4. SOUND AS INFORMATION

It is easy to lose sight of the non-conscious, 'bottom-up' aspect of sound and get carried away by 'top-down' perceptions which seemingly lie closer to our conscious activities and plans. William Johnson seeks to establish a single context for evaluating sound by minimizing its 'bottom-up' qualities. He wishes to prove that sound possesses an 'equal ontological status with the image', and therefore deserves equal aesthetic weight with the image in films and in the terminology used to analyse films.[36] He bases aesthetic equality on ontological distinctness and equality.[37] However, the epistemological issue of sound cannot be so easily bypassed. In which (top-down?) perceptual context is sound to be judged?

Johnson acknowledges that '[t]he one important distinction between sound and image stems from their physical origin [origins?]' and points to the contrast mentioned above where sound appears to come to us directly from its source while light is reflected and appears to characterize various reflected surfaces rather than its source.[38] But then Johnson concludes as follows:

Thus sound tends to be a series of active events that is *experienced* while the image tends to be a static display that is *read*. This distinction enables the two channels to complement each other, carrying large amounts of information [usually] without mutual interference.[39]

Some sleight of hand is at work here. Why is the image viewed as essentially 'static' rather than moving and why is it associated with 'reading' rather than 'experiencing'? One would think that listening to dialogue would be closer to reading than the act of looking at colours. Johnson seemingly embraces the 'river of time' metaphor ('series of active events') but since he carefully qualifies his argument (e.g. 'sound *tends to be* . . .'), one is left in doubt about the strength of his ontological conclusions.

More importantly, the effect of Johnson's argument is to admit an epistemological difference between sound and image (within what I have identified as a 'bottom-up' context) but only to dissolve it within some common denominator which he calls 'information'. According to Johnson, when sound and light are conceived as 'channels' for this information, they somehow function (usually) as perfect complements rendering their (physical?) differences mute. They 'can of course be *made* to interfere with each other,' he says; but, presumably, this merely demonstrates their basic ontological equality.[40] Johnson's analysis is designed to show that sound may relate to the image in only two fundamental ways: its information may confirm, or else be made to oppose, the information carried by the image.[41] Johnson is able to achieve this simplicity of analysis because of his belief that sound and image are perfectly distinct, and yet equally capable of

conveying the same amount and type of 'information'. The units of information may oppose each other but sound and light offer no intrinsic contradiction. Johnson, therefore, has embraced the 'conduit metaphor' which
assumes that language (or the film 'experience', or whatever is meaningful)
is a 'communication' ('channels . . . carrying . . . amounts . . . [with little
noise]').[42] This assumption allows the written title, or the spoken sentence of
dialogue (i.e. concentrated information), to become the prototype for all
sound[43] while the image becomes a light display that must be 'read' for the
abstract (less direct, more removed) information it 'communicates' about
relationships in a story world.

Certainly at some level of generality these assumptions will be true. For
example, if the information we need in a film concerns whether or not
Kristin has arrived home, then a shot during which we hear Kristin an-
nouncing her arrival from off-screen will be equivalent to a shot of Kristin
merely opening the door. On the other hand, at *some* level of analysis there
clearly are differences between these two presentations of the event, and
especially differences among the possible *inferences* arising from the two
presentations. Indeed, for Johnson why could not sound in a given case be
more important than the image? Chasing the elusive concept of 'information' also brings nearer a deceptive equation which links art to someone's
(intentional) 'communication' with a spectator. Instead of a communication
between sender and receiver, it would be better to ask what modes and
means of reference and associated mental operations are pertinent to a
spectator's understanding of a presented event.[44] The use of concepts like
information and 'meaning' only postpones difficult questions about our
perception of aural and visual objects and, in fact, reduces the complexity of
the reference relations which may be perceived in a given film text.

5. SOUND WITHIN EPISTEMOLOGICAL BOUNDARIES

If top-down processing is to succeed in foregrounding sound, and complicating its relationship to visual space in film, then it must be accomplished
through the interplay of epistemological boundaries created within the
perceiving of a text, that is, through the various *levels of narration* posited
by a spectator as being within a narrative.[45] In effect, each level of narration
provides a new context within which sound (and its relationship to time and
motion) is re-evaluated according to both a global strategy of making
prominent the significance of a 'scene' in a 'story world' and a local strategy
of comprehending actions and events. The notion of levels here is based on
the assumption that a narrative fiction typically provides a multiplicity of
distinct and sometimes competing routes by which a spectator gains access
to the significance of the text. If one also assumes that levels of the narration

act concurrently (even if undramatized), then sound and image never really stand alone but only at the intersection of various interpretive strategies which seek (offer) knowledge from the text by generating multiple, and often incompatible, descriptions of the text.

By juxtaposing sound and image drawn from different levels of the narration, one may complicate and delay the matching of sound to a source which is to be made visible. In this way a new object may be designated as a source or an old source may be renamed as a new object. The reason for this flexibility of reference is that a given aural narration may exhibit, say, a different range of knowledge, degree of communicativeness, or degree of self-consciousness from its accompanying visual narration.[46] Here are a few examples: a sound which foreshadows or comments on a diegetic event in an image; a subjective sound with an objective image; a diegetic sound with a nondiegetic image; a sound which is not simultaneous with an image; a sound composed of, or switching among, multiple and different recordings of the same event; a sound which is *analogous* to the sound we imagine an object might make if it were to be heard; a metaphorical sound (e.g. an image of a plate breaking accompanied by the sound of fifteen plates breaking or accompanied by the sound of cymbals or the sound of a woman's scream or the sound of a woman's laugh or silence; or, accompanied by the sound of an animal gnawing, cf. catachresis, neologism); a metaphorical sound retrospectively made literal; a sound with rhythms or associations or other features that outrun a specific object so as to apply selectively to other sorts of objects, even to abstract, rhetorical devices of the film; and, finally, a sound gestalt which is unrecognizable (cf. a Rorschach inkblot).[47] In other words, sound may come to refer to an object (several objects, a kind of object, several kinds of objects, a non-tangible object, an associated object, an unknown thing) in a way that does not depend on, or does not depend only on, attributing a specific identity, location, and visibility to the source.

On this account, sound does not possess an absolute quality; it is measured only with respect to a (global, local) way of knowing. Thus a sound may be heard as part of a spoken word, or heard as an object sound (e.g. a wheel spinning or the whistling of the wind), or heard as music (e.g. a long-held, high-pitched note from an operatic aria), or heard as a peculiar 'whining' noise unconnected to an object (i.e. 'pure' or 'free' sound), or *not* heard when expected. However, to hear the sound as merely disconnected free noise—as a sensory datum the *equal* of any other datum—normally requires great effort because bottom-up processing is closely adjusted[48] to the physics of the middle world which recognizes sound as transitory and fleeting, as produced rather than possessed, and hence as tied to a (vibrating) material object or to a person speaking which light makes appear as a permanent object.[49] Paradoxically, to hear a sound as pure noise requires top-down processing—a conscious effort to decompose the sound into noise that is non-referential (e.g. by reversing the components of the sound or *by repeating* the sound *identically* as in anaphora; cf. 'tick-tick').[50] In this context, disconnected noise is like the light reflected off the motion picture screen which we seldom choose to examine for the properties of the reflective screen, preferring instead to imagine glowing two-dimensional forms on the screen as having been transferred to a new space (and time) where they become familiar, three-dimensional objects in a middle world, reflecting a new light and making new sounds.

The perceptual difficulty in decoupling sound from a lighted object is suggested by the fact that it is extraordinarily rare that a film spectator is led to interpret noise *non*diegetically, that is, as arising from (normally unseen) objects which are not merely off-screen but outside the story world. The rarity of nondiegetic noise in film (as opposed to the pervasiveness of nondiegetic music) testifies to the powerful expectations about visual space and visible objects created by bottom-up processing. By contrast, music and words are sounds which, like the construction of a narrative discourse, are already heavily involved in top-down processing and hence easily conform to the many types of epistemological boundaries that may be created during the reading of a text.[51]

6. SOUND UNDER (WHICH?) DESCRIPTION

In comprehending sound, a particular sound will be made to have a use by a perceiver. The sound will be considered broadly to function as an adjective or a noun, tick-tock or tick-tick. It will also be placed against a specific context or, in the case of film, within a specific level of narration. In short, its potential interactions with the perceiver will be variously elaborated and described. What is meant here by 'description'? In answering this question, it will be found that there are different ways in which a particular sound may be called 'particular'.

Keith Donnellan has proposed that there are two different uses of definite descriptions in verbal language.[52] I believe that these two uses help explain the ways in which a perceiver may understand a sound, not just understand a sentence about a sound. (I am assuming that words, pictures, and sounds may all be used descriptively and that percepts are evaluated within schemata whose function is to represent and organize our knowledge, whether our knowledge is embodied mentally in words or in other ways.) In the 'attributive use' of a definite description, the description is essential, for something is being asserted as being true about (the attributes of) whatever object fits that description. By contrast, in the 'referential use' of a definite description, the description is being used merely to call attention to, or to help bring to mind, a particular object about which something is being said. In the referential use, the description *need not be accurate* (nor need the listener nor even the speaker believe it to be accurate) and, indeed, devices other than a verbal description (e.g. a name or a pointing gesture) might have been used in place of the description so long as the proper object is brought to mind.

Consider, for example, the sentence, 'The bird in the tree is singing,' or, equally, consider simply a sound which is heard by a perceiver in the circumstances described by the sentence. When the descriptive phrase, 'the bird in the tree', is interpreted *attributively*, the phrase logically entails (or at least presupposes) that there is one, and only one, bird which is in the tree which is the subject of the assertion because if the phrase fails to denote one bird or other (e.g. there is no bird or there are two birds which fit the description), or else if the specified bird does not, in fact, possess the attribute of currently singing, then the proposition expressed by the sentence is false (or, alternatively, the state of affairs which was believed to exist when the sound was heard in these circumstances turns out, in fact, not to exist). This analysis of attributive use derives from Bertrand Russell's theory of language.

On the other hand, when 'the bird in the tree' is interpreted *referentially*, the phrase is being used only to pick out some particular thing in a particular situation, to refer to (rather than to denote) a particular object. This analysis of referential use draws upon the work of Peter Strawson. When a description is used referentially, some one thing in particular is being selected whereas in an attributive use there is a less specific presupposition which requires only that there exist some one thing *or other* that (exactly) fits the assertion; that is, the two uses of descriptions are associated with different degrees of 'particularity'. Therefore a referential use may be successful (e.g. the relevant bird may be noticed) even though several birds are singing and even if the bird which is described is not singing: for example, a different bird may be singing in a nearby bush or a very different thing may be making the singing noise (an insect, a boy with a bird whistle, the whistling of the wind). Furthermore, the reference may be successful (and, additionally, something true may have been said) even if the description is mistaken in other ways, or is metaphoric or ironic (e.g. a twig moving in the wind is mistaken for a bird or a chattering squirrel is believed to be a species of bird or the relevant singing bird is in a bush not in the tree; or, the object in the tree is a statue or a person in a costume; or, ironically no bird can be heard singing because the tree and the bush have been cut down). In a referential use, there is no requirement that the listener agree with the speaker's description in order to agree with the 'truth' of what was said. My examples are designed to suggest that in using language referentially (or in thinking about a percept referentially) something other than a literal (denoted) object may be at stake. Making a reference is more complex and mediated than making use of a denotation because the act of referring may involve various kinds of 'mistakes' and 'fictions' as well as precise rhetorical play with *categories* whereas denoting an object and its attributes concerns direct empirical truth. Only where there is nothing to be referred to may the act of referring necessarily fail (e.g. where the sound that is supposedly coming from the direction of the tree is just a ringing in the perceiver's ears).

Donnellan emphasizes that the distinction between the attributive and referential uses is based upon a perceiver's evaluation of a pragmatic situation, not upon syntactic or semantic properties of a given sentence nor on formal sorts of ambiguities. Neither a sentence nor, I would argue, a percept by itself discloses how it should be interpreted. Instead, a particular datum is made to have a use through a description or redescription of its relationship with the perceiver in (under, for) a given set of circumstances.

In order to facilitate the analysis of a film's sound track, I would prefer to rename Donnellan's two categories as follows:

1. *Existential Reference*. This is closely equivalent to Donnellan's 'attributive use' of a definite verbal description. Existential reference connects to my argument that sound is an adjective when heard primarily bottom-up and linked to the 'river of time' metaphor ('tick-tock'). I call this 'existential' reference because the perceiver's goals in listening are closely tied to the identification and to the location (of the attributes and actions) of a depicted physical object.

2. *Nominal Reference*. This is closely equivalent to Donnellan's 'referential use' of a definite verbal description. Nominal reference connects to my argument that sound is a noun when heard primarily top-down and linked to 'chunks of ice' floating on the river of time ('tick-tick'). I call this 'nominal' reference because the perceiver's goals in listening are closely tied only to the *name* that is being used to refer to a depicted object or to *a* name for the object or to a proposed name (i.e. the object is called something or called forth by the description, or heard within a descriptive schema). In this type of reference the sound becomes noun-like and is translated into a categorical concept to be manipulated and transformed mentally (through schemata) in pursuit of goals other than the existential identification of definite attributes of the depicted object.[53] Thus nominal reference may act to summon an unusual or non-tangible quality of the object; or direct us toward a different object which shares some (literal or figurative) quality; or remind us of another object through a logical relationship (e.g. contradiction) or through some chain of association.

Theorists claim to have discovered such basic units of film as sound, motion, rhythm, editing, the camera, photography, shots, images, lightness/

darkness, written titles, time, space, and causation. However, the epistemological complexity of sound (two perceptions of time, two types of perception, two uses of description, two types of reference) raises problems for any attempt to isolate sound as a fundamental unit, or 'dimension', of film; or, indeed, to discover other purported basic units in an effort to create a general definition for the experience of film.[54] Sound under which description is pertinent? Time (rhythm, editing, space, image . . .) under which description is pertinent? Is a 'written title' basically aural, or visual, or something new? Is a 'singing voice' basically music, speech, or noise? Is a sound to be heard existentially or nominally? More importantly, for what length of time is a sound to be heard in one way rather than another: when for example, is it expedient to hear a sound under particular narrative, narrational, and fictive descriptions, and when must these descriptions be changed to make the sound mean in new contexts which are of interest to us while we are experiencing a text, or afterwards while thinking about the experience? And so on.

There is no obvious short cut through epistemology to the fundamental nature of film; nor may we save time by declining to make the trip. We do not hear the world in arbitrary ways even if we may hear it in several ways and even if we may choose ways which conflict with one another. Our perception is tied to the physics of the middle world as firmly as it is tied to the stories, scripts, plans, goals, and activities we pursue in the middle world. No single interpretation for sound will cover all the circumstances. Instead there are merely interpretations which are more or less probable, which more or less fit a goal being pursued in the middle world. A particular sound exists only under one or several descriptions; that is, it may be made particular in more than one way. As discussed earlier, sound may be intrinsically subordinate/supplementary to light ('tick-tock') when perceived in conjunction with a spectator's effort to identify and locate physical objects depicted in a film. Or, sound may be intrinsically dominant/complementary to light ('tick-tick') when, for example, it is described through top-down schemata as independent, ambiguous, or deceptive; or, when described as opposed, tangled, or parallel with light. In analysing the appearance of sound in film, then, one must be careful to specify the perceptual processes, and the descriptions, which are taken as the context for what we will later remember as having heard.

NOTES

1. There are actually two aspects to the argument that film is a 'visual medium'. First, there is a belief that the essence of film is photography and/or a visual experience of the visible and/or a visual experience of the non-visible (for example, a spectator's

visual experience of what is off-screen or non-tangible or spiritual; or, a visual experience which evokes some kind of feeling). Second, there is a belief that an audience will understand the appropriate sort of visual experience as a necessary and sufficient condition for the existence of a 'medium' of performance and/or communication. Rick Altman has referred to the first belief as the 'ontological fallacy' because it was developed and used as a prescriptive standard: film *is* a photographic experience and so a given scene *should be presented* visually. See Altman, 'The Evolution of Sound Technology', in Elisabeth Weis and John Belton (eds.), *Film Sound: Theory and Practice* (New York: Columbia University Press, 1985), 51–2, repr. from 'Introduction', *Yale French Studies*, 60 (1980) (special issue on 'Cinema/ Sound'). See also Altman, 'Introduction: Four and a Half Film Fallacies', in Altman (ed.), *Sound Theory, Sound Practice* (London: Routledge, 1992), 37–9; and letters to the editor by Robert Cumbow and William Johnson in *Film Quarterly*, 39: 2 (Winter 1985–6), 64.

The second belief might be referred to as the 'fallacy of medium specificity' since it might be argued that a 'medium' is not defined a priori but arises within a social context and represents a shared judgement about what properties a material is perceived to have and what materials may properly be grouped together to become an accepted means of discourse. (How materials may be grouped properly, i.e. syntactically or aesthetically, is still another issue.) As society and its technology, and our various responses and memories, change, so too may the 'boundary' of a medium. See, for example, the many suggestive analyses—tied to historical conditions—that Kristin Thompson provides in support of Stephen Heath's conviction that 'Against vision, a materialist practice of film thus proposes and opposes analysis, "analysis by means of image and sound" . . . in which sound is not some supplement to the cinematic essence of the image but, on the contrary, its essential despectacularisation. . . . Reality is to be grasped not in the mirror of vision but in the distance of analysis, the displacement of the ideology that vision reflects and confirms.' Thompson, *Breaking the Glass Armor: Neoformalist Film Analysis* (Princeton: Princeton University Press, 1988), 112. See also Jonathan Rosenbaum, 'Sound Thinking', *Film Comment*, 14: 5 (Sept.–Oct. 1978), 38–40, and his letter to the editor in the Nov.–Dec. issue (14: 6, 79). For a different view of 'medium' and its use as a theoretical concept, see Gregory Currie, *Image and Mind: Film, Philosophy and Cognitive Science* (New York: Cambridge University Press, 1995), 1–16 (sounds 'are incidental accretions so far as cinema itself is concerned', p. 3). See also nn. 11 and 22 below.

2. Compare the distinction drawn by Aristotle between predicates that are 'present in' their subjects and those that are 'predicated of' them. Aristotle says that 'whiteness' may be 'present in' an object because 'colour requires a material basis', even though colour is 'never predicable of anything'. *Categoriae*, ch. 2. Note further that although we speak of a colour as being possessed by its object, the colour that we perceive the object to have is actually the only colour that is *not* possessed by the object because it has been reflected to our eyes rather than absorbed by the object.

3. In a study of 53 languages representing 14 different language stocks from all the major parts of the world, Ake Viberg found that all of the verbs of perception could be arranged into a hierarchy with sight being the most powerful, followed by hearing, touch, taste, and smell. A number of important syntactic, morphological, and semantic characteristics common to all 53 languages can be explained using this approach. 'The Verbs of Perception: A Typological Study', in Brian Butterworth, Bernard Comrie, and Osten Dahl (eds.), *Explanations for Language Universals* (New York: Mouton, 1984), 123–62.

Viberg also discovers that the verb having the prototypical meaning 'see' within a given language has a privileged position in that it commonly can be used in an extended sense as an overall *frame* with which to describe the perceptual activities of the other sense modalities including very general experiences like 'I see' in the sense of 'I understand'. Consider: 'David listened to the record to *see* if it was well-recorded.' The verb 'see' is also closely connected to 'show', 'shine', 'seem', and 'similar' (p. 141). These are convenient facts for theorists who believe that film is essentially a visual medium, and for film critics who develop metaphors based on the visible style or plot of a film, e.g. the visual appearance of a shot, spectacle, a camera look, character vision, loss of sight, photography as illusion, etc. However, as we see in section 3, these insights into sight cannot be so easily mapped into such grand conclusions. On see and seem, see also J. L. Austin, *Sense and Sensibilia*, ed. G. J. Warnock (Oxford: Clarendon Press, 1962), ch. 4, pp. 33–43.

4. The frequency of visible light is on the order of 10^{16} cycles per second as compared to 10^4 cycles per second for audible sound. Light travels at 186,281 miles per second as compared to $\frac{1}{5}$ mile per second for sound.

5. The much longer wavelength of sound as compared with light accounts for Béla Balázs's declaration that 'the specific nature of sound . . . never permits sound to be isolated from its acoustic environment as a close-up shot can be isolated from its surroundings. For what is not within the film frame cannot be seen by us. . . . [By contrast, what we hear in a close-up shot are] the sounds themselves, which can always be heard throughout the whole space of the picture, however small a section of that space is included in the close-up. Sounds cannot be blocked out.' *Theory of the Film: Character and Growth of a New Art*, trans. Edith Bone (New York: Dover, 1970), 211; see also pp. 213–14, 215–16, 53, 54.

6. Laurence E. Marks, 'Multimodal Perception', in *Handbook of Perception*, viii: *Perceptual Coding*, ed. Edward C. Carterette and Morton P. Friedman (New York: Academic Press, 1978), 330–3.

7. On the sounding of certain object interiors, see Don Ihde, *Listening and Voice: A Phenomenology of Sound* (Athens: Ohio University Press, 1976), 70, 98–9. On room tone, see Stephen Handzo, 'Appendix: A Narrative Glossary of Film Sound Technology', in Weis and Belton, *Film Sound*, 395.

8. I have made some minor changes in Metz's examples. Christian Metz, 'Aural Objects', trans. Georgia Gurrieri in Weis and Belton, *Film Sound*, 155–6, repr. from *Yale French Studies*. 'Aural Objects' is an excerpt from 'The Perceived and the Named', trans. Steven Feld and Shari Robertson, *Studies in Visual Communication*, 6: 3 (Fall 1980), 56–68. Note that 'Aural Objects' is from Metz's later psychoanalytic phase of work. It was first published in 1975—the same year as 'The Imaginary Signifier'.

Like Metz, Jean-Louis Comolli concludes that sound in film is dominated by the image though his argument rests on the nature of a dominant ideology, not on the nature of language and perception. See 'Machines of the Visible' in Teresa de Lauretis and Stephen Heath (eds.), *The Cinematic Apparatus* (New York: St. Martin's Press, 1980), 121–42. Kathryn Kalinak reviews many of the ideological and cultural approaches to the nature of sound in *Settling the Score: Music and the Classical Hollywood Film* (Madison: University of Wisconsin Press, 1992), 20–39. See also Roy Armes, 'Entendre, C'est Comprendre: In Defence of Sound Reproduction', *Screen*, 29: 2 (Spring 1988), 8–22. For an unusual critique of 'Aural Objects,' See Allan Casebier, *Film and Phenomenology: Toward a Realist Theory of Cinematic Representation* (Cambridge: Cambridge University Press, 1991), 91–9.

Jean-Louis Baudry employs still another approach in 'The Apparatus: Metapsychological Approaches to the Impression of Reality in the Cinema', trans. Jean Andrews and Bertrand Augst in Philip Rosen (ed.), *Narrative, Apparatus, Ideology: A Film Theory Reader* (New York: Columbia University Press, 1986), 299–318. Baudry asserts that sound, as opposed to light, is intrinsically tied to reality. He says that in cinema 'one does not hear an image of the sounds but the sounds themselves. Even if the procedures for recording the sounds and playing them back deforms them, they are reproduced and not copied. Only their source of emission may partake of illusion; their reality cannot. Hence, no doubt one of the basic reasons for the privileged status of voice in idealist philosophy and in religion: voice does not lend itself to games of illusion, or confusion, between the real and its figurativity (because voice cannot be represented figuratively) to which sight seems particularly liable. Music and singing differ qualitatively from painting in their relation to reality.' (pp. 304–5).

It would seem that Baudry is treating sound as an indexical sign (i.e. meaning derives from the sign's place in a causal sequence). By contrast, drawing on Plato's allegory of the cave, Baudry treats an image as merely iconic (i.e. meaning derives from the sign's resemblance to, or its imitation of, something). In addition, however, Baudry seems to regard an image as arbitrary, like a figure of speech (or a slip of the tongue or dream-work). Both Metz and Stanley Cavell would apparently agree with Baudry that sound is reproduced while light is copied; Metz, 'Aural Objects', n. 7; Cavell, *The World Viewed: Reflections on the Ontology of Film*, enlarged edn. (Cambridge, Mass.: Harvard University Press, 1979), 18–20; but cf. p. 186. For a more recent, penetrating view, see David Alan Black, 'Cinematic Realism and the Phonographic Analogy', *Cinema Journal*, 26: 2 (Winter 1987), 39–50.

9. Note that the 'source' of the sound in this instance is neither the 'wind' nor the 'trees', but a complex object: 'wind-trees'. Such 'contact sound' is the model for almost all of what we hear. Although visual objects, too, are complex in this sense (e.g. the action of incandescent light on the cover of a book), the word 'source' is normally applied in a different way to light, referring only to the emission of incident light, not reflected light. Here our use of language reveals the importance we attach to the effects of light (the 'red' which is reflected from the surface) as opposed to the causes of sound (e.g. the noise produced by walking *in* a boot *on* a floor). That is, the different ways in which we speak about sound and light seem to derive from aspects of our causal reasoning which, in turn, embody a practical interaction with the world.

10. Metz, 'Aural Objects', 156. Metz draws on the work of Luis J. Prieto, *Messages et signaux* (Paris: Presses Universitaires de France, 1966).

11. 'Aural Objects', 155. Metz argues for the primacy of verbal language over, say, the audio-visual: 'Language can say, even if sometimes only with approximation, what all the other codes can say, while the inverse is not true . . . [L]anguage does much more than [translate] vision. . . . To speak of the image is in reality to speak the image; not essentially a [translation] but a comprehension, a resocialization. . . . Nomination completes the perception as much as it translates it; an insufficiently verbalizable perception is not fully a perception in the social sense of the word.' ('The Perceived and the Named', 62–3.) Metz leaves open the possibility that sound might escape its adjectival status if one could somehow live a new (non-Western?) language. See also Mary Devereaux, 'In Defense of Talking Film', *Persistence of Vision*, 5 (Spring 1987), 17–27 ('How we interpret the film's pictures depends in part on what we take the film to say, and that surely depends in part, although not entirely, on what the film's characters say,' p. 26). See also n. 1 above, and section 3 and n. 45 below.

12. I explore some of the complex assumptions underlying Metz's version of linguistic determinism in ' "Here is a Picture of No Revolver!": The Negation of Images, and Methods for Analyzing the Structure of Pictorial Statements', *Wide Angle*, 8: 3/4 (1986), 8–17. Metz would seem to be asserting that our recognition of sound is accomplished through a 'head and modifier' schema where the 'head' represents the source of the sound specified as a visible (lighted) and/or tactile object and the 'modifiers' represent secondary attributes, such as the object's sound and colour (hue, saturation). However, other schemas are available which may lead to different conceptions of the experience of sound. See pp. 11–13.

13. When sound is heard as created and contingent (i.e. tied to a nearby motion-event), it makes the object which is in motion distinctive. Thus sound may serve as a 'signature' for identifying both a particular object and its space. Susan T. Fiske and Shelley E. Taylor argue that the distinctiveness of sound actually has the effect of increasing the power of visual memory in humans. They say: 'The reason for the strength of visual memory is not entirely clear, but one possibility is that visual stimuli do not attract attention as automatically as do other stimuli. That is, a bright flash may not draw attention as quickly as a loud noise. Moreover, processing visual information requires that one actively orient one's eyes toward the stimulus, while processing auditory information does not require that one actively orient one's ears. To compensate for these weaknesses in visual information processing, people may favor encoding of visual cues, as a general strategy . . .' *Social Cognition*, 2nd edn. (New York: McGraw-Hill, 1991), 315–16. Cf. Rick Altman's notion of 'spatial signature' in *Sound Theory, Sound Practice*, 24, 77, 241–6, 252.

Stephen Handel reacts to these aspects of sound as follows: 'Listening puts me in the world. Listening gives me a sense of emotion, a sense of movement, and a sense of being there that is missing when I am looking. I am more frightened by thunder than by lightning, even though I know that thunder is harmless and lightning is deadly. I feel far more isolation living with ear plugs than living with blinders. Listening is centripetal; it pulls you into the world. Looking is centrifugal; it separates you from the world.' *Listening: An Introduction to the Perception of Auditory Events* (Cambridge, Mass.: MIT Press, 1989), xi.

I believe, however, that sound need not always be heard (as above) adjectivally. I argue in section 3 that sound can be heard (and images can be seen) in an entirely different way.

14. See Tom Levin, 'The Acoustic Dimension: Notes on Cinema Sound', *Screen*, 25: 3 (May–June 1984), 62–4 (special issue devoted to the sound track).

15. A match of sound and image in film is called 'synchronized sound', not 'synchronized light' perhaps because sound is perceived (initially) as a duration contingent on the motion of something. It seems more natural to think of sound as a variable, fitting or not fitting a stable object while light seems less variable and tied more closely to the object.

16. Levin refers to the process of matching sound space to image space as 'diegeticising the acoustic' (ibid. 63). He draws on Rick Altman's argument that sound obeys a 'hermeneutic' logic in which various aural questions about the source of the sound are posed in order to be answered by the image. Rick Altman, 'Moving Lips: Cinema as Ventriloquism', *Yale French Studies*, 60 (1980), 74; see also pp. 69, 72, 75.

17. Hans Reichenbach, *Atom and Cosmos: The World of Modern Physics*, trans. Edward S. Allen (New York: George Braziller, 1957), ch. 19, 'Picture and Reality', p. 288. An account of the 'middle world' will be altered when its basic terms are considered within another framework. For example, since Einstein argues that matter is equivalent to energy, space as a distribution of matter might be seen as merely the product of energetic motions and particle interactions. The notion of velocity as 'a "distance" divided by a "time"' might then be re-examined. Can distance and time be measured without movement? According to Einstein, judging distance depends upon the velocity of the measuring device and judging time depends upon an observer's relative velocity. What is absolute for Einstein is the velocity of light in space-time; space and time separately are variable. No other absolute is known within this framework. In these sorts of arguments motion seems to reappear as at least the equal of space.

The quantum world, too, lies outside the middle world. Since the fundamental laws of physics are time-symmetric, the 'arrow' of time does not exist at a microscopic level of description, but rather emerges only at a (middle-world) macro-scopic level in the second law of thermodynamics which states that the entropy (disorder) of an isolated system always increases toward a maximum. See generally, David Layzer, 'The Arrow of Time', *Scientific American*, 233: 6 (Dec. 1975), 56–69; Stephen W. Hawking and Roger Penrose, *The Nature of Space and Time* (Princeton: Princeton University Press, 1996).

18. See e.g. Milic Capek, *Bergson and Modern Physics: A Reinterpretation and Re-evaluation* (Dordrecht: D. Reidel Publishing, 1971), ch. 8, 'Bergson, Reichenbach and Piaget' and ch. 9, 'The Logic of Solid Bodies from Plato to Quine', 65–80 in Part I, 'Bergson's Biological Theory of Knowledge'; Mark Johnson, *The Body in the Mind: The Bodily Basis of Meaning, Imagination, and Reason* (Chicago: University of Chicago Press, 1987).

19. A root metaphor is one which provides a framework for construing a realm of experience. It provides a source for generating a common language of explanation while filtering out alternative philosophical and scientific models. See Stephen Pepper, *World Hypotheses* (Berkeley and Los Angeles: University of California Press, 1942).

20. Heraclitus is not explicitly referring to time; nor is my interpretation accurate or complete with respect to his metaphysics. I have combined several translations of his statement. See Heraclitus, *Fragments: A Text and Translation with a Commentary*, by T. M. Robinson (Toronto: University of Toronto Press, 1987), fragments 12, 91a; cf. 6, 49a, 60, 88.

   In general, theories of physiology from Heraclitus (101a, 118), Plato, and Aristotle to the nineteenth century were committed to the supremacy of sight over hearing; in addition, sight was often associated with the intellect, hearing with the emotions. Hence the imperative, 'fiat lux' ('let there be light'), rather than 'fiat sonus'. See Kalinak, *Settling the Score*, 20–39; Martin Jay, *Downcast Eyes: The Denigration of Vision in Twentieth-Century French Thought* (Berkeley and Los Angeles: University of California Press, 1993), 1–147; Paul Davies, 'The Face and the Caress: Levinas's Ethical Alterations of Sensibility', in David Michael Levin (ed.), *Modernity and the Hegemony of Vision* (Berkeley and Los Angeles: University of California Press, 1993), 252–72. Don Ihde complains that all of Western metaphysics is founded upon the ideal of the mute, stationary, middle-sized, and opaque object; *Listening and Voice*, 3–16, 65–6, 70, 94.

21. See George Lakoff and Mark Johnson, *Metaphors We Live By* (Chicago: University of Chicago Press, 1980), 7–9, 16, 41–5, 65–8, 113, 118; Lakoff and Mark Turner, *More than Cool Reason: A Field Guide to Poetic Metaphor* (Chicago: University of Chicago Press, 1989), 34–49, 86. Using linguistic evidence, Lakoff and Johnson assert that the river of time is usually seen as flowing toward us, bringing the future nearer at the same rate that the past recedes behind. In this image, time is given as singular, linear (as opposed to, say, circular), continuous, regular, objective, and natural, and the observer of time as directly confronting the future, looking ahead and upstream. It might be interesting to study other ways in which individuals visualize this scene. Could the observer face in another direction? Do we think of time as having a sound? How near is the river?

22. The apparently contingent quality of sound in the middle world leads Kendall Walton to formulate 'two significant disanalogies between vision and hearing: In the first place, vision is frequently more effective than hearing as a means of identifying particulars, as a source of *de re* rather than mere *de dicto* knowledge. . . . Secondly, sounds are thought of as standing apart from their sources more easily than sights are, as objects of perception on their own, independent of the bells or trains or speech which might be heard by means of them. A sight is nearly always a sight *of* something, in our experience; a sound can be just a sound.' 'What is Abstract About the Art of Music?', *Journal of Aesthetics and Art Criticism*, 46: 3 (Spring 1988), 352

(Walton's emphasis); see also pp. 358–9. Note that Walton's claims are hedged with such words as 'frequently', 'thought of', 'nearly always', and 'can be'.

One consequence of seeing sound adjectivally (as does Walton above) is that *voice-over* narration in a film will be understood as essentially a kind of gloss or explanation of the image (i.e. as embodying what Walton calls 'mere *de dicto* knowledge') and hence, unlike the image, capable of lying to a spectator. I argue in section 3, however, that sound need not always be heard adjectivally.

The nature of voice-over narration is an important problem for film theory because it bears on questions concerning the essential components of the 'medium' and the extent of non-spoken narrations. See n. 1 above and n. 45 below. On voice-over see e.g. Sarah Kozloff, *Invisible Storytellers: Voice-Over Narration in American Fiction Film* (Berkeley and Los Angeles: University of California Press, 1988), 48–9, 69–71, 109–17, 124–6 ('when words and images absolutely contradict each other, the images seem always to be the truth-tellers,' p. 114) ('[the image-maker] is condemned to constant reliability, constant authority; I can think of no methods by which an image-maker could cast grave or persistent doubts upon his own adequacy or truthfulness,' p. 110); Avrom Fleishman, *Narrated Films: Storytelling Situations in Cinema History* (Baltimore: Johns Hopkins University Press, 1992), 18. Auditory adjectiveness appears in many guises in theories of film; see e.g. Dominique Nasta, *Meaning in Film: Relevant Structures in Soundtrack and Narrative* (Berne: Peter Lang, 1991), 26, 43–7, 89.

23. Levin, 'The Acoustic Dimension', 64 (his emphasis). William Johnson agrees with Levin's statement which suggests that for Johnson, sound and image are perfectly separate but equal. However, the problem remains to specify in which context and for what purpose they are to be taken as 'equals'. See n. 37 below. Johnson, 'The Liberation of Echo: A New Hearing for Film Sound', *Film Quarterly*, 38: 4 (Summer 1985), 5. Johnson expands his argument in 'Sound and Image: A Further Hearing', *Film Quarterly*, 43: 1 (Fall 1989), 24–35.

24. Levin, 'The Acoustic Dimension', 62. Levin's approach to sound offers support for Dominique Nasta's claim that 'Sound dialogue forces real time upon the screen, as it takes the same time for a sentence to be uttered as it does in real life . . .', *Meaning in Film*, 45.

25. Johnson, 'The Liberation of Echo', 6 n. 22.

26. Noël Burch, *Theory of Film Practice*, trans. Helen R. Lane (New York: Praeger, 1973), ch. 6, 'On the Structural Use of Sound', p. 91.

27. For example, Johnson's illustration of an acoustic freeze frame from Bellochio's *Fists in the Pocket* (1966) would require as a larger context that the spectator comprehend the sound as part of a narrative discourse—a 'scene'—in which a record player is the source of an operatic aria heard by a character. As the character dies, the image freezes and a prolonged high note from the aria is heard. Evidently, several complex metaphors are at work involving diegetic and nondiegetic narrations within a narrative fiction. Sound and time may 'stop' but only within certain interpretive contexts which authorize a reformulation of the prolonged high note as an 'instant' of time which may now, in a new frame, be scrutinized for a time independently of its duration elsewhere (where it may not have 'stopped'), thus enabling the spectator to hear it as the final sound of the character's life, the closing of the story, and the end of the film; and/or hear it as a symptom of the character's horror and anguish, or our horror, or some more general paralysis defined through (or inferred from) the story as a whole. Johnson, 'The Liberation of Echo', 6 n. 22.

28. Note that space, like time, is subject to at least two different descriptions according to top-down principles of ordering and bottom-up principles of extent (size, scale, depth). Nelson Goodman compares the extent of a solid object to temporal duration and concludes that '[s]trangely enough it turns out not that time is more fluid than (say) space but rather that time is more static. . . . Thus although there is no change

that does not involve time, there is no change in time.' See 'Talk of Time' in *Problems and Projects* (New York: Bobbs-Merrill, 1972), 219–20. See also Ray Jackendoff, *Semantics and Cognition* (Cambridge, Mass.: MIT Press, 1983), 174 (temporal ordering must be mentally represented in spatial terms) and pp. 150–1 (on the verb 'to see').

Goodman may, however, have underestimated the power of top-down processes to rework temporal duration so that time is perceived to change (speed up, slow down, repeat itself, etc.) according to our specific problems and projects in a cognitive context. I believe that a spectator's experience of time in a film is related to the complexity of juxtaposition allowable under a given descriptive method. More-over, when we remodel a description of time or space to fit a new task in the middle world, then we may also need to rethink our language of 'causality'. See Branigan, 'Here is a Picture of No Revolver!', 10–13, and *Narrative Comprehension and Film* (New York: Routledge, 1992), 20, 26–32, 39–44, 49, 50, 116, 148–9, 148 n. 22, 203.

Bertrand Russell apparently would deny that there are at least two fundamental perceptions of time—order and duration—but only because his notion of 'order' is so restricted as to depend exclusively upon our *acquaintance with contiguity*, i.e. simple consecutiveness, or chronology: what comes before and after. Russell argues that one may establish temporal contiguity to any degree of precision by merely dividing up the duration of a physical event into arbitrarily short segments. However, time is not just periodicity, or ordered periodicity in Russell's sense, but *hierarchical* periodicity. This latter, more complex notion of time helps to account for certain intricacies in our comprehension of both music and language where new sequences are formed by mentally taking elements out of sequence according to top-down schemata. Cf. Ray Jackendoff, *Consciousness and the Computational Mind* (Cambridge, Mass.: MIT Press, 1987), 253–6. Bertrand Russell, *The Problems of Philosophy* (London: Oxford University Press, 1972), 32–3, 87, 102, 146. See generally Goodman, *Ways of Worldmaking* (Indianapolis: Hackett, 1978).

29. Movement of the camera, like sound, may seem to exemplify temporal duration: an expansion, contraction, sliding (motion parallax), or revolving of space often seems to mark the continuous presence of the present. However, like sound, other descriptive schemes (and narrative contexts) applied to a film by a spectator may render camera movement as fragmentary and merely evocative of relationships among fixed positions in a larger matrix; for example, in films by Miklós Jancsó and Jean-Luc Godard. Similar remarks apply to many other 'formal' parameters of film, such as film projection, motion in the image, editing, and the performance of actors. Further-more, the common belief that film images are often, or always, 'in the present tense' is a myth fostered by the use of certain restrictive descriptions and widespread metaphors for time. See Alexander Sesonske, 'Time and Tense in Cinema', *Journal of Aesthetics and Art Criticism*, 38: 4 (Summer 1980), 419–26; Branigan, 'Here is a Picture of No Revolver!', 10–12.

30. My analysis of the expression 'tick-tock' is indebted to Frank Kermode's discussion of the word in *The Sense of an Ending: Studies in the Theory of Fiction* (New York: Oxford University Press, 1967), 44–6. Kermode relies upon Paul Fraisse's *The Psychology of Time*, trans. Jennifer Leith (New York: Harper & Row, 1963), but he does not indicate the relevant passages; see e.g. pp. 72–3, 77–8, 81–4 (vocal utter-ances as a scale against which to measure duration), 89. For suggestive comments about the perception of intervals and the use of metaphors for time, see Fraisse, pp. 128–34, 283–7.

'Tick-tock' is actually a member of a wider class of expressions each of which is composed of two elements that differ only in one vowel sound. I call such an expression a 'harmonic pair'. A detailed discussion of the unusual properties of these expressions—I have found about 45 of them in English—is not appropriate here, except to note that what is striking about these pairs is that each is based on an initial 'i' vowel. Three exceptions—*heehaw, seesaw*, and *teetertotter*—are not really exceptions since the initial vowel is voiced only slightly higher than the 'i' and is equally front and unrounded. I believe that this use of the 'i' vowel in harmonic pairs is connected to more fundamental references to time in English. Steven Pinker discusses this class of words in terms of 'phonetic symbolism' in *The Language Instinct: How the Mind Creates Language* (New York: Harper Perennial, 1994), 166–8.

31. A 'replica' is a new and distinct entity which is similar in all 'important' ways to another entity. What counts as 'important' in defining the similarities which make one thing a 'replica' of another is determined with respect to a stipulated purpose or use within a course of human conduct. Replicas are separate from one another but function equivalently in some contexts. Thus two dimes in my pocket are replicas of each other without becoming either One Dime, or one dime and one perfect imitation (or, perfect forgery) of a dime. Though my dimes may have different mint dates, they are each worth 10 cents in trade. If one is made out of tin, however, it will not sufficiently count as a replica to be a dime in the store.

Roger Brown has shown that locally functioning *non*-linguistic (i.e. cultural) practices correspond closely to our activities of naming and creating conceptual categories with which to organize experience. The act of naming is a discovery of what is taken to be 'important'. See 'How Shall a Thing be Called?' in *Psycholinguistics: Selected Papers by Roger Brown* (New York: Free Press, 1970), 3–15; *Social Psychology* (New York: Free Press, 1965), 318–22 ('There is an isomorphism between naming behavior and other sorts of culturally patterned behavior.'); and *Words and Things* (New York: Free Press, 1958). See also George Lakoff, *Women, Fire, and Dangerous Things: What Categories Reveal about the Mind* (Chicago: University of Chicago Press, 1987). Non-linguistic practices are also crucial in determining whether an entity will be seen as a legitimate replica or as an original (or fake). See Nelson Goodman, *Languages of Art: An Approach to a Theory of Symbols*, 2nd edn. (Indianapolis: Hackett, 1976), ch. 3, 'Art and Authenticity', pp. 99–123.

32. The existence of bottom-up and top-down processes significantly alters the traditional distinction between perception and cognition. Jackendoff, *Consciousness*, 271–2. On the distinction between the two processes, see Howard Gardner, *The Mind's New Science: A History of the Cognitive Revolution*, expanded edn. (New York: Basic Books, 1987), 96–7. See also Barnard J. Baars, *The Cognitive Revolution in Psychology* (New York: Guilford, 1986). For an account of film perception describing some of these processes, see Julian Hochberg and Virginia Brooks, 'Movies in the Mind's Eye', in David Bordwell and Noël Carroll (eds.), *Post-Theory: Reconstructing Film Studies* (Madison: University of Wisconsin Press, 1996), 368–87; Julian Hochberg, 'Representation of Motion and Space in Video and Cinematic Displays', in *Handbook of Perception and Human Performance*, vol. 1: *Sensory Processes and Perception*, ed. Kenneth R. Boff, Lloyd Kaufman, and James P. Thomas (New York: John Wiley and Sons, 1986), 22–1 to 22–64; Virginia Brooks, 'Film, Perception and Cognitive Psychology', *Millennium Film Journal*, nos. 14/15 (Fall/Winter 1984–5), 105–26. See generally David Bordwell, 'A Case for Cognitivism', *Iris*, 9 (Spring 1989), 11–40 (special issue on cinema and cognitive psychology).

My discussion of bottom-up and top-down processes in taken from *Narrative Comprehension and Film*, 37–9, 45–6, 118. It is not immediately clear whether the distinction between bottom-up and top-down processes is coextensive with the distinction between what is on the 'screen'—i.e. what may be an expression of the medium itself—and what is in the 'story'—i.e. what may be translated into other media.

One may extend the notions of 'bottom-up' and 'top-down' processing to cover two different approaches to research and theoretical activity. See e.g. Zenon W. Pylyshyn, 'Metaphorical Imprecision and the "Top-Down" Research Strategy' in Andrew Ortony (ed.), *Metaphor and Thought* (Cambridge: Cambridge University Press, 1979), 420–36.

33. The existence of top-down processes accounts for the fact that what is remembered and what is overlooked in comprehending a narrative film is not a matter of chance. On top-down mechanisms that guide the construction of some narrative and non-narrative experiences, see e.g. Jean Matter Mandler, *Stories, Scripts, and Scenes: Aspects of Schema Theory* (Hillsdale, NJ: Lawrence Erlbaum Associates, 1984). Some forms of cultural knowledge (concerning, for example, going to the movies, attending a birthday party, buying groceries, making dinner, taking a trip, eating at a restaurant, visiting a doctor's office) may be organized as sets of schemata though not necessarily as a narrative schema. See Roger C. Schank and Robert P. Abelson, *Scripts, Plans, Goals and Understanding* (Hillsdale, NJ: Lawrence Erlbaum Associates, 1977); Fiske and Taylor, *Social Cognition*.

34. There was a vigorous debate in the 1930s concerning where the microphone should be placed with respect to the sound source and the camera in order to best integrate sound space and image space for an audience. One theory held that the *loudness* of the sound should be correlated with the position of the camera, the focal length of the lens, and the reverberatory properties of the environment so that a visual object in the background of a shot would never be as loud as it would be if it were in the foreground ('sound perspective'). Note that what is at stake here is not only a systematic variation in loudness and reverberation but its strict correlation to variations in scale throughout a sequence of shots with respect to the positions of various sound sources. An opposing theory held that the microphone should be placed solely to capture the most important sound in the scene and render it clearly intelligible without regard to the position of the camera ('psychological realism', or perhaps, 'narrative perspective').

   Both theories are correct because they are premissed on two different ways of perceiving sound. The first theory favours bottom-up perception, the second, top-down. For example, the second theory would hold that just as size is not absolute, but relative to a visual field (i.e. what seems tiny in the distance may be larger than a nearby object), so also is sound relative to an aural field: a soft sound at a distance may be deemed louder than a nearby whisper. This would allow the distant (softer) sound to be represented initially in a film as louder than the nearby sound *if* one also assumes that what is being represented for an audience is *a particular (often narrativized) attention* to a space, or *a particular desire* (e.g. if I were located an equal distance from both sources . . . ; or, if only I were closer to that object . . . ; or, I believe that a certain character wishes he were closer to that object). See Mary Ann Doane, 'Ideology and the Practice of Sound Editing and Mixing', in Weis and Belton, *Film Sound*, 58–61, repr. from de Lauretis and Heath, *The Cinematic Apparatus*; and Rick Altman, 'Sound Space' in *Sound Theory, Sound Practice*, 46–64. Incidentally, one can find analogues to the above two kinds of perspective—perceptual and narrative—which may be taken as contexts in order to describe the uses of other filmic devices, such as composition, camera movement, and editing, whether or not the devices are being used to represent a character's point of view.

35. On the implications of a modular structure of mind, see e.g. Jackendoff, *Consciousness*; Jerry Fodor, *The Modularity of Mind* (Cambridge, Mass.: Bradford Books/MIT Press, 1983); Howard Gardner, *Frames of Mind: The Theory of Multiple Intelligences* (New York: Basic Books, 1983); Marvin Minsky, *The Society of Mind* (New York: Simon and Schuster, 1986); Margaret S. Livingstone, 'Art, Illusion and the Visual System', *Scientific American*, 258: 1 (Jan. 1988), 78–85; Andy Clark,

Microcognition: Philosophy, Cognitive Science, and Parallel Distributed Processing (Cambridge, Mass.: MIT Press, 1989).

36. Johnson, 'The Liberation of Echo', 4.

37. It is unclear whether Johnson means that sound and image are ontologically equal because they are composed of the same elements (e.g. 'information') or whether he means that they are ontologically distinct, but equal, within some metaphysical hierarchy. He speaks of sound as a 'full and equal partner' of the image (p. 2) which 'deserves equal billing with the image even when its role is inconspicuous' (p. 11). He also endorses Elisabeth Weis's view which he says 'consistently attributes equal importance' to sound and image (p. 2). These formulations may be interpreted in several ways, some of which are not ontological. See also Johnson's reply to a letter by Robert Cumbow, *Film Quarterly*, 39: 2 (Winter 1985–6), 64 ('ontologically equal'), and see n. 23 above.

38. Johnson, 'The Liberation of Echo', 6. The use of the terms 'direct' and 'indirect' are ambiguous and misleading when applied to the phenomena of sound and light for they apply in different ways depending upon which properties of sound and light are at issue. As discussed earlier in the text, there are two fundamental, physical differences between sound and light which lead to them being perceived differently by bottom-up processes.

39. Ibid. 6 (Johnson's emphases; footnote omitted).

40. Ibid. 6 n. 20 (Johnson's emphasis).

41. Ibid. 7. Johnson's categories for analysing sound are few. Sound may be synchronous or asynchronous, on- or off-screen. In such a state, sound may confirm or oppose, strongly or weakly, the information provided by the image. Other writers have offered much richer schemes. See e.g. Siegfried Kracauer, *Theory of Film: The Redemption of Physical Reality* (New York: Oxford University Press, 1960), 102–56; David Bordwell and Kristin Thompson, *Film Art: An Introduction*, rev. edn. (New York: McGraw-Hill, 1997), 315–54. Since it may be an open question what sort of time is signified by a particular sound, juxtaposing sound and image may create various sorts of time-space events. Two methods for analysing the kinds of temporal and spatial articulations of sound and image may be found in Branigan, *Narrative Comprehension and Film*, 39–44, 146–9; and David Bordwell, *Narration in the Fiction Film* (Madison: University of Wisconsin Press, 1985), 74–88 and 99–130.

42. See Michael J. Reddy, 'The Conduit Metaphor: A Case of Frame Conflict in Our Language about Language', in Ortony, *Metaphor and Thought*, 284–324.

43. Like Johnson, Alfred Hitchcock is thinking top-down about sound when he says, 'To describe a sound accurately, one has to imagine its equivalent in dialogue.' François Truffaut, *Hitchcock.*, 5th edn. (New York: Simon and Schuster, 1984), 297.

44. For some alternatives to a communication model, see William Frawley, *Text and Epistemology* (Norwood, NJ: Ablex Publishing, 1987); Edward Branigan, *Point of View in the Cinema: A Theory of Narration and Subjectivity in Classical Film* (New York: Mouton Publishers, 1984); Bordwell, *Narration in the Fiction Film*. On the complexity of reference relations, see Nelson Goodman, *Of Mind and Other Matters* (Cambridge, Mass.: Harvard University Press, 1984), 'Routes of Reference', pp. 55–71.

45. 'Narration' refers not to what is told and happens in a story, but rather to the conditions of the telling—to the overall regulation and distribution of knowledge which determines when and how a reader acquires knowledge from a text, including the invention of (sometimes tacit) speakers, presenters, actors, listeners, watchers, and focalizers who are in a (spatial and temporal) position to know. The use of such a person or agent in a descriptive statement about the reader's 'position' or state of knowledge is merely a convenient fiction which serves to mark how the field of knowledge is being divided at a particular moment during the reading. Narration

concerns the reader's procedural knowledge ('knowing how') of the story rather than his or her declarative knowledge ('knowing that'). Thus conceived, film narration is much more than the device of 'voice-over' narration; indeed, much more than what is heard on the sound track or, for that matter, seen in the image. On narration and its levels, see Branigan, *Narrative Comprehension and Film*, 63–124.

Note that the issue addressed by the concept of narration is not the actual production (recording, editing, mixing) of a sound (or an image) in a film, but its reception and interpretation by a spectator. For example, within a specific frame of reference (narrational level) defined by a story, it may not matter that the sound which is heard in the film as a bird singing by the spectator has not actually been produced by the bird which is seen by the spectator; nor may it matter that the sound may not have been produced by an actual bird. Instead, what matters is how the sound is heard, and described, by the spectator.

46. Here I am using some of David Bordwell's terms for analysing film narration; see *Narration in the Fiction Film*, 57–61. Another approach may be found in George M. Wilson, *Narration in Light: Studies in Cinematic Point of View* (Baltimore: Johns Hopkins University Press, 1986), 4–5. For an overview of the issues involved in analysing narration, see Susan Sniader Lanser, *The Narrative Act: Point of View in Prose Fiction* (Princeton, NJ: Princeton University Press, 1981).

47. On analogous sound, see Burch, *Theory of Film Practice*, 95.

48. As discussed earlier, there are biological reasons for our adaptation to a middle world environment.

49. 'Object sound' is neither the simplest nor the most complex of sounds which we may experience and interpret. Object sound possesses internal structure because we understand it as the product of a *visual, material* object *making* waves in an *elastic* medium. Thus object sound is not a primitive building block of perception but is rather, I believe, a so-called 'basic-level categorization' closely linked to the physical and social world (through bottom-up psychological processes). 'Basic-level' categories are, in effect, a middle world within the middle world and are the basis for both superordinate and subordinate systems of categorization. Thus, for example, a child may learn to call an object a 'dime' because of its use in a store before recategorizing it in a superordinate system as 'money', 'thing', 'metal object', or 'coin'; or, before referring to it in a subordinate system as a '1952 Denver-minted dime' or as a 'scratched dime'. See Roger Brown and n. 31 above. On basic-level categorization see also Lakoff, *Women, Fire, and Dangerous Things*, 31–54, 199–201, 265–71, 296–7; and Stevan Harnad (ed.), *Categorical Perception: The Groundwork of Cognition* (Cambridge: Cambridge University Press, 1987), esp. chs. 9, 16, and 19, 'Perceptual Categories in Vision and Audition' (pp. 287–300), 'Categorization Processes and Categorical Perception' (pp. 455–90), and 'Category Induction and Representation' (pp. 535–65).

50. In Keith Donnellan's terms (discussed in section 6), to hear a sound as pure noise requires a conscious effort to make the sound 'non-attributive'. Such a sound may ultimately refer to a non-tangible object, such as a colour, an idea, a character's mental state, or a future (perhaps foreshadowed) event.

One might speculate that both sound and lightness may be experienced as 'facts' without being related to either a 'source' or an 'object'. There is also evidence that motion may be experienced apart from any object which may be in motion. See Hochberg, 'Representation of Motion', pp. 22–8, 22–30, 22–33. If so, at what stage of our thinking is there 'enough' of sound or light (or motion, space, time) to comprise a mental 'event'—sound or light experienced simply as a percept? Is such an impression truly simple or the result of complex processes? Recent computational approaches to perception suggest that apparently simple percepts have great complexity. See, for example, David Marr's influential argument for a $2\frac{1}{2}$-dimensional representation of space as a stage of visual processing in *Vision: A Computational*

Investigation into the Human Representation and Processing of Visual Information (San Francisco: W. H. Freeman, 1982). The perception of motion in film is based on psychological processes which are still not completely understood, such as flicker fusion, short-range apparent motion, and masking. See Joseph D. Anderson, *The Reality of Illusion: An Ecological Approach to Cognitive Film Theory* (Carbondale: Southern Illinois University Press, 1996), 54–65, 102–3.

51. According to Anderson, music and dialogue acquire their narrational flexibility through the power of *synchrony* to produce and confirm a spectator's recognition of a unified, ecologically significant 'event'. *The Reality of Illusion*, 80–9.

52. My description of the nature of attributive and referential uses is based primarily on the following pages of Keith S. Donnellan, 'Reference and Definite Descriptions', *Philosophical Review*, 75: 3 (July 1966), 285, 289, 290–1, 295–6, 297, 299–302. Saul Kripke examines Donnellan's argument in 'Speaker's Reference and Semantic Reference' in A. P. Martinich (ed.), *The Philosophy of Language*, 2nd edn. (New York: Oxford University Press, 1990), 248–67 ('speaker's reference' and 'semantic reference' approximate Donnellan's 'referential use' and 'attributive use', respectively). I do not develop Kripke's ideas in this essay because he relies heavily on intentionality and communication; his focus is the speaker not the perceiver nor conventions of reception; and he seems to assume that a 'referential use' of a description occurs only through a simple mistake on the part of the speaker—thus leaving unclear how one should analyse descriptions that are fictional, rhetorical, and/or aesthetic. For a comprehensive and sophisticated approach that does not rely upon authorial intention, speech acts, or communication models in dealing with problems of interpretation, see e.g. David Bordwell, *Making Meaning: Inference and Rhetoric in the Interpretation of Cinema* (Cambridge, Mass.: Harvard University Press, 1989).

53. I believe that a third major type of reference is 'fictional reference'. I have argued that such reference involves a certain kind of *in*definite description that bears upon a perceiver's cognitive (though not necessarily emotive) appreciation of a text. Sound is heard fictionally through what might be called 'hyper-top-down' processes which act to defer denotation (existential reference) by routing meaning through intricate sequences and layers of descriptions. See Branigan, *Narrative Comprehension and Film*, 192–217. See generally Murray Smith, 'Film Spectatorship and the Institution of Fiction', *Journal of Aesthetics and Art Criticism*, 53: 2 (Spring 1995), 113–27. For some goals that a perceiver might undertake, other than the existential identification of an object, see main text above at nn. 13 and 33.

54. See Edward Branigan, 'What Is a Camera?', in Patricia Mellencamp and Philip Rosen (eds.), *Cinema Histories, Cinema Practices* (Frederick, Md.: University Publications of America, 1984), 87–107. David Bordwell documents the enormous number of ideas that have been submitted by theorists about the essence of cinema in *On the History of Film Style* (Cambridge, Mass.: Harvard University Press, forthcoming).

PART II
Meaning, Authorship, and Intention

For some years, theories of criticism have been marked by anti-intentionalistic attitudes, disdaining or at least downplaying the relevance of the intentions (and related mental states) of the makers of art objects. Moreover, while structuralist and post-structuralist theory broke with many critical and theoretical assumptions, with respect to the issue of intentionality it is continuous with an important strain of the New Criticism which it displaced as the institutionally dominant paradigm of theory and criticism. The most famous New Critical statement on intention was the influential essay by W. K. Wimsatt and Monroe Beardsley, which characterized criticism focused or dependent on the intentions of the artist as falling foul of nothing less than an 'intentional fallacy'. Of more direct influence, however, in film and cultural studies, have been the arguments of Foucault, Barthes, and Derrida respectively: (1) that authorial criticism which depends on the unearthing of the author's intentions is nothing more than a historically contingent form of criticism; (2) that attention to the intentions of the author amounts to a kind of deification of him, which has the effect of repressing the reader's role in creating meaning; and (3) that the intended meanings of the author are, in any case, subject to the forces of displacement inherent in language; like a postcard, the intended message of the author may or may not arrive intact, or at all, with the reader. The deferral of meaning becomes so omnipresent that the very notions of an originating author and a final destination in the reader become suspect; the activities of agents (authors and readers) become mere epiphenomena in the endless circulation of (linguistic) meaning.

Intentional, author-based criticism, however, has led something of a double life in film studies specifically. The anti-intentional theses alluded to above were made during the very same era when the *politique des auteurs* had a pronounced impact on the study of film. Several attempts were made at reconciling auteur criticism with structuralism—for example, in the form which became known as 'auteur structuralism'. The tradition of author-based criticism, given enormous momentum by the critics of *Cahiers du cinéma* and *Movie*, has stubbornly persisted throughout the period of (post-)structuralist ascendancy. (As David Bordwell once put it, if the author really is dead, critics regularly perform seances in order to speak with him.) Author-based criticism is once more becoming theoretically respectable, and the essays by Livingston and Gaut are among the first to reassess the basis of such criticism, its limitations and strengths.

The two essays take significantly different tacks, however, even if they are both sailing in an intentional direction. Livingston first punctures the claims to historical authority assumed by Foucault's essay, and goes on to investigate the extension of our concept of authorship through a series of imagined case-studies, in each of which the degree and level of control of individual agents in the process of production differs. Livingston argues that contributing some form of agency to the production of an artefact is insufficient to be counted as an author of it; a communicative or expressive intention must stand behind the contribution if we are to view it as an authorial action or 'utterance'. It is in this respect that Livingston differs from Gaut. For both Livingston and Gaut, commercial films are the result of the work of many agents; but for Gaut, the import of this fact is that, typically, films are multiply authored. Though the fact of collaboration is always acknowledged, Gaut's essay is unusual if not unique in that he makes it the foundation of his argument, rather than a decorative qualification. Gaut describes the assumed object of auteur criticism as the 'dominant author' film, that is, a film made through collaboration but largely controlled in expressive and aesthetic terms by a single person. Other films, however, are best understood as the product either of a 'synergistic' collaboration among several significant artists, or of conflict among them. Thus, Gaut argues for a more liberal conception of what is to count as an authorial contribution to a film than does Livingston. Gaut and Livingston agree, however, that the prohibition against reference to intention mystifies and obscures many aspects of films which are of central interest to us. Films, like other representations, may be placed under non-intentional descriptions, but these descriptions alone will not suffice to answer all the questions we may ask of or about them.

If the prohibition against reference to intention tends to denude criticism of much that is of legitimate and often central interest in fiction films, it is equally damaging in the domain of the non-fiction film. Post-structural 'textualism' in this field has emphasized non-intentional definitions, for example definitions based on the ability of film to record a trace or 'index' of real events, by virtue of the light which bounces off objects and then hits light-sensitive emulsion or magnetic tape; or stylistic definitions based on characteristic kinds of technique employed in non-fiction films, such as hand-held camera or the use of 16mm, black and white stock. Efforts to define the non-fiction film through these means collapse, however, as they fail to mark reliably the borders between fiction and non-fiction. The predictable, post-structural response to this state of affairs is to declare the distinction between fiction and non-fiction an unstable one, or even (self-defeatingly) a fictional distinction. Counter-intuitive and absurd as this conclusion is, the textualist is driven to this conclusion because intentionalist avenues of thought have been blocked off from the outset. Theorists deriving inspiration from that nemesis of deconstruction—speech act theory—are not so stymied, however. Both Carroll and Ponech pursue a definition of non-fictional, documentary films based on speech act theories of utterance and assertion (building on earlier suggestions by Carl Plantinga). Carroll's essay develops and defends this core definition in detail. Ponech, working from a similar basic definition, explores its ramifications for understanding different types of documentary film-making practice.

George Wilson tackles a rather different aspect of criticism and the ascription of meaning to films, though there are points of intersection between his argument and those of the other authors gathered in this section. Wilson is concerned to examine the analysis of interpretation given by David Bordwell, in which 'comprehension' is divided from 'interpretation' proper. Wilson argues that, on a theoretical level, such a distinction appears to be merely stipulative; and taking *Bigger than Life* as an example, he argues that it is impossible to maintain in many individual cases. Wilson also argues that the fundamentally linguistic construal or 'meaning' that underpins Bordwell's analysis is mismatched to the task of understanding the kind of meaning or significance we search for in watching a fiction film (or indeed, in engaging with any kind of narrative). When we interpret a narrative, we are searching for the significance or 'meaning' of actions in the context of a character's life, in much the same way as we try to make sense of the actions of real persons. Moreover, this search for significance has an intrinsically evaluative component overlooked in Bordwell's discussion. We are not merely concerned with discerning the semantic or thematic import of a film, whether this is characterized as a 'lesson' or 'moral' or something more subtle and intangible. In this respect, Wilson's emphasis is very different from that in the two essays on non-fiction, which as we have seen make analogies between linguistic and filmic 'utterances'. Implicitly, then, Wilson opposes the description of films as *texts*. This is a stance shared by Gaut, for a different though parallel reason: where Wilson objects to the obscuring of the human significance of filmic narratives by linguistic-textual accounts, Gaut points to the occlusion of the distinctive perceptual and ontological qualities of films which are lost in criticism which treats them as if they were identical with individually authored, literary texts.

5

Cinematic Authorship

Paisley Livingston

Authorship has long been a controversial topic in cinema studies. A central question is whether a 'traditional' conception of authorship should be applied to the cinema, or at least to some significant corpus of films. Although a positive response to that question helped to motivate the inclusion of film studies in the academic curriculum in the 1960s, current scholarly opinion tends to favour the idea that a traditional conception of authorship is not applicable to the cinema, either because this conception is simply false, or because authorship in film is fundamentally different from literary and other forms of authorship. Although author studies are still written and published, it is generally held that the work of an individual film-maker is best understood as figuring within a larger social process, system, or structure, be it a discursive, institutional, national, or international one. Some scholars allow that authorship obtains in instances of independent film production, but not in cases of studio-produced works. Yet even this thesis is controversial, and debate over the topic of authorship continues.

One shortcoming of many discussions of authorship is that insufficient attention is paid to the problem of analysing the 'traditional' conception of authorship that is supposed to be at stake in these debates. Often it seems to be wrongly taken on faith that we already have a strong, shared understanding of what this traditional conception of authorship entails. This shortcoming is apparent in the writings of both anti-individualists and individualists, for neither the champions of 'the great directors' nor the students of system and structure have provided detailed elucidations of the concept of authorship. The current chapter seeks to remedy this situation by doing some conceptual spadework. Section 1 looks at authorship in general and surveys some different strategies of definition. I describe and advocate one well-entrenched way of construing the term and point to some of the problems inherent in alternative approaches. Section 2 turns to the cinema and asks whether there are any good reasons why this notion of authorship

I would like to acknowledge financial support for this research provided by both the SSHRC and FCAR. Thanks as well to Murray Smith for comments on a draft of this chapter.

is not applicable. I focus on the kinds of cases that are often thought to make authorship especially problematic in film, namely, those involving 'industrial' modes of production characteristic of commercial, mass-market cinema. Individual authorship, I claim, does obtain in some such cases, and I discuss the conditions under which this occurs. Section 3 provides a brief discussion of the contrast between anti-realist and realist conceptions of authorship, focusing on the common claim that the cinema is especially suited to the former.

In order to try to forestall some predictable misreadings, let me state at the outset that my goal in what follows is not to defend the idea that solitary artistic genius is the fundamental unit of all valuable cultural analysis. I do, however, maintain that an understanding of individual agency is crucial to the latter. I hold that many films emerge from a process of collective or individual authorship; others may have makers, but no author(s)—at least in the sense I elucidate.

1. WHAT IS AN AUTHOR?

Ordinary usage of 'author' (and of cognate terms in other languages) is today extremely diverse. People are said to be the authors of such disparate items as letters, schemes, mischief, disasters, poems, philosophical treatises, cookbooks, someone's demise, instruction manuals, and so on, and the conditions under which one can become an author of such things are anything but simple. The diversity is even greater if we turn to earlier English usage, including those times when the 'traditional' conception of literary authorship supposedly got constructed and reigned supreme. According to the *Oxford English Dictionary*, both Alexander Pope and William Thackeray would have allowed that one's father could also be called one's author. 'Author' could refer not only to a writer, but to that person's writings. The editor of a periodical was its author. And in another now obsolete usage, 'author' designated the person on whose authority a statement was made, such as an informant.[1]

In light of such diverse usage, if the term 'author' is to serve as a helpful descriptive or explanatory tool in a context of systematic enquiry and scholarly debate, we need a consensus on a more limited and cogent usage. The absence of such a consensus, accompanied at times by a false belief that such a consensus in fact obtains, has fuelled confusion in the theoretical literature on authorship.

An example is the case of Michel Foucault's influential essay on authorship. Many readers of that essay have been surprised to be told that ordinary personal letters (i.e. not those of Madame de Sévigny) have writers, but not authors: 'Une lettre privée peut bien avoir un signataire, elle n'a pas d'auteur;

un contrat peut bien avoir un garant, il n'a pas d'auteur. Un texte anonyme
que l'on lit dans la rue sur un mur aura un rédacteur, il n'aura pas un
auteur.'[2] Yet in everyday French and English, the writer of a letter or contract
is its author. When a French schoolteacher finds an insulting slogan painted
on the wall outside the schoolyard, 'Qui en est l'auteur?' is a question she
may well ask, in spite of Monsieur Foucault's stipulation to the contrary. Yet
it also seems clear that Foucault did not think he was arbitrarily stipulating
a new meaning for 'auteur'; on the contrary, he appears to claim that his
technical usage corresponds to a real phenomenon, the 'author-function' as
constructed in early modern Europe. Foucault hoped to focus attention on
the historical emergence of some particular ways of treating texts, ways
which are not, he claimed, either natural or necessary. He also wanted to
promote some alternative ways of relating to texts. Although these motives
may have been admirable, the flaw in Foucault's strategy is that the initial
conceptual and verbal stipulation in fact vitiates the historical analysis (e.g.
by wrongly stressing discontinuity where continuity is in fact more relevant).
Given the many important counter-examples (ranging from Horace and
Petrarch to Furetière, La Croix du Maine, and Du Verdier), we may conclude
that authorship neither begins nor ends where Foucault says it does.[3]

Where, then, does authorship begin and end? Authorship may be a fuzzy
concept, but it would be helpful to have a better sense of the spectrum
on which it is to be located. What is wanted is a semi-technical notion of
authorship that avoids at least some of the confusion and ambiguity of
ordinary language without merely stipulating a usage that is theoretically
self-serving or historically inaccurate. The failure to find such a notion
makes theoretical debate over authorship in cinema a sterile game. Do we
want to claim that films never have authors? Then let 'author' refer to the
unmoved mover who is alone responsible for every property a film has, and
it follows that no film has an author. Do we want to claim that films always
have authors? Then let 'author' refer to anyone who plays any sort of causal
role in endowing a film with any of its properties, and the authors of any
given film become as numerous as the figures in a medieval master's picture
of the Last Judgement.

As an attempted remedy to this situation, I shall sketch a provisional
definition of 'author' as a term of art in critical enquiry. This definition is
meant to occupy the middle ground between the two extremes just evoked,
and should help set the stage for an exploration of authorship in the cinema.
Consider, then, the following very broad (but not the broadest possible[4])
construction:

author = (def) the agent (or agents) who intentionally make(s) an utterance, where 'utterance' refers to any action, an intended function of
which is expression or communication.

Such a definition is inscribed within, and relies upon, a very widespread and commonplace schema of agency and communication, the philosophical analysis of which is a well-developed yet ongoing project.[5] Some remarks on this definition's basic rationale are nonetheless in order. According to this broad definition, anything that is not an agent, that is, anything that is not capable of action, cannot be an author. For an action to occur, a system's (e.g. an organism's) behaviour must be oriented and proximally caused by that system's meaningful attitudes, such as its desires, beliefs, and intentions. Thus, if a computer is not capable of genuine action because it literally has no meaningful attitudes, then it cannot be an author, even though some of the configurations on its monitor are highly meaningful for some interpreter. The same would be true of the meaningful noises made by a parrot, as long as the bird does not intend to express or convey any attitudes by means of its sentence-like squawks. Expression, which is a matter of articulating or manifesting one's attitudes in some medium, need not be sincere, original, or even skilful for an instance of authorship to occur, but authorship does entail that the expressive utterance is an intentional action.[6] We are not, then, the authors of our dreams or of things muttered in our sleep, because these are not utterances.[7] Communication differs from simple expression in that the agent not only intends to make an attitude manifest, but tries to get this attitude, as well as the relevant intentions, recognized by some audience in the right sort of way. In saying that expression or communication is *an* intended function of an utterance, we allow that the author can act on other kinds of intentions when making an utterance. For example, a speaker can simultaneously intend to make his belief known while also hoping to impress his hearers with a display of eloquence. Note as well that the broad definition allows that more than one agent could be the maker of a single utterance: an utterance can have a collective author. For example, John and Mary jointly draft a letter, or make a video, to send holiday greetings and news to their parents. Finally, it should be pointed out that utterances need not be linguistic: 'utterance' is meant to designate any number of different expressive or communicative actions *or products thereof*, assuming that such products (e.g. objects or artefacts) are identified with reference to the relevant features of their context of production.[8] In the Daimonji Gozan Okuribi festival held in August in Kyoto, huge fires outlining Kanji characters blaze on the slopes of five mountains surrounding the city. The intentional burning of these rather large, fiery words constitutes an utterance following the proposed definition. Fires of the same size and shape accidentally caused by a stroke of lightning would not.

The broad definition of 'author' just surveyed allows that most people are authors a lot of the time simply by virtue of performing unremarkable expressive and communicative actions. The intuitive basis of this approach is simple and, I think, provides good reasons for preferring this definition over other possible ones. We want to be in a position to say, for example, that some of our intentional doings are not a matter of authorship because there is no expressive intent behind them. Utterances, however, belong to a different category. And it makes sense to think that one is the author of one's utterances, even when they are a matter of the most ritualized morning greetings, because one exercises a significant degree of direct control over such behaviour and because one is, as the proximate causal source of that behaviour, in some sense responsible for it. Saying something at what one deems to be an appropriate moment, as opposed to saying some other phrase or nothing at all, is normally something one does on purpose, even if this action does not result directly from an episode of careful, conscious deliberation; to perform such an action intentionally, it is necessary to activate one's linguistic and social know-how. But to be the author of a particular utterance of 'Good morning' addressed to one's co-workers, one need not have invented the phrase or the social practice it fulfils. The broad usage of 'author' I have identified belongs, then, to a pragmatic framework in which the term is used to pick out the agent or agents who function as the proximate cause of utterances conceived of as intentional, expressive actions. Such a pragmatic framework can, of course, be the subject of sceptical doubts and eliminitivist counter-proposals, but it nonetheless remains a deeply entrenched, valuable, and arguably indispensable schema of interaction. It is, moreover, a schema that we frequently apply in discussions of the arts.[9]

In spite of such considerations in favour of a broad notion of authorship, some critics and theorists promote a narrower definition, such as one having nothing to do with utterances, or one restricted to some subset of utterances, such as literary (and other) works of art. The danger with this kind of approach, however, is that such stipulations appear implausible in the light of obvious counter-examples. It is arbitrary and purely stipulative to say that banal, non-artistic utterances have no authors, or to claim that great literary works have authors while pieces of pulp fiction do not. Another problem with such stipulations is that some strong version of aesthetic or hermeneutic intentionalism is built into the very definitions of 'utterance' and 'authorship'. Thus something's being an utterance is deemed equivalent to its having a meaning entirely determined by its author, and to be an author is held to be equivalent to the determination of an utterance's meaning.[10] Others, who oppose this sort of intentionalism, accept that this kind of strong or absolute intentionalism is entailed by authorship, and they deem it important to attack authorship as part of their opposition to that doctrine. It is crucial to see, however, that the cogency of such attacks depends entirely on the soundness of the prior assumption whereby authorship entails some form of overly strong intentionalist constraint on interpretation. If one recognizes that an utterance can be both intentionally produced by someone and have meanings that are not all and only those intended by that person, then it follows that strong intentionalism is not entailed by a broad conception of authorship. We can identify someone as the author of an utterance without having to say that that person has authored each and every meaning (or significance) that the utterance manifests.

Even if my objections to some of the alternatives are granted, it should be recognized that the broad definition just sketched hardly answers all of our questions about authorship. One may argue, for example, that while such a notion is cogent, it does not follow that literary and non-literary conceptions of authorship do not differ fundamentally. And it is the latter, and not the former, that provides the object of Foucauldian and other critiques. Do not the very conditions of *literary* authorship involve social factors that transcend the schemata of individualist pragmatics? An analogous argument focusing on the case of cinema will be taken up in the next section.

2. WHAT IS A CINEMATIC AUTHOR?

A first step in a straightforward approach to the definition of cinematic authorship is to adopt the broad notion of authorship proposed above while replacing 'utterance' with 'cinematic utterance'. One could add that, roughly speaking, an utterance is a cinematic one just in case the agent or agents who produce it employ photographic (and other) means in order to create an apparently moving image projected on a screen (or other surface).[11] Yet even if we assume that this is essentially the right approach to establishing the boundary between utterances in general and cinematic utterances, we must still address ourselves to a serious challenge, which runs as follows. Although the film medium is sometimes employed in ways covered by an everyday pragmatic notion of authorship, the cinema as a large-scale social phenomenon (e.g. the cinema *qua* institution or group of interrelated institutions and social systems) transcends that notion. It is one thing to speak of some individual being the author of the home movie he sent to his parents on the occasion of his father's birthday, but something else entirely to think of Fred Zinnemann or his collaborators as the author(s) of *High Noon* (a Stanley Kramer production that premiered in 1952). Not only does the actual nature of the process of production differ fundamentally in these two kinds of cases, but facts about the distribution and reception of the two utterances make it incorrect to apply the same conception of authorship to them. It is far from obvious how the idea of 'intentionally making an utterance' is to be applied in the case of a film to which many different people have made a number of significantly different contributions. Is Ned Washington, who wrote the lyrics for the ballad heard on the soundtrack, one of the authors of *High Noon*? Can or should an audience react to a Hollywood film the same way that the father responds to the home movie made by his son, that is, with many features of the author's context, character, aims, and activities in mind? The claim, then, is that the making and reception of commercially produced, feature-length films is complex in ways that are obscured by an everyday notion of expressive and communicative action, and thus a concept of authorship based on the latter is seriously misleading with regard to such works, which is what happens when one insists, for example, on thinking of the director as the author of the film.

In response to such an argument, it is important to note that the director is not always the author of an industrially produced motion picture. Only sometimes does a director's role in the productive process warrant the idea that he or she is the film's author. It may be useful to add that some industrially produced films are not accurately viewed as utterances having an author or authors because it is possible that no one person or group of persons intentionally produced the work as a whole by acting on any expressive or communicative intentions. The film may be the unintended result of disparate intentional and unintentional activities, in roughly the same way a traffic jam is the unintended and unwanted 'perverse effect' of many individual drivers' purposeful and accidental behaviour. The same, however, could be said of some small-scale, non-industrial cinematic arte-facts, such as ill-begotten and accidental stretches of 'home movie'. The live issue, then, is not whether all films necessarily do or do not have authors in the broad sense introduced above, for it seems clear that they do not. The question, rather, is whether the kind of authorship we have in mind is absent in *all* (or even many) mass-produced commercial films.

As David Bordwell and Kristin Thompson put it, 'The question of author-ship becomes difficult to answer only when asked about studio production', or more generally, about what they refer to as 'serial manufacture'.[12] Serial manufacture as they describe it is a process that resembles mass manufac-ture on an assembly line because it has a similar hierarchical division of labour. The difference, however, is that the final product is not a replica of a single prototype, but in some sense a unique film, even when it is a derivative instance of a familiar genre. In this mode of production, special-ists with a striking variety of skills and tasks collaborate to create a unique final product. Amongst these specialists are figures who exercise control and provide guidance in function of a more or less schematic overall plan, which may or may not be known to the other contributors. Under what conditions does the product of serial manufacture have an author or authors, and what are the distinguishing features of authorship in such a context? In order to develop and illustrate my response, I shall sketch some 'ideal-typical' examples. I shall begin with a case of a serially manufactured film that has no author.

Case One: An Authorless Film

A rich and famous actor—we'll just call him KK—has a rather 'watery' idea for a film. Acting as both producer and star, KK invests his personal fortune and gets additional financial backing from various sources. It is agreed that KK will be entrusted with artistic control of the project. KK has no talent as a writer. Armed with his kernel idea for a story, he hires three scriptwriters and four script doctors in succession. The script that results from these writers' separate efforts is changed many times during an expensive and chaotic shoot in Hawaii. A first, very talented director who works on the film is fired and replaced when he and KK quarrel. While KK is away doing something else, another team of people start editing the resulting footage into a feature-length film. When the audience at a preview reacts negatively, KK panics and hires someone else to make a number of substantial cuts. KK does not say what those cuts should be, but merely enjoins the editor to 'fix it'. KK is unhappy with the rather incoherent and artistically flawed results, but the production has by now gone way over budget. KK meets with his backers and there is bitter disagreement about what to do. KK wants them to invest more money, but the other backers deem it best to cut their losses. A group of them finally team up to take control; they buy KK out and hire a new director to shoot some additional scenes and supervise the making of a final cut, which is what gets released commercially. A successful ad campaign attracts large audiences to see the result.

Although he had a lot to do with its production and appears throughout the film in the lead role, KK is not the work's author. After all, his contributions to the process of production ended long before the final cut was made. But the project's other financial backers are not the film's authors either. Nor are any of the different writers, directors, or technicians who have worked on the project. The film certainly has makers—lots of them—but no author. Why not? What aspect of authorship is missing from such a case? Bordwell and Thompson point out that authorship is often defined in terms of control and decision-making, and intuitively one wants to say that the project in Case One has got 'out of control'.[13] This seems right, but 'control' can mean many different things in such a context—from the ability to perform certain tasks in a skilled manner, to having and exercising some kind of social authority (such as legal ownership or some form of institutionally grounded power to get others to act on one's instructions). KK, who looks like the closest candidate for authorship in Case One, both has and lacks control in several senses of the word. KK, after all, has the initial idea for the film and acts on it, prompting and guiding other people's efforts to that end. Initially he controls the making of the film in the sense that he has the power to make such relevant decisions as the hiring, firing, and supervision of artists and technicians. When he accepts his partners' offer for a buyout, he agrees to abandon his involvement in, and rights over, the project in exchange for a part of his initial investment. Henceforth he enjoys no decision-making power or control.

Does the exercise of some sort of uninterrupted control, in the sense of the authority to make binding decisions, suffice to constitute cinematic authorship? Not at all, as the following example is designed to show.

Case Two: Authority without Authorship

Big John has made an immense amount of money trading in livestock and decides to invest some of it in the entertainment industry. He hires a producer and director and enjoins them to collaborate on the making of some sort of film, but because he wants to keep an eye on his investment, he stipulates that they must regularly submit their plans and results to him for his approval. This they do, and Big John soon realizes that he has a very poor understanding of this business. Again and again, he finds that he has no informed preferences concerning the decisions that need to be made, starting with the choice of genre and basic story idea. Yet his pride prevents him from admitting this to his employees, so he pretends to engage in careful deliberations before he tells them what to do. Often he simply approves the ideas they submit to him, but sometimes he has to choose between several proposed options, and on many occasions he must settle disagreements between his producer and director, who have strikingly different visions of the film they are making. Big John secretly makes all such decisions by flipping coins. So when the film has been made, Big John has effectively exercised an unchallenged decision-making authority throughout the project, and his random choices have had a significant impact on the work's nature. As luck would have it, the director and producer each get their way about half the time. Neither of them is the film's author, it would seem, but nor is Big John.

Why isn't Big John's decision-making constitutive of authorship? To answer this question, we must return to our basic pragmatic assumptions. Being an author, I have claimed, is intentionally making an utterance, and an utterance is an expressive (and perhaps also a communicative) action, that is, one in which some agent (or agents) intends to make manifest some meaningful attitudes (such as beliefs and emotions). To make an attitude manifest is to do or make something, the cognition of which is likely, under the right conditions, to bring that attitude to mind. For example, Giacomo Leopardi arguably had a number of complex thoughts and feelings in mind when he wrote 'La ginestra', and he intended to fashion this poem so that at least some readers would experience similar emotions and ideas as a result of reading and thinking about it.[14] The attitudes that an author intends to make manifest in an utterance need not, of course, be ones that the agent sincerely holds or feels. In making an utterance, an author acts on an expressive intention, the content of which is a representation of some attitude(s) to be made manifest and of a means of so doing. The content of an intention can be referred to as a 'plan', and in this sense, following a plan—even a very schematic one that subsequently gets fleshed out and altered—is a necessary (but not a sufficient) condition of all intentional action, including the 'authoring' of any utterance.[15] This condition should not be misconstrued as requiring authors to have a perfect mental image of the final utterance in mind, prior to the beginning of the productive process. What the condition does require is that an author have at least a schematic idea of some of the attitudes he or she aims to make manifest in the utterance, as well as an idea of the processes by means of which this utterance is to be realized.

Returning now to the case of cinematic utterances, we may add that the expressive action constitutive of authorship must be performed through the making of an apparently moving image projected on a screen or other surface, which typically requires the production of what we can refer to as a cinematic text (roughly, the final cut or negative of which multiple positive, projectable prints can be made). This cinematic text is the principal means by which some agent intends to make some specific attitudes manifest. In straightforward cases of individual or independent cinematic production, cinematic authorship is a matter of an individual's making such a text as a means to realizing an expressive intention. In the case of serial manufacture, authorship involves not only making such a text oneself, but enlisting the aid of others in making one. A partial analysis of cinematic authorship, then, runs as follows:

> Cinematic author = the agent or agent(s) who intentionally make(s) a cinematic utterance; where cinematic utterance = an action the intended function of which is to make manifest or communicate some attitude(s) by means of the production of an apparently moving image projected on a screen or other surface.

Does Big John in Case Two satisfy these conditions? It is true that a cinematic text gets made, largely as a result of John's action, but it is far less clear that Big John has made an utterance. He does intend to pay to have a film made, and he also intends to exercise a high degree of control over the process of its making. He is the one who makes key decisions, accepting or rejecting the results of decisions made by others. At no point, however, does Big John have any specific attitudes in mind that he intends the cinematic text to make manifest, and when he makes decisions that are relevant to which attitudes the film is likely to make manifest, he acts at random. Big John may very well act on the intention that the film be expressive of attitudes—that is, of some attitudes as opposed to none at all—but he has no plans or aims concerning which attitudes these should be. He does not even act on the paradoxical modernist intention of having his film express his supreme indifference concerning the attitudes his work will make manifest. To make an utterance, one must act on one's plan concerning the attitudes being expressed, which is what Big John fails to do.

Big John is not the author; but what about his producer and director? Theirs is not a case of joint authorship because they have incompatible intentions with regard to the nature of the utterance they are involved in making, and only Big John's random edicts settle their struggle for control.[16] Nor is either of them, taken separately, the film's author. One cannot intentionally make a cinematic utterance unless one makes the cinematic text, and one is not the overall maker of a cinematic text unless one fulfils a particular kind of role in the productive process. What is that role? In cases of serial manufacture, a film's author does not do everything that has to be done for the text to be made, but when the author delegates tasks, he or she does have to have final say over which fruits of other people's labour do and do not get incorporated into the final work. When, during the editing of the film, Big John overrules one of his director's proposals and accepts the producer's idea, the director no longer functions as the film's author. But with the next toss of the coin, the same holds for the producer. So Case two is another instance where there are makers but no authors.[17]

It may be objected here that 'having final say' is somewhat vague, and that an author's authority is not exercised in a vacuum. An author's effective decisions are in many ways constrained by other agents' preferences and actions—or at least by what the author believes them to be. Thinking that the star will be furious and therefore impossible to work with if a certain scene is eliminated, the director decides to include it because he thinks this is the lesser evil. Anticipating the censor's action, the director cuts out an entire sequence. Imagining (quite wrongly) that the audience will require comic relief, the director includes such a sequence. In spite of the external constraints—real or imagined—all such decisions are authorial decisions.

There are, however, cases involving situations where the interpersonal influence is of a different sort. I have in mind cases where a decision relative to an utterance's expressive content is ordained by someone who wields the requisite power (e.g. legal or institutional power) to issue a well-founded ultimatum to the text's maker(s): either you do it, or you are fired and someone else will. 'Well-founded' in this context means simply that the person who makes this threat both has the power to act on it successfully and fully intends to do so if the antecedent condition is not satisfied. Whence another case to be considered.

Case Three: Taking Orders

Jeanne, a talented young film student who has written an ambitious script, meets an encouraging and generous producer. He helps her get the backing she needs for a pet project and appears to offer her the opportunity to make the film she wants to make. With the help of a cooperative and talented crew, she gets all the footage she thinks she needs. But the trouble starts when the producer gets a look at a rough cut. 'This will never sell', he tells her, and he issues an ultimatum: either she cuts out a long, central sequence he finds too difficult for a popular audience, or she will be fired and someone else will finish the film following his plan. A talk with the lawyers convinces her that these are in fact her only two options, and after due reflection, she capitulates. By giving in, she keeps her name in the credits and appears as the film's director. But is she the work's author?

One's judgement concerning such a case is likely to vary in function of the expressive significance of the changes that Jeanne has made in compliance with the producer's ultimatum. Jeanne has chosen to go ahead and make the film under these coercive conditions, so the expressive action of making the film is still hers, but aspects of the film's content are not of her choosing. Whether the global fact of authorship is vitiated as a result depends on the extent to which Jeanne's expressive intentions have been realized. One can readily imagine cases at either end of the spectrum, as well as difficult, borderline examples. It may be best, then, to think of global authorship of a work as a matter of degree. To the extent that the decision the producer imposes on Jeanne is not destructive of her plan for the film, she remains the work's author, even though she has complied to someone else's orders. In a case where her key ideas are sacrificed, Jeanne is hardly, or just barely, the work's author. But a director who has no choice but to accept relatively minor cuts thought of by a producer remains the work's author to a large degree.[18]

Authorship in a context of serial manufacture may usually be a matter of degree, but it need not always be so. I shall now evoke a case of successful individual authorship in such a context.

Case Four: Authorship in the Studio

Many aspects of the making of Ingmar Bergman's 1962 film *Winter Light* are vividly described by Vilgot Sjöman in his book on the subject.[19] Although this was not a Hollywood mega-production, it was not an instance of independent film-making either, for Bergman was working squarely within the Swedish Film Industry's studio system. Yet the division of labour in that context was influenced by Bergman's very special talents and powers. Bergman wrote his own script, did some of the casting, directed the actors, supervised the editing and the sound-mixing, and worked closely with his cinematographer. Bergman also exercised a high degree of control over the choice of locations, props, make-up, and many other technical matters. At no point during the production process did any producer or other figure coercively require him to reverse an artistic decision he had made (although he did often accept other people's advice about possible changes). We are wholly warranted, then, in characterizing him as the author of the work, even though we know that he did not personally create or think up everything that can be seen in the film. For example, when we hear bits of J. S. Bach's music in a Bergman film, we know that Bergman did not compose or perform this music, but we can still recognize him as the author of the film as a whole, as well as of this particular utilization of music in film. He has made the decision about whether to use music at all, and where to put it in the film. He has chosen a particular part of a musical composition, as well as a particular performance of this music, and such decisions function as a significant instance of artistic expression in the overall film (e.g. by conveying Bergman's romantic ideas about the ethical status of some pieces of music).

Bergman, then, is the author of *Winter Light*. He initiated and guided its making, skilfully engaging in many of the diverse tasks involved, while supervising and exercising control over the activities of his collaborators. It is important to add that although Bergman enjoyed a huge measure of authority while making the film, he worked very hard to solicit a collaborative dialogue with his co-workers. For example, part of Bergman's special talent as a cinematic author derives from his ability to help his actors and actresses give remarkable performances. Unlike many film directors, Bergman read through the script together with the performers, analysing and discussing every line in an effort to arrive at a shared understanding of the story and characterizations. In Sjöman's image, Bergman resembled a foreman who showed the building plans to his co-workers, asking for suggestions for changes, and hoping to make sure they grasped the overall plan. The foreman image is apt because it underscores both Bergman's high degree of involvement in the making of the work as well as the help he got from others, but it also depicts him as the ultimate author of the work as a whole.

3. REAL AND UNREAL AUTHORS

So far I have considered authorship as an activity of actual agents. In so far as an interpretation makes claims about authorship, it can be false. There is, however, a rival conception (or family of conceptions) regarding the relation between interpretation and authorship. Following this anti-realist line, interpreters of a film should construct an image of the work's author without being guided by evidence concerning actual processes of production. The interpreter still frames ideas about the attitudes expressed in the work, but does so without asking whether those attitudes were in fact intentionally made manifest by anyone. Instead, the interpreter simply pretends or makes believe that the attitudes expressed in the text were expressed by someone. The make-believe persona that emerges from this sort of interpretative process is referred to variously as the 'real', 'fictional', 'implied', or 'postulated' author.

I find this model of interpretation unattractive, but cannot review here the complex debate between realist and anti-realist approaches to authorship. Instead I shall focus primarily on issues pertaining specifically to the cinema.[20] Two reasons are often given why the cinema is supposed to be especially suited to an anti-realist notion of authorship: (1) an ontological one having to do with the complex nature of cinematic production; and (2) an epistemological one having to do with the difficulty or impossibility of acquiring sufficient evidence about a film's making.

Is it the very nature of film-making that helps warrant the adoption of authorial anti-realism? I think not. Film production is not always qualitatively more complex—or less authorial—than work in other media, so the interpreter must decide, on a case-by-case basis, whether a film has or has not been made in a way that involves individual or collective authorship or some other sort of process. Such a decision requires reference to the evidence concerning real authorship. In cases where it is discovered that individual authorship obtains, why should the interpreter pretend or make believe that the attitudes expressed are those of an author? If I genuinely believe, for example, that Bergman was the author of *Winter Light*, why should I pretend to attribute the film's expressive qualities to the activity of a non-existent, but all-too-Bergmanian, author-surrogate? If, on the other hand, the interpreter discovers that neither collective nor individual authorship obtained, why should we continue to think of the text's expressive qualities as the intended results of an author's activities? An unauthored film can, like a traffic jam or a randomly generated computer message, display various properties that I can dislike or enjoy without having to attribute them to an imaginary maker. So in neither the case of an authored nor an unauthored film does the adoption of a fictional idea of authorship find any special warrant in the specific nature of cinematic authorship.

With regard to the epistemological claim, it is again misleading to suppose that the cinematic medium, or any specific mode of cinematic production, is especially suited to an anti-realist approach to authorship. The evidentiary difficulties surrounding our access to cinematic authorship are not always insurmountable; sometimes the evidence supports reasonable—but of course fallible—inferences about events involved in a work's making.

It is true that often we cannot get all of the evidence we would like to have, and it is logically possible that all of the evidence we do have is misleading. But that is, unfortunately, a familiar truth about all historical knowledge.

A more plausible anti-realist line runs as follows. For various practical reasons, most film spectators simply do not know what went on during the making of the film they are viewing, yet the interpretative process requires them to attribute attitudes and implicit meanings to someone's expressive activity. It would in many cases be a factual error for such viewers to assume that the expressed attitudes were those of the text's real maker(s), so it is best for them simply to make believe that the attitudes expressed are those of a fictional author. Such make-believe cannot be wrong, because it is just a fiction that enhances the viewer's appreciation of the film.

In response, one may argue that knowing about a work of art's production tends to enhance insight and appreciation. To hold that such knowledge is unnecessary or undesirable because it is often unattainable looks like a case of 'sour grapes'. Why not recognize that such knowledge is always desirable, but sometimes out of reach? What is more, we may wonder how the spectator can form an adequate make-believe image of authorship in the absence of evidence about the real author's situation, skills, and activities. Under what conditions would such a spectator be able to make believe that a film had no author, but emerged from a chaotic process involving various people's activities? Textual appearances, which are the anti-realist's sole basis, can be deceptive: a cinematic text that emerges from a chaotic and uncoordinated production could look as though it has been made by a single author, and a work crafted by a single (or collective) author could look like something emerging from an uncontrolled or highly conflictual process. The spectator who fashions a make-believe author on the basis of textual evidence alone is blind to the difference, and can only work with a default assumption favouring authorial control. I contend, on the contrary, that spectators and scholars alike ought to be attuned to such differences in histories of production. In short, critical insight, appreciation, and explanation are better served by an interpretative principle according to which it is the viewer's and critic's goal to arrive at interpretations which match, as opposed to diverge from, the work's features, including those involving its causal history.

NOTES

1. Cognate terms in other languages (e.g. the French *auteur*) are also used in such disparate ways, but I shall not document this claim here.
2. Michel Foucault, 'Qu'est-ce qu'un auteur?' in *Dits et écrits 1954–1988*, ed. Daniel Defert and François Ewald (Paris: Gallimard, 1994), 789–821; citation, p. 798. The

published English translations of this essay are unreliable (e.g. one of Foucault's own footnotes is presented as a translator's comment), and were based on a talk given in the United States, which diverged in interesting ways from the initial French lecture of 1969. I translate the cited passage as follows: 'A personal letter may well be signed by someone, but it still has no author; a contract may have a guarantor, but it has no author. An anonymous text that one reads on a wall when walking down the street will have a writer, but it will not have an author.'

3. The literature on Foucault's historical inaccuracies is quite large. With specific reference to his claims about the author-function, it is instructive to consult the following: Roger Chartier, *L'Ordre des livres: lecteurs, auteurs, bibliothèques en Europe entre le XIVe et XVIIIe siècle* (Paris: Alinéa, 1992), 35–67; Denis Dutton, 'Why Intentionalism Won't Go Away', in Anthony J. Cascardi (ed.), *Literature and the Question of Philosophy* (Baltimore: Johns Hopkins University Press, 1987), 194–209; M. H. Abrams, 'What is a Humanistic Criticism?', in Dwight Eddins (ed.), *The Emperor Redressed: Critiquing Critical Theory* (Tuscaloosa: University of Alabama Press, 1995), 13–44.

4. For a broader notion of authorship of cinematic works, see Berys Gaut's contribution to this volume.

5. I survey a range of topics related to agency and literature in *Literature and Rationality: Ideas of Agency in Theory and Fiction* (Cambridge: Cambridge University Press, 1991). For some background on pragmatic and action-theoretical assumptions, see Paul Grice, *Studies in the Way of Words* (Cambridge, Mass.: Harvard University Press, 1989); Stephen C. Levinson, *Pragmatics* (Cambridge: Cambridge University Press, 1983); François Recanati, *Meaning and Force: The Pragmatics of Performative Utterances* (Cambridge: Cambridge University Press, 1987); Dan Sperber and Deirdre Wilson, *Relevance: Communication and Cognition*, 2nd edn. (Oxford: Blackwell, 1995); Alfred R. Mele, *Springs of Action: Understanding Intentional Behaviour* (New York: Oxford University Press, 1992), and *Autonomous Agents: From Self-Control to Autonomy* (New York: Oxford University Press, 1995).

6. For an analysis of intentional action, see Alfred R. Mele and Paul K. Moser, 'Intentional Action', *Noûs*, 28 (1994), 39–68.

7. Freudians are likely to disagree with this move, but I shall not enter into the tired debate surrounding the soundness of this or that psychoanalytic doctrine. Suffice it to say that dreaming and talking in one's sleep are behaviours devoid of the kinds of planning, deliberation, choice, and effort that accompany successful authorship of even the most banal sort, such as writing a legible and cogent letter to a friend. It is perhaps significant that psychoanalytic discussions of the arts have largely abandoned Freud's interest in creativity and authorship in favour of a one-sided emphasis on the consumer's more passive activity. One reason for this shift in emphasis may be that watching a movie seems analogous to dreaming in ways that using cinematic technology does not.

8. In this regard, utterances are like works. For background, see Jerrold Levinson, *Music, Art, and Metaphysics: Essays in Philosophical Aesthetics* (Ithaca, NY: Cornell University Press, 1990); Gregory Currie, *An Ontology of Art* (New York: St Martin's, 1989); and Levinson's review of the latter in *Philosophy and Phenomenological Research*, 52 (1992), 215–22.

9. For arguments supporting this thesis, see Noël Carroll, 'Art, Intention, and Conversation', in Gary Iseminger (ed.), *Intention and Interpretation* (Philadelphia: Temple University Press, 1992), 97–131.

10. For a straightforward example of this sort of view, see Stanley Fish, 'Biography and Intention', in William H. Epstein (ed.), *Contesting the Subject: Essays in the Postmodern Theory and Practice of Biography and Biographical Criticism* (West Lafayette, Ind.: Purdue University Press, 1991), 9–16. For criticisms of Fish, see

Alfred R. Mele and Paisley Livingston, 'Intentions and Interpretations', *Modern Language Notes*, 107 (1992), 931–49, and George M. Wilson, 'Again Theory: On Speaker's Meaning, Linguistic Meaning, and the Meaning of a Text', in Mette Hjort (ed.), *Rules and Conventions: Literature, Philosophy, Social Theory* (Baltimore: Johns Hopkins University Press, 1992), 1–31.

11. Here I follow Gregory Currie, who similarly declines to deal with verbal (and other) issues related to filmic utterances' relation to television and other possible, related media. See his *Image and Mind: Film, Philosophy, and Cognitive Science* (Cambridge: Cambridge University Press, 1995), 1–16.

12. David Bordwell and Kristin Thompson, *Film Art: An Introduction*, 4th edn. (New York: McGraw-Hill, 1993), 30.

13. Ibid.

14. My argument does not depend on this specific example. For background, however, see John Alcorn and Dario Del Puppo, 'Giacomo Leopardi's "*La Ginestra*" as Social Art', *Modern Language Review*, 89 (1994), 865–88.

15. For background, see Mele and Moser, 'Intentional Action'. Requiring that an agent's A-ing can only be an instance of intentionally A-ing if the agent follows a plan rules out cases of causal deviance and specifies that the content of the relevant attitudes (such as the agent's intention) plays the right sort of role in generating the action. Mele and Moser's thorough analysis also includes clauses ruling out cases where an action is not intentional because its successful realization of the intended state of affairs involves too large an element of luck, or an overly inaccurate understanding of the processes involved.

16. The director and producer do share some intentions, but not the ones necessary for an intentional production of a joint utterance, i.e. those relative to the work's expressive content. For background on shared intention, see Michael E. Bratman, 'Shared Intention', *Ethics*, 104 (1993), 97–113.

17. Nor would I speak of 'multiple authorship' here, unless we follow Jack Stillinger in using that term to refer to cases where more than one agent fashions a text in the absence of any agreement or shared plan. See his *Multiple Authorship and the Myth of Solitary Genius* (New York: Oxford University Press, 1991). For his discussion of cinema, see pp. 174–81. Stillinger rightly suggests that authorship is often dispersed in the industrial process of production, but I cannot agree with his empirically dubious conclusion that 'the idea of director as sole author will not hold up under scrutiny; it is simply not possible for one person, however brilliant, to provide the entire creative force behind so complex a work as a motion picture', p. 179.

18. And as Murray Smith usefully suggests, there is a spectrum of external constraints, at one end of which we find the strongest forms of coercion.

19. Vilgot Sjöman, *Dagbok med Ingmar Bergman* (Stockholm: Norstedts, 1963).

20. For excellent treatments of the topic, see Berys Gaut (this volume) and Robert Stecker, 'Apparent, Implied, and Postulated Authors', *Philosophy and Literature*, 11 (1987), 258–71. I discuss a number of relevant anti-intentionalist arguments in my 'Characterization and Fictional Truth in the Cinema', in David Bordwell and Noël Carroll (eds.), *Post-Theory: Reconstructing Film Studies* (Madison: University of Wisconsin Press, 1996), 149–74.

6

Film Authorship and Collaboration

Berys Gaut

1. TWO PUZZLES

The notion that certain films are authored is one of the most powerful and
pervasive views in current thinking about cinema. The enthusiast, who
looks forward to the film he thinks of as the new 'Scorsese', 'Allen',
'Rohmer', or 'Tarantino', is paying homage to the idea of the director-as-
author. Rooted in the writings of Truffaut and other French critics in the
1950s, the view was transplanted to the United States by Andrew Sarris in
the early 1960s, and dubbed by him 'the auteur theory'. The figure of the
film author, sometimes supposed to have been engulfed by the tides of
semiotics and post-structuralism which swept over film studies in the 1970s,
yet managed to survive, bobbing up again not as an actual person but as a
constructed entity. As Bordwell and Thompson note, the notion of director-
as-author, 'remains probably the most widely shared assumption in film
studies today'.[1]

Yet the notion of film authorship—so appealing to lay intuition and
scholarly understanding alike—is oddly mysterious and deeply elusive. It
has been held that the film author is the director, the screenwriter, the star,
or the studio; that the film author is an actual individual, or a critical
construct; that there is not one film author, but several; the claim of film
authorship has been held primarily as an evaluative one, or an interpretative
one, or simply as the view that there are authors of films as there are authors
of literary works. And each of these claims has been challenged, each
challenge producing a new defence or reformulation of the thesis. One
explanation of this state of affairs, this unclarity in formulation but continuing intuitive appeal, is that the variations of the thesis draw on some core
truths for their appeal. Or is a more sceptical conclusion to be drawn: that
there is no truth to be found in the claim of film authorship, its capacity
endlessly to mutate merely allowing it to stay one step ahead of its critics?
That is the first puzzle of authorship.

If, as I shall argue, there is in fact a core truth in the claims of authorship,

I would like to thank Richard Allen, Paisley Livingston, Alex Neill, and Murray Smith for
their helpful comments on this chapter.

then we face the question of whether any more substantial claims can be added to it. The most fruitful way to answer this question is by addressing a second puzzle. The dominant view of authorship has been that many films have a single author, usually held to be the director. Yet it is a commonplace that most films are highly collaborative, and collaborative in ways that affect their artistic properties: actors, screenwriters, producers, cinematographers, all leave their marks on the way a film looks and sounds. Yet how can there be a single author if there are very many artists involved in film production? How can a film be like a novel where always in principle there could be and usually in fact is a single author? Various strategies have been developed by auteurists to show how this is possible: it will be shown that they all fail. Films we must acknowledge to have multiple authors. The resulting, more substantive authorship theses are, I will show, more theoretically sound and more critically fruitful than the dominant view of single authorship. And the notion of multiple authorship will give us reason to question the literary paradigm that still dominates film studies.

2. VARIETIES OF AUTEURISM

To begin, we need to regiment the gaggle of claims constituting auteurism. Any adequate taxonomy of authorial claims must distinguish at least five dimensions on which they can vary:

1. *The kind of claim.* (*a*) An *existential* claim: when Truffaut made his claims on behalf of the film author, he contrasted the *auteur* with the *metteur en scène*, who merely adds the pictures to a literary text without adding any significantly new dimension of meaning to it. His aims were polemical: to show that there are film artists in the way that there are literary artists.[2] So we can make an existential claim: film artists exist. More particularly, this should be understood to require that certain films are the products of film artists. (*b*) A *hermeneutic* claim formulates the most general claim of auteurist criticism, the kind of criticism that interprets films by construing them as products of their makers (usually taken by such critics to be the director): to interpret a film requires understanding what its maker(s) did. Some more specific versions of this hold that it is the makers' intentions that are relevant to understanding the films, while others deny intentionalism.[3] (*c*) An *evaluative* claim: early auteurists, pre-eminently Andrew Sarris, were concerned largely with the problem of the evaluation of films, which Sarris construed in terms of a 'pantheon' of directors.[4] Such an auteurist might hold that a good film is the product of a good director. But it is under dispute whether there are one or several film artists per film (dimension 5) and also who occupies these role or roles (dimension 4). Moreover, auteurists ought to acknowledge the possibility that a group of

untalented film-makers might inadvertently produce a masterpiece.[5] So the most general version of the evaluative claim would hold that a good film is typically the product of good film-maker(s). Under this general doctrine we can distinguish many variations. For instance, there are different theories about how the film artist makes his film good: either in terms of an expression of his distinctive personality, or in terms of the overthrow of established codes and ways of looking so as to open up new ways of reading and seeing.[6] Clearly, these three kinds of authorial claims—existential, hermeneutic, and evaluative—can consistently be held together.

2. *The ontology of the author.* (*a*) An *actual* person: the kind of entity who is the author was supposed in early auteurism to be an actual individual: John Ford, Jean Renoir, etc. (*b*) A critical *construct*: with the rise of auteur-structuralism in the early 1970s, it came increasingly to be held that the author was a construct, generated by critics in order to grasp and evaluate films better. On this view the critical task is 'to locate an *author of the fiction* who is by no means dispersed but who in "his" notional coherence provides the means for us to grasp the text in the moment of its production before us'.[7] More recent theorists are also often attracted to the picture of the author-as-construct. Stephen Heath writes that 'The author, that is, may return as a *fiction* . . . Grasped thus, the author . . . now becomes part of an activity of writing-reading.'[8]

3. *Authors and artists.* (*a*) *As an artist*: though the literary paradigm was of immense influence on auteurism, early auteurists often did not hold that the author was literally such, i.e. the producer of a *text*. Sarris mentions Shakespeare, Beethoven, and Bach as examples of *auteurs*. On this view, the author is simply an artist.[9] (*b*) *As a (literal) author*: with the rise of interest in semiotics in the 1970s, theorists came increasingly to think of a film as literally a text, for they held that there is a language of film. On this view, the author is literally such.

4. *Occupiers of the authorial role(s).* Theorists have made differing claims over who counts as the author(s) of a film: (*a*) the *director* is favoured by most, including Sarris and Perkins; (*b*) the *screenwriter* by some, e.g. Corliss; (*c*) for some films, the *star* is held by some to be the auteur, e.g. McGilligan and Dyer; (*d*) some theorists favour the *producer* or the studio, e.g. Thomas Schatz.[10] These claims are most naturally construed as being about the author as an actual individual, but their analogues exist for the author as a construct (so one might talk about the implied director, screenwriter, etc.).

5. *The number of authors.* (*a*) *Single authorship*: the dominant view of auteurists appears still to be that there is a single author of a film in most cases (evidently, there will be exceptions where two or more individuals work together very closely, sharing key roles, such as the Coen brothers, or Powell and Pressburger). (*b*) *Multiple authorship*: this view holds that there

are many authors of a film, plausibly occupying some or all of the main production roles (director, screenwriter, actors, cinematographer, composer, etc.), who may or may not be in harmony on the purposes of the production. This view, at least held unambiguously and explicitly, is less common than the claims of single authorship: Richard Dyer seems to hold that it applies to many films.[11]

These five dimensions of variation are logically independent of each other; together a selection of one item from each of them makes up a distinct auteurist thesis.[12] For instance, one can hold that (1a) there is a film author, who is (2a) an actual person, (3b) a literal author, (4a) the director, and (5a) there is just one for a film. Or one can hold that (1a and 5b) there are multiple authors, who (2b) are critical constructs, (3a) are artists rather than literal authors, and (4a–c) are directorial, screenwriter, and star-constructs. Or one can hold that (1b) to understand a film requires understanding what the author did, construing the author as a (5a) single (4a) directorial (2b) construct and (3b) a literal author. Evidently, very many other variations are possible.[13] Within each dimension further subdivisions of options could also be made, some of them already mentioned (e.g. the differences in views over how value is conferred on a film, and the role of intentions in the hermeneutic thesis). Hence the taxonomy could further be refined, but the illustration of the wide variety of authorial claims is sufficient for present purposes.

3. MINIMAL AUTEURISM

This recipe for making up one's own authorial theses, even with the fairly basic ingredients on offer, gives succour to the sceptic who alleges that auteurism is a sham. This sceptic thinks auteurism is so diverse that it escapes criticism simply by changing its formulation: when criticized, a new theory is offered in the place of the old discredited version, a new theory that will in turn eventually be disproved. For the sceptic, the dominance of authorial views is simply a by-product of the fact that they have no fixity. But, contrary to the sceptic, there are some true auteurist theses. Consider the following argument:

   (i) Some films are works of art.
  (ii) Some of these films are non-accidental products of their makers.
 (iii) Non-accidental products that are works of art are products of artists.
  (iv) So, some films are products of film artists.
   (v) So, there are film artists.

The conclusion gives us a version of the existential claim (1), holding for actual authors (2), but underdetermined with respect to formulations of 3,

4, and 5—the artist might in addition be a literal author (if a film is a text), the role or roles occupied are unspecified, and it is open whether there are one or more makers of a film.

This argument—the argument for the *minimal existential claim*—is sound. (i) Some films are works of art: *The Rules of the Game, Rashomon,* and *Pulp Fiction,* for instance, are clear examples of works of art. (ii) The makers of these and many other films did not make them accidentally, but knew what they were doing (as witnessed by their abilities to make other good films, for instance). (iii) It is sufficient to be an artist that one produce a work of art, though not accidentally (someone might fluke a masterpiece, and one might therefore deny that he is an artist).[14] So (iv) those films that are works of art and are non-accidental products of their makers must be the products of artists. And since a film artist is construed here simply as an artist whose product is a film, these artists are film artists. So (v) there are film artists.

This result is not trivial: after all, it is certainly no trivial matter that (i) is true: making films which are works of art is a difficult task, and (ii) many skills, much thought and planning are required to avoid making films with many accidental features. But this is an achievement of film-makers, not of the film theorist. And (iii) rests on a conceptual point about the notion of an artist: conceptual points are not trivial either (or else there would be no informative analyses of concepts). But there is no disguising that the minimal existential claim falls well short of the ambitions of auteurism: it follows conceptually from the existence of films which are works of art and non-accidental products that there must be film artists, but that is all. Even Truffaut's claim that there are film artists whose contribution lies in more than adding pictures to the text does not follow from this.

The *minimal hermeneutic claim* holds that to interpret a film requires understanding what its maker(s) did. This follows from the general claim that to interpret a work of art requires understanding what its maker(s) did, support for which I have given elsewhere, and the point already acknowledged that some films are works of art.[15] The minimal hermeneutic claim accepts (1*b*) and (2*a*), and leaves open the options under the remaining dimensions. Intentionalism does not follow from the minimal claim: there are many aspects of understanding what someone did that go beyond explaining it (even if all explanation is intentionalistic, which may be disputed), such as characterizing the action in various ways, and not all features of actions (or of films) need be intended. So the more informative actual author intentionalistic, or implied author intentionalistic, theses do not follow from this minimal claim.[16] Again, we have got somewhere, but not very far.

The *minimal evaluative claim* holds that a good film is typically the product of good film-maker(s). This claim, by appealing to what is typically the case, allows for the possibility of a fluke masterpiece, and more broadly for a good film which is not the product of good film-maker(s), since its quality results partly through accidental factors, such as unanticipated interactions between untalented collaborators. Good film-makers are those who have non-accidentally produced at least one good film.[17] It follows that a good film typically is the product of good film-makers. This argument is sound, but again its conclusion is not of much use for elaborating film theory and criticism. For instance, nothing follows from it about *how* the makers give the films the value they possess (whether by the expression of their personalities, or by the creation of complex or subversive structures, for example).

These three theses show that there is a minimal core truth in auteurism, in respect of all three kinds of claims listed under dimension (1). That is enough to refute the sceptic, and also explains the ineliminability of some of the intuitions that make auteurism so attractive. But the theses are *extremely* minimal, having very little substantial contribution to make to film theory, and giving very little guidance to critical practice. If this is all that can be shown for auteurism, it is a limp doctrine indeed. The question is, can we specify any of these theses more precisely, cutting down on the indeterminacies, carving out more substantive doctrines? I turn to this task by arguing that all versions of the single authorial thesis (4a) are false.

4. ARGUMENTS FOR SINGLE AUTHORSHIP

As noted above, the dominant view of film authorship has been that there is generally at most one author of a film. We have seen that the second puzzle creates a prima-facie difficulty for this view. Evidently, there are some films, such as Stan Brakhage's *Mothlight*, which are the products of a single individual, but the auteur approach is supposed to apply also and chiefly to what we may dub *mainstream* films—films that have more than one actor, or where the actor is different from the director. Here the fact of collaboration is undeniable.

The pressure to acknowledge multiple authorship is considerable. Indeed, supporters of single authorship sometimes hedge their views with so many caveats about the collaborative nature of film production that they end up embracing convictions that stand in tension with each other. Sarris acknowledges the input of many people besides the director to a film, and holds that 'the cinema could not be a completely personal art even under the best of conditions', but nevertheless thinks that 'Ultimately, the auteur theory is not so much a theory as an attitude, a table of values that converts film history into directorial autobiography.'[18] Victor Perkins gives a convincing and detailed account of the collaborative elements that enter into a film, but nevertheless thinks that the director is 'the author' of the film (i.e. *the* author: there is just one).[19] Thus, two prominent auteurists are prepared to speak of a single author of a film, but display such sensitivity to the complexities of film production that with only a little violence one could represent their positions as multiple authorship views, albeit ones which hold that a worthwhile film has the director as the dominant author. Since my concern here is to establish which, if any, of the more substantive authorial positions is correct, rather than with details of textual exegesis, I will examine the tenability of the pure claim of single authorship, drawing on the work of these auteurists, without seeking finally to determine what their own view is.

The second puzzle—how there can be many artistic collaborators, but only one author—poses a problem for the claims of single authorship. One way to resolve it is by holding that the author is the maker of the film text, all other artists contributing to its non-textual elements (thus we would chose the literary construal of the film artist, on dimension 3). But this supposes that film can be thought of as literally a text, and therefore that film conventions constitute a language, which is a view that should be rejected.[20] And even if we were to think of film as a text, the textual elements, as objects of interpretation, would have to include such items as nuances of acting, of camerawork, and of music that are the contributions of artists other than the director. Thus the claims of others to be literal co-authors, even if films are texts, could not be undermined by this strategy.

More promising are three other strategies available to the supporter of single authorship, to counter the threat that collaboration poses.

1. *The restriction strategy.* Summarizing the view of his classic auteur study, *Hitchcock's Films*, Robin Wood writes that its premiss was that 'the films—insofar as they are significant—belong exclusively to Hitchcock'.[21] Wood's view was therefore that the role of Hitchcock's collaborators did not affect the artistic significance of the film, merely its non-artistic features. The view would be analogous to the claim that an assistant may construct a wooden framework and stretch canvas over it, but the sole artistic input of the artist for the resulting painting is not thereby compromised. Authorial control is restricted to the artistically significant features of works: with respect to these, there is a single artist, the director. More developed versions of the same thought are deployed by Wollen and Perkins. The former distinguishes between the structure of a film, which the director can control, and the 'noise', irrelevant to criticism, which may be produced by actors and cameramen forcing themselves to prominence; the latter argues that a director can make a film his own, despite the contributions of others, by controlling the synthetic relationships which constitute a film's essence.[22]

The restriction strategy in its simple version founders as soon as it leaves port: almost any aspect of a film is potentially artistically significant, so hardly any aspect is left for collaborators to control. Matters such as the placement of sprocket-holes in the film are, it is true, artistically irrelevant. But it is the film as seen and heard which is the object of our artistic attention (of our attention to it *qua* work of art). And virtually everything that we see and hear, produced by a print using adequate projection equipment, is potentially significant in judging the meaning and value of a film. The few exceptions, such as scratches on the print caused by wear and reel-change marks, do nothing to show that actors', composers', or cameramen's contributions concern only artistically irrelevant features. A further basic difficulty with the restriction strategy bulks large, for there is no aspect of the finished film which can be attributed solely to the director's activity by virtue of his directorial role. The director is someone who directs and supervises others. When we survey artistically significant aspects of the film—whether they be the acting, editing, writing, or whatever—we see the results of others' actions, actions supervised by the director and not attributable to him alone. If he is a writer-director, the script may be his; but the script is a single strand in the intricate web of a film. Further, at least one of the acting roles will not be taken by the director in the case of a mainstream film; so there will always be an artistically relevant feature which is not his product alone.

These obstacles to the simple restriction strategy also bar the way to the more sophisticated position of Perkins. Distinguishing between the elements of a film and its synthetic relationships, Perkins holds that the style and meaning of a film are the products of these relationships, which constitute the film *qua* film. Since the director controls the relationships, he commands the artistic terrain of the film. 'Being in charge of relationships, of synthesis, he is in charge of what makes a film a *film*.'[23] But Perkins's auteurist endeavour is not advanced by his distinction between elements and relationships. Though he gives no criterion for distinguishing the two, he does maintain that the director controls the style, meaning, and value of a film by controlling its synthetic relations. So we can understand him as holding that any aspect of the film relevant to these matters concerns not its elements, but its relations. So construed, the difficulties adumbrated above resurface, it being evident that almost any feature of a film should be counted as a matter of its relations: the story, decor, details of the acting, lighting, camerawork, and so on may all be significant determinants of the style, meaning, and value of a film. (Similar considerations undermine Peter Wollen's defence of authorship by distinguishing between 'structure' and 'noise', since his construal of film structure appears to equate it with any aspect of a film which is an object of criticism.) So appeal to the distinction between artistically significant and artistically irrelevant properties of a film will not support any claim of single authorship.[24]

   2. *The sufficient control strategy.* Painters often had assistants who did not just perform tasks such as stretching a canvas over the frame and mixing

paint, but were also given the job of painting in some of the background details; yet we still are prepared to call the resulting painting a Rubens or a Tintoretto. Writers sometimes receive a great deal of help from their editors, not just in removing parts, and tightening structure, but in positive suggestions about new ways to develop the story (Maxwell Perkins's help to Thomas Wolfe in this respect is well known). Or, even more strikingly, consider architecture, where we often consider an architect the sole artist responsible for his buildings, even though they are not built by him personally. Hence the artist need not be someone who has total control, but merely sufficient control, over the artwork. Sufficient control displays itself not just by the artist's direct personal input into his work, but also in the fact that he uses others' talents, absorbing them into his own work.

Perkins deploys this sufficient control strategy: he acknowledges the director's lack of total power over a film, but maintains that he is 'chiefly responsible for the effect and quality of the completed movie', which is enough to make him 'the author' of the film.[25] The director controls a film not just by what he himself invents, but also by what he allows actors, cameramen, and others to do: 'The resulting action "belongs" to the director as much as do the details that he himself suggests.' Hitchcock, for example, was able to cast those actors who best fitted into the design of his films, and so was 'able to absorb the strong personalities of Grant and Stewart into the textures of his movies'.[26]

However, even in the case of paintings, novels, and architecture, if there are others who make a significant artistic difference to the work, then it is only fair to acknowledge them as artistic collaborators, and modern scholarly practice is coming increasingly to do so (consider the attributions of paintings to Rembrandt and workshop, rather than simply to Rembrandt). So appeal to these other arts does not in itself support the claims of single authorship. But in any case it is a weak analogy, since the artistic effects of collaboration are much more important in film than in these other arts. Consider the case of architecture. In those cases where we do not countenance the builders as co-artists with the architect, that is because their contribution, if carried out competently, does not affect the artistic qualities of the building.[27] And that is because the architect can specify precisely enough what they are to do (the sizes of the rooms, the type of materials used for construction and cladding, etc.). There are some film tasks, such as when a director tells an editor to cut a shot after 240 frames, which can be specified exactly, and the collaborator can carry out the order with no room for discretion. But most film tasks are not at all like this, for the dimensions of variation possible in performing the job are immense. This is particularly obvious in the case of acting: think of the innumerable ways in which one can say a line like 'Frankly, my dear, I don't give a damn', the way one can shift the stress to different words, insert pauses of varying lengths, convey vastly different emotions from noble resignation to petty-minded spite. No matter how many takes are used, directorial instructions cannot in practice be fine grained enough to select just one precise way of saying these lines, with an exactly shaded emotional meaning. Any actor will inevitably bring something of his own personality and training to the way he speaks his lines, inflecting them with the nuances derived from verbal mannerism and unique vocal tonalities, colouring his performance with the personal memory and felt experience he uses in imaginatively projecting himself into his role. Given the inability to specify many film tasks exactly, and given this, the uniqueness of human beings, the way their mode of expression inevitably reflects their personalities (their expressive individuality), it is evident that the director's degree of control over the work is not that of the architect's.

Secondly, consider a parallel in literature to the degree of control Perkins gives directors over films: suppose it emerged that Flaubert did not pen all of *Madame Bovary*, but had commissioned several writers to produce individual chapters, had rejected some of their drafts, accepted others with editorial changes, and then inserted passages linking the results together. We would not speak of Flaubert as the sole author of the novel. The book would be a collaborative work, in which Flaubert's was (perhaps) the most important contribution, but where the artistic work of all participants should be duly acknowledged. Moreover, Perkins's talk of others' actions 'belonging' to the director should not be taken to suggest that they belong only to him. Should Stewart decide to read his lines so as to make the character he is playing sound neurotic, and should Hitchcock countenance this interpretation, then Stewart has performed an artistic act, even if Hitchcock also performs such an act by agreeing to accept that interpretation of the role. Nor does the fact that a director can cast actors of his choice in a film make him its sole author. Some actors do have a screen image which the director can employ and inflect, but they are not inanimate objects with a fixed meaning, to be collaged by the director into his film. They are performers, and the exact manner in which they perform will escape precise directorial control. The actors of a film are among its co-creators.

3. *The construction strategy.* The two previous strategies are most naturally construed as about authors as actual individuals. But as noted earlier, the dominant view since the early 1970s has been of the film author as a critical construct. This view bears a striking resemblance to that of many literary theorists and philosophers, who hold that the author should be distinguished from the writer of a text, the former being a mere postulate in terms of which one can interpret the work, the latter being the actual individual who penned its words. In literature the advantages of the distinction are great: one can acknowledge that the author's persona as it appears

in her work may be radically different from her actual character, and can maintain that a work is the product of authorial acts, without being thereby committed to believing that the writer's actual intentions determine the correct interpretation of her work.[28] In film the application of the distinction has, in addition, the advantage of affirming that the constructed author may not be the product of a single actual person, but may instead be the outcome of a collaborative effort between several.[29] Acknowledgement of multiple collaboration in film-making is thus compatible with holding that there is a single postulated author of the film. This construal of the author, then, permits him to lend a welcome helping hand (if only a constructed one) to the single authorship thesis.

The formulation of an authorship thesis as thus construed needs some care. Substituting the notion of the implied author for that of the actual author, the existential thesis would hold that mainstream films sometimes are the products of a single postulated author. But that is incoherent. To talk of the film as a product of an author is to regard the former as an effect of the latter's actions, yet the author as a merely postulated, non-actual, being cannot possess this sort of causal power. Encountering the same difficulty in the case of literature, Nehamas suggests we think of the author as being manifested in the text, and Wilson similarly holds that the implied film-maker manifests himself in his films.[30] Construing the concept of manifestation literally, our problem re-emerges, for merely constructed persons cannot manifest themselves: if I manifest myself to you, I show myself to you; showing is a process by which I bring it about that you see me; and seeing is a causal process. Yet only actual entities can enter into causal relations with real people. Nehamas, however, suggests we understand the author not as a text's efficient, but as its formal cause. But the author as a real person is a text's efficient cause; so if the notion of efficient causation, of the text as product, had no role whatsoever to play in the formulation of the constructivist view, we would have good reason to deny that the postulated entity should be thought of as in any sense an author. In the light of this, a more promising way to capture the auteurist position is as follows: when we talk of the postulated author with certain characteristics manifesting himself in a text, we mean that for the purposes of interpreting and evaluating the text, it should be thought of *as if* it were the product of a single artist with those characteristics (the persona). This formulation preserves the fundamental point that we postulate an author in order to understand and appreciate a text properly (the hermeneutic and evaluative theses are what drive author-as-construct views); it allows the notion of the text as product of the author to figure in the view, as something to be imagined; and it also acknowledges the author to be a construct, a being who is imagined to make the text, with a persona which may be distinct from the real writer's personality. We will, then, construe the constructivist auteurist position as holding that some mainstream films manifest a single postulated artist, and gloss this in the manner just suggested.[31]

In his interpretation of *Letter from an Unknown Woman*, Wilson shows how and why one might appeal to an implied film-maker. The patterns of camera movement and placement, production design, script, music, and acting, he argues, are all crafted so as to create a sympathetic but objective point of view onto the actions and character of Lisa, the film's protagonist, and to give the viewer an insight into her condition which she never herself attains. In light of the wide range of variables which are employed to underpin this vision of Lisa, we here have evidence for the viability and necessity of an implied film-maker: 'It is impossible to escape the impression of an intelligent and sometimes ironic observer, the implied film maker as it were, who is continuously observing with special insight into the wider patterns that Lisa ostensibly describes.'[32]

Can the construction strategy save the single authorship thesis? We should acknowledge a constructed author when we can identify an autho-rial personality, a persona, which may be distinct from that of the actual writer. Clearly there is a Hitchcock persona which emerges in his films. But equally Stewart and Grant have personae—as indeed do Bernard Herrmann and other contributors to Hitchcock's films who are not actors—and these personae are prominent in the films. So, by the criterion of artistic person-ality to which the constructivist appeals, we should acknowledge such films to involve multiple artists.

Moreover, were we to construct just one author for each film, it would be so different from people as we know them that its use to interpret and evaluate films would systematically distort our responses to cinema. Re-sponsible for all aspects of film-making, the author must be manifested in the screenplay, direction, camerawork, musical score, editing, and so forth; so we would have to think of it *as if* it were the being who had done all of these things. What sort of entity could master the full range of these functions? At the very least, it would have to be a genius, whose ability to fulfil the many tasks of film-making exceeded even Chaplin's myriad skills, and the tritest film must be judged an extraordinary achievement, the product of a wonderfully giftéd and strikingly protean talent. Odd as these results are, it is when we apply the constructed author to acting perfor-mances that it yields a true efflorescence of glittering improbabilities. For we have to think of these performances as if they were the products of a single artist: strictly construed, the performers' actions would be the artist's, he would move them in the same way I move my arm. To think of the actors in this way is to forfeit our sense of them as agents, and so radically to distort our experience of mainstream cinema, an experience of seeing repre-sentations of agents performing actions. Moreover, the author must be imagined as capable of moving these performers as we move puppets, a capacity far exceeding human abilities. Who knows what such a being would be like? For the constructivist, interpretation involves seeing what qualities are manifested by a film's implied author: but what might be gained by speculating on the psychology of a kind of super-intelligent octopus, whose tentacles control the myriad machines of cinema and reach into the very souls of actors? Given its unknowable psychology, the signs we take to be those of sympathy towards a character might instead be marks of wry amusement, haughty disdain, vehement fury, or emotions utterly unimaginable to us.[33]

Thus constructivism cannot be employed to defend a single authorship thesis. But Wilson's sensitive analysis of *Letter to an Unknown Woman* is, surely, correct in seeing signs of the intelligent use of scene design, script, music, acting, and camerawork to express a sympathetic view of Lisa. Signs of intelligent production, though, do not require *one intelligence* implicitly to do the producing. Rather than a single implied film-maker being manifested in the film, an implied *group* of film-makers is manifested in it: actors, screenwriters, director, composer, and so on. By virtue of the coordination of their activities to achieve common ends, each manifests sympathy towards the unfortunate protagonist. But one can readily imagine a film where such coordination breaks down, the implied actor showing sympathy for a character towards whom the implied director manifests hostility. The possibility of these conflicts demonstrates the coherence of the view that an implied group is manifested in a film; and only the multiple authorship view can adequately theorize such cases of the film-as-battleground, some real examples of which are discussed below. A mainstream film does not manifest just one implied artist. It manifests very many.[34]

5. ONTOLOGY AND MULTIPLE AUTHORSHIP

Some of the more promising strategies for resolving the second puzzle in favour of single authorship fail. That being so, we should admit that films have multiple authors, for we have seen that many of the collaborators have significant artistic input to a film. The failure of the strategies in favour of single authorship is partly to be explained by a fundamental difference between the ontology of films and literature.

We can approach this issue by contrasting the role of the author-as-construct in film with its role in literature. The persona of Tolstoy as manifested in *Anna Karenina* is very different from the personality of the real man as manifested in his life, and so there is reason to distinguish the former from the latter (though just how sweeping a role this critical construct should play in our understanding of the work is another matter). There is no difficulty in imagining a person with the construct's personality penning the novel: no extraordinary mastery over a wide range of skills and functions would be needed, as it would were a film being made. Nor do actors portray the characters in the novel; so countenancing the single author as critical construct cannot undermine their agency or expressivity, as it does when the single author is introduced into films; nor are the literary author's capacities required to bloat to fantastic proportions so he can be thought of as controlling actors' behaviour. There are thus genuine differences between literature and films, differences which make the construction of an author in the case of the latter inappropriate in a way they do not in the case of the former.

This question of the disparity between literature and film is worthy of careful scrutiny, for the auteurist's guiding principle is that the two art forms exhibit a structural similarity. Moreover, many of the arguments deployed above drew on the element of performance in films to attack the single authorship thesis. But the auteurist will object that theatre similarly involves performances by several actors, yet the playwright's claim to sole authorship goes unchallenged. So what can be said about the relation between literature and film?

Novels, poems, and plays are texts (understanding texts to be semantic entities, rather than simply types of physical marks) produced by writers; but films are moving pictures with sound, which incorporate mechanical recordings of performances.[35] This dissimilarity between literary works and films is reflected in their individuation-conditions: literary works are individuated by their texts (and, perhaps, by their writers and times of composition as well[36]), but films are not so individuated, for radically different films can emerge from the same text: the 1922 film *Nosferatu* and the 1978 film of the same name incorporate roughly the same screenplay, but are remarkably different films. Nor are films individuated by their storyboards, if there are any, for very different photographic shots and different performances by actors can be realizations of the same storyboard. Films are, in fact, individuated by their entire range of acoustic and visual properties, and by the causal sources of these.[37] Further, because of their status as texts, literary works can be performed (novels and poems are performable, by being read out, as was common until fairly recently), whereas films cannot be performed, any more than can pictures or photographs. (The screening of a film is not a performance of it, since one cannot, for instance, talk of a screening being a misinterpretation of a work.) Performances in films are, rather, internal to a work: recordings of performances are part of what make a film what it is.

From these basic ontological differences between literary works and films emerges a difference between the relation of the actor to his role in a play and in a film, which has implications for authorship. There is no difficulty in understanding how Shakespeare can be the sole author of *Othello*, for he can brandish the bardic plume and inscribe the text. That text specifies the character of Othello, granting him a certain range of determinate features (being a Moor, killing his wife, speaking glorious poetry while proclaiming his simplicity) and leaves a set of other features indeterminate within certain bounds (exactly how he rolls the rhapsodies off his tongue, what his movements and facial expressions are as he does so). The latter gives scope for actors to present their varying interpretations, or characterizations, of his character, by determining these indeterminates in some way within their performance (speaking certain lines not with heartfelt fervour, but with neurotic unease). But how Robeson or Olivier characterized Othello does not affect the character himself: that is under Shakespeare's complete control.[38] That the *performance* of a play is collaborative, involving many different actors and a director, then, does not undermine the single authorship of the play itself. But whilst a play specifies its characters by its text, a film specifies them by its acoustic and visual features. These features incorporate recordings of actors' performances, so these performances play a part in specifying the characters portrayed in the film. The film actor, then, co-determines (with the screenwriter, director, or whomever) the character he plays in a film. How he looks and says certain lines are now how that character looks and says those lines; and had a different actor been employed, the character would have been correspondingly different.[39] Imagine a Julie Marston in *Jezebel* played, not by Bette Davis, but by Claudette Colbert.[40]

The implications for film authorship are evident. In theatre, actors' performances are external to the play itself, whereas in cinema (recordings of) their performances are internal to the film. So, despite the collaborative nature of performance, the playwright can exercise complete control over the characters of his play; but it is a vastly more difficult task for a film's putative author to have the same degree of control over the characters of a film. If the author is construed as an actual individual, he would have entirely to determine the acting of all the actors playing the parts, and we have already seen how implausible is the claim that he could do this. If the author is viewed as a critical construct, he is freed from the constraints on what people as we know them can do. But in thinking of him as if he had control over all the performances, as well as of other film-making tasks, both he and the performers must be imagined as radically different from the human beings with which we are familiar. So to do is to speculate on the psychologies of being so dissimilar from the persons who actually make films that we would warp out of all recognizable shape our understanding and appreciation of cinema. Many of the objections to the single author both as an actual individual and as a construct, then, are rooted in the firm and fertile ground of a basic ontological difference between literature and films.

6. THE MULTIPLE AUTHORSHIP VIEW REFINED

The varieties of auteurism distinguished earlier are susceptible to further subdivisions and refinements. To show the attractions of the multiple authorship view, its merits in enhancing critical understanding compared to the single authorship view, it is useful briefly to develop it, and to compare films to other collaborative art forms.

Two dimensions of variation may usefully be distinguished in collaborative artistic activities. The first concerns the degree to which creative power in determining the artistic properties of a film is centralized or dispersed. In some films a person or small group of persons may be the dominant collaborator, having power by virtue of their organizational role or by the force of their artistic presence; in other films there may be a greater diffusion of power between many roughly equal collaborators. The second dimension of variation concerns the degree to which the different collaborators are in agreement over the aims of the film and their role within its production. This can vary from total agreement to complete failure to agree. The latter may produce a shambles of a film, or may generate conflicts which greatly enhance its artistic merit. The collaborators may also either be aware of, or be completely unconscious of, the fact that they are in agreement or in conflict. The variations possible along these two axes, and the interactions between them, can generate complexities within films that the single authorship view cannot adequately theorize.

The possibility most akin to the single authorship view of cinema is when one individual has dominant creative control over a film. The most plausible candidates are writer-directors, such as Ingmar Bergman, Preston Sturges, Quentin Tarantino, and Woody Allen. Others, such as producers (David Selznick) or stars (Mae West), may sometimes wield artistic power—a circumstance that explains the endless, futile debates within the auteurist camp as to the identity of a film's author (the disputes under dimension 4). But, as we have seen, such an individual, even when he or she exists, is not correctly characterized as the sole author of the film. Sturges's great films at Paramount in the 1940s relied on a stock company of actors, for whom he wrote the parts, and whose performances are indispensable to the character and success of his films. Bergman and Allen similarly relied on a talented group of artists: the role of Sven Nykvist, Bergman's director of photography, was crucial to the look of his films. Indeed, some of these films' features, often ascribed to the directors, are more plausibly traced to the work of other collaborators. The comic mood of Allen's films became more serious and less kooky when Diane Keaton was replaced by Mia Farrow, a change of tone partly traceable to their differing skills as comic actresses. The existence of dominant author films explains why the notion of single authorship has appeared plausible to many.

In other films artistic power is more dispersed. The great musicals produced by the MGM Freed unit are testimony to the skills of a wide range of artists, all of whom stamped their hallmarks on the silver screen.[41] Even a film like *Blade Runner*, whose release in 1992 in a 'director's cut' bears witness to the ideology of single authorship, is an extraordinary collaborative venture. Philip Dick's source novel; the radical reworking of that material by David Webb Peoples's screenplay (stressing the futility of revenge, a theme shared with his script for *Unforgiven*); director Ridley Scott's concern with the marginalized and powerless in society (also seen in *Thelma and Louise*); Syd Mead's marvellous visual imagining of a drenched and decayed megalopolis, half postmodern pastiche, half dystopian nightmare; Vangelis's futuristic, ethereal synthesizer score; the worried helplessness of Harrison Ford's acting—the work of all these artists and more combine synergistically to produce a film of great merit.

Rather than rigidly categorizing films by their directors, films should be multiply classified: by actors, cameramen, editors, composers, and so on. The career paths of all cinematic artists need to be traced, showing how their work adapts to new contexts, demonstrating how each interaction alters the ingredients and flavours of the cinematic pot-pourri. Sometimes tracking the trail of a non-director's career will be the best way to follow significant developments in film history: the career of cameraman Gregg Toland, one of the rediscoverers of deep focus photography in the 1930s, can fruitfully be traced, as he developed his technique under William Wyler, and then radicalized it with neophyte director Orson Welles, who for some time was credited with innovations not entirely his own. An increasing amount of serious work is being done on the role of stars and other non-directors in film-making, and the multiple authorship thesis should serve to sustain and enhance the importance of such studies.

The second dimension of variation mentioned above, and in particular the role of conflict between authors, is important in shaping many films. One of the key tropes of contemporary criticism, both of films and of literature, is that of the 'contradictory text', the idea that works may be riven with tensions between their professed ideology and their actual representation of the world, so that the suppressed violence of an actor's performance may detonate the mealy-mouthed pieties of a film's official line. The case for such films is strengthened by tracing their conflicts back to the differing projects of the various collaborators. Yet, ironically, recent criticism has not generally availed itself of this thought; indeed, one of the key sources of the notion of the contradictory film appears to work within a constructivist single author position.[42] Here again the multiple authorship version shows its superiority. *Do the Right Thing*, perhaps Spike Lee's finest film, has in Sal a character who is surprisingly sympathetic, despite his complicity in a racial tragedy culminating in a horrifying murder. Sal is an important element in the film's richness and complexity, and some have hailed him as marking the subtlety of character creation of which Lee is capable.[43] The truth is otherwise: 'St. Clair Bourne's documentary record of the location shoot, *Making Do the Right Thing* (1989), offers an intriguing glimpse into the way an actor can overwhelm an auteur. In a discussion about Sal's character, Lee declares flatly that he thinks Sal is a racist. Aiello disagrees—and on the screen if not in the screenplay his portrayal wins the argument.'[44] Other instances of artistically fruitful disagreement, or of flat confusion, abound: some of the complexity of *Gentlemen Prefer Blondes*, Richard Dyer has argued, can be traced to Monroe's spirited refusal to conform to Hawks's demeaning conception of the character she plays; and the story is well known of the conflicts of purpose between Mayer and Janowitz, and Lang and Wiene, which resulted in the addition of the framing-story to *The Cabinet of Dr Caligari*.

Given the importance of collaboration to film, much can be learned from the critical discourse surrounding other areas of artistic collaboration. Since films incorporate recordings of performances, studies of collaborations involved in performances are particularly germane. Performances of plays, involving the artistic collaboration of playwright, director, actors, and others, provide a useful comparison for thinking about film-making: the ideology of single authorship is noticeably less compelling in theatre studies, where the cult of the director has not (yet) ballooned to the bulbous dimensions it has assumed in film studies.

Musical performances are also collaborative, for the musical styles of all the participants affect the outcome. Particularly illuminating is the comparison of film with jazz. For the most part what matters in jazz is improvised performance, not composition; and just as radically different films can be based on the same screenplay, so can very different improvisations derive from the same tune. Consequently, critical interest centres on the different musical styles, personalities, and interactions of the improvisers in the group, interactions still present even when one member of the group is dominant. The modes of such interplay are complex. A musician's playing may vary in response to that of his collaborators, or his tone may simply sound different in diverse musical contexts: Bill Evans never played better than when working with Scott LaFaro and Paul Motian; in the Miles Davis–John Coltrane groups, the fragility of Davis's tone is rendered more poignant through its contrast to Coltrane's searing attack. The ideal implicit in jazz is one of democratic individualism—of a set of strong musical personalities who converse with each other through their playing, and create music richer than any could make on his own. The multiple authorship theory of films encourages us to look at films the same way as we do jazz: as a product of many individuals, whose work is inflected in a complex manner by their interactions with their colleagues. A film is no more the product of a single individual than is the music of an improvising jazz group.

The multiple authorship view can be seen as stemming from a more general view of film. The dominant paradigm for understanding films has been a literary one. The auteur theory was inspired by the comparison of films to literary works, even though the theory also allowed for structural parallels to paintings and compositional music. The connection between films and literature has also been trumpeted by film semiotics, which argues that films are, or are closely akin to, linguistic texts. The literary paradigm has, I believe, led to serious distortions in our understanding of film, properly regarded as an audio-visual medium, where the exact qualities of images and sounds, dependent on the particular individuals who generated them, are crucial to a film's artistic features. Films are movies, moving pictures which have learned to talk, and are not usefully regarded as text-like. And, as we saw when examining the question of ontology, there are some important differences between films and literary works, even waiving the question of the language of film.

7. THE WAY FORWARD

When we move beyond the minimal authorship theses of section 2, we see that mainstream films have multiple authors (i.e. option 5*b* is correct). We have seen the importance of actors to a film, and considerations for the importance of scriptwriters and for those producers who concern themselves with the actual making of the film could easily be advanced as well. So there is no reason to deny the potential artistic contribution, and therefore co-authorship, of any of those mentioned under dimension 4, or indeed of many others too, such as special effects artists. The artistic importance of various collaborators is likely to vary from film to film, and the multiple authorship theory should be open to the possibility of very many different roles having an artistic input to a film. I have already indicated that the film author should not be thought of as a literal author, for the film is not a text (dimension 3). My continuing to call him an 'author' here is from deference to tradition, not from any conviction that there is a language of film. Given multiple authorship, there is no reason to disallow either the actual or constructed author as playing a role in film (dimension 2). Since multiple actual artists are involved in mainstream films, one incentive for acknowledging constructed authorship is removed. On the other hand, many of these artists have personae, evident in their film 'signatures', whether these be of actorly performance, directorial trademarks, characteristic concerns of the scriptwriter, or whatever. Finally, how does dimension 1 fare? (*a*) We have seen that there are multiple actual and constructed authors of mainstream films: actual authors are causal agents in bringing the film into existence, constructed authors are manifested in the film in the sense indicated. (*b*) To understand a film requires understanding what its actual authors did (putting the minimal hermeneutic thesis together with the multiple authorship thesis). As indicated earlier, this does not entail actual author intentionalism. Indeed, given the existence of multiple authors, the spell of intentionalism is weakened, for we have considered cases where conflicts between collaborators lead to features of the film unintended by any of them. Relevant to interpretation will also be the natures of the constructed authors, for grasping their personae may be an important aspect of understanding the film (recall Wilson's analysis of *Letter from an Unknown Woman*). But, again, this does not entail that implied author intentionalism is a correct general theory of film interpretation.[45] (*c*) A good film is typically the product of good film-makers (putting multiple authorship together with the minimal evaluative thesis). But, again, the existence of multiple authors makes it more likely that what they actually do may diverge from what they were trying to do, and hence that there will be more accidental features in a film (so the importance of the 'typicality' condition is enhanced, for there is more room for the fluke masterpiece than the single authorship view countenances). If we read the evaluative condition in terms of manifestation, so as to cover the case of constructed authors, it is also correct: a good film will typically manifest good constructed film-makers, since we will construct the film-makers as good precisely when they are manifested in a good film that seems not to be produced accidentally. But, again, very many aspects of evaluation go beyond these still fairly minimal evaluative claims.

Thus a number of authorial theses are correct—there are correct ontological, hermeneutic, and evaluative theses formulated in terms of both actual and constructed multiple authors. No version involving single authors or literal authors is true. Some of these more substantive authorial views have interesting implications: we have for instance explored the role of multiple authorship in enriching our understanding of films. More work needs to be done on these lines, in further refining the classification of the different sub-options in the various dimensions, in exploring the questions thus raised: the question of how authors create value in films, the question of the importance of the contributions of different cinematic roles to the value of films, and so forth. Authorship views have suffered from much vagueness and diffuseness in their formulations, leading to an elision of distinct views, and an unclarity in the claims of even eminent auteurists. What we need is a more careful and precise classification and articulation of the options, and a nuanced exploration of the correctness of these more precisely defined positions.

Film authorship should not be rejected in the cavalier fashion in which some critics have dealt with it: but neither should it be defended with the vagueness with which some of its friends have embraced it. Theories of authorship deserve a more careful treatment than they have generally received.

NOTES

1. David Bordwell and Kristin Thompson, *Film Art: An Introduction*, 4th edn. (New York: McGraw-Hill, 1993), 38.
2. François Truffaut, 'A Certain Tendency of the French Cinema', in Bill Nichols (ed.), *Movies and Methods*, vol. i (Berkeley and Los Angeles: University of California Press, 1976).
3. For instance, V. F. Perkins, *Film as Film* (Harmondsworth: Penguin, 1972), is a nuanced defender of the authorial thesis, but he is also a formalist, denying the importance of intentions to meaning (p. 173).
4. See Andrew Sarris, 'Notes on the Auteur Theory in 1962', in Gerald Mast and Marshall Cohen (eds.), *Film Theory and Criticism*, 3rd edn. (New York: Oxford University Press, 1985); and Andrew Sarris, 'Towards a Theory of Film History' in Nichols (ed.), *Movies and Methods*.
5. Perkins acknowledges the possibility of a 'fluke masterpiece', in the sense of a film that is a masterpiece, even though its overall coherence is not due to directorial control, but says that he knows of no actual examples: Perkins, *Film as Film*, 185.
6. See respectively Sarris's remarks on 'the distinguishable personality of the director as a criterion of value' in 'Notes on the Auteur Theory in 1962', 537–8; and Peter Wollen, *Signs and Meaning in the Cinema*, 3rd edn. (Bloomington: Indiana University Press, 1972), 171–2.
7. Geoffrey Nowell-Smith, 'Six Authors in Pursuit of *The Searchers*', in John Caughie (ed.), *Theories of Authorship* (London: Routledge, 1981), 222.
8. Stephen Heath, 'Comment on "The Idea of Authorship" ', in Caughie (ed.), *Theories of Authorship*, 220.
9. Sarris, 'Notes on the Auteur Theory in 1962', 529.
10. Ibid.; Perkins, *Film as Film*, ch. 8; Richard Corliss, 'The Hollywood Screenwriter', in Mast and Cohen (eds.), *Film Theory and Criticism*; see Richard Dyer, *Stars* (London: British Film Institute, 1979), for a discussion of McGilligan and for Dyer's claims about Garbo, Burstyn, and Streisand, pp. 174–5; and Thomas Schatz, *The Genius of the System: Hollywood Filmmaking in the Studio Era* (New York: Pantheon, 1988), introd.
11. See Dyer, *Stars*, on the 'voices model' of film, pp. 175–6.
12. An exception to the 'one item' rule occurs under (4), where if one believes in multiple authorship, more than one item must be selected.
13. There are in fact 180 theses that can be generated on the options given, partly because of the different combinations selectable under dimension 4 on the multiple authorship option.
14. This may be too strong a claim: perhaps one has non-accidentally to produce several works of art in order to be an artist. But this would not materially affect the argument, since there are many people who have produced (caused to come into existence) several films that are works of art.

    What is required for non-accidental production of a work of art? It cannot be that every artistic property of the work is intentionally produced, since that would require an implausible mastery to be ascribed to the artist. So we should hold merely that some large number of a work's artistic properties are intentionally produced; this leaves a good degree of indeterminacy in the application of the concept, as seems correct, but does not affect the argument in the text.

15. See my 'Interpreting the Arts: The Patchwork Theory', *Journal of Aesthetics and Art Criticism*, 51: 4 (1993), 597–609. I there give considerations for the general claim about interpretation (pp. 605–6). This claim is consistent with there being a legitimate role for spectatorial construction: see my 'Making Sense of Films: Neoformalism and its Limits', *Forum for Modern Language Studies*, 31: 1 (1995), 8–23.

16. See Gregory Currie, *Image and Mind: Film, Philosophy, and Cognitive Science* (Cambridge: Cambridge University Press, 1995), ch. 8, for a defence of implied author intentionalism. Currie claims this view is neutral about the truth of auteurism (pp. 258–9), but that is partly because he appears to assume that multiple authorship views are not auteurist views.

17. One might hold that good film-makers must produce several good films: then to retain the truth of the minimal claim, the typicality condition must be weakened to allow for the possibility of one-off good films.

18. Sarris, 'Towards a Theory of Film History', 247 and 246.

19. Perkins, *Film as Film*, 181.

20. For some arguments against the language of film view, see Currie, *Image and Mind*, ch. 4.

21. Robin Wood, *Hitchcock's Films Revisited* (London: Faber & Faber, 1991), 5. This work incorporates the earlier study, originally published in 1965. On the same page Wood writes that his current view is that Hitchcock's films 'do not belong *only* to him'.

22. Wollen, *Signs and Meaning in the Cinema*, 104–5; and Perkins, *Film as Film*, 184.

23. Perkins, *Film as Film*, 184.

24. Recall that Perkins himself may not believe in single authorship: my concern with his arguments is merely to see whether the single authorship thesis can be supported by means of them.

25. Ibid. 179 and 181.

26. Ibid. 181–2.

27. Contrast the role of sculptors on the façades of Gothic cathedrals, where the scope for individual expression does give us reason to talk of many artists.

28. See Wayne Booth, *The Rhetoric of Fiction*, 2nd edn. (Chicago: University of Chicago Press, 1983), esp. 70–7 and 151–3, for the notion of the implied author; and Alexander Nehamas, 'The Postulated Author', *Critical Inquiry*, 8: 1 (1981), 133–49, for a somewhat different view of the author as construct with an account of its implications for interpretation. For our purposes the differences between these views are not germane; and in what follows I shall use 'postulated author', 'implied author', and 'author as construct' interchangeably.

29. ' "John Ford" is as much present in the work of collaborators who made the film with and for the director as in the work of the director (John Ford) in person', Nowell-Smith, 'Six Authors in Pursuit of *The Searchers*', 222.

30. Nehamas, 'The Postulated Author', 145; and George Wilson, *Narration in Light: Studies in Cinematic Point of View* (Baltimore: Johns Hopkins University Press, 1986), 134–9, esp. 134. Wilson points out that his concept is broadly in line with Booth's notion of the implied author (p. 217 n. 11).

31. Currie holds 'that the implied author intends P to be fictional means just that the text can reasonably be thought of as produced by someone intending the reader to recognize that P is fictional' (*Image and Mind*, 245). This is his formulation for literature: it is generalized for film, which is not textual. Since the implied author is used by Currie for interpretative purposes, his suggestion about how to construe the implied author is related to mine, except that he wishes to keep open the possibility of either single or multiple implied authors.

32. Wilson, *Narration in Light*, 123. It is not clear that Wilson should talk of an observer

here, however, since that is presumably someone who is part of the same world as Lisa: the notion of the implied author is of a being that we think of as if it produced the film world, and that requires it not to be a part of it.

33. The supporter of single authorship might reply that on his view actors are still to be regarded as agents, but as agents completely schooled by the author, every nuance of their performance attributable to his tuition. This version, however, runs into the same difficulties of a superhuman film-maker whose psychology is unknowable, and strips actors of the expressive individuality that, as we noted earlier, is so central to our appreciation of films.

34. In his important paper 'Cinematic Authorship' (this volume), Paisley Livingston considers four cases of film-making, and holds that the first two involve no author, the third involves a partial author, and the fourth involves a sole author. On the view defended here, all four cases, assuming they are works of art (even if bad ones), involve multiple authorship (though I agree that Big John as described is not one of the authors in Case Two). Part of our difference here is to be explained by Livingston's use of what I term the restriction and sufficient control strategies; part is to be explained by our different understandings of what an author is. For Livingston a necessary condition of authorship is that the author intends to manifest his attitudes or has communicative intentions. On my view, this is too restrictive, for the notion of the artist is that of the non-accidental producer of a work of art. An artist need not have any expressive or communicative intentions, for he may not intend to communicate, intending the work only for himself, and not all artistic properties are expressive: an artist may intend simply to produce a work with various artistic properties, such as beauty, vibrancy, and aesthetic unity. The difference in our construal of authorship is also linked to different understandings of artistic meaning: on the latter, see my 'Interpreting the Arts: The Patchwork Theory'. However, Livingston and I are at one on the importance of appeal to the notion of agency in understanding artworks, and on the failure of constructivist accounts to shore up theories of single authorship.

35. This is not, of course, to be confused with the claim that films are simply filmed theatre: how the performances are filmed matters a great deal, the resulting images are standardly subject to a great deal of technical manipulation, and what appears in the film includes many non-performance elements, such as special effects.

36. See Jerrold Levinson, *Music, Art, and Metaphysics: Essays in Philosophical Aesthetics* (Ithaca, NY: Cornell University Press, 1990), 63–106. The ontological differences between literature and films remain on this view: a novelist composing a work at a certain time, given the particular text he has produced, could not have composed a different novel using that text, but a director could have produced a different film at a particular time, given a particular screenplay; and evidently it is still true that films cannot be performed, but literary works can be.

37. We need to refer to the causal sources of the images, because we should count as distinct films those which, though identical in all their perceptible properties, are made by different people at different times. Since new copies of films are made by photographing earlier copies, identity of causal source of the images must be understood in terms of the objects which were the source of the images in the first photograph from which later copies were taken.

38. Of course, the actor determines the character-in-performance, i.e. the particular version presented of the character in a particular performance: but the character-in-performance is distinct from the character in the play (for instance, the former exists only for the duration of that particular performance, whereas the latter is not thus temporally bounded).

39. The film actor will, of course, also leave certain features of his character indeterminate—but they will concern such things as aspects of character motivation, rather than the precise intonation or physical appearance of the character.

40. For similar considerations about individuation-conditions and the difference they make to the relation of theatre and cinema actors to their roles, see E. Panofsky, 'Style and Medium in the Motion Pictures', in Mast and Cohen (eds.), *Film Theory and Criticism*, 243; Stanley Cavell, *The World Viewed: Reflections on the Ontology of Film*, enlarged edn. (Cambridge, Mass.: Harvard University Press, 1979), 27–9; and Arthur Danto, 'Moving Pictures', *Quarterly Review of Film Studies*, 4 (1979), 1–21, sections I and III.

41. See the interviews with the participants in the *An American in Paris* ballet in Donald Knox, *The Magic Factory*, an extract from which is reprinted in Mast and Cohen (eds.), *Film Theory and Criticism*, 572–92.

42. The editors of *Cahiers du cinéma*, 'John Ford's *Young Mr. Lincoln*', in Mast and Cohen (eds.), *Film Theory and Criticism*, 695–740.

43. See, for instance, Lisa Kennedy, 'Is Malcolm X the Right Thing?', *Sight and Sound*, 3: 2 (NS) (1993), 6–10, at p. 9.

44. Thomas Doherty, 'Review of *Do the Right Thing*', *Film Quarterly*, 43: 2 (1989–90), 35–40, at p. 38.

45. For an attack on both actual author and implied author intentionalism as all-embracing theories of interpretation, see my 'Interpreting the Arts: The Patchwork Theory', 599–601.

7

Fiction, Non-fiction, and the Film of Presumptive Assertion: A Conceptual Analysis

Noël Carroll

I. INTRODUCTION

In both film studies and the culture at large, there is an area of practice which is typically labelled 'the documentary', or perhaps less frequently, 'non-fiction film'. These labels are roughly serviceable for practical purposes, but they are not always as theoretically precise as they might be. Therefore, in this chapter, I will propose another label for the field—namely, 'films of presumptive assertion'—and I will attempt to define it.[1] In response to this statement of intent, some may worry that my new label and its accompanying definition are stipulative and revisionist. However, I will argue that they track the extension of films that film scholars want to talk about and refer to better than the alternative candidates do.

Current usage of the term 'documentary' to denominate the field in question appears to stem from John Grierson.[2] It was his preferred name for his own practice, and it has been extended by many to cover all work in what might be provisionally earmarked as the non-fiction film. However, when Grierson introduced the term, he had something rather specific in mind. He defined the documentary as 'the creative treatment of actuality'.[3] The notion of *creative treatment* in this formula had a very particular function. It was intended to distinguish the Griersonian documentary from things like the Lumière *actualité* and newsreels.[4]

In contrast to the *actualité* and the newsreel, the Griersonian documentary had a creative dimension by virtue of which it was explicitly conceived to be artistic. In this, Grierson's ambitions paralleled those of other filmmakers and theoreticians of the silent and early sound periods who wished to defeat the prejudice that film could merely function as the slavish and

I would like to thank George Wilson, Paisley Livingston, Gregory Currie, Richard Allen, Murray Smith, Vance Kepley, Ben Brewster, David Bordwell, Carl Plantinga, and Sally Banes for their comments on earlier versions of this chapter. If what remains is flawed, it is probably due to my failing to listen to their sagacious suggestions.

mechanical reproduction of whatever confronted the camera lens. They argued that film could be more than a record of the flow of reality. It could shape reality creatively and, therefore, it deserved to be taken seriously in virtue of its artistic dimension.[5]

One can certainly sympathize with Grierson's aims. However, once we see what is behind his definition of the documentary, I think it is pretty clear that the notion will not serve to demarcate the area of study that often bears its name today. For Grierson's concept is too narrow. It excludes such things as Lumière *actualités* and the videotape of the Rodney King beating—things that most of us, I conjecture, think belong legitimately in the curriculum of courses with titles such as *Introduction to the Documentary Film*.

Needless to say, this is not a criticism of Grierson. He meant to exclude candidates like these from the class of things he called 'documentaries'. And it is his privilege to call what he was doing whatever suits him. Rather, I mean to criticize those who carelessly try to stretch Grierson's notion to cover the whole field. For Grierson's notion of documentary picks out an extension of objects far more narrow than that referred to by most subsequent authors of books on the so-called documentary.

One might say 'so what?' Grierson meant one thing by 'documentary', and now we mean something else by it. But there is at least this problem. Whatever *we* might mean by it is obscure and perhaps equivocal. Thus, we find ourselves in a situation where we have, on the one hand, the relatively precise notion of the documentary that Grierson has bequeathed us, and, on the other hand, another more ambiguous idea. This at the very least courts confusion. I propose to relieve that confusion by granting Grierson his definition for what he was talking about and by introducing a new concept for what we wish to speak about.

Here it might be thought that we already have an alternative ready to hand in the concept of non-fiction. But if the Griersonian label of the documentary is too narrow for our purposes, the notion of non-fiction is too broad. Consider the way in which the couplet fiction/non-fiction divides up a book shop. The novels, short stories, and perhaps plays will be found in the fiction section. Everything else is non-fiction, including children's drawing manuals. But when we consider what is discussed under the prevailing rubric of the documentary film, interactive lessons about the way to draw a flower are not what we have in mind.

Moreover, films like J. J. Murphy's *Print Generation*, Peter Kulbelka's *Arnulf Rainer*, and Ernie Gehr's *Serene Velocity* are not fictions. They tell no imagined story. So, they are non-fiction. But, once again, they are not included in histories of, nor classes concerning, the so-called documentary. Thus, I take it that the suspicion that the category of non-fiction is too broad for our purposes is well motivated.

If I am right in supposing that our presiding labels and concepts are inadequate to our purposes, then the best solution, it seems to me, is to devise a new label, accompanied by a rigorous definition. This sounds very reformist. However, I think that my proposal in terms of films of presumptive assertion—which might more tendentiously be called 'films of putative fact'—does a better job of locating the body of work that concerns those who currently signal their domain of discourse by means of the idiom of the documentary or non-fiction film.

How might one substantiate this claim? One way is to argue that the notion of films of presumptive assertion makes more sense out of the debates that people have in this area of enquiry. For example, major debates over the so-called non-fiction film involve claims about the objectivity of the relevant films and about whether they can refer to reality. But if what we want to talk about includes films like *Arnulf Rainer*—a flicker film—then questions of objectivity and reference to reality fall by the wayside, since it makes no sense to ask of *Arnulf Rainer* whether it is objective or even subjective in its reference to reality. Its images are not fictional, but they are not referential either. It is a non-fiction film, but it stands outside the epistemic questions that obsess documentary film studies. On the other hand, the notion of films of presumptive assertion would not encompass works like *Arnulf Rainer* to begin with, but only films that play what we might call the assertion game, a game wherein epistemic questions of objectivity and truth are uncontroversially apposite.

I will pursue the analysis of films of presumptive assertion in stages. First, I will try to draw a distinction between fiction and non-fiction. Then, I will go on—exploiting what has been said about the fiction/non-fiction couplet—to propose an analysis of films of presumptive assertion (as a subcategory of the non-fiction film). Once I have worked out my analysis of films of presumptive assertion, I will then contemplate a series of problems or questions that my theory is likely to raise.

2. FICTION AND NON-FICTION

The first step in defining the film of presumptive assertion is to draw a distinction between fiction and non-fiction, since the film of presumptive assertion, on my account, is a subcategory of non-fiction. However, many film scholars are likely to regard even this first step as quixotic. For they are persuaded that there is no viable distinction between fiction and non-fiction. They are convinced that it has been, as they say, 'deconstructed';[6] all films can be shown to be fictional.

Christian Metz, for example, has argued:

At the theater Sarah Bernhardt may tell me she is Phèdre or if the play were from another period and rejected the figurative regime, she might say, as in a type of modern theater, that she is Sarah Bernhardt. But at any rate, I should see Sarah Bernhardt. At the cinema she could make two kinds of speeches too, but it would be her shadow that would be offering them to me (or she would be offering them in her own absence). Every film is a fiction film.[7]

Another reason why some film scholars suppose that the distinction between fiction and non-fiction is inoperable is that non-fiction and fiction films share many of the same structures—flashbacks, parallel editing, cross-cutting, point-of-view editing, and the like. And certain mannerisms found in non-fiction films, like grainy footage and unsteady camera movements, have been appropriated by fiction films in order to achieve certain effects—like the impression of realism or authenticity. Thus, on the grounds of formal differentiae, one cannot distinguish fiction films from non-fiction films.[8]

There is also another way to argue for the view that the distinction between fiction films and non-fiction films is unsupportable. Friends of this view, whom we will call 'deconstructionists' for convenience, might suggest the following intuition pump. Presented with a film, it is at least conceivable that an informed viewer—i.e. a viewer fully knowledgeable of film techniques and their histories—might not be able to identify it correctly as a fiction or non-fiction film. All the formal information in the world would not be conclusive. Perhaps the dissection segments of the notorious *Alien Autopsy* are a pertinent example in this respect.

But let us start with Metz's position first. Metz's argument seems to me to be clearly fallacious. In effect, it not only denies the distinction between fiction and non-fiction, but it undermines the distinction between representation and fiction as well. If the reason that a film of Sarah Bernhardt saying that she is Sarah Bernhardt is a fiction is because Sarah Bernhardt is not in the screening room, then an aerial photograph of a battlefield will count as a fiction. But clearly it is not a fiction. It does not represent an imaginary configuration of forces due to the fact that the enemy is not in the room as our General Staff examines said aerial photographs. Armies do not plan counter-attacks on the basis of novels. But that is tantamount to what they would be doing if the aerial photographs were fictions.

Perhaps the proponent of Metz will counter that, even though all representations are fictions, there are different kinds of fictions. The aerial photographs belong to one sort and *All that Heaven Allows* to another sort. But what then distinguishes these different sorts of fiction? Without further argument, it would appear that something like the fiction/non-fiction distinction needs to be reintroduced.

Perhaps it will be said that there are *fictional* non-fictions (the class to which the aerial photographs and *Hoop Dreams* belong) and *fictional* fictions (the class to which *Seven* belongs). But this seems to reinscribe the fiction/non-fiction distinction, rather than to dismiss it. And, furthermore, the aforesaid *fictional* prefixes to these alleged categories do no conceptual work—i.e. make no meaningful contrast conceptually—and, therefore, are theoretically dispensable.

But an even deeper criticism of Metz's argument is that it contradicts the logic of representation. Representations are not equivalent to whatever they represent. This is why we have representations. It is one of the reasons they are so useful. If a map had to be the very terrain it is a map of, it would be of no added pragmatic value when we are lost on the terrain in question. Representations standardly are not what they represent. But in requiring Sarah Bernhardt in the screening room for a film of her *not* to count as fiction, Metz is forgetting (and, indeed, contradicting) what a representation is, as well as conflating representation and fiction.

In response, one might say that what Metz has done is to discover that all representations are really fictions. But one wants to question the nature of this discovery. It certainly does not reflect the way in which we typically deploy these concepts. Maybe Metz is assuming some stipulative redefinition of these concepts. But can Metz defend his stipulative redefinition of these concepts on the grounds that it is useful to construe these concepts his way? I doubt it. Indeed, Metz's reconstrual of these concepts is more likely to cause more confusion than anything else. Imagine how counterproductive it would be to be told that the pictures on a wanted-poster are fictional?

Metz reminds us that when Bernhardt plays Phèdre, there is a person, Bernhardt, standing before us, whereas when we see a movie of the same event, Bernhardt is not present. Fair enough. But what Metz ignores is the fact that the actress, Bernhardt on-stage, is a representational vehicle, indeed a fictional representational vehicle. She represents Phèdre. And there *is* also, in fact, a representational vehicle present in the screening room with us, namely the cinematic apparatus projecting the film of Bernhardt/Phèdre. So far there is no significant theoretical difference between the stage case and the film case in terms of the presence of representational vehicles. Moreover, in neither case is what we literally see a fictional character. What we literally see is a representational vehicle which may present either a fiction or non-fiction. Therefore, the question of the presence or absence of a representational vehicle is irrelevant to deciding a difference in the fictional/non-fictional status of the two cases.

Furthermore, what Metz vaguely calls absence would appear to be an essential characteristic of representations, irrespective of whether the representations are fictional or non-fictional. Thus, Metz seems guilty of a conceptual confusion inasmuch as he conflates representation and fiction.

Let us now turn to the second line of dissolving the distinction between fiction and non-fiction. This 'deconstructionist' attack begins with a series of reasonable observations. Many of the structures of the fiction film are shared by the non-fiction film. It is certainly true that non-fiction film-makers have imitated narrative devices that originated in the fiction film. And fiction film-makers have imitated non-fiction stylistics. Nevertheless, the lesson that those who favour the view that every film is fictional draw from these observations is too quick. They surmise that these considerations indicate that there is no difference between fiction and non-fiction. But another conclusion, equally consistent with the relevant observations, is that the distinction between fiction and non-fiction *does not rest* on a principled difference between the stylistic properties of fictional and non-fictional films.

Consider the analogous case of literature. There are no textual features— linguistic structures, writing styles, or plots—that mark something as a fiction. You might suppose that there are certain structures that could appear only in fiction, such as internal monologues. But, in fact, you can find them in non-fictions such as *Armies of the Night*. Moreover, this problem is necessarily insurmountable, since any linguistic structure, writing style, plot device, or other textual feature that characteristically appears in a fiction can be imitated by the non-fiction writer for a wide range of aesthetic effects.

And, of course, there is the mirror-image problem regarding the fiction writer. He can imitate any of the textual features characteristically associated with non-fiction writing for a broad assortment of purposes, including that of imbuing his fiction with a sense of heightened verisimilitude. So, since non-fiction and fiction authors alike can appropriate any of the formulae or devices associated with fiction and non-fiction respectively, we are compelled to the unavoidable conclusion that fiction and non-fiction cannot be differentiated by pointing to some linguistic or textual features that belong to all and only fiction or non-fiction respectively.

Of course, this is a theoretical rather than a practical problem, since we rarely encounter texts not knowing their status as fiction or non-fiction. Generally, we know before we start reading a text whether it is fiction or non-fiction. We do not adopt the role of detectives, trying to determine whether the story we are reading is fictional or non-fictional. Typically the story comes to us labeled one way or the other. Thus, the issue is theoretical and not practical.

Admittedly, it might be a problem which, though rarely arising, nevertheless could arise. We might find a text from the distant past, about which we possess no contextual information. In such a case, we might look at stylistic and textual features for some evidence about whether the work is fictional or non-fictional. But though this is a way in which we might proceed, such speculation is neither the only evidence we would look for,[9] nor would it be conclusive. Such evidence is at best probable and contingent because of what has already been said—namely, that any non-fictional device can always be imitated by the fiction writer, and vice versa for the non-fiction writer. But the distinction between fiction and non-fiction is ultimately not a matter of probability; it is a conceptual matter.

Yet even the preceding case does not show that there is no distinction between fiction and non-fiction, but only that nothing is conclusively fiction or non-fiction writing on the basis of the textual or linguistic features that it possesses. A text does not, for example, have the status of a fiction by virtue of the textual features it has or has not got. The fictional status of a text is not constituted by its textual features, even if, to a limited extent, the textual features, in some circumstances, might provide us with *some* evidence or clues that we might use to hypothesize its status where it is otherwise unknown.

Another way to make the point is to say that the fictionality of a text is not constituted or determined by its *manifest* textual properties. That is, you cannot tell whether a text is a fiction simply by looking at its linguistic, stylistic, or other textual features. You cannot tell for sure whether a text is fictional by reading it in a decontextualized way, where the only permissible information involves the consideration of its linguistic and textual features. Whether or not a text is fictional depends on its non-manifest (relational) properties (which I will specify further anon). You cannot tell whether a text is fictional in virtue of its manifest properties, inspected in isolation. You have to consider the text in relation to something else—something else that is not manifest in the text; something else that cannot be read off the surface of the text.

As it is with literature, so it is with film. One does not conclusively identify something as either a fiction or a non-fiction film by looking at its manifest structural features. This is not what film-goers do. Like the readers of literature, film-goers generally know whether the film they are about to see has been labelled one way or the other. This information circulates in the film world before the work is seen—in the form of advertisements, distribution releases, reviews, word of mouth, and the like. This is why the previous intuition pump is so contrived and unilluminating. We do not go to films and attempt to guess whether they are fictions or non-fictions. In the largest number of cases, we know ahead of time how to categorize the films in question. Moreover, it is hard to see what motivation practitioners in the institution of film would have to replace the current system with guessing games.

Film scholars are correct in noting the overlapping stylistics of the fiction and non-fiction film. However, they are wrong to understand this as entailing that there is no distinction between fiction films and non-fiction films, and that all films are fictional. Their error is logical. For they presume that if there is no stylistic differentia between fiction and non-fiction films, then there is no differentia whatsoever. But this is baldly a non sequitur. For they have not foreclosed the possibility that there may be differentiae other than stylistic or formal considerations in virtue of which the distinction can be drawn.[10]

Of course, revealing the lacuna in the argument for the reduction of all film to fiction on the grounds that it has failed to preclude the possibility that it has not eliminated all the potential candidates for drawing the distinction, though logically correct, is unlikely to be persuasive, unless it is possible to come up with a plausible alternative candidate for distinguishing fiction from non-fiction. Thus, in order to carry my case across the finish line, it is incumbent upon me to show that there are eminently reasonable grounds for thinking that there is a viable way to make the distinction that the 'deconstructionists' have overlooked, and to defend it.

By denying that one can demarcate fiction from non-fiction on the basis of stylistics, the 'deconstructionist', in effect, is denying that one can determine whether a candidate film is a fiction, for example, on the basis of the intrinsic, manifest properties of the work. I agree. But this does not mean that the distinction cannot be crafted by considering certain non-manifest, relational properties of the works in question. This is the line of argument that I want to pursue. Specifically, I want to argue that we can draw a distinction between fiction and non-fiction on the basis of certain authorial intentions.[11] The authorial intentions I have in mind may, of course, not be manifest in the work, and, moreover, they are relational properties of the work—i.e. properties of the work in relation to the author, and, as we shall see, in relation to spectators as well.

Furthermore, if the analysis in terms of authorial intentions can be defended, then, from the perspective of logic, the burden of proof falls to the 'deconstructionists'. That is, if they still wish to maintain that there is no distinction between fiction and non-fiction, it falls to them to show the error in my proposal.

As I construe the problem, we begin with a presumption in favour of a distinction between fiction and non-fiction. There is a presumption in favour of it because it is deeply embedded in our practices and it is at the centre of our conceptual scheme. It is difficult to see how we can get along without it. But a presumption is not a proof. The presumption must be backed up by compelling reasons. Moreover, as we have seen, the presumption cannot be defended on stylistic grounds. We can imagine fiction films that are stylistically indiscernible from non-fiction films, and vice versa. We cannot 'eyeball' the distinction between the two. That is one indication that the problem before us is philosophical.[12]

Because we cannot 'eyeball' the distinction by looking at a given film, the distinction, if there is one, must rest upon some non-manifest, relational properties of fiction films and non-fiction films respectively. But what can that distinction be?

In order to answer that question, I shall take advantage of what might be called an intention-response model of communication. This approach is frequently employed nowadays by philosophers in order to develop theories of art as well as fiction.[13] The approach is broadly Gricean in its inspiration. Applied to art, it presupposes that an artist or an author, such as a film-maker, communicates to an audience by way of indicating that the audience is intended to respond to his or her text (i.e. any structure of sense-bearing signs) in a certain way, where the reason that the audience has for mobilizing the response or the stance in question is the audience's recognition of the sender's intention that they do so.

This approach is social, at least in the sense that it depends upon certain relations, rooted in our communicative practices, between the senders and receivers of sense-bearing signs. Moreover, if this approach can be applied to the cases of fiction and non-fiction, it will propose a non-manifest, relational property of the texts in question as that which determines the status of the text as fictional or non-fictional. And that is just the sort of property that we are looking for in our endeavour to distinguish fiction and non-fiction films.

Since the Gricean-type intention-response model of communication has provided insights already to philosophers, psychologists, and linguists alike, it seems a reasonable theoretical option to try out, at least hypothetically, though, of course, the hypothesis must be defended subsequently. Thus, applying the intention-response model to the case of fiction, we may begin by hypothesizing that a structured set of sense-bearing signs, such as a novel or a film, is fictional only if presented by an author, film-maker, or sender who intends the audience to respond to it with what we might call the fictive stance on the basis of recognizing the author's, film-maker's, or sender's intention that the audience do this on the basis of recognizing what we might call the sender's fictive intention. A compact, jargonistic statement of the theory, then, is that a structure of sense-bearing signs is a fiction only if it is presented by a sender with the fictive intention that the audience respond to it by adopting the fictive stance on the basis of recognizing the sender's fictive intention that they do so.[14]

Of course, this definition is pretty obscure. It needs to be unpacked—more needs to be said about what is involved in a fictive stance and a fictive intention. What is a fictive intention? It is the intention of the author, film-maker, or sender of a structure of sense-bearing signs that the audience imagine the content of the story in question on the basis of their recognition that this is what the sender intends them to do.

Suppose we are buying a can of lemonade from a vending machine. After we put our money in the machine, we then press one of the selection buttons. Why do we do this? Because we realize that this is what the designer of the machine intends us to do, presupposing that we wish to use the machine in the way it was designed to be used. Similarly, there is a design intention when it comes to fiction—namely, that we imagine the content of the story in question. Moreover, we adopt this attitude when consuming a fiction because we recognize that this is what the sender intends us to do, presupposing that we wish to use the story in the way in which it was designed to be used. So, when we read that Sherlock Holmes lives on Baker Street, we imagine that he lives on Baker Street. Moreover, our mental state or attitude here is one of imagining, rather than, say, one of believing, because we recognize that Conan Doyle intends us to imagine rather than to believe that Sherlock Holmes lives on Baker Street.

Undoubtedly, there may be epistemological questions about the way in which we come to recognize whether the sender's intention is fictive or non-fictive. But we can put them to one side for the moment and come back to them later. For our concern now is ontological, not epistemological, since what we are pursuing is the question of the nature of fiction. It is one thing to say that fiction is constituted by an authorial fictive intention, and another thing to say how we go about recognizing that intention.

In *Metaphor and Movement*, the dance historian Lincoln Kirstein intends us to believe that *The Sleeping Beauty* ballet was produced in 1890, when he presents us with propositions to that effect, whereas in the novel *The Moor's Last Sigh*, Salman Rushdie intends us to imagine that Aurora is a great Indian painter. Moreover, Rushdie does not intend us to adopt this mental state as the result of magic or drugs. He intends that we adopt this mental state on the basis of the recognition that this is what he, the designer of the text, intends us to do with the novel.

With respect to *The Moor's Last Sigh*, one of Rushdie's fictive intentions is that we imagine that Aurora is a great Indian painter. I say *one* of his intentions because he has others—for example, he also intends that we imagine that Aurora is married to Abraham. Furthermore, all these fictive intentions can be subsumed under one, overarching fictive intention—namely, that the reader imagine all the objects, persons, actions, and events that comprise the story of *The Moor's Last Sigh*. In publishing *The Moor's Last Sigh*, Rushdie intends that the reader shall imagine the persons, actions, objects, and events of the story.

Shall here is normative, not predictive. That is, Rushdie's fictive intention prescribes or mandates how we should take his story in order to use it as it was designed to be used. Someone might, of course, mistake it for a history book and come to believe, rather than to imagine, that Aurora was a great Indian painter. Yet that only shows that to prescribe certain behaviour is not to predict behaviour, a fact brought home to God more than once since the time he promulgated the Ten Commandments.

But, in addition, Rushdie's fictive intention does not simply involve a prescriptive component—that the reader shall imagine the content of the story. It also contains what we might call a reflexive, reason-giving component—that the reader imagine the content *for the reason* that he recognizes that this is what Rushdie intends him to do. Thus, Rushdie's fictive intention is that the reader imagine the propositional content of *The Moor's Last Sigh* for the reason that the reader recognizes that this is what he is intended to do.

We have already effectively described what is involved in the fictive stance in the preceding discussion of the fictive intention. The notion of the fictive intention looks at the matter from the author's side of the transaction; the notion of the fictive stance refers to the audience's part of the bargain. The author intends the audience to adopt a certain attitude toward the propositional content of the story. That attitude is the audience's stance.[15] Where the work is a fiction, the attitude or stance is one of imagining. The fictive stance, then, is a matter of the audience's imagining the propositional content of a structure of meaning-bearing signs whether they be of the nature of words, images, or something else.

So far, our analysis says that a structure of sense-bearing signs is a fiction only if it involves the audience's adoption of the fictive stance on the basis of its recognition of the author's fictive intention. However, the analysis contains at least one major obscurity. The fictive stance involves imagination. But what is meant by the notion of *imagining*? This problem is compounded by the fact that the histories of literature, psychology, and philosophy are littered with many different, often non-converging notions of the imagination. So how are we to understand that term in a formula such as: x is a fiction only if the sender intends the audience to imagine the propositional content of x for the reason that the audience recognizes that this is what the sender intends?

The way in which we conceive of imagining here is crucial to the attempt to defeat the 'deconstructionist'. For certain concepts of the imagination are likely to encourage 'deconstruction' rather than to thwart it. For example, one concept of the imagination, found in Descartes's *Meditations* and echoed by Kant in *The Critique of Pure Reason*, is that the imagination is the faculty that unifies perceptions. That is, I have the discrete perception of the front of a building, and another discrete perception of the back of the building. But my mind unifies them as parts of the same building. How is this done? By what we might call the imagination.

But if this is the concept of the imagination that we bring to the preceding analysis of fiction, the prospect of 'deconstruction' looms again, since both the historian and the novelist intend us to mobilize what can be called the

constructive imagination. Indeed, if Kant is right, the constructive imagination is always in play so its operation cannot serve to distinguish anything
involving cognition from anything else.[16]

Of course, there are other major notions of the imagination. One is that
it is the capacity for mental imagery. But this will be of no use to us in
defining fiction, since the audience's prescribed response to a fiction does
not require mental imaging. I can imagine the proposition that Aurora is a
great Indian painter, even if I do not have a mental image of her. And as
well, it is possible for the reader of a history book to have mental images on
the basis of the text.

The imagination has received a great deal less philosophical attention
than mental states such as belief. As a result, the notion has often served as
a catch-all category of last resort. Thus, we have inherited a mixed bag of
faculties and mental functions under the rubric of the imagination. Consequently, if we intend to use the concept of the imagination in our formula
for fiction, we must specify what exactly we take *the imagination* to refer to.
We cannot have either the constructive imagination or the mental-imaging
imagination in mind in our formula for the reasons already given. Instead,
my claim is that the relevant sense of *imagination* for my formula is what I
will call the *suppositional imagination*.[17]

Often in the course of a discussion, we may say something like, 'I'll grant
you *x* for the purposes of the argument.' Or, in a mathematical proof, we
may begin by saying, 'Suppose *x*.' These are examples of what I mean by the
suppositional imagination. In such cases we are entertaining a certain
thought or propositional content—namely, that *x*—without committing
ourselves to it by way of belief. We hold *x* in our mind as, so to speak, a
hypothesis, rather than as an assertion. Or we can say that we are entertaining that *x* as an unasserted thought. To believe *x*, on the other hand, is to
entertain *x* as an asserted thought. The idea here is that we can entertain
thoughts or propositional contents—such as that Aurora is a great Indian
painter—as either asserted or unasserted. To entertain a thought or a
propositional content as unasserted is to imagine it in the sense of the
suppositional imagination. And it is suppositional imagining that is pertinent to the analysis of fiction advanced above.

Fictions, then, in this sense are communications that authors intend the
audience to imagine on the grounds that the audience recognizes that this is
what the author intends them to do. That is, in making fictions, authors are
intentionally presenting audiences with situations (or situation-types) that
we are meant to entertain in thought.[18] The author, in presenting a novel as
a fiction, in effect signals to the reader 'I intend you to hold these propositions (*p*) before your mind unasserted'—that is, 'suppose *p*', or 'entertain *p*
unasserted', or 'contemplate *p* as a supposition'.

Of course, it needs to be added that when an author invites you to imagine the propositional content of a story, he is not providing you with a *carte blanche* to imagine whatever you wish. He is inviting you to imagine *his* story—its propositional content, including what it presupposes and implies. The audience's suppositional imagination is to be controlled imagining, normatively speaking. That is, it is supposed or meant to be constrained by what the author mandates by way of presenting his text. The details of the text control what it is legitimate for the audience to imagine in response to the author's fictive intention.

With this conception of the imagination under our belt, we can say that a structure of sense-bearing signs x by sender s is fictional only if s presents x to an audience a with the intention that a suppositionally imagine the propositional content of x for the reason that a recognizes this as s's intention. This is the core of our proposal of what it is for a text—filmic or otherwise—to be fictional. It constitutes a necessary condition for fictionality, though further conditions would have to be added to bring the formula to sufficiency.[19]

Moreover, once we have the crucial defining condition of fiction in our possession, the formula for non-fiction is also within our reach. We can generate it by negating the core defining feature of fiction. So, a structure of sense-bearing signs x is non-fictional only if sender s presents it to audience a with the intention that a not suppositionally imagine x as a result of a's grasp of s's intention. That is, a non-fiction x is such that it is presented by an author to audience with the intention that the audience recognize that it, the audience, is *not mandated* to entertain the propositional content of the relevant structure of sense-bearing signs as unasserted. This, of course, is only an essential, defining, necessary condition of non-fiction; the complete formula would have to be more complicated.[20]

Inasmuch as this account of non-fiction is simply a negation of the core defining feature of fiction, it encompasses a great many structures of sense-bearing signs, indeed it includes any structure of sense-bearing signs that is not a fiction. Any film, for example, that does not authorially prescribe that viewers entertain its propositional content as unasserted falls into this category. And that will incorporate not only films that mandate that their propositional content be entertained as asserted, but also films that lie outside the assertion game, like Kubelka's *Arnulf Rainer* or Gehr's *Serene Velocity*.

But *Serene Velocity*, I submit, does not tell us anything about how we are to entertain the shots of the hallway that comprise it. Are we to imagine there is such a hallway, or are we to believe it? It really makes no difference to the effect of the film one way or another.[21] It does not mandate that we entertain as unasserted the thought that there is such and such a hallway, since the film-maker is neutral or perhaps indifferent to how the images of the hallway are to be entertained by us. Thus, it is non-fiction, since, for the reasons given, it does not mandate that we imagine that there is such a hallway. The shots of the hallway function purely as stimuli. So *Serene Velocity is not fiction*. But as I claimed earlier, *Serene Velocity* is not at the same time the sort of film that people in the field of the so-called documentary film have in mind. We need a more fine-grained concept than nonfiction in order to capture that narrower extension of films.

3. FILMS OF PRESUMPTIVE ASSERTION

Against 'deconstructionists', we have introduced a principled distinction between fiction and non-fiction. However, as we have seen, the concept of non-fiction that we have defined is broader than what we need for film studies. Nevertheless, I think that we can locate a category, suitable to the purposes of film studies, which is a subcategory of the preceding concept of non-fiction.

We derived our concept of non-fiction by negating the fictive stance component of our concept of fiction. In effect, we characterized non-fiction as the logical contradictory of fiction—that the audience *not* entertain as unasserted the propositional content of the structure of sense-bearing signs in question. That is, the non-fictive stance involves not imagining the propositional content of the text, or, summarily: nonfiction = not the fictive stance. So, we might generate a narrower concept than non-fiction by producing the logical contrary of the fictive stance.

The fictive stance involves entertaining as unasserted the propositional content of the text. An alternative, logically contrary stance, then, is that the audience entertain as asserted the propositional content of the text. In plain English, the mandated audience response to fiction is that the audience imagine the propositional content of the text. An alternative audience attitude is mandated when the author intends the audience to believe the content of the text.

Our concept of non-fiction was essentially negative. It was based on specifying what the author intended the audience to refrain from doing, namely, imagining the propositional content of the text. Our present suggestion is a positive characterization. It specifies what the author intends the audience to do with the propositional content of the pertinent structure of sense-bearing signs. To wit: we are to entertain the propositional content of the relevant structure as asserted thought. This characterization is key to defining the film of presumptive assertion.[22]

With the film of presumptive assertion the film-maker intends that the audience entertain the propositional content of his film in thought as asserted. Thus, in the CBS *Twentieth Century* instalment entitled *Born to Kill*, the audience is not only mandated *not* to imagine that Jeffrey Dahmer and

Ted Bundy were found guilty, but, in addition, the film-makers prescribe that the audience should entertain this proposition in thought as asserted. We might say that in contrast to the case of fiction, the sender of a structure of sense-bearing signs of this sort possesses an assertoric intention which prescribes that the audience adopt an assertoric stance toward the propositional content of the text on the basis of their recognition that this is what the sender intends them to do.

This is a necessary condition for the species of cinema that I am calling films of presumptive assertion. I call them films of *presumptive* assertion not only because the audience presumes that it is to entertain the propositional content of such a film as asserted, but also because such films may lie. That is, they are presumed to involve assertion even in cases where the film-maker is intentionally dissimulating at the same time that he is signalling an assertoric intention. Moreover, in light of this presumption, the films in question are assessed in terms of the standard conditions for non-defective assertion, including: that the film-maker is committed to the truth (or plausibility, as the case may be) of the propositions the film expresses *and* that the propositions expressed in the film are beholden to the standards of evidence and reasoning appropriate to the truth (or plausibility) claims that the film advances.[23]

In the case of the film of presumptive fact, the film-maker presents the film with an assertoric intention: with the intention that the viewer entertain the propositional content of the film as asserted. In order for the film-maker's assertoric intention to be non-defective, the film-maker is committed to the truth or plausibility of the propositional content of the film and to being responsible to the standards of evidence and reason required to ground the truth or plausibility of the propositional content the film-maker presents.

Recognizing the film-maker's assertoric intention, the audience entertains the propositional content of the film as asserted thought. This means that the audience regards the propositional content of the film as something that the author believes to be true, or, in certain circumstances, that the author believes is plausible, and as something that is committed to the relevant standards of evidence and reason for the type of subject-matter being communicated. If the audience believes that the film-maker does not believe the propositional content of the film, despite the fact that the film-maker signals an assertoric intention, they suspect that the film-maker is lying. If the audience member thinks that the film is not committed to the relevant standards of evidence, he suspects that the film is apt to be mistaken, and, in any case, that it is objectively unjustified. Such audience expectations are part of what it is to take the assertoric stance—to entertain the propositional content of the film in thought as asserted.

Stated compactly, then, a crucial, defining condition of the film of presumptive assertion is that it involves an assertoric intention on the part of a film-maker that the audience adopt an assertoric stance to the propositional content of the film, where the audience adopts this stance on the basis of its recognition of the film-maker's assertoric intention. This gives us the core ingredients of the film of presumptive assertion. However, more is required to define the film of presumptive assertion completely. For not only does the audience have to discern and respond to the film-maker's assertoric intentions. It must also grasp the meanings communicated by the film. That is, the maker of a film of presumptive assertion not only intends that the audience adopt the assertoric stance to his film, but he also intends that the audience understand his film. So a complete definition of the film of presumptive assertion involves not only an assertoric intention on the part of the film-maker, but a meaning-intention as well.

In order to accommodate this requirement, let us adopt a Gricean account of what is involved when an utterer means something by x. Let us say that 'a sender means something by x' is roughly equivalent to 'the sender intends the presentation of x to produce some effect in an audience by means of this intention'.[24] Applying this pattern, then, to the film of presumptive assertion, I contend that:

> x is a film of presumptive assertion if and only if the film-maker s presents x to an audience a with the intention (1) that a recognizes that x is intended by s to mean that p (some propositional content), (2) that a recognize that s intends them (a) to entertain p as an asserted thought (or as a set of asserted thoughts), (3) that a entertains p as asserted thought, and (4) that 2 is a reason for 3.[25]

Or to put the matter more succinctly, something is a film of presumptive assertion if and only if it involves a meaning intention on the part of the film-maker which provides a basis for meaning pick-up on the part of the audience as well as an assertoric intention on the part of the film-maker which provides the grounds for the adoption of the assertoric stance on the part of the audience.[26]

In order to appreciate what is involved in this theory of the film of presumptive assertion, it is instructive to compare it to an alternative theory of the way in which we might characterize the so-called 'documentary' film. Using the intention-response model, we might hypothesize a category which can be called 'the film of the presumptive trace'. On this account, the relevant structure of sense-bearing signs is such that the film-maker intends that the audience regard the images in the films as historic traces as a consequence of the audience's recognition that that is what the film-maker intends them to do. Regarding the images as historic traces, in turn, involves entertaining the thought as asserted that the images in the film have originated photographically from precisely the source from which the film claims or implies they originated. Nevertheless, these are called 'films of the *presumptive* trace', since, of course, the film-maker may be dissimulating.

In a fiction film, we see an image of a house and we imagine that it is Tara, the home of Scarlet O'Hara. In the case of the film of the presumptive trace, when we see an image of a tree and we are told something about trees in the Amazon rainforest, we entertain as asserted—so the theory of the film of the presumptive trace goes—that the image of the tree we are seeing is the photographic trace of some tree in the Amazon rainforest. We do not regard the image as the historic trace of some tree in a botanical garden in Brooklyn. We regard it as the historic trace of some tree in the Amazon; nor do we use the image to imagine that there is such a tree. We take the image as having been produced by a camera aimed at a specific tree in the Amazon rainforest.

Moreover, we regard the image in this way because we recognize that the film-maker intends us to regard the image of the tree as an authentic historic trace. In effect, we recognize that the film-maker intends that we regard as asserted the proposition that this image of a tree was photographically produced by some actually existing tree which does or did luxuriate in the Amazon rainforest.

The concept of the film of the presumptive trace is different from that of the film of presumptive assertion. The film of presumptive assertion, for the most part, is broader, since it refers to works where the film-maker possesses any sort of assertoric intention, whereas the film of the presumptive trace refers only to films where the makers have a very particular assertoric intention, namely, that the images be entertained in asserted thought as being historic traces. The notion of films of the presumptive trace captures the 'document' dimension that many associate with the so-called documentary film. One might even regard it as deriving inspiration from the *actualité*. Films of presumptive assertion, on the other hand, not only include *actualités*, but any film made with an assertoric intention, including an animated simulation of the trajectory of a satellite.

Given these two contrasting concepts, the question arises which one we should prefer? Both seem perfectly intelligible. Is one more attractive than the other? Needless to say, in order to answer this, we have to consider the use we wish the concept to serve. If we wish to define the *actualité*, the notion of the film of the presumptive trace does a better—more precise—job of tracking the phenomenon. However, if we want to capture what film scholars generally have in mind when they talk about documentaries or non-fiction films, I think that the notion of the film of presumptive assertion is superior. The reason for this is that scholars in this field have always talked about films where the audience was clearly not intended to regard every shot as the historic trace of its subject.

Consider, for example, the History Channel's film *Nautilus*. Quite clearly not all of the images are historic traces, nor are they intended to be taken as such. In the first part of the film, there is a discussion of nineteenth-century submarines. As the narrator discusses a progression of these early submersibles, we see outline drawings of them superimposed over water; we also see a model of Fulton's submarine, in living colour, likewise superimposed over water. These are not historic traces of antique submersibles, nor are they intended to be so taken. The audience realizes that they are merely illustrations of them. Audience members understand that they are being shown these images in order to gain a sense of what these contraptions looked like.

Similarly, when the narrator of *Nautilus* recounts the sinking of the cruiser HMS *Cressy* by a German U-boat in the First World War, we are shown a shot in colour—of palpably contemporary origin—of a sailor's cap floating to the bottom of Davy Jones's locker. Later, when we are told that a U-boat sank a merchant ship, we see another colour shot, this time of a life-preserver labelled *Falada*, the name of the doomed ship. But the audience does not take these shots as historical documents.

Nautilus is clearly what scholars, and film distributors, are prone to label a 'documentary', but its makers do not intend that the aforesaid shots be regarded as historic traces of the naval engagements in question. The audience understands that they are at best factually based illustrations of something that plausibly happened when, respectively, the *Cressy* and the *Falada* sunk. What the audience is intended to entertain in thought as asserted is simply that the *Cressy* and the *Falada* were torpedoed with lethal effect.

Throughout *Nautilus*, we are shown maps sketching the journeys of various submarines. The audience correctly regards these as informational, but nothing indicates that one is to take these shots as historic traces of actual submariners plotting their courses on authentic naval charts. Moreover, the film has some re-enactments, in colour footage, of what was involved in life in the close quarters of a U-boat. The audience understands that this is not actual archival footage, but only presumptively accurate visual information bringing home concretely to the viewers what the narrator means when he tells them how very cramped the space in a vintage submarine was.

I submit that *Nautilus* is a film that falls into the category that everyone in the field of the so-called documentary wants to talk about. But if we are employing the notion of the film of the presumptive trace to model that category, *Nautilus* would be excluded.[27] Of course, the issue is not simply whether *Nautilus* should be included. Rather, the point is that the techniques to which we have drawn attention in *Nautilus* are pretty common in the so-called documentary film. Thus, if we are trying to capture conceptually what people generally mean by 'documentary' today, then the film of the presumptive trace is too narrow a concept.

The concept of the film of presumptive assertion is a better idea. For it allows that the films in question can involve re-enactment, animation, the use of stock footage, and the like. In fact, a film of presumptive assertion could be comprised completely of animation or computer-generated imagery. For the notion of the film of presumptive assertion merely requires that the structure of sense-bearing be presented with the assertoric authorial intention that we entertain the propositional content of the film as asserted thought. It does not require that we regard the images as authentic historic traces. The notion of the film of presumptive assertion countenances a state of the art, computer-generated programme on the life of dinosaurs as falling under its rubric, whereas it seems to me that such a programme could not be contained in the class of things denominated as films of the presumptive trace.

Unlike Grierson's notion of the documentary, the concept of the film of presumptive assertion encompasses the *actualité*. But in contrast to the concept of the film of the presumptive trace, it also covers much more. It includes every sort of film of putative fact, irrespective of whether those facts are advanced by means of authentic archival footage or by other means. And in so far as it captures this wider domain, it better suits the purposes of film scholars, film-makers, film distributors, and the general public than does the idea of the film of the presumptive trace.

4. SOME OBJECTIONS

In developing the concept of both the film of presumptive assertion and the film of the presumptive trace, I have taken advantage of the intention-response model of communication. Both concepts require that the audience recognize a certain intention of the film-maker. However, many film scholars are apt to reject this type of theorizing, since, like their confrères in other humanities departments, they do not believe that we can have access to authorial intentions, and, therefore, they do not believe that theories of this sort are practicable.

Perhaps the very first thing to say in response to this objection is that it misses the point, since the theory of the film of presumptive assertion is an ontological theory—a characterization of the nature of a certain type of film—and not an epistemological theory about the way in which to identify such films. However, having said that, let me also add that I do not believe that the theory would be impracticable if used to distinguish different sorts of film. And so even though the objection misses the mark, I will attempt to show that the allegation of impracticability is also mistaken.

If film scholars think that the concept of the film of presumptive assertion is compromised because they presuppose that intentions are always un-fathomable, then they need to be reminded that we constantly attribute intentions to others with an astoundingly high degree of success. When someone holds a door open, I take this as a signal of their intention that I walk through it. And most of the time when I make this inference, I am not mistaken. When someone at the dinner table hands me a plate of potatoes. I infer that they intend that it is my turn to take some potatoes. And again I am almost always correct in this. Likewise, when the notice comes from the electrical company, I always recognize that they intend me to pay my bill. And every time I pay my bill in response, it turns out that I was right. Or, at least, they never send my cheque back.

Social life could not flourish if we were not able to discern the intentions of others. We could not understand the behaviour or the words and deeds of others if we could not successfully attribute intentions to them. This is not to say that we never make mistaken attributions of intentions to others. But we are all more successful in this matter than we are unsuccessful.

Consequently, the film scholar who is sceptical of the practicability of the category of the film of presumptive assertion on the grounds that we are incapable of correctly attributing intentions to others, including film-makers, is immensely unconvincing. We do not typically have any prin-cipled problems in discerning the intentions of others. The social fabric could not cohere, unless we were *generally* successful in attributing inten-tions to others. The social fabric does cohere because we are so adept at discerning the intentions of others, including even film-makers. There are no grounds for thinking that, in principle, the intentions of others are unfath-omable. For in fact, they are not.

Moreover, our ability to attribute intentions to others successfully is not restricted to living people. Historians scrutinize the words and deeds of the dead with an eye to determining their intentions. And there is no reason to suppose that they do not often do so successfully. Are historians wrong when they hypothesize that by early 1941 Hitler intended to invade the Soviet Union, or that in 1959 Kennedy intended to run for the presidency? Perhaps Hitler and JFK took some of their intentions to the grave with them. But some of their intentions are certainly accessible to historians. Not all the intentions of historical agents, including film-makers, are ontolo-gically obscure. Historians, including film historians, confront no unscal-able barriers when it comes to surmising the intentions of past persons.

Scholars in film studies and the humanities in general distrust talk of authorial intentions because they believe that powerful arguments with names like the 'intentional fallacy' and 'the death of the author' have demonstrated that authorial intentions either are inaccessible or should be treated as such. These arguments are inconclusive, and I, and others, have attempted to show at length why they are mistaken.[28] However, rather than enter that debate once again, let me now point out that even if the preceding arguments were uncontroversial, they would still not provide grounds for scepticism with regard to the assertoric intentions required for films of presumptive assertion, since the intentional fallacy and the death of the author argument pertain to the interpretation of the meaning of texts,[29] not to their categorization. Thus these arguments, even if they were sound (which they are not) are irrelevant to the question at hand.

According to the intentional fallacy and the death of the author argument, invocation of authorial intention is either illicit, impossible, or impermissible when we are interpreting the meaning of a text. The meaning intentions of the author are, so to speak, out of bounds. But when presenting a work, meaning intentions are not the only intentions at issue. There are also what we might call *categorical intentions*—i.e. intentions about the category to which the relevant work belongs. And these are hardly inscrutable in the way that friends of the intentional fallacy and the death of the author allege the meaning intentions of the author to be. Can anyone doubt that Stanley Kubrick intended *A Space Odyssey* to be regarded as at least belonging to the category of the science fiction film or that John Ford intended *My Darling Clementine* as a western? What grounds are there to suppose that these attributions of intention are mistaken? Surely the reasons for scepticism about the attribution of meaning intentions do not cut against such attributions of categorical intentions.[30] We might argue about the intended meaning of the Star Child in *A Space Odyssey*; but we do not think that the attribution of categorical intentions raises the same kind of epistemological problems. It would take something like the postulation of a Cartesian demon to be seriously sceptical about the attribution of the preceding categorical intentions to Stanley Kubrick and John Ford.

The force of the intentional fallacy and the death of the author argument is that the reference to authorial meaning intentions is either irrelevant or prohibited when interpreting the meaning of a poem. But it is one thing to interpret a poem on the basis of a hypothesis of what an author intends to mean, and another thing to identify a poem on the basis of a hypothesis that poetry is the category in which the author intended to write. Indeed, it may be that in order to be agnostic about authorial meaning intentions even requires that an interpreter know (as he almost always does) that what he is dealing with is intended to be a poem and not a laundry list.

The relevance of this discussion of categorical intentions, I hope, is clear-cut. The assertoric intention of the maker of a film of presumptive assertion is a categorical intention. It is not, therefore, the kind of intention at which either the intentional fallacy or the death of the author argument is directed. Categorical intentions are at the very least more publicly determinable than meaning intentions are supposed to be according to proponents of the intentional fallacy and the death of the author argument. Personally, I do not believe that meaning intentions are as inaccessible as these fashionable arguments allege. But even if (*a big if*) meaning intentions were, that would provide no reason to be suspicious concerning the categorical assertoric intentions of the makers of films of presumptive fact.

Of course, this defence of the practicability of reference to the assertoric intentions of film-makers is rather abstract. It provides a very theoretical reassurance that the assertoric intention is not, in principle, inaccessible. But the conscientious film theorist will want to know in some detail how we go about recognizing the film-maker's assertoric intentions before he or she is willing to grant that my formula is feasible for identifying films of presumptive assertion. So how do we determine that the film-maker has the assertoric intention that we adopt the assertoric stance when we see a film?

Actually, the answer to this question is so obvious that only a film theorist could miss it. Films come labelled, or indexed, as to the type of films they are, and where these labels index the films as 'documentaries' or 'non-fiction films' the audience has access to information about the assertoric intentions of the film-maker.[31] The way in which a film is indexed is a perfectly public matter; there is nothing occult or obscure about it. We have access to the film-maker's assertoric intentions through many routes. There are press releases, advertisements, television interviews, film listings and TV listings, previews, critical reviews, and word of mouth. Moreover, information in the title cards of the film may also be relevant, as in the case of the *National Geographic Society Special—Rain Forest*.

Through many redundant, public channels of communication, the typical viewer knows the kind of film he is about to see. When one chooses to see a film, one generally knows that it is what is called a 'documentary' ahead of time because the film has been indexed and circulated that way. And knowing this much, the film viewer knows that he is intended by the film-maker to adopt what I have called the assertoric stance.

Of course, it is possible that while channel surfing we come across a film whose indexing is not already known to us. Perhaps we ask ourselves, what kind of film is this supposed to be? But we can figure this out pretty quickly—by fairly reliable inference if it is on the Discovery Channel or the History Channel, or, more directly, by looking it up in a TV guide. And we can also wait for the end credits which will generally reiterate information pertinent to indexing the film. Needless to say, we may also use the content, the look, or the sound of the film as evidence about the category to which the film belongs. And this generally works, but, for reasons discussed earlier, a conclusive determination hinges on ascertaining the film-maker's intention through indexing.

Another apparent problem case might be the situation of the film historian who discovers film footage in an archive and wonders what kind of film it is. He cannot be sure by just looking at the film. And let us suppose that the titles are missing. What is he to do? Well, probably what he will do is attempt to find some paper record of it. He will look at newspapers, film histories, memoirs, the records of distributors and film-makers, and the like to find a description of something like the footage he has discovered. He will attempt to identify the footage by appealing to historical data. And in searching for the identity of the film, he will also be searching for its indexing.

Historians have to evaluate, identify, and authenticate documents all the time. Very often they are successful in their endeavours. There is no principled reason to think that a film historian searching for the indexing of a film need be any less successful than any other historian dealing with primary sources of uncertain origin.

Admittedly, it is logically possible that our film historian may never discover the way in which a given film was indexed. Thus, it may turn out that in such cases the assertoric intentions of the film-maker are lost to us forever. What would be the consequences of such cases for the theory of films of presumptive assertion? Not much. First of all, it would not compromise the theory as a definition of films of presumptive assertion because that is an ontological theory. Our inability to determine whether or not the film in question was a film of presumptive assertion would not challenge our claim that the film falls in that category just in case its makers were possessed by an assertoric intention. That we are uncertain of the relevant intention is compatible with the fact that the maker had an assertoric intention, but that we do not know it. The film is or is not a film of presumptive assertion, whether or not we know it is.

Moreover, the practicability of our formula is not unhorsed by the fact that sometimes our formula will leave us with undecidable cases. For, given the phenomenon of indexing, our definition will give us a *generally reliable* way of sorting films of presumptive assertion from other types of film. If there are some cases where there are empirical obstacles to applying the theory, then that does not show the theory is not generally practicable. The theory does not guarantee that we can ascertain with every case whether a given film is a film of presumptive assertion or not. But, nevertheless, it gives us the wherewithal to tell most of the time, and, more importantly, there are not principled reasons to suppose that the formula is not generally reliable. The only problems that may arise are with possible isolated cases where the record of the indexing of the film has been completely obliterated. But this is not likely to occur very often.[32]

In general, then, by virtue of the way a film of presumptive assertion is indexed we recognize the maker's assertoric intention that we entertain the propositional content of the film as asserted thought on the basis of his intention. Thus, when I go into a Blockbuster video outlet and peruse a cassette of *Reptiles and Amphibians*, by Walon Green and Heinz Seilman, I recognize that it is intended to be a film of presumptive assertion, not only because it is in the section labelled 'documentary', but because the information on the sleeve of the cassette iterates this indexing. Moreover, when I put it in my VCR, the title cards indicate that it is a National Geographic Society presentation. As a result, I know that, *ceteris paribus*, the film-makers intend that I entertain the propositional content of *Reptiles and Amphibians* as asserted thought.

Thus, when the film shows and/or tells me that the vine snake of southeast Asia lives in trees, that the Komodo dragon is a really a monitor lizard and that it sometimes eats small goats, that the sea snake's venom is the most toxic, and that, before engaging in ritual mating combat, male tortoises bob their heads, I entertain these propositions as asserted thought, I presume that Walon Green and Heinz Seilman believe these things to be true, and that they are committed to the probity of these propositions in accordance with the canons of evidence and reason-giving appropriate to this type of information.

Were I to learn that Green and Sielman did not believe that these things were true, I would accuse them of lying, even if, unbeknownst to them, these things were actually true. Moreover, if the film-makers were not committed to the appropriate canons of evidence and reason-giving—if they came up with all this stuff about reptiles and lizards by reading tea-leaves—I would have grounds for criticizing the film as a nature film of presumptive assertion. Likewise, the fact that *Roger and Me* knowingly plays fast and loose with the evidence is a bad-making feature of that film, just as if it knowingly advanced propositions that could not be supported by the relevant canons of evidence and reason-giving.

That films of presumptive assertion are beholden to the interpersonal canons of evidence and reason-giving appropriate to the kind of information they convey entails that such films are committed to objectivity. This, of course, does not mean that all, or even most, films of presumptive fact are objective, but only that they are committed to it, which, in turn, entails that their failure to respect the requirements of objectivity provide us with reasons to criticize them *qua* films of presumptive assertion. We may have further reasons to commend such a film—perhaps, its editing is bravura. Nevertheless, the failure to meet its commitment to objectivity, entailed by the assertoric intention that we take an assertoric stance toward it, is always *a* bad-making feature of a film of presumptive assertion, even if, in addition, the film possesses other good-making features. A film of presumptive assertion that fails to meet our expectations with respect to objectivity, which are based on our recognition of the film-maker's assertoric intention that we adopt the assertoric stance, can never receive anything but a mixed critical verdict. If *Roger and Me* is acclaimed as effective anti-capitalist propaganda, outrageous street theatre, or comic high jinks, it should also at the same time be criticized for its failure to respect the evidentiary record.

Of course, in arguing that according to the theory of films of presumptive assertion such films are necessarily committed to objectivity, I am courting rebuke by film scholars. For they believe that it has been conclusively demonstrated that objectivity is impossible in the sort of films I am talking about. Thus, if I maintain that such films are necessarily committed to objectivity, they are likely to respond that, inasmuch as 'should implies can', there is something profoundly wrong with my theory. That is, I contend that makers of films of presumptive assertion, in virtue of their assertoric intention and what it entails, should abide by canons of objectivity. But film scholars are apt to counter that this must be wrong because it is well known that such films necessarily cannot be objective.

Of course, I disagree with this presupposition, and I have argued at great length against it elsewhere.[33] It is not true that such films necessarily always fall short of objectivity because they are selective—a popular argument among film theorists—since selectivity is an essential, non-controversial feature of all sorts of enterprises, such as sociology, physics, biology, history, and even journalistic reportage. Thus, if selectivity presents no special problem for the objectivity of these areas of enquiry, then it is not an a priori problem for makers of films of presumptive fact either. Film-makers, like physicists and historians, may fail to meet their commitments to objectivity. But where that happens it is a matter of individual shortcomings and not of the very nature of things.

Moreover, postmodern theorists who contend that objectivity is impossible in the film of presumptive assertion because it is impossible to achieve in any form of enquiry or discourse champion a position that is inevitably self-refuting. For such theorists act as if they are presenting us with objective reasons that support the truth or the plausibility of their conjectures about knowledge claims in general. But how is that possible if the notion of objective reasons is to be regarded with suspicion? For if all reasons fail to be objective that includes their reasons. So why are they advancing them as objective reasons, and why should anyone believe them?

Likely grounds for rejecting the theory of films of presumptive assertion involve scepticism about the accessibility of authorial intentions and scepticism about the prospects for objectivity. In this section, I have tried to undermine both these anxieties. If my efforts in this regard have been successful, then the theory of films of presumptive assertion is provisionally creditable, and the burden of proof falls on the sceptics to show otherwise.

5. CONCLUSION

In this chapter I have advanced a theory of what I call films of presumptive assertion. It is my claim that this concept captures what people mean to talk about when they speak informally of 'documentaries' and 'non-fiction films'. Whether the theory is successful depends, in part, on how well it picks out the extension of films we have in mind when we use terms like 'documentary'. Undoubtedly, it is up to the reader to see how well my theory tracks usage.

I began developing this theory with the presumption that there is a real distinction in this neighbourhood. I tried to defend this presumption by (1) criticizing the plausibility of 'deconstructionist' arguments to the contrary, and (2) showing that we could develop persuasive theories of fiction, non-fiction, and films of presumptive assertion by employing the intention-response model of communication. In effect, my argument is transcendental in nature. I take it, after clearing away various sceptical arguments, that there are genuine distinctions here to be drawn and then I propose candidates for what I argue are the best ways of making those distinctions. Thus, at this point in the debate, it is up to others (such as the 'deconstructionists') to show either that my distinctions are flawed (logically, empirically, or pragmatically), or that there are better ways of drawing the distinction than mine. Until that time, I propose that what has heretofore been regarded as documentary film in common, contemporary parlance be reconceived in terms of films of presumptive assertion.

Of course, 'films of presumptive assertion' is quite a mouthful. And it does not have a nice ring to it. So, I am not suggesting that we attempt to make ordinary folk replace 'documentary' with this cumbersome locution. We would not succeed, even if we tried. Rather, I am suggesting that for technical or theoretical purposes, we understand that what is typically meant by saying that a film is a 'documentary' is really that it is 'a film of presumptive assertion', unless we have grounds for thinking that the speaker is using the term in the Griersonian sense. The reform I am suggesting is not primarily a linguistic reform, but a theoretical one. Moreover, if other film theorists think that this reform is ill advised, it is up to them to say why.

NOTES

1. Though I constantly refer to film in this chapter, this is really a *façon de parler*. For I also mean to be talking about TV, videotapes, and computer imaging. A more accurate way to talk about the extension of visual media I have in mind would be to speak of *moving images*. But that would not only be cumbersome and perhaps confusing. It would also add even more jargon to an essay that already uses quite enough. Nevertheless, when I refer to film in general in this chapter, it should be understood as referring to moving images of all sorts including TV, video, and CD-ROM. For an account of what I mean by *moving images*, see Noël Carroll, 'Defining

the Moving Image', in *Theorizing the Moving Image* (New York: Cambridge University Press, 1996).

2. According to Chuck Wolfe, by way of Carl Plantinga, the term *documentaire* was widely used in France in the 1920s before Grierson used its English translation to refer to *Moana*.

3. Paul Rotha, *Documentary Film*, 2nd edn. (London: Faber, 1952), 70. This book was originally published in 1935.

4. Brian Winston, *Claiming the Real* (London: British Film Institute, 1995).

5. Showing just this was a pressing issue for early film-makers and film theoreticians. For an account of this ambition, see Noël Carroll, *Philosophical Problems of Classical Film Theory* (Princeton: Princeton University Press, 1988), ch. 1.

6. Throughout this chapter, I have placed terms like 'deconstructed' and 'deconstructionists' in scare quotation marks in order to signal my recognition that some may charge that what I refer to is not strictly Derridean deconstruction. I call the practitioners I have in mind 'deconstructionists' because they wish to erase the distinction between fiction and non-fiction. However, in dismissing this distinction in favour of calling everything 'fiction', these practitioners might be accused by Derrideans of *privileging* fiction.

7. Christian Metz, 'The Imaginary Signifier', *Screen*, 16: 2 (Summer 1975), 47.

8. Michael Renov suggests an argument like this one—among other arguments—in 'Introduction: The Truth about Non-fiction', in his anthology *Theorizing Documentary* (New York: Routledge, 1993). For criticism of Renov's overall position, see Noël Carroll, 'Nonfiction Film and Postmodern Skepticism', in David Bordwell and Noël Carroll (eds.), *Post-Theory: Reconstructing Film Studies* (Madison: University of Wisconsin Press, 1996).

9. Other evidence that we would look for might include the search for mention of this work by historical commentators who might identify it one way or the other, or, at least, suggest the appropriate identification, given information about the context of the work (in terms of its production and/or reception).

10. It also pays to note that there is a second logical error in their argument. For even if it were demonstrated that there is no differentia between fiction and non-fiction films, it would not follow that all films are fictional.

11. Trevor Ponech explores a similar line of argumentation in his chapter in this volume.

12. This view of the nature of philosophical problems is defended by Arthur Danto in his book *Connections to the World* (New York: Harper & Row, 1989).

13. Examples of the intention-response model with respect to art theory include: Monroe Beardsley, 'An Aesthetic Definition of Art', in Hugh Curtler (ed.), *What Is Art?* (New York: Haven, 1983), and Jerrold Levinson, 'Defining Art Historically', in his *Music, Art, and Metaphysics* (Ithaca, NY: Cornell University Press, 1990). Examples of the intention-response model with respect to fiction include: Gregory Currie, *The Nature of Fiction* (Cambridge: Cambridge University Press, 1990), and Peter Lamarque and Stein Haugom Olsen, *Truth, Fiction and Literature* (Oxford: Clarendon Press, 1994).

14. The notion of a 'fictive intention' derives from Currie's *The Nature of Fiction*. 'Fictive stance' is used both in Currie's book and by Lamarque and Olsen in *Truth, Fiction and Literature*.

15. I use the notion of propositional content in its technical sense. It does not refer narrowly to sentences. Propositional content is what is conveyed by a structure of sense-bearing signs, where the sense-bearing signs need not be restricted to sentences of natural or formal languages.

16. It seems to me that a move like this, which film 'deconstructionists' might attempt to emulate, is made by Paul Ricœur in his 'The Interweaving of History and Fiction'.

However, I think that this move is mistaken because Ricœur is trading on the notion of what I call the 'constructive imagination', whereas I maintain that the relevant sense of the imagination for this argument should be what I call the 'suppositional imagination'. See Paul Ricœur, *Time and Narrative*, vol. iii (Chicago: University of Chicago Press, 1985), 180–92.

17. In this I disagree with Kendall Walton, who employs the notion of make-believe. Walton and I might appear to be in agreement, since we both think that fiction involves mandating that the audience imagine. But we have different concepts of imagination. Mine is the suppositional imagination, whereas Walton thinks of the relevant function of the imagination in terms of make-believe. For some of my objections to Walton's notion of make-believe, see Noël Carroll, 'The Paradox of Suspense', in P. Vorderer, M. Wulff, and M. Friedrichsen (eds.), *Suspense: Conceptualizations, Theoretical Analyses and Empirical Explorations* (Mahwah, NJ: Lawrence Erlbaum, 1996), 88; id., 'Critical Study: Kendall L Walton, Mimesis as Make-Believe', *Philosophical Quarterly*, 45: 178 (Jan. 1995), 93–9; and id., 'On Kendall Walton's *Mimesis as Make-Believe*', *Philosophy and Phenomenological Research*, 51: 2 (June 1991), 383–7. Walton's view is stated most elaborately in his book *Mimesis as Make-Believe: On the Foundations of the Representational Arts* (Cambridge, Mass.: Harvard University Press, 1990).

18. Kendall Walton objects to the assimilation of the imagination to the notion of 'entertaining thoughts'. He contends that entertaining thoughts restricts us to occurrent imaginings, whereas in order to follow a narrative fiction the non-occurrent imagination must be employed as well in order to deal with such things as the presuppositions and implications of the fiction. But I worry that this is a matter of quibbling over words. For if I ask you to entertain the thought (unasserted) that Taras Bulba is a man, then, *ceteris paribus*, I am also asking you implicitly to entertain all the presuppositions and implications of that thought. I am asking you to entertain the propositions (unasserted) that he has a heart, a circulatory system, that he requires oxygen, and so on. *Pace* Walton, not everything that you are invited to suppose and that you implicitly suppose need be in the spotlight of the theatre of the mind.

19. One reason that this analysis requires more conditions is because, as stated, nothing has been said about the audience's understanding of the meaning of the structured, sense-bearing signs in question. Thus, a fuller account that takes heed of this would be:

> A structure of sense-bearing signs x by sender s is fictional if and only if s presents x to audience a with the intention (1) that a recognize that x is intended by s to mean p (a certain propositional content), (2) that a recognize that s intends a to suppositionally imagine p, (3) that a suppositionally imagine that p, and (4) that 2 is the reason for 3.

> Undoubtedly this analysis could be further refined. For example, see Currie's *Nature of Fiction*, 33. Though Currie and I disagree on some important points, the structure of my analysis was inspired by his.

20. The complications derive from the same considerations found in the preceding note. A more complete definition of non-fiction would look like this:

> A structure of sense-bearing signs x is non-fictional if and only if x is presented by sender s to audience a where s intends (1) that a recognize that x is intended by s to mean p, (2) that a recognize that s intends them not to entertain the propositional content of p as unasserted, (3) that a does not entertain p as unasserted, (4) that s intends that 2 will be one of a's reasons for 3.

21. I would not wish to deny that *Serene Velocity* might be involved in providing something like an object lesson concerning the impression of movement in film. But it is not material to that object lesson whether the images of the hallway be entertained by way of the suppositional imagination or belief. The object lesson will obtain either way. Thus, since Gehr does not prescribe that we entertain the propositional content of his shots—that here is a hallway—as unasserted, *Serene Velocity* is not a fiction; therefore, it is non-fiction.

22. Though from here on I talk about the film of presumptive assertion, it should be clear that the analysis could be applied more broadly to what we might call either 'texts of presumptive assertion'—like history books or newspaper articles—or what we might call, even more commodiously, 'structures of sense-bearing signs of presumptive assertion'.

23. For a discussion of assertion, see John Searle, *Expression and Meaning: Studies in the Theory of Speech Acts* (Cambridge: Cambridge University Press, 1979), 62.

24. This is the Gricean way of putting it, but, as Richard Allen points out, the relevant effects that the reader should have in mind here are what might be called 'meaning effects'.

25. I say *a* reason here because there may be other reasons as well having to do with the verisimilitude of the image.

26. This analysis shares a number of points with the one proposed by Carl Plantinga in his article 'Defining Documentary: Fiction, Non-fiction, and Projected Worlds', *Persistence of Vision*, 5 (Spring 1987), 44–54. I suspect that, despite the difference in language, our theories are compatible. Plantinga expands on his view in *Rhetoric and Representation in Non-fiction Film* (New York: Cambridge University Press, 1997).

27. Perhaps the defender of the notion of the film of the presumptive trace would deny this, claiming that the makers of the film intend the audience to regard all the footage in the film as historic, but that, in addition, they are lying. I, however, can find no grounds to suppose that the film-makers are trying to mislead the audience about the provenance of the footage described above.

28. See Noël Carroll, 'Art, Intention, and Conversation', in Gary Iseminger (ed.), *Intention and Interpretation* (Philadelphia: Temple University Press, 1992); id., 'Anglo-American Aesthetics and Contemporary Criticism: Intention and the Hermeneutics of Suspicion', *Journal of Aesthetics and Art Criticism*, 51: 2 (Spring 1993).

29. Of course, the intentional fallacy also pertains to the evaluation of texts. But, once again, evaluation is not categorization.

30. Interestingly, Monroe Beardsley, one of the leading progenitors of the intentional fallacy, uses the intention-response model in order to present his theory of art. He, at least, thinks that reference to an artist's categorical intentions is not problematic, while also arguing that reference to an artist's meaning intentions falls foul of the intentional fallacy. He believes that being open to categorical intentions while rejecting meaning intentions is logically consistent, and this leads him to a mixed view—accepting the invocation of authorial intentions for the purpose of categorizing a work, but disallowing it in the interpretation of a work. See Beardsley, 'An Aesthetic Definition of Art'.

31. Indexing is discussed in Noël Carroll, 'From Real to Reel: Entangled in Nonfiction Film', in *Theorizing the Moving Image*.

32. The reader may wonder about a case where a film-maker dissimulates by presenting cooked-up footage, but indexes the film as a documentary. My view is that we regard it as presented with an assertoric intention, since the film-maker has prescribed that the audience entertain its propositional content as asserted thought. It does not become a fiction film because the film-maker has counterfeited the footage. It is still a film of presumptive assertion. But it is a *bad* film of

presumptive assertion because the film-maker has failed to live up to his commitments to the standards of evidence and reasoning appropriate to the subject-matter of the film.

33. See Carroll, 'From Real to Reel: Entangled in Nonfiction Fiction Film', and 'Postmodern Skepticism and the Nonfiction Film'.

8

What is Non-fiction Cinema?

TREVOR PONECH

Some of the most cognitively and practically important questions we can ask of a cinematic depiction concern whether it is a work of fiction or non-fiction, and why it is one rather than the other.[1] These questions pertain to the kinds of effects that film-makers seek to have on us, and the sorts of assumptions they wish us to make about the relation between their movies and extra-cinematic reality. Yet in place of cogent answers to basic queries about the documentary's difference, scholarship for the most part has provided conceptual confusion. In this chapter, I offer a pragmatic account of what it is that causes a movie to be non-fiction. I argue that documentary motion pictures are simply those which result from the film-maker having a particular purpose in mind, namely an intention to produce non-fiction.

My analysis of non-fictional audio-visual communication owes more to speech act theory and the philosophy of action than to cinema studies. Hence it inevitably involves breaking the taboo against publicly committing the so-called 'intentional fallacy'. I shall also be breaking from ideological, ethical-political critiques of documentaries and documentarians—such evaluations being the priority of many theorists eager to make worldly pronouncements in the service of progressive politics. Here I emphasize that I do not believe film aesthetics to be radically autonomous from political, ideological, moral, and economic concerns; what is more, I do hold that critical and empirical enquiry into film's many conceivable links to these spheres is imperative. But I also think we ought to be careful not to conflate two separate research projects. There is, on the one hand, the explanation of why a documentary was made or has just the form, content, properties, and effects that it has—a task which may involve adverting to social-historical, cultural factors. On the other hand, there is the explanation of what makes a given movie a documentary. The latter is my present task.

A wholly non-fictional motion picture need not be wholly factual. It need not contain a single purely objective, unmanipulated representation or statement. It need not be on any particular kind of subject-matter; nor need that which it depicts really exist, more or less as depicted, 'out there' in off-screen reality. Nor is documentary, in my account, defined by the particular conventions or norms—pertaining to form, style, content, truth, or objectivity—according to which it is produced, classified, and/or inter-preted. All of these paths to understanding the nature of non-fiction film, criss-crossing their way through the literature, lead to dead ends.[2] A cin-ematic work is non-fiction if and only if its maker so intends it.

I propose an account of documentary according to the best available hypotheses concerning the nature of human communication. It shall be appropriate to movie media, recognizing practices specific to the generation of cinematic artefacts. I shall say that in producing non-fiction, a communi-cator uses some unit of motion picture footage in an effort to assert that something is (or was, or will be, or could be) the case. Hence:

To perform a cinematic assertion is to employ a motion picture medium, typically consisting of both visual and audio tracks, with the expressed intention that the viewer form or continue to hold the attitude of belief toward certain states of affairs, objects, situations, events, proposi-tions, and so forth, where the relevant states of affairs etc. need not actually exist.

This definition fits a large number of ordinary non-fictions. However, as I eventually will explain, I do not think that it covers every possible instance of the genre.

It is even more important to distinguish my topic from the phenomenon of natural meaning. The thermometer's mercury level means that it is $-21\,°C$. That man's rolling gait means that he is a sailor.[3] These photos mean that there are glaciers in Antarctica. In each case, one object or situation is indicative of another's condition by virtue of how it is objec-tively related to that other state of affairs, due to the nomic and necessary constraints on their relationship.[4] If the man's rolling gait naturally indi-cates that he is a seaman, his gait depends on his being a seaman, but not on his or anyone else's belief that he is a sailor or intention to show that he has this occupation. Moreover, a natural sign's meaning, or, if you prefer, the natural meaning of an item or state of affairs, is purely factual. For x to be a natural sign of y, y must really be the case. The mercury does not mean that it is $-21\,°C$ if a demon makes the thermometer read ten degrees colder than the actual ambient temperature. And the photographs do not naturally mean that Antarctic glaciers look just so if, lacking snap-shots, I show you ones of Swiss glaciers instead, expecting you will not know the difference.

Natural meaning, being objective and informational, is untrammelled by imagination, make-believe, connotation, fantasy, subjectivity, expressivity, figuration, infelicity, insincerity, and all that might converge with fiction. Since movies, unlike drawings or paintings, have this property, why not make it the grounds for identifying non-fiction cinema? We could, for instance, say that a documentary is any unit of photographically produced movie imagery having only or preponderantly natural meaning, leaving it to documentarians and theorists to devise norms of proportionality. We might even want to claim that every movie is, under one description, non-fictional in so far as its pictures are naturally meaningful with respect to how things stand in extra-cinematic reality. I grant that there is no trace of fiction in natural meaning. But defining cinematic non-fiction or stipulating its proto-type on the basis of a-rational, mind-independent indicator relations does not really capture the actual conditions under which even surveillance camera footage becomes a work of non-fiction, versus a natural sign the function of which is more like a thermometer than *Drifters*. Nor does it explain why there is a description under which *Star Wars* is not a documentary. By the same token, it would exclude legions from the realm of genuine non-fiction due to interpretative, rhetorical, figurative, and sometimes misrepresentative properties resulting from their having been moulded by an organizing consciousness. If film theory has taught us one lesson, it is that documentary is no more mind-independent a mode of representation than linguistic discourse.

I argue that the core of non-fiction consists not of an objective indicator relation, but of the *action* of indication, i.e. somebody deliberately and openly indicating something to somebody else. Documentaries acquire their status as such because they are conceived, created, shown, and used with certain definitive communicative purposes in mind. As I say, they are cinematic assertions, naturally meaningful images being among the elements employed by the communicator toward assertive ends.

Let's look at *Trance and Dance in Bali*, produced as part of Gregory Bateson and Margaret Mead's classic anthropological study of character formation in Balinese culture.[5] This short film, silent except for a non-synchronous music track, depicts the *Tjalonarang* (Witch) play, and consists of footage shot between 1936 and 1939 at numerous village dance club performances. The movie begins with a series of titles noting the time and place of the recordings, identifying the makers and their scholarly affiliations, and giving a synopsis of the theatrical action. As the depiction unfolds, we observe a masked Witch ward off the attacks of the Dragon's followers, each armed with a long, sinuous dagger or kris. Sent into a trance by the Witch, the attackers' ballet manœuvres give way to violent posturing: bending backward, throwing their hips forward, and holding their arms straight out and above their chests, the dancers repeatedly mimic the action of thrusting their krises into their own chests.

In offering these images, it seems appropriate to say that the authors' objective is to assert that this ritual performance has the aforementioned features. In other words, they would have us recognize their intention that we adopt certain beliefs concerning the *Tjalonarang* and how it is enacted.

This attribution of assertive intent makes sense, in so far as it is consistent with what we know about their anthropological interests in culture, the circumstances under which the film was made, and their efforts to make it available as an empirical research tool. It coheres better with what we know than, say, the assumption that they wish us to imagine that the movie depicts a ritual, or make believe that a given ritual occurred as portrayed. And it makes more sense than ascribing to them the goal of retelling the *Tjalonarang* fiction primarily for the sake of encouraging their viewers to enjoy imagining the events of that narrative.

Many considerations have no direct, proximal bearing on whether or not *Trance and Dance in Bali* is non-fiction. Two among these are its accuracy and its objectivity. Seized by the imp of the perverse, Bateson and Mead could have somehow indicated that the *Tjalonarang* commemorates the arrival of extra-terrestrial astronauts—a ludicrous falsehood, but not the kind of thing that could cause the film to be fictional. It just so happens that the ethnographers, lacking a record of women dancing with krises, once asked a troupe to break with their customary performance of this play by including female kris dancers, an innovation that became the norm by 1939![6] Having altered their subject-matter, their work's objectivity is likely to be questioned; maybe its content has more to do with the film-makers' ethically questionable, lifeworld-distorting desires than with the facts about Balinese culture. But from the perspective of communicative pragmatics, the act of cinematic assertion needn't by definition be innocent of either bias or hegemony.

We could note that *Trance and Dance in Bali* seems to have been made according to a venerable ethnographic norm against self-referential depictions of the depictors. Perhaps a work's embodiment of, or classification by, some representational convention is one, if not the only, determinant of its non-fictional status. It is important to bear in mind that a convention is not an autonomous, self-generating property or regularity immanent to the work itself. Rather, it contributes to the effective realization of a goal, such as making a movie, only in so far as it coheres with the reasons guiding some person's relevant actions. It plays a mediating role, the agent adapting his work to a convention when he expects that doing so will help to bring about his aesthetic, professional, or communicative ends, like guiding his audience toward a certain conclusion. The author's selective adherence to the standards, rules, or 'codes' associated with this or that variety of documentary— black and white photography, jerky camera movements, voice of God narration, etc.—is thus one subordinal element in a more basic and decisive plan, i.e. fulfilling his assertive intention.

Cinematically asserting that something or other is the case is akin to a constative speech act, such as a speaker performs in making an announcement, uttering a conclusion, recounting an event, describing an object, or predicting an outcome. These acts each exhibit the pattern exemplified by simple linguisitic assertives: a belief is verbally expressed, along with a certain kind of 'illocutionary force', namely the intention that the hearer acquire or maintain a like belief. In writing or saying the following sentence, 'My students all dig Tarantino', I assert the content of that proposition (that my students all dig Tarantino) if I thereby express my (putative) belief that my students all dig Tarantino, and my intention that you, the reader or listener, hold a corresponding belief. According to Kent Bach and Robert Harnish, whose model of constatives I adopt, my utterance is an assertion provided that I make it in such a way that I try to signal to the receiver that I wish to elicit his or her credence in what I have said.[7] To assert is to attempt to give receivers reasons to think that one seeks to produce a certain effect on them, that effect being their recognition of one's intention that they form a given belief. This assertion's content is either true or false of the state of affairs to which it refers. Provided that he or she enjoys a basic linguistic competence and grasps that my making marks or sounds is in fact communicative action, and barring uncertainty as to my sincerity or the operative meanings of certain words ('dig', 'Tarantino'), the receiver is likely to infer that I believe that my groovy young students admire Tarantino, and that I want him or her to have the same belief. This inference is simply the one that best accounts for my linguistic output, in light of the semantic meaning of the utterance, the way in which it is expressed, and the context in which it arises.

In representing the *Tjalonarang*, Bateson and Mead use cinematic techniques to achieve the same definitive goal associated with linguistic constatives. They intend spectators to take the attitude of belief toward their representation's content. By content I mean the extra-cinematic objects, individuals, states of affairs, situations, and events indicated and described in the movie depiction. These items need not be actual or real. Just as one can make verbal assertions about extra-terrestial beings, one can produce filmic assertions about them, even going so far as to use special effects to show what they allegedly look like. Nor, as I said earlier, need a film's description of its depicta be veridical. What is important is that, in steering the spectator's attention toward an audio-visual field and at least some of the observable items in that field, the film-maker takes steps (to try) to bring about on the viewer's part certain determinate perceptions and realizations regarding what objects and so forth are depicted.

In asserting that something or other is the case, cinematic agents typically expect audiences—employing a combination of perceptually derived beliefs about the depiction, non-perceptual beliefs and background knowledge, and inferences—to arrive at particular cognitions regarding not only what is shown on the screen but also how things stand in the world. By choosing to document a given ritual, by making preparations to record instances of it, selectively shooting these events, choosing some of this footage, editing these shots into a sequence, and taking steps to distribute this work, one of the effects intended by Bateson and Mead is to get whoever views the film to notice, for instance, that the *Tjalonarang* ends in convulsive, putative trance states. This is a non-fictional work because its makers openly signal their intention that viewers take the attitude of belief toward this situation.

There are no logical or metaphysical assurances that every cognition arising from non-fiction viewing will always be perfectly accurate. Owing to misperception, inattentiveness, and so on, one could come away with numerous flawed beliefs about what the film-makers wished to show; such spectator errors also could be traced to the unclear or imprecise nature of the representation itself. Likewise, due to their own cognitive limitations, the depiction's ambiguity, or the film-maker's errors or even malfeasance, spectators might form mistaken or unclear ideas about the extra-cinematic world. Due to my own limitations, I still cannot see whether one of the trancers really bites the head off a live chick. But often observers do acquire true and justified beliefs in the wake of viewing documentaries. If you notice that the Witch wears an *anteng*—a cloth sling in which a mother carries her baby—then you've exploited this motion picture to learn a fact about the traditional *Tjalonarang* play.

Much of what I have said hints at a basic agreement with Carl Plantinga, whose intelligent work on the nature of non-fiction merits critical commentary.[8] In a nutshell, he contends that such a movie asserts a belief that given objects, entities, states of affairs, events, or situations actually occur(red) or exist(ed) in the actual world as portrayed. By using the term assertion— which he understands to include non-linguistic asserting with pictures and sounds—Plantinga suggests that cinematic non-fictions are those toward which makers would have viewers adopt the mental stance of belief. But I have reservations regarding his formulation, one being that it is yoked to a questionable clause identifying non-fiction with the expression of truth claims. The first problem here is that, rather than just identifying non-fictions with producers' assertive intentions, Plantinga goes on to stipulate in general terms the content of the typical filmic assertion, namely a belief that the depicted items actually exist(ed) as portrayed. This added stricture is confusing, because it makes it sound as if the expressed belief's content helps make communication, be it linguistic or cinematic, non-fictional. That job is done by the author's expression of illocutionary force, the work's status being secured by the communicator's recognizable indication of an intention that the receiver adopt the attitude of belief.

Secondly, the non-fiction maker need not be at all committed to proclaiming the truth of his depictions. In *Reassemblage* (1982) and *Surname Viet Given Name Nam* (1989), Trinh T. Minh-ha uses complicated stylistic strategies, as well as explicit verbal statements regarding her anti-realist film aesthetics, in an effort to undercut viewer assumptions about the veridical nature of ethnographic films. Even if she is implicitly making a second-order claim for the truth—or, given her entrenched scepticism, 'truth'—of a postmodern account of cinematic representation, it still behoves us to provide a more fitting description of her actual communicative goals. One alternative is to say that her movies fall into the class of 'suggestives': rather than asserting the outright truth of beliefs $B \ldots B_n$ about certain indigenous African peoples or the post-war lot of Vietnamese woman in Asia and North America, the film-maker expresses the belief that there may be reason, but not sufficient reason, to assent to $B \ldots B_n$.

Unfettered truth claims are numerous in verbal as well as cinematic non-fictions. But they neither define nor exhaust membership in the category of non-fiction. Think of such speech acts as prohibitives, which consist of the speaker's expression of (1) his belief that his utterance, in virtue of his authority over the hearer, constitutes reason for the hearer not to engage in a certain conduct and (2) the speaker's desire that because of his utterance the hearer not perform that conduct.[9] A motion picture analogue of a prohibitive could consist of an animated 'No Smoking' graphic—an encircled cigarette figure with transverse bar suddenly superimposed across it, maybe to the accompaniment of a resonant sonic thud. Although this symbolic act implies the fact that some authority does not allow smoking in a given location, to subordinate it to the conceptual category of truth claims obscures the specific communicative function which it is designed to serve. This case leads me to note that the class of cinematic artefacts that are literally not fiction is larger than the class of cinematic constatives. So my own model of motion picture non-fictions has its limitations, since it is only meant to describe, as broadly as possible, the essential pattern—the expression of assertive illocutionary force—embodied by a single, albeit major group of non-fictions.

There is a third degree of confusion triggered by Plantinga's characterization of paradigmatic non-fictions. We might ask, *how* do non-fictions assert beliefs that the depicted items actually exist(ed) as portrayed? What is a film-maker doing when he or she asserts the truth of these beliefs? I am not sure how Plantinga would detail the pragmatics of this activity. But I suspect that claims to truth frequently involve something along the lines of confirmative communicative acts. In Bach and Harnish's taxonomy, these illocutionary acts, like assertions, consist of a speaker's expression of a belief as well as a desire that the hearer form a like belief. Differentiating it from an assertion is the speaker's expression that he has formed (and the hearer should form) the belief as a result of a truth-seeking procedure, such as observation, investigation, or argument.[10] A film-maker, too, might intend viewers to acquire the belief that such and such is the case, for reasons above and beyond the viewers' recognition of the intention that they take that attitude. Often the cineaste expresses the intention that we believe that an object, event, or situation *o* actually exists (as shown) in reality because, in portraying *o*, the maker thereby offers some probative support for belief in its existence. TV news programmes and documentary reports usually exemplify the confirmative schema; not only do producers signal their wish that we take the attitude of belief toward the show's content, they also indicate that this attitude is warranted in light of evidence amassed through enquiry and documentation.

It is useful at this stage to make a distinction between direct and indirect motion picture confirmatives. A hard core of the former would be composed of works in which overall priority is given to the articulation of various focal claims that result from the makers ostensibly having undertaken truth-seeking procedures. Such a film is in a strong sense about the substantiation of these claims. Think of the PBS Frontline documentary *Innocence Lost*, director Ofra Bikel's probe into the conviction of seven day care workers on sexual abuse charges. She and her colleagues are at pains to show that these accusations are the upshot not of careful investigation but of rumour, psychological testing biased toward confirmation, and a general failure to challenge distorted statements coaxed from pre-school age witnesses by police officers and negligent therapists. The film-makers use the cinematic medium to present the results of their background research—the alleged victims' testimony is, for instance, illustrated by actors reading from official transcripts, their voices dubbed over courtroom sketches. Moreover, the medium is itself used to gather evidence, in the form of recorded interviews with parents, jurors, lawyers, therapists, and experts.

Many ordinary non-fictions are not principally devised to verify claims about the world. Yet it is still appropriate to regard them as confirmatives, only in a weaker, indirect mode. Television talk shows are full of information about people's appearances, actions, and utterances. Are we therefore to assume that their main objective is to furnish proof of people's appearances and so forth? On the contrary, it seems to me that these programmes are subordinated to the overriding goal of entertaining spectators with non-fictional images of individuals more or less spontaneously engaging in interactions like gossiping, quarrelling, and confessing. But these and other non-fictions normally embody a standard, naturalistic use of the medium. In executing their specific purposes, they present recognizable, approximately accurate audio-visual images of actual, independently existing objects. Without belonging to the hard core of motion picture confirmatives, they nonetheless fit within a category of indirect confirmatives because, in achieving their particular ends, they satisfy a key presumption pertaining to content: by using the medium in a standard fashion, the producers endeavour to fulfil the audience's expectation that they will be able to see by the depiction what really occurred and how various objects and events actually looked or sounded.

In preparation for a slightly more detailed analysis of the pragmatics of non-fictional cinematic depiction, let me take a moment to summarize and refine some previous points.

The action definitive of much non-fictional cinematic communication is assertion. To make assertions cinematically, agents use motion picture technologies and representational strategies in order to indicate to viewers that they are supposed to take the attitude of belief toward what is represented. The producers at CNN do not want us to imagine that Christiane Amanpour is a correspondent reporting the day's events in some war-torn region; neither do they, nor Amanpour, wish us to make believe that a mortar attack on an apartment building happened roughly as shown. Nor do they wish us to make believe that the footage records the attack in question. Instead, they anticipate that we will pick up a variety of cues that should help us to become attuned to their desire that we adopt an attitude of belief *vis-à-vis* objects, states of affairs, situations, and events either explicitly portrayed or implied by the motion picture.

In making non-fiction, film-makers thus follow what amounts to a rationality heuristic. Motion pictures are composed on the largely tacit but nonetheless operative assumption that audience members, by mobilizing a combination of visual and aural perceptions, background knowledge, and non-perceptual beliefs and inferences, will be more or less able to grasp the movie's content and intended force. When news broadcasters show scenes of apartment blocks under mortar fire, they exploit their viewers' capacity to recognize pictures and sounds of bombardment, as well as their ability to surmise that these recordings are the results of a certain type of causal relationship between the recording equipment and a prefilmic event not caused by the recording process itself. Of course, there is plenty of room for deception here, since perfidious film-makers using special effects or stock footage could take advantage of the fallibility of perceptually derived beliefs pertaining to cinematic representations. Yet a bogus depiction of intensive warfare—made on a Hollywood back lot and passed off as authentic by gun-shy reporters—is for all its falseness no less a work of non-fiction.

A film's content is not always fully manifested in what is explicitly displayed on the screen. Often spectators must ascertain implicit content by making inferences, including reasoning about authorial plans and preferences. Consider *The Thin Blue Line*, Errol Morris's brilliant documentary about a man wrongly convicted of murdering a Dallas policeman. Arguably, Morris wants us to apprehend something to the effect that wishes and prejudices can all too easily undermine the pursuit of truth. At no time is this statement flashed on the screen or uttered by a speaker in so many words. Instead, we are warranted in inferring from the movie's other properties that the director would have viewers form this belief. Given the information related by the interviews and stylized reconstructions of witnesses' testimony—sequences in which the frailty of the charges against Randall Adams is juxtaposed with revelations about the reasons why various people were preponderantly motivated to assist in Adams's conviction rather than test the evidence—a suitable explanation of the movie's rationale would point to the author's interest in exposing the distortion of truth-seeking procedures by self-serving desires.[11]

Film-makers usually expect audiences to marshal perceptions and background knowledge so as to decide whether a work is non-fiction. Now I suspect that at some initial moment—often prior to watching the film itself, given expectations arising from advertising, reviews, programming notes printed in television timetables, etc.—people settle on adopting a global attitude of belief toward many movies and broadcasts. Reconsideration occurs only if this judgement seems to be counter-indicated by some feature of the movie. In any case, documentarians can guide viewers toward an understanding of a work's intentional status by exploiting their audience's attunement to various cues. One cue would be the absence of stereotypical traits of motion picture narrative fictions, for instance, the showing of thespians performing apparently scripted roles, or the breaking down of scenes into sequences of carefully composed and blocked camera angles and shots. On the positive side, non-fictioneers also avail themselves of their public's familiarity with orthodox formats and styles associated with non-fiction, as well as their ability to recognize some films as non-accidentally accurate depictions of actual historical, as opposed to imaginary, events. The inclusion of linguistic cues, like the utterance of assertions by on- or off-screen speakers, is another normal means of expressing the movie's main communicative intent. These markers do not themselves make a work non-fictional; nor are they unequivocal, nomic indicators of authorial intentions. But they do provide evidence that will figure in spectators' reasoning about the author's likely goals. It is in light of our reasoning about why the maker would show us such and such, in this way, that we hypothesize that he must want us to treat the work as non-fiction. This assumption is sometimes the one that makes the communicator's behaviour seem rational and appropriate. Spectators and film-makers are frequently able to achieve a measure of this sort of coordination because of the mutual communicative assumptions that structure and constrain their rapport. For example, viewers tacitly assume that a cinematic artefact is produced with recognizable illocutionary intent, just as its makers tacitly assume that viewers will assume it is made with a recognizable intent.

As I understand it, cinematic assertion consists of the determination of content and the expression of force by cinematic versus, say, specifically linguistic means. By cinematic means, I have in mind the gamut of resources and methods that movie makers have at their disposal for establishing content and indicating the appropriate intentional attitudes to take toward it. Generally speaking, this consists of recording images and sounds, with the further intention of exhibiting this audio-visual package to somebody in the hopes that they will subsequently arrive at certain determinate realizations. This broad description of the process hardly does justice to the variety of devices and elements potentially at play. The tools of contemporary motion picture production include not only photographic, naturally meaningful pictures but also computer-generated imagery. Graphics, animation, intertitles, and subtitles may be used. Cinematic communicators could establish the content of their works by way of *mise en scène*; by camera set-ups, movements, and effects; and by the selection and organization of images and sounds. They might also employ sound recordings of people, present on- or off-screen, communicating linguistically.

Everything that I have said up until now is tied to the assumption that documentary film-making—rather than being random, purposeless, or otherwise a-rational behaviour—is a complicated form of means-ends oriented action having designated effects subserved by various representational strategies. A way of elaborating on this thesis is to explain the link between the content of cinematic non-fictions and practical reasoning, that is, reasoning undertaken to resolve such questions as, 'What do I do now?' or 'How do I achieve *x*?' And one way of articulating this relation is in terms of film-makers' plans with respect to content.

'Plans', according to Michael Bratman, 'are intentions writ large' because they are relatively complex mental states serving to initiate and control conduct.[12] On this view, they have a motivational dimension, since to have a plan to do *x* is to cease deliberating and settle on *x*-ing, either right away or at an appropriate moment in the non-immediate future. Plans also have representational content: having a plan to *x* entails having, and being guided by, some fixed ideas about steps conducive to doing or realizing *x*. These ideas need not be comprehensive. Deciding to devote the weekend to home improvement, I initially leave open the matter of precisely what projects I shall tackle. Yet this partial plan is a crucial filter on further practical reasoning and planning. It rules out some activities (renting half a dozen old movies on video) while admitting others (making a list of what needs to be done, deciding what I can hope to do in two days, going to the hardware store, etc.). As time passes I may fill in additional steps toward my goal's realization, undertaking such reasoning as is necessary to the plan's adjustment and completion. Hence plans characteristically exhibit a hierarchical structure, embedding at first general and preliminary, then increasingly more specific means, sub-plans, and intentions.

Below I distinguish between two main strategies of non-fictional depiction, corresponding to two categories of plans.

Type I Non-fictions

Sometimes producers have only schematic plans and highly flexible commitments regarding what they will depict, hence what cognitive perceptions they expect to trigger. Up to and including the time when their cameras roll, they might simply intend to show whatever it is that ultimately happens to be recorded on the resultant footage. In such cases, cineastes may well be executing highly detailed plans concerning how images will be captured, plans encompassing stylistic considerations, logistics, budgetary constraints, and so on. Nonetheless, one facet of the content of this planning structure—the specification of what, exactly, will (probably) be shown—remains relatively abstract. The incompleteness of plans with respect to cinematic content could be a function of one or a combination of any of three conditions: (1) the environment imposes constraints on the cinematic agent's activities that limit significantly his foreknowledge of what he can expect to depict, and/or his influence over what he expects to depict and/or the means of depiction; (2) the agent prefers to try to minimize his influence over pre-filmic events; (3) the agent is to a greater rather than lesser degree uncommitted to using the motion picture representation to bring about particular realizations and cognitive perceptions on the part of viewers.

Consider the example of observational cinema. In movies like Frederick Wiseman's *Law and Order*, the film-maker is at the outset largely agnostic about what will wind up on the editing machine. Wiseman and his cinematographer, William Brayne, surely planned to represent certain kinds of law enforcement situations, and must have engaged in extensive means-ends reasoning about feasible intermediate steps. They were, for instance, aware of the potential for witnessing police brutality and considered focusing on exposing the violence of the Kansas City officers to whom they had negotiated access.[13] However, it also seems to have been part of their strategy to try to restrict their influence over their subjects' behaviour before the camera, and to put themselves in situations in which they would have incomplete knowledge of precisely what courses of events would unfold. So while Wiseman and Brayne counted on recording activities of, say, the vice squad, they operated under conditions of uncertainty that stopped them from settling in advance on a specific, narrowly conceived intention to secure audio-visual documentation of, say, an officer putting a stranglehold on a prostitute while telling her, 'Go ahead, resist. I'll choke you till you can't breathe.' In this sense their plan embedded a preference for working with a level of abstraction concerning that which would be portrayed in the day's footage.

Of course, adherence to a Type I plan is no guarantee against kinky wayward causation. Although the film-maker might take every step to avoid influencing those under observation, it is not impossible that awareness of the camera could either elicit or discourage subjects' responses. The agnosticism of a Type I schema can also accommodate *kinoki* who are quite sanguine about the chance that their presence may foster certain events. I am thinking of what Erik Barnouw labels *cinéma vérité*.[14] Instead of simply trying to record events, the *vérité* film-maker is a catalyst, in as much as he or she attempts to precipitate or contribute to the pre-filmic situation. Barnouw cites some of Jean Rouch's films as paradigmatic of participant observation. A case in point is *Tourou et Bitti*, during which Rouch, in a voice-over, remarks that he hopes the camera's arrival at a ceremony will provoke a trance. Of course, an intention to try to trigger an event need not betoken a detailed plan regarding the actual features of that which will ultimately transpire, hence be depicted. The film-maker might foresee and desire some of the ramifications of his intervention, yet have only a vague idea of the kind of event that he would like to precipitate.

There is a post-filmic variation on Type I representations. Finding a length of previously recorded motion picture footage, a film-maker or user could hit upon the idea of showing this material to an audience, intending that they take the attitude of belief toward whatever happens to be portrayed. The cinematic agent is still relatively undirective, in so far as he has but a general notion of what he wants to indicate by the image, along with a correspondingly loose idea of what he expects the viewer to see by the footage. Imagine someone who unwittingly leaves his new home video camera on, the apparatus registering a panoramic view of the living room. In the absence of the relevant sorts of intentional attitudes to initiate and guide it, the recording process itself falls short of being an act of non-fictional communication. But after he realizes what has happened, the accidental videographer resolves to send the tape to a relative with a note saying, 'This is how our living room looks.' Hence, downstream from the generation of the video images, he formulates a plan pertaining to what effects he wishes to give rise to by displaying this footage. And this plan calls for nothing more specific than taking steps to give someone perceptual access to the grosser observable features of the room. The agent having played next to no role in the recording process, the movie's content is established by default. While he probably would expect that anyone watching the tape could discriminate a vast array of perceptual items, he lacks a narrow commitment to showing that one of the paintings hangs crooked, or that there are exactly ten CDs stacked by the stereo. Instead of trying to guide the percipient's attention toward a specific region of the depiction, or dictate to him a particular meaning of the image, he is satisfied to take the opportunity to show him the look of the scene.

Type II Non-fictions

Type II works are also shaped by stable structures of authorial choices and preferences. But unlike Type I movies, they result from intentions that are more rather than less restrictive of content. Type II non-fictions correspond to significantly more detailed plans concerning the depiction's discernible audio-visual properties and the facts that viewers are thereby meant to notice. The claim here is not that improvisation, spontaneity, or accident can play no part in the production of such a work; nor am I implying that the film-maker ever achieves full lucidity and complete mastery over all aspects of the cinematic artefact's meaning. Yet a wholly defensible thesis would be that measures are sometimes taken to try to align the documentary's content with that of certain comprehensive plans, instead of allowing it to depend preponderantly on the emergence of unmanipulated, unforeseen, or undesired pre-filmic situations.

The Thin Blue Line would be an instance of documentary's content being finely adjusted to extensive future-directed schemes. Plans regarding blocking, lighting, shot composition, camera movement, the staging of re-enactments, and so forth systematically oriented what is ultimately shown to, and noticed by, spectators. From the pre-production phases through to the shooting and cutting of this noirish film, its depictions were thus designed and achieved with the same meticulousness associated with Hollywood fictions. Of course, that a movie was made in a fashion typical of the fiction film is not itself sufficient reason to conclude that it is essentially a work of make-believe, or is somehow a less straightforward piece of non-fiction. After all, the difference between fiction and non-fiction is one of force, not of style, form, or content. And in the case of *The Thin Blue Line*, it seems that various plans with respect to what would be represented, and how these representations would be constructed, were subordinated to the principal goal of letting spectators know that it is appropriate to take the attitude of belief toward the greater part of that which is either explicitly shown or implied by the depiction. The more general point is that a conceptual distinction between Type I and Type II non-fictions reflects no hierarchy of non-fictional status. That exemplars of the first category are often associated with standard, even institutionally prescribed practices or conventions of non-fiction film-making, issuing in certain stereotypical journalistic or 'pure' documentaries, could be symptomatic of our normative suppositions about what makes for a good documentary, but tells us nothing about the necessary and sufficient conditions for a movie being non-fiction.

Type II plans with respect to content can also be post-filmic, that is, bear directly on how the film-maker or film-user will instantiate content by manipulating footage on which images and sounds have already been registered. For instance, having completed their shooting, documentarians more often than not discriminatingly assemble their material, adding narration, music, or other audio-visual features. To the degree that this processing is done with an eye to precipitating in the viewer certain cognitive perceptions and inferences, that which the movie depicts is at least partly the result of Type II post-filmic plans. The directors of *The Atomic Cafe* evidently appropriated extant audio-visual materials on the basis of comprehensive schemes for combining and altering them with a view to achieving certain meaningful ends. Excerpts from government propaganda films, military training movies, news footage, and music are combined so as to suggest a historical progression of public discourse about the bomb, from adulation to an increasing and perspicacious cynicism.

I have been arguing that a documentary's content depends prominently on the content of various kinds of plans motivating and guiding its author. Moreover, distinguishing between Type I and Type II non-fictions reflects the intuition that there are genuine if not radical differences between, for instance, works of observational cinema and more theatrical documentaries—an intuition that can be developed through an analysis of the cinematic agent's practical reasoning and action. Yet if talk of types of non-fictions is to be illuminating, it is best to locate such categories on a continuum. Instead of looking for mutually exclusive classifications, it makes more sense to situate films somewhere along a gradual progression from minimal to maximal prevalence of authorial intentions. In all likelihood the majority of works are a combination of Types I and II, one or the other kind of plan prevailing at certain production stages. For example, it is fair to say that in Wiseman's *œuvre* Type I plans govern film-making up to and including the recording phase. But in so far as he carefully edits his images—thereby creating certain impressions and pursuing various rhetorical ends—Type II plans also play a key role in his films.

In discussing the pragmatics of communication, I have stressed that both linguistic and cinematic assertion result from a communicator's intention that others recognize his intention that they should adopt the attitude of belief toward some particular content or message. Film-makers put pictures and sounds together so as to signal this reflexive intention, while speakers and writers use words and sentences. Comprehending assertions made in either representational system is not just a matter of knowing a-contextual semantic and compositional rules governing how the indicator elements are arranged. Instead, it requires that the interpreter make judgements about non-conventional factors, namely the rationality of the communicator and the illocutionary force he meant to express by producing a given artefact at a certain time and place.

Much of what now counts as cutting-edge documentary film theory is, of course, antipathetic to my emphasis on purposiveness and pragmatics.[15] An approach such as mine is likely to be regarded by many film theorists as a naive, even sinister commission of the intentional fallacy. After all, communicative intentions are not easily identified. What is more, an ideologically suspect film-maker, such as Leni Riefenstahl, could take refuge in my a-historical, decontextualized analysis of the nature of non-fiction film, saying that it was merely her intention to document the Nazis' Nuremberg rally. But my analysis in no way precludes the coexistence of an intention to make non-fiction with other motivations, like intentions to deceive, deify, spread ethically-politically reprehensible doctrines, arouse emotions of fear and awe, and so on. Moreover, I can think of no good reason why scholars should not investigate a wide range of agential plans and purposes, reference to which might help to explain why a given documentary was produced and why it has the properties that it has.

I add that two substantial philosophical tasks face those sceptical of intention's definitive job. They would be responsible for offering informed arguments supporting the conclusion that movies cannot be assumed to result from agents acting on stable, decisive purposes and plans—where an informed argument is one addressing contrary hypotheses and data emerging from within the best currently available work in such pertinent fields as linguistics, the philosophy of action, and philosophical psychology. Theorists would also need to offer similar grounds for maintaining that it is always or often one reasonable option to doubt that competent spectators have the ability to detect the actual intentions of cinematic communicators. In formulating their arguments, they would want to take into consideration that proponents of an intentionalist approach to defining documentary, while being realists about the causal functions of intentions, need not be aiming for infallible attributions.

To contend that non-fictional motion pictures result from a particular kind of intention is not to assume that it is always immediately clear what the film-maker's aims were. Aside from paying close attention to the cinematic work, it is sometimes necessary to buoy our inferences about authorial goals with extensive background research, marshalling whatever evidence (notes, production documents, letters, interviews, other works in the film-maker's corpus) might be pertinent to reconstructing the proximal intentions giving rise to the movie in question. Even then there is no ultimate assurance that all of our judgements will always be correct. But again, we need not make a fetish of absolute certainty. For an attribution of non-fictional intent to be justifiable, it need only be the case that, in light of argument and currently available evidence, it is more reasonable to believe than disbelieve that the film-maker's activities were indeed subordinated to this end. It is this kind of reasoning about people's rationality and goals that film scholars routinely undertake when they anticipate their colleagues' attendance at planned meetings, decide if students' papers are plagiarized, or determine whether a *Nova* episode on mummification has been misplaced in the horror section of the local video store. Why should we not begin its principled, conscientious extension into the domain of non-fiction cinema studies?

NOTES

1. By motion picture I have in mind live transmissions as well as works recorded on film or video. I should also note that I will on occasion use the term 'documentary' as a substitute for non-fiction motion picture. I am aware that 'documentary' can be, and in some discursive contexts should be, reserved to refer to a specific subcategory of non-fiction. But here I wish to take advantage of its popular use as a synonym for non-fictional depiction in general.

2. A short list of writings relevant to the problem of defining the nature of the non-fictional cinematic depiction might include: Erik Barnouw, *Documentary: A History of the Non-fiction Film*, 2nd rev. edn. (New York: Oxford University Press, 1993); Richard Meran Barsam, *Nonfiction Film: A Critical History*, rev. edn. (Bloomington: Indiana University Press, 1992); Noël Carroll, 'From Real to Reel: Entangled in the Nonfiction Film', *Philosophical Exchange*, 14 (1983), 4–45; Dennis Giles, 'The Name Documentary: A Preface to Genre Study', *Film Reader*, 3 (1978), 18–22; John Grierson, 'First Principles of Documentary', in Forsyth Hardy (ed.), *Grierson on Documentary* (London: Faber & Faber, 1966), 35–46; William Guynn, *A Cinema of Nonfiction* (Rutherford, NJ: Farleigh Dickenson University Press, 1990); Jerry Kuehl, 'Truth Claims', in Alan Rosenthal (ed.), *New Challenges for Documentary* (Berkeley and Los Angeles: University of California Press, 1988); Bill Nichols, *Representing Reality: Issues and Concepts in Documentary* (Bloomington: Indiana University Press, 1991); Linda Williams, 'Mirrors without Memories: Truth, History, and the New Documentary', *Film Quarterly*, 3 (1993), 9–21.

3. This example is one used by Charles Sanders Peirce in discussing what he calls indexical signs. See *Collected Papers of Charles Sanders Peirce*, ed. Charles Hartshorne, Paul Weiss, and A. W. Burks (Cambridge, Mass.: Harvard University Press, 1931–58), ii. 285.

4. My observations on natural indication derive from Fred Dretske's analysis in *Explaining Behavior: Reasons in a World of Causes* (Cambridge, Mass.: MIT Press, 1988), 54–9.

5. A comprehensive discursive as well as photographic survey of Bateson and Mead's research is to be found in their *Balinese Character: A Photographic Analysis*, Special Publications of the New York Academy of Sciences, 2 (New York: New York Academy of Sciences, 1942). For a critical re-evaluation of their work on Balinese culture, see Gorden D. Jensen and Luh Ketut Suryani, *The Balinese People: A Reinvestigation of Character* (Oxford: Oxford University Press, 1992).

6. Bateson and Mead, *Balinese Culture: A Photographic Analysis*, 167.

7. Kent Bach and Robert Harnish, *Linguistic Communication and Speech Acts* (Cambridge, Mass.: MIT Press, 1979), 39–46.

8. Carl Plantinga, 'Defining Documentary: Fiction, Non-fiction, and Projected Worlds', *Persistence of Vision*, 5 (Spring 1987), 44–54; id., 'The Mirror Framed: A Case for Expression in Documentary', *Wide Angle*, 13 (1991), 41–53; id., 'Moving Pictures and Nonfiction: Two Approaches', in David Bordwell and Noël Carroll (eds.), *Post-Theory: Reconstructing Film Studies* (Madison: University of Wisconsin Press, 1996).

9. Bach and Harnish, *Human Communication and Speech Acts*, 47.

10. Bach and Harnish analyse the confirmative as follows. Where *e* is a sentence in some language, *S* is the speaker of that sentence, and *H* is the listener:

> In uttering *e*, *S* confirms (the claim) that *P* if *S* expresses:
> i. the belief that *P*, based on some truth-seeking procedure, and
> ii. the intention that *H* believe that *P* because *S* has support for *P*.

See Bach and Harnish, *Human Communication and Speech Acts*, 43.

11. Here my remarks are meant to reflect Morris's own comments on his goals in making *The Thin Blue Line*. See Peter Bates, 'Truth Not Guaranteed: An Interview with Errol Morris', *Cineaste*, 17 (1989), 16–17; and 'Bill Moyers Talks with Errol Morris', PBS broadcast, 26 Apr. 1989.

12. Michael Bratman, *Intentions, Plans, and Practical Reasoning* (Cambridge, Mass.: Harvard University Press, 1987), 29.

13. Wiseman has discussed his approach to making *Law and Order* in several interviews. On each of these occasions, he comments that his initial desire to 'get the cops' gave way to a wish that police brutality is part of the violent, antisocial behaviour that they face. See ' "You Start off with a Bromide": Wiseman on Film and Civil Liberties', interview with Alan Westin, in Thomas R. Atkins (ed.), *Frederick Wiseman* (New York: Simon & Schuster, 1976), 47–60; Janet Handelman, 'An Interview with Frederick Wiseman', *Film Library Quarterly*, 3 (1970), 5–9; Donald E. McWilliams, 'Frederick Wiseman', *Film Quarterly*, 24 (1970), 17–26. Shortly after finishing *Law and Order*, the film-maker also authored a short article reflecting on some of his experiences in making this movie; see Frederick Wiseman, 'Reminiscences of a Filmmaker: Frederick Wiseman on *Law and Order*', *Police Chief*, 36 (1969), 32–5.

14. Barnouw, *Documentary: A History of the Non-fiction Film*, 253–62.

15. For a representative sampling of some orthodox and influential modes of documentary film theory, readers may consult the essays collected in Michael Renov (ed.), *Theorizing Documentary* (New York: Routledge, 1993).

9

On Film Narrative and Narrative Meaning

George Wilson

1. BORDWELL ON EXPLICATIVE INTERPRETATION

The fortunes of explicative or 'intrinsic' interpretation of works of art have waned dramatically since the heyday of New Criticism. The project of explicative interpretation, under various conceptions, has been the subject of a series of influential attacks. Susan Sontag's 1964 essay 'Against Interpretation' is an early, well-known instance of this sceptical genre, and it has been followed by many others. It is my impression that, as time has gone by, scepticism about explicative interpretation has become the predominate outlook, although I suspect that the sources of this scepticism are various. Some have been convinced by the theoretical arguments of Sontag and her fellow sceptics. Others are troubled in a more diffuse way by their feeling that the practice of such interpretation is not guided by any clear and coherent conception and, correlatively, that the evidential standing of interpretative claims are difficult or impossible to adjudicate. Still others hold that there is simply more valuable work to do in film and literary studies.

In his book *Making Meaning* (hereafter *MM*), David Bordwell has joined in this sceptical tradition, paying special attention to the practice of interpretation in film studies.[1] Reading his book, it is hard to avoid the conclusion that Bordwell is right to have constructed a broad challenge to what has been the dominance of interpretative work in the area. In the course of his discussion, Bordwell offers an overview of past interpretative practice, and the picture he paints is familiar and, on the whole, depressing. Many of the examples of interpretation he describes strike one as unilluminating, unoriginal, and/or poorly argued. He is certainly right in thinking that well-regulated debates about the nature and function of interpretation in film studies are rare at best. The diverse subdepartments of 'Interpretation Inc.' have continued to produce interpretations of one variety or another, largely suppressing the questions that their strategies of analysis raise and ignoring,

I am deeply grateful to the National Endowment of the Humanities and to the National Humanities Center for a grant and for other forms of support that made this research possible.

usually with some disdain, the alternative strategies and objectives of competing approaches. At best, the situation is intellectually unhealthy. At
worst, it would be better if the tradition of explicative interpretation were
simply to die off.

However, it is not clear just what morals Bordwell wants to draw from
his extended historical and theoretical account of interpretation. Throughout much of his discussion, one has the impression that he believes that
there is something badly wrong at the very foundations of interpretative
practice, but the most explicit statements of his conclusions are not terribly
severe. Indeed, he overtly concludes that interpretative studies should be
more carefully, clearly, and responsibly conducted, and he also urges that
there are other kinds of worthwhile large-scale projects which film studies
should undertake.[2] With these and similar recommendations, it is difficult to
disagree. Nevertheless, it seems to me that *MM* is permeated with a deep
sense of scepticism about the coherence or, at least, the fruitfulness of
explicative interpretation, and grounds for such scepticism are easily derived from his discussion, whether he intended that result or not. For
example, hoping to delineate the target of his enquiries, Bordwell begins
with his own formulation of the character of explicative interpretation. But,
as we will shortly see, explicative interpretation, so conceived, *is* a dubious
and probably hopeless endeavour. I will argue, however, that the fault lies
with the formulation, and I will sketch an account whose prospects, it seems
to me, are substantially better.

So we begin with Bordwell's characterization of what explicative interpretation is all about. This forms a part of his larger taxonomy of different
modes of interpretation. He is well aware of the fact that almost any aspect
of our understanding of a film *could* be judged to be the product of some
sort of 'interpretation' or another. He therefore attempts to specify the
hermeneutical enterprises which he intends to investigate in *MM* and to
distinguish these from others with which he will not be concerned. For these
purposes, he sets out to draw a broad division between what he dubs
'comprehension', on the one hand, and what he calls 'interpretation', on the
other.[3] Clearly, his employment of these two terms is meant to be, to a
considerable degree, stipulative.

The objects of 'comprehension', in the case of narrative film, are said to
be 'referential' and 'explicit' meanings. The referential meaning of a film is
composed of the entities, persons, events, and actions within the film's
fictional world, together with the depicted spatial, temporal, and causal
relationships between these items in virtue of which they are imbedded in an
intelligible story (*fabula*). Viewers 'comprehend' a given movie when they
derive, from the ordered manifolds of information provided by the film's
narration, a set of judgements about what is fictionally true in the movie. In
the standard case, it is expected that these judgements will hang together

with enough dramatic coherence to portray the unfolding of a fictional narrative. Beyond this, when viewers grasp some moral, message or abstract theme that is 'explicitly' put forward in and by the film, then their grasping of this content is the comprehension of an 'explicit meaning' of the film. Bordwell suggests, in passing, that referential and explicit meanings together represent a filmic counterpart of 'literal meaning.' His strategy in *MM* is to set these types of meaning and comprehension to one side and to focus on the more problematic topic of interpretation proper.

Interpretation, in Bordwell's usage, gets under way when critics or viewers concern themselves with film meanings that go beyond 'the literal'. Here, once again, he distinguishes two relevant domains: the object of 'explicative interpretation' is said to be 'implicit meaning', and several brands of diagnostic interpretation deal with what he refers to as 'symptomatic meanings' of a film. Since, in this chapter, I will deal only with the questions that Bordwell raises about the former, I will bypass the account he offers of what symptomatic meanings are. However, even with this restriction in place, we will find that there are problems enough concerning what he claims about the nature of explicative interpretation and its supposed subject, implicit meanings.

In introducing this subdivision of meaning, Bordwell says the following:

The perceiver may also construct covert, symbolic, or *implicit* meanings. The film is now assumed to 'speak indirectly.' For example, you might assume that *Psycho*'s referential meaning consists of its fabula and diegesis (the trip of Marion Crane from Phoenix to Fairvale, and what happens there), and you might take its explicit meaning to be the idea that madness can overcome sanity. You might then go on to argue that *Psycho*'s implicit meaning is that sanity and madness cannot be easily distinguished. Units of implicit meaning are commonly called 'themes,' though they are also be identified as 'problems,' 'issues,' or 'questions'. (*MM* 8–9)

However, this passage raises at least as many questions as it answers. First, we are told that implicit meanings are meanings that specific films 'speak' only indirectly, and so, I take it, they are 'covert' in that sense. Second, the character of these meanings is supposed to be thematic, symbolic, and/or to bear on general issues and problems. Both proposals cry out for amplification.

The notion that 'implicit meanings' are indirectly 'spoken' by the film is most extensively elaborated at the beginning of chapter 3. Bordwell explains:

On a summer day, a suburban father looks out at the family lawn and says to his teen-age son: 'The grass is so tall I can hardly see the cat walking through it.' The son construes this to mean: 'Mow the lawn.' This is an *implicit* meaning. In a similar way, the interpreter of a film may take referential or explicit meanings as only the point of departure for inferences about implicit meanings. In constructing those meanings, the critic makes them apparent. That is, she or he *explicates* the film, just as the son might turn to his pal and explain, 'That means Dad wants me to mow the lawn.' (*MM* 42)

This clarification takes us some distance from Bordwell's proposal quoted earlier, but the direction in which it takes us is surprising, given the larger ambitions of his discussion. In the example above, he appeals to the familiar distinction between what the words of a speaker, on a given occasion of use, literally mean, and what the speaker means by uttering the words in question. The latter is a matter of what the speaker meant, i.e. intended, to convey, suggest, or otherwise invoke *by* uttering his words in the relevant conversational context. Construed strictly, the proposed analogy seems to indicate that an implicit meaning of a film segment is a 'content' that *the film-maker* (or: *film-makers*) intended to convey, suggest, or otherwise invoke by constructing the segment, where the segment is already freighted with its particular referential and explicit meanings.

Taken in this way, the account obviously commits the proponent of explicative interpretation to a very strong, unqualified form of interpretative *intentionalism*, i.e. the thesis that every aspect of the meaning of a work is a function of what its creator intended to communicate. And yet, historically, many, perhaps most, explicative interpreters have rejected, in theory and in practice, any intentionalism of this breadth and strength. Moreover, Bordwell himself appears to acknowledge this point implicitly, for, as his discussion proceeds, he attempts to aim his reflections on explicative interpretation at a significantly wider target. It is not easy, however, to see how that target is to be circumscribed. Some of what he says hints at the following idea. It is *the film itself* (or, perhaps, the specific character of the film narration) which implies, i.e. indirectly conveys or suggests, the relevant contents, and it is these 'implied' contents that explicative interpretation seeks to ascribe. Still, whatever greater latitude this idea may seem to offer is gained chiefly through its opacity. After all, it is principally *speakers* who imply things by what they say, and it is unclear that *films* can imply anything at all unless some responsible agent has had the relevant communicative intentions. Assuming that the notion of 'what a film implies' is not to be cashed out in terms of the strong intentionalism mentioned above, then, as far as I can see, there are just two alternative ways in which the putative concept could be articulated.

First, one could fall back on some weaker brand of intentionalism. Thus, if we assume (as Bordwell, by the way, does not) that we can usefully adopt the thesis that narrative fiction films engender either filmic narrators or 'implied authors' or both, then it could be proposed that a film implies whatever its filmic narrator or implied author intended it, by indirection, to convey.[4] Second, it could be proposed that an implied content of a film is any content that can be reasonably *inferred* from the film by competent viewers in the light of the referential and explicit meanings its narration presents. This second proposal is in greater consonance with other positions that Bordwell himself accepts. I will not attempt to adjudicate the merits of these proposals here. Both raise difficult problems. But I do want to insist that *some* account of what a film implies is badly needed if that concept is to be intelligibly introduced. It would take a great amount of work to make either proposal relatively concrete and plausible, and I will leave the matter open.

A second puzzle generated by Bordwell's description of explicative interpretation is the following. No matter how we work out the concept of what it is for a film or a part of a film to 'imply' a content, it will remain the case that a great deal of what Bordwell counts as referential meaning will similarly be implied rather than manifestly shown or stated. As he emphasizes in *Narration in the Fiction Film*,[5] much of what we correctly take to be a part of what has happened in a film's story is necessarily inferred from the action and events that have been 'directly presented'.[6] For example, it will be merely implied in a certain film that, after the murder, the murderer went home and changed his clothes. Thus, at best, it is only a necessary condition for implicit meaning that the content in question be implied or suggested by the film. So, what *more* is required to distinguish implicit meanings from implied referential meanings?

I do not think that Bordwell ever supplies a determinate answer to this question, but the express contrast between 'explicit' and 'implicit meanings' and the examples he gives of each hint at what he seems to have in mind. An explicit meaning, as we have observed, deals with themes, general messages, and views concerning 'problems' and 'issues' raised by the movie, *when* these contents have been directly presented by the film's narration. Hence, it appears that implicit meanings are comparably general and abstract 'statements' that are counted as 'implicit' because they are implied by the movies to whose content they belong. Notice that, in the first passage quoted above, Bordwell takes the proposition 'Madness is indistinguishable from sanity' as his (admittedly hypothetical) example of an implicit meaning in *Psycho*. Therefore, if I read Bordwell correctly, implicit meanings are defined as the product of the kind of narrative transcending content they involve and the fact that they are only indirectly conveyed by the film.

And yet, this conception of explicative interpretation has often been strongly contested, although the issues associated with these debates are delicate and hard to describe incisively. It has been an important tradition, within explicative interpretation, to reject a key feature of the conception that Bordwell delineates. Within that tradition, critics and theorists have insisted that works of art are not, on the whole, in the business of conveying, whether directly or indirectly, general themes or morals or messages. Consequently, it is not the task of interpretation to work out and state what these might be. I take it that the so-called 'heresy of paraphrase' is the view that explicative interpretation aims at a well-motivated formulation of what a work propounds concerning this or that global theme or problem.[7] It is purported to be heretical precisely because it represents an improper conception of the goals and achievements of critical analysis. Perhaps the clearest and most effective statement of this position, in connection with film, is offered by V. F. Perkins in his book *Film as Film*, especially in the chapter ' "How" is "What" '. For example, he states, 'Our understanding and judgement of a movie, then will depend largely on the attempt to comprehend the nature and assess the quality of its created relationships.'[8] 'Created relationships' here subsumes, at a minimum, the dramatic relationships of narrative, the epistemic relationships of narration, and the formal and tonal relationships of style, where all of these are relationships 'internal' to the film. The task of understanding such relationships is emphatically contrasted, in Perkins's discussion, with the dubious endeavour of discovering a constellation of 'messages' that the film has supposedly asserted or implied.

Again, I will not try to work through all of the various large and sometimes foggy issues that arise in this connection. What I hope to do is to illustrate some of the problems, as I see them, of conceiving explicative interpretation along the lines that Bordwell favours, and I will draw some methodological lessons to which those problems point. In particular, I believe that it is a mistake to conceive of the procedures and results of explicative interpretation as if they were distinguishable from attempts to comprehend, systematically and in detail, the stories or fabulas of fiction films. Bordwell, and many before him, have been led astray on this matter by looking to 'meanings' in linguistic contexts as models for the kinds of meanings that explicative interpretation purports to explain.[9] I will sketch a corrective to the emphasis on linguistic and speech act meanings, an alternative that explains why the implicit meanings of a film are inextricable from the network of relationships that constitute a fabula portrayed in film.

To avoid the danger that the claims and arguments I will be developing may seem too remotely connected with the conditions and constraints of critical practice, I will start by sketching a moderately complex interpretation of a reasonably well-known movie, Nicholas Ray's 1956 melodrama *Bigger than Life*. This analysis will provide us with a relatively specific point of reference, and the abstract character of my theoretical position will be mitigated by specific application to my (partial) interpretation of the film.

2. BIGGER THAN LIFE

I will concentrate initially upon an enigmatic scene that takes place late in the movie. But it will be helpful to have before us an outline of the broad narrative context in which it occurs.

The character Ed Avery (James Mason) is an elementary schoolteacher who is seriously under stress from the demands and constrictive circumstances of his professional and domestic life. Furthermore, he is intermittently struck by blinding attacks of pain. At first, the nature of these attacks is mysterious to him and to the audience, but, as the movie gets well underway, his doctors diagnose his seizures as the result of a life-threatening disease of the arteries. To stop the pain, and, beyond that, to save his life, he is directed to take heavy doses of the then new 'miracle' drug cortisone. However, the cortisone has unfortunate psychological side effects: Avery becomes progressively more manic and has growing illusions of intellectual and moral superiority. Hence, the title *Bigger than Life*. In an odd way, he comes to see himself as the spiritual counterpart of his doctors. He thinks that he can diagnose the social and psychological illnesses that afflict him and his peers, and he becomes progressively convinced that he can prescribe the requisite cures. He, in other words, will serve the function, in a larger social context, that his doctors have served for him. In the strange scene to be described, these processes come to a kind of culmination. Avery's son has failed to respond to the strenuous ethical and educational regimen that his father has sought to impose, and Avery is gripped with the unbending conviction that God has told him, as God told Abraham, that he must kill his son. This brings us to the specific scene I want to investigate.

Intending to kill his son, Avery climbs the stairs to the boy's room and enters. But, when he comes into the room, he is stopped in his tracks by the view before him. The audience sees him standing at the open bedroom door, while the son, cross-screen and in the nearer distance, is shown to be kneeling on his bed, facing away from his father. The son is holding an overinflated football, and, slowly and as if involuntarily, he raises it in one hand and extends it, still without looking at him, in Avery's direction. Thus, the boy continues to be turned away from his father as he executes his gesture, but, at the completion of the action, he gradually turns to face his father directly, and, in doing so, he silently regards him with a gaze of surprisingly firm defiance. (This moment in the confrontation is presented in a slightly distorted shot from Avery's point of view.) In response to the boy's action, Avery freezes, seemingly in acute suffering, and presses his body up against the bedroom door. Moreover, his vision is momentarily eclipsed by a tangled field of garish orange. While the father is blinded by this disorienting visual eruption, the son seizes his opportunity and escapes from the room. The abandoned football is left rocking mechanically upon the floor.

I want to stress how puzzling and disturbing this scene is. Nothing in the remainder of the movie does anything to explain Avery's culminating attack of pain. The film proceeds rapidly to its apparently happy ending. Avery almost dies from this final seizure, but he recovers in the hospital and the family re-establishes its original solidarity. But no account is offered of the bout of pain in the son's room. To all appearances, this seizure resembles the earlier attacks that had sent Avery to the hospital in the first place, but, if this *is* a recurrence of his old affliction, then that fact is itself problematic. At the time at which this scene takes place, Avery is heavily overdosed on cortisone, and that fact should make the recurrence of the pain impossible. Of course, it is possible to move on with the story and to ignore the question, but then the plot, thus apprehended, contains a glaring explanatory gap at what is clearly a crucial moment.

And yet, when the movie is viewed again and reconsidered, it is possible to draw together some important strands. This is not the first time in the movie that a question about the character and sources of Avery's pain is raised. In the first part of the film, it remains for some time quite unclear whether Avery's suffering simply is produced by unknown physical causes or whether the suffering is somehow a response to the pressures and perceived humiliations of his life. Naturally, in watching the movie, the audience is inclined to accept, as Avery does, the diagnosis that his doctors reach, but, I am suggesting, it may be that present scene serves the function of reawakening the uncertainty about the true causes of his agony. Perhaps, in the end, it is his conscious or unconscious registration of basic truths about himself and about the conditions in which he lives that is essential to producing the pain he repeatedly undergoes.

There are two basic points to emphasize here. First, the high levels of cortisone in his system at the time in question should block the purported physical causes of such seizures. Second, it very much seems that it is Avery's perception of the scene before him that crucially elicits his paralysed reaction. What he sees, in the first instance, is his son presenting him with the football. And that football has acquired a kind of loaded psychological significance in earlier scenes. Just before Avery goes off to the hospital, it is established that the football has been kept as a pathetic trophy of some minor heroics that Avery had performed in a high school football game. When the father and son take notice of the football sitting on the mantel, Avery observes that over the years it has become dusty and deflated. He orders his son to fetch a pump, and they reinflate it just before he departs to take his 'miracle' cure. It seems clear enough, in this and ensuing contexts, that the newly inflated football is a grotesque counterpart to Avery himself. He also is a shrunken figure who is artificially reinflated by the heavy doses of cortisone.[10]

It is for this reason, I suspect, that he reacts so violently to the later appearance of the football in his son's outstretched hand. The football appears to him as a ridiculous emblem of what he, now (ambiguously) bigger than life, has become. This is the truth that he discerns in the half-darkness of his son's room. And, more than this, the fact that it is his son, the son he has sought to instruct and dominate, who presents him with this image of himself constitutes the most devastating repudiation of his pretension to special authority and moral superiority. As he stands stricken in the doorway, his delusory perspective simply shatters and collapses. It is true that, at the very end of the film, he and his family have come together once more, but, at the same time, this seems to be an equivocal resolution. After all, the conditions depicted at the outset of the movie have not changed. All of the old needs, indignities, and psychological strains will confront him as before.

These proposals mesh, in complicated ways, with other important aspects of the narrative. Although Avery does accept his doctors' diagnosis of his illness, he also holds them in some contempt because they do not recognize the facts that he imagines that he sees so clearly, i.e. the awfulness of contemporary life and the deleterious effects it has on those who lead it. For these more spiritual diseases, *he* will be the teacher/doctor who knows the truth. If I am right in suggesting that the doctors may well have offered him a too simple, overly reductive account of his suffering, then his perception of them has some justice. And, as crazy as his own analyses and prescriptions may be, the movie strongly indicates that there is a core of truth in his reaction to and understanding of his situation at home and in his school. All things considered, it is not obvious what overall judgement is to be made upon these issues. The doctors do seem to be too narrowly focused on purely medical causes, but Avery, although he is, perhaps, more perceptive in sundry important ways, is also unquestionably delusional. A more elaborate analysis would attempt, as far as possible, to sort these rather subtle matters out.

3. MEANING AS SIGNIFICATION AND MEANING AS SIGNIFICANCE

My interpretative conjectures are bound to be controversial, but it is not important to the present discussion that they be accepted. What is important is the kind of content the claims have and the sort of grounds that support them. At the centre of my analysis is the question of what happens to Avery in his son's room and of the causes of his behaviour there. If the story is understood, as it usually is, as a drama that shows the dangerous side effects of cortisone, then, for the reasons given, the scene is likely to seem inscrutable. But, I have argued, it is plausible that, if we take a wider look around, these narrative-based questions may well have surprising answers. However, according to the taxonomy that Bordwell sets up in *MM*, these answers concern only the fabula, the 'referential meaning' of the film, and, as such, fall short of anything that he will count as interpretation. That conclusion, in this case at least, strikes me as strongly counter-intuitive. In some sense or other, these proposals, although directed upon questions about the details of the fabula, *do* offer an alternative conception of the 'deeper meaning' of the film. It is just that they do not take the form of a statement of some supra-narrative theme or message implied by the film.

What we do plainly have is an *explanation*, constructed in terms of the information provided by the movie, of why Avery reacts as he does in the scene in question. What is more, the explanation is a *causal explanation*. The thesis, roughly, is that it is fictional in the film that Avery's behaviour is caused by his recognition of the significance of his son's strange actions. But, for Bordwell, because such causal judgements bear only on the 'referential meaning' of the film, this excludes them from the realm of 'interpretation'. It is precisely this exclusion that seems so dubious.[11] After all, there is a familiar sense in which the *meaning* of an event or action is fundamentally constructed in terms of its place within a relevant network of causality. Let me explain.

When we wonder about the meaning of some salient episode in our lives, we are not supposing, absurdly, that the happenings that make up the episode have some covert semantic dimension that we are seeking to decode. Rather, what we are looking for is a relatively global account of the episode that sets it into significant connections with some of the key events and circumstances that preceded it and, very probably, with some of the chief consequences that ensued. Moreover, the connections in question are primarily causal. How did the episode arise from its antecedents in our lives and what was the upshot of the results that it engendered in its wake? It is true that, when we regard the episode as potentially meaningful, we are not interested in just any scattering of causes and effects. It is our aim to find a surveyable pattern of explanatory connections, a pattern that enables us to situate the episode within a narrative framework that opens it up to plausible perspectives of moral, psychological, political, religious, etc., assessment. The meaning of the episode is just whatever its place in the pattern reveals to us from the evaluative perspectives that we have adopted. We aim for a pattern that resolves, where possible, our engaged perplexity.

This wording may give the impression that we are presented with the highlighted causal sequences, on the one hand, and that they are matched against some system of values on the other. But, of course, this is not the way in which these issues characteristically are posed. The episode is experienced by us as, say, morally problematic in certain fairly specific ways. Suppose, to take a simple example, that I have, by my actions, broken off a long-standing friendship, and I am troubled by what I have done and by its potential implications for the future. The 'narrative given' in such a case is not the bare fact of the rupture, but the fact that the rupture occurred in a manner that concerns me and raises the troubling questions. I hope to be able to find an accurate story, importantly constituted by causal judgements, that casts light on the disturbing aspects of this slice of my history and helps me reach some reasonable evaluation of what has here occurred. In other words, I want my story of the broken friendship both to be true to the facts and to offer a perspicuous *resolution* of the value-inflected questions that worried me in the first place. (Of course, sometimes I may have to settle for an understanding of why no such resolution can be reasonably expected.) When we achieve a story that fits a puzzling episode in what we regard as a satisfying and enlightening manner, then we are likely to speak of having learned something about the 'meaning' of the episode, the meaning that it had in our lives. I highlight these familiar, if somewhat elusive considerations, because they remind us that there is a concept of 'meaning'—a concept of the meaning of events, actions, life segments, etc.—that is clearly tied to, rather than sharply divorced from, the causality of the episodes in question.

The same concept of 'meaning' comes into play when we read or view a work of narrative fiction. In these 'aesthetic' transactions, it is fictionally true of the reader that he or she is learning of some ordered series of real events, and it is part of the standard game of make-believe we 'play', that we are expected and licensed to ask after explanations of why the fictional history unfolds as it does, where these explanations are to be framed in terms of what is implied about the workings of the fictional world.[12] At the same time, we are normally interested in, concerned about, suspicious of, etc., the fictional agents that move that history, and this means that we suppose that the explanations we arrive at will help us assess the character, sensibility, and motivational structure of those agents and arrive at reasonable evaluative judgements both about them and about the things they do and think. In short, we hope to embed their behaviour within a configuration of explanatory relations in a manner that renders it meaningful in the sense described above. In fact, when ordinary readers and viewers ask about the meaning of a story, it is this sense, I believe, that they very often have in mind. They are puzzled by the activities of a character who seems psychologically inscrutable, stumped by what appears to be a significant lacuna in the dramatic development, or doubtful about the ethical implications of a situation that the characters have faced. They lack the sense of a pattern of explanatory connections sufficient to permit an overall assessment of the key dramatic questions that have arisen for them from the work.

In my brief discussion of *Bigger than Life*, I have tried to say enough to yield a sense of how 'meaning', in the present usage, arises in that narrative setting. Although the analysis is originally motivated by the enigmatic nature of Avery's aborted attack upon his son, to make some sense of this I summoned potentially relevant considerations from various parts of the movie. What are we to make of the movie's early emphasis upon the professional and familial pressures to which Avery is subjected? Are the initial attacks of pain correlated, in some manner, with those pressures? What impression are we to form about the various lectures that Avery delivers in which he expresses his view that contemporary life is somehow seriously off the track? And how do we construe the fact that Avery's doctors are depicted as unprepossessing technicians of the body? Related questions proliferate throughout our experience of the film. Admittedly, my brief discussion touched only lightly on these matters. There is a lot of detail that deserves to be worked through, and there are many questions I have not mentioned at all. Nevertheless, it is not simply that my sketch of an interpretation yields up a judgement about the causes of Avery's final bout of pain. It purports to make a beginning at pulling all of these questions about the drama together into an explanatory network that casts light backwards and forwards across the film. The strategy here is one of *re-emplotment*. We take an already familiar series of events, the members of which have seemed integrated into one kind of narrative, and argue that, when they are reordered, re-weighted, and linked to still other events, they actually tell a different and, perhaps, a better story. For *Bigger than Life*, we have attained a new notion of the 'meaning' of Avery's final seizure and of a host of other incidents and actions in the film. It is in this sense that we have an outline of the meaning or meanings of the dramatic developments in the movie.[13]

This, then, is the core of my dissent from Bordwell's characterizations of explicative criticism. We are both willing to agree, with some qualifications, to the platitude that giving an interpretation of a work is providing an account of the work's meaning. But Bordwell, like many other writers on the subject, takes an aspect of linguistic meaning as his paradigm of what it is that interpretation explicates. Sophisticated enough to see that there are stresses and strains in the analogy, he tries to weaken and generalize the analogical relations upon which his account is intended to rely. But, after all the adjustments are made, his reader is left with a dilemma. Either Bordwell is endorsing the 'heretical' claim that implicit meaning is some kind of narrative transcending thematic content conveyed indirectly by a film, or it is entirely unclear that he has given us any substantive account of implicit meaning and explicative interpretation at all. Moreover, if the situation were to be rectified along the lines that I have sketched, then the temptation to draw a strong contrast between the deliverances of explicative interpretation and the contents of the fabula should lapse.

The choice of linguistic meanings as the model for the implicit meanings of films informs and, I believe, distorts other features of Bordwell's conception of interpretative practice. In the middle section of *MM* (chapters 5, 6, and 7), he describes interpretation as a matter of 'mapping' cinematic 'cues' onto the elements of a 'semantic field'. 'A semantic field', we are informed, 'is a set of relations of meaning between conceptual or linguistic units' (*MM* 106), and legitimate mappings from films to semantic fields are primarily determined by institutionally favoured 'schemata' and institutionally sanctioned 'heuristics', 'protocols', and 'routines'. The institutions in question here are the various 'critical institutions' to which film interpreters belong in virtue of their allegiance to one set of explicative 'conventions' or another. But this is to treat interpretation as if it were a task of translation, assigning 'conceptual or linguistic units' to targeted elements of a film's narrative and narration. Represented in this fashion, explicative interpretation appears to be radically and problematically indeterminate, and its methods and objectives seem to lack any rationale beyond the fact that various interpreters adopt them. However, I believe that the worrisome appearances arise largely from the fact that most of the reasonable constraints on interpretation have already been suppressed by the unfortunate selection of the analogy with translation. I will say a bit more about this a bit later.

I initiated my interpretation of *Bigger than Life* by calling attention to and reflecting upon the anomalous character of a particular incident in the film. Bordwell mentions this strategy several times in his book. For example, he says, 'The spectator may seek to construct implicit meanings when she cannot find a way to reconcile an anomalous element with a referential or explicit aspect of the work' (*MM* 9). However, the epistemic substance of these attempts to 'reconcile anomalous elements' and their potential contributions to a work's overall intelligibility and force are never systematically explored. Bordwell, as noted above, tends to treat such anomalies simply as 'cues' that trigger 'ascriptions of meaning' from would-be interpreters. As such, they are treated as if they were on a par with the windows and mirrors in movies that 'prompt' some critics to the ascription of reflexive references to the movie that contains them. I share Bordwell's opinion that most instances of this kind of putative self-referentiality are arbitrary and implausible. In the absence of careful argument, it is a facile way of dealing with the narrative as if it were an allegory—an allegory of its own cinematic construction. Of course, this is not to deny that explicative attempts to resolve apparent narrative anomalies are themselves often carried out in a defective and unconvincing way. But, then, any form of sound argument can have would-be instances that are either well or poorly constructed. The fault, where it exists, will lie with the individual practitioners and not with the nature of the argument form. On the other hand, when explicative interpretation of narrative fiction film aims at the objectives that I have adumbrated earlier, then, it seems to me, the norms that we are able to bring to bear in evaluating the success or failure of such interpretations are rich and substantial. There is promise here of firmer ground beneath our feet.

First, the problems that interpreters face in their endeavours are the same in kind as the problems that ordinary viewers cope with continually in forming the most minimal comprehension of narrative in film. As Bordwell stresses, especially in *Narration in the Fiction Film*,[14] viewers must constantly frame and reframe hypotheses about what is happening in a movie story and about the causes and effects of the occurrences depicted. When we are confronted with an anomalous narrative episode which is especially recalcitrant, we may be forced to the supposition that our questions can be answered only by a markedly more detailed and extensive consideration of what the broader narrative context may reveal. Moreover, when the supposition turns out to be warranted, then the reasoning that supports our resulting claims to understand the puzzling incident will draw more comprehensively than usual upon diverse features of the total film, and the compilation of evidence that we construct may well be more complicated than is ordinarily required. Nevertheless, the kinds of narrative materials that we draw upon and the argumentive structures that we deploy will not be especially recondite or charged with theory. Explicative interpretation, in this mode, will be *continuous* with the activities of ordinary viewers, except, perhaps, on scales that measure the complexity of the evidence assembled. Considered in this light, explicative interpretation is a natural, although sometimes more sophisticated, extension of familiar and absolutely basic strategies by means of which typical audiences comprehend a movie.

Second, consider the important case of what fictionally causes what in a film. We all come to the movies with broad experience of making causal judgements about the real world, and, difficult as they may be to state, we have, through that experience, internalized a variety of norms about how such judgements may be derived and about the standards that render them reasonable or not. In transferring these capacities to the making of similar judgements about fictional causality within a narrative film, we begin by operating from the same base. Of course, particular movies may signal that they are presenting fictional worlds whose causal operations are, in certain ways, importantly different from those of the real world. But this only means that we understand that certain of our familiar norms are to be suspended and others are to be adjusted to suit the case in hand. The likelihood of a reasonable consensus about whether certain sorts of causal judgements are plausible in the narrative context will ordinarily remain strong. Similar remarks apply to fundamental features, other than causality, that order and integrate our fabula constructions.

In *Narration in the Fiction Film*, Bordwell places great importance on an accurate understanding of how actual film viewers process the information supplied by film narration and form the complex of judgements that constitute their comprehension of the fictional world. And certainly, he is right to do so. However, in *MM*, when he turns his attention to problems of film interpretation, he fails to emphasize the difference between the question, 'How does such-and-such a viewer *actually* understand this segment?' and the *normative* question, 'How is it *reasonable* for a viewer to understand the segment?'[15] Plainly, the answers to counterpart questions of these two kinds may diverge significantly, and, as I have described it here, explicative interpretation attempts, in the face of anomaly, to offer plausible and powerful answers to questions of this normative variety. Naturally, ordinary viewers usually assume that their judgements about a film's narrative *are* reasonable. This is a standard which they accept. But, in any given instance, viewers may be mistaken in so assuming, or, at least, it may be false that they have made the most reasonable judgement. Explicative interpretation is or should be an attempt to show that, for the film under scrutiny, more reasonable discriminations and explanatory connections can be made and that it is intellectually, imaginatively, and emotionally worthwhile to do so.

Throughout *MM*, Bordwell presents a dismal parade of wayward interpretations, and this reminds us how often interpreters fail to meet the tests of plausibility and interest in their work. Nevertheless, the many instances of failure give us no good reason for scepticism about the project of explicative interpretation. For all that Bordwell shows, the source of much of the trouble may be simpler. That is, it may be that critics and interpreters are frequently just careless about what questions they mean to be raising about a film and that they do not make their case that it is genuinely reasonable to comprehend a given film in the terms that they propose. This is the more mundane diagnosis that I mentioned previously. I think that it deserves to be taken quite seriously, but Bordwell evinces considerable sympathy with a view that obscures its potential viability.

The view in question, often associated with the work of Stanley Fish,[16] maintains that an interpretation is reasonable only relative to the canons of evidence and 'reasonability' accepted by one 'critical institution' or another and that those canons cannot be reasonably challenged, from within the institution, as long as they have the status of conventions to which the members of the institution conform. Thus, if an interpreter belongs to a critical school that goes in for the practice of reading windows and mirrors in movies as symbols of the movie screen, then his practice is necessarily impeccable from the perspective of his school. Correlatively, the practice is not rationally criticizable by the members of any other school since they are merely the representatives of a different and incommensurable critical practice. Such a position makes it difficult to explain how many interpreters, following some well-established explicative routine, can nevertheless be wrong.

But I have been urging that film viewing and film interpretation do not divide up so sharply into incommensurable schools and practices. To a large extent, we all start out from the norms of reasonable judgement that inform our cognitive processes in ordinary perception, and, in the context of film viewing, we activate our knowledge of the additional norms of basic cinematic exposition. If we were to speak of an 'interpretative community' at this level, then nearly all competent movie spectators belong to it. No doubt this shared foundation of norms will not suffice to resolve *all* of the disputes between different 'critical schools' and between competing explications of a particular film. Still, the epistemic power and complexity of the norms should not be underestimated. Especially in those cases in which we sense strongly that some doctrine of theory or methodology is flawed or that some interpretative proposal is unconvincing, we are able to explain the grounds of our suspicion by appeal to violations of these common norms. There may well be several reasonable ways to view a movie, but the constraints on 'reasonable' viewings are much stronger than the picture of thoroughgoing incommensurability suggests.[17] And interpretative procedures may simply fail, more often than we care to think, to satisfy the constraints to which we are antecedently committed.

In the final chapter of *MM*, Bordwell proposes that film interpretation, as we have known it, should be replaced by a more systematic 'historical poetics'. I am not entirely clear about what his historical poetics does and does not include, but he affirms, for example, that it will incorporate 'explanations [of film construction], of an intentionalist, functionalist, or causal sort' (*MM* 269). Hence, if this remark were to be filled out in certain ways, our disagreements about a positive agenda for film interpretation might not be so great. It would be fine with me if the kind of narrative meaning I have highlighted were to find its natural home within some form of 'poetics' of film. Probably Bordwell would judge that my discussion in this chapter is less an account of the sort of explicative interpretation that past and present interpreters have actually conducted and more a prescription of my own for reforming contemporary critical work. Nevertheless, no matter which description is to be preferred, it is important to point out the liabilities of linguistic models of narrative meaning and to make it plain that an alternative conception is available. Otherwise, I am afraid, the temptations to commit the heresy of paraphrase are with us always, and we will sin and sin again.

NOTES

1. David Bordwell, *Making Meaning* (Cambridge, Mass.: Harvard University Press, 1989). By focusing on Bordwell's influential discussion, it has been possible to achieve a sharper delineation of certain main issues. However, I believe that most of the criticisms I make apply with at least equal force to many others who have written on the nature of explicative interpretation. So, I consider Bordwell's position as an instance of a broader target. Also, my differences with Bordwell on the topic of interpretation should not obscure our extensive agreement on many other subjects.
2. See, especially, his summary conclusions in the final chapter of *Making Meaning*.

3. Bordwell's development of his taxonomy of cinematic meaning is presented in *MM*, chs. 1–4.
4. For a defence of the concept of 'the implied author', in connection with film, see Gregory Currie, *Image and Mind: Film, Philosophy, and Cognitive Science* (Cambridge: Cambridge University Press, 1995), 243–80. Currie argues that the 'intentions' of the implied author of a film ground the correctness and incorrectness of many kinds of interpretative claims about film.
5. *Narration in the Fiction Film* (Madison: University of Wisconsin Press, 1985), 33–40.
6. As anyone familiar with classical philosophical theories of perception would suppose, there are enormous difficulties about what is and is not 'directly presented' (about what is and is not 'epistemically given') in a movie. In the present context, I will ignore these problems altogether, and pretend that, from case to case, we can make reasonable discriminations concerning this distinction. However, in various theoretical and interpretative contexts, our lack of clarity about the matter can become very important.
7. Of course, the classic source of both the phrase and the methodological position is Cleanth Brooks in the essay 'The Heresy of Paraphrase'. It is found in *The Well-Wrought Urn* (New York: Harcourt Brace Jovanovich, 1947), 192–214.
8. V. F. Perkins, *Film as Film* (New York: DeCapo Press, 1993), 116–33. I believe that the present essay can be plausibly read as an elaboration of some of the central themes in Perkins's seminal book. Also, for an admirable, extensive study of narrative comprehension, see Edward Branigan, *Narrative Comprehension and Film* (New York: Routledge, 1992). Branigan is excellent in bringing out both the subtlety and the power of intricate narrative constructions in film.
9. In a similar connection, Berys Gaut speaks of 'the *semantic* paradigm' and its dangers. See his article 'Interpreting the Arts: The Patchwork Theory', *Journal of Aesthetics and Art Criticism*, 51: 4 (1993), 597–609. In n. 8 he acknowledges the influence of discussions with Richard Moran. Moran apparently spoke of 'the *linguistic* paradigm'. I favour Moran's phrase because the use of 'semantic' suggests that erring theorists take as their 'paradigm' the conventional relations of words, phrases, and sentences to their meanings in the relevant languages. Sometimes this is so, but, as we have seen, Bordwell appeals to the speaker's meaning in motivating his account.
10. Later in the movie, Avery uses the football to humiliate his son, and it appears that a part of his motive in doing so is to reinforce the boy's sense of his father's superiority.
11. The importance of the 'games of make-believe' that we play in engaging with a work of art is a major theme of Kendall Walton's *Mimesis as Make-Believe: On the Foundations of the Representational Arts* (Cambridge, Mass.: Harvard University Press, 1990).
12. But doesn't my analysis of *Bigger than Life* illicitly interweave a proposed account of the movie's fabula with various general thematic issues and thereby obscure the fact that Bordwell's concept of 'implicit meaning' does have application in this instance? For example, isn't it a part of my interpretation that the movie implies that middle-class American life in the 1950s was stultifying and that medicine tended to be inadequate to grasp the nature of the resultant suffering?

    The objection is misconceived. First, *Bigger than Life*, given its complexity and ambiguity, is not committed to the simple sample messages mentioned above, and attempts even to *formulate* more complex and plausible alternatives are likely to qualify themselves out of existence. The difficulty of the task would be even more obvious if one were to try to extract suitable general messages from, say, *North by Northwest*, *The Rules of the Game*, and *The Marquise of O*. Second, no matter what general and/or abstract themes one might arrive at, they would be supported by the film only in so far as one was entitled to see the concrete fictional situations in the movie as *typical*, *paradigmatic*, or somehow *emblematic* of the relevant general range of real world cases. As a rule, however, a film does not offer guidance, directly or indirectly, about whether its narrative components have one or another of these functions. Hence, there is no clear sense whatsoever in which the putative generalizations are 'implied' by a given movie. Finally, for the reasons given in the text, my partial exegesis of *Bigger than Life is* an account of 'meaning' in the film, and as such, is full-bloodedly interpretative. Any general morals or messages that the film might suggest to various viewers seem to me to ride piggy-back upon the viewers' understanding of its narrative meaning, and the messages are neither necessary nor sufficient to promote that understanding to the status of 'interpretation'.

13. In this discussion, I have concentrated on questions about the meaning or meanings of a film *narrative*. One objective here has been to reject Bordwell's dichotomy between comprehending the narrative of a film and interpreting the film's meaning. Nevertheless, I realize that comparable observations can and should be made about the various (and sometimes anomalous) functions of film *narration* and features of *film style*. My special attention to narrative should not suggest that I view these other topics as relatively unimportant. In fact, in any particular instance, it is difficult and artificial to disentangle issues about one of these aspects of film from the others. Moreover, queries about 'the meaning of a film' are often intended to call for an explicative account that brings the meaningfulness of the different aspects together within a global perspective that explains their interaction.

14. See esp. ch. 3, 'The Viewer's Activity'.

15. See also Berys Gaut, 'Making Sense of Films: Neoformalism and its Limits', *Modern Language Studies*, 31 (1995), 8–23. Gaut also points out that Bordwell accords insufficient attention to the normative character of interpretative questions. For his criticisms of Bordwell on this score, see esp. pp. 15–16.

16. Especially *Is There a Text in This Class? The Authority of Interpretive Communities* (Cambridge, Mass.: Harvard University Press, 1980).

17. Although it may be true that there are conflicting explicative interpretations of interesting films which maximally tie in terms of overall plausibility and power, given the considerable density and complexity of the material to be accounted for, it is normally very difficult to formulate and support even *one* that does not founder in the light of the available filmic evidence.

PART III
Ideology and Ethics

Over the course of the 1970s, semiotics (the study of signs, as derived from structural linguistics) became wedded to psychoanalysis, a theory of the development of human subjectivity, in the enterprise of understanding the nature and operation of 'ideology'. The inspiration for this undertaking was the work of French Marxist Louis Althusser, for whom ideology was not a mere epiphenomenon of the capitalist mode of production, but central to its maintenance. For Althusser, 'ideology' described the process by which social institutions cultivated individuals compliant to the social system by appealing to their need to be recognized, or acquire a social identity. According to Althusser, institutions call upon the maturing human being to take up social roles and positions. By responding to this 'hailing' the growing human becomes an 'individual', believing, after the fact, that his sense of self-identity is something freely chosen, although in fact he has come to occupy a position determined in advance by the social system. Althusser's suggestion that his description of the formation of the individual was akin to Lacan's account of the 'mirror-stage' (a recasting of Freud's theory of narcissism) was taken up by critical theorists in the humanities, who assimilated the role of 'institutions' in Althusser's theory to the role of representation in the theory of Lacan. The theorization of 'subject position-ing' dovetailed with the analysis of cinematic representation, for cinema seemed at once a model for and a vehicle of subject positioning, as we discussed in the introduction. These theorists argued that the spectator is subject to an 'impression' or 'illusion' of reality at the cinema. His mistaken belief in the literal reality of what is depicted is in some sense necessary for him to comprehend it, that is, for him to be a subject-spectator at all, even though there is a part of himself that knows that his position as a spectator, and, in grander terms, his self-identity, is founded upon illusion. Pyscho-analytic theory alone could explain this state of affairs.

The multiple confusions, ambiguities, and incoherencies that underlie the film theory derived from Althusser's all-encompassing and yet extremely sketchy theory of ideology have now been thoroughly exposed. As Jennifer Hammett's essay makes clear, however, the legacy remains to be properly redressed in the domain where it arguably had the greatest influence: femi-nist film theory. The theory of subject construction allowed feminist theor-ists to argue that cinema (by and large, Hollywood cinema) was patriarchal not simply by virtue of the content of the stories it told—for example, male-centred narratives in which women occupy a secondary role—but by virtue of its very status as representation. The form of commercial cinematic representation, as both model and vehicle of ideology, was not gender-neutral but structured gender relations at the expense of women. For the position of the film spectator who 'identified' with the 'gaze' of the camera and mistook representation for reality was a masculine (patriarchal) one, in contrast to which 'woman' appeared as an object rather than a subject of the gaze. Hammett's verdict on this line of thinking is uncompromising. Feminist film theorists assume that the representation of women can be contested only by revealing the way in which representation structures subjectivity—male and female alike—but this accomplishes nothing for feminism. The assumption is at best trivial, because it only reveals the platitude that we can only understand gender through our representations of it; or at worst, (1) false, in that effective feminist criticism can be conducted by countering pernicious representations of women with progressive ones, or (2) self-defeating, for the only position the feminist can occupy is the male (patriarchal) position, unless she incoherently imagines a place for herself altogether outside representation (feminist essentialism). Post-structuralist and essentialist feminism are each other's idealist and realist mirror image. Feminists, she concludes, should abandon feminist film theory for feminist film criticism. Without denying the strategic, political value of psycho-semiotic film theory in making the pervasiveness of sexist assumptions both visible and a key object of debate, this debate can and should move forward without these theoretical liabilities.

Hector Rodriguez's chapter picks up a question left open by Hammett. Is there an alternative to Althusser's conception of ideology, which in effect identifies ideology with thought itself? Certainly there are a number of such alternative definitions available, in the work of the analytic Marxist Jon Elster, to take one example. Within film theory itself, both Terry Lovell and Noël Carroll have advanced non-Althusserian accounts of ideology. Carroll has argued that ideologies are false beliefs upholding practices of social domination, and that such ideologies can be countered by factual evidence. Drawing on the later philosophy of Wittgenstein, Rodriguez takes issue with this view of ideology—though he notes that Carroll himself has subsequently revised his views—on the grounds that ideologies involve beliefs held in such a way that they are resistant to empirical falsification. Rodriguez does not deny that ideologies may contain demonstrably false beliefs, but argues that this does not account for their distinctive character. Ideologies, he argues, are a particular form of moral picture, a kind that contributes to forms of social domination. As moral pictures, they define how we think and feel about the world in such a manner that their 'truth' lies in the conviction with which they are carried. Ideologies are not so much empirically false, though this is often the case, as morally unjustified. From the perspective of Rodriguez's chapter, then, patriarchal ideology is identified not with representation *per se* but with the articulation of moral pictures that are demeaning and discriminatory towards women. By emphasizing the way in which ideology shapes the way we think and feel about the world, Rodriguez's argument redeems one aspect of Althusser's conception of ideology that the theory of ideology as false belief overlooks.

The 'Althusserian–Lacanian paradigm' had two especially important in-

tellectual consequences for the study of film. First, the equation of representation with ideology reduced aesthetic questions to political ones. Secondly,
the idea that political emancipation could be delivered by certain forms of
modernist, anti-realist film-making reduced the evaluation of both aesthetics and ideology to a rigid and misleading dichotomy between 'classical' or
'dominant' cinema on the one hand, and avant-garde film on the other
hand. The 'Third Cinema' debate that, as Tommy Lott's chapter points out,
frames recent black film theory and criticism, shared the reduction of
aesthetics to ideology and an opposition to Hollywood film. In this context,
however, the opposition to Hollywood was less in the name of a political
modernism than in the name of an independent, anti-imperialist cinema that
would use the aesthetic resources at its disposal, however 'imperfect', for
political ends. The political importance of this opposition to Hollywood by
black film theorists cannot be gainsaid, yet, as Lott argues, the reduction of
aesthetics to ideology and the uncritical valorization of 'independence' are
insufficient for understanding the nature and possibilities of contemporary
black film-making. Black film critics' opposition to Hollywood racism,
however justified, has left black film theorists bereft of an adequate explanatory framework with which to make sense of the aesthetic and ideological
strengths and weaknesses of black film-making within Hollywood: both so-
called 'blaxploitation', and the more recent incursion of black 'independents' like Spike Lee into Hollywood. Lott argues that we should understand
the aesthetic and ideological merits of both commercial and independent
black film-making on their own terms. Through a detailed investigation of
black film criticism, he explores the value of both textual analysis and the
study of audience reception in pursuit of this goal.

10

The Ideological Impediment: Epistemology, Feminism, and Film Theory

JENNIFER HAMMETT

The 'truth' of [women's] oppression cannot be 'captured' on celluloid with the 'innocence' of the camera; . . . What the camera in fact grasps is the 'natural' world of the dominant ideology.

(Claire Johnston[1])

As an advanced representation system, cinema poses questions of the ways the unconscious (formed by the dominant order) structures ways of seeing and pleasure in looking.

(Laura Mulvey[2])

Born under the sign of Althusserian Marxism and Lacanian psychoanalysis, feminist film theory's birthright was a certain account of representation, a semiotic theory already evident in these formative contributions to the field. Beginning with the first premiss of semiology—the non-identity of sign and thing—Johnston reminded feminists that cinematic images are not the traces of a transparent reality, but representations. Meanwhile, Mulvey rehearsed the insight that representations, cinematic images among them, structure our conscious and unconscious relations to the world. As a result, perception itself is always a way of seeing, a function of conceptual categories in no way compelled by the reality they purport to grasp.

Both Mulvey and Johnston went beyond the unassailable claim that cinematic images are not identical with the objects they picture, however. Both identified the constitutive role of language—the fact that knowledge is a function of representation and not the other way around—with the operation of ideology. Feminist film theorists following Mulvey and Johnston combined Althusser's definition of ideology as 'the imaginary

This is a slightly revised and expanded version of 'The Ideological Impediment: Feminism and Film Theory', originally published in *Cinema Journal*, 36: 2 (1997). I would like to extend my sincere thanks to Richard Allen, Dudley Andrew, Gillian Brown, Natasa Durovicova, Rosann Greenspan, Howard Horwitz, David Jung, Margo Kasdan, Murray Smith, my former students and colleagues at the University of Iowa, and the anonymous readers of *Cinema Journal* for their helpful comments on earlier drafts of this article.

relationship of . . . individuals to their real relations of existence'[3] with Lacan's theory of the subject as constituted through language to conclude that representation is coincident with ideology. The perceived result was an epistemological crisis. The fact that we are embedded in language was thought to be the occasion of epistemic inadequacy and the occlusion of the real. Representation, now identified with ideology, was not only alienation, but error.

Feminists were quick to embrace the concept of ideology as a way of affirming that representations generally, and gender representations in particular, are socially constructed and thus subject to change. It is essential to the feminist project that patriarchal gender definitions do not reflect essential, biological differences between men and women. In practice, however, the marriage of representation to ideology severely limited feminism's strategic options. As Laura Mulvey characterized the problem: the 'ultimate challenge' to feminism is 'how to fight the unconscious structured like a language . . . while still caught within the language of patriarchy' (LM 7). In structuring our conscious and unconscious relations to the world, patriarchal representations trap women in an ideological blind alley, according to Mulvey. Debarred by the regime of language from an immediate relation to the real, we construct a simulacrum of the real out of the representational resources of the dominant ideology, according to this argument. Constituted as subjects by patriarchal representations, women do not have the epistemic resources necessary to escape patriarchy.

Of course, most feminist film theorists would insist that we have long since moved beyond Johnston's and Mulvey's vision of a monolithic and effectively limitless patriarchal ideology. And apparently we have. Few today would argue that patriarchal texts invariably position spectators within ideologically complicit structures of identification and desire. Film theorists, feminist and otherwise, now widely acknowledge that texts cannot guarantee their own reception, nor compel spectator acquiescence to their ideological goals and effects. At this point in the debate, the issue is no longer whether we are able to escape the ideological effects of (patriarchal) texts, but how.

Feminist film theorists have suggested two possible mechanisms for evading patriarchal ideology. The first appeals to the radical potential of critical self-awareness or critical distance; the second invokes the authenticity of everyday reality and lived experience. These two strategies for evading the supposedly falsifying effects of ideology approach the problem of circumventing ideology from opposite directions—one idealist, the other realist. The premiss animating them, however, is the same; both the realist and the idealist responses to the reign of representation assume that our embeddedness in language and representation matters. For all their attempts to restrict the scope or diminish the force of patriarchal ideology, feminist film theorists continue to embrace the assumption underlying post-structuralist theories of ideology: they assume that the fact that we know the world only through our representations of it necessarily calls our beliefs about the world into question. I will suggest, to the contrary, that there is no reason to believe that the alienation that characterizes representation necessarily entails error.[4]

From Johnston and Mulvey to the present, the history of feminist film theory is best understood as a series of attempts to escape the epistemological crisis that theories of ideology apparently precipitate.[5] In fact, it could not be otherwise; as long as feminist film theorists hold on to the belief that our embeddedness in language matters, they will continue to manœuvre endlessly within Mulvey's theoretical orbit, pursuing inevitably futile attempts to get outside ideology, outside of representation. As long as they accept the necessary correlation between representation and error, they will remain in ideology's shadow. And yet, as my analysis will show, the inevitable failure of feminist film scholars to theorize an escape from ideology has no consequences for the practice of feminist film criticism and, similarly, no consequences for feminism. Once we abandon the premiss that our embeddedness in language matters, then the need to escape that embeddedness—to achieve a neutral encounter with phenomena—simply disappears. If I am right, feminists can give up the epistemological ambitions of feminist film theory, and pursue feminist critical and political goals unencumbered by fears of the alienating effects of representation.

I. ESCAPING IDEOLOGY: CRITICAL SELF-AWARENESS

The first strategy for avoiding the supposedly falsifying effects of representation turns on the critic's ability to maintain a 'critical distance' from her own historically constructed assumptions, commitments, and beliefs. Indeed, a belief in the emancipatory force of keeping a critical distance from one's beliefs—the notion that a critic must at all times be alert to how her historically constructed attitudes and beliefs condition her critical assessments—has become something of a commonplace among politically committed film scholars. Mary Ann Doane's feminist formulation of this position is exemplary, however, for what it reveals about the logic and structure of this particular attempt to evade ideology.

Perhaps no one more forcefully presents and defends the position that mainstream Hollywood cinema constructs a patriarchal subject than Mary Ann Doane. In 'Masquerade Reconsidered: Further Thoughts on the Female Spectator', Doane cites Freud for the proposition that patriarchal 'texts, especially jokes . . . have a certain psychical force' (MR 50).[6] Similarly, Doane locates in the woman's film of the 1940s 'a certain representation of spectatorship which is *powerful in its effects*' (CO 144, emphasis mine). Opposing herself to theorists who insist on 'the mobility and fluidity of the spectator's relation to the text', Doane maintains that 'feminist criticism must of necessity deal with the constraints and restraints of reading with respect to sexual identity—in effect, with the question of power and its textual manifestation' (CO 145).

Once a theorist has posited the existence of 'constraints and restraints on reading', however, the question of multiple or resistant readings inevitably arises. How does the feminist spectator escape the textual manifestations of patriarchy's power? Like all theorists committed to the existence of textual constraints on reading, Doane is also committed to the possibility of evading those constraints, of eluding the 'psychical power' of patriarchal representations. Accordingly, Doane imagines two possible relationships between spectators and texts—submission and critique. In the difference lies the possibility of a feminist resistance to patriarchal ideology.

As Doane describes it, submissive spectatorship re-enacts the now familiar horror story of a mass audience taken over by the alien (and alienating) forces of mass culture. Demonstrating a candour rare among film theorists, however, Doane may be the first to narrate this story in the first person. She writes, 'Sometimes, when I am subject to a strong desire to laugh and hence "belong" to an audience, or when I am tired, watching late night television, and off my guard, I will find myself laughing at a sexist joke. I "find myself", I am beside myself, I am other' (MR 50). In this narrative of the split subject, Doane represents herself as vulnerable to the power of the mass media, as yearning to merge with a mass audience which is, almost by definition, uncritical. In a scenario reminiscent of *The Invasion of the Body Snatchers*, her vulnerability is physical (she is 'tired', the pod people can complete the replication process only after their human hosts have fallen asleep). And yet, finally, as in the movie, it is her mind that is subject to the alien force (recall 'texts, especially jokes . . . have a certain psychical force').

A similar vision of the coercive power of dominant texts underlies Doane's debate with Tania Modleski over what it means to 'get' a joke. Modleski insists that 'getting' or understanding a joke is not the same as thinking it is funny.[7] While Doane acknowledges the logical distinction between understanding a text and enjoying it, she reserves the term 'getting' for a particular relation between comprehension and pleasure: 'The term "getting" suggests that the effect of the joke must be instantaneous, that [understanding and pleasure] must be simultaneous' (MR 50). Accordingly, some responses to representations—those named by the term 'getting'—are 'instantaneous', 'automatic', 'unthinking', even 'induced'—in effect, out of our control (MR 50).

Thus, Doane commits herself to the belief that patriarchal representations are capable of inducing a spectator's automatic, unthinking assent to patriarchal ideology. Accordingly, spectators who submit to patriarchal representations—to 'power and its textual manifestation'—suffer a loss of agency and of self. At the same time, Doane's account of the 'psychical force' of patriarchal representations leaves open the possibility of another spectator/text relationship: it is possible for the spectator to resist the seductive power of patriarchal representations, as long she remains alert. Like the hero of *The Invasion of the Body Snatchers*, the heroine of Doane's narrative of alien textual power must not fall asleep. As an alternative to the unthinking submission characteristic of reception, Doane proposes 'the critical act' (MR 51).

Thus, Doane insists both on the text's power to restrain reception and on the possibility of staging an escape from that power. According to Doane, reception is bounded by 'constraints on reading, constraints on spectatorship' (MR 51); feminist critique neutralizes those constraints. The difference is 'all a question of timing' (MR 51). While reception is instantaneous, automatic, induced, the critical act takes place '*in a second moment*—a moment made possible by feminist theory' (MR 51, emphasis in the original).

What precisely is the difference between reception and critique, in this view? Put another way, what happens during Doane's second moment to release the spectator from the power of the text and precipitate the shift from response to critique? Whatever else happens, it cannot be that the spectator simply, if belatedly, remembers her feminist commitments and beliefs, since Doane begins with the premiss that the ideology embodied in patriarchal texts overpowers those commitments. If it did not, the necessity for Doane's second moment might never arise in the first place; feminists might reject patriarchal texts just as automatically as others embrace them. A spontaneous, unreflexive, feminist response to texts will not serve Doane's purposes. If the difference between reception and critique is 'all a question of timing', then a spontaneously feminist response would not count as critique.

More than just a metaphor, Doane's appeal to temporality clearly maps the logic of her position. The problem, according to Doane, lies in our susceptibility to the power of representation. Therefore, the solution cannot be thought to lie in submitting to other (feminist) representations. Critique requires an additional step.

Accordingly, the difference between response and critique cannot simply be a function of holding different beliefs. Nor does the distinction between having beliefs and reflecting on them account for the difference, for the simple reason that reflection alone does not necessarily ensure critique. Surely one might just as well affirm one's responses upon reflection as renounce them. That is to say, thinking about our responses does not in itself change them. Although there surely is a distinction between having responses and reflecting on them, reflection alone would not guarantee Doane's second moment its critical edge.

Thus, neither having feminist beliefs nor reflecting on them is sufficient to produce the critical moment. In Doane's view, something more is necessary to loosen ideology's hold on us, something having to do with feminist theory.[8] Further insight into the nature of the critical moment and its relation to feminist theory can be found in Doane's mobilization of the concept of masquerade. According to Doane, the lesson to be learned from the principle of masquerade is that 'the mask is all there is' (MR 47). The only truth that the mask conceals is that there is no truth, in particular, 'no "pure" or "real" femininity' (ibid.).

The critical moment consolidates the lessons of the masquerade. Accordingly, the critical moment is that moment when we realize that language is all there is, that all beliefs, all representations, are equally ungrounded. The call for critical self-consciousness assumes that once we acknowledge our own immersion in historically determined commitments and beliefs, we become less bound by them, more open to opposing viewpoints and to the play of multiple differences. Or, to put it differently, once we recognize that we know the world only as a series of representations, we are better able to represent it differently.

But does the practice of maintaining a critical distance from our commitments and beliefs actually produce the results Doane hopes for? After all, why should the recognition that our beliefs are merely beliefs, our representations merely representations, make us any less committed to them? Granted, our experience of the world is mediated; all we have are representations/beliefs. The goal of obtaining unmediated proof that our beliefs are true, our representations accurate, is beyond our epistemic reach. As a result, we cannot have direct proof that our beliefs are true. But neither can we have any such proof that they are false. Epistemologically speaking, we have no more reason to doubt our representations of the world than to believe them. The fact that our beliefs are precisely beliefs, the fact they are not and cannot be grounded in an unmediated, neutral encounter with the real, does not in itself give us any reason to doubt them.

Indeed, to imagine that it does, to imagine that our representations/beliefs are necessarily suspect because ungrounded in an epistemically privileged, neutral relation to the real, is itself to claim epistemological certainty.[9] Such a claim imagines a position outside historically constituted beliefs where we can have one piece of true, unmediated knowledge, i.e. that all beliefs are untrustworthy. This weak form of scepticism is no more coherent than scepticism in its strong form. If it is impossible to be a radical sceptic—since to insist that 'All knowledge is false' is to insist that at least one piece of knowledge is true (i.e. that all knowledge is false)—it is also impossible to maintain a critical distance from our beliefs. At a minimum, we would have to continue to hold at least one belief closely (i.e. the belief that we can and should maintain a critical distance from our beliefs). Simply put, the call to maintain a critical distance from all beliefs proposes the impossible.

Feminist film theorists are correct in insisting that our knowledge of the world is socially constructed and, therefore, radically contingent. Indeed, the call for critical distance may be nothing more than an injunction to keep this in mind. If so, however, the critical act is an empty gesture. Because our knowledge, our beliefs, are never the product of a neutral encounter with the world, a critical awareness of that fact alone cannot tell us which are true and which false, which to cling to and which to cast off, which to replace and with what. Armed with the certainty that all beliefs emerge within social and historical contexts, we are no better equipped than before to gauge the value of particular beliefs or to weigh their validity against others. To the extent that the critical moment means nothing more than remembering that the world and our representations of it are not identical, then the critical moment has no use value. In sum, while critical distance in the strong sense of radical self-doubt is impossible, critical distance in the weak sense of acknowledging our embeddedness in history and culture is useless.

Like Doane, spectators may indeed find themselves in the grip of contradictory beliefs, beliefs that produce, in turn, contradictory responses to texts. Yet in Doane's view, such responses implicate more than contradictory beliefs. According to Doane, subjectivity is divided between an ideological self and a critical self, the two distinguished by their differing positions *vis-à-vis* beliefs. The ideological self is always already in the grip of alien beliefs; the critical self knows with certainty that the ideological self is constituted as a subject by beliefs that do not originate in the self. Thus, the critical self—the true self—recognizes the believing, ideological self as other. Rather than shifting, contradictory beliefs, Doane imagines a shifting balance of power between the ideological and the critical selves.

But precisely because, as Doane herself recognizes, we comprehend the world only through structures of representation, being distant from one set of beliefs is nothing more than being close to some other set of beliefs. Therefore, the feminist critic is no less constrained when criticizing a sexist joke than when laughing at one, no less 'other' in the critical moment than in the moment of reception. *If there is a difference between the duped spectator and the self-aware critic, it is not in their relationship to their beliefs, but in the content of their beliefs. What is at stake is not differing positions* vis-à-vis *beliefs, but differing beliefs.* The essential difference between spectator and critic lies not in the text's ideological hold over its spectator, nor in the critic's temporal distance from the text; the difference, if any, lies in the spectator and her beliefs.

In saying this, I am not positing the existence of a spectator/subject prior to discourse. It is because the spectator is always in discourse, always the subject of beliefs, that Doane's opposition between the critical moment and the 'restraints and constraints of reading' is a false one. Of course, Doane herself begins with the premiss that our relationship to the world is mediated, that we can never escape the embeddedness in language which is the very condition of our subjectivity. And yet, the suggestion that we can loosen the hold certain representations have on us simply by recognizing them as representations bears witness to her continued commitment to the possibility of at least partially escaping that embeddedness.[10]

Doane's narrative of alien textual power is illuminating in its suggestion that the call for critical distance makes sense only against a background vision of representation as an invading force. Similarly, in evoking the masquerade, Doane reveals a nostalgia for a self empty of beliefs—that is, for a self residing outside of history and outside of culture. As a result, Doane focuses on the nature of our relationship to our beliefs, rather than on the beliefs themselves. However, we do not need, nor can we consistently achieve, a critical distance from our beliefs. What we, as feminists, need to promote is not a different relationship to beliefs, but different (feminist) beliefs. The 'critical moment' is nothing more- or less-than a feminist response to texts, one that is possible at any moment, first, second, or last.

2. ESCAPING IDEOLOGY: THE TRUTH OF EXPERIENCE

Doane's attempt to counter ideological beliefs with critical distance suggests a distrust of representation, a discomfort with the fact that there is no necessary, causal relation between the world and our representations of it. In her effort to circumvent ideology, Doane adopts an idealist critique of representation which denies the very possibility of accurately representing the real. Idealism is not the only option available to theorists seeking to escape ideology's reign over representation, however. Recognizing the inadequacies of an idealist epistemology which denies the possibility of representing the 'truth' of women's oppression,[11] feminist film theorists have more recently embraced its opposite, that is, a brand of realism. These theorists posit a category of knowledge and experience prior to and outside the reach of representation. According to this view, lived experience serves as a check on the falsifying effects of ideology.

Christine Gledhill began questioning the post-structuralist refusal of representation as early as 1978, when she wrote in her influential article 'Recent Developments in Feminist Film Criticism':

A major problem, it seems to me, lies in the attempt to make language and the signifying process so exclusively central to the production of the social formation. Under the insistence on the semiotic production of meaning, the effectivity of social, economic and political practice threatens to disappear altogether.[12]

Political pragmatism drives Gledhill's dissent: according to Gledhill, feminists cannot afford the luxury of an infinite play of meanings. 'From the point of view of the Women's Liberation Movement . . . there are some meanings, associated with the image of women that have to be forcibly rejected' (*RV* 41). Feminists must be willing to pronounce some representations of women false and, by implication, some true, some more oppressive and others, perhaps, less so.

In support of this position, Gledhill points to the ontological gap between representation and referent. As she correctly reminds us, saying 'that language has a determining effect on society is a different matter from saying that society is nothing but its languages and signifying practices'. Though she recognizes that 'social processes and relations have to be mediated through language', Gledhill nevertheless insists on the dangers of 'conflating the social structure of reality with its signification' (*RV* 41).

Gledhill is right to insist on the ontological difference between world and symbol; she errs in supposing that this fact alone resolves the epistemological question of how we come to know that world. To assert that the world exists independently of our representations of it does not prove that we know the world independently of our representations of it. Nonetheless, Gledhill moves from ontology to epistemology when she appeals to 'everyday reality and lived experience' as guarantors against epistemological relativism and the 'endless play of the signifier'. Recognizing the force of the post-structuralist insistence on the mediating role of language, she tries to identify a realm of experience outside language and representation that would provide a source of epistemological certainty. As she avers, 'one must finally put one's finger on the scales, enter some kind of realist epistemology' (*RV* 41).

Like others, Gledhill grounds such an epistemology in the 'real and contradictory conditions of women's existence' (*RV* 44), in the social practices and material conditions that position women 'differently from men in the social formation' (*RV* 42). While exploring the historical links between melodrama and realism, for example, Gledhill repeatedly locates the source of female subjectivity in 'the daily lived experience of the female audience'.[13] As a consequence of their 'daily lived experience', women are able to perceive the 'contradictions arising from the sexual and social positioning of men and women' within Western culture, contradictions not apparent to the male subject (*HH* 10). Similarly, Gledhill contends that because melodrama is 'rooted in the daily, lived experience of women', it is ripe for 'colonization' by female discourse, that is, by a female voice and subjectivity (*HH* 35). Because they are 'drawn from the social realities of women's lives', such discourses are able to 'negotiate a space within and sometimes resist patriarchal domination' (*HH* 37).

Each of these passages posits a correlation between the reality of women's lives and their understanding of that reality. According to this view, the 'real and contradictory conditions of women's existence'—their experiences *in* the world—are a sufficient basis for positing a feminine epistemology—that is, a feminine understanding *of* the world. This attempt to locate a common female subjectivity in the shared material conditions and social practices of women must overcome several hurdles, not the least of which is the difficulty in identifying material conditions and social practices specific to women. Put differently, in order to establish a common female subjectivity, realists would first have to overcome the demographic challenge of proving that women's material conditions across race, class, and ethnicity are sufficiently similar in pertinent ways to produce similar subjectivities.

One possible way of avoiding the issue of demographic diversity is to locate women's commonality in a universal experience of oppression. Catherine MacKinnon, for one, has suggested that all women experience sexual oppression at the hands of men. MacKinnon writes:

Socially, femaleness means femininity, which means attractiveness to men, which means sexual attractiveness, which means sexual availability on male terms. What defines woman as such is what turns men on. Good girls are 'attractive', bad girls 'provocative'. Gender socialization is the process through which women come to identify themselves as sexual beings, as beings that exist for men. It is that process through which women internalize (make their own) a male image of their sexuality *as* their identity as women. It is not just an illusion.[14]

While this approach succeeds in overcoming personal, social, economic, racial, and other barriers to a common female subjectivity, as we shall see, it does so only at a very high price.

In making the experience of sexuality determinative of female subjectivity, MacKinnon suggests that a woman's gender socialization is fundamentally uninflected by other aspects of her experience. Yet even if we assume, for the sake of argument, that women are treated similarly by men—that social practices as regards a woman's sexuality are invariable—that fact alone cannot guarantee that women's subjective responses to those experiences will also be identical. The only way to secure a one-to-one correlation between particular experiences and a common subjectivity is to posit a universal female subject who would always privilege that experience above all others, and respond typically. Regardless of similarities in their experiences, women will respond to identical experiences identically only if they already share a common subjectivity. The argument, advanced by both Gledhill and MacKinnon, that shared material conditions and social practices produce a common female experience of the world is circular; it assumes what it sets out to explain.

Not only is this position circular, it is also, of course, essentialist. Only a single, universal female response, tied to a female essence, could guarantee the move from experience to subjectivity. Ironically, the reason feminists like Gledhill and MacKinnon point to the shared material and social conditions of women in the first place is to discover a basis for female commonality not grounded in a female essence. True, women are often similarly situated—both materially and socially. As a result, their political interests frequently converge. But this fact alone cannot guarantee a similar convergence of subjective response (surely it is not unusual for women to be subjectively unaware of their common interests). Shared material conditions and social practices can be made the basis of a politics; they cannot be made the basis of an epistemology without embracing an essentialism that the initial appeal to material conditions and social practices was designed to avert.

Finally a word about the positivism implicit in Gledhill's realism. Gledhill suggests that in a post-structuralist, post-Enlightenment world the theorist has three options: a now discredited positivism which proclaims the theorist's ability to apprehend the world directly; the now ascendent post-structuralism which exposes the impossibility of the realist project; and a third option which Gledhill associates with the aesthetic project of melodrama:

Taking its stand in the material world of everyday reality and lived experience, and acknowledging the limitations of the conventions of language and representation, [melodrama] proceeds to force into aesthetic presence identity, value and plenitude of meaning. The signifier cannot cover the possibilities of the signified; nor will the melodramatic subject accept the gap between the self, its worlds, and meaning laid bare by the post-structural project. (*HH* 33)

Attempting to stake out an epistemological middle ground—neither positivist nor post-structuralist—Gledhill nevertheless insists that certain categories of knowledge enjoy an epistemically privileged relation to the real. Thus, she retains epistemological immediacy as the measure of truth. As a result, her third option does not differ significantly from the first; she does not abandon positivism, so much as shift its locus of operation. According to Gledhill, we can know with the certainty of direct apprehension the truth of our own experience of the world.

Like Doane's appeal to the liberating force of critique, Gledhill's attempt to privilege experience over representation is unnecessary. Once we abandon epistemic immediacy as a measure of truth, we no longer need to identify an epistemically privileged realm of experience. Gledhill suggests that 'in the face of the limitations of realism exposed by post-structuralism', the proper response is 'so what?' (*HH* 33). As we have seen, however, she does not understand the full force of her own argument. Gledhill's 'so what?' suggests that the representational nature of knowledge is simply not pertinent to the validity of particular representations. However, if the proper response to the reign of representation truly is 'so what?', then that response is always available; it applies not only to knowledge arising out of lived experience, but to all knowledge equally.

Ultimately, Gledhill adopts post-structuralism's suspicion of representation, and of representation's role in structuring consciousness, because she thinks it is possible to escape representation. As I will argue below, however, a third option is, indeed, available. This option would recognize representation's role in structuring the mind's interactions with the world, while refusing the conclusion that representation is necessarily an impediment.

Gledhill is not alone in looking to the historical experience of women to ground a female subjectivity.[15] She may be alone, however, in acknowledging the realism that inevitably underlies such claims, and for that reason her work is particularly revealing. As appealing as it is to think that women's perceptions are united by their common experience of oppression, this position restores the essentialism and positivism that the appeal to common experience was meant to circumvent. Indeed, any attempt to tether response to shared group experiences, whether the group is classified by race, class, gender, or any other category, has the effect of essentializing the characteristic used to identify the group. Fortunately, the success of a social movement such as feminism is not built on epistemological ground.

3. THE IMMATERIALITY OF IDEOLOGY

For the last twenty years, feminist film theorists have struggled to reconcile the supposedly determining force of ideology with the possibility of social change. Despite the recent shift to an emergent historicism,[16] feminist film theorists continue to affirm representation's role in barring our access to the real, a commitment which limits the avenues of change they are able to imagine. Having conceived of the problem as epistemological—having to do with our cognitive relation to the real—they seek epistemological solutions; if ideology governs the representation of the real, then it is necessary to get outside of representation, to a more immediate epistemic relation to the real, in order to escape ideology.[17]

I have identified two complementary attempts to stage such an escape— the recto and verso of a single theoretical sheet of paper. The first relies on the idealist claim that it is possible to achieve a relation to beliefs that is not simply a matter of holding other beliefs. The second relies on the realist claim that certain kinds of knowledge are exempt from the distorting effects of ideology. Both begin with the insight that all knowledge is mediated. Both then try to escape this condition by achieving a more immediate epistemic relation to true knowledge—the idealist to the true nature of beliefs (i.e. all beliefs are untrustworthy), the realist to the true nature of experience. As long as feminist film theorists continue to be committed to the belief that representation is alienation, that our embeddedness in language matters, then the only options available to them are those already fully played out by Doane and Gledhill. Consequently, they are doomed to repeat their errors.

Though Mary Ann Doane and Christine Gledhill occupy important places in the history of feminist film theory, I have been interested in their work primarily as exemplars of a certain logic. Both Doane and Gledhill—both idealists and realists—demonstrate a nostalgia for a world in which the dream of positivism was still thought to be attainable. But there can be no epistemological middle ground. Once we recognize the ontological gap between representation and referent, then there is no getting outside representation, outside language.

My argument challenges the belief that epistemology matters by suggesting that the fact that we cannot get outside representation is without consequences. The logic of representation does not force us, as both Doane and Gledhill believe it does, to succumb to relativism. It might, however, compel us to abandon the project of epistemology, if the goal of epistemology is to make general claims about the nature and sources of true knowledge. The fact that our knowledge is representational tells us nothing whatsoever about whether it is true, or false, or how to go about finding true knowledge; it is, strictly speaking, irrelevant to the truth or accuracy of particular representations/beliefs.

Neither Doane nor Gledhill, however—neither idealist nor realist—entertains the possibility that nothing follows from the fact that we are always within discourse. Lacan aside, it is possible to retain the insight that the subject is split in language, while disavowing the implication that language *necessarily* entails distortion or error. In effect, my argument would drain the Lacanian concept of alienation of any intimation of pathos, any connotation of loss.

Ideologists correctly remind us that the mere fact that we believe our beliefs does not make them true. But neither does it make them false. An ideological, mediated, representational vision of the world is all we shall ever have. As a consequence, there is nothing categorical we can say about representations/beliefs. What we can and must do is argue over the validity of particular beliefs.

4. CONCLUSION

Representation *per se* is not a problem for feminists (though particular patriarchal representations certainly are). In other words, we need not escape the logic of representation in order to achieve the goals of feminism. Feminists cannot and need not achieve either a critical distance from their beliefs or a realist epistemology. What we need in order to challenge patriarchy is not an alternative epistemic relation to the real. To the extent that the struggle is over ideas—that is, over representations—what is needed is not a feminist position *vis-à-vis* representation, but feminist representations. If the problem is generating feminist responses to patriarchal texts, the solution is not and never will be epistemological.

In searching for a feminist response to the reign of representation, feminist film theory has been pursuing a futile and pointless goal.[18] The struggle is not over representation, but over representations—the traditional province of feminist film criticism. There can be no doubt, then, that feminism needs feminist film criticism. The question is whether feminist film critics need feminist film theory.[19]

NOTES

1. Claire Johnston, 'Women's Cinema as Counter-Cinema', in Claire Johnston (ed.), *Notes on Women's Cinema* (London: SEFT, 1973), repr. in Bill Nichols (ed.), *Movies and Methods* (Berkeley: University of California Press, 1976), 214. References are cited in the text as CJ.
2. Laura Mulvey, 'Visual Pleasure in Narrative Cinema', *Screen*, 16: 3 (1975), 7; repr. in Laura Mulvey, *Visual and Other Pleasures* (Bloomington: Indiana University Press, 1989). Also repr. in Constance Penley (ed.), *Feminism and Film Theory* (New York: Routledge, 1988) and in Philip Rosen (ed.), *Narrative, Apparatus, Ideology* (New York: Columbia University Press, 1986). References are cited in the text as LM.
3. Louis Althusser, 'Notes towards an Investigation', in *Lenin and Philosophy, and Other Essays*, trans. Ben Brewster (London: New Left Books, 1971), 164.
4. The critique of ideology that I develop in this chapter extends only to those who would attach consequences to the fact that knowledge cannot be grounded in a direct encounter with the world, that is, to those who equate ideology with the very nature of knowledge. Though I take this to be the majority position, ideology has, of course, been theorized in other ways. Some theorists would strip the term of its epistemological onus, using it descriptively, rather than normatively, to refer to any system of beliefs. Others would use the term to refer to false beliefs characterized primarily by their effects in upholding practices of social domination (see Noël Carroll, *Mystifying Movies: Fads and Fallacies in Contemporary Film Theory* (New York: Columbia University Press, 1988), 73), rather than by their genesis in representation. It is hard to see the utility of the former, while the latter seems to me underinclusive, for reasons slightly different than those suggested by Hector Rodriguez in his chapter in this volume. (Contrary to Rodriguez, I would suggest that empirically defensible beliefs can be enlisted in the cause of oppression.) Nevertheless, neither of these approaches equates representation with error and, therefore, neither is implicated in the argument I make here. Work like Jon Elster's, however, is a different matter. Elster defines ideology in terms of its genesis in society (ideological beliefs, according to Elster, are beliefs 'that have society as their object as well as their explanation')

(Jon Elster, *Making Sense of Marx* (Cambridge: Cambridge University Press, 1985), 464). Although for reasons of space I cannot pursue the argument here, one corollary of the position I present in this chapter is that the genesis of beliefs is logically unrelated to their validity.

5. The repeated reference to Mulvey's ground-breaking article in *Camera Obscura's* 'Spectatrix' volume, particularly by theorists wishing to distance themselves from her positions, testifies to the continuing struggle of feminist film theorists to work within a theoretical world whose boundaries Mulvey and Johnston defined, a world in which representation is defined as alienation, and alienation as error. (See *Camera Obscura*, 20–1. References to this volume are cited in the text as CO.)

6. Mary Ann Doane, 'Masquerade Reconsidered: Further Thoughts on the Female Spectator', *Discourse*, 11: 1 (1988–9), 50. References are cited in the text as MR.

7. Tania Modleski, *The Women Who Knew Too Much: Hitchcock and Feminist Theory* (New York: Methuen, 1988), 26–7.

8. Recall that, according to Doane, the critical moment is made possible by feminist theory.

9. Stanley Fish put it well: 'The project of radical doubt can never outrun the necessity of being situated; in order to doubt *everything*, including the ground one stands on, one must stand somewhere else, and that somewhere else will then be the ground on which one stands' (Stanley Fish, *Is There a Text in This Class?* (Cambridge, Mass.: Harvard University Press, 1980), 360).

10. This position recalls Judith Butler's claim that an awareness of the fact that gender is performative is, in itself, liberating (see Judith Butler, *Gender Trouble: Feminism and the Subversion of Identity* (New York: Routledge, 1990), 146–7).

11. Recall Claire Johnston's dictum, cited above, that 'The "truth" of [women's] oppression cannot be "captured" on celluloid with the "innocence" of the camera' (CJ 214).

12. Christine Gledhill, 'Recent Developments in Feminist Film Criticism', *Quarterly Review of Film Studies*, 3: 4 (1978); repr. as 'Developments in Feminist Film Criticism' in Mary Ann Doane, Patricia Mellencamp, and Linda Williams (eds.), *Re-Vision: Essays in Feminist Film Criticism* (Los Angeles: American Film Institute, 1984), 41. References to the *Re-Vision* version are cited in the text as *RV*.

13. Christine Gledhill, 'The Melodramatic Field: An Investigation', in Christine Gledhill (ed.), *Home is Where the Heart Is: Studies in Melodrama and the Woman's Film* (London: British Film Institute, 1987), 10. References to this work are cited in the text as *HH*.

14. Catharine MacKinnon, 'Feminism, Marxism, Method, and the State: An Agenda for Theory', *Signs*, 7: 3 (1982), 531.

15. Teresa de Lauretis's final chapter of *Alice Doesn't* represents a similar attempt to secure a link between reality and representation by recourse to the concept of experience. On the face of things, de Lauretis's account of experience is a good deal more subtle; for one, she recognizes that both subject and social reality are 'entities of a semiotic nature' (Teresa de Lauretis, *Alice Doesn't: Feminism, Semiotics, Cinema* (Bloomington: Indiana University Press, 1984), 182.) And yet, within de Lauretis's semiotic economy, social practices enjoy a privileged position. According to de Lauretis, 'the significance of [a] sign could not take effect, that is to say, the sign would not be a sign, without the existence or the subject's experience of a *social practice* in which the subject is physically involved' (ibid. 183, emphasis in the original). That is to say, meaning is somehow confirmed, anchored, in the physical reality of social practices. Ultimately, de Lauretis's goal is to affirm the 'mutual overdetermination of meaning, perception, and experience' (ibid. 184), a goal which would be tautological unless practices themselves have a role in determining subjectivity *apart* from structures of meaning.

In the end, however, de Lauretis shifts from a realism reminiscent of Gledhill to an idealism reminiscent of Doane. With Gledhill, she avers that practices partially determine subjectivity; they produce a 'kind of knowledge' (ibid. 158). With Doane, however, she insists that the reality that we come to know through experience is a patriarchal one. Epistemological realism is therefore insufficient. Echoing Doane, de Lauretis insists that 'the original critical instrument' of feminism is self-consciousness (ibid. 185). The thrust of my argument has been to demonstrate that both de Lauretis's realism and her idealism are as unnecessary as they are futile.

16. The recent turn by feminists to reception studies, for example, reflects theoretical commitments similar to both Doane's and Gledhill's. Thus, theorists of reception claim, on the one hand, that knowledge of texts in unattainable and, on the other, that there is a necessary link between the lived experience of spectators as women and the way they read particular films. For the former, see Janet Staiger, *Interpreting Films* (Princeton: Princeton University Press, 1992). For the latter, see Elizabeth Ellsworth, 'Illicit Pleasure: Feminist Spectators and *Personal Best*', *Wide Angle*, 8: 2 (1986).

17. Doane, at least, would deny this. In 'Masquerade Reconsidered', she expressly rejects the notion of an alternative 'female epistemology' valorizing 'closeness, nearness, or presence' (p. 46). I have argued, however, that the logic of her binary distinction between reception and critique necessarily commits her to her own alternative epistemology, one that in her case valorizes distance and critical separation, rather than closeness and presence, but one that offers the feminist theorist a privileged relation to the real, nonetheless.

18. This has not been feminist film theory's only goal, of course, although it has been a major one. Feminist film theory's other major set of concerns revolves around questions of female ontology. Space limitations prevent a full treatment of this branch of feminist film theory here, though it seems to me that ontological feminist film theory often becomes entangled in questions of epistemology, and thus falls prey to one of the two errors I critique above. Moreover, apart from epistemological issues, the question of whether it is possible to locate or identify a female ontology, though a question of potentially great interest to feminists, is essentially an empirical question, and not a theoretical one.

19. The fact that many feminist theorists are also insightful critics does not necessarily provide an answer. For example, Mary Ann Doane's book-length critical work *The Desire to Desire* powerfully and persuasively identifies and describes 'a certain *representation* of female spectatorship' (Mary Ann Doane, *The Desire to Desire: The Woman's Film of the 1940s* (Bloomington: Indiana University Press, 1987), 8. Emphasis in the original). As an examination of the way the woman's film of the 1940s 'represents and re-presents' a certain vision of femininity (ibid. 176), Doane's work adds significantly to our understanding of the workings of patriarchy. Because they focus on particular representations, her conclusions are unassailable on theoretical grounds, precisely because they are not theoretical. Understanding the meaning, the significance, and even the appeal of these particular representations, however, does not depend on a theory of 'power and its textual manifestations'.

The same could be said of Gledhill's readings of melodrama, and of Mulvey's readings, in 'Visual Pleasure and Narrative Cinema', of classical Hollywood cinema, Sternberg, and Hitchcock. For example, Mulvey's most important critical insight— that in classical Hollywood cinema men look and women get looked at—can be read as a contingent generalization from empirical fact. As such, it does not depend on her theoretical claim that, within the patriarchal symbolic order, 'the female form . . . speaks castration and nothing else' (LM 6). In fact, it is not clear how this sweeping theoretical generalization could account for Mulvey's own, more subtle readings of the meaning of the female form in *Marnie*, *Vertigo*, and *Rear Window* (LM 15).

Ideology and Film Culture

HÉCTOR RODRÍGUEZ

INTRODUCTION

This chapter sketches an argument on behalf of the claim that ideology critique is a species of moral persuasion, mainly concerned with the normative evaluation of certain ways of thinking, feeling, and acting that have a bearing on our social institutions. There is a moral dimension built into the concept of ideology, as that concept is characteristically used in critical film theory. Ideology is often described as something undesirable or unworthy, something that has to be criticized. In many cases, then, the question 'What is ideology?' also means 'What does a critic of ideology do in criticizing ideology?'

One important answer to this question emphasizes the role that erroneous propositions play in ideological thinking. Ideologies are in this view comprised of false beliefs whose falsehood is in some sense caused or fostered by practices of domination. The beliefs are false because they have been distorted by a pattern of social power. Call this the 'false consciousness' model. According to Richard W. Miller, this approach faithfully reflects the impetus of classical Marxist theory. Miller argues that both Marx and, especially, Engels described ideologies as false ideas whose deficiencies are 'a product of *truth-distorting* social forces'.[1] Film scholars have sometimes upheld this model. According to Noël Carroll, for example, ideologies are false beliefs that uphold some practice of social domination, as in the statement 'all black men want to rape white women'.[2] And Terry Lovell has similarly defined ideology as 'the production and dissemination of erroneous beliefs whose inadequacies are socially motivated'.[3] In this account, ideologies belong to a class of statements that make factual claims. They are in other words comprised of assertions. Assertions have a propositional content that describes a state of affairs as being the case. Their validity can be checked by appealing to inductively acquired evidence, or by challenging the logical consistency of their premises. Specifically, ideologies are false assertions that help uphold or rationalize a practice of social subordination.

For their comments and encouragement, I would like to thank Richard Allen, Murray Smith, John Champagne, Jenny Kwok Wah Lau, and Paisley Livingston.

Consider the example of a free-market conservative who believes that the welfare state is overburdened and top-heavy. This person could defend her view by asserting that social services account for the largest portion of the US Federal budget. The endorsement of an extreme version of laissez-faire capitalism would here go hand in hand with an empirical assertion which can readily and straightforwardly be compared with the relevant evidence. Budget figures in fact reveal military spending to be the largest item.[4] It is important to note, however, that factual beliefs alone seldom suffice to justify one's approval or disapproval of social services. A conservative may after all consent to the fact that welfare is not the largest budget item while nonetheless holding on to the view that the state ought not to help the poor. To define ideological thinking as comprised *exclusively* of false assertions is, I will argue, to misrepresent the role that they play in our lives. It is not unreasonable to hold political convictions that cannot be meaningfully supported or falsified by facts. In contrast to the false consciousness model, I describe ideologies as patterns of thought, feeling, and conduct which *may, but need not*, include defeasible beliefs. Of course, ideologies are often expressed as assertions, or at least can be paraphrased as assertions. But I want to argue here against the philosophical commonplace that assertions always and everywhere advance empirical propositions. Assertions have many uses, some of which involve falsifiable claims while others do not. Whether a proposition requires evidence or not depends on its place within a broad network of human experiences and concerns. To describe ideologies as false beliefs is to abstract from these various uses and erect what I take to be a reductive view of the role that thoughts play in particular contexts of human emotions, convictions, intentions, desires, and practices. I will criticize this definition of ideology not only by presenting arguments against it, but also by sketching an alternative framework in what I take to be a compelling and persuasive form.

FALSE BELIEFS?

Consider another statement, 'women are less rational than men'. Is this a falsifiable proposition? How could one present evidence against it? Perhaps one might point to women who are quite adept at logical thinking, according to various standards. But would that be enough to dissuade someone who believed in the inferior mental powers of women? Could such a person not simply reply that those individual women are exceptions, or that, while they do seem rational, a close look at their everyday behaviour would invariably reveal that they tend to act on impulse? It is an important aspect of such assertions that those who uphold them do not always engage in empirical testing. Rather, propositions of this nature seem to be of a special kind which expresses convictions and values rather than describing states of affairs. Political and social controversies are not always, perhaps not centrally, settled by appealing to inductively acquired evidence. Whoever states that women lack full powers of ratiocination is in many instances expressing a commitment, and commitments are not characteristically supported by facts; rather, they are distinct ways of seeing, understanding, evaluating, and otherwise relating and responding to facts.[5] If we do persuade someone to give up the view that women are irrational, we have not thereby merely altered his factual opinions about the world: we have modified the way he sees and interacts with women.

A proponent of the false consciousness model could nonetheless reply that this line of argument is trivial and misleading. The fact that factual information may fail to persuade others to change their views does not necessarily mean that the views themselves are not falsified. Any theory of ideology worth its salt must surely admit the possibility that in many cases no amount of evidence will suffice to modify someone's political beliefs. The false consciousness thesis can perhaps be construed as follows: factual evidence constitutes the sort of argument that ought to persuade a person who proceeds rationally. To be sure, it frequently happens that our passions (wishful thinking, for instance) prevent us from rationally assessing beliefs. We may continue to uphold a political ideology simply because it satisfies a wish for safety, power, pride, and so on. But this does not mean that a belief like 'women are less rational than men' is not in principle falsifiable. If I am only making the trivial comment that inductive evidence sometimes fails to convince, then my objections are obviously beside the point.

My argument is not, however, an empirical description of the practical difficulties of persuading another. I am advancing a grammatical claim about what counts as an ideological belief in our ordinary language. This kind of belief need not involve factual claims. The point is that the notion of falsification may not always make sense here. Although our moral commitments are often expressed in propositional form, they are not characteristically based on inductive evidence. They do not always furnish information. They often express an attitude to reality from which, so to speak, nothing is missing, quite unlike a hypothesis that requires factual support. They do not stand outside reality but rather help to define a whole way of living. Moral beliefs comprise an integral part of the fabric of a person's or a community's experience. In order to understand the significance that an ideology has for someone, we generally reconstruct how it hangs together with the individual convictions of the person and of other like-minded persons, how it is combined with various other thoughts, emotions, and actions, or how it may fit into a ritual of a custom or an institution. We seldom rely on protocols of inductive verification. Evidence will often fail to convince because factual information is not a necessary ground of ideological belief.

Proponents of the false consciousness model could reply that, in describing ideologies as 'false beliefs', they do not necessarily mean 'false when compared with factual evidence' but also, and more broadly, 'ambiguous, vague, derived from faulty premisses, or based on unsound inferences'. A belief can be considered false when, for instance, it incorporates muddled, imprecise, or poorly defined concepts. But it is by no means evident that justified moral convictions should be expressible in clear and precise terms. What is striking about this way of putting things is of course the fact that ideological beliefs are described as subject to logical norms. But what could it possibly mean to demonstrate that a person's way of life is logically incoherent? As Paul Johnston has persuasively argued, it is difficult to specify the logical considerations that could possibly prove the rightness of acting in one way rather than another.[6] The very concept of acting incoherently does not seem to make sense here. Of course, false consciousness theorists could insist that their theory of ideology refers to ideas rather than ways of life, and ideas can be straightforwardly assessed in accordance with logical standards. But this is precisely what I take issue with. Whether an idea, or a cluster of ideas, is falsifiable or not depends on its relationship to a particular field of human experience. To detach it from that background is to misrepresent its import. In such a case, *the beliefs being criticized are simply not the beliefs that people actually believe in.* This is of course not to deny that it may sometimes matter whether a belief lacks inductive support or logical coherence. But the question of whether it does actually matter can only be assessed on an ad hoc basis by considering in detail the particular context of human thoughts, activities, and attitudes in which the belief plays its role. It seems pointless, if not downright misleading, for philosophers to believe that they can settle the matter in advance.

This line of argument brings out what I take to be another important weakness of the false consciousness account, or at least many versions of it. According to its proponents, the question of whether a thought is ideological cannot be settled by noting the role that it plays, or is meant to play, in a given social context. To demonstrate that an assertion has been put forth in order to justify a practice of social domination is not a sufficient criterion of the ideological status of that assertion. In addition, critical theorists should treat ideas as rational claims by testing their empirical adequacy and logical cogency regardless of their social origins or purposes.[7] The underlying assumption here is that a belief can be rationally evaluated without taking into account its place within a field of human practices and concerns. But I am not persuaded by this way of approaching the matter because the fact that a belief plays a role in a situation of domination may in some instances be enough to warrant our criticism of it. It is often very difficult to evaluate the worth of a political belief, or even to understand what the belief really means, without taking into account the context of its use. The meaning of a political idea may be given precisely by its connection to a broad range of activities and experiences, and these will in some instances include a background of social institutions. Statements like 'black men want to rape white women' and 'women are less rational than men' characteristically mean what they mean in contexts of discrimination. The meaning of these assertions is partly constituted by their position within social practices.[8] Think of someone who only manages to see a single scene from a particular film, the ending for instance: that person would probably be able to follow the dialogue and more or less grasp what it is that the characters are doing, but she has not understood the action in the same way as someone who has seen the entire film. Important pieces of the context will be missing, which is precisely what happens when ideological assertions are detached from the background practices and concerns that give the point to political beliefs.

My claim is not simply that whoever adheres to an ideology is thereby pretending to make, or fictionally making, truth-claims. Rather, these assertions do not always function as truth-claims for the person who utters them. To be sure, it is often possible to specify what should count as evidence for and against a political or social belief by, for instance, compiling statistics or designing tests of various sorts, thus establishing clear defeasibility conditions. It is an important feature of ideologies that they can often be transformed into truth-claims. But this does not entail that they already contained truth-claims to begin with. There is a confusion here, which Pierre Bordieu has brought out in an anthropological study influenced by Wittgenstein. The confusion consists in treating our patterns of conduct, our everyday ways of thinking and living in the world, as rational products subject to logical laws and inductive protocols. Bordieu's favourite example is Plato's question as to whether 'it was the earth that imitated woman in becoming pregnant and bringing a being into the world, or woman that imitated the earth'.[9] In trying to furnish a logically consistent account of religious beliefs, Plato misses precisely what is distinctive about those beliefs, the complex ways in which they are woven into the fabric of everyday experience. The bias for logical order does not necessarily clarify the main features of our commitments but rather tends to distort the role that they play in the texture of our lives. For the aims and concerns of moral convictions are directly connected to, expressed by, patterns of human conduct that need not fit the requirements of any logical paraphrase. Plato's confusion, which Bordieu terms the 'scholastic fallacy', recalls the definition of ideology as false consciousness, an approach which makes our political and social commitments answerable to inductive standards. In contrast, I argue that, while ideologies may include factual assertions, and to this extent the definition does correctly capture *one* extremely important aspect of the phenomenon at hand, truth-claims are characteristically *not* the foundations on which all the other elements of the ideology rest. Rather, propositions are usually connected with overlapping networks of emotions, convictions, and activities. An important consequence of this line of argument is that our rational beliefs are not, and should not be required to be, the final ground of our conduct. Human actions are not everywhere bound by reasons. They are rooted in fields of experience that may not be entirely dependent on rational considerations. A critic of ideology has to recognize that arguments sometimes leave untouched the core of an opponent's political beliefs, which is the way these beliefs ramify into a whole way of life.[10]

To be sure, critical theorists do often use the terms 'true' and 'false' in assessing rival political frameworks. Ideology critique frequently amounts to the exclamation 'But in all truth things are not really like that!' It is, however, important to remind ourselves that this expression, which seems to me aptly to describe what critical theorists tend to do, contains exclamation marks: the point of ideology critique, I would suggest, lies precisely in those exclamation marks. The enterprise of critical theory is in many cases akin to a startling gesture, like shaking someone who holds what we believe to be inappropriate or flawed attitudes. What is often asked of the other person is not that she should give up a factual opinion but that, she should substantially modify, or sometimes radically change, her ways of seeing and living. The concepts of falsehood and truth are being used in a rather special sense here. In some instances, a successful critique of ideology brings about a thoroughgoing and fundamental transformation, something akin to a religious conversion. To replace a Christian ethic with a socialist or anarchist one, to give up homophobic or patriarchal sentiments, or to acquire an active interest in the emancipation of an oppressed people, frequently involves a basic change in one's attitudes towards the world. A belief is in such instances true ('compelling' might be a better term) if it persuades us to see the world in a new light and to act in accordance with this new way of seeing and feeling: if we come to feel at home in this particular moral framework. Truth is here shown by the capacity of a belief to modify how we look and act, not by appealing to inductive protocols. The truth of the picture is shown by our response to the picture. This is the kind of commitment that Wittgenstein had in mind when he noted that moral beliefs 'will show, not by reasoning or by appeal to ordinary grounds for belief, but rather by regulating for all in his life'.[11] In other cases, however, ideology critique may be more piecemeal, addressing a particular commitment without completely altering the whole fabric of a person's experience. We may, for instance, convince an environmental activist that free-market capitalism does not foster ecological balance. In this case, the person has incorporated a socialist commitment into a prior set of political convictions without necessarily effecting a total change in her general ways of thinking and acting. In this piecemeal kind of persuasion, inductive evidence is more likely to play an important role than in the more spectacular 'conversion' cases. And there are intermediate cases which are more deeply rooted in one's enduring traits of character than a mere factual belief but can nonetheless be given up without a total conversion: some forms of sexism may perhaps be described that way. We may even embark on a particular critique in order to reaffirm or illuminate our own political commitments rather than to change someone's opinion. But it is my central contention that none of these instances must always and everywhere depend on factual information or logical norms.

MORAL PICTURES

Proponents of the false consciousness model could reply that my line of argumentation only reasserts a dubious distinction between fact and value. But nothing said thus far rules out the possibility that moral evaluation could sometimes mainly depend on the truth or falsehood of a belief, and to that extent I do not claim that questions of fact are always irrelevant to, or independent from, questions of value. There need not be a sharp demarcation between factual and normative matters, but this does not mean that the distinction is entirely without value. My point is that the practice of ideology critique does not necessarily rest on judgements of truth and falsehood; even when it does, it is precisely as a moral matter that the falsehood of a belief interests the critical theorist. False consciousness theorists could nonetheless reply that there is a compelling account of what morality is which emphasizes questions of truth and falsehood. The assessment of evidence is arguably more central to the enterprise of morality than I have allowed for. To describe ideology critique as a moral enterprise is compatible with the assertion that ideology critique rests on the assessment of factual evidence. The account I have in mind here circumscribes the moral domain in terms of the concept of action, narrowly understood as the domain of rational deliberation and choice. Morality would therefore involve patterns of decision-making that involve the application of general norms and principles to particular circumstances. Those norms and principles may be said to guide action, in the sense that they help us choose an appropriate goal in the light of our beliefs about the situation at hand. Morality would consist in finding the proper way to hook general principles up with the concrete facts of a particular situation. This view would therefore assign the procedures of rationally assessing factual information a central role in the moral domain. For example: given the hypothetical principle that sentient beings should not be harmed, and given a definition of what counts as sentience, then the question of whether a camel should or should not be harmed would partly depend on whether there are general facts about camels which fit the general description of a sentient being. From this standpoint, which may be termed the 'principles-facts' account, it is arguably misleading to sharply separate fact and value. If I understand him correctly, Noël Carroll sometimes seems to endorse a similar model, although it is by no means clear whether he upholds the principles-facts account as a general description of what morality is or simply as one possible type of moral deliberation.[12]

In any case, I would suggest that, in so far as the principles-facts account makes ethical practice a function of logical deliberation, it is reductive as a general description of what morality is, for reasons which Cora Diamond has persuasively outlined. Patterns of moral conduct are not always based on deliberation and choice, or on the concrete application of general rules and principles. To overemphasize the relationship between abstract norms and the activity of deciding what to do is to produce an impoverished account of morality.[13] Moral visions can also inform, for instance, the way one smiles or refrains from smiling, the differences between one's public and private behaviour, or the way one relates to and moves about the spaces one inhabits. What counts in such instances is not necessarily how a general norm helps us decide between alternative courses of action in the light of factual information, but how a vision of the good is expressed in the texture of our conduct. I am using the phrase 'texture of our conduct' to include not only patterns of rational decision-making, but also habits and gestures, styles of thinking and feeling, turns of speech, conceptions of aesthetic order or beauty or pleasure, patterns of theatre-going, as well as conceptions of costume, architecture, and food—all those enduring traits of culture and/or character, those ways of acting and living that manifest underlying attitudes towards the world, towards ourselves, and towards others. The point is also the emotional and imaginative quality, the richness and sincerity and complexity, the overall tonality and creativity, of one's moral work and one's enduring traits of character: the manner in which we, for instance, listen to the concerns and values of others, or attend to the subtle nuances of a particular situation, or respond to complicated shifts in our own passions.

In a similar vein, contemporary philosophers working within an Aristotelian understanding of virtue, such as for instance Martha Nussbaum and Nancy Sherman, have emphasized the capacity for 'discernment' or 'ethical perception' as a key component of moral conduct.[14] Discernment takes place before or alongside action. The term describes our quality of attention and response to the particular features of a situation. As Sherman glosses it: 'Discerning the morally salient features of a situation is part of expressing virtue and part of the morally appropriate response . . . In this sense, character is expressed in what one *sees* as much as in what one *does*.'[15] And Nussbaum notes that moral insight 'is not simply intellectual grasp of propositions; it is not even simply intellectual grasp of particular facts; it is perception. It is seeing a complex, concrete reality . . . with imagination and feeling.'[16] Discernment is an important aspect of morality, which goes beyond the mere application of general rules or the assessment of propositions.

I propose to use the expression 'moral pictures' as a term of art to refer to the underlying configurations of moral thought, perception, and feeling expressed in our actions. The expression is meant to highlight the extent to which morality is (1) not necessarily a rule-dependent domain but also a matter of practical discernment and responsiveness, and (2) not necessarily the product of conscious reflection but also of enduring traits of character. Of course, it *is* possible to devise general maxims to cover everyday attitudes, something like 'do not be arrogant when giving moral advice' or 'always try to understand how others feel about things before judging them', but our ordinary concept of morality does not require the application of such abstract principles or general rules to particular cases. We can of course always organize our moral commitments into a comprehensive doctrine in order to, for instance, explain their import to someone from another culture or to a young person from our own, or to attain a clearer sense of what matters most in our own life, or to clarify the moral stakes of a particularly painful dilemma, or to see whether our spontaneous patterns of conduct are undesirable and for that reason worth changing. But the ability explicitly to formulate and apply rules derived from abstract principles does not exhaust the entire field of moral practices. Morality is not simply a matter of applying general norms to particular circumstances. It also includes the capacity to express, in the enduring fabric of our conduct, a sense of what is valuable. And this practice need not be governed by, or subject to, either explicit rules or tacit presuppositions. What I am suggesting is that, rather than factual beliefs, the concept of ideology often designates the styles of perception and feeling that come together as moral pictures.

Ideologies are distinct configurations of moral thoughts, emotions, and practices that play a part in a situation of domination. Loosely speaking, domination occurs whenever an agent or group of agents place another group in a subordinate or marginal position, the most common form being the imposition of restrictions on access to resources or opportunities. Domination in the relevant sense is often institutionalized, by which I mean that it is systematically sustained by the rules or practices of a community or organization, as in laws denying women the right to vote. In using the term 'domination' as opposed to a more neutral word like, say, 'authority', I am of course also suggesting that this form of power is in some sense morally

unjustifiable. Certain controls over infants, for instance, are perhaps justified exercises of power. A central aim of ideology critique therefore consists
in assessing the legitimacy of a practice of subordination. Some, but only
some, moral pictures sustain one's adherence to patterns of unwarranted
domination. The conviction that women are too emotional or irrational to
participate in political activities, and should therefore be legally prevented
from voting, fulfils the main criteria of ideology. The belief supplies a
background of thoughts and emotions in relation to which it makes sense to
commit oneself to an institution or set of institutions that unjustifiably
subordinates a group of people.

MORAL REASONS

An important consequence of the framework I am proposing contends that
moral discussions are not necessarily settled by appealing to any grounds of
independent assessment, such as facts about reality. There is no neutral way
of adjudicating between different moral standpoints: whenever one criticizes a moral picture, one does so from the perspective of an alternative
moral claim, of another way of seeing and living in the world. This conclusion of course has important consequences for critical theory. In adopting a
set of political commitments, left-wing critics do not proceed on the basis of
value-free empirical facts any more than their conservative opponents. The
difference between the left and the right is often one of moral commitment
rather than access to more information. Whenever one argues that, say,
conservative criticisms of the welfare state are contemptible, narrow-
minded, and harmful, one proceeds from a (socialist or liberal) moral
standpoint rather than from neutral evidence. The evaluation of a moral
position is itself a moral activity.

This conclusion, however, seems to deprive ideology critique of its rational force. If moral convictions do not necessarily follow from information about reality, and if, more generally, our political commitments do not
completely depend on rational considerations, then there can be no neutral
way of adjudicating between different moral standpoints. Someone may
hold the same factual information that we do while nonetheless choosing to
act differently, not out of ignorance but on the basis of an alternative set of
convictions and concerns. Is there no cogent way to offer objective arguments for or against a particular set of political convictions? As Carroll has
rightly noted, the concept of ideology has a 'pejorative force. Ordinarily we
do not want our ideas and our thinking corrupted by ideology.'[17] In order
to explicate the concept of ideology, it is important to specify precisely
according to what critical standards any given belief should be evaluated
and criticized, and to provide concrete illustrations of ideology at work in

the cinema. Having stipulated that ideologies should be rationally criticiz-able, Carroll himself goes on to argue that to criticize them is to falsify them. Refusing to make political disagreements non-rational, he rightly wants to hold on to the view that critical theory is a matter of considered reflection. There are, then, very good reasons why he stipulates that ideologies must be false beliefs.

My argument contends that political beliefs are characteristically rooted in ways of life which are not everywhere bound by reasons: but it does not follow that reasons play absolutely no part in our lives, or that political disagreements are in every respect unreasonable. I do argue that reasons do not mainly consist of facts, but this does not mean that no reason of any kind whatsoever can be meaningfully given in defence of a political belief. To criticize, say, corporate capitalism is not to express an arbitrary opinion, but to put forth a strong conviction which one takes to be right. Commitments advance the moral claim that certain responses, certain ways of thinking and acting and feeling, are appropriate to particular situations: that, say, outrage and political activism are in some sense desirable responses to racial segregation or economic exploitation. This claim can sometimes include factual information. My sympathy towards a capitalist whose property has been seized by a new revolutionary govern-ment is likely to change if I acquire information about his prior exploitation of workers. But facts do not always function as inductive evidence in the usual sense; they are often exemplars of a way of seeing and living. In alerting a bigot to the suffering that racial segregation has brought about, for instance, one may use figures, dates, and other historical data, but the point is the emotional attitude embedded in the presentation of those facts, the effort to bring the other person to see the moral outrage that is racism. The information may illustrate the suffering brought about by segregation, and the moral concern, anger, and activism that should follow from the acknowledgement of that suffering. Instead of furnishing information, these facts help to guide one's way into a particular apprehension of our predica-ment as social beings, bringing out a distinct way of responding to states of affairs. In the context of moral controversy, evidence is often used to illustrate a certain conception of what it means to be human, of the proper ways to regard and interact with others, of the nature of ethical dilemmas, of the place that moral values occupy or ought to occupy in our life and tradition, and so forth. In arguing that moral pictures are not mainly comprised of factual claims, then, I do not mean to suggest that they are for that reason not rationally criticizable. It is possible to bring out, say, the emotional deficiencies of a person's beliefs without appealing to criteria of falsehood: one may point to her apathy, detachment, rigidity, narcissism, love of power, or insensitivity to the suffering of others.

Narrative fiction can itself criticize an ideology by presenting an alternative moral picture, a different set of feelings and attitudes. Consider, for instance, film historian Charles Musser's description of *The Pawnshop* (Charles Chaplin, 1915). Chaplin's actions throughout the film 'undermine work as productive labor' by either destroying tools of labour or transforming them into objects of play: 'Cleaning the balls from the pawnshop symbol, he bounces them off the head of his co-worker; and when he sweeps, he sweeps a piece of string into a straight line and walks on it as if it were a tightrope.'[18] The film consistently reduces wage labour to an object of anger, violence, contempt, or ridicule and, in so doing, represents those emotional responses as singularly appropriate to the suffocating, oppressive conditions of everyday menial work. A moral picture is here expressed by the emotional texture of fictional situations, by the ways in which the viewer is invited to react with liberating laughter at Chaplin's revolt against wage labour. The behaviour of the tramp passes a moral judgement on a social practice. Of course, it is possible to reconstruct this judgement as an assertion, something like 'Wage labour is suffocating,' and it may perhaps be sometimes valuable to put things this way, but such a paraphrase simply fails to capture what is distinctive, indeed powerful, about the vision embodied in the film: its playful, anarchic disregard for social rules and the barely contained anger that it projects. *The Pawnshop* rules out any complacent idealization of the predicament of a worker while mocking the suffocating discipline of wage labour. Chaplin's film exemplifies the fact that, precisely because there is a way of using the imagination to criticize the emotional underpinnings of a political or social belief, narrative fiction can unfold a practice of ideology critique. There is an important use of story-telling that makes a contribution to the enterprise of critical philosophy. *Drugstore Cowboy* (Gus Van Sant, 1988), for instance, criticizes the repugnance shown by many right-wing politicians towards drugs by sympathetically showing the painful experiences that may foster or sustain addiction. The film-makers tend to view the story from the perspective of a group of addicts themselves. Narrative fiction here provides a paradigm of a mode of looking at a particular predicament from the standpoint of a participant rather than a detached observer, and it is here that its critical import lies.

A narrative film can criticize an ideology by expressing a paradigm of discernment that runs counter to dominant forms of representation. *Jeanne Dielman, 23 Quai du Commerce* (Chantal Ackerman, 1975), for instance, is a critical feminist film that redeems certain daily experiences normally excluded or denigrated in a patriarchal culture. The plot records in meticulous detail the obsessively repetitive daily routines (shopping, cleaning, cooking, and so on) of a middle-aged woman. This narrative to my mind incorporates a moral aim, that of bringing the viewer to attend carefully to an individual woman's everyday experience. The repetition of similar events

throughout the film, the confinement of the story to a few, often claustro-
phobic, middle-class locations, the careful observation of the woman's
mounting desperation and anxiety with a static camera and long takes, all
evoke a sense of time and place at once hopeless and suffocating. The formal
composition of the film is governed by a moral aim respectfully to represent
a woman's quotidian experiences, precisely those which are seldom shown
in commercial cinema, as worthy of careful, loving attention in their own
right. Once again, these aspects could be summarized into straightforward
assertions and maxims, something like 'ordinary housewives lead a monoto-
nous, confined life' or 'we ought to respect and acknowledge her efforts to
create her own space', but this sort of paraphrase of course leaves out
precisely the texture of the experience of viewing the film: not only the sheer
tenacity of the protagonist's daily efforts to stake out a space of her own in
such dreary circumstances, but also the film-maker's careful, loving attention to these efforts. In this context, the most valuable contribution of a
critic is precisely the willingness to describe the quality of attention, the
point of view, conveyed by the formal structure of narrative fiction. Narrative fictions can project configurations of human conduct, thought, and
feeling that come together as distinct ways of living.[19]

In his recent work on the political implications of the cinema, Carroll has
refined his concept of ideology, bringing it closer to the alternative framework I am here proposing. Following Ronald de Sousa, Carroll draws our
attention to the presence of 'paradigm scenarios' embodied in the stories
people create, disseminate, and consume. The force of these scenarios lies in
the ways objects and situations are depicted in connection to sets of emotions.[20] Stories provide paradigms of ways of feeling, and it is the ongoing
encounter with such scenarios that helps to shape our emotional attitudes.
In this context, a film may reinforce, refine, or challenge the dominant
paradigm scenarios of a culture. Carroll's main focus is the representation
of women and the ways in which, for instance, they are depicted in accordance with a very narrow range of images: the dichotomy of virgin and
whore is an obvious illustration. Carroll now contends that, in addition to
propositional beliefs held assertively, ideologies may also include emotional
attitudes as well as non-propositional categorial frameworks, 'ways of
carving up phenomena'.[21] What is important to recognize is that ideologies
do not refer exclusively to beliefs, but also to ways of feeling, acting, and
seeing.[22] In Carroll's refined definition, ideologies are either false or, *in some
sense*, epistemically defective (misleading, ambiguous, or otherwise unwarranted) ideas or frameworks that uphold a system or practice of social
domination. I am prepared to accept this formulation, provided that the
expression 'epistemically defective' be broadly construed in moral epistemological terms. Whereas epistemology in a narrow sense studies the
conditions or procedures for the justification of factual statements and

beliefs, moral epistemology studies the justifiability of normative statements and patterns of conduct. It addresses itself to such questions as: can moral beliefs be true or false? And, if not, does it make sense to justify or criticize them? Broadly speaking, then, a belief is epistemically defective if it can be shown to be *in some sense* unjustified. Throughout this chapter, I will continue to use the term 'unjustifiable' rather than 'epistemically defective' to avoid the impression that ideology critique need always involve the assessment of factual information.[23]

AN EXAMPLE

John Millius's *The Wind and the Lion* (1975) strikingly shows how an individual film can express an interlocking network of morally undesirable social pictures, including not only explicit thematic messages but also ways of feeling and acting embedded in the choice of narrative genre. Before turning to this example, however, it is worth emphasizing that my overall account of ideology does not privilege textual analysis over reception studies. It is to my mind legitimate to discuss an individual film as the product of an author, or a group of film-makers, or as the product of a social context, or as a combination of those factors. But it is also illuminating to consider the ways in which different viewers consume or use films in everyday reception situations. My broad approach is indifferent to the ongoing debates between text-centred and audience-centred film scholars. I would only suggest that the matter is best approached on a case-by-case basis. In some instances, ethnographic research at the reception end may be far more illuminating than textual interpretations. John Champagne has called our attention to an important example. Gay porn parlours where viewers characteristically engage in various sexual practices during screenings obviously invite a more ethnographic approach: after all, the films themselves, which few people actually watch, are only a pretext for a wider field of activities.[24] In most instances, however, I would conjecture that both text-centred activities and reception research can fruitfully complete and illuminate one another. At any rate, the following example should be taken as a modest illustration of the aims and concerns of critical theory rather than a defence of the practice of textual analysis. For reasons of space, my analysis will not be a comprehensive one.

The plot of *The Wind and the Lion* follows an episode of US military intervention in what is now often called the 'Third World': the ambivalent struggle and mutual admiration between President Theodore Roosevelt and Moroccan rebel fighter Raisuli. Millius's main achievement as a film-maker consists in building a convincing and compelling relationship between two historical figures who never actually meet. Separated by the Atlantic Ocean, they only hear about each other's great deeds. The interconnection of their lives despite their vast geographical distance of course marks them as players within an encompassing global political environment of colonial intervention and resistance. Characters in the film often compare this military intervention with other instances of US expansion, particularly the Panama Canal, thus depicting the Moroccan conflict as a particular example of the broader aims and interests of US expansionism. Made in the shadow of the Vietnam war, *The Wind and the Lion* endeavours to justify the military subjugation of Third World nations at a time when that subjugation was being increasingly contested both inside and outside the USA. The film-maker's aim can be reconstructed as a solution to the following problem: how to rationalize the military violence that underpins foreign intervention. The film realizes this aim by depicting modern history as an enterprise carried out by great men who stand out from the mediocre crowd by virtue of their courage, honour, foresight, audacity, virility, and even a touch of madness. Roosevelt himself suggests that the price of individual greatness is loneliness: 'The road traveled by great men is dark and lonely, and lit only at intervals by other great men.' The superhuman dimension of both Roosevelt and his enemy Raisuli is underscored by heroic situations (bear hunting, riding, slaying enemies, executing daring escapes) that bring out the dauntless strength and unshrinking impetuousness of both protagonists. Great men are those who, in Roosevelt's words, recognize that 'nothing in this world is certain' and squarely face this existential predicament by risking their own lives. Only by overcoming all fear about the future can human beings realize their full potential as human beings and thus stand out from the quietly mediocre, docile existence of the crowd who remain timidly apprehensive of anything different or new. This self-realization can only be achieved through action and struggle, because it is only in battle that human beings can continually test themselves by risking everything they have.

The Wind and the Lion therefore describes the individual's capacity for self-perfection through violence as the fundamental moving force in international politics. The film justifies the violence of modern colonialism by inviting the viewer to see foreign policy in terms of a warrior ethic, as an arena for the self-realization of great men. This picture underpins a form of Social Darwinism according to which might makes right because victory testifies to the valour, fortitude, and intelligence of the victor. Millius defends this approach by invoking and idealizing certain historical facts, such as Roosevelt's 'big stick' doctrine, his hunting trips and love of the wilderness, and his well-known espousal of a Social Darwinist outlook. One of the film's most sympathetic American characters, the brash and impetuous captain Jerome, vehemently defends the value of military intervention by quoting Roosevelt's dictum: 'We are the greatest power, we carry the biggest stick ... we must seize the [Moroccan] government at bayonet point.' Military interventionism in northern Africa is therefore depicted as a test of the evolutionary superiority of some nations and national heroes over others. Whereas Moroccan society has remained static, trapped in an unchanging way of life, the United States embodies the vigour, majesty, and dynamism of historical progress. In pop existentialist terms, American culture is not; it becomes. In the film's coda, a respectful letter written by the defeated Raisuli to his victorious doppelgänger Roosevelt describes the American struggle against Morocco as a struggle between history and stasis: 'You are like the wind, and I like the lion. You form the tempest, the sand stings my eyes, and the ground is parched. I roar in defiance but you do not hear. But between us there is a difference. I, like the lion, must remain in my place. You, like the wind, will never know yours.' John Millius uses narrative fiction as a pattern of argument for an entire way of living that exalts imperial intervention by depicting it as an evolutionary test of epic courage wherein the forces of modern history must inevitably destroy the anachronistic remnants of traditional culture.

The confrontation between Raisuli's 'primitive' desert forces and Roosevelt's modern military technology foreshadows the struggle between native American warriors and the US cavalry in the later western *Geronimo* (1992, Walter Hill), also scripted by Millius. The film-maker's use of extreme long shots of the vast, arid Moroccan landscapes throughout *The Wind and the Lion* recalls the generic iconography of the American western, described by Robert Stam and Ella Shohat as a 'dry, desert terrain [that] furnishes an empty stage for the play of expansionist fantasies'.[25] Millius mobilizes a tradition of American painterly images, exemplified by Frances Palmer, which connects the national identity with a sense of landscape, rooted in the epic adventure of westward expansion.[26] The film depicts military intervention in the 'Third World' in terms of the conquest of the West, mobilizing one of the most insistent political tropes of American political culture: the violent domination of virgin or primitive land by hunters and Indian fighters. In a famous phrase not quoted in Millius's film, Roosevelt had praised the 'iron in the blood of our fathers' which had domesticated the frontier and brought America to a dominant position in the international arena.[27] Narcissistically projecting the iconography of the American West onto the oriental world of north Africa, *The Wind and the Lion* regards imperialism as an expression of the epic competitiveness and expansionism putatively characteristic of the national soul. In the film, Roosevelt uses natural metaphors to describe the national character: 'The American grizzly bear is a symbol of the American character: strength, intelligence, ferocity—a little blind and reckless at times, but courageous beyond all doubt. Another trait [is] loneliness. . . . The world will never love us. For we have too much audacity, and we are a little blind and reckless at times.' It is obvious that Roosevelt's assertions do not mainly convey factual information but rather bring out a picture of foreign policy that idealizes the putative audacity and strength of his nation. The ideological work of the film consists precisely in this idealization. *The Wind and the Lion* therefore presents a kinder vision of imperialism that justifies US foreign policy without dehumanizing its opponents. Millius wants to show respect and admiration for the struggles of Third World liberation movements, while proving that such respect is compatible with an ongoing commitment to First World military intervention. Moroccan rebels do have a grandly epic charm, but they must give way to the (American-dominated) forces of historical evolution.

The ideological aim of the film is embedded in the narrative structure. The plot opens with the kidnapping of US citizen Eden Pedicaris and her children by Raisuli. Eden's relationship to her captor evolves from initial hostility and distrust to wholehearted admiration for his unflinching virile courage. This love is shared by her children, who gradually begin to wear bedouin clothing and praise Raisuli's dauntless boldness. Having destroyed the sheltered, edenic tranquillity of their mansion, Raisuli becomes the children's ideal, heroic father, introducing them to the more fulfilling world of violent struggle. In contrast to this masculine epic world, the mother is associated with the pastoral seclusion of her domestic space: her name, Eden, obviously suggests an idyllic withdrawal from history, which in the film means the world of epic combat, a restful paradise which Raisuli destroys with masculine vigour. It had to be destroyed, of course, because it was deeply confining, cutting her children and her own self off from the possibility of risk and adventure. Raisuli's mission is precisely to educate the family into the violent, competitive ethos that alone makes life worth living. At the same time, the film retains a refreshingly comic attitude towards Raisuli's lovable, and at times charmingly naive, bravado, allowing Eden and her children occasionally to laugh at him without, however, undermining his overall heroic stature. Using slow-motion images, point-of-view shots, and majestically slow dollies, Millius persuasively renders the way the children see and admire their hero. *The Wind and the Lion* vividly recreates the texture of youthful tales of exotic adventures, a world reminiscent of novels by Emilio Salgari and Karl May, suggesting that, in order to achieve our full potential as human beings, we need a certain openness to the sense of wonder and amazement expressed in children's fantasies about wilderness adventures. In those fantasies is expressed a general refusal to dry up in a mediocre existence, an existence without risk and without value. What the film gives us is not only a set of ideas but also a certain way of looking at the men who make history from a child's point of view, an attitude that idealizes the capacity to face tremendous odds with determined self-confidence.

Broadly speaking, then, the ideological aim of *The Wind and the Lion* is to bring the viewer to see history as a heroic arena where adventurous characters realize their full human potential by boldly putting their lives on the line. The film defends a social picture according to which history is made by great patriarchs who, having overcome the widespread human fear of uncertainty and risk, undertake impetuously virile and dangerous actions. Greatness means strength, boldness, and nobility, which are said to be the underlying motives of US military intervention and, more generally, the fundamental traits of the national character. Particularly important here is the connection between American nationalism and a certain vision of the landscape rooted in the generic iconography of the Western and orientalist fantasies of north Africa as a backdrop of imperial adventure. It is certainly possible to argue that the film's depiction of Moroccan history is factually inaccurate, but this line of argument to my mind misses what is distinctive about the film-maker's ideological intent. Millius invites us to see colonial history in terms of a moral picture that endeavours to legitimize his country's foreign policy by idealizing military conquest as the expression of an existential confrontation with risk and death. This picture, which mobilizes a broad repertoire of orientalizing images, many of them derived from the conquest of the American frontier and from the iconography of colonial adventure, systematically overlooks the patterns of systematic exploitation and abuse imposed on colonized peoples, as well as the economic institutions and interests that encourage and subsidize military expansion.

THE AIMS OF CRITICAL FILM THEORY

This description of *The Wind and the Lion* is meant to illuminate what I take to be the main goals and concerns of critical theory. A critic of ideology brings out the pictures that undergird a certain pattern of social and political commitment, so as to reveal something morally undesirable about those pictures and that commitment. I am arguing that, whenever critical theorists describe a particular film or set of films, or a practice of film exhibition and distribution, as ideological, they characteristically proceed by reconstructing the social pictures that govern or undergird those patterns of film-making or exhibition or distribution in order to show how these pictures underpin such morally undesirable patterns of institutionalized domination as colonial conquest.

Having outlined the main features of ideology, and illustrated them with a cinematic example, it is now important to recognize that my account has a modest aim: to provide a clear description of a practice with which we are already familiar. I only claim to survey the distinctive concerns and strategies that already animate the enterprise of critical theory as it is practised by many film scholars. My goal is to reconstruct what critical theorists are already doing, in such a way as to clearly map out their goals and protocols. I do not, of course, claim that critics of ideology would always agree with my description of their own work. What critical film scholars believe they are doing need not correspond to what they are actually doing. It is conceivable for theorists to give erroneous or one-dimensional accounts of their own practices, in the same way that, say, a linguist who is perfectly capable of forming intelligible sentences could nonetheless produce a misleading theory of what it is to make meaning. One reason to command an overview of the goals and protocols of ideology critique is precisely because critical theorists themselves sometimes give confused accounts of their own practices. One of the most widespread confusions is the extension of a legitimate insight beyond the proper scope of its application. Because a felicitous formulation illuminates a wide range of social or cultural practices, theorists can be seduced into believing that it covers all possible practices, as in the Althusserian claim that subjectivity is everywhere ideological because it involves processes of narcissistic projection and identification.

In order to show the accuracy of my account, I now conclude by describing two familiar examples of ideology critique from the closely connected fields of film studies and mass communication theory. I will not contend that these authors are correct in drawing the conclusions that they draw (although I believe that for the most part they are) but, rather, that the framework I have outlined faithfully captures their core aims and interests. The point of the following remarks is to show that my approach accurately describes the distinctive concerns and procedures of critical film theory.

Mary Ann Doane has suggested that many Hollywood melodramas picture women as pathological, as prone to hysteria or narcissism or frigidity and thus in need of a male psychiatrist who subjects them to forms of clinical observation, classification, diagnosis, and cure. This picture, expressed in films like *The Lady in the Dark* (Mitchell Leisen, 1944), *Now Voyager* (Irving Rapper, 1942), or *The Snake Pit* (Anatole Litvak, 1948), depicts women as subject to forms of scientific control and supervision. Moreover, the women's psychological deficiency in those films often manifests itself in a pathological inability to care for their own appearance; they often look overweight, unkempt, and dirty, so that '[the]"cure" consists precisely in the beautification of body/face'.[28] What is diagnosed in the patients is, in other words, their failure to fulfil rules of feminine behaviour; these rules demand that the woman should model her conduct on the expectations and desires of the men around her. By thus describing the pictures underpinning a group of Hollywood films, Doane also undermines the rationale behind those films, in that the putative representation of a medical or scientific cure is shown to be part of a situation of institutional-ized domination.

My second example is derived from the work of John Berger, and Stuart Ewen and Elizabeth Ewen, who have traced the role of glamour in both mass media advertising and the Hollywood star system. 'The state of being envied', writes John Berger, 'is what constitutes glamour.'[29] According to this analysis, many Hollywood films and mass media advertisements rely on stars and models who are depicted as possessing intensely enviable at-tributes. Glamour projects a social picture, a way of seeing and responding to the world, wherein happiness depends on the judgements of others, on the acquisition of idealized qualities that others would also desire for themselves. In the rhetoric of advertising, the goal of being envied requires that persons transform themselves by buying particular products, thus partaking of what Stuart Ewen and Elizabeth Ewen call 'consumption as a way of life'.[30] This social picture underpins and purports to justify a style of conduct that requires the mass production of consumption goods, and it does so by defining self-improvement in relation to the desires and expecta-tions of others, thus encouraging a diminished, impoverished sense of personal autonomy.

Doane, Berger, and Ewen and Ewen share a common set of goals, concerns, and protocols. They characteristically describe a certain way of life as expressing or defending a social picture designed to justify such forms of institutionalized domination as patriarchy and capitalism, which justification is in some sense false or morally undesirable. A critic of ideology rearranges the way we think of a particular activity, or set of activities, by forcing us to confront aspects of our pictures that had been previously overlooked or underplayed. What critical theory invites us to consider is the extent to which a picture involves erroneous or unjustifiable rules of institutionalized domination. The enterprise of ideology critique in the field of cinema studies is a moral practice underlain by an interest in clarifying and evaluating the desirability of our social commitments and beliefs. By challenging the legitimacy of particular styles of conduct and imagination, critical film scholarship addresses itself to our moral awareness. In this way, theory becomes an ethical practice that shakes us from our complacency and encourages a fresh apprehension of familiar social phenomena.[31]

NOTES

1. Richard W. Miller, *Analyzing Marx: Morality, Power and History* (Princeton: Princeton University Press, 1984), 46.

2. Noel Carroll, *Mystifying Movies: Fads and Fallacies in Contemporary Film Theory* (New York: Columbia University Press, 1988), 73.

3. Terry Lovell, *Pictures of Reality* (London: British Film Institute, 1980), 31.

4. Noam Chomsky, 'Rollback, Part I: the Recent Elections, the State of the Nation', *Z Magazine* 8: 1 (1995), 24.

5. Cf. Cora Diamond's excellent *The Realistic Spirit: Wittgenstein, Philosophy, and the Mind* (Cambridge, Mass.: MIT Press, 1991), 310.

6. Paul Johnston, *Wittgenstein and Moral Philosophy* (London: Routledge, 1989), 67.

7. A proponent of this view is Richard Allen in his otherwise excellent work *Projecting Illusion: Film Spectatorship and the Impression of Reality* (New York: Cambridge University Press, 1995), 15.

8. I am only advancing a local point about a few examples of ideological assertions. I am not advancing an argument about language use in general. My point is therefore not that making meaning is necessarily a social activity.

9. Pierre Bordieu, *Outline of a Theory of Practice*, trans. Richard Nice (Cambridge: Cambridge University Press, 1977), 155–6. See also, Pierre Bordieu, *In Other Words*, trans. Matthew Adanson (Stanford, Calif.: Stanford University Press, 1990), 112.

10. Note, however, that it is not impossible in principle, although it may be very difficult in practice, for people who uphold different convictions to find common ground and communicate intelligibly about topics of shared concern. Nothing said here leads to the conclusion that different moral standpoints are always and everywhere incommensurable.

11. Ludwig Wittgenstein, *Lectures and Conversations on Aesthetics, Psychology and Religious Belief*, ed. Cyril Barrett (Berkeley and Los Angeles: University of California Press), 54.

12. Noël Carroll, *Theorizing the Moving Image* (New York: Cambridge University Press, 1996), 123.

13. Diamond, *The Realistic Spirit*, 373–6.

14. See the essays collected in Martha Craven Nussbaum, *Love's Knowledge: Essays on Philosophy and Literature* (New York: Oxford University Press, 1990), 148–67. More recently, Nancy Sherman has outlined a similar argument in *The Fabric of Character: Aristotle's Theory of Virtue* (Oxford: Clarendon Press, 1989), 3–4, 28–55.

15. Sherman, *The Fabric of Character*, 4–5.

16. Nussbaum, *Love's Knowledge*, 152.

17. Carroll, *Mystifying Movies*, 73.

18. Charles Musser, 'Work, Ideology, and Chaplin's Tramp', *Radical History Review*, 41 (1988), 50.

19. See for instance A. R. Louch, *Explanation and Human Action* (Berkeley and Los Angeles: University of California Press, 1969), 103.

20. Carroll, *Theorizing the Moving Image*, 268.

21. Ibid. 279.

22. To speak of categorial frameworks can nonetheless lead to the misleading conclusion that the meaning of a belief can be grasped independently of the circumstances of its use by an individual or a group of individuals. This is a minor point which, in any case, Carroll is probably willing to concede.

23. Now, I am not sure that I would wholeheartedly subscribe to the cognitivist assumptions of Carroll's approach. He argues (ibid. 268) that paradigm scenarios make it possible for us to 'gestalt' particular situations: 'Given a situation, an enculturated individual attempts, generally intuitively, to fit a paradigm scenario from her repertoire to it.' But, in any case, Carroll has modified his original model in a promising direction. He now admits that emotions can play a central role in ideological thinking. For an important implication of this is that ideologies can be criticized for their emotional deficiencies rather than their epistemic shortcomings.

24. John Champagne, 'Disciplining the (Academic) Body: Film Studies, Close Analysis, and Pornography,' paper delivered at the Seventeenth Annual Ohio University Film Conference, Nov. 1995.
25. Ella Shohat and Robert Stam, *Unthinking Eurocentrism: Multiculturalism and the Media* (London: Routlege, 1994), 116.
26. For a succinct and informative discussion of the nationalistic uses of landscape, see Stephen Daniels, *Fields of Vision: Landscape Imagery and National Identity in England and the United States* (Cambridge: Polity Press, 1993), 174–99.
27. Quoted in Michael Rogin, *Ronald Reagan: The Movie, and Other Episodes in Political Demonology* (Berkeley and Los Angeles: University of California Press, 1987), 188.
28. Mary Ann Doane, *The Desire to Desire: The Woman's Film of the 1940's,* (Bloomington: Indiana University Press, 1989), 41.
29. John Berger, *Ways of Seeing* (London: Penguin, 1972), 131.
30. Stuart Ewen and Elizabeth Ewen, *Channels of Desire* (New York: McGraw Hill, 1982), 24.
31. Cf. John Wisdom, *Philosophy and Psychoanalysis* (Berkeley and Los Angeles: University of California Press, 1969).

12

Aesthetics and Politics in Contemporary Black Film Theory

TOMMY L. LOTT

At a recent film conference Spike Lee criticized the minstrelsy in black television programmes, a criticism levelled not only at white producers, but also at black producers who perpetuate certain entertainment practices that aim to demean black people.[1] In the case of a white film-maker the allegation of minstrelsy amounts to a charge of anti-black racism, whereas a black film-maker is charged not only with serving the interests of racists, but also with the violation of an ethical norm in African-American culture that proscribes acts of self and group denigration. This proscription is an important reason questions regarding the aesthetic merit of a black film sometimes are treated as inseparable from questions regarding the film's political perspective.

The practice of evaluating a black film's aesthetic achievement primarily by reference to its political ideology is a critical counterpart to the counter-hegemonic stance against Hollywood produced films taken by the independent black film movement of the late 1960s led by black film-makers from the UCLA School. The political orientation of this group of black independents was influenced by revolutionary Third World film-making. Guided by Julio Garcia Espinosa's concept of 'imperfect cinema' they practiced an American version of Third Cinema.[2] One of the chief tenets of the Third Cinema manifesto is that a film's aesthetic orientation is not politically neutral. According to Espinosa, '[I]f art is substantially a disinterested activity and we're obliged to do it in an interested way, it becomes an imperfect art. In essence, this is how I use the word imperfect. And this I think isn't just an ethical matter, but also aesthetic.'[3] The 'imperfect cinema' advocated by Espinosa was the model for the UCLA School's endeavour to provide an alternative to Hollywood's inauthentic images of black people.[4]

The anti-Hollywood stance of the UCLA School was, without a doubt, warranted by the film industry's racism. Nevertheless, a consequence of adopting this stance has been that aesthetics and politics are almost always treated as inseparable in the critical assessment of a black film's strengths and weaknesses. I want to draw into question the idea that the aesthetic achievement of a black film is indistinguishable from the ideology it embraces. Black film critics are often in a position to appreciate the aesthetic achievement of a film even when that film's political perspective is problematic, or to notice a film's aesthetic shortcomings, despite its powerful social message. Such moments suggest that there are separable political and aesthetic criteria for evaluating a black film. I argue further that the political, or aesthetic, value of a black film is not to be equated with its status as independently produced. Different films display strengths and weaknesses with regard to their political orientation, aesthetic orientation, or their reception by a black audience. Hence, there is no single fixed criterion that can be generally used to appraise black films. Audience reception is a strength of mainstream black films and political and aesthetic orientation are strengths of Third Cinema, but in either case both political and aesthetic criteria come into play.

The idea that genuine opposition to the aesthetically coded racist ideology in Hollywood films can only be expressed through overt contestation, and rejection, of films styled after Hollywood movies has influenced the general practice among black film critics of positioning modernist films by black independents over realist Hollywood films. This idea is misleading to the extent that it suggests that every modernist independent black film is counter-hegemonic and that every realist studio film is a form of minstrelsy. A too rigid distinction between studio-produced and independent black films has often been a source of confusion regarding the aesthetic value of films that have been produced by both groups of film-makers. The conventions of Hollywood film-making have strongly influenced the aesthetic make-up of mainstream films by black film-makers because their films are slated for mass consumption. Independent black film-makers have more freedom to experiment with the aesthetic features of a film because they are not constrained by the market influences that shape Hollywood movies.

Black film scholars interested in contemporary black cinema have had to come to grips with the fact that some of the most promising black independents have entered the Hollywood studios. Independent black film-makers from the UCLA School, such as Julie Dash and Charles Burnett, have not been reticent about capitalizing on the recent studio interest in black films.[5] Moreover, since the success of Spike Lee, many black independents no longer see their Hollywood affiliation as antithetical to the movement's earlier goal of making politically challenging films that are supported by the black community. The growing number of Hollywood movies by independent black film-makers seems to demand a more nuanced black film commentary than the standard critique of Hollywood that was fostered by earlier blaxploitation era films.

I want to consider several recent endeavours to meet this demand. First I critically examine the prevailing notion of independent black cinema to show that in many cases this notion involves a commitment to a Third Cinema paradigm of black film-making. Some critics, however, have relied on other paradigms such as Melvin Van Peebles's *Sweet Sweetback's Baadasssss Song* and Bill Gunn's *Ganga and Hess* to define independent black cinema. But the political and aesthetic value of *Sweetback* has been a matter of controversy among critics, many of whom have appealed to considerations regarding black audience response to ground their appraisals. I turn to this debate to consider the standing among critics of a film-maker's intention and the film text in relation to its reception by a black audience. I maintain that, in cases of disagreement regarding a black film's political or aesthetic value, the film-maker's intention and the film text cannot be ignored. I conclude that the appeal to black spectatorship is too problematic and cannot be used to override a concern with the content of a film.

THE DEFINITION OF INDEPENDENT BLACK CINEMA

In *Redefining Black Film* Mark Reid elevates the critique of Hollywood movies to the level of a critical theory of black film. He separates feature-length movies about black people into three fundamental categories: comedy, family, and action. He then analyses a selection of films that represent blackface, hybrid, and satiric hybrid variants within each category. According to Reid the African-American film image has amounted to nothing more than 'comedy subtypes' and 'their facsimiles in other genres'.[6] His conception of African-American cinema, articulated primarily in terms of minstrelsy, contrasts sharply with the diaspora paradigm of independent black film he wants to endorse. Because, for Reid, the legacy of minstrelsy is a defining element of African-American cinema, his distinction between studio-financed, -produced, or -distributed films and those that were independent of this kind of white control is the cornerstone of his revisionism.[7] He offers us a quasi-essentialist notion of independent black cinema as film-making controlled by black film-makers.

The opposition of black independents to Hollywood-style film-making sometimes has been taken to mean that a black film-maker must seek complete economic self-reliance. Some commentators seem especially worried that unless a black film-maker is completely autonomous and not dependent on Hollywood's financial resources, skilled technicians, advanced technology, and extensive distribution networks, he will lose control. This worry about black film-makers losing control over their films led Reid to embrace a concept of independent black cinema that rigidly excludes films by Oscar Micheaux and Melvin Van Peebles because they were either financed, or distributed, by whites.[8] For Reid, an independent black film-maker loses control whenever his or her film is either co-financed, co-produced, or distributed by a studio.

To see that Reid's notion of control does not exhaust all of the variables that shape a film's political perspective or aesthetic form, suppose that an independent black film-maker, such as Julie Dash, were to gain enough control over a studio-financed project to make exactly the film she would have made as an independent. In his appraisal of Spike Lee's films Reid seems to respond to this suggestion with the following claim, 'I argue against the assumption that a black director, even with final-cut privileges, can guarantee a re-vision of the filmic image of black womanhood in particular and the black experience in general.'[9] But since this absence of a guarantee applies to independent films as well, Reid has given no reason to prefer them over studio films by black directors with final cut privileges.[10] His demand for a revised black film image displays a concern with the aesthetic consequences of white control, yet his contention that studio-affiliated black film-makers have always produced 'tendentious' minstrel images is not historically well grounded. He condemns a priori any film touched by Hollywood hands as aesthetically defective, but from the standpoint of historical practice there simply is no clearly marked aesthetic divide between independent and studio-affiliated films.

Independent black film-makers often have done whatever it takes to make their films. Reid's statement that 'there are some black filmmakers who resist the calls of fame and increased production budgets' portrays the plight of black independents having to make films with virtually little financial support as noble acts of artistic autonomy.[11] But this leaves us to wonder how his stipulation requiring such a rigid separation from Hollywood could be a defining element of independent black cinema when it clearly goes against the grain of what African-American film-makers do to survive. His theory allows him to position films that satisfy his notion of independent black cinema as having greater political and aesthetic value based solely on the criterion of a film-maker's oppositional strategy of eschewing studio affiliation. This view, however, does not leave room for other more subversive strategies by film-makers who have opted to work in Hollywood studios.

By direct contrast with Reid's diaspora paradigm Ed Guerrero's notion of independent black cinema emerges from his critical examination of the Hollywood image of black people.[12] Guerrero tailors his view of independent black cinema to fit his historical account of Hollywood cinema, a history comprised primarily of the periods before and after the blaxploitation era. Although he endorses the achievements of black independents only as one among many modes of resistance chosen by black film-makers, he nevertheless relies on misleading dichotomy between films by black independents and films by black film-makers working in Hollywood.

Unlike Reid, Guerrero maintains an accommodationist view of the relation between Hollywood and black independents, while recognizing
the oppositional function of independent black cinema. He speaks of
the black independent movement of the 1970s as having 'laid a clear
political, philosophical, and aesthetic foundation for an ongoing cinematic
practice that challenges Hollywood's hegemony over the black image'.[13]
He praises film-makers from the UCLA School for their endeavour to create
'an emergent, decolonizing, antiracist cinema that in its images, sounds,
aesthetics, and modes of production has attempted to reconstruct the
world on the screen from black points of view cast in liberating images
and new paradigms'.[14] These remarks regarding 'liberating images' and
'new paradigms' refer to the modernist aesthetic orientation of Third
Cinema film-makers. Guerrero's endorsement of this concept becomes
problematic, however, when he includes under its rubric the first films of
Spike Lee (*She's Gotta Have It*, 1986) and Robert Townsend (*Hollywood
Shuffle*, 1987).

Guerrero's move to extend the Third Cinema concept of independent
black cinema to include these films is facilitated by his discussion of the
tactics of 'guerrilla cinema financing'. He does not consider the possibility
that the use of guerrilla tactics to finance a film does not always yield a film
that counts as Third Cinema. According to Spike Lee's own testimony, the
topic of black female sexuality in *She's Gotta Have It* was selected because
of its commercial potential. The film itself was a replacement for a less
commercial film (*Messenger*) he initially had begun to shoot.[15] Robert
Townsend's film *Hollywood Shuffle* is fashioned after a series of *Saturday
Night Live* skits about movie clichés and racial stereotyping. Although it is
undeniable that these films contain elements of resistance, Guerrero goes
too far in proclaiming them 'the two productions in the mid- to late 1980s
that have best realized the projections and hopes of black critics,
filmmakers, and audience alike'.[16] The satire of Lee and Townsend, which
aimed for a crossover market (dominated at the time by Eddie Murphy),
was a far cry from the 'liberating images and new paradigms' of Third
Cinema. Guerrero acknowledges that they represent a new group of 'cross-
over' black independents who are more than willing to provide a black voice
that speaks in the language of Hollywood cinema, yet he mistakenly
conflates Lee's hybrid and Townsend's imitative film-making styles with the
alternative practices of Third Cinema.

By contrast with the notion of 'guerrilla' cinema focusing on Lee and
Townsend advanced by Guerrero, Toni Cade Bambara presents a notion
that centres on the subversive achievements of Bill Gunn, a blaxploitation
era film-maker.[17] Gunn's film *Ganja and Hess* is a studio production (albeit
subversive) that is closer to the Third Cinema aesthetic orientation of the
UCLA School than the independent productions of Lee and Townsend.[18]

Bambara wants to distinguish commerically oriented black independents from what she calls 'conscious Black cinematistes'. Spike Lee is excluded from the latter because he represents the new generation of black film-makers 'who regard the contemporary independent sphere as a training ground or stepping-stone to the industry, rather than as a space for contestation, a liberated zone in which to build a cinema for social change'.[19] In the light of what has happened to films by radical black film-makers such as Bill Gunn, Bambara cautions against studio-produced films on both ideological and aesthetic grounds. She raises the question of whether films by former black independents who work in Hollywood have been co-opted by commercial influences. This worry about co-optation is the basis for the view that black independents, *by definition*, cannot be studio-affiliated.

When Manthia Diawara reasserts the definition of independent black cinema as 'any Black-produced film outside the constraints of the major studios' he complicates this widely held view by selecting, as paradigms, films by Melvin Van Peebles and Bill Gunn, both of whom worked in Hollywood as a means of financing their films.[20] Diawara cites *Sweetback* and *Ganja and Hess* as illustrations of two different aesthetic orientations by independent black film-makers. Without realizing he has selected two cases that do not fit his definition of independent black cinema, Diawara employs these different paradigms of guerrilla film-making to illustrate the aesthetic value of both realist and modernist styles. Diawara's selection of *Sweetback* as a paradigm of independent black cinema indicates that some critics are willing to recognize that a black film can have political value regardless of its aesthetic orientation. In the light of Diawara's move to canonize *Sweetback* and *Ganja and Hess* the blanket condemnation of all blaxploitation era films for reproducing denigrating Hollywood images of black people must be reconsidered.[21]

Reid draws upon a wide variety of diaspora black film-making practices to construct his notion of independent black cinema. He overlooks the fact that African-American film-making also has included a wide variety of practices. Since the late 1960s there has been a dialectical relation between the Hollywood studios and independent black film-making that has thrived on an interplay much more complex than the rigid dichotomy between studio and independent-produced film allows. In addition to the Third Cinema group at UCLA, composed of film-makers who worked outside the Hollywood studios, there was another group of black documentary film-makers who also were actively involved in the black independent movement. For two years (1968–70) these film-makers worked in network television producing politically conscious films for *Black Journal*, a monthly PBS news magazine programme.[22] Some black independents, such as Melvin Van Peebles and Bill Gunn, were involved in the making of studio films

during the blaxploitation era, while others, such as Fred Williamson and
Jamaa Fanaka, formed film companies to produce their own action genre
films. This plethora of black film-making practices suggests that the political
and aesthetic differences among black independent films cannot be captured
by a single paradigm. The definitions of independent black cinema offered
by both Reid and Guerrero assume that the financial autonomy of a black
film-maker will guarantee films that have certain political and aesthetic
features. Guerrero's concept of independent black cinema conflates important differences between several African-American film-making paradigms,
while Reid's concept narrowly excludes many of them.

THE *SWEETBACK* DEBATE AND BLACK SPECTATORSHIP

Commentators often require black film-makers to assume the time-
honoured 'burden of representation', which imposes a duty to uphold a
'positive' image of black people and, at minimum, to avoid perpetuating
denigrating images. This expectation was an underlying factor in the moral
controversy surrounding the use of inverted images in blaxploitation action
films. The ambiguous political status of these inverted images has prevented
many studio films, in the minds of some critics, from having political and
aesthetic parity with films that display the more symbolic imagery of Third
Cinema.[23] In the case of blaxploitation era films, the estimate of their
aesthetic value seems also to have influenced the appraisal of their political
value. Many blaxploitation era film-makers were deemed reactionary because of their borrowings from Hollywood conventions, yet their detractors
have frequently overlooked important political and aesthetic differences
between their films in favour of considerations regarding black audience
response.[24] The appeal to audience response as a basis for the evaluation of
a black film is motivated by a desire to account for both the objectionable,
as well as the subversive, elements in studio films that have a hybrid, or
polyvocal, text. But in controversial cases, to what extent should considerations pertaining to black audience reception outweigh other criteria? I will
insist that the intention of the film-maker and the content of the film cannot
be ignored as a basis for determining the value of a politically ambiguous
film such as *Sweetback*.

It is worth noting that considerations regarding audience reception apply
best to mainstream black films, because they have had a much greater
appeal to black audiences. Although many explanations can be given of the
lack of a black audience for independent black cinema, aesthetic considerations are paramount.[25] The aesthetic parameters of a work of entertainment
slated for a mass market are quite different from those that govern independent productions. Films by the UCLA School avoided using traditional

Hollywood narratives, whereas these narratives were used frequently with inverted racial coding in blaxploitation era Hollywood films.[26] In responding to Gerima's criticism of *Sweetback's* Hollywood style, Van Peebles makes a simple point regarding aesthetic values and black audiences that must be well taken. The question of how best to reach black audiences with a socially conscious message, he pointed out, may require a black film-maker to consider differences between a Third Cinema aesthetic orientation and the mainstream aesthetic orientation from a marketing standpoint.

One much celebrated danger of allowing marketing concerns to dictate the aesthetic orientation of a black film is that the use of Hollywood conventions almost always results in the co-optation of the film's political message. Indeed, the black hero formula for many blaxploitation era films was supplied by *Sweetback* despite Van Peebles's intention. The disagreement between St Clair Bourne and Haile Gerima over the political value of *Sweetback* was expressed in terms of the film's mainstream aesthetic orientation.[27] Van Peebles was criticized by Gerima for using the Hollywood narrative of the rugged individual in which the black male hero is a sexual figure who abuses women. With regard to the narrative strategy of *Sweetback*, Gerima accused Van Peebles of allowing commercial concerns to influence the film's political perspective, whereas Bourne understood it to be subversive and defended Van Peebles against this criticism on political grounds. Of special interest here is the fact that both Gerima and Bourne appealed to the reading of the film by black spectators from different standpoints to support their respective appraisals.

It is somewhat ironic that the blaxploitation formula adopted by Hollywood was supplied by an independent black film-maker who aimed to subvert the Hollywood entertainment codes with a politically conscious message.[28] The co-optation of *Sweetback's* political statement by the subsequent rash of macho action films has overshadowed Van Peeble's subversive intention. Guerrero sides with the critics of *Sweetback* who disallow the appeal to Van Peebles's intention to override their concern with how the film was read by black audiences. He seems to be concerned that to permit such an appeal would justify too much in blaxploitation era films that is questionable. It would allow, for instance, Gordon Parks, Jr.'s argument that *Superfly* was *intended* to be an anti-drug film to stand uncontested by those who believed it was an inducement for black youth to enter the world of crime.

Diawara's favourable assessment of *Sweetback* suggests that he believes it has a political orientation that can be distinguished from some of its blaxploitation sequels such as *Superfly*.[29] Unfortunately he does not specify the criteria by which we can so readily distinguish between the political orientation of *Sweetback* and the political orientation of *Superfly*. Complete acceptance of Diawara's assessment is hindered by the moral controversy surrounding the use, in both films, of 'bad nigga' narratives that portend the fate of the black male lumpenproletariat. It was, after all, the creative incorporation of black urban folklore in these films that resonated with such a large segment of the black audience.[30] Despite the popularity of these films with black audiences the use of the black male criminal as a heroic figure of resistance has been a source of much criticism.[31]

After noting that the political orientation (i.e. class background) of the viewer was a factor in the commentary on *Sweetback*, Guerrero reports Huey Newton's famous 'revolutionary' analysis of *Sweetback* to indicate the black urban male lumpenproletariat reading of the hustler character as a deconstruction of the positive image that was typically modelled on a black bourgeois ideal of the ever-striving, upright Negro.[32] He points out that the 'positive image' in Hollywood films was read by the post-Civil Rights generation as an overcompensation for the racist stereotypes. He then cites a quite different reading of *Sweetback* by black nationalist critic Haki Madhubuti, who denied Newton's claim that the film was about the development of revolutionary consciousness. Although Guerrero easily disqualifies the opinion of *Ebony* magazine critic Lerone Bennett, because of Bennett's strong middle-class bias, he is less inclined to dismiss Madhubuti's reiteration of Bennett's view. Does the criticism of *Sweetback* stand when it is seconded by a voice that is taken to represent equally the interests of the black male lumpenproletariat? It is somewhat disappointing that Guerrero does not even attempt to specify any criteria by which to judge the success, or failure, of the attempt by Van Peebles (and Gordon Parks, Jr.) to deconstruct, or subvert, the Hollywood crime genre by imposing on it a narrative from the expressive tradition of black urban males.

Guerrero takes the polemic between Gerima and Bourne to indicate a stalemate in so far as the assessment of *Sweetback's* political statement regarding black male oppression is concerned. He instead criticizes the structural absence of black women's perspectives on the film's treatment of gender, citing the unremarked rape scene as a lapse in male criticism.[33] He concludes that the subsequent devaluation of black women in blaxploitation era films is due to 'the figure of the sexploitative pimp, hustler hero of the then-rising genre'.[34] Yet he does not consider the fact that the typically anti-women stance of the classic 'bad nigga' narratives in black folklore, as well as the general ambiguity these narratives assume when appropriated for political purposes, derives from their inherently nihilistic outlook.

There is no doubt that the 'bad nigga' narratives of blaxploitation era films such as *Sweetback* and *Superfly* were blatantly sexist, yet by comparison with some of the narratives in classic black male folklore, the hustler characters in these films are rather mild in their relations with women.[35] The male protagonist in *Sweetback*, a worker in the underground sex industry, is portrayed by Van Peebles to be as much a victim of sexual abuse as the women he abuses. In *Superfly*, Priest is a drug dealer because he does not have the heart to be a pimp. I do not cite these concessions to mainstream values in these films to appease Guerrero's concern with the treatment of women. Rather, I want to draw attention to a more fundamental issue at stake, namely, the question of whether the nihilistic aspects of these films conveys an ideology that is inconsistent with the development of a social consciousness conducive to *collective* political action.[36] Guerrero does not notice that this question includes a concern with the treatment of women, for it involves a broader issue of whether 'bad nigga' narratives can be used by a film-maker to convey a sense of community.

Critical reflection on *Sweetback* has been dominated by the general issue of how a controversial black film text, with morally objectionable content, is read by black spectators. The appeal to audience reception, however, cannot account for some of the important political and aesthetic differences between *Sweetback* and other blaxploitation era films. In some films such as *Superfly* the film-maker's intention seems to have boomeranged as a consequence of the incongruity of the film's visual endorsement of the black gangster lifestyle and the socially conscious statement against it that was presented in the dialogue. The 'bad nigga' figure in *Superfly* is used to recode a traditional Hollywood crime narrative, whereas in *Sweetback* this figure is used to subvert the genre. As commentators have noted, the street-wise protagonist in *Superfly* displays very little political consciousness. With reference to the content of *Superfly*, Brandon Wander found it inexcusable that in a film about a black drug dealer by a black director the socially pressing issue of drugs in the black community is never raised.[37] This stands in sharp contrast with *Sweetback*, in which the portrayal of the transformation of the political consciousness of a black criminal figure was a basis for Huey Newton's interpretation. The use of the 'bad nigga' figure gave both films a special appeal to black urban audiences, but the political message of *Superfly* supports the status quo, while the political message of *Sweetback* challenges it. Motivated by the success of *Sweetback*, many blaxploitation era films relied on images drawn from black urban folklore to enhance their appeal to black audiences. The political and aesthetic value of these films cannot be decided strictly by appealing to black spectatorship. Although this appeal may justify a moral concern regarding the widespread exploitation of vernacular representation in Hollywood films, each film's appraisal must also take into account its ideological frame, as well as the film-maker's aesthetic strategy.

THE LIMITS OF RECEPTION-BASED CRITICISM

Thus far I have examined black spectatorship from the standpoint of the positive audience reception given to films that, by drawing upon black urban folklore, explicitly seek to elicit the allegience of black audiences. However, critics have also investigated forms of reception where the way in which the text is received explicitly or implicitly contests the intentions of the film-maker. One of the most interesting applications of reception-based criticism has been in cases where the intention of a film-maker is understood by black spectators to be problematic; nonetheless the film is appropriated and given a political meaning that differs from that intended by the film-maker. Feminist commentators who advocate this practice have rarely considered the response of black spectators to blaxploitation era films, although some have devoted considerable attention to black women's responses to Steven Spielberg's *The Color Purple*.[38] Jacqueline Bobo provides an account of the manner in which many black women 'read through' Spielberg's film to reconstruct a meaning that was ideologically different from what was intended by the film-maker.[39] She outlines the mechanisms of ideological construction employed by Spielberg to show how his negative portrayals of black women (for example, Sofia's overbearing matriarchal figure and Shug Avery's victimization by her own insatiable sexual appetite) were reconstructed by black women spectators. According to Bobo black women spectators relied on the sensibilities they have cultivated to survive domination and oppression in everyday life to resist the pull of the film and extract a meaning that differs from the mainstream values Spielberg depicts. Bobo draws a rather surprising conclusion from her study. A Hollywood film that is blatantly and irretrievably racist, as well as one that is only patronizing and negative, should be protested and criticized, unless there is a black audience who embrace it. Then it should be 'analyzed and assessed for the benefits that can be derived from it'.[40]

If we apply Bobo's analysis of the relation of black women spectators to *The Color Purple* to the relation of black male spectators to *Sweetback*, concern with the treatment of women in Van Peebles's film seems misconstrued. The ghetto characters in blaxploitation crime films such as *Superfly*, *Black Caesar*, *Hell up in Harlem*, and *The Mack* were employed as film versions of urban black male folklore. In keeping with Bobo's stipulation, why not suppose that black male spectators (and others) who enjoyed these films had the capacity to 'read through' the text in a manner similar to the way black women spectators were able to 'read through' Spielberg's film? If Bobo wants to argue that it is all right from a feminist perspective to endorse a film that perpetuates a problematic image of black women when black women spectators have appropriated it and given it a different meaning, then a similar argument must be allowed regarding black men and *Sweetback*.

Bobo's account of reading through the text can be used to explain how conversion themes were incorporated into the 'bad nigga' narratives of films such as *Sweetback* and *Superfly* and read by black male spectators.[41] In the case of films that have ambiguous texts, such as *The Color Purple* and *Sweetback*, the appeal to black spectatorship does not override the use of other criteria such as the film-maker's intention, or the film's content, for all three elements are a part of the process of reading through a film.

Commentators have attempted to account for the resistive elements in studio-produced black films by considering them as texts that stand in a dialogic relation with readers who interpret them.[42] Diawara explains this relation in terms of the *rupture* that transpires when a Hollywood narrative constructs a racist image of black people with which the black spectator is unable to identify. Bobo's account focuses on the *identification* that transpires despite such a construction. Trouble arises when we consider instances in which divergent readings of the same film occur among black spectators. Some black women resisted what they found to be objectionable in *Sweetback*, just as some black men (such as Huey Newton and the Black Panthers) read through it. Similarly, some black men resisted what they found objectionable in *The Color Purple*, whereas some black women read through it.

By reference to several features of contemporary Hollywood narratives that include blacks, Diawara attempts to support his thesis that the dominant cinema situates black characters primarily for the pleasure of white spectators. He cites the mechanism of transferring villainy from the Klan to the black soldiers that was used in *A Soldier's Story* (1984) to illustrate how the pleasure afforded by identification is denied to black spectators. He refers to a similar feature of *The Color Purple* to illustrate further how this rupture transpires. Unfortunately, his assimilation of the chase sequence in *The Color Purple* to the Gus chase sequence in *The Birth of a Nation* does not take into account gender differences among black spectators. Depending on whether the spectator is male or female, this scenario can be a source of either identification, or resistance. Without assuming a one-to-one correlation it seems that class and gender are factors that have influenced divergent readings by black spectators of mainstream films such as *The Color Purple*.

What about the potential of a film to employ certain mechanisms of ideological construction to engender ambivalence in spectators? This issue was brought to light, somewhat inadvertently, by Henry Louis Gates, Jr. in his discussion of Isaac Julian's film *Looking for Langston*.[43] Gates points out that Julian's film is clearly not meant to be an examination of Hughes's sexual life. Instead, the point of his 'act of cultural retrieval and reconstruction' is to represent issues of gender and desire by constructing a counterhistory in which black gay identity can be expressed. Gates notes that Julian's avant-garde style in *Looking for Langston* presents more than an uncritical act of reclamation. It is not only used to rewrite the history of that cultural moment, but compels spectators to participate in this rewriting by invoking the present. Gates mentions the scene in the film where the audience sees a shot of Mapplethorpe photos projected on a backdrop while a white man walks through them. With regard to the intended contrast of Julian's image of 'masculinity unmasked' with Mapplethorpe's 'Primitivist evocations', he claims, 'Indeed, this may be the film's most powerful assault on the well-policed arena of Black masculinity.' But there are other possible readings of this scene.

Kobena Mercer has spoken from a more complex black gay perspective regarding Mapplethorpe's 'troublesome black male nudes'.[44] Mercer had earlier criticized Mapplethorpe's work for aestheticizing the stereotype into a work of art. Several years later he proposed to recontextualize his account of the aestheticization of racial difference. Specifically, he revised the assumption that fetishism is necessarily a bad thing. Mercer realized that Mapplethorpe's images engendered ambivalence: on the one hand he resisted identification with the black men depicted as sex objects for white fantasy, while on the other he shared the same desire to look. Recognizing his own feelings of envy and rivalry, Mercer concludes, 'I would actually occupy the same position in the fantasy of mastery that I said was that of the white male subject!'[45]

One of the advantages of reception-based criticism, which ultimately reveals its greatest shortcoming, is the manner in which it can be employed to accommodate very complex readings of film texts to account for cases in which black spectators identify with contradictory standpoints represented in a film. Mercer cites the polyvocal quality of Mapplethorpe's photographs to ground his identification with both object and subject of the white male gaze. With a similar concern in mind Michelle Wallace argues for a conjunction of race and gender in feminist film theory.[46] She reports her experience of having identified both with the Rita Hayworths and Lana Turners as well as with the Butterfly McQueens and Hattie McDaniels. This fact, she claims, attests to the need to view racial identity as problematic and to expand our conception of it rather than abandon it. According to Wallace, 'It seems crucial here to view spectatorship not only as potentially bisexual but also multiracial and multiethnic.'[47]

What about the fact that the sight of negative portrayals of black women on the screen by Butterfly McQueen and Hattie McDaniels caused some black female spectators to turn away as a gesture of resistance? bell hooks offers a quite different account of the response of black female spectators toward the screen representation of black women such as Sapphire in *Amos 'n' Andy*.[48] hooks employs Diawara's account of the resisting spectator to argue that, unlike Miss Pauline Breedlove in Toni Morrison's *The Bluest*

Eye, not all black women spectators 'submitted to that spectacle of regression through identification called for by Hollywood'.[49] She insists that 'From "jump," Black female spectators have gone to films with awareness of the way in which race and racism determined the visual construction of gender.'[50] In opposition to the claim by Michelle Wallace, hooks maintains that 'Black women were able to critically assess the cinema's construction of White womanhood as object of phallocentric gaze, and choose not to identify with either the victim or the perpetrator.'[51]

Where Wallace emphasized a process of identification with Hollywood narratives that demean black women, hooks focuses on black women spectators resisting any such identification and (in a manner similar to Bobo's notion of 'reading through' a text) instead creating alternative texts based on their own experience. This disagreement between hooks and Wallace over the question of whether black women spectators experienced identification or rupture in such cases indicates the major shortcoming of reception-based criticism, namely, its reliance on quasi-empirical claims, and a priori arguments, regarding the responses of black spectators. This objection has even greater application in the case of independent black films where criticism that relies on an account of the responses of black spectators has even less application. Unlike other critics who largely appeal to audience reception to ground their appraisals of studio films Reid applies his account of audience reception to independent black cinema as well.

Reid maintains that audiences are not passive, inert receptacles absorbing monologic meanings from a screen, but instead are engaged in dialogue with a film. By reference to their own cultural frame audiences continually reinterpret what is depicted on the screen in ways different from the intended meanings. He uses the idea of spectators actively reinterpreting texts to explain how blacks could laugh along with whites in cases such as *Amos 'n' Andy.* With blacks as the ridiculed objects this blatant form of blackface minstrelsy required a racist audience positioning. Reid acknowledges that if blacks saw humor in *Amos 'n' Andy,* then apparently they laughed for a different reason from whites, which implies that there was a different reading of the programme by black and white audiences. He tells us, 'When a comedy film objectifies blacks, it produces both pleasure and pain for both racial groups but such feelings are not of the same quality and, therefore, must be differentiated.'[52] Reid wants to say that black audiences resisted while white audiences assimilated the racism in *Amos 'n' Andy* but is prevented from doing so by one of the provisions in his account. He points out the various responses available to white audiences. 'In the production and reception of minstrel and hybrid minstrel comedies, whites can produce racial myths, believe myths that support their imagined racial superiority, or feel maligned by the production of these myths and create an oppositional form of reception.' He then goes on to point out that blacks are permitted 'only the last two of these choices, both of which require black spectators to use oppositional strategies of reception.'[53] These remarks suggest that Reid thinks both black and white spectators can resist a racist film discourse; consequently, he cannot hold that resistance is a distinctive feature of black audience response to *Amos 'n' Andy*. But what about the black spectator's identification with the programme? He is unable to specify what distinguishes the experiences of black and white audiences in this case because his account does not rest on empirical grounds.

Difficulties of this sort stem from Reid's tendency to vacillate on the issue of whether black cinema is intended for a black audience. His insistence that a film about black people must be controlled from writing to distribution by black people in order to count as independent black cinema does not quite agree with his claim that 'The theory I am proposing assumes an interracial audience.'[54] To allow an interracial audience at the reception end of the film-making process is inconsistent with disallowing interracial participation at the production-distribution end. He concedes that studio action films were made for a black audience, but when discussing diaspora films by black women his view seems to shift. He states,

> The recognition and shared productivity of the postNegritude project results from the active participation of an 'interested' audience that decodes the black subject by using discourse that surround and construct representations of gender, race, class, sexuality, and nation. An 'interested' audience scrutinizes the incorporation of these images (and how they reflect individuals and the community). Through this shared postNegritude recognition, black audiences will question their own (and, by implication, others') interpretations.[55]

Reid moves very quickly from talk about an 'interested' audience to talk about a black audience without making clear how the two are related. For instance, does the 'interested' audience have the 'shared postNegritude recognition' Reid attributes to black audiences? Moreover, Reid's attribution of this ideological orientation to black audiences seems wholly prescriptive, for he seems inclined not to appreciate the empirical nature of the question of whether black movie-goers have it or not.

In the controversy surrounding films such as *Sweetback* and *The Color Purple* critical appraisals that aimed to defeat moral objections to the alleged racist and sexist content in these films were based on the fact that these films had been appropriated and read differently by a politically conscious segment of black men and women spectators. Most of Reid's comments regarding audience reception of independent black films are couched hypothetically. He tells us that 'Black womanist films that depict nonsexist men may threaten the psychologic desires of certain feminists— for example, separatists who deplore any feminism that includes men' and 'Certain pan-Africans might view black feminism as a threat to black communal solidarity.'[56] This leaves us to wonder how, in fact, black womanist films have been received by black audiences. Although Reid acknowledges that a black womanist film may provoke any of several modes of reception, he nonetheless focuses on resistance, allowing the possibility of oppositional readings by black audiences. As I have already noted in connection with Reid's account of black audience response to *Amos 'n' Andy*, he offers us a theory that is not well suited to explain the black spectator's experience of identification. Here we must suppose that the mechanisms of ideological construction (identified by feminist critics) come into play so as to produce resisting spectators.

With regard to black independent films, Reid does not explain how we are supposed to understand a black spectator's experience of rupture, rather than identification. In his discussion of Spike Lee's films Reid speaks as if all of the various modes of reception are not possible. He cannot be taken seriously, however, if he meant that Sharon Larkin's *A Different Image* is more polyphonic than Spike Lee's *Do the Right Thing*, for he allows that even the grossly exploitative studio action films were polyphonic. More-over, the claim that a black film text allows an oppositional reading should not be confused with a claim that it has in fact been so read by black spectators. Reid maintains that 'spectatorship is a physical phenomenon' yet he has failed to come to grips with the fact that there is not much of a black audience for the black womanist films he cites. Box office receipts and video sales and rentals suggest that Spike Lee's films are being assimilated by large black audiences while there is no evidence that Sharon Larkin's pan-African womanist representations are even known to them. Reid has given us a top-down view that prescribes, more than it describes, the responses of black audiences.

Reid's application of reception theory to independent black films aims to support his commitment to a diaspora paradigm of black cinema. He assigns to diaspora film-making the function of educating black audience by producing films that are an alternative to Hollywood-styled films. This function is in keeping with the aesthetic goal of Third Cinema. He shares the aesthetic concerns of other critics, such as Gerima and Bambara, who have objected to studio films because they believe the commercial exploitation of recoded images by the studios often reproduces a mainstream frame of reference. There is an important sense in which *Sweetback* set up its own co-optation by employing Hollywood hero mythology. This does not entail, however, that Van Peebles's endeavour to draw upon black urban folklore to recode a Hollywood image, or that other ghettocentric mainstream films, lack political and aesthetic value. Instead it suggests a need for the less commercial orientation of Third Cinema.

The aspirations of black people are often misrepresented when they are framed to accord with the views of the white mainstream. Critics have objected to the recoding of a negative portrayal of black people through inversion because this practice often reiterates an ideology designed to maintain white hegemony. Third Cinema representations of black people are presented from a wholly black cultural perspective instead of through the racist frame imposed by studios on many mainstream films. Critics have advocated the alternative aesthetic of Third Cinema because it offers black spectators relief from studio films that rely primarily on an inversion of racial codes—a structural feature that positions black spectators to view themselves from a mainstream perspective. The recent 'narrowcasting' of mainstream markets by television and film studios has created new opportunities for black film-makers to make films that appeal directly to black audiences. In the future the distinction between the aesthetic and political orientations of black films will no longer place such a great emphasis on their status as independent or studio-produced. The prescriptive criteria of Third Cinema are no longer the sole basis for evaluating Hollywood cinema, which must be dealt with on its own terms without reducing criticism to moral judgement. When it is empirically grounded, reception-based criticism provides a different way of assessing the value of a black film, but we must be wary of a priori claims that rely on reception theory to legitimize the opinion of the critic.

NOTES

1. Pan-African Cinema Conference, Tisch School of the Arts, New York University, New York, 28 Mar. 1994.
2. 'For an Imperfect Cinema', in Michael Chanan (ed.), *Twenty-Five Years of the New Latin American Cinema* (London: British Film Institute and Channel 4, 1983), 28–33. In a later commentary Espinosa invokes a concept of authenticity, which he tells us is 'an image without make-up that is nonetheless more attractive', to preserve a distinction between bad film-making and alternative film-making. 'Meditations on Imperfect Cinema . . . Fifteen Years Later', *Screen*, 26: 3–4 (May–Aug. 1985), 94.
3. 'Meditations on Imperfect Cinema', 94.
4. For discussions of the Third Cinema movement and the UCLA School see Ntongela Masilela, 'The Los Angeles School of Black Filmmakers', in Manthia Diawara (ed.), *Black American Cinema* (New York: Routledge, 1993), 107–17; Clyde Taylor, 'The LA Rebellion: New Spirit in American Film', *Black Film Review*, 2 (1986), 2; Teshome Gabriel, *Third Cinema in the Third World: The Aesthetics of Liberation* (Ann Arbor: UMI Research Press, 1982); and Jim Pines and Paul Willemen (eds.), *Questions of Third Cinema* (London: British Film Institute, 1989).
5. In a recent interview Dash stated, 'We need films financed by Hollywood. We deserve them, and it's long overdue. Filmmaking is a business venture. It's not a charity; we have stories to be told, and studios have money to be made,' *Wide Angle*, 13: 3–4 (July–Oct., 1991), 117.
6. Mark Reid, *Redefining Black Film* (Berkeley and Los Angeles: University of California Press, 1993), 43.

7. With such a heavy emphasis on the influence of minstrelsy, however, more needs to be said about the relevant discontinuities between African-American and diaspora black film-making, given that there has been less of a minstrel influence outside the American context. Reid uses the term 'black' interchangeably with the term 'African-American', as though there are no significant differences between film-making in Africa, America, Australia, Europe, and the Caribbean. It makes no sense, however, to speak of 'independent' black film-makers in these countries in quite the same way as we speak of black independents in the United States. Reid evades discussing the quite different political and economic influences on black film-making practices in countries such as Cuba and Britain. For a discussion of independent black cinema in Britain see Reece Auguiste, 'Black Independents and Third Cinema: The British Context', in Pines and Willemen (eds.), *Questions of Third Cinema*, 212–17. For a discussion of Cuban film-making see Ana M. Lopez and Micholas P. Humy, 'Sergio Giral on Filmmaking in Cuba: An Interview', in Michael T. Martin (ed.), *Cinemas of the Black Diaspora* (Detroit: Wayne State University Press, 1995), 274–80 and Michael Chanan, *The Cuban Image* (London: British Film Institute, 1985).

8. Although what Reid means by 'control' is far from clear, some of his remarks indicate different criteria. For example, he tells us that, 'the Micheaux films produced after his company's 1929 re-incorporation cannot be considered black independent films, according to my definition, because black independent films must be produced by black-controlled film production companies'. He goes on to stipulate that, 'Although *Sweetback* was independently produced by a black, I do not consider it a black independent film. It was distributed by Jerry Gross's Cinemation Industries, a mini-major distribution company and the parent company of Cinecom theatres.' According to Reid, 'Van Peebles intensified the eroticism of his film in order to make it appeal to Cinemation.' *Redefining Black Film*, 17 and 82.

9. Ibid. 93.

10. In fact some studio-financed films by black directors with final cut privileges have done better at fulfilling Reid's demand for a revised image (e.g. Bill Duke's *Deep Cover*) than some non-Hollywood films under black control (e.g. Jamaa Fanaka's *Penitentiary* series).

11. Ibid. 125. He misses the point of Oscar Micheaux's crafty business deals to stay afloat. Two of America's finest independent black films, Julie Dash's *Daughters of the Dust* and Charles Burnett's *To Sleep with Anger*, were both studio-distributed and shown on PBS television stations. Along with these non-commercial films, Reid's narrow criteria would exclude other historically significant films such as Spencer Williams's *Blood of Jesus*, Bill Gunn's *Ganga and Hess*, and Ivan Dixon's *The Spook Who Sat by the Door* as independent black cinema because of the film-maker's studio affiliation in each case.

12. Ed Guerrero, *Framing Blackness* (Philadelphia: Temple University Press, 1993).

13. Ibid. 137.

14. Ibid.

15. See Lee's remarks in an interview with Nelson George in Spike Lee, *Spike Lee's Gotta Have It* (New York: Fireside, 1987), 38.

16. Guerrero, *Framing Blackness*, 138.

17. In her essay 'Reading the Signs, Empowering the Eye: Daughters of the Dust and the Black Independent Cinema Movement', in Diawara (ed.), *Black American Cinema*, 118–44.

18. Gunn was hired by a Hollywood studio to make a black horror film, but his intention was to gain access to the resources Hollywood offered black film-makers. The expectation of the studio was that Gunn's film would follow the pattern of other low-budget black films and reap inordinate profits. He instead made two socially

conscious films, *Ganja and Hess* (1973) and *Stop!* (1975), that were never released by the studios, but have circulated on the college–museum–film festival circuit. (Bambara ought to have told us how Gunn managed to pull this off twice!) See Manthia Diawara and Phyllis R. Klotman, 'Ganja and Hess: Vampires, Sex, and Addictions', *Black American Literature Forum*, 25 (Summer 1991).

19. Diawara (ed.), *Black American Cinema*, 137.
20. In his essay 'Black American Cinema: The New Realism', ibid. 7
21. See, for example, the criticism of Brandon Wander and Thomas Cripps. Brandon Wander, 'Black Dreams', *Film Quarterly*, 24: 1 (Fall 1975), 2–11; Thomas Cripps, *Black Film as Genre* (Bloomington: Indiana University Press, 1979), 128–40.
22. See St Clair Bourne, 'Bright Moments', *Independent Film & Video Monthly*, 11: 4 (May 1988).
23. Many blaxploitation era films were not action films. Guerrero identifies a category of positive image films that were produced in 1972. He notes that, during the black film boom 1970–3 only 47 of the 91 films were modelled on the blaxploitation action formula. He cites *Melinda, Sounder*, and *Buck and the Preacher* as examples.
24. Wander's analysis is filled with several gross misreadings due to this failure. Cripps expresses a worry about the film's influence on urban youth, but ambivalence is revealed in his statement that 'Of all the "blaxploitation" movies, *Sweetback* was most able to convey a dirt poor ghetto ambience with startling conviction.' Cripps, *Black Film as Genre*, 140.
25. See Clyde Taylor, 'Black Films in Search of a Home', *Freedomways*, 23: 4 (1983), 226–33.
26. Julie Dash's *Illusions* seems to be an exception. She used a *film noir* style to engage in a visual satire of Hollywood's portrayal of the 'tragic' mulatto who passes for a white woman. As the title suggests, the film is about subversiveness (deception) in the film industry.
27. This claim refers mainly to the use of the Hollywood hero mythology, for it is clear that Van Peebles's film was not meant to be a mainstream Hollywood film. His technique is influenced by his background as a European film-maker as well. As Cripps has noted, Van Peebles employed the social realism of *film noir* to engage in hyperbole. See his *Black Film as Genre*, 134–5.
28. In a colloquy on *Sweetback* that included St Clair Bourne, Haile Gerima, and Pearl Bowser, Van Peebles denounced the manifesto of the Third Cinema movement and argued that the blaxploitation formula was the most effective strategy to reach an otherwise unreachable black audience. Gladstone Yearwood (ed.), *Black Cinema Aesthetics* (Athens, Oh.: Ohio University, 1982), 53–66. See also Melvin Van Peebles, *The Making of Sweet Sweetback's Baadasssss Song* (New York: Lancer Books, 1971), 14.
29. It should be noted that Diawara does not discuss *Superfly*. I am interested in a more general question of the extent to which his analysis would apply to other films in this genre.
30. See Renee Ward, 'Black Films, White Profits', *Black Scholar*, 7: 8 (May 1976), 13–24; Jacqueline Bobo, ' "The Subject is Money": Reconsidering the Black Film Audience as a Theoretical Paradigm', *Black American Literature Forum*, 25: 2 (Summer 1991), 421–32; and Guerrero, *Framing Blackness*, 96–9.
31. For a discussion of the pitfalls of using the black heroic figure see Gladstone L. Yearwood, 'The Hero in Black Film: An Analysis of the Film Industry and Problems in Black Cinema', *Wide Angle*, 5: 2 (1982), 42–51.
32. St Clair Bourne also claimed that the negative criticism of *Sweetback* was class related. Yearwood, *Black Cinema Aesthetics*, 56. For Newton's analysis see Huey P. Newton, 'He Won't Bleed Me', in his *To Die for the People* (New York: Writers and Readers Publishing, 1995), 112–47.

33. Guerrero overlooks the commentary by Brandon Wander, who maintained that Sweetback not only raped women, but also was raped. *Film Quarterly*, 24: 1 (Fall 1975), 9.
34. Guerrero, *Framing Blackness*, 91.
35. Robin D. G. Kelly reports on the perpetuation of 'bad nigga' narratives in Hip Hop culture in 'Kickin' Reality, Kickin' Ballistics: The Cultural Politics of Gangsta Rap in Postindustrial Los Angeles', in Eric Perkins (ed.), *Droppin' Science: Critical Essays on Rap Music and Hip Hop Culture* (Philadelphia: Temple University Press, 1994). For a selection of these narratives see Daryl Cumber Dance, *Shuckin' and Jivin'* (Bloomington: Indiana University Press, 1978), 224–46. See also H. Nigel Thomas, *From Folklore to Fiction: A Study of Folk Heroes and Rituals in the Black American Novel* (New York: Greenwood Press, 1988), 71–9.
36. This was a question raised by Haile Gerima at the Ohio University Colloquy. Yearwood, *Black Cinema Aesthetics*, 61. See also Wander, 'Black Dreams', 9.
37. Wander, 'Black Dreams', 7.
38. See, for instance, Cheryl B. Butler, 'The Color Purple Controversy: Black Woman Spectatorship', *Wide Angle*, 13: 3–4 (July–Oct. 1991). One exception to my claim regarding feminist neglect of blaxploitation era films is Jane Gaines's essay 'White Privilege and Looking Relations: Race and Gender in Feminist Film Theory', *Screen*, 29: 4 (Autumn 1988), 59–79.
39. In her essay 'Reading through the Text: The Black Woman as Audience', in Diawara (ed.), *Black American Cinema*, 272–87.
40. Ibid. 287.
41. If the popularity of the Hughes brothers's *Menace II Society* is any indication, it seems that 'bad nigga' narratives that retain the nihilism of classic black urban folklore resonate more with black audiences than those that attempt to be morally uplifting.
42. Many were influenced by Laura Mulvey's classic essay 'Visual Pleasure and Narrative Cinema', *Screen*, 16: 3 (Autumn 1975), 6–18.
43. In his essay 'Looking for Modernism' in Diawara (ed.), *Black American Cinema*, 228–302.
44. Kobena Mercer, *Welcome to the Jungle* (New York: Routledge, 1994), 171–219.
45. Ibid. 193.
46. In her essay 'Race, Gender and Psychoanalysis in Forties Film: *Lost Boundaries*, *Home of the Brave* and *The Quiet One*', in Diawara (ed.), *Black American Cinema*, 257–71.
47. Ibid. 264.
48. In her essay 'The Oppositional Gaze: Black Female Spectators', in Diawara (ed.), *Black American Cinema*.
49. Diawara (ed.), *Black American Cinema*, 293.
50. Ibid. 294. hooks does not discuss the fact that among the audience for *Amos 'n' Andy* there was rupture along lines of class as well as gender. See Thomas Cripps, 'Amos 'n' Andy and the Debate over American Racial Integration', in John E. O'Connor, *American History/American Television: Interpreting the Video Past* (New York: Frederick Ungar Publishing Co., 1983), 33–54.
51. Diawara (ed.), *Black American Cinema*, 295.
52. Reid, *Redefining Black Film*, 25.
53. Ibid.
54. Ibid. 42.
55. Ibid. 113.
56. Ibid. 115. Reid adopts this notion of black womanism from Alice Walker. According to Walker a black womanist, like white feminists, loves and prefers other women and

women's culture, but, unlike white feminists, she also loves men and children and is not a separatist. See Reid, *Redefining Black Film*, 109 and Alice Walker, *In Search of our Mother's Gardens* (New York: Harcourt Brace Jovanovich, 1983), p. xi.

PART IV
Aesthetics

Many early or 'classical' film theorists responded with enthusiasm to the aesthetic possibilities of the new medium of cinema, either in terms of its ability to fulfil traditional aesthetic criteria (Rudolf Arnheim), or by celebrating precisely those qualities that some arbiters of taste disparaged: the mechanical basis of the image (Béla Balázs, Jean Epstein, Walter Benjamin) and its use of popular, generic forms (Erwin Panofsky, the Surrealists, Robert Warshow). However, as a marginal branch of what is sometimes regarded as a marginal area of analytic philosophy, the aesthetics of film received little attention from analytic philosophers prior to the recent wave of interest of which this anthology is a part, with the notable exception of a handful of authors like Cavell, Khatchadourian, Scruton, Sesonske, and Sparshott (see the items listed in the bibliography). Moreover, overtly aesthetic questions have had a low priority for most semiotic film theorists, who have tended to reduce aesthetic questions to ideological ones, as we noted in the introduction to the last Part. The chapter by Tommy Lott in the previous part, however, demonstrates how a concern with the political and ideological aspects of texts is quite compatible with a sensitivity to their aesthetic qualities; and with the advent of so-called 'neo-formalist' film theory (pre-eminently in the work of David Bordwell and Kristin Thompson), aesthetic issues have again become central.

One of the beneficiaries of this renewed attention to aesthetics has been the study of film music (indeed, film sound in general), and Peter Kivy's chapter here stands as another contribution to this domain of study. Kivy's chapter poses a question which arises out of the convergence of the debate in film studies concerning the functions of sound and music in film, with a consideration of the history of musical forms: why does the practice of musical scoring persist as standard in the cinema after the advent of synchronous sound, while the parallel practice of musical melodrama (in the technical, musicological sense: 'spoken drama with musical accompaniment') died away soon after its invention in the late eighteenth century? Kivy's question is of particular interest to film scholarship for two reasons. First, it demonstrates how conceptual questions may arise out of and are interrelated with empirical—in this case historical—ones. Conceptual analysis is not the desiccated, abstract practice it is sometimes depicted as by its detractors. Secondly, Kivy's analysis sheds a new light on the debates around melodrama in film studies since he is concerned not with the 'blood and thunder' popular theatre of the nineteenth century that is the usual reference-point, but with the much more specific (and short-lived) musical melodrama, and its bearing on cinema. Kivy's question is a precise and novel one: it enquires after not merely the 'aesthetic function' of musical scoring in sound film (the expression of mood and of character states) but its specific 'filmic function'. What is it that music in film does which seems to make it necessary even after the original grounds of its necessity (the absence of speech in silent film) have disappeared? Kivy's conjecture is that, even with the addition of synchronous sound, filmic representation lacks the expressive fullness of live theatrical performance.

Flo Leibowitz returns to an issue that was central to early film theorists: the expressiveness of the cinematic image. She begins by considering the various ways in which films can be expressive in their visual style and then goes on to evaluate the pertinence of various accounts of expressiveness, developed in relation to other arts, to expressiveness in movies. She focuses on three candidate theories: the psychoanalytic, 'historical-agent' theory of Richard Wollheim, developed in relation to painting; the 'imagined persona' account posited by Bruce Vermazen, an account with claims to generality but whose model is oratory; and a theory based on ascribing intentionality to the work of art itself, rather than either a real or imagined expressive agent, developed by Stephen Davies in relation to music. Leibowitz argues that Wollheim's theory is an important, rational revision of the Romantic account of artistic expression: even though the artist's intention is significant in understanding the expressive qualities of a painting, the artist need not be supposed to have been experiencing the emotion in creating the painting which is expressive of it. Nevertheless, she still finds vestiges of the 'Romantic caricature' in Wollheim's account (art is the expulsion of unhappiness), and argues that a wider range of motivations for artistic expressiveness, including relatively 'impersonal' ones, must be recognized, particularly (if not uniquely) in the case of film-making (in this connection, readers may also wish to consult Berys Gaut's chapter on authorship and collaboration in Part II). In her commentary on Vermazen, Leibowitz moves still further away from an account of expressiveness tied to an expressive agent, for she argues that, at least in the case of films, positing an 'imagined persona' who is responsible for the expressive qualities of a movie is redundant. She follows Davies in arguing that, as in the case of music, expressive qualities, and the intentionality they are necessarily linked with, can be ascribed more economically to the appearance of the artwork itself. Like the chapters in Part II, then, Leibowitz brings back intentionality into the fold of respectable (indeed, essential) film critical concepts.

Deborah Knight takes up another concern of early film theorists, one that has been addressed more recently by a number of writers in the analytic tradition: the aesthetic appeal of popular genres. She does not address the question of 'art' directly, but focuses instead upon a supposed paradox of genre or 'junk' fiction consumption, anatomized by Noël Carroll in the following way: assuming that consumers of such fiction are rational, why would they repeatedly engage with texts whose outcomes they know in advance (precisely because they are generic and highly formulaic)? Carroll solves the paradox by claiming that genre texts—like any narrative text—engage viewers in the cognitive activities of testing out hypotheses concerning the likely outcome of the action. Knight, however, argues that the 'paradox of junk fiction' is not so much false as ill-conceived: there is nothing irrational about consuming genre texts because not every text is exactly the same as every other, and genres are not absolutely fixed categories. Moreover, Knight argues that some problematic assumptions that inform the paradox posited by Carroll also inhabit his solution. Carroll assumes that narrative comprehension involves grasping cause–effect relations in a linear plot structure and ignores the dimension of 'entelechial causality', that aspect of narrative comprehension which is concerned not simply with how a plot develops but with how all the actions are understood as part of an overall 'configuration'. Through a detailed examination of a number of film genres and genre films, Knight argues that entelechial causality is central for understanding genre fictions in which the 'horizon of expectations' is explicitly framed.

13

Music in the Movies:
A Philosophical Enquiry

PETER KIVY

'Natura abhorret vacuum.'

The two major forms of 'talked' drama, movies and plays, are sharply distinguished in numerous ways, as artistic practices. But one of the most notable and, I shall argue, most mystifying of these ways is in regard to *music*. For the presence of music in a spoken play is a rare occurrence— although there is a tradition for it—whereas what is rare in the cinema is the *absence* of music. The movies have had, almost from the very beginning, a running musical background. And whereas it is fairly clear what the reason for that was in the silent era, it is by no means obvious, as I shall suggest later on, why music endured in its peculiar relation to the cinema with the advent of the talkies.

What I aim to do in this chapter is, first, to show what the roots of movie music are, in the tradition of Western art music: in particular, music for the stage. I shall argue that, in spite of the marked difference in technological resources, the basic aesthetic practices of music in the movies are of a piece with a musical tradition that goes back at least as far as the invention of opera at the close of the sixteenth century.

Second, I aim to show that consideration of the specific musical practice music in the movies most closely resembles, indeed is a species of, namely, eighteenth-century 'melodrama', suggests to us a puzzle as to *why* the former was an artistic failure that quickly withered on the vine, and why the latter endured after the advent of sound film: after, that is, the condition that made the *raison d'être* of music in the movies *obvious*, no longer obtained; why, in other words, music in cinema outlived the necessity of its apparent function in the silent film.

In the end I shall venture the most tentative conjecture as to why music in the movies has endured, while its analogue in spoken plays, namely, melodrama, was a palpable aesthetic non-starter. But my conjecture is

I am extremely grateful to Richard Allen, Noël Carroll, Peter Sacks, Alex Sesonske, and Murray Smith, who have all read earlier versions of this chapter, and provided useful and generous comments. They have tried as hard as they could to save me from my ignorance and folly. Where they have failed, the blame is entirely mine.

offered with the utmost diffidence. And anyone is free to offer another. What, I think, cannot be avoided is the question to which my conjecture responds.[1]

I. SOME HISTORICAL BACKGROUND

For present purposes the beginning of music for the theatre, as we know it, can be located in the 'invention' of opera as we know it, at the very close of the sixteenth century. Of course music for the theatre does not spring out, fully armed, in 1597—the date of *Daphne*, which tradition calls the 'first' opera. There was theatre before 1597, and music in it, going back, no doubt, to the ancient Greeks. But this is not the place, nor am I the person to undertake the stupendous task of presenting a history, if such a thing is even possible, of the musical theatre.

In any case, the musical techniques that developed with startling speed in the first years of the seventeenth century, and the operatic forms they had evolved into by the close of the eighteenth, provide, essentially, the full aesthetic arsenal from which film music has drawn its weapons. So there it is convenient for us to begin.

A group of the Italian nobility, intellectuals, poets, composers—the so-called Camerata—brought what we know as 'opera' into the world, in Florence, at the beginning of the seventeenth century. Under the theoretical guidance of Vincenzo Galilei, father of the great Galileo, the composers Jacopo Peri and Giulio Caccini began composing a kind of musical declamation for solo voice, which they called *stile rapresentativo*—the style of the actor—and which was meant to represent in music the emotional tone and cadence of the human speaking voice.

By 1608—the date of the first great operatic masterpiece, Monteverdi's *Orfeo*—the *stile rapresentativo* had evolved into a dramatic representation of human declamation unsurpassed in its sensitivity to the expressive nuances of speech. As a musical rendering of human utterance it remains still, in Monteverdi, one of the most artistically successful.

Yet at the very outset, opera (or *dramma per musica*) had built into it a tension that has characterized the operatic enterprise to this day. For as successful as the *stile rapresentativo* was as a dramatic vehicle, it failed to satisfy what might be called our desire for the 'pure musical parameters'. It was 'music' but it was not *music*. It does not reward the kind of musical expectations we bring to the 'closed' musical forms, either of the seventeenth century or of the centuries before and after. The tension between the demands of dramatic declamation and those of the pure musical parameters has defined the driving force of opera and opera 'reform', opera theory, and opera criticism, from the very beginning to the present moment.[2]

By the end of the seventeenth century a highly successful 'compromise' was reached between the 'dramatic' and the 'musical' in the form of the so-called 'number opera'. So successful was this compromise that it endured as a going concern past the middle of the nineteenth century, and produced such exemplary operatic achievements as the *opera seria* of Handel, the comic masterpieces of Mozart and Rossini, and, still in fairly recognizable form, the great works of Verdi's early and middle periods.

In its most 'unpolluted' form, in the eighteenth century, number opera consists of a chain of separate musical movements, 'numbers', each of which displays a closed musical form. These musical numbers, principally aria, duet, trio, the larger ensemble, and chorus, are separated by *secco recitative*, which is to say, a rapid, conversational parlando with little or no musical interest—'minimal music', if you will—through which the plot is advanced by 'conversation' and 'soliloquy', accompanied solely by keyboard, as in Mozartian *opera buffa*, or keyboard and instrumental bass, the 'basso continuo', in baroque *opera seria*.

What is of special interest for us, and not yet mentioned, is a musical technique somewhere betwixt and between the fully closed operatic 'numbers' and the connective tissue of the *secco recitative*, music's limiting case, so to speak. I am referring to what is usually called, in English, 'accompanied recitative'. In accompanied recitative, the singing voice has full orchestral support, but retains its declamatory, non-melodic character, although with highlighted musical and expressive interest.

The star performer, in accompanied recitative, is the orchestra. And it functions in two ways: both as dramatic and expressive background to the singing voice, and as a musical interlude between appearances of the singing voice, in which it serves as dramatic and expressive commentator on the sentiments of the singer, in whatever character he or she represents. In one kind of accompanied recitative the orchestra is silent while the singer declaims, only entering when the singer falls silent. In another kind, the orchestra provides a running accompaniment to the singing voice. And in a third, the two above-mentioned are combined, the orchestra sometimes being present while the singer declaims, and sometimes silent.

The accompanied recitative, then, is a powerful as well as flexible medium for musico-dramatic expression. And as such, it endured in clearly recognizable form throughout most of the nineteenth century.

But in addition to its indispensable dramatic role in opera, accompanied recitative gave birth, in 1770, through the fertile brain of Jean-Jacques Rousseau, to the strange, short-lived theatrical phenomenon known as 'melodrama' (or, sometimes, 'monodrama'). In France it was still-born. In Germany it had a brief yet noteworthy career, attracting, among the immortals, no less than Mozart, Beethoven, and Carl Maria von Weber. And it surfaces now and again (in Debussy's *Martyrdom of Saint Sebastian*, for example). It yet lives, probably unbeknownst to most of the practitioners, in movie music. To a brief discussion of this 'exotic' art form I now turn my attention.

2. MELODRAMA

Even as late as the eighteenth century, although opera had been a going concern for more than 100 years, many still thought of it as, in Dr Johnson's famous description, 'an irrational entertainment', and still had trouble with dramatis personae who sang rather than spoke. Conversation in musical tones seemed an absurdity, though conversation in blank verse, or even rhymed couplets, did not. (I dare say many sophisticated theatre-goers today still feel the same way.)

Melodrama was an answer to that difficulty, keeping the music in the pit, speech on the stage. It was, in other words, spoken drama with musical accompaniment. The idea of film music, then, existed fully fledged, some 100 or more years before the invention of moving pictures.

The first such production, *Pygmalion*, words by Rousseau, whose idea it was, music by one Horace Coignet, was performed in Lyons, in 1770. The French let it alone. But in 1772, Anton Schweitzer wrote new music to a German translation of Rousseau's words, and had it performed in Weimar. Goethe loved it. So did Germany. The love affair was brief, however, as we shall see.

Melodrama, as a separate dramatic form, had its first and only 'master' in Georg Benda. Benda was a composer of real talent, if not genius; and his melodramas, *Medea* and *Ariadne auf Naxos*, so impressed Mozart, in 1778, that he wrote to his father: 'I think that most operatic recitatives should be treated in this way—and only sung occasionally, when the words *can be perfectly expressed by the music.*'[3]

It is more than mildly interesting—indeed prophetic—that Mozart, from the start, did not see melodrama as a separate dramatic entity, but as a dramatic technique: a substitute, *in opera*, for accompanied recitative. And it is also worth noting that Mozart perceived immediately what the origin and nature of melodrama was. Again to his father, in the same letter:

You know, of course, that there is no singing in it, only recitation, to which the music is like a sort of obbligato accompaniment to a recitative. Now and then the words are spoken while the music goes on, and this produces the finest effect.[4]

Thus, as Mozart immediately perceived, melodrama is accompanied recitative with spoken instead of sung declamation. The 'opera sceptic' has what he wants: spoken conversation rather than the 'absurdity' of conversation in song.

One further point in Mozart's letter to his father deserves special notice. Melodrama, like accompanied recitative, from whence it came, made use of *both* the declamation without and the declamation with accompanying music. That is to say, sometimes the voice declaims between 'comments' and 'preludes' of the orchestra; and sometimes it declaims with orchestral accompaniment. It was the latter that most charmed Mozart. ('Now and then the words are spoken while the music goes on, and this produces the finest effect.') It is the latter that film music has been able to exploit beyond anything Benda could have attempted. I think that for this reason Mozart would have loved the movies.

Why, then, did melodrama, in spite of captivating the man some would argue is the greatest composer the stage has ever known, fail to flourish even in that great composer's hands? Looked at from one point of view, the answer is all too obvious. Looked at as a solution to *the* problem of opera, the problem of reconciling music with drama, melodrama fails. For it fails to *be* music: it fails to give a full-blooded musical experience. Opera is drama-made-music.[5] Melodrama is drama with . . . well, with a musical *texture*. It never became, in the hands of Benda or anyone else, drama-made-music. It did endure well beyond the eighteenth century, indeed into the twentieth, as one dramatic technique within opera, as well as within other musical forms, the stirring dungeon scene in Beethoven's *Fidelio* being the best-known and perhaps greatest example. But as a separate 'operatic' enterprise it did not survive beyond its first incarnations.

But why view melodrama as 'opera' at all—as, that is, a *musical* form? Why not, rather, view it as a genre of spoken drama, as, in fact, films are viewed—spoken drama with music? Film, after all, is not viewed as a musical form but as a form of spoken drama, its musical track to the contrary notwithstanding.[6]

But viewed in this way—viewed, that is, as spoken drama with a musical 'background'—melodrama becomes deeply puzzling in its rapid demise, because its modern counterpart, the talky, has retained *its* musical 'background' beyond its *obvious* purpose, which is to say, to fill the vacuum of silence in the silent film. (More of that in a moment.) So theatrical melodrama withered on the vine, while filmic melodrama flourished (and flourishes). *Why?* That is my puzzle. And to solve it we must now turn to film music itself.

3. THE VACUUM OF SILENCE

Even in its most primitive form, as a more or less improvised piano accompaniment consisting of bits and pieces from the classical and semi-classical repertoire, music in the movies was doing the same things as it was and had been doing in opera and melodrama from at least the eighteenth century, indeed, was speaking the same dramatic and expressive 'language'. And if one should ask the question what the purpose of musical accompaniment was in the silent film *after* it ceased to be that of drowning out the projector's noise[7] (if that ever *was* its purpose) then one correct answer would be: to do all of the things for the silent moving picture that it does for sung drama, i.e. opera, or the spoken drama, i.e. melodrama: to, in general terms, provide an expressively and dramatically appropriate musical fabric. I am going to call this multiple function of music in the cinema its 'aesthetic' function, or, where I am more specific, its aesthetic functions (in the plural). And the point is that music in the silent cinema shares this aesthetic function, or these aesthetic functions, with music in opera and melodrama as well.

There is, however, another sense to the question of music's function in the silent cinema. When asked with this other sense intended, what the questioner wants to know is why music, given its internal function in the silent movie, is there in the first place. Why was an expressive and dramatic background wanted, or needed, in the silent film? That is the sense to the question, after the aesthetic function of music within the silent film is given. Call what *this* question is seeking music's 'filmic function'. What is the filmic function of music in silent cinema?

The answer seems to me obvious enough, and ought to be completely uncontroversial. The filmic function of music in the silent movies is to fill the *vacuum of silence*. It serves *some* of the functions of speech and, marginally, even of the other sounds of the world: storms, battles, and so forth. But principally it serves the function of speech. And if one wonders why *music* was chosen for this role, the answer must be, what else? It was already in place, it was easily assimilable, and it had a 200-year tradition of serving just such dramatic functions in opera and spoken drama.

Were these new or startling ideas, or were they less than perfectly obvious, I might be inclined to dilate upon them at greater length. But they are neither new nor startling, and so I need say little to make my point.

In a spoken play, an actor communicates to an audience with sound and visual appearance. And when he speaks, he communicates both with the matter of his speech, and, of course, with the tone and inflection of his voice. In dumb show he only has gesture, countenance, and bodily behaviour at his disposal. Speech is denied him. He cannot communicate in sound.

Music can help to make up for that deficit. It not only adds the dimension of sound to the silent screen world, but, more importantly, it adds the dimension of *expressive* sound. It cannot give the silent actress the *matter* of words, but it can give the *emotive expression*. And, indeed, because it comes in company with a visual image of expressive behaviour, it can, as Noël Carroll has insightfully pointed out, do so with far greater specificity than it could do as music alone. As Carroll puts it: 'Wedding the musical system to the movie system, then, supplies the kind of reference to particularize the broad expressivity of the musical system.'[8]

There seems to me, then, to be no very great mystery about what the filmic function of music is in the silent movie. It adds the dimension of sound to a silent world. More importantly, it adds the dimension of sonic *expression* that in a world of sound is the office of human utterance and human speech. But now along comes the talking picture, and at a stroke the rules of the game are changed forever, the vacuum of silence filled up. The cinema possesses, with the coming of sound, all the expressive resources of the spoken theatre—and more. For it then possesses not merely the expressive resources of articulate speech and inarticulate utterance— the word and the groan—but all of those sounds, unheard in the theatre, that the technique of the soundtrack can provide: thus, not merely the word and the groan, but the heartbeat and footstep.[9] (I will say more of this later on.)

My question—the question of this chapter—is *why* the music plays on when the sound comes in? If the filmic function of music, in the silent era, is to fill the vacuum left by the total absence of expressive sound, why does it outlast its function when the full resources of expressive sound fill that vacuum in the era of the talking picture?

What's the problem?, the sceptical reader well may ask. If pasta substitutes for meat during Lent, that hardly suggests that *after* Lent we will want to give up pasta altogether. Why not have both? Why not meatballs *and* spaghetti? And, by parity of reasoning, why not have speech, sound, *and* music in the movies? The Lent of silence may be over, but there is no reason therefore to give music up, when it makes such a rich aesthetic contribution to the enterprise—richer than ever, indeed, with the added technological resources of the perfectly coordinated music track.

This answer may satisfy some. But anyone who knows the historical roots of film music in eighteenth-century melodrama will remain *un*satisfied by such a facile answer to our question. For the failed promise of Georg Benda's intriguing experiment, even in the hands of the great Mozart himself, whose magic touch in the musical theatre has never been surpassed, gives us to wonder why the selfsame experiment, two centuries later, in the talking picture, should have been such a rousing success.

4. GHOSTS

Perhaps the best-known, as well as the most bizarre, attempt to explain the filmic function of music in the talking film is that of Hanns Eisler and Theodor Adorno in their 1947 book *Composing for the Films*.

Eisler and Adorno eschewed the obvious, and, in my view, obviously correct, answer to the question of music's role in the silent film, namely, that it is a substitute for human vocal expression, both linguistic and inarticulate. The reason for that seems fairly clear. They wanted an answer to that question that would hold good for the presence of music in the talking film as well; and it is not at all obvious how the expressive role music plays in silent film can possibly also be the reason for its presence in the talky, since what it is a substitute for, talk, is no longer absent.

For that reason, I suspect, Eisler and Adorno sought a less obvious role than expression for music in the silent film—a role that they saw as possible for it in the sound film as well. Of music in the silent era, they wrote: 'The pure cinema must have had a ghostly effect like that of the shadow play—shadows and ghosts have always been associated. The major function of music . . . consisted in appeasing the evil spirits unconsciously dreaded.' The role of music in the silent film play, then, was 'to exorcise fear or help the spectator absorb the shock'.[10]

Furthermore, according to Eisler and Adorno, the ghosts persisted into the era of sound, although we now had talking ghosts. (An even more frightening prospect perhaps?) Thus, '*the talking picture, too, is mute.* The characters in it are not speaking people but speaking effigies. . . . Their bodiless mouths utter words in a way that must seem disquieting to anyone uninformed.'[11]

Well, so if the ghosts remain, the need for musical exorcism remains as well. 'The sound pictures have changed this original function of music less than might be imagined.'[12] The magic is still wanted, and music is still there to provide it. That, in brief, is the ectoplasmic theory of Eisler and Adorno.

Noël Carroll makes rather quick work of rejecting Eisler and Adorno's proposal; and although there *are* two grains of truth in it (as will become apparent later on), I have no reason to go beyond Carroll's refutation of their proposal as it originally stands. Carroll writes of their account of music in the silent film:

their theory seems based on pretty flimsy evidence. They claim that film spectators feel discomfort viewing cinematic images *because* we find them ghostly. . . . Informal evidence for this might be that audiences are often restless during silent films, unaccompanied by music, and frequently complain about the silence. But perhaps we should take spectators at their word. . . . Perhaps it is the *silence* that strikes them and not some putative fear of ghosts.[13]

As for the talky,

pace Adorno and Eisler, one does not encounter comparable complaints with sound films. There is, to my knowledge, no evidence for believing that spectators respond to sound films in the way Eisler and Adorno say they do. . . . Adorno and Eisler base their analysis on postulating a state in the spectator that has no basis in the data of film viewing.[14]

Having dismissed the proposal of Eisler and Adorno in this wise, Carroll has a positive proposal of his own to make that merits serious consideration. In his answer to the question of music's function in the cinema, Carroll offers a number of suggestions as to what I have been calling its *aesthetic* function that are, it appears to me, right on the money. But in so far as they are not answers to the question of music's *filmic* function, they need not concern us here.

However, Carroll does offer one suggestion that I would characterize as addressing the filmic function of music; that is, why the expressive resources of music are utilized in film, as opposed to theatre. Carroll's answer is what might be called a 'sociological' one.

Movies are a means of popular expression. They aspire for means of communication that can be grasped almost immediately by untutored audiences. Another way of putting this is to say that moviemakers seek devices that virtually guarantee that the audience will follow the action in the way that the filmmaker deems appropriate.[15]

It being the case, therefore, that movies are for a 'popular' audience, the musical track is necessary as an expressive prop to assure a correct expressive reading by the unsophisticated viewer. Thus, 'given the almost direct expressive impact of music', its presence in the movies 'assures that the untutored spectators of the mass audience will have access to the desired expressive quality and, in turn, will see the given scene under its aegis.'[16]

I do not have any doubt at all but that Carroll's conjecture is altogether correct as a partial answer to the question of music's filmic function. I strongly suspect, however, that it cannot be the whole answer for the following reason. Were the filmic function of the musical track only to give the unsophisticated movie-goer an expressive aid, I believe there would have evolved a genre of cinematic 'high art' where the musical track would have been dispensed with, since such a genre would be aimed at a sophisticated audience which, on Carroll's hypothesis, would not require it. Film-makers, after all, aim at different levels of audience sophistication with different films. And whereas the general run of Hollywood movies was and is aimed at a mass audience, 'art films' of various kinds are not, necessarily; yet these films for sophisticates do not lack musical tracks. To the contrary, where one would expect, on Carroll's hypothesis, a decline in the prominence of the music, there is frequently an increase in musical quality and involvement, producing such memorable scores as that for Olivier's *Hamlet*, to name but one outstanding example.

Thus, although I by no means reject Carroll's 'sociological' answer to the question of music's filmic function in the talky, I think that it must be amplified with another, which holds not merely for unsophisticated movie audiences but movie audiences *tout court*. And to that answer, my answer, I now turn my attention.

5. THE VACUUM OF SOUND

I said in my discussion of Eisler and Adorno that there are two grains of truth in their theory, bizarre though it is. They are, I think, first, that what I call the filmic function of music must be more or less the same for both sound and silent film and, second, that this function must have something to do with the way they characterize the personages of the sound film, namely, as 'speaking effigies'. But it is my view, as we have seen, that the filmic function of music in the silent era was to fill an expressive gap produced by the vacuum of silence. And if, as I also think, it performs the same filmic function in the sound film, then it follows that some gap or other must still remain even after the vacuum of silence has been filled up by speech.

If I am right, then, that something essential is still missing from cinema, even with all the resources of the modern soundtrack in place, which the musical track must be seen as filling in for, what can that 'something' be? I propose a simple answer: again, as in silent film, it is some aspect of *human expression* which the 'speaking effigies' cannot provide.

There is some evidence for this in the very nature of theatre music itself, as it has been constituted at least since the beginning of the seventeenth century, particularly in the opera. For although it would be a serious mistake to suggest that music has only one purpose in opera, and other forms of musical theatre, the dominant one has always been as a medium for the representation and expression of the emotive states of mind of the dramatis personae. This fact is so well known as to require no argument here. Emotive expression in the musical stage is to be found, primarily, neither in word nor gesture, but in *music*. Film music, for the most part, shares this role, as Carroll has pointed out: its primary purpose is always expressive: expressive of the dominant emotion or emotions of character or scene.

But that in itself is not enough to demonstrate convincingly that the expressiveness of music in the sound film is there to fill a gap. It may *suggest* that possibility. However, the sceptical reader will naturally want to know exactly what the gap is in expression or why one might have reason to believe there is one, besides the mere presence of expressive music.

In silent film the expressive gap is obvious: it is the gap left by the absence of all the emotive expression accomplished by the human voice. But in the talking picture all of that emotive expression is restored: for there the actor and actress have ceased to be dumb, have regained all of the expression of which the noise-making human animal is capable. But does the talking filmic *image*, Adorno and Eisler's speaking effigy, have all of the resources of human expression *tout court*? I suspect it does not. And although I cannot provide an iron-clad argument for it, I can at least suggest wherein my suspicions lie.

To begin with, let me return again, for a moment, to the hypothesis of Eisler and Adorno. In the course of developing their unlikely explanation of music in the movies based upon a fear of the image, they emphasize the lack, in cinema, of a third dimension. The characters of film, they write, are 'endowed with all the features of the pictorial, the photographic two-dimensionality, the lack of spatial depth'.[17]

I cannot believe, actually, that the two-dimensionality of the screen image can be mined for very much. We scarcely perceive the screen image without depth, any more than we do the picture space of Renaissance painting. But to follow out their theme, perhaps there is, metaphorically speaking, a 'dimension' lacking in the filmic image that music is there to compensate for, if not substitute for, even when the image speaks. I think that there is; and what it is I hope to explain.

Everything philosophical analysis has revealed to us in recent years about the concept of human emotive expression, and the reading thereof, testifies to how fragile it really is, when one wants to get beyond the very basic emotions like fear or anger or happiness into the more subtle distinctions: how dependent on what the 'intentional objects' of the emotions may be.[18] We know how difficult it is to read human emotive expression, except in the most general terms, out of real context, and in the absence of the emotional setting.

Well, this is nothing to the present purpose, it will be doubtless objected, because in the sound film all the disambiguating cues are present, as they are in 'real life'. But does it have *all* of them? It is not, after all, 'real life'. Of course, it will be replied, neither is legitimate theatre 'real life'. What does spoken theatre have that the talky lacks? That is the question.

Well one thing spoken theatre has that even sound movies do not is the *real presence* of human beings. Does that make a difference? Let me suggest that we have at least some prima-facie evidence and some anecdotal evidence as well in favour of its really mattering for the communication of emotion whether we confront a talking filmic image, a 'speaking effigy', or the real presence: an actor or actress in the flesh. We have some reason to think—I do not say it is overwhelming or conclusive—that being in the real presence of the speaker, even in the public ambience of the legitimate stage, provides a more intimate expressive connection and more subtle expressive cues than can be got in the movies, isolated in darkness, from a talking image. And the reason for that reduction in power and connection seems to

me completely unmysterious, even if the nuts and bolts are not well understood. Nor does it have aught to do with ghostly metaphysics, but with the
perfectly reasonable conjecture that a physically present human being offers
more expressive cues than a moving photographic image, even though it
talks.

But what are these additional expressive cues, it will fairly be asked, that
the real presence exhibits and the film lacks? My altogether disappointing
answer is that I do not know, though I hope to amplify that answer
somewhat in some of my following remarks. So I must allow, at this point
in the argument, that the sceptical reader may well say of my conjecture
what Noël Carroll said of the theory of Eisler and Adorno: 'based on pretty
flimsy evidence.' Yes, that is so. Yet it is not based on no evidence at all. And
it is, I submit, an eminently sensible conjecture that accords well with our
ordinary experience of human expression and interpersonal transactions.
Who does not feel the relative remoteness of the electronic or filmic image,
as compared to the real presence of a human being, where emotive communication is concerned? Doubtless, many of the emotive cues are experienced
but semi-consciously, if consciously at all. (More of that anon.) But who
doubts that they are there?

Well, perhaps that last rhetorical question is the result of a quite unjustified confidence. Doubtless there are doubters. What more can we say to
dispel their doubts?

6. A SECOND OPINION

As I have said, I offer my hypothesis with regard to the filmic function of
music tentatively, and probably with as many misgivings as the reader who
receives it. And perhaps one way to remove at least *some* of the misgivings
(I doubt if I can remove them all) would be to present an alternative
hypothesis, a second opinion that may seem inviting at first, but turns out
to be not so attractive as it first appears. Here, then, is another proposal for
the filmic function of music in the talking film. It is less 'elegant', more
complex than the first, but, maybe because of that, more convincing to those
who do not share my intuition of a remaining expressive vacuum in the
talky. I shall argue, however, that it has problems of its own that render it,
at least as I perceive things, less plausible than the more simple and elegant
one it is meant to replace.

Assume, for starters, that my account of the filmic function of music in
the silent era is, on the whole, correct, that, in other words, music is filling
the expressive vacuum that the absence of human, emotively expressive
speech creates. Assume further, if you like, although I do not think it is
essential to the proposal, what might be called a principle of musical

'squatter's rights'. Once music was firmly in place in the movies, it would have tended to stick, unless there were some powerful force to evict it after the advent of sound. It was solidly entrenched and therefore a familiar element in the motion picture, whose removal would have itself caused feelings of angst, dislocation, and deprivation of an expressive element the viewer had come to expect.

Furthermore, in suggesting the analogy between talking film and spoken theatre, it may well be objected that I ignored another analogy, every bit as obvious and valid, between talking film and silent film. For, after all, the talking film, unlike spoken theatre, provides opportunities for what might be called 'scenic intervals', which will be empty of people, and therefore empty of speech—perhaps, indeed, empty of sound altogether. Music, so the argument might go, is needed to fill the sound vacuum that remains in the gaps between talking—gaps that hardly ever exist in legitimate theatre.[19]

The problem I have with this suggested alternative explanation is that it provides no reason for why the music is not reserved solely for the gaps: why, that is, it accompanies speech as well, which it manifestly does in so many sound films. Nor, it turns out, does it even explain, really, why it should accompany the scenic gaps either.

The problem we began with, remember, was why melodrama did not survive as an autonomous artistic practice where its twentieth-century descendant, the sound movie with music, did. Melodrama is a form of drama in which words are spoken, with musical accompaniment, opera a form of drama where the words are sung and musically accompanied, theatre a form of drama from which music is all but absent, sound cinema a form of drama where the words are spoken with musical accompaniment a good deal of the time. Opera, theatre, and sound cinema have survived and flourished, melodrama has not, apparently because spoken words with musical accompaniment was not an artistically viable enterprise. Why, then, is it an artistically viable enterprise in sound cinema? That is problem, and it remains, whether or not music does have the filmic function of filling the gaps of silence between the episodes of talking: filling, that is, as it does in silent cinema, the vacuum of silence.

But, furthermore, it turns out to be false even that, as a filler of the gaps between episodes of dialogue, music has the filmic function, as it does in silent cinema, of filling the vacuum of silence left by the absence of speech. For the scenic gaps between dialogue are either, in life, themselves silent, for example, a city asleep, or a quiet landscape; or they are noisy in life, for example, a city awake with traffic, or a prairie alive with cattle. If the latter, then the soundtrack provides the appropriate sonic background; if the former, the absence of sound is not what I have been calling the vacuum of silence at all, because there was no sound to begin with. The vacuum of silence is a sonic space with the sound sucked out, as in silent cinema. But the silence of the world is truly represented by the silence of the screen; and there should be no felt need for music to fill in that silence at all.

Is there a felt need for music to fill the silence of a silent world? If so, and it seems that there is, since music obtrudes even there, then even *there* there must be a vacuum. But what does a filmic representation of a silent city, or a silent landscape, lack that its real-life counterparts possess? Could it be that some subtle expressiveness, in some way analogous to the expressiveness that, on my hypothesis, is lost in the transfer from the real human presence to the filmic image, is also lost in the transference of in-life silent scenes to their filmic representations? Well, after all, our non-peopled world—the world of mountains and fields, animals and plants, machines and artefacts—has expressive properties of its own, does it not? Or is that too improbable a hypothesis to entertain? And does the filmic image of these creatures and things also lack a subtle essence that music has come to restore?

Even more puzzling still, music is even present, more often than not, in gaps that are full of noise, that is to say, in noisy landscapes. So even where the city is awake with traffic, or the prairie alive with cattle, the sounds of traffic and cattle seem not to suffice. Even here the sound of music is felt to be required. Even here, where sight *and* sound are made present, with all of the technical resources the cinematographer and sound engineer at our command, the expressiveness of music seems to be wanted. What else can it be wanted for but some subtle essence of expressiveness that these impressive resources lack? The chase without the music of the chase? Unthinkable!

In any event, far from solving the problem of music's filmic function in sound cinema, the theory of the gaps (if I may so call it) raises a problem just as puzzling, if not more so, than the one it fails to solve. And so I will leave it for someone else, perhaps, to make more of than I have been able to do, returning to my original hypothesis, for the purpose of further elucidation.

7. A REFINEMENT

Now I am not, of course, suggesting that emotive expression, *tout court*, fails to be captured by the filmic or photographic image. Indeed, there is strong evidence that facial configurations, in particular, are universal in the species, and, clearly, transfer quite adequately from the real presence to the photographic or even painterly image. The research of Paul Ekman, for example, has made this quite apparent. But it has also made quite apparent how limited the universal emotive repertory is. Ekman writes in this regard:

The evidence of universality in emotional expression is limited to the emotions of happiness, surprise, fear, anger, disgust, and sadness. We expect that there are also universal facial expressions for interest and, perhaps, shame. There may be other emotions for which there is also a universal facial expression, but probably not many.[20]

Thus, to the extent that the filmic image relies on facial expression, it is limited to a rather small and unsubtle repertory of emotions. Indeed beyond this, even speech does not seem to be the major, or at least the sole, means of divining human emotion. For human beings, generally, do not, so to say, wear their hearts on their sleeves, and tend to 'manage' their emotive expressions, as Ekman puts it, which is to say, they to a certain extent mask or control the revelation of their inner states. Nevertheless, emotive expression tends to 'leak' through the control system; and, Ekman has concluded, 'there is more leakage in body movements than in either words or facial movement'.[21] But even body language, apparently, is not of itself the basic key to the reading of human emotions. Indeed, the key turns out to be very complex. Ekman writes:

The estimate that emotion is present is more likely to be correct when [among other things]

— The response system changes are complex, when it is not just a facial, or skeletal, or vocal, or coping response, but a combination;
— the changes are organized, in the sense of being interrelated and distinctive for one or a combination of emotions.[22]

What emerges, then, from Ekman's work is that recognition of the human emotions, in any of their subtlety, is a matter of recognition of extremely subtle cues, well beyond the obvious ones of facial expression, body movement, or even speech. We are, either by nature, or nurture, or both, finely tuned to these cues; and if they are absent, our ability to recognize emotions in others will be dislocated.

Now it is clear that the sound film captures all of the gross parameters of emotive expression, notably facial configuration and speech, that convey, when unmasked, the basic repertory of human emotions. What Ekman's work suggests, though, is that human beings, because of the dual phenomena of management and leakage, are attuned to far more subtle cues than those. I hypothesize that it is these more subtle cues that may be lost in the filmic image, even when it speaks, and the absence of which the audience 'feels', 'senses', 'intuits' as an emotive vacuum, a vacuum that, I have been arguing, music helps to fill. Or, perhaps another way of putting it, it warms the emotional climate, even though it cannot substitute for the emotive cues that are lost.

Of course the legitimate theatre cannot, any more than can the cinema, present to its audience *all* of the subtle emotive cues of which I speak. For the stage actor no more than the movie actor is really angry when he 'expresses' anger, in love when he 'expresses' love, *pace* the 'method' (and other such myths, which may be true in theory but impossible in practice). Many of the cues that evade our management may be unknown to us, and some that are not, beyond conscious control. But those that the actor can reproduce, either by 'art' or by 'instinct', are going, so I am suggesting, to be harder to pick up out of the real presence. Thus the cinema will, to appropriate Plato's image, be at two removes from emotive reality, an image of a pretence. And it is the image of the pretence that, so I am arguing, is most in need of the emotive enhancing of which music is so eminently capable.

That last remark merits amplification. It is certainly not in music's power to fine-tune emotive expression beyond the offices of human language. Indeed, the shoe is on the other foot, as I have argued elsewhere: language, in vocal music, fine-tunes musical expression, for music's expressive repertory, without the assistance of linguistic props, not coincidentally, in my view, is pretty much that of Ekman's catalogue of facial expressions.[23] Thus what music adds to the emotive pot is not a functional equivalent for what expression the talking filmic image may lose but provides expressive oomph for that expression that remains: the sadness is sadder, the happiness happier. To adduce an analogy, the uncle cannot replace the mother, but he can become an additional father, if you will, strengthening the father that is already there. The loss remains, but is less keenly felt because what remains has been amplified.

Now at this point in the argument a comment is perhaps in order concerning not what might be lost to expression when we go from the real presence to the filmic sound image, but what might be *gained*, through both cinematographic techniques of all kinds, and the techniques of the soundtrack, which is not, of course, nor need be just a recording of the same sounds that would be heard in the theatre, or even in life, but sounds that we could not hear although they are nevertheless there, and perhaps of expressive use.[24]

Let me adduce an example of each. Perhaps the most obvious example of visual advantage which cinema has over the theatre is the close-up. And since so much expression of the grosser variety, of the basic emotions, is displayed in the face, the expressive contribution of the close-up is obvious. I can get closer to a person's face in the filmic image than I can ever get either in theatre or in life.

As for sound, let me just mention an old chestnut: the beating heart. The sound of another's heartbeat is something of course that one almost never hears in life, under usual circumstances, or in the theatre at all. But it is easy enough to do, and has been done more than once, to give the impression, through the soundtrack, of hearing a person's heartbeat. And a fast, loud heartbeat, when other cues are in place, is a dead giveaway to, and a standard cinematic icon for, *fear*.

Now both the visual close-up, and the sound close-up (if I may so call it), can be, then, expression-enhancers. But the question is whether they help to fill the expressive vacuum of which I have been speaking: the vacuum occupied in life, and, at least partially in the theatre, I have been arguing, by those subtle cues alluded to by Ekman and others. The answer seems to me to be negative. Here is why.

The visual and sound close-up are, of course, artistic devices. But the subtle emotive cues are 'in-life' occurrences; and our emotive sensibilities are tuned, either by nurture, or nature, or both, to those in-life occurrences. Few get within three inches of another's nose, in life, no one lays her ear on his chest, unless one is a doctor or a lover. No: the subtle cues of which Ekman and others have written are perceived in everyday human encounters and situations. Thus the cues they may fail to encounter in the movies cannot be substituted for by the visual and sonic close-up, nor will their feeling of lack, of something missing in the expressive canvas, be assuaged by them.

In short, the visual and sonic close-up, and other cinematic and sonic techniques of the movie, perform much the same function, when they are being used expressively, that music does. They reinforce the gross emotive cues that are already there: they do not—cannot—replace the ones that are, on my hypothesis, absent.

But this suggests the objection that if the expressive function of these cinematic and sonic techniques duplicates this same expressive function of music, then that expressive function cannot be the explanation for why music should be there. Music would seem to be distinctly *de trop*. Who needs it?

Well, although I think it is perfectly true that the filmic function of music is, to a certain extent, reinforced by other cinematic techniques, both visual and sonic, the ubiquitousness of the musical medium, its ability to be present almost everywhere, to seep into every crevice, makes it the prime mover in the enterprise of filling the expressive vacuum. Close-ups come and go; music endures. Indeed the overwhelming presence of music, almost everywhere, almost all the time, speaks of its pride of place *in this particular regard*.

This of course is emphatically not to say that music has pride of place in the cinema *tout court*. If that were the case, cinema would be recognized, like opera, as a basically musical art, which, needless to say, it is not. All I am saying is that in this particular filmic function of filling what I have been calling the expressive vacuum, music has pride of place. In narrative, of course, cinematic technique, both visual and auditory, is the basic machinery, and music almost impotent to help. Its peculiar genius here, as in opera, song, and liturgy, is *expressive*. What else it can do is a matter of perennially unresolved controversy, on which I am on the side of the 'minimalists'.

Thus, to sum up this part of the argument, I have been urging that although other elements of cinematic technique, both visual and aural, can, to a certain extent, perform the filmic function of music, namely, to fill the expressive vacuum by reinforcing those expressive cues that are in place, they are far less suited to this task than music which, in this particular respect, has the lion's share, by natural right. That, in any case, is my conjecture, which I offer, as I have said before, in the spirit of conjecture alone.

8. WHEN THE MUSIC STOPS

I have, so far, been talking about the *musical presence* in both silent and sound cinema. But at least a brief comment, perhaps, is in order about those rare occasions in the talking picture where music is absent altogether. What might the significance be of that? In particular, what might the significance be, for my argument, of films in which music is intentionally omitted completely, for expressive purposes, as surely is done from time to time?

Two films of recent memory, *The China Syndrome* and *The Birds*, have been suggested to me as examples of films that 'do not possess a musical score, and yet . . . are not expressively underpowered'.[25] Indeed, one might make the even stronger claim that, far from the lack of a score rendering them 'expressively underpowered', it renders them expressively super-charged, beyond even what an expressive musical score might provide. For the perceived absence of music itself has an expressive power uniquely its own.

This is perfectly true, and *The Birds*, it seems to me, exemplifies the expressive impact of musical absence in a really quite stunning way, in that the naked sound of the birds, without musical accompaniment, is rendered all the more ominous. But worthy of note though the absence of a musical score is, as an expressive (and dramatic) technique, it is something of a red herring here, if, at least, it is intended as a criticism of the view that music's filmic function is to fill an expressive vacuum, *The Birds* and its ilk being incontrovertible instances of film's impressive expressiveness in the complete absence of a musical accompaniment.

The reason such an argument fails is that the expressive effect of music's occasional absence from film is parasitic on its almost universal presence. Only when the presence of music is so familiar as to be completely taken for granted can withholding it from all (or part) of a film produce the stark expressive effect that Hitchock attains in his avian horror story. The great opera composers well knew this, which was why melodrama could be used, *but sparingly*, as an occasional dramatic technique in a sung work, where the disappearance of music altogether, and the sudden intrusion of the speaking voice, could produce such expressive effects as Beethoven accomplished in the dungeon scene of *Fidelio*, the emptiness of the spoken voices underscoring the emptiness of the subterranean galleries through which Rocco and Leonore descend.

But from the expressiveness of music withheld one can scarcely argue for the expressiveness of film without music altogether. For only against the canvas of music as a ubiquitous expressive part of film generally can the silencing of music have the expressive effect it does. If all cinema were without music, the absence of it in *The Birds* would neither be noticed, nor have any expressive effect at all.

9. AN EXPERIMENT AND A CONCLUSION

Before I come to my conclusion, one other feature of my hypothesis that it seems to me might make it more attractive to the sceptic, and which perhaps deserves mention, is that it might very well be verifiable in experience—a characteristic perhaps unexpected in a conjecture offered as part of a 'Philosophical Inquiry'. It is not difficult to imagine different audiences confronting the same film or film excerpt, with and without the musical track, or a filmed scene, and the same scene 'in the flesh'. Nor is it difficult to imagine ways of canvassing such audiences as regards their respective 'readings' of expressive content or the emotional reactions towards it. My expectation is that there would be significant differences in these readings and reactions bearing out my hypothesis.

Of course my hypothesis might be defeated; if it were, though, another would be needed. For it seems to me the question this hypothesis is meant to address will not dissolve, nor will it be answered by the quite reasonable task of investigating further the aesthetic functions of music in the sound film. Its filmic function will yet remain mysterious to anyone who gives serious thought to the history of eighteenth-century melodrama, and to the history of the cinema which, whether for the reason suggested, or some other, has not recapitulated it, but evolved into the most popular combination of music and spoken drama in the history of either.

I offer my conjecture with not a little diffidence, and have said it often enough to have begun to sound like Uriah Heep. But I press my *question* in the strongest possible terms. Until we understand not merely the aesthetic functions of music in the movies (many of which we do already), but its filmic function as well, we will fail in essence to understand what is arguably the most important artistic event and practice for our century—certainly the most widely influential, for better and for worse. And music, I emphasize, *is* of the essence of the modern cinema—not merely an inessential accompaniment. That its continued presence has amply demonstrated. If we do not understand music's filmic function in cinema, we do not understand cinema itself.

NOTES

1. A brief word here is in order on the use of the familiar word 'melodrama'. As musicologists use the term, it refers *specifically* to the genre of drama that consists in spoken words with musical accompaniment, of which Georg Benda's works are the prime (and almost lone) example, and to the technique that survived as a rare occurrence within opera and other sung dramatic works. It should not be confused with the term as used to refer to the popular nineteenth-century vaudeville plays, with musical accompaniment, although, needless to say, the latter use of the word must surely have developed from the former. It is the latter use, clearly, that led to the current use of 'melodramatic' to mean 'sensational' or 'overwrought' drama, which these nineteenth-century vaudevilles frequently were, I use the term as the musicologists do, my argument being founded on that use, and the musical works to which it refers. That music in the movies may have had its origin and model in nineteenth-century melodrama, as Murray Smith has suggested to me, I would not want to deny, for it is hardly part of my argument that the first makers of movies were students of eighteenth-century musical practice, or the art of melodrama as an operatic technique, in Beethoven, Weber, and their ilk.
2. On this see Peter Kivy, *Osmin's Rage: Philosophical Reflections on Opera, Drama and Text* (Princeton: Princeton University Press, 1988), part I.
3. Mozart to his father, 12 Nov. 1778, *Letters of Mozart and his Family*. trans. Emily Anderson (New York: Macmillan, 1938), ii. 937.
4. Ibid.
5. As I have argued in *Osmin's Rage*.
6. Of course there are exceptions, like *Alexander Nevsky*, where the music is so impressive and so woven into the cinematic fabric that we are tempted to call them truly 'musical' works. But such exceptions are rare, at least in my experience and on my accounting.
7. Irwin Bazelon, *Knowing the Score: Notes on Film Music* (New York: Van Nostrand Reinhold, 1975), 13.
8. Noël Carroll, *Mystifying Movies: Fads and Fallacies in Contemporary Film Theory* (New York: Columbia University Press, 1988), 220–1. Other recent studies of film music, all of which discuss the role of music in expressing emotional states, include Claudia Gorbman, *Unheard Melodies: Narrative Film Music* (Bloomington: Indiana University Press, 1987); Kathryn Kalinak, *Settling the Score: Music and the Classical Hollywood Film* (Madison: University of Wisconsin Press, 1992); Caryl Flinn, *Strains of Utopia: Gender, Nostalgia and Hollywood Film Music* (Princeton: Princeton University Press, 1992); and Royal S. Brown, *Overtones and Undertones: Reading Film Music* (Berkeley and Los Angeles: University of California Press, 1994). Gorbman also provides a discussion of the persistence of film scoring after the introduction of synchronous sound, 53–69.

9. I omit mention of the stream of consciousness that the voice-over of the soundtrack can provide, because the drama possesses that (although perhaps less 'naturally'?) in the monologue—witness the substitution of voice-over for spoken soliloquy by Orson Wells and Sir Laurence Olivier in *Macbeth* and *Hamlet* respectively.

10. Hanns Eisler and Theodor Adorno, *Composing for the Films* (London: Dennis Dobson, 1947), 75.

11. Ibid. 76.

12. Ibid.

13. Carroll, *Mystifying Movies*, 215.

14. Ibid. 216.

15. Ibid. 223.

16. Ibid. 223.

17. Eisler and Adorno, *Composing for the Films*, 76.

18. I refer here to the growing literature on the so-called 'cognitive' theory of the emotions, which emphasizes the role of belief and object in the forming of human emotions. A useful bibliography of this and other work on the emotions can be found in Amelie Oksenberg Rorty (ed.), *Explaining Emotions* (Berkeley and Los Angeles: University of California Press, 1980).

19. The alternative that I am presenting and criticizing here was suggested by Richard Allen.

20. Paul Ekman, 'Biological and Cultural Contributions to Body and Facial Movement in the Expression of Emotions', in Rorty (ed.), *Explaining Emotions*, 97. In adducing the work of Ekman I am responding to a suggestion of Murray Smith's, although I am drawing a favourable conclusion for my hypothesis, whereas, I think, he expected the opposite.

21. Ibid. 89.

22. Ibid. 87.

23. On this see Peter Kivy, *The Corded Shell: Reflections on Musical Expression* (Princeton: Princeton University Press, 1980).

24. I am responding here to a suggestion by Murray Smith with regard to both visual and sound techniques, and to a request for more about sound techniques from Peter Sacks.

25. Murray Smith, in a private communication.

14

Personal Agency Theories of Expressiveness and the Movies

FLO LEIBOWITZ

In this chapter, I examine three theories of expressiveness proposed by three philosophers and consider the applicability of each to expressiveness in movies. One of these philosophers, Richard Wollheim, understands expressive qualities in paintings in terms of a person whose expression the painting is. For Wollheim, this person is the actual (historical) artist.[1] Thus considered, one would expect few explanations of expressive qualities to be more intuitive. However, I argue that when Wollheim's theory is extended to movies, it produces accounts of movie production that do not fit the facts, and that this is a consequence of the notion of projection, the notion on which the theory rests. Subsequently, I discuss the applicability to movies of two other theories of expressiveness. One of these is offered by Bruce Vermazen, whose theory is intended as a theory of narrative and non-narrative art and depends on an imagined authorial persona.[2] I argue that Vermazen's theory is unsuitable to movies, too, although for different reasons from Wollheim's theory. Last, I examine Stephen Davies's theory of expressiveness in music. This theory assumes that musical expressiveness may be understood without referring to any personal agency. Instead, the theory holds that music has its own intentionality, even though musical artworks are objects and not persons.[3] I argue that this theory provides a promising model for addressing expressiveness in movies, even though it does not address a visual or narrative art. It should be evident that I assume that the theories of expressiveness presented by recent philosophers may be expected to apply to movies, or, in the case of theories addressed to particular art forms, they may be expected to provide model approaches to expressiveness in movies.

The expressive qualities of movie music and movie acting have been acknowledged elsewhere, and I will not emphasize them here.[4] While I recognize that movies employ characteristic expressive devices, I recognize also that movie images do more than record the acting of the actors. Hence, I present examples of movie images which are expressive in virtue of camera movement, slow motion, colour scheme (the expressive use of black and white film stock and colour film stock), and, to a lesser extent, expressive *mise en scène.*[5] I will not give a complete catalogue of expressive images, since that would require more space than is available here. Rather I present what I take to be typical cases of expressive movie images. I emphasize expressiveness in *movies* (that is, commercial entertainment fiction films) because movies are a familiar kind of film art. The expressive devices of movies overlap to some extent with those of other kinds of film, for example, non-fiction films, art cinema, and silent movies, and I am willing to assume that we can learn a great deal about expressiveness in film by looking at examples from any one of these types.[6] There are potential complications to this assumption that are not addressed here. For example, there may be expressive qualities that appear more often in one of these kinds of film than in another. But even if this turns out to be the case, I do not think this outcome is problematic, since my task is to indicate that there is expressiveness in movie images, and to discuss the significance of this for the theories of expressiveness that have been presented by recent philosophers.

I turn now to expressiveness in movies. *The Wizard of Oz* is about the adventures of Dorothy and Toto, but that is not all there is to know about why it looks the way it does. Similarly, Van Gogh's painting *Wheat Fields and Crows* depicts wheat fields and crows, but that is not all there is to know about why it looks the way it does. A movie is expressive in virtue of the way it looks, just as the painting is expressive in virtue of the way it looks, and understanding the expressiveness of movies is as much a part of understanding the art of cinema as understanding the expressiveness of paintings is part of understanding the art of painting. Movie images may have expressive qualities in virtue of several techniques. Some of the most common examples of expressiveness in movies make use of camera movement. Consider for example, the buffalo hunt in the movie *Dances with Wolves*. In the buffalo hunt scene, the camera appears to be riding on horseback through a herd of stampeding buffalo, just as the hunters do. The camera moves through the herd (or appears to) and it shakes, as if the ground were shaking. This way of shooting the scene gives it an expressive quality: the camera's movements make it appear to be excited (cameras do not actually get excited, since they are not people) and so the camera's movement expresses excitement. As a result, so does the movie scene it was used to make. The excitement of the scene was enhanced by movement of objects within the frame, for example, the horses, the riders, and the buffalo, and these moving objects were seen from close range.

Let us consider another example of expressive camera work. It occurs during the aeroplane daydream scene in *The Best Years of our Lives*. This is an unusually complex scene and it includes several shots that are notable individually, as well as together.[7] In one of these shots, the camera's movement makes it appear to be taking off, as if it were an aeroplane. It is an attention-getting shot that expresses the excitement of flying, and it may even arouse in the audience the physical sensation of take-off. In this way, Fred Derry's daydream of flying is made especially vivid. This shot is an example of the dependence of expressive techniques on the narrative line for appropriateness. In expressing excitement, the shot reminds us of the meaning that flying held for Derry and how it once gave him purpose. Since a theme of the movie is the personal dislocation brought about by the end of the war, Fred Derry's loss of purpose is very relevant, and had the movie been made as a celebration of victory, the aeroplane scene would seem less motivated. The take-off is not filmed from the cockpit, where Derry is sitting; rather it is filmed from outside the plane.[8] However, we can tell that the shot has to do with Fred Derry because of what we have seen and heard already (e.g. Fred sitting in the cockpit) and what we see and hear after (e.g. a workman calls out to ask what he is doing there). Thus, the movie's narrative line makes it possible for this complicated expressive shot to be intelligible to the viewer. The sceptical viewer may say that the aeroplane take-off arouses excitement, and thus watching the movie is an engaging experience. My reply is that the image arouses excitement on the basis of expressing it. I do not mean that the audience is excited by the discovery that excitement, as opposed to some other mental state, is expressed. Rather I mean that recognizing the excitement in the movie may lead in turn to a mirroring emotional response.

Some movie scenes have become famous for their use of slow motion, for example, the finales of *Bonnie and Clyde* and *The Wild Bunch*. Slow-motion scenes in the former do not tell the audience that Bonnie and Clyde are falling to the ground more slowly than dying people normally do. Rather these images express a sense of crisis. 'The sense of crisis' as I use it here is an emotion. People experience this emotion, for example, right after a car crash or athletic injury, or right after hearing that the bank has foreclosed on the mortgage. It is not fear, because it is not based on the anticipation of harm. In this case, a significant harm has already occurred. In the movies mentioned, slow motion was used to show the violent deaths of important characters, and hence the device made narrative sense. But there is no necessary link between slow motion and scenes of *violent* death. Rather the link is between slow motion and a matter of gravity. In recent years, a secondary use of slow motion in movies has emerged: gory deaths are slowed down so that the audience may gawk at the details. This does not appear to be an expressive use of slow motion. These scenes are like the replay of a key play in a sports broadcast: in both cases, the event of interest is shown in slow motion so that the audience may see better what happened. It is merely an aid to attention.

The overall colour scheme of a movie is often used expressively, and typically the colour scheme is chosen or evolved with this purpose in mind.

For example, the Technicolor used in the 1938 version of *Robin Hood* expresses playfulness. Stanley Cavell has said that the colour reminded him of the illustrations in children's books.[9] Colour expresses playfulness in *The Wizard of Oz* as well. Here, however, part of the movie is colour and part of it is black and white, and, in the end, both colour schemes were used expressively, to express opposing qualities. The audience realizes this when the colour scheme is changed. What quality does black and white express in this context? It isn't seriousness and it isn't boredom, because these are too strong to be the opposite of playfulness. I think this elusive quality is matter-of-factness, or the matter-of-fact attitude. The objects in the black and white images are to be taken for granted. At the end of the movie, black and white images still express matter-of-factness, but there is a change in the film's point of view. Now ordinariness is to be valued ('There's no place like home').[10]

Black and white colour schemes do not always express the same thing. *Don't Look Back* and *Schindler's List* were also made in black and white, but in neither of these does black and white express the same qualities that it did in *The Wizard of Oz*. In *Don't Look Back* the audience was expected to think of black and white in the context of low-budget movie-making of the 1960s (the time of the concert tour depicted) and thus its look is expressive of unpretentious artistic motives. *Don't Look Back* might not have been made by people whose artistic motives were of that sort, but this is the attitude its look is meant to express.[11] In *Schindler's List*, black and white is meant to be appreciated in historical context, too, although it is a different context. In the black and white scenes, the movie looks like the dramas that were made during the 1940s. There are period clothes and automobiles in it, and they are shot and lighted so they look in *Schindler's List* much as they do in period movies. It is sometimes supposed that the look of black and white expresses nostalgia, and I think that is right as long as this is understood as nostalgia for period movies, that is, for the kinds of heroism that they celebrated or perhaps for the artistry in the movie-making of that time. There are awful events depicted in *Schindler's List*, and it is hard to be nostalgic about awful things. Alternatively construed, the images in *Schindler's List* might be supposed to look like old photographs do, and thereby invest the film with the quality of a family album. Seen this way, the film's look is expressive of the feelings that you get when you look at photographs of relatives you have never met, but about whom you may have heard stories.[12]

Not every feature of a movie image is expressive, and that is one reason the concept of expressiveness remains an interesting one. For example, camera movement is not always expressive. Sometimes, a character may be centred in the frame simply to direct the viewer's attention to him and the camera may move as the character does just to keep him centred in the frame. Not all uses of colour are expressive uses, either, even when colour is used artfully. Consider, in this connection, the beginning of *Written on the Wind*, a sequence which is shown under the opening titles and credits. The sequence previews the movie's central characters and issues, and it uses a combination of expressive images and other techniques. The cameos of the Hadley family members (the playboy drunk, the tramp sister, the suffering but faithful wife) depend on expressive gestures. There are also images of the mansion entry with moving shadows and blowing leaves, and on the soundtrack the sound of the wind is heard. These compositions express emotional desolation. However, there are also images in the sequence that draw analogies, and an image that draws an analogy need not be expressive in addition. Toward the beginning of the title sequence, Kyle Hadley's yellow sports car pulls up beside the stucco columns of the family mansion. The resulting composition is a snapshot of pretentious tastes (we see, in fact, two generations of pretension, younger and elder) and, in the sequence overall, these tastes are being compared to the larger insensitivities that the movie is about. The colour and design of Kyle's car serves a purpose, in informing the audience that Kyle Hadley has flashy taste, but the image of the car need not have expressive qualities in order to do this.[13]

In the remainder of this chapter, I discuss the extent to which some recent theories of expressiveness accommodate expressiveness in movies. I turn first to Richard Wollheim's book *Painting as an Art*, which presents one type of personal-agency theory of expressiveness. Wollheim emphasizes the role of the historical (or actual) painter, and one striking feature of Wollheim's model is how robust an agency this painter is. His painter has a significant amount of control over the expression process, and the painter gets the painting to look the way it does (or tries to get it to look that way) in order that it express a particular emotional quality. For this painter, art-making is a form of strategic thinking. Wollheim writes that the hand of a painter is the hand 'in the service of the eye: In the case of the painter who is an artist the expressive gesture of the hand comes to adapt itself to the look of the mark it will deposit, and the look of the mark to the expressive way in which the eye will perceive it.'[14]

For Wollheim, a painter need not actually experience the expressed emotion at the time of painting in order for his or her painting to express it. The painter may remember having that emotion, or may simply think about its meaning, but, in any case, deliberation or reflection on the emotion is part of the expressing process. Wollheim denies that the relationship between an emotion and a painting that expresses it is just like the relationship between an emotion and its bodily expression. He maintains that the bodily expression of emotion is a response to a currently felt emotion, rather than a response to a reflection on that emotion, and so it is unlike painting. For example, consider dropping your jaw in surprise. You do not drop your jaw

as a result of thinking about what surprised you, rather, you just drop it.
Moreover, Wollheim argues, what one expresses in painting is a response to
an ongoing condition, not a transient one. So while you may drop your jaw
in surprise on a single occasion, you would not paint a painting on that
basis. You might paint a painting if the *memory* of that event persisted, but
that is another matter.[15]

Wollheim's account of expressiveness depends on the notion of projection, which is a psychological process of the painter. In *Painting as an Art*,
painting is a process with many parts, and so is the process of projection
itself. According to Wollheim, a painting is a prop in an elaborate imagining
of the painter's (the 'phantasy' of projection) which reshapes the way the
artist experiences the world. Wollheim writes of projection that:

On the first tier, there is the initiating phantasy which, as we have already seen, is
entertained on the occasion of some emotion or feeling that the person wants either
to rid himself of, or to retain and preserve. Fear of, or fear for, the emotion
stimulates anxiety, and it is in order to allay this anxiety that projection is set in
train. The initiating phantasy represents the emotion as being expelled from the
body and then spread or smeared across some part of the world, and the primitive
nature of the mental functioning to which projection belongs is revealed in the highly
physical or corporeal way in which (as this description of its content makes clear) the
expulsive phantasy envisages mental phenomena. Emotions are in effect envisaged as
bits or products of the body which can be spewed out or excreted and then deposited
in the world. But the primitive nature of projection is also revealed in the enduring
effect that the initiating phantasy has over the person who invokes it . . . For having,
in phantasy, expelled the emotion, the person then finds set up in himself a disposition to phantasize which leads him to experience the world in a certain way. He is
led to experience the world as permanently modified by this event. The expulsive
phantasy dyes the world, and it is this dye that gives the world its new projective
properties.[16]

Despite the vividness of this account of projection, there are several
reservations one might have about this picture. For one thing, projection
thus construed would be unsatisfying in the case of projecting a sad emotion; but if it is not satisfying, projection loses its point. The problem is that,
for the painter, making the sad painting is a symbolic expelling of sadness
out of his or her person.[17] As a consequence, the painting stands as a vivid
reminder of that sadness, but this ought to be the last thing the painter
wants. When a person wants to stop being miserable about something it is
typically more effective simply to get away from it. Alternatively, and with
more difficulty, a person may rethink the meaning of this misery-making
thing and then move on to other matters. In either case, reminders are not
especially useful. There seems to be more point in projecting into the world
something you fear to lose, rather than something you want to lose, because
of the physicality with which the operation of projection is infused.

Wollheim acknowledges that people engage in projection in those kinds of cases (that is, in cases of feared loss), and that creates a more consistent picture of projection. However, that does not remedy the concern I am raising here, which is the apparent implausibility of the theory and not its internal consistency.

On Wollheim's model of projection a painter may paint a sad painting when he or she is not actually sad, but we do not have to say that he or she is therefore making an insincere work. In this way, the model steps away from the Romantic caricature which requires that an authentic artist feel the emotion that the artwork expresses while the art-making is going on. This is an advantage. Yet the distance between the artist and the sadness (or other psychological state) expressed is not entirely abolished, for if it were, projection would become unmotivated. This is the basis for another reservation about the projection model of expressiveness. On this model, projection is motivated by anxiety, and that seems unduly restrictive of the range of psychological states which people experience and which the arts express.

Wollheim's model supposes further that the curiosity behind art-making is always curiosity about oneself. This is too strong. While it is useful to a model of artistic activity to suppose that painters and other artists are motivated by forms of curiosity, Wollheim's model says more. The general idea at work in *Painting as an Art* seems to be that painters paint because they have a need to come to terms with some aspect of their personal experience. But even if this is true of painters, it is unlikely to be true of a commercial entertainment movie. Movie-makers may be emotionally invested in the work they do, but ongoing issues in their personal lives need not be the basis of this investment. A writer may write an original screenplay because he thinks the characters, of whom he had fleeting images, would make a good movie; that is, because there was an engaging artistic project in it. It does not have to be because the writing was a means of thinking through some personal conflict. In fact, artists for whom satisfaction comes from using art to come to terms with personal concerns are likely to be uncomfortable in the Hollywood production system, which is organized along industrial lines. A cinematographer, an art director, and even a director commonly contribute to movies whose themes are not of their own invention. Moreover, movies are made by groups of artists, and the individuals in the production line do not necessarily share the same personal histories. In this respect, a production group is not very different from work groups in other industries and offices.

Production by groups introduces further obstacles to extending Wollheim's thinking to movie-making because the activity of projection that Wollheim describes seems applicable to the mind of an individual, but not to group decision-making. There are some options for extending the notion of projection to groups, but the options are not promising. For example, group therapy is a collective response to anxiety and it is one in which reflective thinking plays a role; in that way, it shares some of the features of individual projection. So perhaps a movie studio conference operates like a therapy group. The comparison fails, however, because therapy group members do not share a joint project beyond the therapy group, and the makers of a movie do. The therapy group members are dealing with the same issues, or they think they are, but each is concerned first and foremost with personal consequences. In this respect, they are engaged in a form of mutual aid in the service of their individual projects (in this case, their personal growth). By contrast movie-makers in conference are engaged in a shared project, the movie, to which their individual projects are subordinated.

This is troubling. *Painting as an Art* offers a model for the analysis of expressiveness in artworks in terms of the actual art-maker. But this model did not generalize to movies because of the nature of movie-making. How then may we understand pictorial expressiveness in movies? An alternative model of expressiveness has been given by Bruce Vermazen, who proposes that an expressive work of art is to be understood as the expression of an imagined utterer, or persona, rather than as the expression of an actual or historical artist. This is another personal agency theory of expressiveness, only here the expressing agency is an imaginary person and not a real one. Vermazen's imagined utterer is conceived purely in terms of its function: it is the agency whose mental properties the expressive object expresses. It appears to be consistent with his account that the imagined utterer be an imagined group or committee; it need not be an imagined individual. However, even if that is how the theory works, it is not a good theory of expressiveness in movies. This is because, once the move is made to an imagined utterer, the issues change substantially, and other movie-related weaknesses arise.

Unlike Wollheim, Vermazen embraces a concept of expression that likens everyday expressive behaviour to expressive art. For Vermazen, to express is to provide evidence for the mental life of an expressor: that is what the term means, and that is why his theory preserves this notion even though it bypasses actual historical expressors. He writes: 'The analysis of expression for the case of expressive objects comes to this: an object expresses a mental property if and only if the object is evidence that an imagined utterer of the object has that mental property.'[18] With this account, he maintains, expression in art, speech, and behaviour are all of a piece, and, in his view, this is a useful unification. Nevertheless, Vermazen's model is a risky one, because it sacrifices an appealing feature of historical-artist theories of expressiveness. Historical-artist theories offer an intuitive explanation of why it is that expressive artworks are engaging. The explanation is that audiences are connected via expressive artworks to expressing persons. When the expressing agency is an imaginary person, however, this connection loses its intuitiveness. Mind-melding through artworks is appealing, but mind-melding with imaginary artists makes no sense.

For Vermazen, expression in an ordinary spoken or written English sentence is the model case. He says that oratory, an artful form of speech, presents an especially clear example of expression according to his model. He writes:

Suppose I am asked to say a few words at a memorial for martyrs to a cause I have adopted. I may not feel the same degree of passion now that I felt at the news of their death, but I want somehow to convey the earlier emotion to my audience, and not just describe it. So I write a speech such as an unusually eloquent and composed person would have uttered under the influence of that emotion, and I deliver it. This unusually eloquent and composed person is the persona, the utterer to whom, if I am successful, the crowd will attribute the emotion I wanted to convey. They will probably also attribute the emotion to me, and even identify me with the persona, if they are naive about oratory. But we who are in on the trick know that at this moment, it is only imaginary that there is a speaker feeling the relevant emotion.[19]

An oration, the expressive object in this case, depends, then, on an imagined person to whom the state of mind expressed in it is attributed.

It is true that movie and theatre audiences separate the real actors from the characters they play in much the same way that the orator's audience separates the oratorical persona from the actual person speaking. So perhaps Vermazen's model has some application to expressiveness in acting. However, movies are not merely recordings of stage plays. They are narratives, as orations are, but there is no compelling reason to see them as mediated by an implied author or other imagined person. For this reason, Vermazen's model overly complicates the process of accounting for expressiveness in movies. David Bordwell has argued that implied authors are superfluous for understanding movie narration. He writes:

No trait we could assign to an implied author of a film could not more simply be ascribed to the narration itself: it sometimes suppresses information, it often restricts our knowledge, it generates curiosity, it creates a tone, and so on. To give every film a narrator or implied author is to indulge in an anthropomorphic fiction. . . . [film] narration is better understood as the organization of a set of cues for the construction of a story. This presupposes a perceiver, but not any sender of a message.[20]

Recently, Gregory Currie has disagreed, arguing that 'narratives obstruct, mislead and manipulate us by their selective presentations of events. But no text, no sequence of visual images, can do those things; such things require agency. Most of the ways we describe narrative make no sense if we cut narrative off from the agency which produced it.'[21]

Currie suspects that rejections of the implied author are based on a mistaken assumption which he calls the Imagined Observer Hypothesis.

According to this hypothesis, a movie viewer imagines that he or she is viewing the action from within the space of the movie, rather than from the viewer's seat in the movie house. This hypothesis, Currie surmises, invites the mistaken notion that no agency is responsible for the images the viewer receives.[22] My response to Currie is that the quoted passages indicate that intentionality, rather than personhood, explains the kinds of things that narratives do. If attributing intentionality to movie narratives were justified, then we could explain the things that movie narratives do without resorting to implied authors, and without resorting to the Imagined Observer Hypothesis.

The notion that objects of any kind possess intentionality may seem strange at the outset. However, in the next section of the chapter, I will discuss a model of expressiveness in which intentionality is attributed to musical pieces, and in which the course of a musical piece and the things that musical pieces do are understood in this manner. I will then propose, although on preliminary grounds, that we attribute intentionality to movies. Music is not a visual art, and so a comparison of musical expressiveness with movie expressiveness may seem odd. Moreover, music does not need to represent anything, and theories of musical expressiveness typically take untexted music as the model musical case. Nevertheless, one recent treatment of expressiveness in music invites the comparison of movies to music in several respects.

Stephen Davies attributes expressiveness to music while referring this expressiveness to no expressing personal agency. Davies observes that when we listen to music, we attend to sounds and hear what they express, and on this basis we attribute expressive qualities to the music. He argues further that we do not require an implied composer or musician in order for this attribution to make sense. Why is this so? First, Davies identifies what he calls the 'emotion-characteristics in appearance' that there are in human behaviour. He observes in this context that a person may look sad, but not actually feel sad. He observes further that we can tell that the person looks sad on the basis of his or her appearance, because there are qualities of a person's appearance that we identify as sad-looking. Davies maintains that when we listen to music we think in a similar way, in that we identify music as sad on the basis of its sound (that is, on the basis of its aural appearance). Just as there are sad-looking faces, there is music that sounds sad. But, Davies also maintains, in identifying sad music we do not assume that there must be some fictional person, for example, an implied composer or musician, whose sadness is being expressed. Rather, he believes, we ascribe the sadness to the music in virtue of its sound.

This provides a model for thinking about expressive movie images. Earlier in this chapter, several different expressive images were discussed. Some of these images were expressive in virtue of camera movement, some were expressive in virtue of slow motion, and some were expressive in virtue of colour scheme. In all these cases, we emphasized the way the expressive device in question makes the resulting images look. Using Davies's approach as a model, we can understand why the audience attributes the expressive qualities to the movie in every case. Consider the images that expressed excitement: we would say that the audience sees the excitement in the image in virtue of the way camera movement makes it look, and on this basis attributes the excitement to the movie. There is no need to assume that there is some implied director (or, in this particular example, an implied cinematographer) whose personal excitement it is. Similarly, we would say that in the slow-motion cases, the audience sees the sense of crisis in the image because of the way slow motion makes it look, and on that basis attributes the sense of crisis to the movie. Finally, in the colour scheme cases, we would say that the audience sees sadness or playfulness in the images because of the way the colour scheme makes them look, and on that basis attributes the sadness or playfulness to the movie. In all these cases, the model leads us to the same thing: when we watch a movie, we see what its component images express in virtue of the way they look, and we attribute these expressive qualities to the movie. We do not need an imagined person to whom we attribute the expression in order to make sense of those qualities.

There is more. While Davies's account of musical expressiveness does not rely on an expressing personal agency, it assumes that musical pieces (the expressive objects in this case) have intentionality. Concerning the organization of musical pieces, Davies writes that

Music displays the type of intentionality which is characteristic of human behavior. Unlike an explanation of the movements of a machine, an explanation of the movement of music is incomplete if it refers merely to causal mechanisms and the composer's intentions. Much more to the point in such an explanation is an account of the *reasons* why the musical movement takes the course that it does. We say, for example, 'This section develops the preceding motive and foreshadows the melody which follows'. The reasons for the musical movement are to be sought in the music itself.[23]

I propose that movies have intentionality on similar grounds. First, there are reasons why a movie takes the course it does, just as there are reasons a musical piece takes the course it does. Moreover, the reasons why a movie takes the course it does are to be sought in the movie itself, too. Even the musical case given as an example has a movie counterpart: to know that a scene in a movie develops a particular narrative theme and foreshadows what is to follow is to give a reason for the scene's inclusion. The example, applied to movies, is suggestive in additional ways. If a movie can foreshadow events and develop them without a personal agency, then it can presumably also obstruct, mislead, and manipulate the audience by selective presentation of events (Currie's examples) without one, too.

There are, of course, remaining conceptual questions. Consider, for example, Davies's account of audience responses to music. Davies maintains that the typical and simplest response to the emotion expressed in a musical work is to feel that emotion yourself. While he concedes that we can respond to music in other ways that we may consider more sophisticated and which involve more than mirroring some feeling, he considers this mirroring response to be the basic one, and it is something that listeners must overrule or override in order to respond in more intellectual ways. By contrast, Davies says, when we respond to a representational painting, there is no feeling to override. Suppose now that Davies is right in what he says here. What form does the movie counterpart of this idea take? Perhaps it is that a movie normally arouses in the viewer the qualities that its look expresses. But is that really the case? And even if it is the case, is this mirroring response the primary response to the movie or is it a sophistication, as Davies says it is in painting? These are questions which I have not addressed here.

Like Wollheim's approach to painting, and like Vermazen's general theory, Davies's approach to music treats the qualities of the expressive object as real qualities of the object. Like these other theories, it explains why we refer to expressive qualities with psychological predicates, that is, predicates which refer to mental states and activities. But Davies's account of musical expressiveness depends on no expressing personal agency. Still, it explains why expressive artworks engage us. In responding to these artworks, Davies's theory tells us, we are responding to the appearance of human subjectivity. This is an intuitively satisfying explanation and thus a further asset. I do not mean here that we are responding to a mere appearance or superficiality. Rather, the notion operating here is that we detect the expressive qualities of artworks with our sensory equipment (e.g. we hear them or see them, and that is how we come to be aware of them), and, in this way, Davies's theory assumes that we have sensory access to conceptually complex qualities. Further, in assuming no personal expressing agency, Davies's approach may help us conceive of movies, which are both narratives and expressive objects, in a unified way. This is a highly appealing combination of features for dealing with expressiveness in movies. For these reasons, Davies's treatment of musical expressiveness provides a useful model for movie expressiveness, and merits further exploration in this connection.

NOTES

1. Richard Wollheim, *Painting as an Art* (Princeton: Princeton University Press, 1987), 43–100. Wollheim's views on expressive qualities, along with the views of the other

two philosophers discussed in this paper (see nn. 2 and 3), are considered in Jerrold Levinson's collection on *The Pleasures of Aesthetics* (Ithaca, NY: Cornell University Press, 1996), ch. 6.

2. Bruce Vermazen, 'Expression as Expression', *Pacific Philosophical Quarterly*, 67 (July 1986), 196–224. Readers of Vermazen's article may find illuminating two preceding treatments of expressiveness: Alan Tormey, *The Concept of Expression* (Princeton: Princeton University Press, 1970) and Guy Sircello, *Mind and Art: An Essay on the Varieties of Expression* (Princeton: Princeton University Press, 1972).

3. Stephen Davies, 'The Expression of Emotion in Music', *Mind*, 89 (Jan. 1980), 67–86. See also the extended treatment in Stephen Davies, *Musical Meaning and Expression* (Ithaca, NY: Cornell University Press, 1994). Several preceding theories of musical expressiveness are discussed there. Readers of Davies may find illuminating what is sometimes called the contour theory of musical expressiveness in Peter Kivy, *Sound Sentiment* (Philadelphia: Temple University Press, 1989).

4. On movie acting, see James Naremore, *Acting in the Cinema* (Berkeley and Los Angeles: University of California Press, 1988). Some recent accounts of movie music include Claudia Gorbman, *Unheard Melodies: Narrative Film Music* (Bloomington: Indiana University Press, 1987); Caryl Flinn, *Strains of Utopia: Gender, Nostalgia and Hollywood Film Music* (Princeton: Princeton University Press, 1992); Kathryn Kalinak, *Settling the Score: Music and the Classical Hollywood Film* (Madison: University of Wisconsin Press, 1992); Jeff Smith, 'Unheard Melodies? A Critique of Psychoanalytic Theories of Film Music', in David Bordwell and Noël Carroll (eds.), *Post-Theory: Reconstructing Film Studies* (Madison: University of Wisconsin Press, 1996), 230–47; and Jerrold Levinson, 'Film Music and Narrative Agency', in Bordwell and Carroll, *Post-Theory*, 248–82.

5. In my discussion of 'Movie Colorization and the Expression of Mood', I discuss some of these devices in a related context. The present chapter develops the basic notions of 'Movie Colorization': that movies employ characteristic expressive practices and that expressive work is done by the look of movie images. 'Movie Colorization' appeared in *Journal of Aesthetics and Art Criticism*, 49 (Fall 1991), 363–5. It is reprinted in Alex Neill and Aaron Ridley (eds.), *Arguing about Art: Contemporary Philosophical Debates* (New York: McGraw Hill, 1994), 48–52.

6. By 'art cinema' I do not mean the European art cinema, e.g. the films of Bergman and Fellini, rather I mean what is sometimes referred to as 'experimental cinema' e.g. the films of Mekas, Brakhage, Conner, and Deren. I use the term 'art cinema' to indicate that the mass art/high art distinction applies in film, and that a film is not necessarily an instance of mass art just because it is a film.

7. There is an extended and illuminating discussion of the aeroplane scene in Edward Branigan, *Point of View in the Cinema: A Theory of Narration and Subjectivity in Classical Film* (New York: Mouton Publishers, 1984), 135–8. Numbered illustrating plates are referred to in these pages. I am indebted to Branigan's book for this example.

8. Ibid. 137.

9. Stanley Cavell, *The World Viewed* (Cambridge, Mass.: Harvard University Press, 1979), 81. It may be supposed that the colour expresses some quality of fantasy or the imaginary. However, not all imagined scenarios are playful in the way the story of Robin Hood is, and so I prefer the first characterization.

10. Noël Carroll has attributed matter-of-factness to Jasper Johns's sculpture *Painted Bronzes*, which looks like two cans of Ballantine Ale. I think his point here is that matter-of-factness, the expressive quality of these ordinary-looking items, is to be seen in contrast to the expressive qualities of traditional fine art sculpture, e.g. marble nudes. Noël Carroll, *Philosophical Problems of Classical Film Theory* (Princeton: Princeton University Press, 1988), 71–2. Ch. 1 of this book contains an analysis of

Rudolf Arnheim's theory of expressiveness and of his application of it to film. The example mentioned here is given in this context.

11. *Don't Look Back* is a non-fiction film. In including it here, I have made an exception to my stated emphasis on fiction film.

12. Readers may be aware that *Schindler's List* is not filmed entirely in black and white. For example, there is a colourized image (or what appears to be one) toward the beginning, which depicts a sabbath observance. The image has a golden-yellow hue and is softly lighted, and this is perhaps expressive of warmth, in the psychological sense, and contentment. The epilogue, which is set in the present day and is not presented as fiction, uses ordinary movie colour.

13. For this example, I am indebted to Thomas Elsaesser's analysis of *Written on the Wind* in 'Tales of Sound and Fury: Observations on the Family Melodrama', in Christine Gledhill (ed.), *Home is Where the Heart is: Studies in Melodrama and the Woman's Film* (London: British Film Institute, 1987), 43–69.

14. Wollheim, *Painting as an Art*, 89.

15. The specific example is my own. I have offered it in order to illustrate Wollheim's concerns.

16. Ibid. 84.

17. This is the case for both the simple and complex forms of projection distinguished by Wollheim. Among other things, they have somewhat different consequences. In complex projection, the quality the painting ends up with as a result of projection is not the same quality the artist projected, although sometimes the same predicate is used to refer to both qualities. In other words, a sad painting does not require a sad artist, although it does require that the sadness is in the artwork which expresses the qualities because the artist put those expressive qualities there.

18. Vermazen, 'Expression as Expression', 207.

19. Ibid. 199.

20. David Bordwell, *Narration in the Fiction Film* (Madison: University of Wisconsin Press, 1985), 62.

21. Gregory Currie, *Image and Mind: Film, Philosophy, and Cognitive Science* (Cambridge: Cambridge University Press, 1995), 247.

22. Ibid. 248.

23. Davies, 'The Expression of Emotion in Music', 75.

15

Aristotelians on Speed: Paradoxes of Genre in the Context of Cinema

Deborah Knight

Two of the hoariest questions that philosophy could ask about generic movies are these. Considering primarily the films, and since generic movies are parts of popular culture, philosophy could ask, *But are genre movies art?*[1] Of course, given the proliferation of learned discourses about popular culture including movies, many aspects of popular culture have become part of a learned culture, at least as objects of study, and indeed many popular movies have achieved the sort of canonical status that other disciplines reserve for classical works in their fields. Or philosophy could ask, *But is this behaviour—i.e. watching genre movies—rational?*[2] Being a question about behaviour, it is primarily concerned with movie audiences, but since it is also a question about the rationality of watching *genre* movies, some of the concerns that motivate the first question spill over into the second. Given the usual philosophical prevarications around the term, 'rational',[3] one senses a lingering suspicion about the reasoning abilities of those individuals whose tastes run to popular texts, as well as a suspicion about the nature of the popular texts themselves.

I do not intend to ask or answer the first question. But I will examine one recent rehearsal of the rationality question with respect to generic fictions. In 'The Paradox of Junk Fiction',[4] Noël Carroll considers whether, perhaps, the successive consumption of generic fictions might just not be rational. By offering an account focusing on the ongoing cognitive work of genre consumers, he concludes that we need not despair of the rationality of those who consume junk.

In the first section of the chapter, I support Carroll's contention that the alleged paradox is a false one and the worry therefore unfounded. But my support is not the sort that Carroll would prefer, since what I argue is that

A previous version of this paper was published as 'Making Sense of Genre', in *Film and Philosophy*, 2 (1995), 58–73. I am grateful to the editor, Kendall D'Andrade, for allowing me to revise it for this volume.

Thanks to Richard Allen, Sue Campbell, Noël Carroll, Alan Casebier, Murray Smith, and especially George McKnight, as well as audiences at Queen's University, Kingston, and Carleton University, Ottawa. I also gratefully acknowledge the support of the Social Sciences and Humanities Research Council of Canada.

the paradox as he constructs it is not merely false, it is misconceived. The very framing of the alleged paradox fails to deal adequately with the relationship between genre broadly construed, the particular texts which are collected under any particular generic heading, and the expectations which audiences bring to generic texts. Carroll's strategy is to answer the rationality question by showing how it could make sense that readers and viewers continue to read or watch new examples of familiar genres. So, over and above the question of paradox, there is Carroll's account of the cognitive activities of those who read or view generic texts, and in the second section of the chapter I turn to this. In the third part, I discuss three different genres—mystery/detection, romantic comedy, and action films—to suggest that Carroll's main argument about cognitive activity is inadequate as a general account of what is involved in understanding generic films. Finally, I draw together the conclusions of each of the previous sections. Since Carroll's paradox of junk fiction is not properly a paradox of rationality— at least as Carroll conceives the paradox (section 1), since, *contra* Carroll, story-focus, plot-focus, and genre-focus are all interdependent aspects of our comprehension of generic narratives (section 2), and since the cognitive activities of spectators—in particular, their expectations—are not primarily driven by the particular story but by expectations about genre and plot as they are realized in the particular text (section 3), I conclude that Carroll's positive account of cognitive activity as a way of making sense of the successive consumption of generic fictions returns us to the initial point of paradox.

I. PARADOX, WHAT PARADOX?

In 'The Paradox of Junk Fiction', Noël Carroll asks, 'How can we be interested in consuming stories that we already know? How is it rational? Or, is it simply irrational?' For Carroll, the paradox of junk fiction is a cognitive one. Any junk fiction reader or viewer is antecedently familiar with the general story form upon which each new particular instance performs a variation. So the reader or viewer 'must in some sense know the standard story already', and one comes to know the standard story by 'reading around in the genre' (PJF 226). We (apparently) read or view each of a succession of generic fictions for the story, yet because these are, after all, *generic* fictions, it is a story we already know. The sorts of stories that provoke the suspicion of cognitive paradox or irrationality are deemed to be familiar, frequently repeated—in a word, formulaic. It is the formulaic character of generic texts that suggests the possibility of paradox in the first place.

Indeed, for many critics, what makes genre genre—what makes junk

junk—is the conjunction between form and formula. It is taken for granted that there is an important sense in which, unlike learned fictions, genre just tells *the same story* over and over again. This is a different matter from using the same form over and over again, as for instance the form of the sonnet or the form of the epistolary novel. The claim that genre tells the same story seems to be a claim to the effect that ordinary genres (which I will use as a term to describe such groupings as westerns, horror films, screwball comedies, police procedural thrillers, and so forth[5]) *each tell one story*. This is a claim about form and content, not just form. It is false. Just why it is false requires some careful discussion of particular films in the context of the genres whose conventions they employ.

A familiar way of glossing what distinguishes generic fictions from non-generic fictions is to note what they do not have that learned fictions do have. Some might say that everything that marks literature *as* literature is missing in action films, Harlequin romances, comic books, and so forth: for instance, the moral complexity of action, the depth and intricacy of character psychology, the skilled and subtle use of language which serves as more than a simple medium of communication (and similarly for cinematic and televisual *mise en scène*). It is impossible to make this case universally in the context of cinema, since many revered generic movies are thought to demonstrate such characteristics. I could make the case that we do find moral complexity of action, developed character psychology, and skilled *mise en scène* with respect to paradigm films from various ordinary genres, say, *My Darling Clementine* or *The Left-Handed Gun* (for the western), *The Maltese Falcon* or *Murder, My Sweet* (for the hard-boiled detective); but I can also anticipate a rejoinder to the effect that they are much less sophisticated in these areas than, say, Renoir's *La Règle du jeu* or Fellini's *Otto e mezzo*.

One who associates genre with mere repetition of some pregiven formula would doubtless maintain that what goes missing in generic fictions is nearly everything that makes the learned study of narratives worth doing—where the paradigm for learned study is the canonical text, the great work which reveals to us an author's or director's moral vision. What is concealed from attention by this urgent focus on the great work (especially when augmented by notions of the moral vision of the author/director) is the narrative structure of such texts. For we do not get learned or canonical fictions independently of the narrative form that is so completely unconcealed in genre. What, exactly, is unconcealed in genre? In a word, emplotment, here understood not merely in terms of story structure, but story structure based around a complex interrelationship of thematic, iconographical,[6] and narrational cues and conventions.

The question raised by genre, then, concerns the relationship between the particular generic text and the genre(s) of which it is an instance. Carroll's claim to dissolve the paradox of generic fiction appears at just this point. While acknowledging that audiences will have a certain familiarity with the genre(s) of which any generic text is a part, Carroll proposes dissolving the paradox by turning attention from the genre to the particular text.

Carroll wants to distinguish his answer to the question about the relationship between the particular generic text and the genre of which it is an instance from the answer offered by Thomas J. Roberts in *The Aesthetics of Junk Fiction*.[7] Roberts's answer is that 'genre reading is system reading' (*AJF* 150–1). System reading involves reading with a genre focus rather than a story focus. For Roberts—and Carroll grants this—reading with a genre focus does not involve cognitive paradox since what we are reading for, and within, is the generic system itself. To read for the genre means that, when we read any particular generic work, we read (at least) two texts or two discourses: we read the work in front of us as a particular story, and at the same time we read the genre-as-text *through* the text at hand. In doing so, we might be more concerned with the moral vision of the genre than of the particular text's author.

Reading with a genre focus is similar to reading a parodic text *as* a parody. With parody as with genre, we read with our memories of other texts, but also with our expectations. If we read a parodic text with no awareness of that text *as* a parody, then whatever else is going on, *we* are not reading a parody. We are reading something *written* as a parody, but *we* are not reading a parody. Comparably for generic fictions: to view (say) a western without *any* sense of the western as genre means that, whatever else is going on, *we* are not watching a western, and this despite the fact that the movie was *made* as a western.

While Carroll acknowledges that fans, connoisseurs, academics, and others might read successive generic fictions with a view to the genre-as-system, he does not accept that system reading is the basic level of engagement with generic fictions. He proposes that the 'more basic mode' does after all require 'focus[ing] on the story, not upon the genre of which it is a part' (*PJF* 231). What Carroll evidently means is that the 'more basic mode' of engagement is one in which the reader (who it appears is neither fan nor connoisseur nor academic nor critic—which raises the question of who is left?) reads *for the plot*. This brings Carroll to suggest that 'there is a core phenomenon of reading junk fiction where the consumer knows the story-type and derives justifiable satisfaction from the fiction, but not because he/she is reading in a system' (*PJF* 231). While Carroll accepts that the reader or viewer must have some background sense of what to expect of the genre in question, he denies that reading-within-a-system is the distinguishing feature of basic genre reading. He also suggests that what preserves the rationality of the genre-consumer is a *justifiable* satisfaction that is keyed *to the particular text* and is not keyed to the particular text's position in the constellation of texts which comprise the genre. If this is correct, then the 'core phenomenon' certainly cannot extend to any sense of how the particular text might stand at the intersection of a range of differing generic concerns. But it is far from clear that a generic text can be neatly isolated at the level of story from the genre (or genres) of which it is part. And many generic texts are, to use Steve Neale's term, hybrids, exemplifying aspects of different genres in the same text.[8]

Carroll opposes reading-for-the-story to reading-within-the-system because he takes the latter to be just a case of 'comparative reading' (PJF 231). Carroll seems to think that to read within the system of science fiction or Gothic horror or the western is explicitly to compare a particular work with the broader conventions and formulae of the genre, or explicitly to compare it to some paradigm work of that genre. Comparative reading suggests *studied* comparative treatment of the fiction at hand relative to the genre, as though a particular work were somehow independent of the generic system and could be judged in relation to it in terms of 'variations, subversions, echoes, expansions . . . convergences, contrasts, and extensions within the story type' (PJF 231). This semi-independence from the system is what would allow for comparison. But reading-within-a-system need not be reduced to comparative reading; it involves seeing the particular generic work as itself part of the generic system. And the generic system is broader than the ordinary genre which serves most efficiently to classify it. A work could be handily classified as a western yet clearly be a romance (in the sense of a quest) which in turn combines aspects of drama and epic, suspense and comedy: consider John Ford's *The Searchers*. Reading within the system involves reading both instance and genre through the text at hand. It involves thinking of genre as both a process and a structure, while simultaneously thinking of the particular text as a contribution to and a (potential) modification of the genre (or genres) in question. If this is right, then reading in the system is, after all, a necessary component of reading any particular generic text, since arguably we would not be reading genre if we were not reading story and story type simultaneously, through each other.

Carroll's paradox of genre is not persuasively framed as a paradox of rationality. I am doubtful that any reader or viewer of generic fiction actually believes (*p* and not *p*)—i.e. *I know this story* and *I don't know this story* (or any suitable variation). It is certainly no paradox to know the type but not know the token. Genre tokens cannot be identical to their types, since one thing available within the type is a range of conflicting and sometimes contradictory options for the development of any particular story.[9] For instance, though the gangster usually dies or is caught, he might instead—as in Scorsese's *Goodfellas*—wind up condemned to life as an ordinary person thanks to a witness protection programme. In the meantime, while tokens are always tokens-of-a-type, it is far from obvious how we would describe the type of the comic vampire film, of which *Love at First Bite*, *Buffy the Vampire Slayer*, and *Dracula: Dead and Loving It* might be tokens. Nor is it obvious that consuming successive examples of any particular genre is an action that is generally undertaken against each reader's or viewer's better judgement—i.e. *Since I already know the story, it's a waste of my time to see this new film, but I'll watch it anyway*. And even if some genre viewers do act occasionally against their better judgement—I occasionally watch films I do not think it makes sense for me to spend time watching—this hardly seems to be the general situation when people decide to watch a new example of a familiar genre. The paradox as Carroll frames it is a false one.

Indeed, the idea that readers or spectators antecedently 'know' the story (i.e. the story-type) is itself deeply misleading, in two respects. It puts what Wittgenstein has encouraged us to think of as an undue metaphysical burden on the idea of 'knowing': better to say that standardly readers of generic works are familiar with, or have been exposed to, or recognize, some key narrative, thematic, and iconographical features of genre without in any philosophically loaded sense *knowing* the genre. A second problem with the idea that we antecedently know the story (i.e. the story-type) is the implication that, for any genre, the story-type is in a neat way self-identical, fixed, prescribed, invariant, and singular. But this cannot be the case. Reading around in a genre will tell us that any genre—both as structure and as historical process—may 'be dominated by repetition, but [is] also marked fundamentally by difference, variation and change' (QG 56). For all genres, the story-type is, in Hans Robert Jauss's felicitous, hermeneutical phrase, a 'horizon of expectations'.[10] The story-type includes a range (though not necessarily a terribly broad range) of possibilities from which the particular text makes a selection. If we are engaged with a text which offers the co-presence of different generic types (i.e. thriller and romance, romance and comedy, horror and parody, screwball comedy and irony), the range of possibilities broadens accordingly.

Carroll's suggestion that this 'most basic mode' of reading generic texts dissolves the paradox is mistaken. For there is no paradox of rationality (which, I admit, is also Carroll's point), at least until it can be demonstrated that a viewer holds contradictory beliefs or acts against her better judgement. It is a prevarication with respect to the term 'story' to suggest that familiarity with story-type equals knowledge of the particular story, since in each case a particular story will make decisions as between the various options available within the story-type. This prevarication points to the need to think through all that is involved in the notion of 'genre', and in the notion of 'story-type'. And it is worth doing this, since it will allow us to consider Carroll's positive recommendations concerning generic comprehension and self-rewarding cognitive activities. In the next section, I develop a broadly Aristotelian position concerning narrative, specifically generic narratives. Showing how inexorably story, plot, and genre are interconnected will allow me to criticize the notion of 'transactional value' worked out in terms of story-focused self-rewarding cognitive activities and their putative satisfactions.

2. GENRE, STORY, PLOT

The Aristotelians include, among others, Northrop Frye, Paul Ricœur, Bert States, Thomas Sobchack, and Peter Brooks. What I am calling a broadly Aristotelian line on narrative focuses on plot-based, agent-centred narratives. To consider the question of how such narratives work involves turning our attention away from the description or evaluation of the story or content or message of any particular narrative and toward the form of narrative. It is a main contention of Aristotelians that narrative comprehension—our ability to understand anything *as* a story—depends upon our ability to recognize narrative form or narrative structure.

The Aristotelian line about narrative structure is itself familiar. I think it is uncontroversial that when we recognize something as a story, it is probably because of the co-presence of a variety of canonical features including characters, settings, actions, and events. But we do not just have characters, settings, actions, and events; as Aristotle put it long ago, we have an *emplotted* course of action with a beginning, a middle, and an end. Emplotment is the term used by Frye and Ricœur to translate the Greek *muthos*. *Muthos* as emplotment does not describe the static structure of some plot or other, but, as Ricœur remarks, is instead 'an operation, an integrating process'. It is 'the work of composition which gives a dynamic identity to the story recounted'.[11] Emplotment concerns not just the compositional activity of the novelist, film-maker, tragedian, or other author; it concerns as well the compositional activity of the reader or viewer in coming to understand any narrative. Emplotment involves 'the synthesis of heterogeneous elements'. This, as Ricœur reminds us, requires both the 'synthesis between the events or incidents which are multiple and the story which is unified and complete', and the synthesis that 'organizes together components that are as heterogeneous as unintended circumstances, discoveries, those who perform actions and those who suffer them, chance or planned encounters, interactions between actors ranging from conflict to collaboration, means that are well or poorly adjusted to ends, and finally unintended results' (LIQ 21). Narrative form negotiates between the expected and the unexpected, between the foreseeable and the unforeseen. So a canonical story structure must already be one with much latitude for the accommodation of unexpected and/or unintended—and so, at one level, *unpredictable*—incidents and events.

What counts as a canonical story structure? David Bordwell suggests that a canonical story structure goes 'something like this: introduction of setting and characters—explanation of a state of affairs—complicating action—ensuing events—outcome—ending'.[12] What makes this general structure worth calling canonical is that, as empirical research into narrative comprehension demonstrates, the ability to recognize something *as* a story, and the ability to *retell* a story, both decline if there are significant departures from this general story schema. But we do not need to turn either to psychological research into narrative comprehension or to the literary study of narrative structures (i.e. to narratology) to get a picture of what a canonical story structure amounts to. Roberts has found Algis Budrys's splendidly Aristotelian seven-part description of a story in a science fiction fanzine. A story features:

(1) a protagonist with a
(2) problem in a
(3) context in which his
(4) efforts to solve the problem are a succession of revelatory failures which lead up to a
(5) precipitating event which makes inevitable a
(6) solution followed by a
(7) reward.[13]

Clearly, this is not the one-and-only canonical story structure. Still, it is immediately recognizable as a story schema. Like Bordwell's simpler version, we find here just what we would expect: characters who are involved in purposive actions with a view to solving or resolving a problem or anomaly in an initial situation or context. This version emphasizes the fact that characters have differing degrees of centrality to any narrative, and that standardly the central character is a particular sort of narrative figure, a *protagonist*, around whose actions and reactions the plot develops. Further, we discover here something about the peculiar logic of standard narratives, which depend upon peripety—those divulging or precipitating events which, as Budry remarks, *make inevitable* some particular resolution. And that which is *made inevitable* as a solution often comes in the form of a reward. Canonical story schemata are repeated across nearly all generic fictions. When we think about a canonical story schema, what we are actually talking about is a plot. So despite the tendency of narratology to make distinctions between story and plot along the lines, for example, of the Russian Formalists' distinction between *fabula* and *syuzhet*, when we recognize something as a story, what we are recognizing is an *emplotted story, a muthos*. We *expect* that generic fictions will be organized in terms of just such recognizable story schemata. Arguably, one of the things with which we are already familiar when we set out to read or view a new instance of generic fiction is this basic plot schema. So our expectations begin with the idea that some such story structure will be the framework for the particular generic text.

Thomas Sobchack, perhaps the most Aristotelian of writers on the topic of film genres, suggests that we 'conside[r] the fictional genre film as a single category that includes all that is commonly held to be genre film'.[14] Cutting through the iconographical and other differences separating the ordinary genres—separating science fiction from gangster from musical, and so forth—Sobchack discerns a common structure to the films ordinarily thought of as generic. The common feature is plot structure. Perhaps Sobchack overpraises the earliest (and now canonical) examples of any ordinary genre, calling these 'classical' and criticizing subsequent films within that ordinary genre for dissipating 'the power and purity of the original' by 'embroider[y] and decorat[ion]' (FG 104–5). He also laments those generic films which violate the conventions of closure, especially those that end in a state of moral ambiguity, where for example the villain gets away unpunished. But he is certainly right to emphasize that *the* most predictable and familiar aspect of genre is not, after all, the permutations of the particular generic film or even the conventions of the ordinary genres but the overarching plot structure exploited by generic fictions.

The basic form of plot is clearly *dramatic*, indeed 'blatantly' so (FG 102). But genre films are also indebted to the *melodramatic*.[15] Characterization by broad moral type, emotionally charged incidents, calculated pacing of sequences for emotional effect, uses of voice and music, and so on, have melodramatic ramifications in genre films. What genre films are not, Sobchack insists, are imitations of actions-in-the-world.[16] If generic plots have any mimetic function, if they can be said to imitate anything, what they imitate is *other plots, other fictions* (FG 104).[17] Indeed, we might argue that generic fictions are organized around those uniquely dramatic *and melodramatic* narrative moments when the unexpected, accidental, unintended, or even catastrophic event that *could not have been predicted*—at least on the basic level of a causal sequence of actions—turns out to have been inevitable after all.[18]

The plots at issue here have a striking feature, often discussed in the literature of narratology. We can think of it in terms of a double order of causality.[19] The two orders are, roughly, the causal order of sequence and the entelechial order of configuration.[20] The first involves the notion of a linear-causal plot structure, a structure which respects chronological (i.e. linear) order and a cause–effect relationship between actions in an ongoing sequence. The second involves how a whole narrative is comprehended as the configuration of that sequence of actions. Entelechial causality is historical and retrospective, which is another way of saying that it is teleological.

The first order is concerned with how things might develop, where the plot action might go; the second is concerned with everything that has led the plot to the particular situation which marks its closure. Entelechial causality is the dramatic and melodramatic mode of causality *par excellence*. It is the mode that shows how, given a plot structure where the end is prefigured in the beginning, the beginning a trope of the ending, events which are not part of the sequential chain of intended actions come to have causal significance for the characters in question. Thinking in terms of entelechial causality allows us to see that the emotional and melodramatic aspects of generic plots are as much parts of the story as the sequence of plot incidents because they both contribute to the orientation of our expectations. Further, we see that emotional and melodramatic moments in generic films often arise because of those unexpected, unintentional, or chance events and actions which, it turns out, are not random (though, at the level of sequence, they are presented as random), but central to the configuration of the plot at hand. With uncanny economy, generic fictions make present for us this basically entelechial narrative structure.

And economy is crucial, not trivial, in considering such fictions. Carroll remarks that best-sellers aspire to be page-turners; Sobchack adds that engrossing genre films feel shorter than they are. Not only is the plot *right there*; the moral qualities of the characters are, also, *right there*, the sense of drama or urgency *right there*. One rarely has to sort out the moral align- ment of genre characters, because there is virtually no distance between character and moral attributes. How else could we talk so effortlessly about heroes and villains?[21]

Like Carroll, Sobchack believes that our primary interest in generic plots concerns what is happening and what is going to happen. This is not a rejection of the centrality of entelechial organization in generic plots. Rather, it is a recognition of how economical entelechial organization has become in the genre movie: 'the elements presented in the exposition at the beginning are all clearly involved with the inevitable conclusion,' Sobchack writes, adding, 'Only those scenes that advance the plot are permitted.' Our directedness toward what is happening and what is going to happen under- scores our expectations about the general, generic course of events as well as our interest in, and alignment with, certain characters and their activities. Of course, in certain genres (the thriller, the horror film, action films), what we should be expecting is the unexpected.

Let us now return to Carroll's notion of a basic mode of engagement which focuses on plot action for the particular story we are reading or watching. Carroll's 'basic mode' is a story-token-focused account of the reader's or viewer's interest. Correctly guessing 'What is going to happen next?' allows her to derive 'justifiable satisfactions' by reading for the plot. These satisfactions, in order to be justifiable, must themselves be cognitive or rational. They depend upon the reader's ability to make correct predictions about the ongoing development of the particular plot. Justifiable satisfactions will be calculated in terms of correct cognitive judgements (which Carroll distinguishes from associated judgement-types, including moral judgements and emotional judgements). A justifiable satisfaction is a cognitive-rational satisfaction because the reader is actively engaged in thinking through the permutations of plot. (I suspect that, if he were to say more about the sorts of moral and emotional judgements that are appropriate to generic fictions, we would discover that there is a cognitive-rational bias in these as well.) Carroll proposes that a reader derives 'transactional value'—i.e. justifiable satisfaction—when she is able to exercise and apply her interpretative powers while reading the story (PJF 234). This 'self-rewarding cognitive activity' occurs when 'our inferences and interpretations are correct' relative to the particular story (PJF 235).

This 'basic mode' allegedly allows for 'self-rewarding cognitive activities' which a reader or viewer enjoys if she can make correct story-token-focused predictions about what is going to happen next in an ongoing generic course of events. This makes sense of the ongoing consumption of new instances of generic fictions, thus dispelling the suspicion of irrationality because the reader or viewer turns out to be engaged in worthwhile cognitive activity with respect to each new instance of the familiar genre. But I am extremely dubious about the notion of 'self-rewarding cognitive activities' keyed to the successful prediction of action. I do not believe that we can hive off expectations about the genre from expectations about how a particular plot will unfold. As I will argue in the next section, not only is Carroll's contention not properly transgeneric; it also fails to deal with the interconnection between particular plot and the generic frameworks that constrain and shape our engagement with particular plots. What is behind these objections is a concern with Carroll's too limited account of narrative comprehension in the context of generic fictions.

3. ARISTOTELIANS IN ACTION

Carroll remarks that the paradox of junk fiction 'disappears when we are thinking of what is called classical detective fiction' (PJF 33). I am inclined to think that it disappears not just for classical detective fiction but also for mystery stories in general, whether a traditional 'mystery' story or not: some romances and a fair amount of soap opera work on the principal of an enigma or mystery, for instance a secret from the past. The crossroads between mystery and detection is so clearly tied to the interconnection of what Barthes calls the code of action and the code of enigma[22] that it is hard to see how any reader or viewer could simply passively run her eyes over the words or images of such a fiction and *not* form hypotheses about how things will go, hard to imagine how she could *fail* to participate in 'a continual process of constructing a sense of where the story is headed' by 'envisioning or anticipating the *range* of things ... that are apt to happen next' (PJF 235). Indeed, for those who enjoy fictions which centre on resolving a mystery or explaining an enigma, the idea of ongoing cognitive activity seems essential to following the story at all. And arguably, it is doubtful that we could say that a reader or viewer *understood* the mystery if she failed to attend to it in these ways. Detective stories, as Frank Kermode remarks, often exhibit a 'specialized "hermeneutic" organization'[23] which focuses attention on clues and the possibility of ordering them so as to produce a solution; but this is indeed a *specialized* organization, one not necessarily employed by other ordinary genres. Yet even as we say this, we might overlook two equally common features of mystery or detective narration: the early presentation of salient information *without disclosing its saliency*, so that we will only figure out afterwards that *that* was a clue after all, and the related strategy of planting false clues (red herrings) to lead us to make wrong guesses about the criminal, the crime, the motive, and so forth.

So the example of detection and mystery—introduced to support Carroll's notion that spectators are cognitively active in predicting the range of things that are likely to happen next—is actually a problem for Carroll. The sorts of cognitive activities demanded of those who want to follow and understand such fictions are not merely anticipatory, and certainly not focused on correctly guessing 'What will happen next?' There is a retrospective aspect to understanding mystery or detective fictions. We cannot be certain what the mystery *is* until we are able to explain just what has happened. In fictions centred around the mysterious or the enigmatic, our understanding of the fiction is always subject to correction and revision.[24] The mystery can only be solved when we discover what actually happened. This will standardly involve reinterpreting or redescribing a prior situation or sequence of events. Understanding a mystery is not simply a prospective undertaking, requiring us to forecast what will happen next. It involves rethinking what we take to have happened, and what counts as relevant to our understanding of what has happened. So, in order to 'follow' the plot of a mystery or a detective fiction, we do not merely hypothesize about the range of possible *future* actions; we also have to hypothesize about what seems to have happened in the past. Those different possibilities about what the past events and actions were will produce different views about what the current course of events is, and will have different implications for what we anticipate happening in the future. It is much harder to see that anything this involved is needed to understand fictions from other ordinary genres.

According to Carroll, the sort of cognitive activity required of genre viewers is one that finds us situated at the forward edge of the developing plot, thinking toward—and making predictions about—what is going to happen next. Taking as an example *Sleepless in Seattle*, Carroll suggests that when 'the heroine finds the boy's knapsack, the viewer tracks the action in terms of the question of whether our heroine and our heroes will meet or pass each other on the elevators' (PJF 235). This example seems innocent enough. But it is far from innocent: the scene in question is the concluding one of the film, the scene we have all been waiting for, the scene in which our heroes and our heroine receive their reward, namely, each other. What allows us to track the action is our generic directedness toward their meeting at the previously established rendezvous point, the Empire State Building on Valentine's Day. We do not even entertain questions such as, 'Will Tom Hanks say farewell to Meg Ryan at the outskirts of town and ride back into the wilderness?' (a good guess for a classical western) or 'Will Meg Ryan, realizing that there is nobody left to kill the monster, drive a stake through Hanks's heart?' (a good guess for Gothic horror).

Carroll suggests that viewers track the action in terms of the question whether or not our heroes and our heroine will meet, once Meg Ryan has arrived at the deserted observation deck and found the knapsack that Hanks's son has conveniently forgotten. But the very framing of the question misrepresents the range of options available at this point in the plot. Even Carroll grants that their eventual meeting is generically assured; but the implication that there is a significant likelihood that they will *not* meet here is not a reasonable one. Of course, if we were witnessing an action in the world rather than the final few minutes of *this particular* romantic comedy, then, it is true, we might suppose that the two will either meet here or miss each other. And whether considering real life or romantic comedy, we can hope for a certain resolution (their meeting) while worrying about whether it will happen or not. But *in terms of this plot*, could Hanks and Ryan miss each other? No.

The governing tropes of this film (especially the tropes concerning magical signs and fateful coincidences), its melodramatic structure, its established relation to but significant differences from the repeatedly mentioned *An Affair to Remember*, its utter lack of irony, and the generic inevitability of the union of the correct couple collectively configure the scene at the Empire State Building as one where *they cannot fail to meet*. And indeed they cannot fail but to meet *on the observation deck*. The scene Carroll chooses is one which is entelechially predetermined. Why the meeting cannot fail to happen has already been clearly and unmistakably established. It has been made perfectly evident to us that Sam (Hanks) needs a new wife, and that his son Jonah will be the matchmaker, the creator of the successful union. Further, it has been made perfectly evident to us that

Annie (Ryan) is the perfect mate for him. Annie falls in love with Sam upon first hearing his voice, as he tells Dr Marcia, the radio phone-in therapist[25]—and all of listening America—the story about how much he loved and still misses his wife. And Sam falls for Annie on first sight, when she passes him without realizing it at the Seattle airport. In the meantime, meddling by both Jonah and Annie's best chum has ensured at least the possibility that Sam and Annie will meet. Indeed, even before they both arrive in New York, not only do *we* know that they are the correct couple, and not only does each of them already have a sense that they are somehow fated for each other, but they have very nearly met, in an otherwise quite preposterous scene outside Sam's Seattle waterfront home. There, with Annie in the middle of the road and traffic on both sides, they have *seen each other and said hello.* So given all this and Jonah's decision that they should meet on Valentine's Day at the Empire State Building's observation deck, there is no entelechial option left but for them to meet.

Now, Carroll has said that viewers will track the action in terms of the question whether the two will meet (i.e. on the observation deck) or pass each other on the elevators. But consider the (melo)dramatic construction of the film as it approaches its conclusion. Annie has already almost run herself out of time to get to the rendezvous. Dusk has fallen on New York. Sam has caught up with Jonah at the observation deck—not to meet Annie but to reclaim his son. After waiting for hours, even Jonah has given up hope that Annie will arrive. Annie, at the last possible moment, sees the huge Valentine's Day heart blocked out in red-lit windows up the side of the Empire State Building. On the basis of this contingent event ('It's a sign!'), she dashes across town. Sam and Jonah finally leave as the observation deck closes. Annie wins permission to go up to the deck even though it has just closed. As audience, we know that she has missed Jonah and Sam. Our involvement with this plot means that we are for a moment saddened; the possibility of the happy ending has been thrown into question. But Annie finds the knapsack. The string of magical coincidences has not yet ended. With this as background, is it *reasonable* to suppose that the inevitable meeting will occur anywhere but where it does? The film *has* to unite the two on the observation deck. Arguably, it would violate its own narrative logic—a logic that includes the conventional last-minute coincidences of melodrama—*and* lose its audience's emotional commitment if it failed to have the meeting occur where Jonah desired it to.

Let us see where these reflections on mystery/detection and romantic comedy have got us. It seems that, at least if we are interested in figuring things out for ourselves, we might indeed track the action of a mystery or detection film by forecasting or predicting what will happen next. Like the detective figure, we will search the narrative for clues and motives, and thus perhaps make predictions that may turn out to be correct, and such correct predictions (hunches, guesses, hypotheses) might indeed provide us with what Carroll describes as justifiable cognitive satisfaction. (Of course, we do not have to play this game; we can simply wait until the identity of the criminal is revealed to us.) But this is not all we do, for in the case of mystery and detection, in order to entertain expectations about what is going to happen, we will also have to have formed hypotheses about what has *already* happened. Narrative comprehension in such a case is not simply forward-looking. We have also seen that, at least for some romantic comedies, following the plot does not depend upon the formulation of hypotheses in the same way as following the plot of a mystery. In some romantic comedies, our ability to track action is just as effectively accomplished by means of our generic expectations rather than plot-specific predictions. Generic expectations, including expectations that acknowledge the entelechial causality of generic plots, seem to be more basic to following generic films than story-specific predictions. Let's consider this possibility with respect to a third genre, the action film.

Delayed (but ensured) gratification of hoped-for romantic union is a key plot device of the romantic comedy; ongoing gratification through the orchestration of suspense and tension is crucial to successful action films. Romantic comedy requires the regulated introduction of events which the central characters do not know about and that occasionally viewers also do not know about—usually in the form of actions taken by third parties intended to help bring about or prevent the desired resolution; action films involve the regulated introduction of events which the audience cannot expect and which are moreover events which pose serious threats to those characters with whom we have been aligned and toward whom we feel allegiance.[26] The perpetual risk of danger or the unexpected, properly modulated, produces the sort of suspense and tension that the action film requires.[27]

Finding ourselves on the forward edge of the plot of an action film such as *Speed*,[28] are we likely to be concerned with making predictions (let alone correct ones) about particular events or actions? Arguably not, and for reasons that—perhaps unexpectedly—parallel the account of romantic comedy just considered. At most points in most generic narratives, there are not really *that* many possible ways in which the sequence of events *could* proceed, given the genre and the particular unfolding of the plot in question. Often we are faced with two-place disjunctions—roughly, either some event will happen or it will not. So in the opening sequence of *Speed*, Jack (Keanu Reeves) and his partner will rescue the folks trapped in the elevator or they will not. That is: Jack and his partner will guess that the person who has rigged the elevator with explosives will explode the device anyway, whether or not the ransom is met, and so they will have to devise a strategy that will rescue the trapped passengers. Given all this, either they will rescue the passengers or they will not. A spectator might hope that the rescue will be successful but doubt, all things considered, that it could be.[29] After all, how *do* you rescue passengers caught in an express elevator several floors from the nearest emergency panel in the face of a bomber threatening to explode a second device if he does not receive an enormous ransom? And once we get to a two-place, either/or disjunction, viewers might 'predict' how the action will unfold. Or, recognizing the urgency of the situation and being on the forward edge of a fast-moving episode, they might wait to see how events unfold without predicting things one way or the other.

But which viewer will guess, as Jack does, that the villain intends to (and will) explode the bomb anyway? And which viewer will guess *the strategy* Jack devises to try to rescue the passengers? Jack's correct intuition about the bomber, his ability to work out an *unguessable* means of saving the passengers, and the pressure of too little time, are what makes for the fascination and suspense of this sequence. If viewers were in general correctly able to guess *these* parts of the plot's development, it would only be evidence of a bad plot.[30]

What we are considering here, after all, is the opening sequence of an action film. This is the sequence that establishes Jack, not just as any old protagonist, but as an action hero. As an action hero, his abilities within the fictional world are significantly greater than those of other characters, and certainly greater than ours are in the actual world. We must be shown that Jack can bend the circumstances of the fictional world to his will. Everything about how the rest of the film will unfold depends upon how the elevator rescue plays out. In our position on the forward edge of the plot, we might initially think that it is an open question whether the hostages will be rescued. This is a real question, since minor characters are often killed in action films.

When we first see the group which emerges from the boardroom meeting, it is possible that they will be killed. But as we proceed through the sequence, the possibility that the hostages will die is reduced to zero. Not only will Jack act successfully to rescue most of those trapped in the elevator, he will rescue *all* of them. He *has* to rescue all of them, because he is at serious risk of death or maiming himself during the final instants when the last passenger stands petrified in the elevator, too terrified to move. But even she (finally!) does what Jack tells her, takes his hand, and is pulled to safety as the second explosive detonates and the elevator is sent careering down dozens of storeys to the inevitable thunderous crash in the basement. The action hero will risk his own life to make sure every last innocent person is rescued, and all passengers must be rescued in order to establish the hero as an action hero. Entelechially, there is no other choice.

Action films depend upon the manipulation of affective response. This is achieved through reversals of expectation. Consider the alarming moments that cross-cut between the bus, barrelling through congested LA traffic, and two women pedestrians, one pushing a baby carriage. The cross-cutting establishes for us what neither the pedestrians nor Jack and Annie realize: that there is likely to be an accident. And our emotional investment in this scene is of course intensified because it is a *baby carriage*. At the last moment, Annie (Sandra Bullock) realizes that a collision is unavoidable. Like Annie, we are shaken, devastated. But then the reversal (since, after all, Annie could not have harmed a baby): yes, the bus collided with the carriage, only the baby carriage did not have a baby in it, but instead a collection of old pop cans. Everyone breathes a sigh of relief.

But the baby carriage sequence, as a reversal of expectation, only anticipates the next significant reversal. The problems for the bus in the city—given that it cannot slow down below 50 m.p.h. without detonating the bomb on board—are overwhelming. News that they can get onto the freeway suggests that, finally, some control can be regained which will give Jack time to deal with the general situation of the bomb and the hostages. Getting around the near-impossible right-hand turn is tricky but successful. So given the principle of reversals, just when it looks like things are going to be okay, and the characters, along with the audience, experience again the euphoric release of tension typical of such moments when success has been torn from the teeth of what ought reasonably to have been disaster—we discover *what we could not have expected or even guessed*: that the freeway has not been completed, that there is (yes!) an unfinished overpass which the bus must *jump*, since it cannot either stop, turn, or exit. We could not have guessed that there would be a great gaping hole in the freeway. But even at that moment of celebration as the hostages on the bus cheer Annie's driving and hug each other, anyone who is at all familiar with the genre could predict that, at any second, *something* is bound to go wrong.

So if by 'cognitive activity' Carroll means that, once the bus reaches the apparent security of a long stretch of highway, we hypothesize that something bad is going to happen, then there would be general agreement. I take it, however, that Carroll means something much more strictly keyed to the particular film, something much less generic than the guess that 'something bad is going to happen'. He has to mean something more keyed to the particular film, since otherwise we are back at the point of paradox, watching a film where, because of our familiarity with the genre, we know what is going to happen next (namely, *something bad*). In action films, you are not expected to guess just what is going to happen next. Surely it would detract from the pleasure of action films if, in a regular fashion, you *could* guess what is going to happen next; it would deprive you of the pleasure of anticipating further calamities, a pleasure keyed to the certainty that there will be more of them, and to the surprise that you cannot always foresee what they will be. All you need to know is that *something* is going to happen; and given the escalatory plot structure of action films, you can also guess (correctly) that you will not have to wait long for whatever it is to happen.

So I am not persuaded that cognitive activities involving story-specific correct guesses about just what is going to happen next, or even about the range of things that are likely to happen next, are the basic mode of engagement with particular generic narratives. In the case of mystery/ detection, the generic guess that *somebody* dun it, and we will eventually find out who, is as good a guess as any. At the level of narrative comprehension, however, even sorting out just what crime has been committed, and for what reason, is possible only within and because of generic constraints. In the case of the action film, the generic guess that something bad is about to happen will serve quite well to fuel our anticipation, and is unlikely to be disappointed. In the romantic comedy, the generic guess that the romantic couple will be united is also the only relevant guess worth a mention, and it, too, is unlikely to be disappointed. These are the guesses that allow us to track the action, because these are the guesses that recognize what counts as action within each genre. And in each case, a generic guess will usually be splendidly self-rewarding, without having to be keyed to the actual development of the particular generic plot. Generic guesses are not guaranteed, of course. But arguably, without them, we would have little ability to orient ourselves to the particular generic narrative. Which is only to say, with Steve Neale, that our expectations about any particular generic text are *themselves* constitutive parts of, and expressions of, the genre or genres in question.

4. CONCLUSION, WITH A LINGERING PARADOX

I have been arguing, among other things, that the sorts of guesses that deal with the range of things that could plausibly happen in the plot of a generic film are themselves as generic as the particular generic film. The range of things that are apt to happen in *Speed* are things that are only apt to happen *because* it is an action film and not a mystery or a romantic comedy. As soon as Carroll gives the nod to the idea that spectators are busy making inferences about the *range* of possible occurrences, then I think he winds up espousing a view of the interpretation of particular generic texts that squares with Roberts's 'reading within a system' approach from which he wishes to distinguish his own view. What counts as 'the range of possibilities of action' is one that is largely determined *by the genre(s)* rather than within the constraints of the particular text.

Do we watch action films like *Speed* or romantic comedies like *Sleepless in Seattle* just to guess *what* is likely to happen next, or to feel some sort of self-rewarding *cognitive* gratification when we do? I doubt that, in the main, viewers watch generic films to make cognitive, moral, or emotional judgements (and in any event, this would be a matter for social psychology). Certainly we do not watch generic fictions in order to make moral judgements. We do not need to make them; the genre film makes them for us. With generic fictions, by and large we are not in doubt about moral questions (even apparent counter-examples are only apparently so: for instance, *film noir*). We watch *Speed* because it delivers progressively escalating action, suspense, and romance. We watch for the pleasure of the overt 'action'; some will, in addition, watch for the pleasure of anticipating the union of the romantic couple. We may also watch for the pleasure of built-in moral judgements: for example, for the opportunity to see the villain perform a sequence of progressively more heinous acts and then get what is coming to him. But this is hardly a case of making a moral judgement.

Nor am I persuaded that, in general, we watch generic films to guess what is going to happen next—and this despite the fact that our temporal engagement with narrative art forms directs our attention toward what is going to happen next. Indeed, making correct guesses seems a slim cause for satisfaction. Given the 'page-turning' character of generic fictions, the actual range of relevant inferential options is pretty clearly limited, and arguably so are the sorts and range of cognitive activities required of the reader or viewer. If, as Carroll claims, the transactional value for readers and viewers of generic fictions derives from the 'self-rewarding' character of their interpretative activity—that so often the interpreter can guess correctly about how things will unfold—it seems at least worth emphasizing that what counts as a reasonable guess in the context of particular generic fictions is a guess *keyed* to our expectations about the genre and constrained by the entelechial structure of the narrative in question. The likelihood of such directed guesses being seriously mistaken is only evidence of the degree to which we are unfamiliar with the conventions of the ordinary genre or subcategory, or the eccentricity of the film relative to its generic conventions, as we see for example in Gillian Armstrong's *My Brilliant Career*, a romantic comedy which refuses to unite the romantic couple at the end. However, as soon as we admit guesses that are keyed to expectations formed thanks to our familiarity with each ordinary genre's 'preordained forms, known plots, recognizable characters, and obvious iconographies',[31] we realize that most of our general, generic guesses will be pretty much on the money most of the time. This seems slim cause for satisfaction.

Indeed, extremely unsophisticated generic guesses about future action will often turn out to be right in the long term even if they are wrong in the short term. Jack might not actually kiss Annie until the final scenes of *Speed*, so I might have to wait a while for my guess that they will kiss to be rewarded. He did not, for instance, kiss her after she successfully pulled the bus around the near-catastophic right-hand turn onto the highway. Nor did he kiss her after they escaped from the bus (an exploding 747 interrupted the otherwise romantic moment). In one sense, if I had guessed at each point that they would kiss, I would have been disappointed, or at least not 'rewarded'. But satisfaction is guaranteed with genre; the deferral of the inevitable provides the additional pleasure of prolonged anticipation.

Following the entelechial causality of the plot at hand cannot be a matter of *predicting* what will happen next or even a matter of predicting the *range* of things that are apt to happen next in the context of this particular story. Prediction hardly seems the correct word to describe what we both hope for and have every reason to expect. It also hardly seems the correct word to describe guesses about the *range* of things apt to happen next, especially where that range comes down to either/or alternatives. Carroll's claim that the viewer's satisfaction derives from the self-rewarding cognitive activity of making correct predictions about future actions in the ongoing plot is tantamount to suggesting that, as Umberto Eco puts it, 'we are satisfied because we find again what we had expected'. Eco continues: 'We do not attribute this happy result to the obviousness of the narrative structure but to our own presumed capacities to make forecasts.'[32] Perhaps viewers are so satisfied, but I submit that this is just not quite a rational sort of satisfaction, after all.

NOTES

1. For those who doubt that such—well—*arcane* questions are still asked by philosophers of art these days, consider the review of the new journal *Film and Philosophy* written by James O. Young and published in the *ASA Newsletter*, 15: 3 (Winter 1996), 3–4. Among other animadversions, Young notes that 'few of the essays here treat films as objects of aesthetic contemplation. Words like "beauty", "aesthetic value", and even "art" seldom, if ever, appear in these essays. This is, perhaps, not surprising, since many of the films discussed, including *Back to the Future*, *Home Alone*, *Terminator II* and slasher movies, have little or no aesthetic value.' One senses here that, for Young, genre films are the very antithesis of 'supreme' works of art (p. 4), and that many genre films are ones he would simply dismiss as bad films.

2. There are no end of rationality-related worries for philosophers with respect to film fictions and indeed fictions generally. As Alex Neill has noted in 'Empathy and (Film) Fiction', in David Bordwell and Noël Carroll (eds.), *Post-Theory* (Madison: University of Wisconsin Press, 1996), 'Ancient questions as to how and why it is that we can respond emotionally to characters and events which we know

to be fictional, and whether it is rational to do so, have in recent years resurfaced' (p. 175).

3. For instance, there is rationality considered primarily in terms of optimal calculation of means to achieve ends ('means-ends rationality'), rationality understood in terms of being able to make sense of some behaviour or action by showing it to be intelligible and in that sense reasonable (even where it might not be an optimal calculation of means to achieve ends), and there is rational in the sense of optimal deductive reasoning.

4. Noël Carroll, 'The Paradox of Junk Fiction', *Philosophy and Literature*, 18: 2 (Oct. 1994), 225–41. References to this article appear in brackets in the text as PJF.

5. I employ the notion of 'ordinary genres' to distinguish these sorts of familiar groupings from the four main categories of generic emplotment identified by Northrop Frye in *Anatomy of Criticism: Four Essays* (Princeton: Princeton University Press, 1957) as tragedy, comedy, romance, and satire/irony.

6. The terrific importance of iconographical features for visual narratives, notably cinematic ones, is emphasized by Thomas Sobchack, 'Film Genre: A Classical Experience', *Film Genre Reader* (Austin: University of Texas Press, 1986), 102–13. References to Sobchack appear in the text as FG.

7. Thomas J. Roberts, *An Aesthetics of Junk Fiction* (Athens, Ga.: University of Georgia Press, 1990). References to this book appear as *AJF*.

8. Steve Neale, 'Questions of Genre', *Screen*, 31: 1 (Spring 1990), 45–66. References to this article appear in the text as QG.

9. E. D. Hirsch's suggestion, in *Validity in Interpretation* (New Haven: Yale University Press, 1967), that it is better not to think of genres in terms of types is probably a wise one. Here I keep the term 'type' while agreeing with Hirsch that a generic type is not one that predetermines its tokens, but is rather a system abstracted from its various tokens.

10. Cited by Neale, QG 56.

11. Paul Ricœur, 'Life in Quest of Narrative', in David Wood (ed.), *On Paul Ricœur: Narrative and Interpretation* (London: Routledge, 1991), 20. References to this article appear in the text as LIQ.

12. David Bordwell, *Narration in the Fiction Film* (Madison: University of Wisconsin Press, 1985), 35.

13. Budrys also offers a version of this schema for stories with villains as central characters. These stories involve '(1) a protagonist with a (2) problem in a (3) context in which his (4) efforts to solve the problem are a series of revelatory increasing successes which lead up to a (5) precipitating event which makes inevitable a (6) failure followed by (7) punishment'. He adds: 'Clearly, these are the same thing'— i.e. these are recognizable every time as *stories*. The quote appears in Roberts, *AJF* 90.

14. Sobchack, FG 114.

15. Thomas Elsaessar's article 'Tales of Sound and Fury', *Film Genre Reader*, 278–308, is the *locus classicus* for the discussion of the melodramatic aspects of family melodrama, but his concerns with the audience's emotional identification with these generic films, the importance of plot structuring, the role of voice and music, *mise en scène*, and iconography have implications for the study of other ordinary genres.

16. Roberts notes the interanimation of contemporary social, political, and other concerns, as well as the interpellation of current idiomatic language, slang, and 'technologese' into generic fictions, but this is not to be confused with 'imitating reality'. Neale remarks that some ordinary genres, for instance 'gangster films, war films and police procedural thrillers ... dra[w] on and quot[e] "authentic" (and authenticating) discourses, artefacts and texts' while other genres (science fiction, horror) 'make less appeal to this kind of authenticity' (QG 47).

17. This point has previously been made by Northrop Frye in *Anatomy of Criticism*, 95.
18. For an engaging recent discussion of peripety, see Bert O. States, *The Pleasure of the Play* (Ithaca, NY: Cornell University Press, 1994), 86.
19. See, for example, the discussion in Peter Brooks, *Reading for the Plot: Design and Intention in Narrative* (Cambridge, Mass.: Harvard University Press, 1992), 18. Others have drawn attention to this doubled feature of narrative; Brooks cites, for example, Jonathan Culler's notion of the 'double logic' of narrative (p. 28). Both writers are mentioned in relation to this notion in Gerald Prince's *A Dictionary of Narratology* (Lincoln: University of Nebraska Press, 1987).
20. States makes this distinction using the terms 'empirical' and 'entelechial' causality; I have decided against employing 'empirical causality' only because it is a phrase that philosophers might quibble about.
21. As Sobchack has noted, in terms of our iconographically cued ability to recognize heroes and villains at a glance, typecasting is a virtue, not a fault. He cites John Wayne as the westerner; we could develop comparable accounts of such figures as Meg Ryan, Tom Cruise, Nicholas Cage, Sharon Stone . . . Things are not always just good or evil in genre. Still, occupying positions toward either end of the moral scale is consistent with the melodramatic tendencies of genre films.
22. Roland Barthes, *S/Z*, trans. Richard Martin (New York: Hill & Wang, 1974). The two codes in question are the proairetic and the hermeneutical; the other three concern the semes, the symbolic, and the cultural.
23. Frank Kermode, 'Secrets and Narrative Sequence', in W. J. T. Mitchell (ed.), *On Narrative* (Chicago: University of Chicago Press, 1981), 83.
24. George McKnight and I discuss detection narratives in 'The Case of the Disappearing Enigma', forthcoming in *Philosophy and Literature*, 21: 1.
25. The device of the radio phone-in show, and the absurdity of the pretence that this is at all related to therapy, is actually a striking feature of *Sleepless in Seattle*. It is the sort of feature that Thomas Roberts would note secures the reciprocal position of a junk text *vis-à-vis* its contemporary mediascape. And little wonder that, after the release of the film, the idea of the lonely widower was spun off for an episode of *Oprah*. On the subject of Dr Marcia, Jenny Turner—in a nicely jaundiced review of the film—correctly catches the function of such a figure with the British expression 'agony aunt' (*Sight and Sound*, 3: 10 (Oct. 1993), 53).
26. These terms are central to Murray Smith's argument against a reductive view of spectatorial 'identification' in his *Engaging Characters: Fiction, Emotion, and the Cinema* (Oxford: Clarendon Press, 1995).
27. This is a point Carroll has already developed in his article 'Toward a Theory of Film Suspense', *Persistence of Vision*, 1 (Summer 1984), 65–89, where he proposes that suspense develops in relation to two possible, logically opposed outcomes to a set of events, such that one outcome is morally correct but unlikely, while the other is evil and likely.
28. As an action film, *Speed* is certainly distinguishable from many others in the genre, notably those that serve as the usual vehicles for stars such as Schwarzenegger, Stallone, and van Damme. *Speed* is an *unspectacular* action film. The action is (just about) plausible on a daily level, unlike, say, *Terminator II*. The inspiration for the situation comes from the newspapers, not from comic books. Our action hero is a professional police officer, not some superhuman figure. The film does not depend on extravagant special effects but is, in the main, quite modestly shot (though the subway train crash is nice).
29. A structure of expectations consistent with Carroll's theory of suspense.
30. As Sobchack has remarked (FG 108), generic heroes 'can do what we would like to be able to do. They can pinpoint the evil in their lives as resident in a monster or a villain, and they can go out and triumph over it. We, on the other hand, are in a

muddle. We know things aren't quite right, but we are not sure if it is a conspiracy among corporations, the world situation, politicians . . . ; but whatever it is, we can't call it out of the saloon for a shoot-out or round up the villagers and hunt it down.'
31. Ibid. 105.
32. Umberto Eco, *The Limits of Interpretation* (Bloomington: Indiana University Press, 1990), 86.

PART V
Emotional Response

Consult any commercial screenwriting manual and it will indicate that one of the writer's highest priorities is to engage the spectator's emotional response. Yet the task of investigating and understanding our emotional response to films has, until recently, been largely ignored by academic writing. Carl Plantinga offers an explanation of this neglect. The intellectual tradition of political modernism that framed the discourse of contemporary film theorists militated against serious investigation of the emotions for three reasons. First, it inherited from Brecht a suspicion of emotional response as something inimical to the cultivation of critical faculties in the spectator. Secondly, film theorists cast emotional response within the framework of a psychoanalytic theory of desire and pleasure, subordinating emotions as such to what they regarded as more fundamental psychic processes and dynamics. Thirdly, the same body of film theory tended to characterize our emotional response to fictions on the basis of their formal properties alone. The result was a conception of the role of emotions in our response to fiction which was both negative and reductive.

Drawing on work in both cognitive science and recent philosophy of mind, Plantinga argues that a cognitive approach to the emotions offers a way of taking the role of emotions more seriously than it has been taken in most contemporary film theory. In Plantinga's usage 'cognitivism' is distinctive by virtue of its challenge to the traditional distinction between reason and passion, and its emphasis on the place of reason within emotional response. Plantinga, following Murray Smith, emphasizes the range and complexity of our emotional responses to films and the different roles emotions may play in our lives. Once this complexity is recognized, we can begin to investigate the ethical implications of emotional response. Plantinga examines in detail the case of sentimentality in the movies.

However, political modernists are not alone amongst academic theorists in having neglected the emotions. David Bordwell, who has advanced an impressively detailed cognitive theory of narrative comprehension that explicitly contests psychoanalytic and semiotic theories of film, marginalizes the emotions as well. In Bordwell's case, though, this arises from a methodological imperative to narrow his scope of enquiry, rather than from a mistaken characterization of the nature of emotion. However, focusing on the account of classical narration developed by Bordwell in conjunction with Kristin Thompson and Janet Staiger, Dirk Eitzen argues that Bordwell's failure to address the emotions distorts his understanding of classical cinema. While Bordwell offers a perspicuous description of the 'transparent', goal-oriented narrative that defines the classical mode of story-telling, this is not the primary explanation of the existence and persistence of the classical mode. To be sure, classical narration does maximize our comprehension of the story; but it does so in order to maximize the range and intensity of our emotional responses. Where emotional response can be delivered in other ways, the economy of classical narration will be sacrificed. For Eitzen the case of comedy is exemplary in this regard: a major genre of classical cinema, it displays Hollywood's willingness to sacrifice narrative transparency and drive for the sake of delivering laughs.

The analysis of emotional responses to fiction in contemporary philosophy has focused upon the so-called 'paradox of fiction'. How can we have an emotional response to characters in fictions when we know that those characters do not exist? The illusion theory of fiction provides one answer: we mistakenly believe, for the duration of our engagement with the fiction, that the characters do exist. Once this theory is abandoned—as Noël Carroll, Gregory Currie, and Smith have all argued it must be—there are several plausible alternatives. Among these is the 'thought theory' of emotional response, which argues that we are moved by imagining or entertaining in thought the characters and events of fictions. Murray Smith presents here an elaboration of such a theory, focusing on the role of 'imagining from the inside', or 'central' imagining, in generating empathic emotions. Imagining 'from the inside', he argues, is a particular kind of imagining in which we simulate the beliefs and emotions of characters, as if we were those characters in the situations in which we see them depicted. Smith begins by discussing the relationship between such 'central' imagining, and the contrasting form of 'acentral' imagining in which we simulate belief in the events and characters of the fiction, but not 'from within' any character's perspective. He also discusses certain techniques, like the point-of-view shot, which are usually assumed to elicit central imagining, and limns the very specific conditions under which these devices may be said to perform this function. Through reflection on his own earlier work and on Currie's *Image and Mind*, he argues that, while central imagining cannot be made the basis of a theoretical understanding of imagination and emotion prompted by fiction films, neither can it be eliminated from such theories.

Malcolm Turvey argues against the 'thought theory' of emotional response as it has been taken up by both Smith and Carroll as an alternative to illusion theories of representation. While the thought theory correctly severs the idea of our emotional response to fiction films from our belief in the existence of the objects depicted, Turvey argues that it does so at the price of failing to acknowledge the sensory basis of our response to films. In an essay that complements Richard Allen's chapter on perception earlier in the volume, Turvey argues that thought theories of emotional response to film arise only from the prior assumption that there is a paradox about responding to fictional entities, but that this paradox itself arises only because the thought theorist assumes that because fictional entities are not physically present they cannot be seen. Drawing on a detailed examination of Wittgenstein's comments on aspect perception, Turvey suggests that, on the contrary, we can speak of seeing even where what we see is not a physical object. It is therefore not necessary to claim that we entertain the fiction in thought in order to have an emotional response to it. According to Turvey, we simply respond emotionally to what we see.

16

Notes on Spectator Emotion and Ideological Film Criticism

Carl Plantinga

Many of us occasionally practise ideological criticism, when we consider the ideological issues raised by viewing films. We often believe that films have moral and ideological significance and that they are not merely consumed, discarded, and forgotten but have psychological and cultural effects. Whether it be concern with screen violence, racism, Oliver Stone's revisionist histories, or the promotion of shallow emotional lives, ideological criticism appraises the moral and ideological import of experiences offered by films.

The purpose of this chapter is not primarily to chart a particular ethical position toward the emotions mainstream films are designed to elicit, but to suggest how emotions should be understood in ideological criticism. That being said, I do argue for one substantive ideological claim—that while we should certainly be aware of the rhetorical uses of spectator emotions, it makes little sense to condemn such emotions *tout court*. I begin by criticizing two tenets of ideological film criticism widely assumed in film studies. The first, deriving from Bertolt Brecht, argues that experiencing emotion in mainstream films is inherently mystifying and politically regressive, because emotion clouds a certain kind of critical judgement. The second tenet, a legacy of neo-Freudian film theory, assumes that the critic can make universal claims about the ideological effect of various formal strategies, irrespective of a film's propositional content.

The chapter goes on to characterize spectator emotion, with a view toward conceptual clarification. It argues that the *kind* of emotional experience a film offers, and not emotion *per se*, is a proper target of ideological investigation. It holds that a cognitive approach to emotion is useful in describing kinds of spectator emotions. In its second half, the essay examines two families of screen emotions—(1) sentiment and sentimentality, and (2) the emotions which accompany screen violence—to demonstrate how spectator emotion is related to ideological criticism.

Thanks to the editors, Richard Allen and Murray Smith, for their helpful comments on an earlier draft of this chapter.

IDEOLOGICAL STOICISM

At least since Plato, critics have worried about the affective nature of art. The pleasurable affect and emotion elicited by films has also been a central concern of film criticism. Some critics presume a duality between an emotional response deemed naive, self-indulgent, or even perverse, and an intellectual, vigilant, cognitive response based on reason and critical judgement. An emotional or pleasurable experience is often thought to be harmful or naïve of itself, while an alienated, distanced response becomes the mark of a knowing spectator.

Both the neo-Brechtian and neo-Freudian approaches in film theory distrust the affective pleasures offered by mainstream films. While Brecht and neo-Brechtians characterize emotion negatively, in 'common sense' terms, neo-Freudians refer to pleasures resulting from the arousal and fulfilment of unconscious desire. Such 'desire' is not for this or that narrative outcome, or for any explicit referential occurrence; rather it relates to 'the symbolic circulation of unconscious wishes through signs bound to our earliest forms of infantile satisfaction'.[1] I classify these views as forms of *ideological stoicism* because they call for a retreat from affective experience *tout court*—be it emotion or pleasure—on moral principle. For both Brecht and many neo-Freudian theorists, this retreat must occur through distancing and alienating techniques which short-circuit emotion, pleasure, and 'desire', and thus allow reason to work, unencumbered, in the landscape of our minds.

The facile duality between reason and emotion lies as the unspoken premiss behind many discussions of affect and the spectator, as though emotion must be 'bridled' or 'mastered' to allow reason to function adequately. This duality animates much of Bertolt Brecht's writing about the epic theatre, and since Brecht's ideological criticism has become a model for critical theory, the legacy of this dualism lives on. Brecht embraces a traditional Western perspective in his distrust of the 'soft' emotions; he expresses contempt for the 'scum who want to have the cockles of their hearts warmed' at the theatre.[2] At times Brecht seems to castigate both emotion and empathy as inherently problematic in theatre spectatorship. He writes, for example, that feelings 'are private and limited', and that reason is 'fairly comprehensive and to be relied on' (15). He promotes a distanced and alienated spectator response which encourages psychic distance and critical judgement rather than involved experience, as though involvement and judgement were mutually exclusive, and alienation were inherently superior to affective participation.[3]

Brecht's stoicism has limits, however. Elsewhere, Brecht clearly realizes that this simplistic emotion/reason duality will not hold and that the proper target of his criticism is not emotion *per se* but emotional experiences *of certain types*. He says that the goal of the practitioner of epic theatre must not be to eliminate emotional experience but to encourage the spectator to 'adopt a critical approach to his emotions, just as [he] does to his ideas' (101). Brecht's followers have sometimes ignored the subtleties he recognized, in part because Brecht merely alludes to this critical approach rather than describing it in any detail. Brechtian concepts such as alienation or distancing, plus his frequently drawn, moralistic opposition between 'feeling' and 'reason' (e.g. 37), reinforce the simplistic duality that, in his better moments, he realized is superficial.

Brecht wished to encourage a kind of judgement whereby the spectator takes a critical perspective toward the play. Rather than empathizing with characters or experiencing the emotions the play intends to elicit, the spectator should consider and criticize the larger social and cultural forces the play presumes. Brecht's perspective can be criticized from many directions. Notice that Brecht values a kind of alienated, intellectualized response to the theatre, as though there were no legitimate place for compassion, sympathy, empathy, or any of the emotions which might warm the 'cockles' of one's heart. A feminist critique, expanded on below, could well take this as a masculinist response to discomfort with those emotions sometimes denigrated as feminine, or an assumption of the importance of the political and the triviality of the personal. If Brecht's claim is that we must encourage plays which raise social consciousness, we have no quarrel. If he means to eliminate a whole class of spectator responses, then we must question him.

Brechtian theory also neglects the extent to which critical judgement of the sort Brecht recommends is not only compatible with an emotional response congruent with the play's intentions, but is also often implicated in it. For the cognitivist, emotions have reasons, or objects. For example, the object of my fear could be a lion I imagine to threaten my life. The object of my shame might be the obnoxious behaviour of a friend or relative at a social gathering. *Spectator* emotions also have objects or reasons. Some spectator emotions seem especially designed to accompany a Brechtian sort of critical response. The amusement which emerges from satire, for example, contributes to the spectator's questioning of the object of the satire.[4] In *Dr Strangelove or; How I Learned to Stop Worrying and Love the Bomb* (1964), the target of the satire is the American military-industrial complex. The brilliance of the concluding sequence stems in part from the mixed emotions it fosters. As the sympathetically portrayed pilots approach their target, the suspense and excitement build. The film encourages us to share that excitement, despite our simultaneous knowledge that the mission is misguided and its consequences, should it succeed, apocalyptic. Thus *Dr Strangelove* throws into question every war film which celebrates blind patriotism, heroism, and doing one's duty, and it asks, 'To what end?' Here my amusement depends on my judgement of the film's social and political representations. Moreover, *Dr Strangelove* simultaneously displays the attractiveness and the folly of the actions it represents, eliciting mixed emotions which encourage reflection.

The Brechtian might reply that the amusement that satire elicits is a special case of what might be called an *estranged* emotion, one which encourages a critical view of the characters and events. Thus these are emotions *against* the characters and not what could be called *congruent* emotions, or those felt in sympathy with them. The neo-Brechtian might hold that we must not reject all spectator emotions, and certainly not estrangement emotions, but that congruent emotions are inherently mystifying and manipulative.

Congruent emotions, however, may also encourage self-examination and critical judgement about social and political factors in a film or play. My compassion is elicited while viewing *El Norte* (1983) because I appraise the situation of the protagonists, for whom I have sympathy. My appraisal includes recognition of the unjust social systems in which the characters find themselves. In part, my compassion *depends on* recognizing their plight and the reasons for it. My response may cause me to question or even change my former attitude toward the kinds of events depicted. (Or, conversely, I may conclude that the film is misleading; this would probably interfere with any compassionate response.) In any case, my compassion (or its lack) and my judgement are simultaneous and interdependent, and my critical judgement is compatible with my experiencing congruent emotions.

The neo-Brechtian could argue that films such as *Dr Strangelove* and *El Norte* are the exception, and that Hollywood products like *Pretty Woman*, which *do* mystify the social relations they embody, are the rule. We can grant that point. Many films use emotions in harmful and manipulative ways. Nonetheless, what films such as *Dr Strangelove* and *El Norte* show is that the ideological critic must not condemn spectator emotion *per se* but should examine the *kind* of emotional experience a film offers and the way spectator emotions function in the film's rhetorical project.

Much of contemporary film theory and criticism emerges from a Brechtian-Marxist perspective, but it is also one steeped in neo-Freudianism. Rather than talk of emotion, we hear of 'pleasure' and 'desire'. For Freud, the enjoyment of literature results from the release of tensions by allowing us to enjoy 'our day-dreams without reproach or shame'.[5] Day-dreaming through reading literature or viewing art enables us to confront and symbolically overcome deep-seated conflicts, stemming not from our contemporary exterior world, but from the traumas of childhood development, repressed and relegated to the deep recesses of the unconscious.

An influential strain of neo-Freudianism in contemporary film theory holds that while avant-garde art may have therapeutic benefits, the pleasures of mainstream film viewing are deleterious. These pleasures both arise from and encourage regressive or perverse psychic processes in the spectator. Depending on the theorist, the spectator is characterized as a sadistic voyeurist, fetishistic scopophiliac, regressive narcissist, transvestite, masochist, or a combination of the preceding.[6] Jean-Louis Baudry, for example, argues that mainstream films foster a psychic regression to infantile stages of development, characterized by blissful illusions of homogeneity. Laura Mulvey, in her well-known 'Visual Pleasure and the Narrative Cinema', finds the visual pleasure films offer to be sadistic, scopohilic, and voyeuristic. The intention of her essay, she writes, is to 'destroy' that pleasure by analysing it. Gaylyn Studlar, on the other hand, finds masochism rather than sadism to be the foundational spectator pleasure.[7] What Freud once reserved for the mentally troubled, this kind of theory uses to characterize normative activities, such as mainstream film viewing. While it would be foolish to reject these claims without some consideration (it is possible that our culture is at least in part 'mad'), the evidence for such positions is not strong.[8]

While Brecht tends to dismiss emotion as mystifying, neo-Freudian theory sometimes posits particular psychic phenomena as *essential* to film pleasure, such as masochism for Gaylyn Studlar and voyeurism and scopophilia for Laura Mulvey. I have argued elsewhere that there exists no single, essential pleasure in viewing mainstream films, but rather many varied pleasures.[9] Surely the emotions, pleasures, and affect generated at the cinema are more complex than the above theories imply.

As a substantive ideological theory, ideological stoicism is suspect due to its conceptual shortcomings.[10] Given the limitations of ideological stoicism, together with a contemporary understanding of the relationship between judgement and emotion, it is incumbent upon the stoicist to provide compelling arguments for taking the eliciting of all spectator emotion to be inherently unethical.

IDEOLOGICAL FORMALISM

Ideological formalism, the belief that specific film forms and styles have inherent, universal ideological effects, often accompanies ideological stoicism, though the two are logically separable. The ideological formalist may characterize various techniques as inherently *progressive* when they counter spectator effects claimed to be inherently *regressive*. Much of the weight of neo-Brechtian and neo-Freudian theory, as practised in film studies, is thrown toward advocating the short-circuiting of affective, pleasurable response thought to cause regressive effects. For example, if continuity editing, or its related concept 'suture', is thought to 'bind' the spectator into an illusionistic discourse, then, all things being equal, any technique which creates discontinuity will be seen as inherently progressive. Similarly, when coherence, closure, and linear narratives are thought to position a bourgeois subject, then fractured, digressive, and open narratives will be seen as emancipatory in encouraging estrangement rather than absorption.[11]

Mainstream cinema is often thought to involve illusionism, a kind of epistemic delusion in which the spectator forgets or fails to notice that a film is a constructed representation; hence alienation and reflexive techniques restore a critical perspective. In relation to the documentary, Bill Nichols writes that realist techniques are incapable of representing the 'magnitudes' and complexities of the world. As Nichols claims, 'Reflexivity and consciousness-raising go hand in hand because it is through an awareness of form and structure and its determining effects that new forms and structures can be brought into being [and the spectator realizes that what *is*] . . . need not be'.[12] Thus ideological formalism assumes that kinds of textual strategies have inherent ideological effects. In Nichols's case, reflexivity goes hand in hand with consciousness-raising, apparently independent of propositional content.

Those who promote reflexivity often recognize the limits of ideological formalism, even while embracing it implicitly. Realism is often opposed to reflexivity as a retrograde style. However, Nichols recognizes that reflexivity is not always progressive, and others have identified both 'progressive realism' and 'conservative' and 'postmodern' reflexivity.[13] The unspoken premiss of much left ideological formalism is that reflexive and defamiliarizing strategies must be accompanied by left content and function to count as progressive. Nonetheless, reflexivity has accrued the aura of inherent progressivism, however much its presence in *The Letterman Show* and *Beavis and Butthead* would undermine such an assumption. In the same way, a realist documentary such as Barbara Kopple's *Harlan County, USA* (1976) has more progressive ideological significance than the reflexive programming we see on mainstream television. We must be sceptical of ideological formalism, of the claim that any formal strategy, considered independently of propositional content and rhetorical purpose, has an inherent ideological significance. While ideological stoicism fails to account for the complexity and diversity of spectator emotion, ideological formalism mistakes the issue as one of film form rather than film function. Various forms may have ideological tendencies, but form in itself never fully determines spectator emotion or ideological effect.

THINKING ABOUT SPECTATOR EMOTION

V. F. Perkins notes that because when we view films 'our satisfaction is so directly involved, our experience is the more likely to contradict the film-maker's statement wherever the meaning which he offers is less attractive than the one which we can take'. He gives the example of *The Bridge on the River Kwai* (1957), in which screenwriter Carl Foreman's dialogue repeatedly argues the futility of war and the hollowness of victory, while the film's emotional dynamics invite us 'to share in the excitements, tensions and triumphs offered by the action.'[14] The film establishes a contradiction between what is said to be futile and felt to be magnificent.

We need a language and a method to enable us to understand better the spectator's involvement in movies. I suggest the utility of a broadly cognitive approach, simply because it ties spectator emotion not only to private feelings and/or physiological responses, but to cognition—inferences, appraisals, judgements, hypotheses, etc. This approach to emotion was not born with cognitive theory, narrowly considered. While the cognitive science movement rose during the 1970s, the cognitive approach to emotion dates back at least to the ancients. Aristotle defines emotions as kinds of feeling caused by kinds of thinking. He defines fear, for example, as 'a sort of pain or agitation derived from the imagination of a future destructive or painful evil'.[15] A cognitive approach, broadly considered, allows for differences in methodology and assumptions in the tradition of piecemeal theorizing advocated by Noël Carroll and others.[16] The cognitivist assumptions here, for example, differ from mainstream cognitive science of the early 1980s, which bracketed emotions in relation to cognition and modelled the human mind after the electronic computer.[17]

A cognitive approach will be useful, in the first instance, because it transcends reductive characterizations of emotion. Much recent philosophy and psychology of the emotions has rejected the traditional assumption that emotion is the enemy of reason and critical judgement. It was once commonly thought that emotions were coextensive with feelings. Currently, many philosophers and psychologists would agree that no particular felt physical state represents either a necessary or sufficient condition for a specific emotional state. A cognitive approach holds that an emotional state is one in which some physical state of felt agitation is caused by an individual's construal and evaluation of his situation.[18] In other words, my galvanic skin response and heart palpitations cannot define my emotions; what *particular* emotion I experience depends on my cognitions about my situation.[19]

Not only does thinking accompany and in many cases determine emotion, but emotions can themselves be rational or irrational. In the realm of practical reason, emotional response in some cases *just is* a rational (or appropriate) response to an event or circumstance, while lack of emotion may in some situations be irrational. Ronald de Sousa claims that emotion can be rational because it has the ability to guide reason, to make salient what needs attending to in a specific situation, and to initiate a response.[20]

If we accept this, then we must grant that some emotions may be beneficial to the self and society. The relevant ideological issue then becomes not emotions *per se*, but distinguishing those which are benign or beneficial from those which are manipulative or harmful. While we should be suspicious of the manipulative nature of emotions, as Brecht is, a contemporary understanding of emotion leaves little ground for condemning emotion *tout court* as the enemy of reason.

Moreover, rather than positing universal ideological effects for film forms and styles, we should more usefully relate film form to narrative representations and to the kinds of cognitions and emotions such forms encourage. The fundamental tenet of a cognitive approach is that the spectator's affective experience is dependent on cognition, on mental activity cued not only by film form but also by story content. In viewing films, cognition would include inferences, hypotheses, and evaluative judgements. It is no great innovation to claim that spectator affective experience relates to theme, narrative information, story structure, character—all film elements which the spectator must perceive, think about, and evaluate. It is curious, then, that film theory has tended to neglect 'content' in its descriptions of spectator response, and has failed to theorize the place of cognition in spectator emotion.

To develop such an approach, we must first describe the film viewing situation. Emotion in film viewing can be understood only in light of the context in which it occurs—consisting of the situation of the spectator in the theatre or before a monitor, the spectator's understanding of that situation, and various physiological, cognitive, and emotional responses to the images and sounds and what they represent. Psychoanalytic film theory has typically explained the impression of reality and the affective intensity of movies by an appeal to epistemic illusion. We mistake the image for what it represents, or mistake an absence for a presence. However, we do not require the concept of illusion to account for spectator experience, and in fact, as others have argued, a description of our engagement with fictions as epistemically illusory would seem to require that spectators behave differently from the way they do.[21] Contrary to most theories of illusion, the spectator must have a consistent awareness that what he views is artificial and that he is outside the fictional world. As Perkins writes, we 'enter the film situation but it remains separate from ourselves as our own dreams and experiences do not'.[22]

When we view a fiction film we participate in a ritual designed by the institutions that bring us movies.[23] When we assent to the narrative of a film and become 'absorbed' or 'immersed', we accept an emotional role. We entertain the fiction in our imagination, and it moves us, yet we have a consistent background awareness of its artificiality. This concurrent and dual awareness might be compared to that of an actor who may experience emotions similar to those of the character he plays, but who cannot relinquish his sense of a self separate from the role. This dual and concurrent awareness enables the actor to *act* the role, since a loss of awareness of the acting situation would also entail loss of the ability to act the role.[24] Similarly, a spectator who loses awareness of his ritual situation would have a harder time sitting still when pursued by the Tyrannosaurus Rex in *Jurassic Park*, or abiding any narrative event which, in absence of an awareness of its artificiality, would cause unbearable emotional stress.

If our response to film events cannot be characterized as one of epistemic illusion, then how do we account for the affective power of movies? In other words, why am I moved by Charles Foster Kane's predicament, if I understand that he does not exist? 'Pretend theory' and 'thought theory' are the two main explanations of emotional responses to fiction offered by contemporary philosophy. The 'pretend theory' derives from Kendall Walton and Gregory Currie, who argue that our responses to fiction involve 'make-believe' or a kind of pretending.[25] The 'thought theory', on the other hand, simply proposes that we can have real affective responses not only to actual events but also to those we imagine.[26] For example, I may wince when I imagine someone's big toe being smashed by a hammer or feel sadness when I imagine the death of a loved one. I cannot parcel out the differences between these views here. They both offer plausible explanations of how our responses to fiction might be characterized in the absence of epistemic illusion.

Murray Smith argues that the cinema blends on the one hand, complex narrative scenarios with which we engage imaginatively and, on the other, a striking sensual and perceptual experience not found in literature.[27] Moreover, the photographic and sonic qualities of this experience, although representing fictional and sometimes fantastical events, can have a remarkable quality of perceptual realism.[28] Faced with moving photographs of a toe being smashed (coupled with the appropriate crunching noise), the perceptual realism of the representation makes my wincing almost involuntary.

We 'enter' the fictional world in part through developing a bond of allegiance with one or more characters. This orients us toward the narrative events and is essential in eliciting the desired emotional response. Whether we laugh or cry or feel suspense during a scene often depends on our estimation of its significance for characters.[29] Smith describes what he calls a structure of sympathy, consisting of three aspects: (1) the viewer's recognition of character traits and emotions, (2) alignment with characters through perceptual and epistemic means (point-of-view structures or voice-over narration, for example), and (3) an allegiance toward characters that is based on a moral evaluation.[30]

Critics sometimes assume that character identification is an either/or phenomenon, such that either we identify with a character, in which case we unproblematically lend him our complete allegiance, or we do *not* identify and take an attitude ranging from antipathy to indifference. Some notions of identification attribute a kind of identity of thought and emotion between spectator and character, during which the spectator loses a sense of separate selfhood. Smith's analysis of the structures of sympathy shows that our response to characters is typically exterior, from the standpoint of an evaluating self outside the fictional world, that our perceptual or epistemic alignment with characters does not necessarily imply allegiance toward them, and that, as a key component in determining emotional response to a scene, our allegiance with a character (or antipathy toward him or her) may be complex, ambiguous, and may change over the course of the narrative. If our engagement with a character is conflicted, then our emotions and judgements will be so as well.

In mainstream films, allegiances with and antipathy toward characters orient us. What we are oriented *toward*, and respond to, are characters in narrative situations. Emotional response both inside and outside the theatre depends in part on our evaluation of a situation or scenario. For example, two persons stand in a dark alley. A figure approaches from the shadows. Person A recognizes him as a friend and responds with relief, while Person B thinks him a sinister-looking stranger and becomes fearful. Clearly, these different emotional responses depend on contrary evaluations of the situation. Richard Lazarus argues that emotions can be differentiated according to various relational themes or ways a situation relates to an individual. Anger occurs when I recognize a demeaning offence against me or mine. Guilt arises when I believe I have transgressed a moral imperative. Jealousy comes from resenting a third party for the loss of, or threat to, another's affection or favour. Sadness occurs when we experience an irrevocable loss.[31]

A film also presents a continuously evolving narrative situation, a script or scenario, for the appraisal of the audience. We experience diverse emotions based on these paradigmatic scenarios. One may be curious during a mystery, feel suspense during a thriller, be sad during an unhappy ending, be fearful when the jeep is chased by the Tyrannosaurus Rex in *Jurassic Park*, be shocked during the murder sequence of *Psycho*, be compassionate and angry during *El Norte*, or be sentimental when Rock Hudson restores Jane Wyman's sight and the lovers look forward to a promising 'tomorrow' in *Magnificent Obsession*.[32] It is unlikely that a narrative scenario will elicit a single emotion; more often our response is mixed and complex. In *Rear Window*, for example, an audience may experience a mixture of interest, curiosity, and guilt about Jeff (James Stewart) spying on his neighbours. Thus emotional response depends not only on film form and style but also on narrative 'content'—our evaluation of character, narrative situation, theme, etc.

One issue still to be addressed is spectator difference. Many film scholars have rejected the model of the spectator as passive and defenceless against a film which 'positions them'. Among some, more or less empirical investigations of the spectator or of contexts for spectatorship have replaced straight theoretical explanations. The relevant issues then become not how films determine spectator response but what spectators bring to a film that influences their response, and how contextual factors delimit spectator responses and interpretations.[33] Emotion research not only in philosophy, but in psychology, anthropology, sociology, history, and other disciplines, offers significant potential to expand on such studies, by showing how cultural factors influence emotional response.[34]

However, when we justifiably reject the claim that films *determine* spectator response, we should not characterize films as 'blank pages' or 'empty receptacles' and spectator response as wholly determined by contextual and individual factors. When viewing a film, spectators may have a wide variety of responses. Yet any examination of spectator psychology must assume that one important kind of response will be congruent with the implicit intentions of the film, even while recognizing the possibility of incongruent and even oppositional responses. It should not be a matter of determining whether text or context is most important, as though one should reign supreme. Audience response lies at the intersections of individual and general spectator characteristics, specific context, and textual cues.

SPECTATOR EMOTIONS AND IDEOLOGY

Contemporary film critics have written as though viewers were 'positioned' by films. Such claims are rooted in Lacanian and Althusserian theories of the individual as the intersection of exterior social forces. The theory of 'subject positioning' implies that human choice has no place in film viewing, and that the passive viewing subject is wholly determined—subjected and positioned—by textual operations. Part of this idea seems plausible. It *is* true that when the viewer becomes absorbed in a film, and allows himself to experience congruent emotions, he takes on what could be called an 'emotional role' or position.

We rarely view films indiscriminately, but decide what films to view in part for the kind of experience they offer. This sometimes has little to do with aesthetics; while I may admire Martin Scorsese's *Raging Bull* as a work of art, I may nonetheless limit my viewings because its brutality and graphic violence disturb me. Alternatively, the sentimental pleasures of films such as *Mr Holland's Opus* could offer the kind of experience I seek, even if I do not expect a first-rate film. The emotional roles movies afford are not only something to which we are subjected; we choose to subject ourselves to them.

Hollywood has concocted various means for advertising the kind of emotional role each film offers—through genres which repeat similar experiences, sequels, the typecasting of stars, previews, and advertising. Whether a movie will offer a story of hatred and revenge, 'dangerous' sex, family melodrama, the pleasures of curiosity associated with mystery, or the ironic distance combined with graphic violence of a Quentin Tarantino film, we often have a general sense of the kind of experience it may offer, before we view the film.[35] Some of my female students report having difficulty getting their male friends to see what are derogatorily called 'chick flicks'; these films offer experiences these young men think inappropriate or uninteresting for males. In fact, one could characterize Hollywood genres in part according to the basic emotional responses they afford. The melodrama offers sentiment, the horror film elicits what Noël Carroll calls 'art horror',[36] certain westerns satisfy vengeance, comedies amuse, mysteries encourage curiosity and suspense, adventures excitement, etc.

However circumscribed by social convention, we nonetheless choose from a diverse palette of emotions at the cinema, ranging from compassion and pity to vengefulness and contempt. Amidst this diversity, I should like to examine two kinds of experiences with a view toward initiating a discussion of their ideological import. They are, first, sentiment and sentimentality and, second, the emotions which accompany screen violence. My purpose is not primarily to take a particular ideological stance toward these. Rather, I wish to show how we might think of emotion in relation to ideology without resorting to ethical formalism and stoicism. Emotion, as these examples show, depends on *and* informs belief.

SENTIMENTALITY

It is sentimentality, rather than vengeance, contempt, or hatred, that has sparked the most interest among aestheticians, and suffered the heaping scorn of critics. While sentimentality (*false* or *unearned* sentiment) is often the object of condemnation, even sentiment more broadly considered (any tender, romantic, or nostalgic response) is also held under suspicion. Sentiment is most often associated with the family melodrama and especially the 'woman's film'. Perhaps the most influential strain of film melodrama criticism, established by Thomas Elsaesser, holds that 'sophisticated family melodramas' such as those of Douglas Sirk (e.g. *Magnificent Obsession, All That Heaven Allows, Written on the Wind, Imitation of Life*) are self-consciously Brechtian and distance their audience mainly through the irony of exaggerated *mise en scène* and extravagant endings.[37] However accurate Elsaesser's claims are in relation to Sirk's intentions, this line is unpromising for us because it implicitly assumes, in Brechtian fashion, that the congruent emotions of melodramas are illicit, and that social criticism or critical judgement must come through distancing and alienation. While it is a contingent fact that many melodramas are socially conservative (in which case congruent emotions would parallel the text's ideology) I see nothing inherent in the form or in the emotions melodramas elicit to determine that they will necessarily embody any particular ideological position.

Critics such as Molly Haskell argue that the denigration of sentiment is related to a devaluation of the kinds of narrative concerns which elicit sentiment, such as love, romance, loss of virginity, etc., and discomfort with the kinds of pleasures such films offer. From this perspective come references to 'the weepies', 'wet, wasted afternoons', wish fulfilment, and glorious martyrdom. As Haskell writes, contempt for the women's film is a general cultural attitude, 'conveyed in the snickering response of the supermale, himself a more sophisticated version of the little boy who holds his nose and groans during the hugging and kissing scenes'.[38]

Psychoanalytic attempts to explain the appeal of melodrama resort to broad dichotomies between feminine and masculine desire, and, unpromisingly, tend to ally femininity (and 'feminine' emotions) with hysteria, early stages of childhood development, etc. Robert Lang, for example, puts the 'feminine' on the side of Lacan's Imaginary and Freud's pre-Oedipal stage, and the 'masculine' on the side of the Symbolic and thus language. Melodrama is a 'feminine' form because it is 'allied' with the Imaginary: 'It is towards bliss, the shattering of boundaries, the subversion of the Symbolic, in music, all moments of excess, nonsense, perhaps all emotion itself.' Underlying this dichotomy is the traditional reason/emotion split, associating masculinity with reason, and femininity with emotion and the irrational. In this case, however, the latter is valued against the former. As Lang writes, the 'melodrama is a crusade against the Symbolic function's *inhibiting* imperatives'.[39] Mary Ann Doane locates the pleasure of melodrama in a desire for the condition of desiring itself and points as evidence to its representation of love as a barely controlled hysteria. Thus the melodrama raises from the unconscious that ineffable condition of unconstrained desire.[40]

One trouble with these accounts is that they draw sharp dichotomies between the masculine and the feminine. Although they emerge from a feminist perspective, they ally the feminine with irrationality and the ineffable and thus work to preserve harmful stereotypes. These accounts also trivialize what melodramas are about—the issues Haskell claims are defined as women's issues—by downplaying them. We need not appeal first to unconscious processes to understand the spectator emotions elicited by melodrama. Stories of love and relationships have an affective basis in the kinds of characters and narrative situations they represent, in the spectator's appraisal of those elements, and in relation to the film's manner of representation.

Claims and prejudices against sentimentality are by no means universally accepted, and the debate underscores the complexity of appraising the ideological nature of any spectator emotion. Philosopher Robert C. Solomon argues that 'there is nothing wrong with sentimentality', and that the prejudice against sentimentality and soft emotions 'is an extension of that all-too-familiar contempt for the passions in Western literature and philosophy. Our disdain for sentimentality is the rationalist's discomfort with any display of emotion.'[41] In *Mr Holland's Opus*, one scene finds Holland (Richard Dreyfuss) before a large audience, singing (or rather, intoning) John Lennon's 'Beautiful Boy (Darling Boy)' to his deaf son. A *New Yorker* film critic calls the scene a 'slow-torture concert sequence', illustrating Solomon's contention that sentimentality causes discomfort in some of us.[42] Yet Solomon's argument tends to collapse sentiment and sentimentality, as though sentiment were coextensive with the maudlin and mawkish; those who find immorality in sentimentality do not necessarily condemn all sentiment.

Recognizing the sexism which devalues 'feminine' concerns and emotions goes some way toward combating masculinist prohibitions against warming one's heart cockles. But it does not help us to distinguish appropriate sentiment from sentimentality or, more bluntly, good sentiment from bad. If we agree that sentimentality is 'unearned' emotion, then, in principle at least, there must be the earned sort as well. How does one tell the difference?

What is completely lacking in film studies discussions of melodrama is any sustained consideration of the nature and consequences of sentiment and sentimentality as spectator emotions. Here philosophy can clearly be of use. False or unearned sentiment has been maligned as not only distasteful but immoral. 'Being sentimental', Mary Midgeley writes, 'is misrepresenting the world in order to indulge our feelings.' It is a 'howling self-deception', she goes on, and a 'distortion of the world'.[43] Mark Jefferson adds that sentimentality is grounded in a fiction of innocence, emphasizing the 'sweetness, dearness, littleness, blamelessness, and vulnerability of the emotion's objects'.[44] And as Anthony Savile writes, sentimentality not only requires the idealization of the object but also contributes to self-righteousness or self-deception in encouraging a 'gratifying image of the self as compassionate, righteous, or just'.[45]

If we grant that sentimentality idealizes its object, we still must know why that makes it immoral and ideologically dangerous. Jefferson claims that sentimentality impairs one's moral vision, especially when the objects of sentimentality are persons or countries. As an emotional response, it is based in an often wilful determination to disguise and idealize the actual nature of the object, to ensure the narcissistic and pleasurable emotional response that sentimentality brings. Moreover, as both Midgeley and Jefferson claim, sentimentality is implicated in a brutality stemming from vilification rather than idealization. As Jefferson writes, the 'unlikely creature and moral caricature that is someone unambiguously worthy of sympathetic response has its natural counterpart in a moral caricature of something unambiguously worthy of hatred'.[46] Thus sentimentality may contribute to an emotional culture that also produces animosity toward a vilified other.[47]

It is one thing, however, to say what sentimentality *is* and another to determine whether a particular scene or film is sentimental. Since it involves charges of misrepresentation, distortion, and self-deception, sentimentality is a matter of interpretation. In *City Lights*, Chaplin's character falls in love with a blind flower vendor, who thinks him a benevolent millionaire. Through many trials and tribulations, he raises the money needed for an operation to restore her sight. After a stint in jail, he is set free and discovers that she can now see. Now running a flower shop, the cured woman offers the ragged tramp a coin. After touching his hands and face, she realizes who he is. Her look of disappointment is followed by Chaplin's poignant smile, and the film ends.

If her response had been one of unambiguous joy in rediscovering her benefactor, and the film had implied the usual romance 'happily ever after', then it would clearly be sentimental, a self-deceptive denial that economic class, power, and appearances do compromise romantic love. However, the film implies that although the tramp's love is sincere and selfless, his social standing will probably interfere with any future relationship. On this interpretation, *City Lights* escapes sentimentality. Yet matters are not so simple, and the cynic might reply that the scene is nonetheless sentimental in its representation of the tramp's love as blameless, sweet, vulnerable, and pure. Through our allegiance with the tramp and our experience of congruent emotions, we celebrate a gratifying image of ourselves as compassionate, righteous, and just—because we recognize his selfless love in a cruel world and respond to it emotionally. My point is not to come to a final determination about whether *City Lights* is or is not sentimental. Rather it is to suggest that this type of discussion is useful because it relates emotion to belief and value.

Emotion is a process. The ideological criticism of spectator emotion must consider not simply individual occurrences of spectator emotion, but the trajectory of responses a film elicits. Any spectator emotion, whether 'good' or 'bad' in itself, can be used for unfortunate rhetorical ends. That is, if we grant that sentiment is in itself ideologically neutral or

In this scene *Unforgiven* problematizes our reaction to violence on a thematic and affective level, by presenting a narrative event which withholds the typical justifications of violence, and the pleasures violence affords the spectator. Unfortunately, the climactic shoot-out at the end of the film participates in the same myth of regeneration through violence that the typical western promotes and which the film had criticized up to that point.

Screen violence is prevalent in part because it is a sure method to generate affect, and the pleasurable affect films typically use to promote screen violence in turn ensures that the practice will continue. Violence has become such a prevalent subject in mainstream film that many of us consider it a 'natural' subject for the movies. We must reclaim our sense that we may legitimately demand more humane popular art, less dependent on spectator emotions such as simplistic contempt and vengefulness.

THE RHETORIC OF SPECTATOR EMOTION

A 'weak' social constructionist approach to emotion would argue that although some emotions may be 'natural' or universal, our emotional lives are learned and culture-bound. Cognitive approaches to affect are useful in charting the paradigm scenarios, or emotion schemata, into which a culture 'educates' its members.[50] The cognitive approach also suggests how films might figure into that process, by creating, altering, and/or promoting scenarios for behaviour and emotional response. Narrative schemata such as the revenge plot of the *Death Wish* series can become stereotypes just as character types can, presenting a 'script' for vengefulness. Noël Carroll suggests that paradigm scenarios in film may also affect male emotional responses to women. For example, what Carroll calls the '*Fatal Attraction* scenario', tends to 'demote the ex-lover to the status of an irrational creature and to regard her claims as a form of persecution'.[51]

Through repetition and promotion (making the scenario seem natural, morally correct, or in accordance with 'advanced' tastes and attitudes), narrative paradigm scenarios influence our emotional lives. Our emotional experience at the movies may affect our ways of thinking and thus reinforce or alter the emotion schemata we apply to actual situations. Our responses to films depend on our culture's moral order and can function to prescribe and proscribe thought, feeling, behaviour, and values.

In this chapter I have argued for a cognitive approach to the rhetoric of spectator emotion. My discussion of sentimentality and screen violence is meant to suggest how such an approach would begin a discussion of the ideological import of spectator emotions. Spectator emotions have a powerful rhetorical force because they involve thinking, belief, and evaluation. In fact, one cannot have spectator emotions without the kinds of evaluations that relate narratives to our ideological concerns.

NOTES

1. Robert Stam, Robert Burgoyne, and Sandy Flitterman-Lewis, *New Vocabularies in Film Semiotics* (London: Routledge, 1992), 124.
2. *Brecht on Theater*, ed. and trans. John Willet (New York: Hill & Wang, 1964), 14. References to Willet's translation are made parenthetically within the text.
3. See also Murray Smith, 'The Logic and Legacy of Brechtianism', in David Bordwell and Noël Carroll (eds.), *Post-Theory: Reconstructing Film Studies* (Madison: University of Wisconsin Press, 1996), 130–48.
4. Here I am bracketing the question of whether amusement is, strictly speaking, an emotion. It is at least an affective state, and thus has the same rhetorical potential as screen emotions proper. For those interested in this debate, see Robert Sharpe, 'Seven Reasons Why Humor is an Emotion', and John Morreall, 'Humor and Emotion', both in John Morreall (ed.), *The Philosophy of Laughter and Humor* (Albany: State University of New York Press, 1987), 208–24.
5. Sigmund Freud, 'The Relation of the Poet to Day-Dreaming', in *Creativity and the Unconscious* (New York: Harper & Row, 1958), 44–54.
6. See Berys Gaut, 'On Cinema and Perversion', *Film and Philosophy*, 1 (1994), 3–17.
7. See Jean-Louis Baudry, 'The Apparatus: Metapsychological Approaches to the Impression of Reality in the Cinema', Laura Mulvey, 'Visual Pleasure and the Narrative Cinema', and Gaylyn Studlar, 'Masochism and the Perverse Pleasures of the Cinema', all in Gerald Mast, Marshall Cohen, and Leo Braudy (eds.), *Film Theory and Criticism*, 4th edn. (New York: Oxford University Press, 1992), 690–707; 748; 773–90.
8. The most thorough critique of contemporary 'apparatus' theory is found in Noël Carroll's *Mystifying Movies: Fads and Fallacies in Contemporary Film Theory* (New York: Columbia University Press, 1988).
9. I propose an account of the pleasures of the cinema in 'Movie Pleasures and the Spectator's Experience: Toward a Cognitive Approach', *Philosophy and Film*, 2 (1995), 3–19.
10. While philosophy cannot presume that an appeal to conceptual clarification will *resolve* a debate about ethical stoicism, this says little against either philosophy or conceptual clarification. It does reveal much about the intransigence of our ethical beliefs.
11. For a useful commentary on these issues, see Dana Polan, 'A Brechtian Cinema? Towards a Self-Reflexive Film', in Bill Nichols (ed.), *Movies and Methods*, vol. ii (Berkeley and Los Angeles: University of California Press, 1985), 661–72.
12. *Representing Reality* (Bloomington: Indiana University Press, 1991), 67.
13. Stam *et al.*, *New Vocabularies in Film Semiotics*, 202. For a more extensive discussion of reflexivity in non-fiction film, see ch. 10 of my *Rhetoric and Representation in Non-fiction Film* (Cambridge: Cambridge University Press, forthcoming).
14. *Film as Film: Understanding and Judging Movies* (Middlesex: Penguin Books, 1972), 149.
15. *On Rhetoric*, trans. George A. Kennedy (New York: Oxford University Press, 1991), 139.
16. 'Prospects for Film Theory: A Personal Assessment', in *Post-Theory*, 37–68.
17. For an account of the assumptions of mainstream cognitive science of the last decade,

see Howard Gardner's *The Mind's New Science: A History of the Cognitive Revolution* (New York: Basic Books, 1985), 5–7.

18. A discussion of what he calls the cognitive/evaluative approach to emotion is found in Noël Carroll's *The Philosophy of Horror* (New York: Routledge, 1990), 24–7.

19. Philosophical discussions of the cognitive theory of emotion can be found, for example, in W. Lyons, *Emotion* (Cambridge: Cambridge University Press, 1980); and Robert M. Gordon, *The Structure of Emotions* (Cambridge: Cambridge University Press, 1987).

20. *The Rationality of the Emotions* (Cambridge, Mass.: MIT Press, 1987). Of course, emotion can also lead us astray. The claim is that emotion and reason are not necessarily opposed, not that they are never opposed.

21. For critical discussions of the notion of illusion, see Carroll, *The Philosophy of Horror*, 63–8; and Murray Smith, 'Film Spectatorship and the Institution of Fiction', *Journal of Aesthetics and Art Criticism*, 53: 2 (Spring 1995), 113–27. Richard Allen argues that we should preserve a form of the notion of illusion in his *Projecting Illusion: Film Spectatorship and the Impression of Reality* (New York: Cambridge University Press, 1995).

22. *Film as Film*, 140.

23. Smith, 'Film Spectatorship and the Institution of Fiction'.

24. I have heard anecdotes about stage actors who 'forget' they are acting, momentarily 'become' their character, and cease to follow the script or play to the audience. Such incidents are rare, however, and an actor prone to such behaviour would soon be unemployed.

25. See Gregory Currie, *The Nature of Fiction* (Cambridge: Cambridge University Press, 1990), and Kendall Walton, *Mimesis as Make-Believe: On the Foundations of the Representational Arts* (Cambridge, Mass.: Harvard University Press, 1990).

26. See Peter Lamarque, 'How Can We Fear and Pity Fictions?', *British Journal of Aesthetics*, 21: 4 (Autumn 1981); id., 'Fiction and Reality', in Peter Lamarque (ed.), *Philosophy and Fiction* (Aberdeen: Aberdeen University Press, 1983); id., 'Bits and Pieces of Fiction', *British Journal of Aesthetics*, 24: 1 (Winter 1984). Also see Carroll, *The Philosophy of Horror*, 79–88.

27. 'Film Spectatorship and the Institution of Fiction', 118–20.

28. On the homologies between perceiving photographic images and natural perception, see Stephen Prince, 'The Discourse of Pictures: Iconicity and Film Studies', *Film Quarterly*, 47: 1 (Fall 1993), 12–24, and Paul Messaris, *Visual Literacy: Image, Mind, and Reality* (Boulder, Colo.: Westview Press, 1994). Point-of-view editing and moving photographs of facial expressions, both specific to film and television, also play a central role in the expression and evocation of emotion.

29. Alfred Hitchcock points out that emotional response does not *require* allegiance with a character, but is aided by such allegiance; 'A curious person goes into somebody else's room and begins to search through the drawers. Now, you show the person who lives in that room coming up the stairs. Then you go back to the person who is searching, and the public feels like warning him, "Be careful, watch out. Someone's coming up the stairs." Therefore, even if the snooper is not a likable character, the audience will still feel anxiety for him. Of course, when the character is attractive, as for instance Grace Kelly in *Rear Window*, the public's emotion is greatly intensified.' François Truffaut, *Hitchcock* (New York: Simon & Schuster, 1983), 73.

30. *Engaging Characters: Fiction, Emotion, and the Cinema* (Oxford: Clarendon Press, 1995). Smith's division of the structure of sympathy neatly separates significant and distinct aspects of character identification. My only quibble is with the term 'recognition'. Smith holds that the spectator constructs the character through a series of inferences. My inclination would be to term the phenomenon 'disclosure', since the film reveals emotional information about a character through facial expression, gesture, voice, music, lighting, and a host of other devices. In other words, while

allegiance is something the spectator lends the character, alignment and disclosure (or what Smith calls recognition) are more or less functions of the film more than activities of the spectator. Alex Neill argues that spectators *empathize* with characters, and, furthermore, that such empathy may have beneficial effects, in 'Empathy and (Film) Fiction', in Bordwell and Carroll, *Post-Theory*, 175–94.

31. *Emotion and Adaptation* (New York: Oxford University Press, 1991).

32. See my 'Affect, Cognition, and the Power of Movies', *Post Script*, 13: 1 (Fall 93), 10–29.

33. See, for example, Jackie Stacey, *Star Gazing: Hollywood Cinema and Female Spectatorship* (London: Routledge, 1994); Charles J. Maland, *Chaplin and American Culture: The Evolution of a Star Image* (Princeton: Princeton University Press, 1989); Janet Staiger, *Interpreting Films: Studies in the Historical Reception of the American Cinema* (Princeton: Princeton University Press, 1992); Eric Smoodin, ' "Compulsory" Viewing for Every Citizen: *Mr. Smith* and the Rhetoric of Reception', *Cinema Journal*, 35: 2 (Winter 1996), 3–23; Jacqueline Bobo, 'Reading through the Text: The Black Woman as Audience', in Manthia Diawara (ed.), *Black American Cinema* (New York: Routledge, 1993), 272–87.

34. For a broad survey of such research, see Michael Lewis and Jeannette M. Haviland, *Handbook of Emotions* (New York: Guilford Press, 1993), esp. Peter N. Stearns, 'History of Emotions: The Issue of Change', 17–28; Geoffrey M. White, 'Emotions Inside Out: The Anthropology of Affect', 29–40; Keith Oatley, 'Social Construction in Emotions', 341–52; Richard Sweder, 'The Cultural Psychology of Emotions', 417–34; Carolyn Saarni, 'Socialization of Emotion', 435; Leslie R. Brody and Judith A. Hall, 'Gender and Emotion', 447–60.

35. A former student told me that she had viewed *Steel Magnolias* at least twenty times, and that during each viewing she had a similar emotional experience. Certainly for her, the experience offered her a sought-after pleasure, or perhaps a cathartic or palliative effect.

36. *The Philosophy of Horror.*

37. 'Tales of Sound and Fury: Observations on the Family Melodrama', *Monogram*, 4 (1972), 2–15; repr. in Christine Gledhill (ed.), *Home is Where the Heart is: Studies in Melodrama and the Women's Film* (London: BFI, 1987), 43–69; and Marcia Landy (ed.), *Imitations of Life: Film and Television Melodrama* (Detroit: Wayne State University Press, 1991), 68–91.

38. *From Reverence to Rape: The Treatment of Women in the Movies*, 2nd edn. (Chicago: University of Chicago Press, 1987), 13, 154.

39. *American Film Melodrama* (Princeton: Princeton University Press, 1989), 27, 228.

40. *The Desire to Desire: The Woman's Film of the 1940s* (Bloomington: Indiana University Press, 1987).

41. 'In Defense of Sentimentality', *Philosophy and Literature*, 14 (1990), 305.

42. James Wolcott, 'The Love Bug', *New Yorker* (29 Jan. 1996), 93.

43. 'Brutality and Sentimentality', *Philosophy*, 54 (1979), 385.

44. 'What is Wrong with Sentimentality?', *Mind*, 92 (1983), 524.

45. Quoted from Savile's *The Test of Time* (Oxford: Clarendon Press, 1982) in Marcia Muelder Eaton, 'Laughing at the Death of Little Nell: Sentimental Art and Sentimental People', *American Philosophical Quarterly*, 26: 4 (Oct. 1989), 273.

46. Jefferson, 'What is Wrong with Sentimentality?', 527.

47. Sentimentality may be the flipside of racism as well as brutality. Consider the combination of racism and sentimentality in the films of D. W. Griffith, for example. His sentimental portrayal of women in *Broken Blossoms* and *The Birth of a Nation* does seem implicated in his racist portrayals of African-Americans and Asians. Both require misrepresenting the nature of kinds of human beings.

48. Noël Carroll writes of this type of second order response in *The Philosophy of Horror*, as does Murray Smith in 'Film Spectatorship and the Institution of Fiction'.

49. *Gunfighter Nation: The Myth of the Frontier in Twentieth-Century America* (New York: Harper Perennial, 1992), 1–28.
50. See, for example, Hazel Markus and Shinobu Kitayama, *Emotion and Culture* (Washington: American Psychological Association, 1994).
51. 'The Image of Women in Film: A Defense of a Paradigm', *Journal of Aesthetics and Art Criticism*, 48: 4 (Fall 1990), 357.

17

Comedy and Classicism

DIRK EITZEN

The classical Hollywood cinema was given its most comprehensive definition a decade ago in *The Classical Hollywood Cinema*, a massive tome by David Bordwell, Janet Staiger, and Kristin Thompson.[1] Thanks in large part to this work, coupled with Bordwell's influential theoretical treatise *Narration in the Fiction Film*, published the same year, most film scholars have become accustomed to thinking about mainstream American fiction films in a particular way: as driven by protagonists' needs and desires, organized overwhelmingly around the goal of presenting a clear and coherent fictional world, and focusing viewers' attention almost exclusively upon story outcomes.[2]

There are, however, certain very important tendencies in the classical Hollywood cinema that do not fit easily into this scheme. Comedy is one of these. The comic impulse has always been one of the mainstays of the movies. This is evident not just from the comic genres, which have always been very popular. Even so-called serious movies and non-comic genres are often freighted with comic bits. This goes back to the very beginnings of the entertainment film business and it continues today. And yet, this, historically important impulse often runs against the grain of the kind of narrative that, according to Bordwell, Staiger, and Thompson, characterizes the classical Hollywood movie.

On the whole, Bordwell, Staiger, and Thompson's argument is very persuasive. Most classical American fiction films do look and behave the way they suggest. The theoretical and historical framework they provide for their conception of the classical Hollywood movie is particularly compelling. The purpose of this chapter is to see whether their influential model of the classical Hollywood cinema can be altered or stretched in some way to accommodate the comic impulse.

In Bordwell, Staiger, and Thompson's model, the classical fiction film pivots on the psychologically plausible actions of protagonists as they encounter problems while trying to achieve specific goals. The movie continues as long as one problem leads to another; when the protagonists achieve

I am grateful to Emily Wartchow for her assistance in conducting research for this chapter and to Franklin & Marshall College for supporting her research with a Hackman scholarship.

their main goals, the movie quickly concludes. The principal functions of editing, camera work, and *mise en scène* are, first, to make the protagonists' predicaments clear to viewers and, second, to depict the actions of characters in a way that seems to flow logically, although not completely predictably, from their predicaments, creating a linear chain of apparent cause and effect. Chance elements that short-circuit the impression of causality are minimized. Presentational style is generally subordinated to the logic of cause and effect, except where authorized by the familiar plot patterns of particular genres, as in the case of the song and dance numbers in musicals.

Even though *The Classical Hollywood Cinema* provides a wealth of new historical evidence and theoretical support for this conception of the mainstream American fiction film, the basic conception itself is not new. Bordwell quotes a 1920 manual for would-be screenwriters that lays out the rules: 'Plot is a careful and logical working out of the laws of cause and effect. The mere sequence of events will not make a plot. Emphasis must be laid upon causality and the action and reaction of the human will.'[3]

The spectator in this system is motivated chiefly by suspense. The text creates 'gaps', putting a protagonist into a clear predicament but holding back information about possible solutions or likely reactions, forcing the spectator to make guesses or hypotheses about what will happen next. 'Each sequence, every line of dialogue, becomes a way of creating or developing or confirming a hypothesis; shot by shot, questions are posed and answered.'[4] The questions posed by the plot, because they overwhelmingly concern protagonists' likely reactions to the predicaments in which they find themselves, can be reduced to just one: 'What is this character going to do now?' The chief 'task' of a classical Hollywood film is to prompt spectators to attempt to answer this question. Generally, viewers are permitted to predict correctly the general course of protagonists' actions (because it is 'logical'), even though the action is fleshed out in unanticipated and occasionally surprising ways. Spectators are caught up in the process of guesswork, anticipation, and partial satisfaction. This 'game' is the glue that holds the classical Hollywood film together.

If this theory is correct, we must presume that spectators are interested in seeing how characters can act in original yet 'logical' ways to overcome obstacles and achieve their goals. Spectators take some pleasure in making guesses about how characters will react to predicaments and in seeing how their guesses are confirmed or confounded. Although Bordwell, Staiger, and Thompson do not say so explicitly, this does appear to be their presumption.

It is not generally recognized how thoroughly Darwinian the theoretical underpinnings of Bordwell, Staiger, and Thompson's history of Hollywood are. So-called evolutionary accounts of film history have not been terribly popular among film scholars since Jean-Louis Comolli attacked them in the

1970s, so Bordwell and Thompson took pains to say that their history of Hollywood is not an evolutionary account.[5] Nonetheless, it is clear that it is. At its centre are the two famous mechanisms of evolution postulated by Darwin: blind variation and selective retention.[6]

Blind variation is essentially the process of trial and error. Earlier histories of Hollywood were often a chronicle of invention. For example, some clever individual figured out how to do a match-on-action edit and, *Voilà!*, everyone did match-on-action edits. Bordwell, Staiger, and Thompson take pains to show that the development of the classical Hollywood cinema did not work that way. 3-D, for example, is an invention that failed. It was the system, not the inventiveness of individuals, that determined the course of long-term trends. It was the system that determined whether or not particular innovations survived and spread. To be sure, film-makers and inventors tinkered with cinematic devices and techniques for particular reasons. Still, they could never fully anticipate the impact of their tinkering. Some innovations succeeded; some failed. That is the nature of blind variation.

Selective retention is the means by which certain of these variations are propagated. In biological evolution, the mechanisms for this are genetic reproduction and environmental winnowing, popularly known as 'survival of the fittest'. Bordwell, Staiger, and Thompson demonstrate that the Hollywood movie industry was extraordinarily effective at reproducing successful innovations. Whenever something proved profitable—a new production technique, a new kind of storyline, a new style, or whatever—the industry was quick to attempt to capitalize on it again. Studios reproduced formulae that they had found to be particularly profitable—star vehicles and genres, for example. Organizations like trade unions and the Academy worked to develop, standardize, and spread tried-and-true techniques. The opposite is also true. News about 'failures'—box-office flops, unprofitable techniques, profligate directors, and the like—spread very quickly throughout the industry. As a result, successful innovations caught on and spread; failures were quickly abandoned. That is the nature of selective retention.

The result of the mechanisms of blind variation and selective retention is that persistent pressures in an environment determine the course of change in species in that environment. For example, if on an isolated island in the Galapagos there are a lot of flowers that produce nectar that goes uneaten, that creates a kind of pressure in the environment. It is an unfilled 'niche' in the ecosystem. This niche might last indefinitely. If, however, by chance, a pair of broad-billed finches on the island happens to have long-billed, nectar-sipping offspring, this pre-existing niche makes it very likely that they will thrive and multiply. The environment is not the source of change. Nevertheless, it determines the shape of long-term change. This is the key to Darwin's theory.

The same principle is the key to Bordwell, Staiger, and Thompson's account of the classical Hollywood cinema. Whatever the source of individual innovations such as the musical genre and noir-style lighting, it was pressures in the social and economic system that determined whether and in what form they survived. Even though at any given moment there was a lot of variation within the system, the overall shape both of the Hollywood film industry and of its output was determined by persistent pressures in the sociocultural environment.

That, in broad strokes, is the theory. Here we come to the historical particulars. According to Bordwell, Staiger, and Thompson, there were basically two pressures that characterized the classical Hollywood system. The first was a continual push to maximize profits. Given two ways of achieving any goal—two competing techniques, styles, directors, organizational structures, or whatever—it was always the more profitable one that won out, all other things being equal. If a more expensive technique beat out a less expensive one it is invariably because, in the long run, it proved to be more profitable. The second pressure was more encompassing, since it ultimately determined which techniques, styles, and so on, proved most profitable. That pressure was a predilection among audiences for a particular kind of story-telling: story-telling that is organized around the psychologically motivated actions of a few characters, that is relatively transparent and coherent, and that moves more or less without interruption toward a situation in which the protagonists' desires are satisfied.

Although Bordwell, Staiger, and Thompson's account of the classical Hollywood style is supposed to be primarily descriptive, within the theoretical framework described above, it serves a crucial explanatory role, as well. The shape of the classical Hollywood cinema is not merely the way movies happened to be. It is the indirect result of audience preferences. What accounts for the consistencies in the classical Hollywood style is that audiences were predisposed toward a particular kind of narrative entertainment, a particular kind of pleasure.

Although *The Classical Hollywood Cinema* is silent about the source of this pleasure, Bordwell speculates briefly about it in *Narration in the Fiction Film*. The pattern of response that he sees as typical of the classical fiction film is most compatible with a theory of pleasure in which affect is bound up with expectation and its delayed fulfilment.

When we bet on a hypothesis, especially under the pressure of time, confirmation can carry an emotional kick; the organism enjoys creating unity. When the narrative delays satisfying an expectation, the withholding of knowledge can arouse keener interest. When a hypothesis is disconfirmed, the setback can spur the viewer to new bursts of activity. The mixture of anticipation, fulfillment, and blocked or retarded or twisted consequences can exercise great emotional power.[7]

But the particular source of the pleasure is not crucial to an evolutionary account of the Hollywood style. All that is important is the supposition that audiences were predisposed toward some particular kind of narrative and that this predisposition acted as a relatively constant criterion of selective retention in the sociocultural environment in which Hollywood movies evolved—a persistent pressure in the system, so to speak. That is just what *The Classical Hollywood Cinema* supposes.

What movie audiences wanted, what they were most eager to pay for, and what therefore proved most profitable, was a kind of movie that involved them, with as few distractions and in as concentrated a fashion as possible, in anticipating and observing the goal-oriented actions of characters in a predicament. The main pleasure of the movies, for most viewers, was the pleasure of wondering, 'What is this character going to do now?' That pleasure, according to this view, is what the classical Hollywood cinema evolved to serve up. New stylistic techniques, like expressionistic lighting, and elements borrowed from other entertainments like song-and-dance numbers, had to be made compatible with viewers' overriding interest in the question, 'What is this character going to do now?' Anything that distracted from that question, like disorienting montage, action-halting exposition, or self-conscious stylishness, was eventually minimized or jettisoned, because it proved less profitable than a more transparent, story-centred, action-oriented narrational style. This tendency—a tendency to make form and style slaves to the requirements of transparent story-telling—is supposed to be what chiefly characterizes the classical Hollywood cinema.

The problem is that there are a number of impulses that seem persistently to distract from the question 'What is this character going to do now?' and that, nevertheless, recur again and again in Hollywood movies. Far from being minimized or jettisoned, these elements appear to have been deliberately exploited throughout Hollywood's history. One of these is spectacle. Hollywood movies have always been full of unnecessary violence and gratuitous flesh, chases that do not lead anywhere, ostentatiously lavish sets, amazing stunts, whiz-bang special effects, and so on. The pleasure of these moments has very little to do with wondering what a character is going to do next. It seems to be tied up with a more visceral, less cerebral sort of pleasure. The same is true of melodrama. There are moments in nearly every Hollywood movie where the forward action of the story basically stops so that viewers can watch characters emote. Close shots of faces usually have less to do with what a character is going to do next than with what he or she is feeling at the moment. Music in Hollywood movies works the same way. Yet close shots and music are typical of the classical Hollywood style. Comedy is another of these impulses.

The case of comedy is particularly interesting. While spectacle and melodrama are not exactly part of the cause-and-effect structure of narrative, they can make perfect sense within it. Strong emotions tend to be psychologically motivated by characters' situations and needs. Sensational violence, sex, or special effects can easily serve to advance the goal-oriented movement of the plot. In contrast, jokes, odd or exaggerated behaviours, parody, and other comic devices routinely arrest and interfere with the linear movement of narrative. Gags, in particular, have a notorious tendency to divert attention from the goal-oriented action of characters. Admittedly, in the first decades of the classical Hollywood cinema, there was a move from slapstick, in which the narrative was often scarcely more than the spatial proximity of a series of physical gags, to character-centred comedy, in which gags tended to arise from a narrative throughline, to more situation-based comedy, such as screwball, in which comic elements are relatively diffuse and thoroughly implicated in a goal-oriented narrative structure. Still, in even the most tightly woven narrative, comic elements often seem to be a disruptive force.

A scene from near the beginning of *Bringing up Baby* (1938) serves as a good illustration of this. David Huxley (Cary Grant), a palaeontologist, has been hobnobbing with wealthy acquaintances in order to try to secure a research grant. His efforts to appear dignified, intelligent, and deserving are repeatedly thwarted by disastrous accidental encounters with a beautiful but completely scatterbrained society lady, Susan Vance (Katherine Hepburn). In this scene, he arrives at a fancy restaurant, dressed in tails. His purpose is to meet with the lawyer of a wealthy woman who is interested in his research. Susan also happens to be at the restaurant. She is talking to the bartender about a trick with an olive and, in the process, she drops one. David, who happens to walk by a moment later, steps on the olive, slips, and takes a classic pratfall. When David finds that Susan is, once again, the source of his embarrassing mishap, he tries to put some distance between himself and her, but she pursues him to apologize. This would-be apology leads to another embarrassing accident and another attempted apology, and so on.

Finally, Susan tears David's dinner jacket. In exasperation, David tells her bluntly to get lost. Susan turns on her heel and stomps off, in a huff. But David has inadvertently been standing on the trail of her dress and, when Susan walks away, she leaves the back of her skirt behind, exposing her undergarments. Appalled, David pursues her, to save her from embarrassment. But because Susan is angry, she talks right through his attempted warnings, and David is too flustered to make her problem clear to her. Instead, he tries to shield her derrière from public view with his body, his hat, and by backing her up against the wall, behaviours which merely add to Susan's indignation. Susan eventually discovers her embarrassing plight for herself. In a panic, she asks David to walk out of the restaurant behind her, pressed against her backside to shield it from public view. David chivalrously obliges. Diners in the restaurant stare and titter. David's lawyer acquaintance, in the lobby with friends, looks on dumbfounded.

This is a very tightly constructed bit of narrative. The thing that moves the scene forward is the question, 'What is this character going to do now?'—specifically, for most of the scene, 'What is David going to do now to get rid of Susan?' The thing that sustains the scene (and, indeed, the movie) is David's failure to get rid of Susan. The thing that ties the scene together is a neat sequence of cause and effect: an accident leads to an attempted apology which leads to another accident, and so on. But the thing that makes the scene funny is something else, entirely: namely, that the scene unfolds in ways that are incongruous, unexpected, and surprising. As often as not, these have very little to do with the question, 'What is this character going to do next?'

For example, when Susan drops an olive, it seems completely incidental to the plot. The plot—Susan's discussion of an olive trick with the bartender—looks like a bit of character development. It is only after David slips on the olive that it takes on story significance. It is this surprising turn of events that is funny. Instead of compelling us to look forward to anticipate what is going to happen next, David's fall on the olive impels us to look backward, reassessing something that happened earlier in the scene. Later, when David does his little dance, trying to shield Susan's behind from public view with his body and his hat, it is the oddity of his behaviour, which is at the same time completely 'logical' and completely at odds with 'normal' behaviour, that is comic. This extended physical gag essentially brings the story to a halt. Besides, because it violates our expectations about what is likely and plausible, it calls attention to itself as a bit of comic performance. At the end of the scene, when Susan walks the whole length of the restaurant with David pressed to her backside, it is our recognition of both the social awkwardness of the fictional incident and the sexual innuendo in the text that makes the moment comic. What is funny about each of these moments is somewhat different, but in each case it has very little to do with the question, 'What is this character going to do next?'

These three gags are fairly typical of the humour in classical Hollywood comedy. Because of their unpredictability, they tend to complicate viewers' efforts to figure out what is going to happen next. Because they violate viewers' expectations about what is plausible and likely, they tend to call attention to themselves. Because they focus attention backward, on characters' reactions to surprising misunderstandings and mishaps, rather than forward, on characters' goals, they tend to interrupt the impetus that drives the narrative. The very exaggerations and incongruities that make these moments funny also tend to interfere with the impression of a plausible and coherent fictional world.

The tension between the comic impulse and narrative has been the focal point of much of the theoretical discussion about film comedy. Some of this discussion is neatly summarized in several essays in the recent anthology *Classical Hollywood Comedy*.[8] Most positions fall along a spectrum between the view that comedy and narrative are totally incompatible impulses to the view that they are different but complementary. At one end of this spectrum is Donald Crafton, who writes, with respect to slapstick, 'the separation between the vertical domain of slapstick (the arena of spectacle I will represent by the metaphor of the thrown pie) and the horizontal domain of the story (the arena of the chase) was a calculated rupture, designed to keep the two elements antagonistically apart'.[9] At the other end is Jerry Palmer, who argues that a comic situation is one in which a character's behaviour makes sense in terms of the narrative but is at the same time odd or incongruous in terms of the narrative, so it is only in terms of the narrative that a comic situation can be understood.[10] In more or less the middle is Kristine Brunovska Karnick, who suggests that humorous moments in comedies such as *Bringing up Baby* do make story sense but in unexpected and incongruous ways, which disrupt the smooth unfolding of the fiction and call attention, as well, to formal and aesthetic features of the text.[11]

It is not necessary, for the purposes of this chapter, to stake out a position on this theoretical spectrum. All that is necessary is to recognize one point on which Crafton, Palmer, Karnick, and most other theorists of comedy would agree. What makes us laugh at movies—pratfalls, jokes, exaggerations, incongruities, the violation of conventions, silly and unexpected behaviour, and so on—generally has very little to do with our interest in the goal-oriented actions of characters. It has very little to do with the question, 'What is this character going to do now?' Yet, according to Bordwell, Staiger, and Thompson's model of the classical Hollywood cinema—probably the reigning model—our interest in this question is precisely what organizes and drives classical Hollywood movies.

There is clearly some sort of interest or desire in audiences that comic moments, like those in the above-described scene from *Bringing up Baby*, are attempting to tickle. Since the classical Hollywood cinema is full of such moments, we must assume that the comic impulse has always been an important pressure in the Hollywood system. And yet, there seems to be precious little room for it in Bordwell, Staiger, and Thompson's evolutionary account.

In discussing the example of Buster Keaton's *Our Hospitality* in their book *Film Art*, Bordwell and Thompson assert that every moment in classical Hollywood comedy helps to unify the narrative and move it forward. They offer, as an example of this, a recurring squabble between an anonymous husband and wife whom Keaton passes on the road. The first time, Keaton tries to protect the wife, only to be thrashed by her for butting in. The second time, Keaton gives the couple a wide berth. Still, the wife aims a kick at him as he passes.[12] Bordwell and Thompson maintain that the repetition of the element unifies the narrative. It defines a particular space within the diegesis and it also relates, as a motif, to the theme of southern hospitality. Bordwell and Thompson fail to point out, however, that the squabbling couple is also a gag—an added, unexpected element thrown in— a digression from the central story that, like Keaton's whole gag-filled train trip from north to south in the same movie, is an end in itself. The squabbling couple is not in the movie because it advances the story. It does not. Nor is it in the movie because it illuminates Keaton's character's goals and motives. It does not do that either. It is in the movie because it is supposed to be funny.

In *The Classical Hollywood Cinema*, Bordwell, Staiger, and Thompson say very little about comedy. They evidently regard it as a counter-current that is not representative of the mainstream. They suggest that gags and other elements that distract from the narrative of classical Hollywood movies tend to be vestiges of earlier entertainments. In the early years of the movies and, again, in the first years of the sound film, movies borrowed comic actors and routines from the stage. This, plus the familiarity of audiences with stage and prose comedy, established certain expectations about comic movies that persisted through genre conventions. All of this is true. Nevertheless, it does not explain why people enjoyed comic skits on stage in the first place. Nor does it account for the longevity of the comic impulse, which is still evident today in all kinds of movies.

Another possible explanation for comedy found in *The Classical Hollywood Cinema* is that certain non- or anti-narrative elements in the classical Hollywood cinema appealed to the 'connoisseurship' of particular audiences. As odd as this sounds, it does seem to apply to some kinds of comedy. For example, *Wayne's World* is designed to make a particular group—the *Saturday Night Live* crowd—feel like insiders on a whole string of inside jokes. Nevertheless, the odd behaviour, jokes, pratfalls, and gags that are at the heart of classical Hollywood comedy are generally designed to have very broad appeal.

So, although Bordwell, Staiger, and Thompson explain certain things *about* comedy, they do not manage to account for the comic impulse. They do not account for the incontestable fact that audiences have always liked comedy and been willing to pay for it in movies, even when it runs against the grain of narrative.

How can we resolve this problem? One way would be to conclude that there are all sorts of desires and pleasures that shaped the classical Hollywood cinema. There is the pleasure of narrative, which Bordwell conceives to be something like the pleasure of working on a puzzle in anticipation of finding a solution. Besides this, there are the libidinal pleasures of looking at spectacle, violence, and sex. Besides all of those, there is the pleasure of relating to the emotions of others—vicarious experience, as it is sometimes called—which seems to be at the heart of melodrama. And, as I have been arguing, there is the peculiar pleasure of comedy. All of these may well have exerted a shaping influence on the evolution of the classical Hollywood cinema.

For all the attractions of this smorgasbord of pleasures, it lacks the economy of Bordwell, Staiger, and Thompson's model. A more crucial failing is that, although it accounts for differences within the classical Hollywood cinema, it hardly accounts for the striking uniformities. The big advantage of Bordwell, Staiger, and Thompson's account is that, even if it fails satisfactorily to explain secondary impulses such as spectacle and comedy, it does account for the dominant formal tendencies of the classical Hollywood cinema. This is something the smorgasbord alternative cannot do.

The ideal explanatory model, therefore, would be one that postulates a single dominant impulse, such as an interest in the goal-oriented action of characters, which within an evolutionary framework accounts for *both* the undeniable tendency in the classical Hollywood cinema toward narratives that are organized around psychological causality *and* the counter-currents evident in comedy, spectacle, and melodrama. I wish to propose such a model, or a blueprint of it.

What the average movie-goer seems to want most of all from movies is not narrative *per se*, but strong and concentrated affective responses. Movies can provide a powerful emotional kick in a safe context. I submit that this is what mainstream audiences have always been most eager to pay for in movies—not just the pleasure of seeing a problem through, but the concentrated experience of emotions that are not often triggered in day-to-day affairs: sadness, horror, fear, arousal, the happiness associated with the climax of a romance, the thrill of having survived a brush with death, and the funny side of personal inadequacies or social humiliation. I submit that this is the pressure that most influenced the shape of the classical Hollywood cinema.

Bordwell, Staiger, and Thompson's description of the classical Hollywood cinema is correct, as far as it goes, but their implied explanation is a second-order explanation. An interest in the goal-oriented action of characters did indeed shape Hollywood movies, but the reason for this is that depicting the goal-oriented action of characters is one of the most reliable and effective ways of generating emotional responses in movie audiences.[13] A particular kind of narrative evolved in Hollywood, not primarily because it was intellectually stimulating and easy to follow, but because it dished up emotionally charged events in the most economical fashion, All of the formal qualities that we have come to associate with the classical

Hollywood cinema—invisible editing, naturalistic sets, facial acting, non-diegetic music, chronological structure, and so on—make it particularly easy for viewers to perceive and project emotional responses.

On the other hand, one can make a movie that has all of the elements that Bordwell, Staiger, and Thompson attribute to classical Hollywood fiction—goal-oriented characters, a self-effacing style, a coherent fabula, and all the rest—that is still as dry as sand. Yet, strikingly, this is not what evolved in Hollywood. What evolved are stories that are full of sex, violence, melodrama, fast action, suspense and surprise, fantasy and horror, and, as I have been pointing out here, comedy. The transparent style evolved because, in most instances, that style gives the most emotional bang for the buck. But where another kind of emotional bang could be obtained by sacrificing narrative transparency, as in the case of comedy, there was evidently little hesitation in putting transparency aside.

This hypothesis explains the tendency in the classical Hollywood cinema toward a transparent style and plots organized around the goal-oriented actions of characters. It allows for the possibility that spectators derive a great deal of pleasure or emotional satisfaction merely from the 'game' of controlled expectation and partial fulfilment, as Bordwell supposes. But this hypothesis also accounts for comedy, spectacle, melodrama, horror, 'connoisseurship', and the other common non-narrative gratifications of popular movies. Furthermore, it explains why we can find the same movie enjoyable twice in a row—something problem-solving theories of narrative, like Bordwell's, have trouble explaining. We can experience the same emotions the second time through, even if we already know what is going to happen.

It must be said, here, that some important philosophers of comedy have argued that humour is not an emotional response. Henri Bergson, for example, maintained that laughter and emotions are downright incompatible.[14] Since then, however, there has been a considerable amount of psychological evidence that humour is, indeed, an emotional response, with all the concomitant somatic symptoms: faster pulse, shallower respiration, increased galvanic skin resistance, and so on.[15] Humour is most often associated with social situations in which there is embarrassment, tension, aggression, or the violation of norms or taboos—intrinsically emotionally charged situations.[16] But that is a topic for another essay. The point here is simply that the case of classical Hollywood comedy makes it most likely to suppose that, historically speaking, the primary psychological attraction of movies for most viewers has not been merely the pleasure of seeing a story unfold. It has been the pleasure of experiencing an emotionally charged event. In this respect, it is more like taking a roller-coaster ride than working on a puzzle.

We might test this hypothesis by going back and resifting the historical evidence, including the films themselves, which it makes sense to suppose are the product of evolutionary forces. In my previous mention of the development of Hollywood comedy, my analysis of a scene from *Bringing up Baby*, and my passing reference to the analytical work of other scholars, I have offered the briefest overview of such a project. We might also work in the opposite direction. Instead of describing the shape of the classical Hollywood cinema and proceeding to speculate about the pressures that shaped it, we might describe the structure of emotional responses and proceed to speculate about whether that may account for the various tendencies evident in the classical Hollywood cinema. Ed Tan undertakes such a project in a new book, *Emotion and the Structure of Narrative Film*.[17]

From psychologist N. H. Frijda, Tan borrows a theory of emotions that conceives them primarily in terms of their functions.[18] Emotions are a kind of judgement that takes control of and guides reasoning in situations that touch on an individual's 'concerns'. A concern is anything that a person perceives to have important consequences for his or her well-being. For example, because our social well-being hinges upon our ability to interpret correctly another person's emotional state, the perceived emotional state of another person is almost automatically a concern of ours, as well. How real, urgent, and consequential a concern is perceived to be governs the strength of the response; the nature of the situation determines the kind of response.

There are two steps to any emotional response, in this theory. The first is that a particular situation is flagged as especially relevant, which pushes it more or less irresistibly to the foreground of attention. The second is that deeply ingrained dispositions to particular kinds of action are more or less automatically initiated. Anything that triggers a 'concern' is therefore rather like waving a red flag at the proverbial bull: it almost irresistibly draws the bull's attention, and it makes the bull want to charge. It is those same two kinds of response in humans that, according to Tan, characterize an emotional response.

Not all emotional responses are pleasurable. Sadness and horror, for exemple, are distinctly unpleasurable sensations. But the release from emotional tension is always pleasurable, Tan argues, and the promise of this pleasure is what makes sadness and horror in movies not only tolerable but worthwhile. To push the bull analogy a bit further, a red flag presumably irritates a bull, but if the bull were able to trample the red flag into the dust, disposing of the irritant would produce pleasure so intense that it might make the irritant seem worthwhile. This is analogous to what traditional feature films routinely do, according to Tan: they hold out red flags to the bull, as it were, along with the assurance that, eventually, the bull will have the satisfaction of being able to trample them. The primary 'action tendency' generated by the traditional feature film, therefore, is not the equivalent of the bull's inclination to charge the red flag, it is the equivalent of the bull's hypothetical inclination to court the frustration of chasing the flag around for a spell, in view of the eventual emotional pay-off. The primary action tendency is, in a word, 'interest'. Our interest in an entertainment film and our willingness to sit through dull and occasionally uncomfortable moments is generated and sustained by the promise of eventual emotional rewards.

Tan's model of cinematic pleasure, like Bordwell's, is a quasi-economic one: viewers make an investment of effort and attention with the expectation that this will eventually be amply compensated by some sort of cognitive reward. Anticipation is therefore the key to the structure of the classical fiction film, for Tan as for Bordwell. But for Tan, what we anticipate is not primarily solutions to problems, but emotional pay-offs. The release of tension provided by narrative closure and formal completeness is one of the most important of these, but there are many others, including surprise, spectacle, sympathy, a sense of mastery, a sense of safety, the affirmation of one's values, and the sense of being part of a group. So, Tan's research on emotions leads him to the same conclusion as my study of comedy, which is that classical Hollywood movies are structured mainly as 'emotion machines'.

There is one other way one might test this hypothesis. That would be to perform controlled experiments. It is interesting to note that Tan, who is Dutch and influenced by the 'text linguistics' of scholars such as T. A. van Dijk, bases his conclusions in part upon his own psychological research. American, British, and French humanists, for the most part, have a marked aversion to the idea of performing psychological experiments as part of their research. Be that as it may, if one did decide to do psychological testing to determine whether or not Hollywood movies do in fact function as 'emotion machines', the ideal test subject might be someone who cannot experience emotions.

Imagine a person who does very well in every kind of standardized test of intelligence—language, problem-solving, moral judgement, you name it—a person who can follow a story with no trouble, yet who cannot experience emotion. My guess is that such a person simply would not appreciate much of what goes on in the classical Hollywood cinema—like comedy, for instance—because it hinges on emotional responses, not simply narrative transparency.

Incredible as it may seem, such people do exist. They are people who have suffered damage to particular areas of the frontal cortex. Neurophysiologist Antonio Damasio describes his work with a number of them in a recent book, *Descartes' Error*.[19] These patients show no impairment in any of the standardized tests of reasoning, including tests that require them to weigh complex moral issues, yet they simply cannot cope with ordinary tasks in what Damasio calls the personal and social realms of life. They can tell and understand stories (Damasio gives examples of this), yet they experience and exhibit little emotional response to them. They follow the chain of cause and effect without any problem, but without doing what we often call 'getting it', in human and emotional terms.

For example, one particularly icy winter morning, a patient arrived at Damasio's office. When Damasio asked him about the drive, he responded that it had been quite ordinary, although it had required some attention to the mechanics of driving on ice. Into a discourse on the mechanics of driving on ice, the patient interjected the story of a driver ahead of him, that very morning, who had skidded on a patch of ice, panicked, hit the brakes, and careened into a ditch. The patient negotiated the same patch of ice an instant later, calmly, surely, and dispassionately. Damasio reports that the patient recounted this tale 'with the same tranquillity with which he had obviously experienced the incident'.[20] He turned the incident into a narrative—a narrative intrinsically bound up with the business of 'problem-solving'—but without really 'getting it'.

On the basis of neurophysiological and clinical evidence, Damasio argues that emotion is a very primitive kind of response, deep rooted in the brain, that involves monitoring one's somatic states. Certain kinds of reasoning, especially those having to do with what Damasio calls the social and personal realm—the kinds of reasoning involved in engaging someone in conversation, sustaining a relationship, doing a job, and (I suppose) enjoying a Hollywood movie—are intrinsically bound up with, in fact based upon, these primitive visceral and emotional responses.

The responses Damasio chiefly refers to are excitement, fear, anxiety, and sadness, but he also mentions humour in passing, at several points. Damasio's patients seem to be able to engage in particular kinds of humour: gallows humour, sarcasm, irony, and the kind of wit we call 'dry', meaning emotionally flat. These are all kinds of humour one might engage in without a smile, without exhibiting any kind of emotional reaction. I suspect that more visceral, less cerebral kinds of comedy—slapstick and the comedy of romantic attraction, for example—would elude his patients.

The kind of problem-solving that Bordwell claims is at the heart of the classical Hollywood narrative proceeds pretty independently of emotional responses. We have a character in a quandary who proceeds to work in an orderly and reasonable way to solve his or her problem. Our interest in this process is governed by curiosity, an intellectual attribute in which Damasio's patients seem to have no shortcomings.

Certain kinds of comedy are evidently fully compatible with this kind of problem-solving. For example, one cognitive mechanism that has traditionally been held to explain humour is 'incongruity resolution': a problem is posed and a solution offered which, while fitting, is also incongruous or completely surprising. This is the essence of the riddle. It is also the essence of the comic plot twist. The fundamental response to this kind of humour is surprise. Its natural counterparts are curiosity and suspense, to the extent we conceive suspense as a purely intellectual expectancy, shorn of the emotional underpinnings of anxiety and arousal.

So, much of comedy is perfectly compatible with the system Bordwell, Staiger, and Thompson describe: a system based on audiences' willingness to pay for the opportunity to engage in intellectual expectancy. The triple ending of *Wayne's World*, for example, brings the narrative to conclusion, but in an unconventional, unanticipatable way. Even though its self-reflexivity calls attention away from what Bordwell calls the story (the realm of who does what to whom) and directs attention to the movie's plot (that is, the way the story is told), it is not at all incompatible with the basic mechanism of problem-solving. But this is not all there is to Hollywood comedy. It is not even what is most typical of Hollywood comedy. What is most typical is not merely the violation of expectations, but the violation of personal dignity and social convention: slipping on an olive, inadvertently exposing one's undergarments, behaving in sexually suggestive ways in a formal public setting, and so on.

Humour is one natural, evolved response to emotionally charged social situations. We laugh to defuse a threat or an insult. We laugh in response to feelings of personal inadequacy or failure, especially when we are in public. We laugh when we are embarrassed or when someone else is embarrassed. Contrary to popular belief, the classical Hollywood cinema is not primarily about happy endings; it is about just such emotionally charged personal and social situations. It is about skirting or surviving a series of potential disasters. We know the movie is over when there is no longer any imminent danger of embarrassment or pain. We enjoy happy endings because they give us a pleasurable sense of affirmation, hope, and security, but we do not go to movies primarily for the endings; we go for the process of getting there. The classical Hollywood cinema is primarily about *deferred* happy endings or sustained emotional high points. It is primarily about seeing characters squirm in dangerous, painful, or embarrassing situations.

Since humour is a natural, evolved human response to dangerous, painful, or embarrassing situations, it is quite natural that humour is part of Holly-wood movies. All we need to do to make a place for it in the classical Hollywood system that Bordwell, Staiger, and Thompson theorize is to reconceive the primary pressure that shaped the system as the pursuit of powerful emotional responses in a safe context, rather than the pursuit of narrative problem-solving. This has the fringe benefit of making the system compatible with spectacle, melodrama, and horror, and the other non-narrative attractions of movies. It also makes a certain amount of historical sense, because it aligns the Hollywood cinema more closely with amusement park attractions, variety shows, video games, non-fiction television, and other popular non-narrative entertainments.

I happened to mention to an acquaintance outside the academy that the central conclusion of this essay was that people go to movies to experience strong emotions. Her response was, 'Well, that's obvious, isn't it? Naturally that's why people go to movies!' I had to admit that my conclusion does seem rather obvious. Yet, remarkably, aside from Tan's very recent book, there is precious little published film theory that supports this conclusion. Psychoanalytic theorists have written a great deal about the *desire* attached to movies, but that is something different from emotions. When we speak of emotional impulses, we are talking not about libidinal urges, but about conscious gratifications. We like comedy because it makes us laugh. We like melodrama because it makes us cry. We like sex and violence because they arouse and excite us. And so on. Regardless of the source of these feelings, it is their manifestations in awareness that prompt us to go to movies. And these manifestations are a topic that film theorists have scarcely broached. So, the final conclusion of this chapter has to be a plea to explore further the possibility that what the classical Hollywood cinema is fundamentally about is not the production of a certain kind of narrative but, rather, the production of certain kinds of emotion.

NOTES

1. David Bordwell, Janet Staiger, and Kristin Thompson, *The Classical Hollywood Cinema: Film Style and Mode of Production to 1960* (New York: Columbia University Press, 1985).
2. David Bordwell, *Narration in the Fiction Film* (Madison: University of Wisconsin Press, 1985).
3. Francis Taylor Patterson, *Cinema Craftsmanship* (New York: Harcourt, Brace & Howe, 1920), 5, quoted in *Classical Hollywood Cinema*, 13.
4. *Classical Hollywood Cinema*, 39.
5. Comolli attacked André Bazin's 'evolutionary' history of the technological development of cinema for being a straight-line affair, driven by constant imperatives. Comolli later came under attack himself, from Rick Altman and others, on similar grounds. In a 1983 essay, Bordwell and Thompson themselves attack 'evolutionary' accounts of history and, in response to a critic who accuses *The Classical Hollywood Cinema* of such an error, Kristin Thompson wrote, '[The book] contains *no* discussion of "the evolution of specific techniques." . . . Changes, yes; evolution, no.' It is important to note that none of these discussions of so-called evolutionary accounts of history reflects a proper understanding of Darwinian evolutionary theory (which is briefly described in the body of this chapter). See Jean-Louis Comolli, 'Technique et idéologie', *Cahiers du cinéma*, begun in no. 229 (May 1971) and continued in subsequent issues; André Bazin, 'The Myth of Total Cinema' and 'The Evolution of the Language of Cinema', in *What is Cinema?* vol. i, trans. Hugh Gray (Berkeley and Los Angeles: University of California Press, 1967), 17–40; Rick Altman, 'Toward a

Theory of the History of Representational Technologies', *Iris*, 2: 2 (1984), 111–26; Kristin Thompson and David Bordwell, 'Linearity, Materialism and the Study of Early American Cinema', *Wide Angle*, 5: 3 (1983), 4–15; and Kristin Thompson, 'Wisconsin Project or King's Projection', *Screen*, 29: 1 (1988), 52.

6. For a more thorough and detailed explication of *The Classical Hollywood Cinema*, its relation to evolutionary theory, and the attacks on both, see Dirk Eitzen, 'Evolution, Functionalism, and the Study of American Cinema', *Velvet Light Trap*, 28 (Fall 1991), 73–85.

7. *Narration in the Fiction Film*, 39–40.

8. *Classical Hollywood Comedy*, ed. Kristine Brunovska Karnick and Henry Jenkins (New York: Routledge, 1995).

9. Donald Crafton, 'Pie and Chase: Gag, Spectacle and Narrative in Slapstick Comedy', in *Classical Hollywood Comedy*, 107.

10. Jerry Palmer, *The Logic of the Absurd: On Film and Television Comedy* (BFI: London, 1987), 147 ff.

11. Kristine Brunovska Karnick, 'Commitment and Reaffirmation in Hollywood Romantic Comedy', in *Classical Hollywood Comedy*, 126–30.

12. David Bordwell and Kristin Thompson, *Film Art: An Introduction*, 4th edn. (New York: McGraw-Hill, 1993), 176.

13. As Murray Smith argues in a recent book, *Engaging Characters* (Oxford: Clarendon Press, 1995), our interest in the characters in movies inevitably produces emotional responses, since we cannot help interpreting characters' appearance and behaviour in evaluative and affective terms. One of the main contentions of *Engaging Characters* is that observing and construing characters is the key to the way viewers make sense of narrative films. This seems very likely. On the other hand, the depiction of characters is not the sole means by which movies produce emotions. Even where characters are featured, our emotional responses are not always mediated by our impressions of them, as Smith seems to suggest at points. For example, the chaotic battle scene in Kenneth Branagh's *Henry V* is emotionally charged because we are hard-wired to have a powerful emotional reaction to violent conflict, even if we do not know or care about the participants as individuals. We respond emotionally to the whole *situation*. This response is as immediate and direct as the vertigo we experience at the edge of a cliff. Our understanding of the situation does not have to be filtered through our imagination of the experiences of particular characters in the scene. This is especially evident in certain kinds of comedy, such as the scene in Chaplin's *Gold Rush* where the Little Tramp almost bumps into a bear without realizing it. The situation is funny even though (maybe even *because*) it does not matter what the Little Tramp is thinking or feeling at the moment. Of course, in the case of *Henry V*, our comprehension of the young king's goals, his personal courage, and the long odds his army faces raises the stakes and therefore our emotional response to the battle scene. I would argue that to raise the stakes in this fashion is the primary function of character development in classical Hollywood movies. Smith does not make this point in so many words, but it is completely compatible with his arguments.

14. Henri Bergson, 'Laughter: An Essay on the Meaning of the Comic', in Wylie Sypher (ed.), *Comedy* (Garden City, NY: Doubleday, 1956).

15. See, for example, R. Langevin and H. I. Day, 'Physiological Correlates of Humor', in J. H. Goldstein and P. E. McGhee (eds.), *The Psychology of Humor: Theoretical Perspectives and Empirical Issues* (New York: Academic Press, 1972).

16. This has been shown by anthropological and sociological research, and is supported by studies with infants and apes. See, for example, J. Radcliffe-Brown, 'On Joking Relationships' and 'A Further Note on Joking Relationships', in *Structure and Function in Primitive Society* (London: Cohen & West, 1952); Herbert J. Levowitz, 'Smiles and Laughter: Some Neurologic, Developmental, and Psychodynamic Con-

siderations', in Maurice Charney (ed.), *Comedy: New Perspectives* (New York: New York Literary Forum, 1978); and Mahadev L. Apte, *Humor and Laughter: An Anthropological Approach* (Ithaca, NY: Cornell University Press, 1985).

17. Ed. S. Tan, *Emotion and the Structure of Narrative Film: Film as an Emotion Machine* (Mahwah, NJ: Lawrence Erlbaum Associates, 1996).
18. Tan draws primarily upon Frijda's *The Emotions* (New York: Cambridge University Press, 1986).
19. Antonio R. Damasio, *Descartes' Error: Emotion, Reason, and the Human Brain* (New York: G. P. Putnam's Sons, 1994).
20. Ibid. 193.

Imagining from the Inside

MURRAY SMITH

Close to the beginning of *Dead Calm* (1989), directed by Phillip Noyce, a character climbs on board a deserted boat drifting on a calm sea. He looks around cautiously, accompanied only by the gentle sound of the boat's creaking wooden frame. The calm is broken by a loud noise; our protagonist (John Ingram, played by Sam Neill) turns his head to see a large, heavy pulley swinging directly towards him—or more precisely, directly into his face. We know this because his sight is rendered for us through a POV shot—a shot which mimics the optical point of view of a character. And in this POV shot, the pulley flies fast and directly at the camera. My reaction to this shot on a first, unprepared viewing, was a visceral flinching, as if the pulley were about to clock me in the face. (Informal testing on various friends and audiences suggests that my reaction is not idiosyncratic.) As such, the sequence seems emblematic of the ability of films to create the illusion that I (the spectator) am a character in the story world, faced with the dilemmas and experiences of (in this case) the protagonist; or, more cautiously, that I am brought to imagine 'from the inside' the character's experience. In more common parlance, I may be said to empathize with the character—though, as we will see, there are subtle distinctions which the term 'empathy' (in its everyday sense) glosses over.

Informal commentary on the cinema, as well as more formal theorizing about it, has often supported the idea that films can astound and terrorize in this way because of their purportedly unrivalled capacity for perceptual and cognitive illusion. In this chapter, however, I will not be concerned with the notion of illusion; it has been defended, and, to my mind, much more successfully criticized.[1] Nevertheless, there are residual questions about the 'power of cinema', raised acutely by the kind of experience I recount above, which still have to be answered. The two questions I will focus on here are: what is the place of imagining a character 'from the inside' in engaging with a fiction? And, what is the function of POV, and other striking devices like sudden movements and loud noises, with respect to imagining a character's

Thanks to Richard Allen, Paisley Livingston, Carl Plantinga, and Greg Smith for grappling with and commenting on earlier versions of this essay.

experience 'from the inside' in our engagement with cinematic fictions? In the course of addressing these questions, I will also be reflecting on certain arguments regarding imagination and emotional response in my book *Engaging Characters*.[2]

The idea of imagining 'from the inside'—indeed, the phrase itself—is one that crops up in the work of both Kendall Walton and Richard Wollheim, and both accord it an important place in their accounts of imagination, representation, and art. Walton, for example, cashes in his notion of 'participation' in a fictional story in terms of imagining the events and actions of the story from the inside. Wollheim argues that to imagine from the inside is to imagine *centrally*, a phenomenon he contrasts with *acentral* imagining, in which one imagines a situation 'from no-one's standpoint'.[3] Gregory Currie makes a similar distinction between *personal* and *impersonal* imagination.[4] For both Wollheim and Currie, imagination is a matter of *simulation*: to imagine is to simulate having beliefs, attitudes, emotions, etc, other than those one really possesses, running our normal mental processes ' "off-line", disconnected from their normal sensory inputs and behavioural outputs'.[5] And just as there is a difference between, on the one hand, believing that something is the case, and, on the other hand, believing that one sees or hears or otherwise experiences some event, so there is a difference between imagining that something occurs (impersonal, or acentral imagining) and imagining experiencing that occurrence from the inside (personal, or central imagining).[6]

For Wollheim, when we imagine from the inside, either we ourselves or another person (or character) can be the 'protagonist' of our imaginative project—I could, for example, imagine myself climbing on board the *Victory*, or I could imagine being Nelson and climbing on board the *Victory*. Walton wonders whether imagining from the inside can amount to 'imagining being' a person or character other than oneself in this sense. He suggests that there is something intrinsically self-referential about imagining, just as there is about intending.[7] Imagining 'from the inside' another person or character's experience has to be routed through, as it were, a self-imagining; 'Rather than imagining oneself to be Eddie or a frog, the spectator might imagine having perceptual experiences of certain sorts, ones one takes it to be fictional that Eddie or a frog is experiencing.'[8] A distinct though related worry of some theorists is a certain scepticism regarding the 'depth' of the feelings we are said to share with a character when we adopt them as a protagonist, that is, imagine what we take to be their experience from the inside. 'Empathy' and 'imagining being' seem to imply a kind of total replication of a character's experience, and to some, such a replication seems unlikely.[9] However, as we will see, to imagine from the inside does not require such a total replication of a character's experience at a given moment. To use more of Wollheim's terminology, central imagining can be

more or less 'plenitudinous'. In David Mamet's *Homicide* (1991), for example—a film I will be discussing in more depth—there are moments when
the film invites us to imagine a character's embarrassment, without inviting
us to imagine the throbbing sensation he presumably feels from a recent
blow on the back of the head. Imagining from the inside is frequently—
perhaps even necessarily—partial.

These differences aside, Walton and Wollheim agree that imagining experiences from the inside—including but not limited to imagining perceptual experiences, like seeing—is an important aspect of our experience of
representational art. Alex Neill has also made a strong case for taking this
kind of imagining very seriously, in the context of our actual interactions as
well as those with characters in fiction films. Among other supporting
arguments, Neill points out that simulating what we take to be the beliefs and
other mental states of other persons—imagining from the inside, in other
words—is a basic part of our capacity to understand, predict, and explain
the behaviour of others.[10] If this is true, it would be bizarre if imagining
from the inside, or empathizing as he calls it, did *not* play some role in our
experience of fiction films. Currie, however, in spite of his incorporation of
these arguments concerning the pervasiveness of simulating-the-states-of-
others, argues that such imagining is only of peripheral importance in our
experience of fiction films. In particular, he contends that the role of
imagining seeing—a species of imagining from the inside—in relation to our
experience of fiction films, has been much overstated.[11] Thus, there are both
marked differences and similarities in the accounts of imagination provided
by Currie, Walton, and Wollheim. All acknowledge, however, the existence
of imagining from the inside—a phenomenon that I will also refer to,
depending on which of the various accounts is uppermost at a particular
point in the argument, as central imagining and personal imagining.

TWO CLARIFICATIONS

In *Engaging Characters*, I advance a framework for the analysis and understanding of character, 'identification', and emotional response to cinematic
fictions (much of the framework also applies to fictions in general). Although this framework incorporates both imagining from the inside—or
central imagining, as I call it there—and POV, I am not satisfied that it got
these matters quite right. So I will indulge in this essay in having another go.
My analysis of 'character engagement'—the phrase I use to denote all those
aspects of interacting with a fiction which bear in some way on the characters of the fiction—begins with Wollheim's distinction between central and
acentral imagining.[12] Engaging with a fiction, I argue, typically involves
both acentral and central imagining, though any central imagining that we

engage in is ultimately framed by acentral imagining. In a typical film viewing, we might centrally imagine this character's experience at this point in the film, that character's experience at another point; and at other points we may be imagining the scenario 'outside' any character's perspective, that is, acentrally. Moreover, our experience of the film as an emerging whole must be understood in terms of acentral imagining: I might imagine from the inside Ingram's experience of the pulley swinging towards him, but as I continue to watch the film my knowledge of the larger situation—Ingram's wife Rae stranded on another boat with a madman while Ingram climbs on board the deserted ship—supersedes my imagining, from the inside, that moment in Ingram's experience. My central imaginings are, to adapt a term from Noël Carroll, *assimilated* into a broader, acentral perspective on the situation.[13] And this kind of overarching knowledge, of the experience of several characters in disparate locations, cannot be imagined from the inside. Central imagining might be prompted locally, but our global response is acentral. Engaging with fictions thus involves a mix of central and acentral imagining. What is less clear is the precise place and function of the central imagining, and the degree to which textual structure (in which I include everything from large-scale narrative structure to the minutiae of stylistic usage at a particular point in the film) determines the nature of our imagining; these are the issues I aim to clarify here.

In my account of character engagement, I posit three levels of narrational *structure* under the rubric of acentral imagining: recognition (the identification and assignment of traits to characters); alignment (the revelation of the actions and psychological states of characters); and allegiance (the evaluation of characters, especially morally but in other ways as well—according to notions of taste, for example). Under the rubric of central imagining, I posit three *processes*: emotional simulation (simulating the emotional states of a character by imagining their experiences from the inside), affective mimicry (mimicking the affective states of characters in an involuntary fashion, prompted by facial and vocal cues),[14] and autonomic responses (reacting in reflex fashion to represented events in the same way as a character does—as, for example, in the startle response, in which we jump at sudden loud noises or rapid, unexpected visual movements). There are two respects in which the description I have just given benefits from conceptual clarification—concerning the relationship between textual structure and psychological process, and concerning the relationship among simulation, mimicry, and autonomic responses.

As I set this framework out in *Engaging Characters*, the distinction between textual structure and psychological process is blurred, or rather treated as if the two were always identical: that a particular kind of textual structure determines a particular kind of psychological response (note the implied equivalence, in the preceding paragraph, in describing acentral 'structures' and central 'processes'). In some cases this is true. Since the startle response is hard-wired, so long as we are functioning normally, a loud bang on the soundtrack will inevitably result in a startled reaction. Also, if a film-maker wants to make the viewer's experience of the story world match that of a deaf character, and he removes all diegetic sound from the soundtrack, then he has determined that aspect of the viewer's perceptual experience (as in particular scenes in Abel Gance's *Un grand amour de Beethoven* [1935] and Joseph Lewis's *The Big Combo* [1955]). But with respect to 'higher-level' psychological processes—like central imagining—textual structure does not, at least not in all circumstances, wholly determine psychological process. Of course, textual structure directs and constrains our responses: minimally, a film must align us to some degree with a character—that is, provide us with knowledge of a character's actions and felt experience—if our central imagining is to be motivated or 'authorized'. But there is nothing in the *Dead Calm* sequence which *determines* that it will be centrally imagined by the viewer, even if there is casual evidence that this happens for some viewers. So, rather than arguing that there are two sets of textual structures which neatly match up with two distinct types of imagining (central and acentral), I now argue that all of the textual devices and structures (recognition, alignment, allegiance, and any other ones we may posit) represent for us the events of the narrative in certain ways, which may then trigger either acentral or central imagining (or indeed certain other psychological responses, which are not appropriately labelled 'imaginative'—but that takes us on to the second clarification). I will, however, argue that certain kinds of textual structure may foster or predispose us to imagine in one way rather than another, as distinct from determining the nature of our imaginative response.[15]

The second clarification concerns the relationship between central imagining and the concepts I connect with it: emotional simulation, affective mimicry, and autonomic responses. In a review of *Engaging Characters*, Berys Gaut writes: 'Central imagining is held to include not just simulation of other's mental states, but also mimicry, affective and physical, and autonomic responses, such as being startled. But mimicry need not involve exercise of the imagination, and autonomic responses certainly cannot, or else they would not be autonomic.'[16] Gaut is quite right to spot some fudging here. So I would now recast the relationship among these concepts, and the phenomena they describe, in the following way. Emotional simulation is essentially a species of central imagining, which focuses on our imaginings of the *emotional* states of others, rather than the entire range of possible embodied experiences. Affective mimicry and autonomic responses are not forms of imagining, for the reasons Gaut states, but they are appropriately connected with central imagining and simulation because they often function as aids or prompts to such imagining and simulation.

They are examples of textual devices which foster central imagining, without mandating it. Jumping at a loud bang or a sudden movement, or mimicking an expression rendered in close-up, are not imaginative but autonomic and sub-intentional responses; but along with other aspects of the film, they may help us to imagine vividly, from the inside, some situation or experience. This is a point I will expand on below, with some examples.

What about POV? Where does that textual device fit into this thicket of structures and imaginative responses? As part of the effort in *Engaging Characters* to resist vague claims about how we 'identify' with characters in watching films, I argued against the widely accepted view that a, if not the, primary function of the POV shot is to inculcate 'identification' between the looking character and the spectator.[17] This still seems to me to be correct. However, there *is* something to the intuition that POV is connected with 'identification', beyond the minimal concession that such shots necessarily forge perceptual access (that is, they allow us to see what a character sees from the spatial position of the character). I will argue that POV shots can function as powerful prompts to central imagining, though not in quite the same way as devices prompting mimicry and autonomic reactions. If we look at how POV shots work in context, this will become clear.

POV shots typically work in a two-part structure involving not only a POV shot but a reaction shot. The POV shot itself shows us what the character is looking at, from her spatial location; the reaction shot tells us something (often quite a lot) about the nature of the character's attention to the object (the facial expression of the looking character typically gives us at least some indication of the psychological state of the looker: interest, anger, fear, or whatever). And of course, the context of these shots in the larger narrative will usually allow us to specify further the subjective state of the character.[18] What the POV shot itself does—*and does in a way that no other shot can*—is to render certain aspects of visual experience. By so rendering the visual experience of a character, the POV shot is apt to prompt us to imagine seeing as the character does (imagining seeing being, once again, a specific type of central imagining). Moreover, as part of a larger sequence involving complementary reaction shots—and shots of other sorts—the POV shot plays a role in developing *multifaceted alignment* with a character: a situation in which we have not only perceptual access (the POV shot shows us what we are to imagine a character sees), but a sense of what the character thinks and feels (through the reactions shots, and indeed the way the shots are edited, juxtaposed with music, and so forth—in short, the way the whole is expressively orchestrated). In such cases, the POV shot works to promote central imagining as a part of a larger structure of multifaceted alignment.[19] This formulation gives POV its due, recognizing its unique role with respect specifically to imagining seeing, without falling into the fallacy of POV—the assumption that POV shots somehow wire us directly into the mind of a character. This fallacy arises from abstracting the POV shot from its context, and assuming that it works in glorious isolation. The fact that the POV shot can act as a prompt to central imagining only in context differentiates it, as a device, from those that prompt mimicry and autonomic reactions. Though all three devices tend to foster central imagining, mimicry and autonomic responses do not require this kind of contextualization.

Now, I think, we can begin to see how the sequence from *Dead Calm* might solicit central imagination so effectively. It develops just this sort of multifaceted alignment, and enhances it through devices which are apt to trigger autonomic and mimicking responses. Ingram's approach to the larger boat is rendered by an alternation of POV shots and reaction shots, showing us how the bow of the boat looms up into his vision, and how the bright sun forces him to squint as he looks up at the rigging. We are given a precise sense of what he sees and hears, and because we have also been restricted to what he knows about the boat, our thoughts about the boat are likely to match his in many respects. As he climbs aboard the boat, a medium shot follows him from behind as he moves cautiously along the deck, the framing gradually tightening into a close-up. At this point the sudden loud thump is heard from off-screen, causing Ingram to swing around and face the camera—naturally enough, facially expressing shock/apprehension—at the same moment that we start in our seats. Cut to the POV shot showing the pulley swinging directly into the camera, and so rapidly growing larger in the frame—a visual correlate to the shock of the sound. Cut back to the previous framing, showing Ingram ducking fractionally before the pulley swings into view, again filling the frame. The sequence thus confronts us with a barrage of techniques designed to evoke, and invite us to centrally imagine, Ingram's experience (which are nevertheless probably found to be more compelling as a prompt to central imagining by some spectators than others).

I have concentrated on this sequence from *Dead Calm* because it uses POV within a structure of multifaceted alignment, as well as drawing on affective mimicry and the startle response, in a particularly telling fashion. I should add, though, that neither POV nor any other individual device is essential to the prompting of central imagining. A POV shot is not essential to the prompting of central imagining because the target of the central imagining may not be a perceptual state, but, for example, an emotional state. POV may be particularly effective in rendering how a character sees, and so enabling our imagining from the inside how the character sees, but it is not particularly useful in evoking, say, a character's joy or humiliation or anxiety. Emotional simulation certainly does not need a POV shot in order to be prompted.[20]

Homicide provides a pertinent example of this sort of case. Detective Bobby Gold has been distracted from a case in which he is enthusiastically involved, by another case involving an old Jewish woman who has been murdered in her candy store, situated in a black neighbourhood. The family of the woman believe the murder to be an act of anti-Semitic persecution, and their fears are heightened when the dead woman's daughter-in-law believes she hears a gunshot outside their apartment. Against his will, Gold is compelled to investigate this incident, in large part because he is (by birth, rather than practice) a Jew. Angered by what he believes to be the paranoia and undue influence of the Jewish family, he reluctantly and sceptically checks around their apartment. At one point, he takes a call from his partner regarding the other case, in a room which he believes he alone occupies. The narration of the film maximizes our subjective access to Gold, through framing and dialogue; it also restricts us to his range of knowledge, as in *Dead Calm*. Along with the fact that Gold has been presented sympathetically up to this point, this strategy predisposes us to centrally imagine Gold's emotions—his frustration and anger at the demanding and entitled attitude of the Jewish family. All of this occurs without the use of POV shots or shock effects (though affective mimicry—the involuntary, low-level mimicking of Gold's expressions, and thus of the affects they express—may again play a role here). We will return to this scene from *Homicide* after considering the implications for my argument of another view of imagining in the cinema.

CURRIE ON 'PERSONAL IMAGINING' AND POV

Gregory Currie's recent study of film overlaps in many places with my own study, particularly with respect to the role of imagination in our experience of cinema. However, while there is a significant degree of convergence between our arguments with respect to imagination and POV, some of the details of Currie's argument tend to pull in just the opposite direction to the revisions and refinements of my argument discussed above. I want to examine Currie's argument, then, as the strongest argument against the kind of position I have set out above, in which central imagining plays an important role in our experience of films, and in which POV plays an important role in prompting one variety of such imagining, namely, imagining seeing.

Currie's contrast between personal and impersonal imagining is, as we have seen, very similar to the contrast between central and acentral imagining. One of Currie's most controversial proposals concerns in particular imagining seeing. To imagine seeing something is to imagine seeing something from some particular vantage-point in the story world. Currie argues, correctly in my view, that a widespread assumption in film theory is that viewing a film involves imagining seeing from the perspective defined by the camera's position. The Imagined Observer Hypothesis, as he calls it, has been regarded as a major factor in the power of cinema. What we are to imagine seeing is given directly to us by the camera's field of vision; this directness accounts for the sense of 'immediacy' that is (purportedly) the unique possession of cinema.

Currie argues that this is a seriously mistaken view, and suggests instead that our experience in the cinema is defined by perceptual but impersonal imagining.[21] Our imagining is 'perceptual' in that it depends primarily on our visual capacity to recognize objects—we recognize a shot of a horse using the same capacity we would use in recognizing a real horse. However, the fact that the imaginative prompt is visual, and perspectival, does not mean that we must imagine that the position from which the object is represented is occupied by an agent, and that we are to imagine from the inside that agent's perceptual experience.[22] As Wollheim remarks, in a way that chimes very much with Currie's argument: 'mental imagery, taken in isolation, abscinded from the thoughts and intentions that motivate it, is no sure guide to the mental processes of which it is the vehicle.'[23] In short, perceptual imagining does not entail imagining seeing.

Another distinction Currie makes, apparently of less significance, is that between 'primary' and 'secondary' imagining. Primary imagining is simply imagining what is true in the fiction. In *Anna Karenina* it is true that Anna commits suicide; in *Dead Calm* it is true that our protagonist almost gets hit in the face by a pulley. Secondary imagining refers to imagining that we undertake in order to work out what we should imagine is true in the fiction. This comes into play where 'what we are primarily to imagine is the experience of a character'.[24] Where a fiction focuses on the quality of a character's experience, imagining what the character thinks and feels is often integral to the process of working out what is true in the fiction, since not everything is or indeed can be literally spelt out—for aesthetic as well as logical reasons:

What the author explicitly says, and what can be inferred therefrom, will constrain our understanding of the character's mental state. It will set signposts and boundaries. But if these are all we have to go by in a fiction, it will seem dull and lifeless. It is when we are able, in imagination, to feel as the character feels that fictions of character take hold of us. This process of empathetic reenactment of the character's situation is what I call secondary imagining.[25]

This seems to me persuasive in and of itself; but it is not clear how this coheres with Currie's larger claim that imagining in response to films is overwhelmingly impersonal imagining.[26] For it is clear from the quoted passage that 'secondary imagining' is, or at least typically is, personal

imagining (and might therefore involve imagining seeing, which is a species of personal imagining). So the question is: how does Currie reconcile the importance he attaches to personal imagining (under the guise of secondary imagining) here, with his argument that spectatorship in the cinema is characterized by impersonal imagining? (This echoes, of course, one of the questions posed by this essay as a whole, as much to myself as to Currie: if we grant that experiencing fictions involves both types of imagining, how are they related?) Moreover, there is something odd about tagging 'empathetic re-enactment' (central imagining, in my terms) 'secondary', given the important role Currie gives it in the passage quoted above. Here central imagining is integral, rather than merely instrumental (as the adjective 'secondary' implies), to the power of at least a certain kind of fiction. And this worry applies to fictions in general, not merely cinematic fictions, as the hierarchy between primary and secondary imaginings is one that applies to all fictions. Currie may underestimate the importance of personal imagining to fiction in general, not merely to fiction films.

What about the role of POV with respect to imagining in the cinema? In the section where he most explicitly focuses on POV, Currie argues that it has been accorded an unduly high value in film theory, and that the concept of POV has become overextended as a result of the mistaken application of a 'psychologistic' principle to film—the principle 'that the content of the cinematic image is [standardly] to be interpreted as the content of *someone's* visual experience'[27]—a close relative of the Imagined Observer Hypothesis. Perhaps recognizing the widespread assumption that POV shots instil 'identification' between the looking character and the viewer, Currie seems to be aware—though he never states this—that the POV shot might be seen as a counter-example to his cinema-as-impersonal-imagining thesis. If we were to identify with a character on the basis of a POV shot from that character's vantage-point, that would surely mean that we would imagine seeing the diegesis from just that vantage-point. So Currie is eager to demonstrate how the subjective content of the POV shot can be accounted for by sole reference 'to the character's experience, not to our own'. Discussing the POV shot in *Spellbound* in which we see Dr Bruloff through the bottom of a glass as Ballantine drinks from it, Currie writes:

We are not required to imagine that *we* see Dr Bruloff from Ballantine's perspective or any other. In general, subjective shots function to help us imagine what a character's experience is like, not to imagine ourselves being that character and having that experience.[28]

In short, theories of cinema which place POV at the centre are barking, indeed positively climbing, up the wrong tree.[29]

It is not surprising that Currie should find such theories so uncongenial.

If we look at his argument against the Imagined Observer Hypothesis, we find an example of POV (from Hitchcock's *Vertigo* (1959)) as an accepted challenge to his theory. The shot is one of Hitchcock's celebrated simultaneous dolly-zoom combinations, in this case rendering the vertiginous sensations of Scottie (James Stewart) as he peers down the convent stairwell. Currie admits that this is a case of 'imagining seeing', but the force of the example is held in check by the fact that it is an 'extraordinary' case that cannot be made the basis of a theory of cinema.[30] I do not think it can either, but I think it raises more problems for Currie's theory, and more issues of interest, than he grants.

What is it about the shot that makes Currie accept this as an example of a film fostering 'imagining seeing'? Presumably it is the unusual play with perspective within the shot, given that elsewhere, when he discusses POV shots, he stresses their failure adequately to mimic perception (and so foster imagining seeing).[31] The queasy sensation (which results from a shrinking of apparent depth while size remains constant) so effectively renders Scottie's experience, he implies, that it would be foolish to argue that the shot does not instil or at least encourage imagining seeing (and imagining experiencing vertigo). But it is not clear why or how the zoom-dolly effect is in *principle* different from the framing of a shot from a character's position in terms of its ability to render effectively a visual experience. Surely the zoom-dolly effect is no more an exact replication of how vision appears to one experiencing vertigo than is a POV shot an exact replication of ordinary vision. Why does the zoom-dolly effect 'give the effect of a vertiginous experience'[32] and the framing of a shot from a character's position not give the effect of seeing from that position? Without an argument demonstrating that one can distinguish the two cases, there is nothing to stop us generalizing from Currie's own description of the effect of the shot from *Vertigo*, to POV shots in general.[33] Combining the minimal, and I think incontestable, claim that the POV shot provides information about a character's visual experience ('what a character's experience is like'), with Currie's own arguments about the importance of 'secondary' personal imagining, the implication that POV shots may foster 'imagining seeing' seems inescapable. And once POV shots are accepted as being capable of fostering 'imagining seeing', the notion that it is only 'extraordinary' shots which achieve this begins to look suspect (even if we define POV shots very strictly, and exclude partial and metaphorical POV shots, as he urges we should).

In the last few paragraphs, I have been arguing that POV shots represent a problem for Currie because they seem so readily and well explained by the Imagined Observer Hypothesis (even if other types of shot are not). The reader might conclude from this that my argument about POV is being mounted not only for its own sake, but in order to rehabilitate the Imagined

Observer Hypothesis. This is not my goal here, even if there clearly are problems with Currie's wholesale rejection of imagined seeing. I can afford to be agnostic on this question, because the correctness (or otherwise) of Currie's critique of the IOH does not, in fact, affect my argument concerning the important place of central/personal imagining in film, nor of the role of the POV shot in fostering imagining seeing, odd as this may seem. If the IOH is correct, then there is clearly no problem with my argument on imagining seeing and POV: imagining ourselves seeing as the character sees on the basis of a POV shot just becomes a subtype of the general form of cinematic imagining, that is, imagining that we are an observer seeing from the vantage-point of the camera.

Perhaps more surprisingly, if the IOH is wrong, my arguments about POV and imagining seeing can still be sustained. This is so because there is a way of reconciling the rejection of the Imagined Observer Hypothesis, and the apparently incompatible claim that POV shots encourage us to imagine seeing what the character sees—though it involves a most serpentine (and unparsimonious) series of connections. It works like this. Films provide us with visual and aural representations. These prompt perceptual imagining (as defined above, 420). On the basis of POV shots, we may then engage in secondary, personal imagining, including imagining seeing what a character sees. (This then feeds back into primary, impersonal imagining—imagining what is true in the story world.) So, Currie's framework allows for imagining seeing, and being prompted to do so by POV shots, but not directly, and only instrumentally.[34] These two routes from POV shots to imagining seeing can be summarized in the following way:

IOH true: POV shot > imagining seeing

IOH false: film > perceptual imagining > secondary imagining, e.g. imagining seeing

To recap the argument so far: central imagining—or what Currie refers to both as 'personal imagining' and 'empathetic reenactment'—seems to play a more significant role in our appreciation of fictions than Currie overtly allows for two reasons. First, because 'secondary imagining' is not merely instrumentally important for determining what is true in the fiction, but intrinsically important in many fictions ('fictions of character'). This applies to fictions regardless of the medium in which they are told. Secondly, in relation to specifically filmic fictions, POV shots may play a role in fostering imagining seeing. And this remains true whether we regard this as happening directly, or indirectly through a circuitous series of connections. For both POV shots in fiction films, and fictions in general, may foster personal imaginings, even if the Imagined Observer Hypothesis is in general wrong. Moreover, as *part of* a structure of multifaceted alignment, POV shots may also foster a richer form of personal imagining than merely imagining seeing—imagining a complex of actions, thoughts, and feelings, as in the sequence from *Dead Calm*.

WHY BOTHER WITH ACENTRAL IMAGINING, THEN?

So central/personal imagining is an important kind of response we have to at least fictions of character. Imagining a character 'from the inside' is a major part of the appeal and interest of such fictions. This is rarely the whole story, however: responding appropriately to such fictions involves both central and acentral imagining, interwoven with one another. The concept of central imagining is necessary but not sufficient in understanding our experience of fictions of character. The difficulties of claiming that central imagining alone provides an adequate conceptual framework can be summarized by noting that fictions of character typically provide us either with too much, or with too little, information for central imagining to be sustained throughout the duration of such a fiction. Let me explain this perhaps mysterious statement with some more examples.

The development of the sequence from *Homicide* discussed earlier is instructive in this regard. We left Bobby Gold talking on the phone with his partner, cursing the Jewish family. To be exact: 'fuck 'em and the taxes they pay . . . eh, not my people baby, *fuck* 'em . . . with so much anti-Semitism the last four thousand years we must be doing *somethin'* to bring it about.' As Gold utters these words, he shifts his position and the granddaughter of the murdered woman is revealed to be sitting—still unbeknownst to Gold—in the room. Now, if we have been brought to imagine from the inside Gold's feelings up to this point, as suggested by the earlier analysis, something occurs here which complicates this. In place of the exclusive alignment with Gold, the film momentarily, if minimally, provides us with more information than Gold possesses, by revealing the granddaughter to us before Gold becomes aware of her presence. In doing this, the film focuses our attention on the clash of perspectives between Gold and the granddaughter, on the dramatic irony of the situation, and as such elicits acentral imagining.[35] *Homicide* is entirely typical in this respect. In either minor or major ways, fictions always break absolute alignment between character and viewer.[36]

If *Homicide* demonstrates the way in which a film might demand something other than a centrally imaginative response by giving us 'too much' information, a film like *Dead Man Walking* (Tim Robbins, 1996) shows how providing 'too little' information can have a similar effect. Part of the power of the film lies in the way that it inculcates—if it is successful—imagining from the inside aspects of Mathew Poncelet (Sean Penn)'s experience, as he waits on death row convicted of murder. It is indeed an unsettling, but potent and fascinating, experience to imagine awaiting execution. Part of what we imagine here is Poncelet's feeling of utter powerlessness in the face of a system that seeks his execution, in spite of what may be injustices in his treatment. But again we come up against the limits of the concept of central imagining, *on its own*, as an analysis of our experience of fictions of character. For much of the duration of the film, Poncelet denies that he murdered either of the two victims. He admits to assaulting them, but claims that the trigger was pulled by his older associate. This older associate has plea bargained his way off death row, Poncelet claims, by dishonestly laying the blame on him. Given our knowledge of the American justice system—including preconceptions derived from other dramatized representations of it, like the earlier film *I Want to Live!* (Robert Wise, 1958)—this is plausible; at least, it is as plausible as the possibility that Poncelet is lying. Given that this aspect of the fiction is in doubt, we cannot *just* imagine centrally what it feels like to be Poncelet, because we do not know for certain what beliefs we should be simulating. At the very least, our central imagining is severely circumscribed by this lack of certainty. Of course, one way in which we might try to puzzle out what really happened is through central imagining on the basis of what we do know about him and the events surrounding the murders, which increases as the film continues (this is what it means to say that imagining from the inside functions instrumentally). But, so long as we remain in doubt over major questions (did Poncelet shoot one or both of the victims? did he rape the female victim? has he deluded himself into believing that he did not?), our central imagining must be partial, tentative, and temporary.[37] In this way, central imagining in the context of our experience of fiction should not be taken to amount to 'imagining being', if that is defined as a complete replication of the experience of a character. So long as we are attending to the fiction—rather than using it as a jump start for a private reverie—we will always be 'brought back' or deflected from sustained and 'deep' central imagining.[38]

There is no single logical, psychological, or aesthetic formula which will tell us what the 'right' balance of acentral and central imagining is, either as something an artist aims to elicit or as a perceiver's elicited response. Consider, though, as a contrast to both *Homicide* and *Dead Man Walking*, Larry Clark's *kids* (1996). One of the reasons that this is such an uncomfortable film to watch—at least, for adults to watch—is that it does everything it can to evoke the mindset of a group of manipulative, selfish, sexist, immature teenage characters. In evoking the values and attitudes of this group, in large part through multifaceted alignment with the main characters Telly (Leo Fitzpatrick) and Casper (Justin Pierce), the film encourages us to centrally imagine (some of) their experiences. The focus on these characters is not unrelieved—in terms of alignment, the film alternates between Telly and Jennie (Chloe Sevigny) (a girl that Telly has seduced and infected with AIDS), as she discovers her condition, numbs herself with drugs, and attempts to track Telly down. Nevertheless, one feels imaginatively trapped within a narrow and distasteful mindset in watching the film; and if we centrally imagine the states of mind of the teenage protagonists at least part of the time, this sense of claustrophobia is intensified. *Dead Man Walking* evokes the terror of the murderer on death row, but also the sorrow and righteous hatred of the victims' parents, and the compassion and forgiveness of Helen Prejean (Susan Sarandon). *kids* restricts itself almost wholly to teenage libido, fear, and desolation.

How one evaluates these different films and the manner in which they elicit different forms of imagining is an issue that I cannot hope to resolve here. By way of conclusion, however, it is important to note the general value of central imagining where it occurs, no matter how partial, tentative, and temporary. One facet of its value is that the force of dramatic conflicts is enhanced if we centrally imagine the perceptions, thoughts, and feelings of the characters involved. I do not mean by this that acentral imagining cannot lead to intensely felt emotions, as intense as any we might experience through central imagining. Rather, I mean that central imagining adds a qualitatively different kind of emotion—an imagined, self-directed emotion, rather than an imagined, other-directed emotion; imagining being on death row and dreading one's own execution, rather than imagining (from the outside, acentrally) Mathew Poncelet and his plight. Such emotions are crucial to the larger psychological and social value of fictions: we come to a better understand of both ourselves, and others, through such central imagining. As Walton puts it, 'In order to understand how minorities feel about being discriminated against, one should imagine not just instances of discrimination but instances of discrimination against *oneself*; one should imagine *experiencing* discrimination.'[39] The presence of such 'self-'directed emotions in this way enriches or enhances our overall experience of fictions. The emotions of central imagining add yet more zest to the already emotion-laden broth of acentral imagining in which they float, though they do not make a soup alone.

NOTES

1. Over the last decade, a number of deflationary accounts of the power of cinema have been developed, which reject the idea that cinema standardly creates an illusion of reality, the efficacy of the illusion being its source of power. See, for example, Noël Carroll, *Mystifying Movies: Fads and Fallacies in Contemporary Film Theory* (New York: Columbia University Press, 1988); Gregory Currie, *Image and Mind: Film, Philosophy, and Cognitive Science* (New York: Cambridge University Press, 1995);

and my own remarks in 'Film Spectatorship and the Institution of Fiction', *Journal of Aesthetics and Art Criticism*, 53: 2 (Spring 1995). In the chapter following this one, Malcolm Turvey questions the cogency of my alternative account of emotional response to the fiction film, so I should say a word here by way of response to his argument. Turvey's intricate conceptual analysis of 'seeing', inspired by Wittgenstein's remarks on the subject, certainly raises a number of astute and pertinent questions for the 'thought theory' of emotional response to cinematic fictions. I will restrict myself here to a brief comment on what seems to be the underlying point of disagreement—that is, on the relationship between perception and cognition. Though I accept that the phenomenology of 'seeing' in different contexts is very different, as Turvey's analysis suggests, I find the radical separation of perception and thought implicit in his chapter hard to swallow. What we see in a cinematic fiction is surely constantly contextualized by the kinds of thoughts we have about what we are seeing: what's that character looking at off-screen? Why is she smiling all of a sudden? What's that strange object at the top of the screen? (Oh, a microphone, that's a mistake.) These are all things that we have to work out—think about—in the course of simply understanding a film. (So perhaps understanding a film is rather like Wittgenstein's description of seeing a schematic figure in various ways, which 'demands *imagination*' (445).) Moreover, if seeing a (fictional) world in a film is sufficient to explain why we might respond emotionally to what we see, presumably seeing something is in general sufficient for an emotional response to it. But surely our seeing things—in reality or in representations—just does not exist in isolation from various cognitive activities ('thoughts') which accompany them. I might (i) see someone shot on the sidewalk in front of me, (ii) see my nephew firing a toy gun at a friend, (iii) see a film in which someone gets shot on a sidewalk, (iv) encounter a happening in which I see someone get shot on the sidewalk, and then realize that this is a fiction. In all of these cases, we see something; but that hardly seems sufficient in explaining exactly how we respond (emotionally) to what we see, which involves contextualizing and 'interpreting' what it is that we see. Turvey seems to acknowledge these sorts of differences in his discussion of fiction at the end of his chapter, in which he argues that such differences can be adequately captured in the language of behaviour. The commitment to psychological explanation itself, then, seems to be the crux of Turvey's objections to the 'thought theory'. In spite of this disagreement, Turvey's article is valuable even for cognitivists in pointing up the need to clarify 'how imaginative activity and the spectator's physical perception of the concrete cinematic image are integrated' (435), as Turvey puts it.

2. Murray Smith, *Engaging Characters: Fiction, Emotion, and the Cinema* (Oxford: Clarendon Press, 1995).

3. Richard Wollheim, *Painting as an Art* (London: Thames & Hudson, 1987), 103.

4. Both are influenced in making this distinction by Bernard Williams, 'Imagination and the Self', in *Problems of the Self* (Cambridge: Cambridge University Press, 1973).

5. Currie, *Image and Mind*, 144. For another relevant discussion of simulation in relation to films, though in connection with what I am calling here acentral imagining, see Richard J. Gerrig and Deborah A. Prentice, 'Notes on Audience Response', in David Bordwell and Noël Carroll, *Post-Theory: Reconstructing Film Studies* (Madison: University of Wisconsin Press, 1996).

6. Currie, *Image and Mind*, 166; Wollheim, *Painting as an Art*, 103.

7. Kendall L. Walton, *Mimesis as Make-Believe: On the Foundations of the Representational Arts* (Cambridge, Mass.: Harvard University Press, 1990), 28.

8. Walton, *Mimesis as Make-Believe*, 344; cf. 34. On this issue, Wollheim's position varies somewhat. *Painting as an Art*, 103, seems to argue for the possibility of 'imagining being' in a way that Walton excludes; *On Art and the Mind* (Cambridge,

Mass.: Harvard University Press, 1974), 82, however, articulates a more cautious position, akin to Walton's if not identical with it.

9. Richard Allen has made this point to me.

10. Alex Neill, 'Empathy and (Film) Fiction', in Bordwell and Carroll, *Post-Theory*, 175–94. See also my own *Engaging Characters*, 96–8. For important discussions of simulation, see Robert M. Gordon, *The Structure of Emotions: Investigations in Cognitive Psychology* (Cambridge: Cambridge University Press, 1987), ch. 7, and Alvin Goldman, *Liaisons: Philosophy Meets the Cognitive and Social Sciences* (Cambridge, Mass.: MIT Press, 1991), ch. 1.

11. Currie contrasts his position with those of Walton and Wollheim in *Image and Mind*, 169.

12. Roughly, and in more commonplace terms, empathy and sympathy. Using these more commonplace terms, however, can create confusion.

13. Noël Carroll, *The Philosophy of Horror; or, Paradoxes of the Heart* (New York: Routledge, 1990), 95–6.

14. For a recent study which finds evidence for what I am calling affective mimicry, as an element of the larger phenomenon of 'emotional contagion', see Lars-Olav Lundqvist and Ulf Dimberg, 'Facial Expressions are Contagious', *Journal of Psychophysiology*, 9 (1995), 203–11.

15. Carl Plantinga raises a related a question regarding textual structure and psychological response: 'while allegiance is something the spectator lends the character, alignment and disclosure (or what Smith calls recognition) are more or less functions of the film more than activities of the spectator' (this volume Ch. 16, n. 30). There is a strong intuitive plausibility to the idea that our responses on the level of allegiance are more variable and less textually determined than are our responses on the levels of recognition and alignment. However, I think this intuition arises from the greater pragmatic difficulty of controlling a perceiver's responses on the level of morality and emotion, not from an ontological difference in the type of response. That is, the maker of a film will just as surely attempt to determine our moral and emotional response to a character (finding a star attractive, for example), as they will attempt to control which character we attend to at a given moment (an aspect of alignment) or what traits we perceive in a character (an aspect of recognition, or 'disclosure'). And this would include cases where the text deliberately allows ambiguity about a character's moral status—this would be comparable, on the level of alignment, with a device (like wide framing and deep staging) that allows us to determine which of several points of action to attend to. In other words, texts may attempt to marshal our responses to greater and lesser degrees with respect to all three levels of textual structure, allegiance no less than alignment or recognition.

Though I recognize the intuition that drives Plantinga's proposal, to accept it would be to make an untenable distinction between aspects of the text which are just immutably 'there', and require no response on the perceiver's part, and aspects of the text which depend entirely on the perceiver's response, with the text providing only the most minimal prompt ('allegiance is something the spectator lends the character'). Every aspect of textual structure requires some form of psychological response, though of course such responses range from the reflex to the highly reflective.

16. Berys Gaut, review of *Engaging Characters*, *British Journal of Aesthetics*, 37: 1 (Jan. 1997), 96–7.

17. The position I argue against is exemplified by, for example, Paul Messaris, *Visual Literacy: Image, Mind, and Reality* (Boulder, Colo.: Westview Press, 1994), 33, 137, 157.

18. Edward Branigan, *Narrative Comprehension and Film* (London: Routledge, 1992), ch. 5 (esp. 145, 157); and Noël Carroll, 'Toward a Theory of Point-of-View Editing: Communication, Emotion, and the Movies', *Poetics Today*, 14: 1 (Spring 1993), 123–41.

19. Cf. Walton, 'On Pictures and Photographs', this volume, 63.
20. Cf. Wollheim, *Painting as an Art*, 183.
21. Currie, *Image and Mind*, 185.
22. This mounts a challenge to the notion of illusory identification at an even more general level than my own thesis, in that it questions not only the idea of identifying with characters in the story world, but the idea that we imagine looking at the fictional world directly (regardless of whether or not a given shot can be assigned to a character). See also Currie's comment, in his chapter in this volume, n. 19.
23. Wollheim, *Painting as an Art*, 103.
24. Currie, *Image and Mind*, 153. Again there is a parallel here with my own framework, in which I argue that central imagining may function as a mechanism for determining what is to be acentrally imagined.
25. Ibid. 153.
26. Except in the case of certain 'extraordinary' shots, an aspect of Currie's argument I discuss below.
27. Ibid. 193.
28. Ibid. 179–80; my emphasis.
29. See also Currie's sceptical remarks on POV and identification, ibid. 174–6. Currie's sympathy for the realist ontology associated with André Bazin and Maurice Merleau-Ponty is evident here; prescriptivism aside, compare his attitude to subjectivity in cinema with Merleau-Ponty, 'The Film and the New Psychology', in *Sense and Non-sense*, trans. Hubert L. Dreyfus and Patricia A. Dreyfus (Evanston, Ill.: Northwestern University Press, 1964), 58.
30. Ibid. 170–1.
31. The shot representing Ballantine's POV, 'like most shots of its kind, is quite unrealistic because it fails to capture the binocular nature of ordinary vision' (ibid. 180 n. 18). See also 195.
32. Ibid. 170.
33. Indeed, a footnote at the end of the passage analysing the nature of our response to the POV shot in *Spellbound* states that 'in order to imagine appropriately concerning the character's experience, we may have to imagine having that experience ourselves, thereby engaging in a simulation of the character's experience' (ibid. 180 n. 19). This is in direct contradiction of his earlier statement that 'Watching this shot does not incline me in the least to imagine myself doing or being either of these things' (175). Confusion over the status of secondary imagining—whether it should be regarded as integral or merely instrumental—seems to be the source of this contradiction.
34. On this account, cinematic fictions are no more (or less) likely to prompt imagining seeing than are written fictions, because secondary imagining can take off just as well from symbolic imagining (prompted by words) as from perceptual imagining. The counter-intuitive nature of this last claim may count as another reason to be sceptical of the framework that lead us to it.
35. This should not be confused with the idea that we suddenly cease to have an emotional response to the scene; rather, the claim is that we cease to experience an empathetic emotion (simulating or imagining the emotional states of a given character) but instead experience 'sympathetic' emotions—emotions based on judgements of the characters, but not simulating *their* emotions (as, for example, in pitying a deluded or ignorant character, or being repelled by a happily violent character).
36. In addition to the shift away from exclusive alignment with Gold that I discuss in the main text, something else happens here that, arguably, undermines central imagining. Though Gold has been presented as a likeable character up to this point in the film, his anti-Semitic diatribe may well provoke a moral aversion in the spectator which hinders or blocks central imagining. See Richard Moran's discussion of the phenomenon of 'resistance' to imagining beliefs and attitudes which in some way

offend or repel us, in 'The Expression of Feeling in Imagination', *Philosophical Review*, 103: 1 (Jan. 1994), 95–106.

37. This accords with Walton's argument that one need not imagine either the conjunctions or the implications of the things that one does imagine ('On Pictures and Photographs', 62; see also Neill, 'Empathy', 187). If I am correct that partial central imagining is not only possible, but typical, at least in the context of engaging with fictions, this poses another problem for Currie's rejection of the Imagined Observer Hypothesis. Currie cites shots from extraordinary locations, like outer space, as anomalies for the IOH. For is it plausible that we imagine floating in an oxygen-less vacuum whenever we see an establishing shot of the earth as seen from space? Currie is surely right to suggest that it isn't. If *partial* imagining is the norm, however, to imagine seeing from a vantage-point need not involve us in imagining breathing etc. from that vantage-point. In other words, such shots would no longer count as problems or anomalies for the IOH. Currie considers but rejects the idea of imagining seeing cut off from imagining the concomitants of the vantage-point in question, but he does not consider the other factors which, I believe, make the idea of partial imagining a compelling and necessary refinement of our understanding of imaginative engagement with fictions.

38. By 'deep' I mean 'fully plenitudinous', in Wollheim's jargon: see 413–14, above. This is related to an aspect of Wollheim's account of central imagining as it applies to painting. Wollheim argues that in coming to imagine from what he calls the 'internal spectator's' perspective, the (real) external spectator ceases to attend to the surface of the canvas, and thus to an aspect of the experience of viewing paintings which is indispensable ('twofoldness'). Wollheim argues that it is because of this 'danger' that the same paintings which foster central imagining also contain devices for breaking the hold of such imagining, and return us from 'imagination to perception' (*Painting as an Art*, 166). The parallel, then, between my argument here and Wollheim's is that in each case there is *more* to the experience than central imagining accounts for—either dramatically, in terms of the perspectives of other characters and the narrator, or perceptually, in terms of an awareness of the facticity of the representation.

39. Walton, *Mimesis*, 34; see also Neill, 'Empathy', 189, 192.

19

Seeing Theory: On Perception and Emotional Response In Current Film Theory

Malcolm Turvey

> It is certainly not the least charm of a theory that it is refutable: it is with precisely this charm that it entices subtler minds.
>
> (Friedrich Nietzsche)

I

Murray Smith and Noël Carroll have recently proposed similar theories of the spectator's emotional response to fiction films. These theories are designed to overcome the conceptual problem raised by the 'paradox of fiction', namely the paradox of the spectator responding emotionally to what he knows does not exist. Smith and Carroll both begin by postulating the existence of a mental faculty to explain why it is that spectators appear to respond emotionally to cinematic representations of fictions. Smith calls this mental faculty the 'imagination', while Carroll refers to it more cautiously as, quite simply, 'thought'. According to their theories, the spectator does not in fact respond emotionally to the cinematic representation of fiction at all. Rather, he responds emotionally to the 'thought' or 'imaginative scenario' that is produced in his mind by the cinematic representation of fiction he perceives. 'The argument', writes Smith:

is, then, that spectators—perceivers of fiction in general—do not lose consciousness, as the various metaphors of delusion suggest, but rather *imaginatively entertain* the propositions and imagery of fictional texts. . . . The fiction prompts an imagined scenario; it does not induce a mysterious stupor in the perceiver. Cinematic spectatorship—like the apprehension of fiction in general—is best understood as an imaginative activity in this sense.[1]

For Carroll, 'Thought contents can generate genuine emotion.'[2] In the case of the horror film, it is therefore the thought of the fictional monster—

I would like to thank Richard Allen, Frances Guerin, and Murray Smith for their invaluable comments on earlier drafts of this paper.

caused by the cinematic representation of the fictional monster on the screen—that in turn causes the spectator to feel 'art-horrified'.

Smith and Carroll therefore identify a mental entity as the causal agent of the spectator's emotion during his viewing of fiction films. They then go on to define this mental entity through an analogy with the general human capacity to be moved by thoughts without believing in the truth of those thoughts. According to Smith and Carroll, it is the assumption that there is a necessary connection between belief and emotion that has misled previous film theorists. Instead, as Carroll argues: 'Both beliefs and thoughts have propositional content. But with thoughts the content is merely entertained without commitment to its being the case; to have a belief is to be committed to the truth of the proposition.'[3] Just as one can be moved by a thought without believing in it, so the spectator can respond emotionally to the thought produced in his head by the cinematic representation of fiction without falsely believing in the truth of the fiction. One does not, therefore, have to believe in the existence of the monster to be able to be art-horrified at the thought of it. As Smith puts it: 'The virtue of the imagination theory is that it removes belief. . . . The argument identifies a mistaken premise— that we must believe in x in order to respond emotionally to x—in the statement of the problem itself.'[4] By making this conceptual distinction between 'thought' or 'imagination', and 'belief', Smith and Carroll succeed in providing a theoretical explanation of the spectator's emotional response to cinematic representations of fictions that does not depend upon the account of epistemic deception and perceptual illusion that has dominated contemporary film theory. The spectator has neither to believe in the existence of the fictional referent of the cinematic representation, nor perceptually experience the fictional referent as physically present in the cinematic image and soundtrack, in order to respond emotionally to it. Instead, he responds emotionally to the 'thought' or 'imagination' of the fictional referent that is produced in his mind by the cinematic representation of the fictional referent being perceived. It is therefore this curious mental entity— 'the imagined scenario' or 'thought'—to which the spectator responds emotionally 'without commitment to its being the case', rather than the cinematic representation itself.

II

Smith and Carroll's theories are certainly salutary because they sever the conceptual marriage between belief and the spectator's capacity for responding emotionally to fiction films that has plagued contemporary film theory. However, by postulating a mental entity, namely 'thought' or the 'imagination', as the primary causal agent of the spectator's emotional response, these theories necessarily relegate the spectator's sensuous perception of the concrete cinematic representation to a subsidiary or secondary role. When examined closely, this relegation appears highly implausible because it does not accord with standard intuitions about the essential importance of the concrete cinematic representation within the grammar of the spectator's emotional response to fiction films.

This implausibility can be exposed in a number of ways. To begin with, the subsidiary role assigned to the concrete cinematic representation does not correspond with certain ordinary language descriptions of the experience of fiction films in which the expression of an emotional response is firmly tied to the sensuous perception of the cinematic image as a concrete entity. To speak of being struck, overwhelmed, saddened, or horrified *by* a film, to express the feeling of total absorption, rapt attention, or loss of consciousness *in* a film, to venerate films, like photographs and paintings, as special, fetishized objects in their own right, is to describe a sensuous experience in which the film itself, as a concrete object, plays a major if not determining role. The theories proposed by Smith and Carroll cannot, I would suggest, explain these types of descriptions of cinematic experience because they place an abstract intermediate entity—'thought' or 'imagination'—between the spectator and the film, and argue that the spectator responds emotionally to this abstract, mediating entity rather than the concrete cinematic image. The cinematic representation itself is relegated in their theories to the role of a mere causal 'prompt', to use Smith's word, for the mind. It becomes neutral, perceptual data or information used by the mind to construct an abstract, mental scenario to which the mind then responds emotionally. According to the logic of their theories, the spectator should therefore describe his emotional experience quite differently. Instead of being saddened by a film, he should always speak of being saddened by his 'thought' or 'imagination' because it is not the film to which he is responding emotionally at all, but rather the imaginative scenario or thought unfolding within his head. It is almost as if the prototypical spectator of these theories is blind to the film itself.

The implausibility of this relegation of the role of the concrete cinematic representation can also be pointed to by pushing one of its most important ramifications to its logical extreme. This ramification concerns the claims for medium specificity that have been historically prevalent within film theory. Most contemporary film theorists identify a physical entity as the primal causal agent of the spectator's emotional response, namely the cinematic medium itself. According to many contemporary theorists, the cinema is the only medium in possession of attributes with enough 'iconic' power to engender a perceptual illusion in which the spectator perceptually experiences the fictional referent of the cinematic representation as 'present' or 'real'. This perceptual illusion in turn induces the spectator to believe in the existence of the fictional referent. It is this false belief in the existence of the fictional referent that causes the spectator to respond emotionally to the fiction film, as if he were responding emotionally to a real person or event. This contemporary theory of the spectator's emotional response is therefore medium specific in its dependence upon the attributes of the cinematic medium as a physical entity to explain the spectator's emotional response. Smith and Carroll, however, identify an abstract mental entity or process as the primary causal agent of the spectator's emotion. They argue that the spectator's emotional response to fiction is dependent upon a general mental capacity to be moved by an 'imagination' or 'thought'. In doing so, they thereby divorce the spectator's capacity to respond emotionally to fiction from the unique attributes of the cinematic medium as a physical entity. Like any other medium capable of representing fiction, the cinema simply provides concrete representations of fictions that cause the spectator's mind to engage in imaginative activity. This imaginative activity and the emotional response it gives rise to are therefore independent of the sensuous properties and powers of any medium, including the cinema. As Smith argues, 'Fiction films perform the same imaginative functions as fictions in other media.'[5]

This ramification of Smith and Carroll's theories is certainly, once again, salutary because it dispenses with the definition of cinematic perception as a form of perceptual illusion which causes the spectator's emotional response. However, the logic of this ramification can be pushed to the conclusion that there is no space at all within their theories for the spectator's perception of the sensuous particularities of the cinematic medium to influence or determine his imaginative or emotional response. Instead, his imaginative and emotional response should be identical whatever medium is used to represent a given fiction because, according to the logic of their theories, the spectator's imaginative experience and emotional response is independent of the sensuous particularities of any medium. For example, his imaginative and emotive experience should be essentially unchanged whether he views a hypothetical fiction film or reads the shooting script upon which it is based. In both cases, he is receiving the same information about the same fiction which allows him to construct the same abstract, imaginative scenario. When pushed to this conclusion, these theories ultimately seem to conceive of any hypothetical fiction film as an abstract schema or form of data that is independent of the sensuous attributes of the cinematic medium. The spectator should not, accordingly, make any qualitative distinctions between media upon the basis of the emotive and imaginative power of a specific medium—between, for example, *Rear Window* and the shooting script upon which it is based.

Smith, aware of the implausibility of this ramification of his theory, attempts to pre-empt it by sketching a role for the sensuous particularities of the cinematic medium within the spectator's imaginative and emotional experience:

On the one hand, fiction films present us with complex narrative scenarios, which we are required to engage with imaginatively in order to experience fully; on the other hand, the cinema is built upon an 'apparatus' which can, in certain limited ways, generate the perceptions and sensations which we would *expect* to experience in the fictional scenarios it prompts us to imagine. . . . a spectator might be revolted by an image of a severed limb, while not revolted by reading a description of a severed limb, because the former offers an approximation of the sensory experience as an imaginative prompt, while the latter relies wholly on our ability or willingness to imaginatively represent a verbal description (that is, to form a mental 'image' of the severed limb).[6]

Smith therefore relies on the familiar argument that the cinema as a visual medium can be distinguished from verbal media because it 'approximates', however crudely, perceptual or sensory experience. Yet, as this quotation indicates, he is unable to demonstrate how the spectator's perception of the sensuous particularities of the cinematic medium actually influences or determines his imaginative response. On the contrary, as the example of the severed limb reveals, physical perception and mental imagination seem to be mutually exclusive activities for Smith. In this example of the severed limb, Smith argues that the cinematic medium, unlike verbal media, is able to generate the emotional response of revulsion because it approximates 'the sensory experience' of perceiving the severed limb. Although he does not explain why, he implies that this happens because verbal media rely wholly upon the reader's mental efforts to entertain the thought of the severed limb, while the cinema requires less mental effort on the part of the spectator because it approximates the sensory experience of the severed limb. The power of verbal media to generate an affect is therefore weak in comparison to the cinema, which is able to approximate the immediacy and emotional impact of sensory perception. This distinction between media upon the basis of whether they generate emotion through physical perception or mental imagination demonstrates clearly that Smith conceives of the two as separate activities which operate in inverse proportion to each other. When there is a greater degree of perceptual 'approximation' as in the cinema, the 'work of the imagination is . . . lessened'[7] in the production of an affect. But when there is an absence of such perceptual 'approximation' as in verbal media, the imagination is fully responsible for generating an affect. Not only, therefore, does Smith fail to demonstrate how imaginative activity and the spectator's physical perception of the concrete cinematic image are integrated, but he also contradicts the logic of his own argument. For he seems to be arguing, at least in this example, that the cinema entails less of an imaginative activity on the part of the spectator than verbal media, and indeed that it is the perceptual experience of the cinematic representation of the severed limb, rather than the spectator's imaginative activity, that causes the emotional response of revulsion. According to this example, the cinema seems to be a medium which can generate an emotional response upon the basis of its sensuous particularities rather than the spectator's imaginative efforts. Smith therefore fails to pre-empt the objection that his theory allows no space at all for the spectator's perception of the sensuous particularities of the cinematic medium to influence or determine his imaginative response. Instead, he ends up demonstrating that these sensuous particularities and the spectator's imaginative activity are mutually exclusive.

If we push the logic of this ramification even further, the relegation of the cinematic representation it entails appears even more extreme. For Smith and Carroll's theories appear to lead inexorably to the following conclusion: if the spectator responds emotionally to an abstract thought about the fiction that takes place in his head, then that response can occur at any time, independently of viewing a film. Once assimilated, spectators can carry the perceptual data about the fiction received from the film around with them, and use it to entertain an imaginative scenario at any time they so decide. The relegation of the cinematic representation to the level of a mere perceptual 'prompt' for the imagination in their theories therefore actually frees the spectator's emotional response entirely from the moment of film viewing. The cinematic representation itself, consequently, totally drops out of the spectator's experience of emotional response if we push the logic of their theories this far.

Smith and Carroll would probably disagree, however, with such an objection. Although it may well be true that the spectator can continue to entertain thoughts and feel emotions about a given fiction film long after he has left the movie theatre, both would probably argue that the spectator's emotions are more *intense* at the moment of film viewing. Carroll, for example, includes this passage in his description of the spectator's emotional response to horror films:

Further evidence for the claim that we can be frightened by the content of our thoughts can be marshaled by reflecting on the ways in which one might attempt to deflect one's consternation during an especially unnerving horror film. One can avert one's eyes from the screen, or perhaps direct one's attention from the quadrant occupied by the object of our excitement. . . . what one is doing in all these cases is distracting oneself from the thought of what is being portrayed on the screen.[8]

Carroll's argument here is that once the spectator blocks the access of perceptual data from the screen then his 'thought' about the monster either disappears or lessens in intensity, thereby enabling him to avoid unpleasant emotions. This argument, however, demonstrates very clearly that Carroll conceives of the 'thought' in the spectator's head as some kind of abstract mental copy of the concrete cinematic representation which imprints or inscribes itself on the spectator's mind at the moment of film viewing. According to this argument, when the cinematic representation of a fiction is absent from sight, then the thought of that fiction is absent from the mind, and when it is present, the thought is as well, thereby generating emotion. Smith implies the same causal mirroring of cinematic representation and 'imaginative scenario' in his use of the word 'prompt' to describe the relation between the two. It should be noted in passing that by postulating such a causal relation between the cinematic representation and the spectator's 'thought', the mental process of responding to fiction begins to appear less like a cognitive activity than a state of mental passivity.

Smith and Carroll can, therefore, only ultimately tie the spectator's imaginative activity to the temporal moment of viewing a film by postulating a direct, causal relation between concrete cinematic representation and abstract imaginative thought, and then conceiving of the latter as some kind of internal copy, inscription, or transmigration of the former. This explanation certainly begins to account for how the cinematic representation functions as a perceptual 'prompt' for the spectator's imaginative activity. It explains how the perceptual data from the concrete cinematic representation enter the spectator's mind. However, it does not provide an explanation for why this imaginative activity leads to an emotional response that is more *intense* during the perceptual experience of the concrete cinematic representation. *Why* does the *direct* perception of the concrete cinematic representation enable the spectator to have a more *intense* emotional response at the moment of film viewing, when it is not the cinematic representation at all that causes his emotional response but rather the abstract thought or imagination in his mind? Smith and Carroll's theories do not provide an answer to this question. This is because, I would suggest, the claim that the spectator's emotional response is more intense while viewing a film ultimately points to a qualitative difference between the spectator's emotional response in the direct presence of the cinematic representation and the spectator's emotional response in its absence. Whereas Smith and Carroll's theories are premised upon an analogy between the capacity to be moved by abstract thoughts and the spectator's capacity to be moved by concrete cinematic representations of fictions, the claim that the spectator's emotional response is more intense while viewing a film reveals a fundamental *disanalogy* between these two experiences, namely, quite simply, the essential importance of the sensuous perception of the concrete cinematic representation in the latter. Indeed, Carroll's own acknowledgement that spectators do seem to respond with more emotional intensity when they are perceptually attending to the concrete cinematic representation of the monster seems inadvertently to indicate, like Smith's example of the severed limb, that the concrete cinematic representation is just as much responsible for the spectator's emotional response as any putative mental activity on his part. Thus, the postulation of the direct causal relation between concrete cinematic representation and abstract 'thought' or 'imagination' does not so much succeed in tying the spectator's emotional response to the moment of film viewing as in pointing, once again, to the essential importance of the concrete cinematic representation within the grammar of the spectator's emotional response to fiction films.

In summary, by identifying a mental entity or process as the causal agent of the spectator's emotion, the theories proposed by Smith and Carroll drive a firm wedge between the spectator's sensuous perception of the concrete cinematic representation of a fiction and the 'thought' or 'imagination' of that fiction to which the spectator responds emotionally. Having done so, it becomes impossible to integrate them back together again. The role of the concrete cinematic representation is necessarily relegated to the implausible position of merely providing abstract information about the fiction at hand. Meanwhile, any attempt to satisfy the demands of intuition and specify a greater role for the concrete cinematic representation within the grammar of the spectator's emotional response simply results in contradictions or confirms the mutual exclusivity of imagination and perception. Why, therefore, do Smith and Carroll resort to a theory of the spectator's mental activity that necessarily and counter-intuitively relegates the role of her physical perception of the concrete cinematic representation? Why do they place an abstract intermediate entity—'thought' or 'imagination'—between the spectator and the film, and argue that the spectator responds emotionally to this abstract, mediating entity rather than the concrete cinematic image and soundtrack?

We can perhaps discover the answer to this question by undertaking a brief conceptual investigation into the assumptions about the nature of the cinematic experience that underpin Smith and Carroll's theories. These assumptions are nowhere explicitly articulated by their theories. However, we can unearth them through a conceptual investigation into their theories by starting with the obvious fact that Smith and Carroll employ theories of the spectator's *mental* activity to explain his apparent emotional response to the cinematic image and soundtrack. If the spectator appears to be responding emotionally to the cinematic representation of fiction, Smith and Carroll assume that this must be because the spectator's *mind* is subjectively supplying or adding a special mental entity or process to his objective perceptual experience of the image and soundtrack *qua* material entities. They therefore call upon a theory of this special mental activity of supplying a component to the objective perceptual experience of the cinematic representation that will allow the spectator to respond emotionally to it, a special mental component or supplement that is not present objectively in the cinematic representation itself.

From this perceived necessity to employ a theory of the spectator's mental activity, we can immediately infer the set of more general formative assumptions about the nature of the cinematic experience that entail such an explanation. First, the claim that only a theory of a special mental activity can explain the spectator's emotional response to cinematic representations of non-existent, fictional referents must be premissed upon the assumption that such an emotional response is not possible purely on the basis of the spectator's perceptual experience of the cinematic representation. In other words, for Smith and Carroll's theories, the spectator's sensuous perception of the cinematic image and soundtrack lacks the essential component that gives rise to an emotional response, a component that is instead supplied subjectively by the spectator's mind.

Second, behind this argument must lie the further assumption that the fictional referent or object of the spectator's emotional response—namely, the diegesis populated by characters, fictional objects, and fictional events—is not only physically and materially absent from the cinematic representation due to its fictional and therefore non-existent status. Rather, more importantly, the fictional referent must also be *perceptually* absent from the cinematic representation *qua* objective entity and, consequently, from the spectator's objective perceptual experience of the cinematic representation. For this theory, ontic non-existence entails perceptual absence. The spectator necessarily cannot objectively perceive the diegesis *in* the image and soundtrack, according to this theory, if the diegesis is fictional and non-existent. For if, indeed, the diegesis as fictional referent of the spectator's emotion could be both ontically non-existent yet perceptually present *in* the cinematic representation, available to the spectator's ears and eyes, no theory of the spectator's special, subjective mental supplement would be required to explain his emotional response. One would not have to postulate the necessary mental occurrence of an 'imagined scenario' or a 'thought' prior to and enabling the spectator's emotional response to the cinematic representation. The spectator would not have to 'think' of or 'imagine' the fictional scenario before feeling emotion. Instead, if the diegesis was perceptually present *in* the cinematic representation, he would be able to respond with emotion directly to the cinematic representation of the diegesis itself on the basis of an objective perceptual experience of that cinematic representation while being fully aware that the fictional referent or diegesis is ontically non-existent and therefore materially absent. No special, mental process would be required to explain his ability to do so.

Finally, at the core of this spiral of arguments must lie a basic assumption about the spectator's objective perceptual experience of the cinematic representation itself, namely a definition of cinematic perception. If the fictional referent of the spectator's emotion—the diegetic world of the fiction denoted by the cinematic representation—is materially and perceptually absent from his objective, sensuous perception of the cinematic representation, its place occupied instead by a subjective mental supplement, then this objective sensuous experience can consist only of a direct, literal perception of the image and soundtrack as purely material entities, namely as the movement of light, shadow, shape, colour, and noise (or 'sense data', to use the language of cognitive psychology), stripped of the diegesis itself. The diegesis cannot be perceptually present in the image and soundtrack. According to this definition of cinematic perception, the spectator does not objectively perceive the fictional referent of his emotions, namely the fictional world of the diegesis populated by fictional objects, characters and events. He does not objectively see or hear the diegesis, because the material absence or ontic non-existence of the fictional referent entails perceptual absence. Instead, he can only objectively see and hear the image and soundtrack as purely material entities that represent or denote the diegesis which is itself materially and perceptually absent. If the fictional referent of the spectator's emotion—the diegesis—was somehow perceptually present in the cinematic representation *qua* objective, material entity, then no theory of the spectator's special mental activity would be required to explain emotional responses to cinematic representations. Rather, the fictional referent of the spectator's emotion would again be accessible via his objective perceptual experience of the cinematic representation, and he would be able to respond emotionally to the image and soundtrack themselves without the intervention of a special mental process or entity.

Smith and Carroll therefore resort to theories of the spectator's special mental activity, I would suggest, because of a definition of cinematic perception that is buried deep beneath their theories. In a sense, they are *forced* by this definition to identify a mental activity as the causal agent of the spectator's emotional response. For once cinematic perception is defined as the objective perception of the cinematic image and soundtrack *qua* purely material entities, stripped of the diegesis, then the cinematic representation cannot function as the causal agent of the spectator's emotions. The spectator cannot respond emotionally to the cinematic representation of a fiction if the referent of his emotions—the diegetic world of the fiction—is neither materially nor perceptually present in the image and soundtrack. Thus, Smith and Carroll provide him with a mental replacement for the materially and perceptually absent fiction, a 'thought' or 'imaginative scenario' which stands in for the absent fiction and is built out of perceptual data about the fiction provided by the cinematic representation. No wonder, therefore, that their theory relegates the concrete cinematic representation to a subsidiary role in the grammar of the spectator's emotional response to fiction films, promoting the spectator's mind in its place. For it conceives of the image and soundtrack as merely providing data about an absent fictional diegesis which it is the mind's responsibility to reconstruct.

We have located the rationale for these theories of the spectator's mental activity within a certain definition of cinematic perception. In the light of the implausibility of the subsidiary role to which these theories relegate the concrete cinematic representation, it is therefore, perhaps, worth investigating this definition of cinematic perception itself to see whether it is defensible. Such an investigation may perhaps lead to a different understanding of cinematic perception, thereby hopefully opening the way to a conceptualization of the spectator's emotional response to fiction films that is free of some of the problems I have pointed to in Smith and Carroll's theories.

III

One philosopher who provides us with the conceptual tools for an examination of this definition of perception is Wittgenstein, and it is therefore his investigation into the use of the verb 'to see' in section xi of part II of *Philosophical Investigations* to which I now turn. Wittgenstein, of course, does not refer to *cinematic* perception as such. However, he does consider a variety of visual experiences involving images because of the pertinence of these experiences to his argument that 'seeing' is not a single, monolithic concept. For Wittgenstein, 'seeing' is 'tangled' and it contains 'hugely many interrelated phenomena and possible concepts'.[9] One of the major philosophical errors that he is concerned with exposing is the assumption that a word such as 'to see' refers legitimately to only one experience and therefore has a single correct or proper definition which renders all other uses of the word 'to see' erroneous and improper. Perhaps the central aim of section xi is to demonstrate instead that 'the concept of a representation of what is seen' together with 'the concept of what is seen' are 'very elastic' (*PI* 198).[10] Wittgenstein asserts:

There is not *one genuine* proper case of such description [of what is seen]—the rest being just vague, something which awaits clarification, or which must just be swept aside as rubbish. . . .

It is the same when one tries to define the concept of a material object in terms of 'what is really seen'.—What we have rather to do is to *accept* the everyday language-game, and to note *false* accounts of the matter *as* false. The primitive language-game which children are taught needs no justification; attempts at justification need to be rejected. (*PI* 200)

According to Wittgenstein, it is only when a single definition of seeing is imposed upon the diversity of phenomena that together make up the category of visual experience that 'conceptual confusions' tend to occur. Thus, the fact that Smith and Carroll's theories are premissed upon a single definition of cinematic perception may well be one reason why they give rise to the problems I have already identified.

Wittgenstein begins his investigation into the verb 'to see' with an unusual visual experience which he calls 'noticing an aspect' or 'the dawning of an aspect', and he gives several examples of it.[11] For instance: 'I suddenly see the solution of a picture puzzle. Before, there were branches there; now there is a human shape. My visual impression has changed and now I recognize that it has not only shape and color but also a quite particular "organization". My visual impression has changed' (*PI* 196). And another example: 'I contemplate a face, and then suddenly notice its likeness to another. I *see* that it has not changed; and yet I see it differently' (*PI* 193). The paradox of using the verb 'to see' to describe this curious experience is obvious. On the one hand, the object of sight remains materially unchanged in both these examples of aspect-dawning. Nothing is physically added or taken away from the 'picture puzzle' or the 'face' to change its appearance. And yet, the words we use to describe the experience of aspect-dawning, words such as 'see', 'object', and 'it looks different now' which are drawn from the repertoire of visual vocabulary, all seem to indicate that this is precisely what has happened during aspect-dawning, that indeed the object does seem to have changed materially in front of our eyes during this experience. We now seem to see it differently, as if it had somehow become a different object. 'The expression of a change of aspect is the expression of a *new* perception and at the same time of the perception's being unchanged,' summarizes Wittgenstein, and he elucidates this paradox by asking the beholder who has experienced aspect-dawning to represent the difference between his old and new perception of the picture-puzzle. The beholder is, of course, unable to do so using a drawing or some other type of representation. A drawing of the picture-puzzle prior to the dawning of the aspect will be identical to a drawing of the puzzle once the aspect has dawned. Similarly, in the case of noticing the 'likeness' between two faces, the aspect of 'likeness' cannot be represented using images of the faces concerned. 'The one man might make an accurate drawing of the two faces', observes Wittgenstein, 'and the other notice in the drawing the likeness which the former did not see' (*PI* 193).

Thus, we are introduced to the strange and mysterious concept of the aspect. On the one hand, the aspect of 'likeness', for example, cannot be pointed to or represented directly, using an image or verbal description, in the same way that the material properties of an object can be. The aspect belongs to a different dimension of visual experience from material properties such as colour and shape, which can be pointed to, copied, and described with ease. Thus, it seems to be something invisible, immaterial, or abstract, something beyond the perception of material properties and entities. Wittgenstein therefore removes the visual experience of aspect-dawning from the concept of perception, distinguishing it from the 'perception' of material properties such as shape and colour. Aspect-dawning, he states, 'is not part of perception. And for that reason it is like seeing and again not like' (*PI* 197).

And yet, in a curious way, the aspect nevertheless appears to be materially present within the image or object concerned. It seems to *presence* itself, becoming materially incarnated in the image or object during the visual experience of aspect-dawning. The aspect is something that we appear to experience visually on a sensuous, perceptual level, even though we cannot in fact point to it or represent it, beyond the vague suggestion that it is a type of 'organization'. It is this strange ambiguity of an entity that is both present and absent, material and immaterial, visible and invisible, that prompts Wittgenstein's investigation into this curious experience. The question that Wittgenstein is asking, the question to which he insistently returns again and again, is the question of why we use the word 'to see' to describe this visual experience of an entity that is neither a material property of an object nor can be represented on a material level. 'But this isn't *seeing*!' insists one interlocutor in response to the experience of aspect-dawning. 'But this is seeing!' demands another. And Wittgenstein, in arguing for the diversity of visual experiences that constitute seeing, replies: 'It must be possible to give both remarks a conceptual justification. But this is seeing! *In what sense* is it seeing?' (*PI* 203).

The question of the nature of the aspect is, therefore, impossible to answer directly, precisely because the aspect initially seems to be a mysterious entity that is beyond the reach of both image and language. It cannot be represented. It can neither be directly shown, pointed to, nor described, and instead seems to emerge in the gap between word and image, which both seem to fail in their mutual imbrication to represent it directly. Wittgenstein is well aware of the impossibility of direct access to the aspect, and he therefore approaches it indirectly by attempting first to specify what the aspect is *not*, through a critique of psychological explanations of aspect-dawning. I will not attempt within the confines of this chapter to provide an account of Wittgenstein's concept of the aspect. Instead, I will focus on Wittgenstein's refutation of psychological explanations for aspect-dawning. This is because the definition of perception that Smith and Carroll apply to cinema—namely the sensation of the image and soundtrack as purely material entities consisting of light, shadow, shape, colour, and noise—constitutes the objective component of the psychological explanation for aspect-dawning that Wittgenstein refutes. I will argue, using the conceptual tools provided by Wittgenstein, that aspect-dawning does not involve the addition of some sort of subjective mental entity, such as a thought or interpretation, to the beholder's objective perception of the image as a material entity consisting of light, shadow, shape, and colour. In other words, the aspect cannot be explained *psychologically* as a subjective mental entity. Much more important for our purposes, however, is the ramification of Wittgenstein's refutation of the psychological explanation of aspect-dawning for conceptualizing the perception of images. For once the aspect is shown *not* to be a subjective mental addition to the beholder's objective perception of images, then we are forced to broaden our conception of what the beholder does in fact 'see' in an image. We are forced, in other words, to conclude that the perception of the image as the sensation of material properties is only *one* way in which the beholder 'sees' images. It is for this reason, I will argue, that the wholesale application of this concept of perceiving images to cinematic perception which we have unearthed beneath Smith and Carroll's theories of emotional response is mistaken.

At first sight, a psychological theory of vision may seem eminently capable of explaining the curious phenomenon of aspect-dawning in the emphasis such a theory places on the mental or cognitive processes involved in all perceptual acts. To explain the visual experience of the famous image of the duck-rabbit, for example, such a theory would probably begin by arguing that we must distinguish between the objective material properties of the duck-rabbit figure perceived by the beholder in the form of 'sensory data', and the subjective visual impression, 'picture', or representation of the figure which results from the mental processing or organization of these 'sensory data'. The experience of shifting between the duck-aspect and rabbit-aspect can thereby be explained as an example of the mental process of shifting between one subjective 'picture' of the sensory data to another and back again. However, Wittgenstein quickly points to the inadequacy of this type of explanation. For if it were true that the beholder's subjective visual impression of the duck-rabbit consisted of a 'picture' or 'copy' or inner 'materialization' of the external figure of the duck-rabbit, and that it is this 'materialization' that changes or shifts during the experience of aspect-dawning, then this beholder should be able to depict or describe the changes in his inner 'materialization' in the same way that changes in an external 'picture' might be described. However, the beholder is, of course, unable to do this precisely because it is not the material properties of the duck-rabbit—whether considered as external figure or internal mental 'picture'—that change during the shift of aspects. Rather, it is the overall 'organization' or 'aspect' which changes, and this cannot be pointed to or described in the same way that material properties such as colour, shape, and line can. If the beholder's subjective visual impression is construed as being an internal mental 'copy' or 'image' of an external object or figure, and therefore similar to a 'picture', then it cannot be used to explain the phenomenon of shifting aspects. To use Wittgenstein's words:

If you put the 'organization' of a visual impression on a level with colours and shapes, you are proceeding from the idea of the visual impression as an inner object. Of course this makes this object into a chimera; a queerly shifting construction. For the similarity to a picture is now impaired. (*PI* 196)

The second type of explanation or theory that would probably be offered by a psychologist for aspect-dawning is somewhat more tenacious. We will call this the mental interpretation theory of vision. This theory argues that we do not have to conceive of the beholder's subjective visual impression of the image of the duck-rabbit figure as a mental 'image' or 'picture'. Rather, we can conceive of it as a mental *interpretation* of the material properties of the duck-rabbit figure. This explanation takes as its model the conscious visual experience which Wittgenstein refers to as 'seeing-as'. In this experience, images of schematic figures such as abstract cubes or triangles can be interpreted and seen as many different objects depending upon the behold-er's 'imagination' or textual information accompanying the figure. An image of a bare triangle, for example, can be interpreted and seen as 'a triangular hole, as a solid, as a geometrical drawing; as standing on its base, as hanging from its apex' (*PI* 200). Any beholder would be inclined to describe this visual experience of seeing-as in relation to the triangle by saying something like, 'Now I am seeing the triangle as a triangular hole, now as a solid, now as a geometrical drawing.' According to this explanation, the material figure which we objectively perceive in the form of sensory data, consisting of line and shape, changes its aspect because we mentally process or interpret this sensory data in different ways in our subjective minds. We supply a different mental thought content or process to the sensory data received from the image of the bare material figure on each occasion of a change of aspects. 'So we interpret it, and *see* it as we *interpret* it,' says Wittgenstein, summarizing this position (*PI* 193). 'You can think now of *this* now of *this* as you look at it, can regard it now as *this* now as *this*, and then you will see it now *this* way, now *this*' (*PI* 200). It should be noted that it is the objective component of this definition, namely the definition of the objective perception of the image as the sensation of its material properties, which is presupposed by Smith and Carroll's theory of the spectator's emotional response.[12]

Wittgenstein certainly does not deny the role of thought in the specific experience of seeing-as engendered by images of bare, schematic figures such as abstract cubes and triangles. 'To see [an] aspect of the triangle', he asserts, 'demands *imagination*' (*PI* 207). However, what can be objected to is the use of this model, which refers to the very specific, conscious visual experience of seeing-as, to explain vision *in toto*. Such a use of this model would take the form of a claim that vision in general consists of an objective perception of bare, material reality as sensory data, combined with a subjec-tive mental interpretation or organization of these sensory data by the mind of the beholder. According to this model, any visual impression is the product of a direct, objective, sensuous perception of material properties such as colour and shape plus an indirect, subjective, mental interpretation or process which the beholder's mind supplies.

One way of challenging the use of this visual experience of seeing-as by the psychologist as a model for explaining vision *in toto* is by examining the descriptions and representations offered by beholders of their standard visual experiences in order to demonstrate that the mental interpretation theory of vision does not accord with our behaviour during these standard visual experiences. That is, we do not behave as if we are engaged in the mental activity of interpreting sensory data provided by our physical environment during standard visual experiences. In point of fact, as Wittgenstein suggests, we actually exhibit behaviour that indicates precisely the opposite. For example, according to the logic of the mental interpretation theory of vision which takes as its model the visual experience of seeing-as, all beholders should describe their standard visual experiences of all objects using expressions similar to those employed to describe the visual experience of seeing-as in relation to the image of the schematic triangle. This is because, if the mental interpretation theory of vision is applicable to vision *in toto*, then beholders are always engaged in the mental activity of indirectly interpreting the sensory data they objectively and directly perceive. They therefore should always visually experience seeing-as. And just as the beholder describes his specific experience of mentally interpreting the image of the schematic figure of the triangle by saying 'now I am seeing it as a triangular hole, now as a solid, now as a geometrical drawing', he should also describe his standard visual experiences using similar expressions. For example, he should say of his visual impression of a fork something like 'Now I am seeing the fork this way, now that way, or I could see it like this, or like that.'

Wittgenstein, however, points to the fact that, when confronted by unambiguous objects such as a 'fork' under normal perceptual conditions, any beholder, when asked the question 'what do you see?' will respond unhesitatingly by saying something like 'it's a fork'. Such a beholder will not say of the fork, 'now I am seeing it as a fork', as he might say of the schematic drawing of the triangle which he is seeing-as, 'now I am seeing it as a triangular hole.' Instead, the beholder unhesitatingly, immediately, and necessarily reaches for a certain description of the kind of object he is seeing, rather than pausing over the different mental interpretations of the sensory data he can plausibly offer, as he should do according to the mental interpretation theory of vision. He immediately says of the fork, for example, 'it's a fork'. Moreover, he uses this type of description out of necessity, because it would in fact be impossible for him to interpret and see the fork as a fork or as any other kind of object under normal perceptual conditions. We cannot *will* ourselves to see, interpret, or describe a fork as a fork. Rather, under normal perceptual conditions, we can only use the word 'fork' to describe our visual experience of the kind of object that a fork is. We cannot decide to interpret and see the image of the fork as a knife, for example, and nor, therefore, can we say 'Now I am seeing the fork as a knife.'

Thus, according to the descriptions offered by beholders, we do not and cannot standardly experience seeing-as when we look at objects. Now, the most important ramification of this argument for our purposes is its purchase on the domain of perceiving images. For Wittgenstein, the beholder's descriptions of his standard visual experiences of images also reveal that seeing-as is absent from these experiences. When confronted by an unambiguous image of a lion or any other object, the beholder does not behave as if he is subjectively interpreting the material properties of the image that he objectively perceives. He does not say, 'Now I am seeing it as a lion.' Says Wittgenstein, 'But I cannot try to see a conventional picture of a lion *as* a lion, any more than an F as that letter' (*PI* 206). Instead, when shown the 'conventional picture of a lion', the beholder will unhesitatingly reply 'It's a lion,' or 'It's a picture of a lion,' in response to a question about his visual experience. Wittgenstein calls this standard, unhesitating response to images ' "continuous seeing" of an aspect' or 'regarding-as', and he explicitly spells out the criteria for regarding-as in relation to the example of the beholder's response to the image of two hexagons:

Someone tells me: 'I saw it at once as two hexagons. And that's the *whole of what* I saw.' But how do I understand this? I think he would have given this description at once in answer to the question 'What are you seeing?', nor would he have treated it as one among several possibilities. In this his description is like the answer 'A face' on being shewn [a picture-face]. (*PI* 204)

Here, the fact that the beholder responds 'at once' to the question, and the fact that he does not see the two hexagons as one response among several he may give to the image he is being shown—he does not say, for example, 'Now I see it as two hexagons'—demonstrates, for Wittgenstein, that he is directly seeing the aspect of the two hexagons in the image, instead of indirectly interpreting the material properties of the image, as the mental interpretation theory of vision would argue. In opposition to the multiple responses and temporal duration that are indicative of the mental activity of interpretation during seeing-as, necessity and temporal instantaneity are the criteria, for Wittgenstein, of regarding-as as a dimension of standard visual experiences of images. These criteria indicate that, during such standard visual experiences, we do not distinguish between a direct, objective perception of the material properties of an image, and the aspect *qua* indirect, subjective interpretation which we supply mentally. In our spontaneous, immediate, everyday response to the question 'What is that?' we unhesitatingly refer to the aspect we are seeing in the image because we immediately and directly *see* the aspect *in* the image. Our behaviour during standard visual experiences of images therefore seems to indicate that we do not only see material properties when we look at an image, as Smith and Carroll seem to assume. Nor do we indirectly interpret the material properties of an image in order to produce a meaningful visual impression. Consequently, the aspect which we see in an image cannot be a mental entity, an indirect, subjective interpretation supplied by the mind of the beholder following the direct perception of the material properties of the image. It is not something we *think*. Rather, it is something that beholders *see* directly and instantaneously *in* images. We directly see aspects in images instead of indirectly supplying them *to* images, according to the behaviour and descriptions of beholders. The concept of regarding-as therefore demonstrates that both the objective component of the mental interpretation theory of vision—namely the sensation of the material properties of the image which Smith and Carroll apply to cinematic perception—as well as the subjective component of mental interpretation, are not manifested during our standard visual experience of images at all. Thus, those visual experiences in which the material properties of the image and the aspect *qua* mental interpretation are sundered, such as the dawning of an aspect or the experience of seeing-as in relation to the schematic cube or triangle, must be *exceptional* experiences. To use the experience of seeing-as to explain vision *in toto* is therefore a mistake, and is an excellent example of the way in which the theorist, according to Wittgenstein, tends to impose a single definition of vision upon the diversity of experiences that are described by the verb 'to see'.

At this point, the psychologist who is faced with strong evidence that his mental interpretation theory of vision does not, seemingly, accord with the beholder's behaviour during standard visual experiences might react by postulating the existence of a subconscious. That is, he might defend the mental interpretation theory of vision in the following way. Beholders do not manifest the objective and subjective components of the mental interpretation theory of vision during their standard, habitual visual experiences because, during these experiences, we are so used to interpreting sensory data mentally that this process happens spontaneously and non-consciously, outside the reach of consciousness. During standard visual experiences, we do not experience this indirect mental process of interpreting material properties consciously, even though it does occur in some recess of our conscious mind, namely the subconscious or non-conscious, because this process happens too quickly due to habituation and repetition, and therefore escapes conscious attention. Indeed, the psychologist would probably argue that it is precisely this dimension of non-consciousness that constitutes standard visual experiences. Our behaviour during standard visual experiences does not, therefore, exhibit the mental process of interpretation, according to the psychologist, because of the habitual, non-conscious nature of this process.

Such a psychologist would also be fully aware, however, that, in order to legitimize his postulation of the non-conscious nature of this mental inter-pretative activity during standard, habitual visual experiences, he must be able to point to at least some exceptional, non-habitual visual experiences during which this non-conscious mental activity of interpretation becomes manifest. He must be able to point to examples of exceptional visual experiences during which the beholder's behaviour does exhibit the usually non-conscious activity of supplying an aspect *qua* mental interpretation to the material properties of an image. For without the existence of these exceptional visual experiences, he will be forced into the position of arguing for the existence of a mental process that is not exhibited during the course of *any* visual experience at all. Such a mental process would not *stricto sensu* be subconscious or non-conscious, hidden by the habitual nature of standard visual experiences. For if it were, it would become manifest during non-habitual or non-standard visual experiences. Rather, it would be a more than *un*conscious mental activity in the sense of never being mani-fested or exhibited during any visual experience, and therefore unavailable to consciousness or observation at any time. The psychologist would, con-sequently, be in the position of arguing for the existence of a mental process that does not accord with any observable phenomena at all. Rather, such a mental process would be one that is postulated in spite of all observable evidence contradicting its existence from the realm of both standard and exceptional visual experiences. Such a theoretical position would be akin to a psychoanalyst who continues to postulate the existence of the subjective mechanism of unconscious desire in the absence of any observable phenom-ena that such a mechanism might be called upon to explain, such as a symptom or dream—an impotent and indeed nonsensical position for any psychological theory.

The psychologist would, therefore, have to point to non-standard visual experiences during which this process of mentally interpreting sensory data becomes manifest, in order to legitimize his mental interpretation theory of vision. And indeed, Wittgenstein provides several plausible examples of such non-standard visual experiences which the psychologist could use to illustrate his theory, namely the examples of 'seeing-as' which involve images of schematic figures and the duck-rabbit. These are seemingly non-standard, conscious, and observable visual experiences during which the beholder's mental process of interpretation is exhibited. In other words, they are visual experiences during which the aspect *qua* the beholder's subjective mental interpretation is seemingly divorced from his objective perception of the material properties of the image of the figure in question. In the case of the schematic figure of the triangle, for example, the beholder first perceives sensory data from the bare figure, and then proceeds to interpret and see it according to the dictates of his imagination or textual information that surrounds the figure. The triangle, it might be remembered, can be interpreted and seen as 'a triangular hole, as a solid, as a geometrical drawing; as standing on its base, as hanging from its apex' (*PI* 200), and any beholder would be inclined to describe this visual experience of seeing-as by saying something like, 'Now I am seeing the triangle as a triangular hole, now as a solid, now as a geometrical drawing.' The same would be true, according to the psychologist, of the non-standard visual experience of the duck-rabbit, during which the beholder flip-flops between two different subjective interpretations of the objective figure, saying now that 'It's a duck', and now that 'It's a rabbit'.

Wittgenstein does not deny the role of mental interpretation in the specific visual experience of seeing-as in relation to images of bare schematic figures such as the triangle. However, the example of the duck-rabbit demonstrates that the mental interpretation theory of vision cannot explain *all* visual experiences of seeing-as in which an aspect is sundered from an image. As a beholder, I can regard the duck-rabbit simply as a duck or a rabbit, and can fail to experience the shift between the two aspects. If so, I will report that 'I see a duck', or 'I see a rabbit', and this will demonstrate that I am regarding the duck-rabbit unhesitatingly and unthinkingly as either a duck or a rabbit. If, however, I experience aspect-dawning and flip-flop between the duck-aspect and the rabbit-aspect, I will describe my visual experience very differently. I will say 'Now it's a duck,' or 'Now it's a rabbit,' therefore using a very different form of expression. The psychologist might attempt to explain this visual experience by arguing that it is caused by the ambiguous sensory data provided by the figure. We see and interpret the figure as either a duck or a rabbit because the sensory data support both interpretations, thereby exhibiting the usually non-conscious, spontaneous process of mental interpretation and causing perceptual uncertainty and hesitancy. If, however, we examine this visual experience more closely, we realize that it does not constitute an illustration of the psychologist's mental interpretation theory at all.

The most important characteristic of the duck-rabbit figure is the reaction of *surprise* it engenders in the beholder. In the examples of seeing-as in relation to schematic figures, in which the beholder's imagination alights upon different, additional ways of seeing the figure of the box or triangle, no reaction of surprise is manifested because of the beholder's own mental agency in the production of this experience of additional ways of seeing the figure. The beholder is not surprised during the visual experience of seeing-as in relation to schematic figures because he himself alights upon different, additional ways of seeing the figure of the cube or the triangle through the use of his imagination or contextual information. Indeed, the beholder, in his descriptions of this visual experience, will inscribe his agency into these descriptions. He will say, 'Now *I* am seeing the figure as a box', for example. In the case of the duck-rabbit figure, however, the beholder's reaction of surprise is manifested in his curious ascription of agency to the figure itself. He says, for example, 'Now *it's* a rabbit, now *it's* a duck.' For Wittgenstein, this demonstrates clearly that, unlike the visual experience of seeing-as in relation to schematic figures, the experience of aspect-dawning proper does not involve any thought or imagination at all. He writes of the duck-rabbit:

I should never have thought of superimposing the heads like that, of making *this* comparison between them. For they suggest a different mode of comparison.
Nor has the head seen like *this* the slightest similarity to the head seen like *this*—although they are congruent. (*PI* 195)

In true aspect-dawning, an aspect is found *in* the image itself independently of the beholder's imagination or mental interpretation. In other words, as Wittgenstein says above of the figure of the duck-rabbit, an aspect in aspect-dawning is never something the beholder would *think* of finding in the figure in question, and this is why the aspect, when discovered, causes surprise. Therefore, the beholder does not alight, using his imagination, upon the duck or rabbit aspects as possible ways of seeing the figure of the duck-rabbit, nor does he mentally interpret the material properties of the duck-rabbit figure in these ways. This absence of the imagination, or what the psychologist would call the process of mental interpretation, is further demonstrated by the fact that even when he is mentally aware that there are other aspects to be seen in a figure, the beholder is not necessarily able to see them. For example, if he is regarding the figure of the duck-rabbit as a duck, and is simultaneously aware that the figure can also be seen as a rabbit, the beholder is not necessarily or immediately able to see it as a rabbit. Nor is he able to see the solution of a picture-puzzle, even if he knows it is there. Rather, the rabbit-aspect and the solution to the picture puzzle are things the beholder must go *in search of in the figure*. They are things the beholder *has to look for*, even if he knows they are there. In the visual experience of seeing-as in relation to schematic figures such as boxes or triangles, the various aspects that a figure can be seen-as are ones that originate outside the figure, in the context or the beholder's imagination. They do not presence themselves within the figure, as the aspect does in true aspect-dawning, independently of the beholder's mental agency. It is this characteristic of the presencing of the aspect within the figure which ultimately accounts for the paradox of aspect-dawning with which we began this section. It might be recalled that when we experience aspect-dawning, for example in relation to the picture-puzzle, we describe this visual experience as if the picture-puzzle itself had changed materially in front of our eyes, even though we know that no such material change has in fact occurred in the physical object. According to Wittgenstein, we do so precisely because the aspect that dawns is not something that we supply mentally to the figure in question. It is not the product of our mental agency, imagination, or the mental activity of interpretation. Rather, the aspect is something that seems to presence itself or emerge within the figure in question independently of the beholder, and it is for this reason that we describe this visual experience as if the figure itself had changed physically, thereby attributing agency to it. If the aspect were the product of our mental agency, a way of seeing the figure alighted upon by our imaginations or a thought content that we added mentally to the sensory data provided by the figure, then we would neither be surprised at the visual experience of aspect-dawning, nor would we describe this experience as if the figure in question had changed materially in front of our eyes.

The duck-rabbit example in all its brilliance and complexity therefore demonstrates that the mental interpretation theory of vision cannot explain *all* examples of seeing-as in which aspect and image are sundered in a conscious visual experience. Indeed, it cannot account for precisely that specific and unique visual experience of seeing-as which it was originally called upon to explain, namely aspect-dawning. The experience of aspect-dawning shows that the aspect is something that the beholder directly sees in an image. For if he did not see the aspect, then he would be unable to experience aspect-dawning. Furthermore, he would not be inclined to describe the image in which the aspect dawns as if it had changed materially before his eyes. Rather, he would describe his visual experience of aspect-dawning as if his own mental interpretation had changed, as he does during the experience of seeing-as in relation to images of schematic figures. More importantly, as the duck-rabbit example testifies, the aspect in aspect-dawning cannot be conceived of as a mental entity that is added to the material properties of an image. Instead, it is something that emerges within the image itself, independently of the beholder's mental agency. The non-standard visual experience of aspect-dawning therefore demonstrates that the beholder has the capacity to see an aspect in an image independently of the mental process of interpretation.

The importance of this demonstration for our purposes lies, however, in its ramifications for the beholder's *standard* visual experiences of images. For it legitimizes Wittgenstein's claim that the beholder standardly has the capacity to see an aspect in an image independently of a mental interpretation. In effect, aspect-dawning is a non-standard, conscious visual experience that provides conceptual grounds for the claim that the beholder standardly sees an aspect in an image without any mental process of interpreting the material properties of the image. It is for this reason, and not because of the putative subconsciousness of mental interpretations, that he does not manifest any such mental process in his behaviour or his descriptions of his standard visual experiences. The psychologist, of course, could protest that it is only the non-standard visual experience of aspect-dawning that his theory fails to explain. He could continue to argue that the beholder does not manifest the mental process of interpretation during his standard visual experiences of images because of the subconscious nature of this mental process. However, if the aspect cannot be conceived of as a *mental* entity in the non-standard, conscious visual experience of aspect-dawning in which aspect and image are sundered, then there is no *logical* reason why it should be conceived of as an *unconscious mental* entity during standard visual experiences of images in which aspect and image are not sundered apart. The psychologist's attempt to explain Wittgenstein's concept of regarding-as using a theory of the subconscious or non-conscious therefore falls apart, because his mental interpretation theory of vision cannot explain *all* visual experiences in which the aspect is consciously experienced independently of the material properties of the image.

I make no pretence here to have elucidated Wittgenstein's concept of the aspect. However, Wittgenstein's refutation of psychological explanations for aspect-dawning does provide us with a powerful critique of the singular definition of cinematic perception as merely the sensation of the material properties of the image. This is the definition, I have suggested, upon which Smith and Carroll's theories of emotional response are premised. If we apply to cinematic perception itself the logic of Wittgenstein's concept of regarding-as in relation to images, then we are forced to broaden our definition of cinematic perception beyond the mere sensation of the material properties of the image. It is certainly true that the cinematic spectator can perceptually attend to the material properties of the cinematic image, as abstract films amply demonstrate. However, he can also see the cinematic image in a different way, one that is captured in Wittgenstein's investigation into the verb 'to see' by the concept of regarding-as: 'we *regard* the photograph, the picture on our wall, as the object itself (the man, the landscape, and so on) depicted there' (*PI* 205). Applying the logic of regarding-as to cinematic perception, the fictional diegesis becomes something, like Wittgenstein's picture-face and duck-rabbit, that the spectator can see *in* the cinematic representation. And as the duck-rabbit example illustrates, his ability to do so cannot be explained by the mental interpretation theory of vision. It cannot be explained, in other words, by separating his visual experience into an objective component that consists of the sensation of the material properties of the image, and a subjective component consisting of the mental interpretation of those properties.

Richard Allen elsewhere in this volume addresses the larger implications for film theory of this broadening of the definition of cinematic perception. For us, however, this broadening of the definition of cinematic perception has implications for Smith and Carroll's theories of the spectator's emotional response to fiction films. It will be recalled that, in the second section of this chapter, I pointed to the implausible relegation of the spectator's sensuous perception of the concrete cinematic image within the grammar of the spectator's emotional response to fiction films that the theories of Smith and Carroll necessarily entail. I suggested that this implausible relegation happens because of the firm wedge that Smith and Carroll drive between the spectator's sensuous perception of the concrete cinematic image of a fiction and the 'thought' or 'imagination' of that fiction to which the spectator responds emotionally. I also suggested that Smith and Carroll are forced to postulate a mental entity—namely 'imagination' and 'thought'— as the causal agent of the spectator's emotional response because of their definition of cinematic perception as the sensation of the image and soundtrack as purely material entities stripped of the fictional diegesis, a definition that is buried deep beneath their theories. However, once the spectator is conceived of as regarding the fictional diegesis *in* the cinematic representation independently of any mental process, then a theory of his emotional response to the cinematic representation of fiction that postulates a *mental* entity as the causal agent of his emotional response is no longer a necessity. The emotional response of the spectator to cinematic representations of fictions, which for so long has troubled 'subtler minds' within film theory (to borrow Nietzsche's felicitous phrase), loses its aura of enigma and paradox when removed from the definition of perception as the sensation of the material properties of an image and placed against the background of the concept of regarding-as. Instead, in his ability to regard the cinematic representation as the fictional diegesis, the spectator is able to respond emotionally and directly to it without the need on the part of the theorist to postulate a special, mental event or mechanism to explain his ability to do so. As Wittgenstein himself summarizes in the example of the beholder's response to the picture-face: 'In some respects I stand towards it as I do towards a human face. I can study its expression, can react to it as to the expression of the human face' (*PI* 194). In the same way that the beholder, who is regarding the picture-face as a human face, can 'react' to it as if it were the expression of a genuine human face, so the cinematic spectator can respond emotionally to the cinematic representation which he is regarding as the fictional diegesis. And, as Wittgenstein indicates by the qualification 'in some respects', the spectator's ability to do so does not entail a belief in the material and ontic presence of the diegesis in the cinematic representation. No such supernatural belief is required to enable the experience of responding emotionally to images.

This does not mean, of course, that Smith and Carroll's theories are erroneous. Rather, it simply means that their theories are not generalizable. One reason for the spectator's emotional response to a fiction film might well be that he is sometimes consciously engaged in the mental activity of thinking about or imagining the fiction that he is watching. I might well, for example, be moved by Winona Ryder's superb performance in the recent *Little Women* to explicitly and consciously 'think about' or 'imagine' how sad I would feel if I lost my own sister as I sit in the movie theatre gazing up at Ryder. However, such a mental activity is not *necessary* for the spectator to respond emotionally. The analogy that Smith and Carroll draw between responding emotionally to a fiction film and being moved by a thought is therefore not wrong. Rather, it only accounts for one way in which the spectator might respond emotionally to a fiction film.

To summarize the logic of Wittgenstein's investigation for film theory and theories of emotional response: using the concept of regarding-as in relation to cinematic representations of fictions, we can effectively remove the mistaken premiss that the ontic non-existence and material absence of the fictional diegesis also entails its perceptual absence. As a result, the intermediate, mental entity postulated as the causal agent of the spectator's emotional response by the theories of Smith and Carroll is no longer a conceptual necessity. Instead, the spectator can be conceived of as responding with emotion to a fiction film upon the basis of his direct perception of the fictional diegesis *in* the concrete cinematic representation. Such a re-conceptualization of the spectator's emotional response overcomes the implausible relegation of the concrete cinematic representation within the theories of Smith and Carroll by according with standard intuitions about the importance of the concrete cinematic representation within the grammar of the spectator's emotional response to fiction films.

Smith and Carroll might, however, still insist that, even though the spectator has the capacity to regard a cinematic representation as its fictional referent, a theory of the spectator's mental activity is still required in order to explain his capacity to respond *emotionally* to it. In other words, Smith and Carroll might argue that regarding a cinematic representation as its fictional referent is not sufficient to enable the spectator to respond emotionally to it because a fictional referent does not exist. The spectator must also engage in some kind of mental activity, in addition to the perceptual activity of regarding the cinematic representation as its fictional referent, in order to respond emotionally to it because a fictional referent is not real. Wittgenstein himself, it is true, does not explicitly investigate emotional responses to images of fictional referents. The question of whether the duck-rabbit or the picture-face are images of fictional referents does not explicitly enter into his investigation. However, although I cannot properly address this potential objection within the confines of this chapter, I will briefly attempt to pre-empt it by clarifying my argument further.

Smith and Carroll, it might be remembered, derive their theories of the spectator's emotional response from an analogy with the general human capacity to be moved by thoughts without believing in the truth of those thoughts. Just as one can be moved by a thought without believing in it, they argue, so the spectator can respond emotionally to the thought produced in his head by the cinematic representation of fiction without falsely believing in the truth of the fiction. As Carroll argues: 'Both beliefs and thoughts have propositional content. But with thoughts the content is merely entertained without commitment to its being the case; to have a belief is to be committed to the truth of the proposition.'[13] I have suggested that this analogy is inappropriate because of the essential importance of the concrete cinematic representation within the grammar of the spectator's emotional response to fiction films. However, in doing so, I am not refuting the conceptual validity of this analogy. As I have already acknowledged, it is salutary because it severs the conceptual marriage between belief and the spectator's capacity for responding emotionally to fiction films that has plagued contemporary film theory. Rather, I am merely *extending* into the material world of concrete representations of fictions the propositional attitude towards thoughts that Carroll refers to above as 'to entertain'. Just as one can 'entertain' a thought 'without commitment to its being the case', to paraphrase Carroll, so one can 'entertain' a concrete cinematic representation of a fictional referent 'without commitment to its being the case'. I am arguing, therefore, that the spectator's capacity to 'entertain' a cinematic representation of a fictional referent does not require the postulation of an intermediate, *mental* entity such as a 'thought' or 'imagination' in order to be understood. The propositional attitude that Carroll refers to as 'to entertain' should not be conceived of as a *mental* process or entity in the case of the spectator's emotional response to fiction films. Instead, it should be conceived of as the way in which we *behave* towards concrete representations of fictions within our form of life. In making this argument, I am merely following the spirit of Wittgenstein's general claim in his later philosophy that verbs such as 'to believe', 'to understand', and so on, should not be conceived of as 'occult' mental processes or entities within the mind. Rather, these are verbs which refer to the complex variety of ways that we *behave* towards objects, events, and people within our form of life. Thus, my argument ultimately entails a modification, as opposed to a rejection, of the basic conceptual insight at the heart of Smith and Carroll's theories of the spectator's emotional response to fiction films. Rather than 'entertaining' the 'imagination' or 'thought' produced in the spectator's mind by the concrete cinematic representation and then responding emotionally to it, the spectator can directly 'entertain' and respond emotionally to the concrete cinematic representation of the fictional referent. He has the capacity to do so because he *regards* the concrete cinematic representation *as* the fictional referent it represents.

NOTES

1. Murray Smith, 'Film Spectatorship and the Institution of Fiction', *Journal of Aesthetics and Art Criticism*, 53: 2 (Spring 1995), 118.
2. Noël Carroll, *The Philosophy of Horror, or, Paradoxes of the Heart* (New York: Routledge, 1990), 81.
3. Ibid. 80.
4. Smith, 'Film Spectatorship and the Institution of Fiction', 118.
5. Ibid. 114.
6. Ibid. 119.
7. Ibid.
8. Carroll, *The Philosophy of Horror*, 80.
9. Ludwig Wittgenstein, *Philosophical Investigations*, trans. G. E. M. Anscombe (Oxford: Blackwell, 1958), 199–200. All references to part II of *Philosophical Investigations* are given in the text in the form of the abbreviation *PI*.
10. It is the work of the contemporary visual artist Gary Hill that most clearly exemplifies this crucial Wittgensteinian point about 'seeing'.
11. The following paragraphs are partly indebted to Stephen Mulhall's stimulating account of 'aspect-dawning' in *On Being in the World*: *Wittgenstein and Heidegger on Seeing Aspects* (London: Routledge, 1990).
12. Wittgenstein's model of 'seeing-as' in relation to images of schematic figures closely approximates in its outline the standard theory of perception offered by cognitive psychology. Two film theorists who invoke this theory of perception are David Bordwell, *Narration in the Fiction Film* (Madison: University of Wisconsin Press, 1985), 30–3, and Edward Branigan, *Narrative Comprehension and Film* (New York: Routledge, 1992), 33.
13. Carroll, *The Philosophy of Horror*, 80.

Select Bibliography

The items listed here represent those works from or influenced by the analytic tradition—broadly defined—which we consider to be of significance in the study of film. The bibliography is based upon works referred to within the chapters in this volume, though we have added some related works, so that it might function as a fairly extensive, though not exhaustive, bibliography. For the sake of cohesion, we have not included items which, though important to individual chapters in this volume, fall outside the ambit of the analytic tradition; information on such references can, of course, be found in the notes to each chapter.

ABRAMS, M. H., 'What is a Humanistic Criticism?', in Eddins (ed.), *The Emperor Redressed*, 13–44.

ADORNO, THEODOR W., ALBERT, HANS, DAHRENDORF, RALF, HABERMAS, JÜRGEN, PILOT, HARALD, and POPPER, KARL R., *The Positivist Dispute in German Sociology*, trans. Glyn Adey and David Frisby (London: Heinemann Educational Books, 1976).

ALLEN, RICHARD, 'Representation, Illusion, and the Cinema', *Cinema Journal*, 32: 2 (Winter 1993), 21–48.

—— *Projecting Illusion: Film Spectatorship and the Impression of Reality* (New York: Cambridge University Press, 1995).

ALTIERI, CHARLES, *Act and Quality: A Theory of Literary Meaning and Humanistic Understanding* (Amherst: University of Massachusetts Press, 1981).

BACH, KENT, and HARNISH, ROBERT, *Linguistic Communication and Speech Acts* (Cambridge, Mass.: Harvard University Press, 1979).

BEARDSLEY, MONROE C., *Aesthetics: Problems in the Philosophy of Criticism* 2nd edn. (Indianapolis: Hackett, 1981).

—— and WIMSATT, W. K., 'The Intentional Fallacy', in W. K. Wimsatt with Monroe Beardsley, *The Verbal Icon: Studies in the Meaning of Poetry* (London: Methuen, 1954), 3–18.

BORDWELL, DAVID, *Narration in the Fiction Film* (Madison: University of Wisconsin Press, 1985).

—— 'A Case for Cognitivism', *Iris*, 9 (Spring 1989), 11–40.

—— *Making Meaning: Inference and Rhetoric in the Interpretation of Cinema* (Cambridge, Mass.: Harvard University Press, 1989).

—— 'A Case for Cognitivism: Further Reflections', *Iris*, 11 (Summer 1990), 107–12.

—— and CARROLL, NOËL (eds.), *Post-Theory: Reconstructing Film Studies* (Madison: University of Wisconsin Press, 1996).

—— and THOMPSON, KRISTIN, *Film Art: An Introduction*, 4th edn. (New York: McGraw-Hill, 1993).

BRAND, PEGGY ZEGLIN, and KORSMEYER, CAROLYN (eds.), *Feminism and Tradition in Aesthetics* (University Park: Pennsylvania State University Press, 1995).

BRANIGAN, EDWARD, *Point of View in the Cinema: A Theory of Narration and Subjectivity in Classical Film* (New York: Mouton, 1984).

——*Narrative Comprehension and Film* (New York: Routledge, 1992).

BRATMAN, MICHAEL, *Intentions, Plans, and Practical Reasoning* (Cambridge, Mass.: Harvard University Press, 1987).

BRUBAKER, DAVID, 'André Bazin on Automatically Made Images', *Journal of Aesthetics and Art Criticism*, 51: 1 (Winter 1993), 59–67.

BUCKLAND, WARREN (ed.), *The Film Spectator: From Sign to Mind* (Amsterdam: Amsterdam University Press, 1995).

CARROLL, NOËL, 'The Power of Movies', *Daedalus*, 114: 4 (Fall 1985), 79–104.

——*Philosophical Problems of Classical Film Theory* (Princeton: Princeton University Press, 1988).

——*Mystifying Movies: Fads and Fallacies in Contemporary Film Theory* (New York: Columbia University Press, 1988).

——*The Philosophy of Horror; or, Paradoxes of the Heart* (New York: Routledge, 1990).

——'Art, Intention, and Conversation', in Iseminger (ed.), *Intention and Interpretation*, 97–131.

——'Cognitivism, Contemporary Theory, and Method: A Response to Warren Buckland', *Journal of Dramatic Theory and Criticism*, 6: 2 (Spring 1992), 199–219.

——'Film, Rhetoric, and Ideology', in Salim Kemal and Ivan Gaskell (eds.), *Explanation and Value in the Arts* (Cambridge: Cambridge University Press, 1993), 215–37.

——'Toward a Theory of Point-of-View Editing: Communication, Emotion, and the Movies', *Poetics Today*, 14: 1 (Spring 1993), 123–41.

——'The Paradox of Junk Fiction', *Philosophy and Literature*, 18: 2 (Oct. 1994), 225–41.

——'Critical Study: Kendall L Walton, *Mimesis as Make-Believe*', *Philosophical Quarterly*, 45: 178 (Jan. 1995), 93–9.

——'Nonfiction Film and Postmodern Skepticism', in Bordwell and Carroll (eds.), *Post-Theory*, 283–306.

——*Theorizing the Moving Image* (New York: Cambridge University Press, 1996).

CASEBIER, ALLAN, *Film and Phenomenology: Towards a Realist Theory of Cinematic Representation* (New York: Cambridge University Press, 1991).

CAVELL, STANLEY, *The World Viewed: Reflections on the Ontology of Film*, enlarged edn. (Cambridge, Mass.: Harvard University Press, 1979).

CURRIE, GREGORY, *An Ontology of Art* (New York: St Martin's Press, 1989).

——*The Nature of Fiction* (New York: Cambridge University Press, 1990).

——'Visual Fictions', *Philosophical Quarterly*, 41: 163 (Apr. 1991), 129–43.

——'McTaggart at the Movies', *Philosophy*, 67 (1992), 343–55.

——'Impersonal Imagining: A Reply to Jerrold Levinson', *Philosophical Quarterly*, 43: 170 (1993), 79–82.

——'The Long Goodbye: The Imaginary Language of Film', *British Journal of Aesthetics*, 33: 3 (July 1993), 207–19.

Currie, Gregory, 'Interpretation and Objectivity', *Mind*, 102 (1993), 413–28.

—— 'Imagination and Simulation: Aesthetics Meets Cognitive Science', in M. Davis and T. Stone (eds.), *Mental Simulation* (Oxford: Blackwell, 1995).

—— 'Unreliability Refigured: Narrative in Literature and Film', *Journal of Aesthetics and Art Criticism*, 53: 1 (Winter 1995), 19–29.

—— *Image and Mind: Film, Philosophy, and Cognitive Science* (New York: Cambridge University Press, 1995).

—— 'Film, Reality, and Illusion', in Bordwell and Carroll (eds.), *Post-Theory*, 325–44.

—— 'Realism of Character and the Value of Fiction', in Mette Hjort and Sue Lavers (eds.), *Emotion and the Arts* (New York: Oxford University Press, 1996).

Damasio, Antonio R., *Descartes' Error: Emotion, Reason, and the Human Brain* (New York: G. P. Putnam's Sons, 1994).

Danto, Arthur, 'Moving Pictures', *Quarterly Review of Film Studies*, 4: 1 (Winter 1979), 1–21.

Davies, Stephen, 'The Expression of Emotion in Music', *Mind*, 89 (Jan. 1980), 67–86.

—— *Musical Meaning and Expression* (Ithaca, NY: Cornell University Press, 1994).

De Sousa, Ronald, *The Rationality of Emotion* (Cambridge, Mass.: MIT Press, 1990).

Devitt, Michael, and Sterelny, Kim, *Language and Reality: An Introduction to the Philosophy of Language* (Cambridge, Mass.: MIT Press, 1987).

Diamond, Cora, *The Realistic Spirit: Wittgenstein, Philosophy and the Mind* (Cambridge, Mass.: MIT Press, 1991).

Donnellan, Keith S., 'Reference and Definite Descriptions', in A. P. Martinich (ed.), *The Philosophy of Language*, 3rd edn. (New York: Oxford University Press, 1996), 231–43.

Dretske, Fred, *Explaining Behaviour: Reasons in a World of Causes* (Cambridge, Mass.: MIT Press, 1988).

Dummett, Michael, *Origins of Analytical Philosophy* (Cambridge, Mass.: Harvard University Press, 1994).

Easterlin, Nancy, and Riebling, Barbara (eds.), *After Poststructuralism: Interdisciplinarity and Literary Theory* (Evanston, Ill.: Northwestern University Press, 1993).

Eddins, Dwight (ed.), *The Emperor Redressed: Critiquing Critical Theory* (Tuscaloosa: University of Alabama Press, 1995).

Eitzen, Dirk, 'Evolution, Functionalism, and the Study of American Cinema', *Velvet Light Trap*, 28 (Fall 1991), 73–85.

Elster, Jon, *Sour Grapes: Studies in the Subversion of Rationalilty* (Cambridge: Cambridge University Press, 1983).

—— *Making Sense of Marx* (Cambridge: Cambridge University Press, 1985).

Feagin, Susan, 'Imagining Emotions and Appreciating Fiction', *Canadian Journal of Philosophy*, 18 (1988), 485–500.

Freeland, Cynthia A., and Wartenberg, Thomas E. (eds.), *Philosophy and Film* (New York: Routledge, 1995).

GAUT, BERYS, 'Interpreting the Arts: The Patchwork Theory', *Journal of Aesthetics and Art Criticism*, 51: 4 (1993), 597–609.

——'The Paradox of Horror', *British Journal of Aesthetics*, 33: 4 (Oct. 1993), 333–45.

——'On Cinema and Perversion', *Film and Philosophy*, 1 (1994), 3–17.

——'Making Sense of Films: Neoformalism and its Limits', *Forum for Modern Language Studies*, 31: 1 (1995), 8–23.

GOLDMAN, ALVIN, *Liaisons: Philosophy Meets the Cognitive and Social Sciences* (Cambridge, Mass.: MIT Press, 1991).

GOMBRICH, E. H., *Art and Illusion: A Study in the Psychology of Pictorial Representation* (Princeton: Princeton University Press, 1961).

——*The Image and the Eye: Further Studies in the Psychology of Pictorial Representation* (Ithaca, NY: Cornell University Press, 1982).

——HOCHBERG, JULIAN, and BLACK, MAX, *Art, Perception and Reality* (Ithaca, NY: Cornell University Press, 1982).

GOODMAN, NELSON, *Languages of Art: An Approach to the Theory of Symbols* (Indianapolis: Hackett, 1976).

GORDON, ROBERT M., *The Structure of Emotions: Investigations in Cognitive Psychology* (Cambridge: Cambridge University Press, 1987).

GORMAN, DAVID, 'From Small Beginnings: Literary Theorists Encounter Analytic Philosophy', *Poetics Today*, 11: 3 (Fall 1990), 647–59.

GRICE, PAUL, *Studies in the Way of Words* (Cambridge, Mass.: Harvard University Press, 1989).

GRODAL, TORBEN KRAGH, *Moving Pictures: A New Theory of Film Genres, Feelings, and Cognitions* (Oxford: Clarendon Press, 1997).

HAACK, SUSAN, *Evidence and Inquiry: Towards Reconstruction in Epistemology* (Oxford: Blackwell, 1993).

HACKER, P. M. S., *Wittgenstein's Place in Twentieth Century Philosophy* (Oxford: Blackwell, 1996).

HANSON, KAREN, 'Provocations and Justifications of Film', in Freeland and Wartenberg (eds.), *Philosophy and Film*, 33–48.

HARMAN, GILBERT, 'Eco Location', and 'Semiotics and the Cinema: Metz and Wollen', in Marshall Cohen and Gerald Mast (eds.), *Film Theory and Criticism*, 2nd edn. (New York: Oxford University Press, 1979), 234–6, 204–16.

HJORT, METTE (ed.), *Rules and Conventions: Literature, Philosophy and Social Theory* (Baltimore: Johns Hopkins University Press, 1992).

HYMAN, JOHN, *The Imitation of Nature* (Oxford: Blackwell, 1989).

——(ed.), *Investigating Psychology* (New York: Routledge, 1991).

——'The Causal Theory of Perception', *Philosophical Quarterly*, 42: 168 (1992), 277–96.

ISEMINGER, GARY (ed.), *Intention and Interpretation* (Philadelphia: Temple University Press, 1992).

JAMESON, DALE (ed.), *Philosophy Looks at Film* (New York: Oxford University Press, 1983).

JARVIE, IAN, *Philosophy of the Film: Epistemology, Ontology, Aesthetics* (London: Routledge & Kegan Paul, 1987).

KHATCHADOURIAN, HAIG, 'Remarks on the Cinematic/Uncinematic Distinction in Film Art', in *Music, Film and Art* (New York: Gordon Breach, 1985), 133–9.
—— 'Space and Time in Film', *British Journal of Aesthetics*, 27 (1987), 169–77.
KIVY, PETER, *Osmin's Rage: Philosophical Reflections on Opera, Drama, and Text* (Princeton: Princeton University Press, 1988).
—— *Sound Sentiment* (Philadelphia: Temple University Press, 1989).
KNIGHT, DEBORAH, 'Theory of Action and the Interpretation of Cinematic Narratives', *Stanford French Review*, 16: 2 (1992), 197–213.
—— 'Women, Subjectivity, and the Rhetoric of Anti-humanism in Feminist Film Theory', *New Literary History*, 26: 1 (1995), 39–56.
—— 'The Rhetoric of Theory: Responses to Toril Moi', *New Literary History*, 26: 1 (1995), 63–70.
LAKOFF, GEORGE, *Women, Fire, and Dangerous Things: What Categories Reveal about the Mind* (Chicago: University of Chicago Press, 1987).
LAMARQUE, PETER, and OLSEN, STEIN HAUGOM, *Truth, Fiction and Literature* (Oxford: Clarendon Press, 1994).
LEIBOWITZ, FLO, 'Movie Colorization and the Expression of Mood', *Journal of Aesthetics and Art Criticism*, 49 (Fall 1991), 363–5; repr. in Alex Neill and Aaron Ridley (eds.), *Arguing about Art: Contemporary Philosophical Debates* (New York: McGraw Hill, 1994), 48–52.
—— 'Pornography and Persuasion', *Philosophy and Literature*, 18 (April 1994), 118–23.
—— 'Apt Feelings, or Why "Women's Films" Aren't Trivial', in Bordwell and Carroll (eds.), *Post-Theory*, 219–29.
LESLIE, ALAN M., 'Pretense and Representation: The Origins of "Theory of Mind" ', *Psychological Review*, 94: 4 (1987), 412–26.
LEVINSON, JERROLD, *Music, Art, and Metaphysics: Essays in Philosophical Aesthetics* (Ithaca, NY: Cornell University Press, 1990).
—— 'The Place of Real Emotion in Response to Fictions', *Journal of Aesthetics and Art Criticism*, 48 (Winter 1990), 79–80.
—— 'Seeing Imaginarily, at the Movies', *Philosophical Quarterly*, 43: 170 (1993), 70–8.
—— 'Film Music and Narrative Agency', in Bordwell and Carroll (eds.), *Post-Theory*, 248–82.
—— *The Pleasures of Aesthetics* (Ithaca, NY: Cornell University Press, 1996).
LIVINGSTON, PAISLEY, *Literary Knowledge: Humanistic Inquiry and the Philosophy of Science* (Ithaca, NY: Cornell University Press, 1988).
—— *Literature and Rationality: Ideas of Agency in Theory and Fiction* (Cambridge: Cambridge University Press, 1991).
—— 'Film and the New Psychology', *Poetics*, 21 (1992), 93–116.
—— 'The Poetic Fallacy', in Eddins (ed.), *The Emperor Redressed*, 150–65.
LOVELL, TERRY, *Pictures of Reality* (London: British Film Institute, 1980).
MARTIN, EDWIN, 'On Seeing Walton's Great-Grandfather', *Critical Inquiry*, 12 (1986), 769–800.
MAYNARD, PATRICK, 'The Secular Icon: Photography and The Functions of Images', *Journal of Aesthetics and Art Criticism*, 12: 2 (Dec. 1983), 155–69.

——'Drawing and Shooting: Causality in Depiction', *Journal of Aesthetics and Art Criticism*, 44 (1985–6), 115–29.

——'Talbot's Technologies: Photographic Depiction, Detection, and Reproduction', *Journal of Aesthetics and Art Criticism*, 47: 3 (June 1989), 263–76.

——*The Engine of Visualization: A Philosophical Primer of Photography* (Ithaca, NY: Cornell University Press, 1997).

MELE, ALFRED R., *Springs of Action: Understanding Intentional Behavior* (New York: Oxford University Press, 1992).

——*Autonomous Agents: From Self-Control to Autonomy* (New York: Oxford University Press, 1995).

——and LIVINGSTON, PAISLEY, 'Intentions and Interpretations', *Modern Language Notes*, 107 (1992), 931–49.

MESSARIS, PAUL, *Visual Literacy: Image, Mind, and Reality* (Boulder, Colo.: Westview Press, 1994).

MIDGELEY, MARY, *Heart and Mind: The Varieties of Moral Experience* (London: Methuen, 1981).

MORAN, RICHARD, 'The Expression of Feeling in Imagination', *Philosophical Review*, 103: 1 (Jan. 1994), 75–106.

MULHALL, STEPHEN, *On Being in the World: Wittgenstein and Heidegger on Seeing Aspects* (London: Routledge, 1990).

NEILL, ALEX, 'Fear, Fiction and Make Believe', *Journal of Aesthetics and Art Criticism*, 49: 1 (Winter 1991), 48–56.

——'Empathy and (Film) Fiction', in Bordwell and Carroll (eds.), *Post-Theory*, 175–94.

NOVITZ, DAVID, *Knowledge, Fiction and Imagination* (Philadelphia: Temple University Press, 1987).

NUSSBAUM, MARTHA CRAVEN, *Love's Knowledge: Essays on Philosophy and Literature* (New York: Oxford University Press, 1990).

PAVEL, THOMAS, *The Feud of Language: A History of Structuralist Thought* (Oxford: Blackwell, 1989).

PEACOCKE, CHRISTOPHER, 'Depiction', *Philosophical Review*, 96 (1987), 383–410.

PERKINS, V. F., *Film as Film: Understanding and Judging Movies* (Middlesex: Penguin Books, 1972).

PETERSON, JAMES, *Dreams of Chaos, Visions of Order: Understanding the American Avant-Garde Cinema* (Detroit: Wayne State University Press, 1994).

PETTERSSON, ANDERS, 'On Walton's and Currie's Analysis of Literary Fiction', *Philosophy and Literature*, 17: 1 (1993), 84–97.

PLANTINGA, CARL, 'Defining Documentary: Fiction, Non-fiction, and Projected Worlds', *Persistence of Vision*, 5 (Spring 1987), 44–54.

——'The Mirror Framed: A Case for Expression in Documentary', *Wide Angle*, 13: 2 (1991), 41–53.

——'Film Theory and Aesthetics: Notes on a Schism', *Journal of Aesthetics and Art Criticism*, 51: 3 (Summer 1993), 445–54.

——'Movie Pleasures and the Spectator's Experience: Toward a Cognitive Approach', *Film and Philosophy*, 2 (1995), 3–19.

PLANTINGA, CARL, 'Moving Pictures and Nonfiction: Two Approaches', in Bordwell and Carroll (eds.), *Post-Theory*, 307–24.

—— *Rhetoric and Representation in Non-fiction Film* (New York: Cambridge University Press, 1997).

PONECH, TREVOR, 'Visual Perception and Motion Picture Spectatorship', *Cinema Journal* (forthcoming, Fall 1997).

PRINCE, STEPHEN, 'The Discourse of Pictures: Iconicity and Film Studies', *Film Quarterly*, 47: 1 (Fall 1993), 16–28.

RICŒUR, PAUL, 'Life in Quest of Narrative', in David Wood (ed.), *On Paul Ricœur: Narrative and Interpretation* (London: Routledge, 1991).

RORTY, AMÉLIE OKSENBERG (ed.), *The Identities of Persons* (Berkeley and Los Angeles: University of California Press, 1976).

—— (ed.), *Explaining Emotions* (Berkeley and Los Angeles: University of California Press, 1980).

SCHIER, FLINT, *Deeper into Pictures: An Essay on Pictorial Representation* (New York: Cambridge University Press, 1986).

SCRUTON, ROGER, 'Photography and Representation' and 'Fantasy, Imagination and the Screen', in *The Aesthetic Understanding: Essays in the Philosophy of Art and Culture* (London: Methuen, 1983), 102–26, 127–36.

SESONSKE, ALEXANDER, 'Aesthetics of Film', in George Dickie, Richard Scalfani, and Ronald Robin (eds.), *Aesthetics: A Critical Anthology* (New York: St Martin's, Press, 1977), 583–90.

—— 'Time and Tense in Cinema', *Journal of Aesthetics and Art Criticism*, 38: 4 (1980), 419–26.

SHERMAN, NANCY, *The Fabric of Character: Aristotle's Theory of Virtue* (Oxford: Clarendon Press, 1989).

SHRAGE, LAURIE, 'Feminist Film Aesthetics: A Contextual Approach', in Hilde Hein and Carolyn Korsmeyer (eds.), *Aesthetics in Feminist Perspective* (Bloomington: Indiana University Press, 1993).

SMITH, MURRAY, *Engaging Characters: Fiction, Emotion, and the Cinema* (Oxford: Clarendon Press, 1995).

—— 'Film Spectatorship and the Institution of Fiction', *Journal of Aesthetics and Art Criticism*, 53: 2 (Spring 1995), 113–27.

—— 'The Logic and Legacy of Brechtianism', in Bordwell and Carroll (eds.), *Post-Theory*, 130–48.

SNYDER, JOEL, and ALLEN, NEIL WALSH, 'Photography, Vision, and Representation', *Critical Inquiry*, 2: 1 (Autumn 1975), 143–69.

SPARSHOTT, FRANCIS, 'Basic Film Aesthetics', in Gerald Mast and Marshall Cohen (eds.), *Film Theory and Criticism*, 3rd edn. (New York: Oxford University Press, 1985).

SPERBER, DAN, and WILSON, DEIDRE, *Relevance: Communication and Cognition*, 2nd edn. (Oxford: Blackwell, 1995).

TALLIS, RAYMOND, *Not Saussure: A Critique of Post-Saussurian Literary Theory* (London: Macmillan, 1988).

TAN, ED S., *Emotion and the Structure of Narrative Film: Film as an Emotion Machine* (Mahwah, NJ: Lawrence Erlbaum, 1996).

TAYLOR, CHARLES, *Human Agency and Language: Philosophical Papers 1* (Cambridge: Cambridge University Press, 1985).

——*Philosophy and the Human Sciences: Philosophical Papers 2* (Cambridge: Cambridge University Press, 1985).

VERMAZEN, BRUCE, 'Expression as Expression', *Pacific Philosophical Quarterly*, 67 (July 1986), 196–224.

WALTON, KENDALL, 'Fearing Fictions', *Journal of Philosophy*, 75: 1 (Jan. 1978), 5–27.

——'Transparent Pictures: On the Nature of Photographic Realism', *Critical Inquiry*, 11: 2 (Dec. 1984), 246–77.

——'Looking again through Photographs: A Response to Edwin Martin', *Critical Inquiry*, 12 (1986), 801–8.

——*Mimesis as Make-Believe: On the Foundations of the Representational Arts* (Cambridge, Mass.: Harvard University Press, 1990).

——'Seeing-In and Seeing Fictionally', in James Hopkins and Anthony Savile (eds.), *Mind, Psychoanalysis, and Art: Essays for Richard Wollheim* (Oxford: Blackwell, 1992), 281–91.

WARBURTON, NIGEL, 'Seeing through "Seeing through Photographs"', *Ratio*, New Series 1 (1988), 64–74.

WICKS, ROBERT, 'Photography as a Representational Art', *British Journal of Aesthetics*, 29: 1 (Winter 1989), 1–9.

WILKERSON, T. E., 'Pictorial Representation: A Defense of the Aspect Theory', *Midwest Studies in Philosophy*, 16 (1991), 152–66.

WILLIAMS, BERNARD, 'Imagination and the Self', in *Problems of the Self: Philosophical Papers 1956–72* (Cambridge: Cambridge University Press, 1973), 26–45.

——*Ethics and the Limits of Philosophy*, 3rd edn. (London: Fontana, 1993).

WILSON, GEORGE M., *Narration in Light: Studies in Cinematic Point of View* (Baltimore: Johns Hopkins University Press, 1986).

——*The Intentionality of Human Action* (Stanford, Calif.: Stanford University Press, 1989).

——'Again Theory: On Speaker's Meaning, Linguistic Meaning, and the Meaning of a Text', in Hjort (ed.), *Rules and Conventions*, 1–31.

WITTGENSTEIN, LUDWIG, *Philosophical Investigations*, 2nd edn., trans. G. E. M. Anscombe (Oxford: Blackwell, 1958).

WOLLHEIM, RICHARD, *On Art and the Mind: Essays and Lectures* (Cambridge, Mass.: Harvard University Press, 1974).

——*Art and Its Objects*, 2nd edn. (New York: Cambridge University Press, 1980).

——*The Thread of Life* (Cambridge: Cambridge University Press, 1984).

——*Painting as an Art* (London: Thames & Hudson, 1987).

WOLTERSTORFF, NICHOLAS, *Worlds and Works of Art* (Oxford: Clarendon Press, 1980).

——*Art in Action* (Grand Rapids, Mich.: Eerdmans, 1980).

Index